·'· ·'· · ·ncluding railroad rates,
‸s of

STUDIES IN ECONOMIC HISTORY

MEN, CITIES, AND TRANSPORTATION

VOLUME I

*Published in coöperation with the Committee on
Research in Economic History, Social Science
Research Council*

LONDON : GEOFFREY CUMBERLEGE
OXFORD UNIVERSITY PRESS

MEN
CITIES AND
TRANSPORTATION

A Study in New England History

1820–1900

EDWARD CHASE KIRKLAND

HARVARD UNIVERSITY PRESS

Cambridge, Massachusetts

1948

PRINTED AT THE HARVARD UNIVERSITY PRINTING OFFICE
CAMBRIDGE, MASSACHUSETTS, U.S.A.

In memory of

A. H. K.

who loved trains
and New England

PREFACE

Here, inquisitive reader, is no chronicle of all the railroads in New England. That task has been done elsewhere and done admirably.[1] To others, curious why I selected the period, 1820–1900, let me reply that my study begins logically with transportation on the eve of the railroad and ends, equally logically, when the two great systems, now controlling New England, had come into being. The story of eight decades, wherein New England shifted from a network of waterways and roads to one of steel rails and railroad consolidation, is here complete except for one character, the electric lines. In their early years such lines were a part of urban rather than regional development; the history of their larger importance would have been cut in half by the time scheme of this book.

When I first undertook this study I hoped, perhaps whimsically, to rescue New England history from the colonial era. As time has passed the connection of New England with these volumes has become, in a way, purely accidental. Although the transportation systems here described had peculiarly regional characteristics, the setting has become for me of minor concern. My main interest has turned to the growth and functioning of transportation as a business enterprise. I hope this emphasis has elements of such desirable novelty that it may give a new turn to the writing of transportation history. It is time for us to subordinate the phases of promotion and construction and explore, more fully than we have hitherto, the problems of rates, services, securities, technological changes, government policy, labor and management. To the fashionable query as to what I have tried to prove, I regret I can formulate no fancy answer. I have simply sought to treat the New England transportation system as a human response to the changing needs and ambitions of that area. In my judgment that response was creditable and successful.

And now before the pleasant task of acknowledgments, let me insert a word about bibliography. For a work of this type, based

---

[1] George P. Baker, *The Formation of the New England Railroad Systems* (Cambridge: Harvard University Press, 1937).

upon the materials used, a formal list of books would have been neither possible nor particularly valuable. I have, therefore, handled this matter in footnotes. In every chapter the first time a work is cited I have given the customary data about it. It has not seemed necessary to provide this information for government publications. Congressional documents, in addition to other identifying marks, have been given, in parentheses, their serial numbers.

The list of institutions and individuals who have courteously aided the progress of this study is regrettably too long for a preface. I owe, however, special gratitude to Mr. Howard L. Stebbins, the librarian of the Social Law Library, for permission to use its collections; to Mr. Robert H. Haynes for the many privileges granted in the Harvard College Library; and to the staffs of the Dartmouth College Library, of the Massachusetts State Library, and of the Library of the Harvard Graduate School of Business Administration, all of which have, in their distinctive fashions, been models of helpful service.

To the Social Science Research Council I am indebted for a grant to initiate my study of New England capitalists and to its Committee on Research in Economic History for the publication of these volumes. I should hasten, however, to absolve them of either conceiving this study or of directing its course. Miss Ruth Crandall has skillfully read proof. My research assistants, the late Dr. Hunter D. Farish of the Williamsburg Restoration, and Dr. Robert F. Byrnes, now of Rutgers University, both did dull work with enthusiasm. Dr. Arthur H. Cole has read the proof, made suggestions, and over the years stimulated many of my inquiries. The improvements are his, the remaining errors mine. The contributions of my wife, Ruth Babson Kirkland, in matters of research and routine have been so numerous that her name ought to share the title page. Let me conclude with an expression of gratitude to the President and Boards of Bowdoin College, a small college wise enough to realize that scholarship is essential to teaching and generous enough to assume the obligations such insight involves.

E. C. K.

March 30, 1948

CONTENTS

Water Transportation

Consolidation and Control

Railroad Workers

ILLUSTRATIONS

VOLUME I

Stations by H. H. Richardson *facing p.* 391

MAPS

VOLUME I

VOLUME II

MEN, CITIES, AND TRANSPORTATION

I

NEW ENGLAND'S DOMESTIC MERCHANT MARINE

"That Boston must always be a considerable place of commerce and go on to increase with a steady and certain growth for a long period of time to come, seems evident from the following circumstances: It is the natural center of a district whose population at present exceeds a million, which is gradually increasing. This population is thriving, industrious, and consuming; the District of Maine and the provinces of Nova Scotia and New Brunswick, which lie in front of it, and will always have an active trade with it, are in a state of progressive development, that is yet susceptible of a very wide extension; and it is the center of the great nursery of seamen, and of the business of ship-building. — It is the chief market for all the various products of the fisheries, and of salted provisions; its harbor is safe, commodious, and connected immediately with the sea; it is the place of export for many valuable manufactures, long and solidly established; it is in possession of a very large moneyed capital." — William Tudor, Letters on the Eastern States (1820), p. 100.

I

New England is different. But her cultural condescension, her unmistakable accent, her zealous ancestor worship — traits which have for decades put "foreigners" on the defensive — are not so important for this history of transportation as the fact that, more than most regions in the United States, she possesses natural or strategic frontiers. Salt water washes her eastern and southern

edges; Lake Champlain and the Hudson River form her western
boundary, for every proper New Englander knows that the twenty
mile strip between the Hudson and the nominal western boundaries
of the New England states really belongs to New England; and
even the international boundary on the north is in New England
more natural than when as a parallel of latitude it traverses with
no logic other than direction the prairies and the mountains of
the West. Over a century ago Timothy Dwight in his *Travels
in New-England*, a four-volume compendium of piety, pedantry,
and acute observation, referred lovingly to New England as
"this country." Geographically, he was right.

Although New Englanders saw no necessity for making such a
claim, the face of their country mirrored in a miniature and
slightly distorted fashion that of the great nation of which it
was a part. Like the United States, it had an Atlantic coastline,
with an array of seaports; Boston was New England's New York
and Providence its Baltimore. Stretching inland just far enough
to get away from east winds and the tang of salt air, was a narrow
coastal plain, a zone less than 300 feet above sea level; then
came a tumble of hills and mountains, New England's Appalachian
chain. In northern New Hampshire this range reached in the
White Mountains the highest peaks of New England — Timothy
Dwight cautiously calculated that Mount Washington might be
12,729 feet high, approximately twice its actual elevation as later
determined. Several steep-sided notches, however, traversed the
White Mountain massif and inexorably shaped the routes followed
in turn by wagons, railroads, and endless lines of humming mo-
tors.[1] From the White Mountains the chain slopes southward
until in southern Connecticut and Rhode Island it finally fades
away. Numerous small, sharply defined river valleys cut into
this barrier from both sides, and around its southern terminus,
as around the Georgia tip of the Appalachians, trade and travel
could reach the interior by the coastal plain.

The Connecticut River was the New England Mississippi. To
be sure it thrust east and west no great arms like the Ohio or the

---

[1] Timothy Dwight, *Travels in New-England and New-York* (New Haven:
S. Converse, 1821), II, 161–164.

Missouri, it traversed no limitless prairie plains, but from a source at the northern tip of New Hampshire to its end in Long Island Sound, New England's Gulf of Mexico, the Connecticut formed a great central river valley. This "beautiful river," as Timothy Dwight called it, like the Mississippi was a means of transportation and, after it entered Massachusetts, flowed through level and fertile lowlands. "An almost perfect plain extends each side of the river, with every inch of soil cultivated — the ground covered and groaning under the weight of its rich but honest burden. . . . The far brought Connecticut, that here lords it in the very lap of luxury, comes sluggishly meandering on the perfect parallel to Hogarth's *line of Beauty*." [2]

West of the Connecticut rose New England's Continental Divide. Its northern range, the Green Mountains, with the precision and orderliness of a blueprint, marched from Canada to Massachusetts. Although its summits were lower than the Whites, stretched faintly visible to the east, most of the passes were higher and the approach sharper. Then from northern Massachusetts to southern Connecticut, this sharply defined ridge merged into a broken plateau whose elevation and width formed a greater barrier to movement than the uplands east of the Connecticut. Though a comparison of these ranges to the Rockies perhaps seems ludicrous to a later generation, early nineteenth century travelers from the coastal plains of New England were overwhelmed by their awful ruggedness. Benjamin Silliman, America's earliest virtuoso of science, described the ride through the Berkshires as comparable to one through a "western wild." Another less famous Connecticuter announced that the scene at Bellows Falls, Vermont, was "hideous" — a "ragged, jagged, perpendicular, chaotic mass of mountains seems to totter as you ride beneath them" and at Montpelier, the capital of the state, he saw the "mountains, like modern Alps, towering in the air, ... You almost feel shut up from the world, imprisoned, and in fact are strongly impress'd with your relative situation to the

---

[2] Charles W. Eldridge, "Journal of a Tour through Vermont to Montreal and Quebec in 1833," *Proceedings of the Vermont Historical Society*, New Series, II (1931), 54; Dwight, *Travels*, II, 338.

Battencas of Switzerland." [3] Finally these western mountains sloped away to Lake Champlain and the Hudson, the Pacific coast of the New England country.[4]

II

Until man took to air in flight, the lay of land and water determined the course of travel and transportation. In the eighteen twenties, as it had been for two centuries, New England's coast line and coastal traffic were the bases of its domestic commerce. Improved highways had not challenged their authority; no network of canals or railroads had yet undermined their commercial suzerainty. If it is not too presumptuous for a landlubber and an historian to divide the ocean, as kings and popes have done, New England's coastal waters fell into two areas, separated by the flat, bent arm which Massachusetts thrusts eastward into the sea. Although vessels sailed around Cape Cod regularly and in flotillas, it lengthened every sea journey from southern New England to Boston and put commerce in jeopardy as well. Maps, like that of the United States Engineers in 1903, show shipwrecks as thick as black flies along the outer edge of the Cape, and statistical soothsayers have announced that, if all these lost ships were placed stem to stern, they would form a continuous wall between Chatham at the Cape's elbow to Provincetown at its finger tips.[5] North of the Cape stretched a coast, deep cut with harbors but exposed to the full attack of the Atlantic until, beyond Portland, fiords, islands, and great estuaries shattered the monotony of an ordered shore and made a thousand havens. South of the Cape commerce faced easier circumstance. Though there were rips and giant shoals, channels dangerous in a fog, and though the squeamish dreaded the roll of a vessel off Point Judith; Nantucket Sound, Vineyard Sound, Buzzards Bay, Nar-

[3] Benjamin Silliman, *Remarks Made, on a Short Tour between Hartford and Quebec in the Autumn of 1819* (New Haven: S. Converse, 1820), p. 38; Eldridge, "Journal of a Tour through Vermont," pp. 60, 65.

[4] John K. Wright, "Regions and Landscapes of New England," *New England's Prospect: 1933, American Geographical Society, Special Publication* no. 16 (New York: American Geographical Society, 1933), pp. 14–49.

[5] Henry C. Kittredge, *Cape Cod, Its People and Their History* (Boston and New York: Houghton Mifflin Company, 1930), pp. 208, 230.

ragansett Bay, and Long Island Sound gave a comparatively sheltered navigation. New York City could have the commerce south of the Cape; north of it Boston ruled the waves.

The figures of coastwise arrivals and clearances for the Massachusetts metropolis understated considerably the extent of this commerce since they were prone to ignore the regular arrivals of packets and the presence of smaller vessels. Still they must suffice. In 1825 the arrivals in the coastwise trade were 2,592; while no great increase took place in the remainder of the decade, by 1835 they were 3,879 — roughly three times the number of foreign entrances.[6] A large proportion was employed in the commuting traffic between Boston and its maritime neighbors scattered from Portsmouth, New Hampshire, to Provincetown at the tip of Cape Cod. Not for a moment, however, must the reader assume that the commerce of the north and the south shore was one. Cape Cod was remote from Boston; before the day of the railroad or the motor car, the land journey thither was so arduous and prolonged that "most wise men on the Cape knew the way to China by sea better than they did the way to Boston by land." Cape Codders turned early, therefore, to the construction and navigation of regular packets for the Boston route. Owners and towns fostered an intense rivalry over the speed and safety of their respective lines and the comfort and luxury of their furnishings. No competition could assume in advance, however, the length of the journey; it might last anywhere from six hours to two days. But commodities were as important as passengers. Whether by packet or no, vessels brought fish and oil and salt from every port, though Duxbury was the busiest of all shippers. Plymouth sent nails and hollow ware; and, in the fall, cargoes of onions mingled their odor with that of cod and mackerel. None rivaled, however, the sloop *Sally* from Bristol, Rhode Island, whose 18,000 bunches of onions must have laid a broad scented trail around the whole Cape.[7]

[6] *P. P. F. De Grand's Boston Weekly Report of Public Sales and of Arrivals,* 1824, 1825, *passim; Hunt's Merchants' Magazine and Commercial Review,* XXI (1849), 668.

[7] Kittredge, *Cape Cod,* pp. 232–236; *De Grand's Boston Weekly Report,* 1824, 1825, *passim.*

From the neighborhood ports north of Boston it was so much easier and more certain to travel by stage that passenger travel by sailing vessel was comparatively infrequent. Nevertheless these northern places — Gloucester, Marblehead, Portsmouth, Newburyport, and Salem — had their packets; Salem, indeed, had no less than seven coasters each of which made fifteen trips a year to Boston. In this freighting business, some commodities — boots and shoes, potatoes, apples, cider, cordwood, and fish — were of native production; but more frequently the consignments described in the maritime lists were the goods assembled by the far-flung foreign commerce of these still thriving coastal towns. Marblehead should have sent cod, it sent sugar; Gloucester should have sent salt fish, the sloop *Gloucester-Packet* arrived with 128 casks of claret wine and the sloop *Betsy* with 220 bushels of pepper. Newburyport sent molasses as well as country produce; Portsmouth, coffee as well as potatoes and butter; and Salem reached her epitome by combining the exotic of the East with the prosaic of the New England in the cargo of one of her regular traders, the *Lark*. Boots, shoes, cheese, and nails jostled citron, almonds, cocoa, "5 casks Gum Arabic, 1 case Silk Velvet, 44 sacks Feathers, 6 cases Alabaster Ornaments. . . . 182 boxes Macaroni." [8]

At Portsmouth, the most important of these near northern ports, commerce began to assume the color of the down-East trade. Where that charmed region actually began was somewhat of a puzzle; certainly by Portland where the slow arc of the shoreline bent definitely toward the sunrise. It ended with the New Brunswick and Nova Scotia British Maritimes, almost severed from one another by the double-fanged Bay of Fundy. In this area Portland had a clear lead in domestic as well as in foreign commerce; the trade of the Kennebec from Bath to Augusta was sufficiently great to justify packet services to Boston; and then the recorded coasting traffic — for wood and lumber coasters did not report to its customs — jumped to Quoddy, where

---

[8] *De Grand's Boston Weekly Report*, 1824, 1825, *passim;* Report of the Joint Committee of Railways and Canals on the Eastern Railroad, Massachusetts *Senate Documents*, 1833, no. 133, p. 10.

Eastport prospered by reason of its fortunate proximity to the Bay of Fundy and the Maritimes. Direct and open trade between these British Provinces and the United States was possible only for certain commodities or for certain times, since the attempts of the two countries before 1830 to manage this commerce for their own interests, accompanied as such methods always are with restrictions and reprisals, had raised smuggling to a profession. An ill-defined frontier, islands owing disputed allegiance, waters inadequately patrolled — all gave happy advantages for the illegal exchange of the goods both parties desired.[9]

Before the day of the railroad, down East was far enough from Boston to provide for sailing vessels a considerable passenger traffic. At best this was an uncomfortable method of travel. Even the passenger packets put into harbor at the slightest sign of danger; and a convivial captain was prone to seize this excuse when the possibility of "unbounded capers till ye morning breakfast time" offered itself to him. Under the circumstances a journey from Boston to Boothbay might take eleven days.[10] Often the master of a lumber coaster "took passengers at 'nine shillings for going, and two and three-pence a day for grub'; and huddled them, male and female, into a cabin without staterooms, partitions, or even curtains to the berths. His cook was a never washed, never combed boy, who wore his father's trousers and nobody's shoes; and was proud of the mysteries of making bread by mixing Indian meal with water, and stirring them up with a black iron spoon; of mincing fish with potatoes and warming them with pork fat; and of making, for a treat on Sunday, a salt meat soup. Those who paid 'for going and for grub' were taxed a pint or a quart of 'the West India' for every harbor new to them between the port of departure and destination, and were put under liberal contribution for the gallons that were now and then provided in order 'to raise a fair wind.' "[11]

---

[9] *De Grand's Boston Weekly Report*, 1824, 1825, *passim;* G. S. Graham, "The Gypsum Trade of the Maritime Provinces," *Agricultural History*, XII (1938), 211–223; *Hazard's United States Commercial and Statistical Register* (Philadelphia: W. F. Geddes, 1840), I (1839), 30.

[10] G. W. Rice, *The Shipping Days of Old Boothbay* (Portland: Southworth-Anthoensen Press, 1938), pp. 60–62.

[11] "Timber Trade of Maine," *North American Review*, LVIII (1844), 334–335.

From Portland, as from the north-shore towns of Massachusetts, came articles collected in the foreign trade and then reshipped in the coastal trade. It dispatched more molasses to Boston in the first eight months of 1825 than Havana, Martinique, or Surinam; only the shipments from Matanzas surpassed it and that by less than two hundred gallons.[12] The State of Maine and the Maritimes were, however, really a frontier region. They sent up to the rest of New England fish and potatoes, leather and oats, or perhaps $75,000 in specie to maintain a balance at the Suffolk Bank.[13] Already certain raw material trades had developed. "Prime Eastern Hay," as it was later called, found a ready market.[14] Eastport, the willing accomplice of the Maritimes, shipped tons of grindstones — for the best came from the Bay of Fundy or Pictou — and dirty grey cargoes of plaster or gypsum to replenish with calcium the tired acres of New England farms. "How many farmers some years ago laughed when they saw their neighbours putting plaster on their land," wrote the Boston *Centinel* in 1820, "and now we see the farmers doubling their crops by using it." [15]

Maine was the forest of New England. In the twenties her lumbermen had not yet been driven to cutting spruce, a mere forest weed; the state still deserved its sobriquet "The Pine Tree State." Its cutters were felling the pumpkin pine, its rivermen hurrying the logs down the magnificent rivers to the bustling mills, and scores of vessels loaded plank and board, box shooks and shingles for Boston and other New England ports. The industry was not yet at its peak; nor had Bangor yet become the unquestioned queen of the trade. York and Kennebunk, Hallowell, Bath, and Gardiner on the Kennebec, and Portland were as well the suppliers of New England.[16] Of the last port, Elijah

---

[12] *De Grand's Boston Weekly Report*, 1825, p. 763.

[13] *Ibid.*, 1824, 1825, *passim*.

[14] F. S. Chase, *Wiscasset in Pownalborough* (Portland: Southworth-Anthoensen Press, 1941), p. 413.

[15] Graham, "The Gypsum Trade," pp. 209–211.

[16] Richard G. Wood, *A History of Lumbering in Maine*, 1820–1861 (Orono: University Press, 1935), pp. 214–215, 220; M. Greenleaf, *A Survey of the State of Maine in Reference to Its Geographical Features, Statistics, and Political Economy* (Portland: Shirley and Hyde, 1829), pp. 247–251.

Kellogg, Bowdoin graduate, homespun minister, and writer of boys' books, gave a picture in his *A Strong Arm:* "Then at Portland, on a January morning about sunrise, you might have seen lively times. A string of board teams from George Libby's to Portland pier; sleds growling; surveyors running like madmen, a shingle in one hand and a rule-staff in the other; cattle white with frost, and their nostrils hung with icicles; teamsters swearing and hallooing; Herrick's tavern and the shops in Huckler's Row lighted up and the loggerheads hot to give customers their morning dram." [17] But pine wasn't the whole story. From ash, oak, and birch the mills fashioned staves and headings, axe handles, oars, and bed posts and shipped them to Massachusetts.[18] Maine also was New England's wood box. To keep Boston alone warm and to cook her meals required 120,000 cords of wood, of which a sixth was "country wood," the remainder, coming by sea, was mostly "eastern wood." [19] While to be chopped down only to be burned was ignominious, perhaps it was more dignified to travel to Boston as cordwood than as potashes, the very relic of a relic. Though in the twenties the Maritimes contributed their pittance of cordwood, they were more important for bituminous coal shipped through Sydney at the eastern end of Cape Breton Island or Pictou on the southern shore of the St. Lawrence. As the anthracite trade from Pennsylvania grew dizzily in the later twenties and thirties, Boston became an anthracite city. Until then she imported bituminous from Great Britain or Nova Scotia; the latter shipments were greater.[20]

III

Between the ports along the southern shore of New England, there was a busy interchange of goods. One standardized route

[17] Elijah Kellogg, *A Strong Arm*, p. 147, quoted in R. G. Wood, *A History of Lumbering in Maine*, pp. 219–220.

[18] *De Grand's Boston Weekly Report*, 1824, 1825, *passim*.

[19] *Report of the Board of Directors of Internal Improvements of the State of Massachusetts on the Practicability and Expediency of a Rail-Road from Boston to the Hudson River, and from Boston to Providence* (Boston: Boston Daily Advertiser, 1829), p. 34.

[20] *Hunt's Merchants' Magazine and Commercial Review*, VI (1842), 475; *ibid.*, VIII (1843), 549.

was that between the Connecticut river ports on the one hand and New London on the other. Aside from local interchanges, vessels outbound from the river for the West Indies trade sailed first to New London to complete their cargoes and stopped there on the way back to lighten vessels in preparation for the battle of bucking the Connecticut's sandbars.[21] Rhode Island was a New England Netherlands. Although her inhabitants had built no sea-walls, dikes, or canals, a Baptist God endowed the state with Narragansett Bay and magnificent salt-water rivers; and the merchants and shippers of Providence, Bristol, Warren, and Newport had the wit to use them.[22] In their more distant trades, however, southern New England turned to New York. The magnetic pull of propinquity could not be denied. Just before 1820 Norwalk, only forty-eight miles from New York, had six regular packet vessels plying to the city and the remainder of her coasting fleet, ten sloops and schooners, sought generally the same destination. From New Haven's "very respectable commerce," six or seven packets went regularly to and from New York.[23] Over 50 per cent of the trade of the Connecticut Valley, if the entrances and clearances of vessels were any test, was with New York.[24] The cluster of ports on the Thames estuary did not break the pattern, for New London had four packet vessels plying to New York, and the major part of Norwich's coastal fleet traded thither. With Rhode Island New York's attraction began to weaken. Providence had a foreign trade of its own and its coastal traffic was more diffused. In 1835 arrivals from Rhode Island at the Port of New York totaled only thirteen schooners and twenty-eight sloops.[25] They simply complemented the steamers.

Westward bound cargoes through Long Island Sound still bore witness to the undifferentiated and undeveloped economy of New England. Granite from Haddam paved the streets of New York;

[21] Margaret E. Martin, *Merchants and Trade of the Connecticut River Valley, 1750–1820* (Northampton: n. d.), p. 60.

[22] John C. Pease and John M. Niles, *A Gazetteer of the States of Connecticut and Rhode-Island* (Hartford: William S. Marsh, 1819), p. 326.

[23] *Ibid.*, pp. 108, 185.

[24] Martin, *Merchants and Trade of the Connecticut*, pp. 58–59.

[25] Pease and Niles, *A Gazetteer*, pp. 142, 148; R. G. Albion, *The Rise of New York Port, 1815–1860* (New York: Charles Scribner's Sons, 1939), p. 397.

the easily shaped brownstone or "freestone" of Chatham built its houses. There was an immense provision trade. Stamford in a single year sent 100,000 bushels of potatoes; port after port sent butter, cheese, meat, and grain; to give a meal a climax or to make life bearable, Connecticut dispatched its liquors, cider, brandy, rum, and gin, the last an article in the distillation of which the state achieved distinction. The fisheries added contributions. Connecticut River sent shad of better quality than any other in the United States, New London the mackerel and cod of its smack fisheries, and port after port the succulent oysters of the Sound. To keep New York warm as well as fed, these coastal fleets carried to that market their cords of split oak, walnut, and chestnut.[26] They brought back the assorted articles, dry goods, crockery, wines, hardware, and flour, which the "great emporium of the United States" either manufactured or collected through her own foreign and domestic commerce. And the captains, if they had leisure, were glad to oblige by doing errands for their townsfolk.[27]

Northern New England also had a hand in the commerce of the ports below Cape Cod. Between Boston and Nantucket there was a constant flow of ships bringing barrels of sperm oil, boxes of sperm candles, and whalebone for the twenty firms distributing the products of the whaling industry. New Bedford's trade, it was said, was two-thirds with Boston, one-third with New York. With Rhode Island, though there was a packet service with Providence, connections around Cape Cod were inferior to the coach and wagon overland trade. But it paid to ship Bostonward from Connecticut ports wheat, corn, oats, and provisions and between Hartford and Boston there was a considerable traffic for which gin, freestone, and cordwood provided the bulk commodities.[28]

[26] Pease and Niles, *A Gazetteer*, pp. 13–14, 142, 148, 160, 165–166, 184, 193, 196–197, 277–279, 284–285.

[27] Martin, *Merchants and Trade of the Connecticut*, p. 60; Albion, *Rise of New York Port*, pp. 124–126.

[28] *De Grand's Boston Weekly Report*, 1824, 1825, *passim; Twenty-seventh Annual Report of the Boston Board of Trade, . . . January 1, 1881* (Boston: James F. Cotter & Co., 1881), pp. 19–20; Pease and Niles, *A Gazetteer*, p. 13; *Report of the Board of Directors to the Stockholders of the Boston and Providence Rail-Road Company, Submitting the Report of their Engineer* (Boston: J. E. Hinckley & Co., 1830), p. 46 note

While Boston thus invaded New York's preserve, the latter retaliated by sailing boldly into Boston's backyard. In 1825 a packet line was established between Portland and New York. Long since lumber schooners from Maine had found New York a good market; and vessels had carried grindstones and gypsum from Quoddy and fish from the Maritimes to the Hudson as well as to the Charles.

This urban rivalry, however, was fruitful rather than stultifying.[29] New York was the greatest figure in Boston's coastal trade and Boston was the greatest factor in New York's. In 1835 there were 494 arrivals at New York from Boston and 667 at Boston from New York.[30] The mainstay of the trade was the packets. Though it required imagination and courage to establish the first regular trader just after the Revolution, the trade was so well established by the mid-thirties that there were four distinct lines each of which dispatched two vessels a week from both Boston and New York eight months of the year. Since packets generally traveled full, an additional flotilla of sloops and schooners, owned in New York or Boston or along the Connecticut shore or on Cape Cod, participated in the traffic; and larger vessels, ships and brigs, driving north from southern ports, repaired to New York for additional cargo or shipments to take the place of the cotton, sugar, and tobacco which they left on Manhattan. In a trade as dense as this everything went by water. One third of the Boston-bound packet cargoes was flour. Leather for the nascent shoe industry was another regular traveler. Mackerel, during the fishing season, was one third of the return cargoes, while, month in and month out, domestic manufactures provided a quarter. As for the rest, there was the interchange of varied imports and articles of domestic production — teas, wines, dry goods, crockery, and "particularly those descriptions of merchandise which are designed to supply the retail trade of the city, and which are wanted immediately after being purchased."[31] The long manifests read like an inventory

[29] Albion, *Rise of New York Port*, pp. 129–133.

[30] *Ibid.*, p. 397.

[31] Acts of Incorporation and a Report of a Committee of the Citizens of Norwich, *Worcester & Norwich Rail-Road Company, 1835* (n.p., n.d.), pp. 28–30.

of early nineteenth century civilization. The vessels irregularly engaged on this route likewise carried miscellaneous cargoes; but, if such were not to be secured, they loaded like the sloop *Spartan* with 2,000 bushels of corn, 400 bushels of rye, 800 bushels of oats, and 2 sacks of feathers! This rich commerce was so varied and great, however, that masters rarely had to resort to the common fill-alls of thinner trades — rags, junk, and feathers.[32]

The trade with Philadelphia and Baltimore was a watered imitation of that with New York, a general merchandise trade but less extensive. Baltimore, however, as the premier flour market of the American world and a great grain port, sent northward whole cargoes of flour.[33] And by the late twenties Philadelphia rapidly developed a commerce in anthracite coal. Improved river navigation and canals brought down to her docks Lehigh, Schuylkill, and eventually Lackawanna coal. In 1822 four vessels sufficed to transport this dark and useful commodity to other centers; in 1835 the trade required a fleet of 2,361.[34] But New England had other sources of fuel, and regarded this interloper with a native caution. She required instruction in its utility for iron-making and for domestic use. Early in 1825 P. P. F. De Grand was writing, "LEHIGH COAL is, I understand, used, with great success, in almost every parlor in Philadelphia and New-York and in very many Iron-works, in Pennsylvania. How long will Massachusetts be backward in availing herself of its superior advantages?"[35] Twelve years later Boston was receiving coastwise 80,557 tons of anthracite.[36]

With Baltimore the South began; with the turgid rivers of Virginia it was unmistakable. Here was an immense provision trade, particularly with the trilogy of great river ports — Alexandria, Fredericksburg, and Richmond. Approximately of equal

---

[32] *De Grand's Boston Weekly Report*, 1824, 1825, *passim*.

[33] *Ibid.*, 1824, 1825, *passim*; C. B. Kuhlmann, *The Development of the Flour-Milling Industry in the United States* (Boston and New York: Houghton Mifflin Company, 1929), pp. 46–47.

[34] *Hunt's Merchants' Magazine and Commercial Review*, VIII (1843), 547–559; *ibid.*, XVI (1847), 205–206.

[35] *De Grand's Boston Weekly Report*, January 22, 1825.

[36] *Hunt's Merchants' Magazine and Commercial Review*, VIII (1843), 549.

importance in Boston's commerce, they shipped northward flour, wheat, corn, and oats, seasoned with tobacco, cigars, and at least one cargo of 1,000 bushels of sweet potatoes, a welcome variant to the thousands of white tubers Boston collected from Bridge-port to Eastport. The other Virginia cargo was bituminous coal. Perhaps the small amount taken by New England was Virginia's fault. "In Virginia, it is true, that the bituminous mines were long since opened," commented a writer in 1841, "but the trade has been carried on in an easy, careless, unenterprising manner, so characteristic of that venerable commonwealth, that we can scarcely wonder it has grown into the currency of a proverb, that 'Old Virginny never tires.' "[37] Wilmington and Washington of North Carolina meant tar and turpentine, and Charleston added to its miscellaneous cargoes tierces and half tierces of rice and bales of cotton. The other cotton ports were Savannah, Mobile, and New Orleans, to the last of which commercial power shifted as the cotton kingdom moved in the early thirties to the black sods of Alabama and Mississippi. At this new commercial emporium of the South, Philadelphia and New York both got a headstart on Boston, but when the New Englanders moved in they conquered. Though the oldsters might keep their advantage in the provision trade of sugar, molasses, and grain, Boston wrested the leadership in the New Orleans cotton trade. In 1830–1831 New York took 55,737 to Boston's 36,327 bales; in 1835–1836 the respective figures were 29,604 to 37,084. In 1835 Boston's cotton receipts from all ports were 90,109 bales.[38] For back cargoes New England shipped cotton goods, boots and shoes, and merchandise culled from the import trade. Bulk commodities to balance the southern ones were, however, not yet forthcoming. Lumber ship-ments rarely went south of New York; the commerce in granite paving stones, blocks, and columns had hardly begun; but Fred-erick Tudor in a classic New England imaginative enterprise

---

[37] *De Grand's Boston Weekly Report*, 1824, 1825, *passim;* J. Blount, "The Coal Business of the United States," *Hunt's Merchants' Magazine and Commercial Review*, IV (1841), 70.

[38] W. F. Switzler, *Report on the Internal Commerce of the United States. . . . January 30, 1888*, Treasury Department, Bureau of Statistics, pp. 285–287; *Hunt's Merchants' Magazine and Commercial Review*, I (1839), 189, 283; *ibid.*, III (1840), 454–456; *ibid.*, XX (1849), 215.

had defied temperatures and the skeptics by sending ice through warm waters not only abroad but also to Charleston, Savannah, and New Orleans. By the mid-thirties his experiments had met with success and others were entering the trade. The ingenuity of the shipping and marketing arrangements was paralleled by the large scale cutting operations on the fresh water ponds about Boston. Cheap ice and low freights discouraged the appearance elsewhere of imitators.[39]

IV

Even New England's shorter voyages were no mean journey. Portland lay 110 miles from Boston; New York 180 from Fall River. The genuinely long trades crossed distances that in Europe would have made their commerce international; New York was 300 miles from Boston, Savanah 919, and New Orleans 1,918.[40] Logically voyages of such length should have required large vessels; actually factors of geography and trade worked in the opposite direction. Coastal commerce sailed in shallow waters. The harbors of North Carolina, Georgia, and Florida were notoriously shoal; in New England a port as great as Providence was obstructed until the fifties by a huge shoal covered by only 4½ feet of water; and many a trade compelled vessels to dock at wharfs straddling, when the tide was out, over mud flat and grassy marsh.[41] Coastal commerce sailed in circumscribed waters. The long trades ended in Delaware and Chesapeake Bay or the estuaries of southern rivers; commerce between New York and Providence or Boston had to pick its way through the often crowded waters or straitened channels of Long Island, Vineyard, and Nantucket Sounds or of Narragan-

[39] *Boston Board of Trade. 1857. Third Annual Report of the Government, Presented to the Board at the Annual Meeting on the 21st of January, 1857* (Boston: Rand & Avery, 1857), pp. 79–80; Henry Hall, *The Ice Industry of the United States with a Brief Sketch of Its History and Estimates of Production in the Different States*, Tenth Census of the United States, 1880, XXII, 2.

[40] Report of the Commissioner of Navigation. . . . June 30, 1901, *House Documents*, 57 Cong., 1 Sess., no. 14 (s.n. 4311), p. 366.

[41] John H. Morrison, *History of American Steam Navigation* (New York: W. F. Sametz & Co., 1903), p. 286.

sett and Buzzards Bays; Portland had a magnificent harbor giving at once to the sea, but other down-East ports lay inland along island-studded bays or narrow rivers. Such conditions placed a premium upon vessels of slight draft, upon ease in handling, upon quickness of maneuver. The small, assorted cargoes, the limited capital of shipowners, the anxiety to avoid big risks — these, too, strengthened the preference for small ships. The coastwise arrivals in Boston in 1825 included, therefore, only 23 ships, square-rigged, three-masted; but of brigs there were 215, of sloops, 977, and of schooners, 1,292.[42]

The brigs, a compromise vessel for their two masts were square-rigged, had a transitory popularity. Not as large as a ship, they served well for the trade to the West Indies interlocked with that along the Atlantic coast. The sloops were shallow vessels with a single mast. Though their rig was a fore-and-aft one, often a square sail was set higher on the mast; in any case the sails could all be handled from the deck. To hold them on their course against the wind, builders along the Hudson and in southern New England had equipped the sloop with a centerboard, dropped down through a well in the hull when the boat was under way; drawn up, it permitted the sloop to traverse shallow waters. Fitly enough, Hartford was always referred to as the head of sloop navigation on the Connecticut; Troy won the same appellation on the Hudson. In the trades between Boston and Cape Ann, Cape Cod, and southern New England, the sloop was supreme; in the commerce between New York City and Boston they outnumbered the schooners two to one. Occasionally one even strayed as far as Fredericksburg, Charleston, or Eastport, but in these longer trades the schooners were showing their superiority. The schooner had two masts; in spite of variants, with square fore-topsail or fore-and-main topsails, it was mainly fore-and-aft rigged. The line of its hull, designed to harmonize speed and capacity, made it a magnificent merchant vessel. Most of its sails could be handled from the deck; they were quickly shifted; the crews were small.[43]

[42] *De Grand's Boston Weekly Report*, 1825, *passim*.
[43] *Ibid.*, 1825, *passim;* Howard I. Chapelle, *The History of American Sailing*

Between Boston and New York, sloop and schooner sometimes covered the distance in three days, often in five. In the mid-thirties the packets averaged four and a half. To both Philadelphia and Richmond, times were fourteen or fifteen days; to Charleston, with no bay or river navigation involved, ten; the run to New Orleans took twenty-five. In days of sail, however, such averages were meaningless; speed depended upon weather and upon season. Indeed the coastal trade as a whole had throughout the year an ebb and flow. Winter congealed it and spring unloosed a torrent of commerce. Coastwise arrivals at Boston in May were four times those of January. Partly the seasonal character of production explained this cycle. Coal and cordwood, ice and lumber, were summer shipments; the trade in grain, flour, apples, and potatoes began with the autumn harvest; cotton sailed north at full tide from January to March. But winter was a time of frozen harbors, iced vessels, and of snow-freighted gales. Rates reflected the season. On the New York packets, which halved their sailings during these four inhospitable months, freights rose from seventy-five cents above their summer levels to $1.75 and $2.00 a ton.[44]

Since these coasting craft were small vessels — sloops, schooners, and brigs ran from 50 to 200 tons and the Boston-New York packets averaged 140 — they could be built anywhere on the shore where proper timbers and skilled workers could be brought together. The task was easy in the twenties. New England had forests, oak and pine, close to the sea or along its rivers, a natural avenue of transportation for ship lumber. Craftsmen were everywhere and professional designers were unnecessary when construction was rule-of-thumb. Shipyards bustling with traveling cranes and equipped with ways long enough to reach the horizon were unnecessary. So the building of coasting vessels was widely dispersed. New York and Boston yards might turn out the ships and quality vessels; the river ports of Connecticut,

Ships (New York: W. W. Norton & Company, 1935), pp. 219–249, 296–300; John G. B. Hutchins, *The American Maritime Industries and Public Policy, 1789–1914* (Cambridge: Harvard University Press, 1941), p. 216.

[44] *De Grand's Boston Weekly Report*, 1824, 1825, *passim; Worcester & Norwich Rail-Road Company, 1835*, p. 29.

the towns of Narragansett Bay, the rivers of Massachusetts from
Fore River to the Merrimack, and that dynamic newcomer, the
State of Maine, launched the unsung coaster.[45]

V

Meanwhile the steamboat had invaded New England's coastal
commerce. Though Boston did not have a steamboat line to any
port south of Cape Cod until the fifties nor a steamboat connection with New York until after the Civil War, steam navigation
to the ports of Maine was on a sound basis by 1835 and along
the more sheltered coast of southern New England a multitude of
lines were already caught in a desperate competition. Narragansett Bay and Long Island Sound formed with the Hudson River
the nursery of steam navigation on the Atlantic seaboard. There
was a constant interchange of personnel. On the Hudson, Fulton
and Livingston, grantees of a steamboat monopoly on the waters
of New York, ran the first commercially successful steamboat in
America. Later these enterprising pioneers, either directly or
indirectly, became interested in lines to Connecticut and Rhode
Island. They set a fashion. The great steamboat buccaneers
of the Hudson River — George Law, Elisha Peck, Daniel Drew,
and Cornelius Vanderbilt — at one time or another entered the
competitive cockpit of southern New England navigation. There
was also a constant interchange of vessels. Boats tried out on
the Hudson River were placed on the runs to southern New England ports; vessels, failing to make money on Long Island Sound,
returned to the river. And at New York City, the fulcrum of this
commerce, the yards along the East River fashioned the hulls of
these first steamboats and her skilled engine builders provided
the machinery.[46]

Steam navigation on Long Island Sound began with the *Fulton*.
Built in 1813 from plans by Robert Fulton, her projectors in-

---

[45] Albion, *Rise of New York Port*, pp. 303–305, 406–409; Hutchins, *The American Maritime Industries*, pp. 179, 183, 208–209, 216; Samuel E. Morison, *The
Maritime History of Massachusetts, 1783–1860* (Boston: Houghton Mifflin Company, 1921), pp. 96–105, 255.

[46] Albion, *Rise of New York Port*, pp. 148–151.

Fulton (1813–14), Long Island Sound

Portland (1835), a Down Easter

PIONEER STEAMBOATS

Gridley Bryant   Thomas H. Perkins

FOUNDERS OF THE GRANITE RAILWAY

A Decorative Conception of the First Train on the
Boston and Lowell Railroad

tended her for the Sound and introduced certain technical innovations to meet the different conditions of navigation. Her hull, no longer scow shaped, was given a deep rise and a keel was employed to strengthen it and to prevent the undulating motion of the deck characteristic of many previous boats. Her machinery, "a little less . . . than is now put in a cotton mill," took considerable space and its operation, along with the connections to the paddle wheels, was exceedingly noisy. A single mast, sloop-rigged, made it possible to utilize wind as an auxiliary power. While the War of 1812 and the blockade of New York kept the *Fulton* tethered to the Hudson, early in 1815 with the peace she clattered forth on her first trip to New Haven and demonstrated that a steam vessel could defy the currents of Hell Gate and the perils of deepwater navigation. She soon settled down to a regular schedule of eight to twelve hours each way. Her fare was six dollars. Three years later the *Fulton* ran from New Haven to New London and Norwich whence a stage line connected with Boston; the *Connecticut*, also under license from the Fulton-Livingston monopoly, covered the New Haven-New York run.[47]

The arrival of these vessels, however, angered Connecticut men who wished to run their own steam vessels to New York. The new system of tranportation, they said, meant that "Every port may, on this new plan, have its Steam-Boat; and mercantile men may be enabled to watch the New-York market, and avail of its fluctuations, as those do, who live there." Connecticut ports could become middlemen between the interior merchants and New York supply houses. The only obstacles to the realization of this vision were "the proud monopolists of New York, the rich and able lawyers, and the wealthy individuals who compose the company."[48] Harkening to their pleas, the Connecticut legislature, in imitation of New Jersey, passed a law in 1822 excluding from the waters of the state all vessels owned by the New York monopoly or operating under license from it. The owners of the

[47] Morrison, *History of American Steam Navigation*, pp. 337–338.
[48] *Facts and Considerations on the Question Why Is Steamboat Navigation Interesting to Connecticut?* (Hartford: George Goodwin & Sons, 1819.)

Fulton and the *Connecticut* thereupon inaugurated a new service by sending these vessels to Providence, a port hitherto served by sailing packets to New York. Already the conventional pioneer, the *Fulton*, had on an excursion tempted the terrible seas off Point Judith and demonstrated the feasibility of the route. Slow and expensive as the first steamer was, the owners of the packet sloops proposed to hamper its competition through legislation, either heavily taxing passages on steamboats or preventing their landing at Rhode Island ports. The legislature did not respond. The *Fulton* thus had the distinction of inaugurating steam service to three of the most important ports in southern New England.[49]

On March 2, 1824, the Supreme Court in Gibbons *v.* Ogden declared the Fulton-Livingston monopoly unconstitutional. The response in southern New England was immediate. Lines, like that from New Haven which had run boats toward New York as far as it could in Connecticut waters and then transferred its passengers to stages, or like that from Hartford which had planned a terminus in New Jersey, now went directly to New York City; and Connecticut within fifteen months chartered six steamboat companies to add sailings from Bridgeport, Norwalk, Norwich, and Stamford.[50] Two years later there were at least eight lines on the Sound with Hartford and Providence the most important destinations. On the eve of the railroad, contemporary observers asserted that these steamboats were annually carrying 135,400 passengers — undoubtedly an inflated figure; no estimates of the considerable freight traffic are available.[51] At the

[49] Charles H. Dow, *History of Steam Navigation between New York & Providence, Compiled . . . . under the Direction of D. S. Babcock, Esq., President of the Providence & Stonington Steamship Co.* (New York: Wm. Turner & Co., 1877), pp. 6–8.

[50] Morrison, *History of American Steam Navigation*, pp. 339–340; *Resolves and Private Laws . . . of Connecticut from . . . 1789 to . . . 1836*, pp. 1108–1109, 1112–1113, 1119–1121, 1123–1124.

[51] *Badger and Porter's Stage Register; Containing a Full Account of the Principal Lines of Stages, Steamboats and Canal Packets in the New England States and the State of New-York: Their Hours of Departure and Arrival — Towns through Which They Pass — Proprietors' Names — Fares — Distances of Routes &c.* (Boston: American Traveller, 1826), pp. 18–19; Memorial of a Number of Citizens of New York, *Senate Executive Documents*, 26 Cong., 2 Sess., no. 133 (s.n. 377), pp. 4-6.

same time the pattern of operation had been fixed. It was one of competition.

Though at the greater ports, like Hartford and Providence, public opinion or advertising usually acknowledged one company as the leader — it was denominated "the line" or sometimes "the old line" — there was continuous rivalry. Smaller places, when traffic offered profits, also tempted interlopers. For these competitive outcasts the rewards were certain and considerable. The "old lines" bribed them to desist, or bought their vessels, or absorbed personnel and ships into their own organization. A darker shadow fell upon these unquiet arrangements in 1835. In the previous year the harassed steamboat owners of the Hudson induced Cornelius Vanderbilt, for a consideration, to deny himself the pleasure of competing on that river for ten years. He now transferred his talents to the navigation of Long Island.[52] As one of his fulsome biographers put it, "His foible was 'opposition'; whenever his keen eye detected a line that was making a very large profit on its investment, he swooped down on it and drove it to the wall by offering a better service and lower rates." [53] Alone or in alliance with his brother Jake, he tried Bridgeport, Providence, and Hartford. The entrenched interests struck back. The old line at Hartford in 1836 advertised its *Bunker Hill* as "This is the boat most confidently recommended, for safety, despatch, and good treatment to travelers. The *Lexington* and *Cleopatra* run on the route oppositely, without much system and at any price from $1 to $3." [54]

But competition, coupled with the technical progress to which it was a spur, lowered fares, shortened running times, and increased the ease of travel. In 1822 the *Fulton* and *Connecticut* charged for the New York and Providence run $10 and took from eighteen to twenty-seven hours for the journey. In 1835 the *Lexington*, Vanderbilt's new boat, went "through by daylight" in a little less than twelve hours and a half; her fare was

[52] Wheaton J. Lane, *Commodore Vanderbilt, An Epic of the Steam Age* (New York: A. A. Knopf, 1942), pp. 60–61.

[53] Gustavus Myers, *History of the Great American Fortunes* (Chicago: C. H. Kerr & Company, 1909–1910), II, 110.

[54] *Badger and Porter's Stage Register* [1836], p. 29.

$4.00.[55] At the same time the size and luxury of the Long Island steamboat increased. The *Fulton*, a noisy, unattractive vessel of 327 tons, was 134 feet long. Although completely decked over, she had no staterooms for the sixty passengers who filled her to capacity; they slept in a general cabin in the hold. Twenty-one years later, in 1836, the *Massachusetts*, the *"ne plus ultra"* of comfort, convenience, elegance, and speed, made her first voyage. A boat of 713 tons, 202 feet long, she had magnificent interior appointments. Her spacious principal cabin was uninterrupted by pillars; in it 175 people could sit down for dinner at long parallel tables. Later the males could clamber into the 112 fixed berths that bordered the cabin or sleep in the 100 temporary berths erected in the middle of the floor; ladies retired to the 60 fixed berths in the ladies' cabin.[56]

In comparison with the developments on the Sound, steam navigation north of Cape Cod was literally a second-hand performance. The original plans for it were, indeed, characterized by largeness of vision, for vessels were to run from Boston to Portland and on subsidiary routes. But by 1817 when the *Massachusetts*, a small vessel built in Philadelphia and propelled by oars rather than paddle wheels, arrived in Massachusetts Bay, these hopes had boiled down to the simple project of a steamboat from Salem to Boston. Even this moderate expectation was delayed while the engineer repainted the vessel, took it apart, and redesigned it, and while the citizenry and owners speculated on the possibility of profit from the enterprise. Finally, early in July, it made its first trip to Boston, covering the twenty-odd miles in three hours. Later voyagers found the motion of the boat pleasant and the oars were esteemed ingeniously superior to paddle wheels since they were not required to lift a weight of water on the up-stroke. Still the project was a failure. The *Massachusetts* broke the Massachusetts Steam Navigation Company, proving a "dead loss" to her "adventurers." At the end of a year of operation the vessel was sold south. Wrecked

[55] Dow, *History of Steam Navigation between New York & Providence*, p. 7; Morrison, *History of American Steam Navigation*, pp. 265, 270.
[56] Dow, *History of Steam Navigation between New York & Providence*, p. 7; Morrison, *History of American Steam Navigation*, pp. 271–272, 338.

in New Jersey, her parts were salvaged and reincorporated in a second *Massachusetts* in 1820. The Rev. William Bentley of Salem had no difficulty in accounting for the catastrophe: — "The certainty of reaching Boston in two hours at two thirds of the distance by water, gives every advantage to the Stage. We have 21 miles to the Town & then all the inconveniences of entering & leaving the boat when 13 miles may carry us to the bridge from the entrance of the Turnpike & we can be taken up & put down at the places we may chuse." [57]

By 1835 the exhibit of steamboat navigation on Massachusetts Bay was certainly unimpressive. Attempts to establish lines to Salem, Marblehead, Plymouth, and Newburyport had all failed. Various vessels, all of them built south of Cape Cod, had run since 1817 to Nahant. In 1828 regular service to Hingham was inaugurated by the *Lafayette*, New York built, and in 1835 to Portsmouth by the *Citizen*, one of Vanderbilt's discarded Staten Island ferries. In general, steam vessels, unless the termini of their runs — for example, Nahant or Hingham — were with difficulty reached by land, could not compete with the stages; nor indeed with the sailing packets which were often faster. Certainly Boston, as compared with New York, suffered from her lack of a great inland river like the Hudson, upon which to develop a commercially profitable steam navigation.[58]

Meanwhile promoters turned their attention to the possibilities of steamboat connections between Boston and the ports of Maine. In 1822 a group of Maine men of whom Captain Seward Porter, a sloop captain, was the most important, obtained a charter for the Kennebec Steam Navigation Company. This concern, with a capitalization of two hundred shares of no par value, was granted a fourteen-year monopoly of steam navigation on the Kennebec River if during the more clement months of the year it ran a vessel three times a week between Bath and Augusta and twice a

[57] William Bentley, *The Diary of William Bentley, D.D. Pastor of the East Church, Salem, Massachusetts* (Salem: The Essex Institute, 1914), IV, 405, 457–462, 467–468, 547; Francis B. C. Bradlee, "Some Account of Steam Navigation in New England," *Historical Collections of the Essex Institute*, LV (1919), 1–12.

[58] Bradlee, "Some Account of Steam Navigation in New England," pp. 13–18, 24–25, 115–117, 124; Portland *Press*, November 9, 1863.

week between Augusta and Waterville.[59] The following year, in connection with this privilege, the proprietors placed on the run between Boston and Bath by way of Portland the first of a succession of second-hand boats, the *Patent*. This vessel of two hundred tons, already tried out around New York and the victim of a boiler explosion, could make the trip between Boston and Portland, a distance of 110 miles, in 17½ hours against a head wind. Later, assisted by Boston capital, the company extended its services along the Maine coast as far as St. John, New Brunswick. Although this corporate experiment wound up its affairs in 1828, the Porter family maintained a privately-owned steamboat service to Portland and the Kennebec and continued to try other ports. The roster of their vessels, some of which they purchased from competitors, reads like a graveyard of steam navigation on Long Island Sound. The *Connecticut*, the partner of the *Fulton* in the first line to New Haven and Providence, and the *Chancellor Livingston* and the *Charter Oak* were all hand-me-downs from southern New England. When the Cumberland Steam Navigation Company, in which the Porters were again the leaders, in 1834 built the *Portland*, the first of that name, for the Boston-Portland run, even she was powered by the engine of the former *Chancellor Livingston*.[60] About the same time Boston capitalists built for the Bangor travel the first completely new boat, the *Bangor*, ever to come to the Maine coast. She was too novel. After a brief service she sailed to the Mediterranean where she lived out her span flying the Turkish flag.[61] By the mid-thirties this chaotic period of experiment and promotion was quieting down; the owners of the various lines composed their quarrels, and reduced steam navigation down East to a temporarily stable system. Portland was its center. Between that city and Boston there were daily overnight sailings; at Portland connections were made for Bath and other Kennebec

[59] *Private or Special Laws of the State of Maine from 1820 to 1828 Inclusive,* I, 167–171.

[60] Morrison, *History of American Steam Navigation,* pp. 386–389; Bradlee, "Some Account of Steam Navigation in New England," pp. 117–188, 257, 264–265.

[61] *History of the Boston & Bangor Steamship Co. Formerly Known as Sanford's Independent Line, (1823–1882)* (Boston: T. R. Marvin & Son, 1882), pp. 11–12.

River ports, for Bangor, for Eastport and St. John. The Boston-Portland fare, once $5.00, now dropped to $3.00, and the Boston-Bangor rate was $7.00.[62]

VI

Separated from the East by mountains, western New England naturally directed its travel and trade to the Hudson River and Lake Champlain. For waterborne traffic both were magnificent. Except when it was frozen during the winter, a period that ranged within the decade 1825–1835 from 50 to 125 days, the Hudson was navigable 157 miles from its mouth.[63] Though at its southern extremity Lake Champlain might degenerate into a sluggish stream bordered by lowlands fit only "to produce fever and ague" and its northern end shoal into marshes, most of its 126 miles was superbly navigable. Indeed, at its widest part the scene was "so similar to Long Island Sound" that Benjamin Silliman could hardly persuade himself "that it was fresh water." [64] Still the Lake, in the variety and extent of its commerce, could not be compared to the Hudson. At the latter's mouth stood the metropolis of the nation; an array of ports, Peekskill, Newburgh, Poughkeepsie, and Kingston, stretched along the lower river; above the village of Hudson, "ship navigation" was impossible but sloops, in spite of rapids and silted channels, continued on to Albany and Troy near which a dam built some distance into the stream extended navigation in some seasons a few miles farther to the villages of Waterford on the west and Lansingburgh on the east bank. While all these places had civic ambitions, Albany and Troy, but six miles apart, strove most desperately to engross each other's commerce, including that of New England, and carried their rivalry to the pitch of fanaticism. A New Yorker wrote of the citizens of Troy, "No matter where they come from, or what have been their previous habits, the moment they become resi-

---

[62] *Badger and Porter's Stage Register* [1836], p. 28.

[63] *Hunt's Merchants' Magazine and Commercial Review*, II (1840), 346; Thomas F. Gordon, *Gazetteer of the State of New York. . . . with a Map of the State, and a Map of Each County* (Philadelphia: T. K. and P. G. Collins, 1836), p. 646.

[64] Silliman, *Remarks Made, on a Short Tour*, pp. 180, 188, 189.

dents of this place they are *Trojans*. They not only look well to
their own individual interests, but imbibe the same spirit of
enterprise which they find prevailing, and unite as one man in
sustaining the interests, and advancing the prosperity of Troy.
It is, in fact, a sort of community by itself — like Lubec, or
Hamburg, or any other of the free cities of the ancient Hanseatic
league — belonging to the Confederacy, it is true — but always
minding the main chance for itself." The same could be written of
the citizens of Albany, the Albanians. Though Trojans and Albanians bickered over the merits of menus in their respective ho-
tels and over the size of their respective female academies, they
buckled down with greatest zeal to the battle for manufacturing
and commercial supremacy.[65] No matter how "traditionally" the
trade of the north and east belonged to Troy, Albany envied and
craved it; no matter what superiority Albany possessed in the
trade to the west, Troy manifested a "disposition . . . to monop-
olize the whole." [66]

At the wharves of the two cities the clustered masts of sailing
vessels showed that in the twenties sail was still commercially
more important than steam. Sailing vessels handled the business
along the Hudson and to New York. Similar vessels, many New
England owned, distributed products from Albany and Troy
along the New England coast and returned with West Indian
goods, manufactured articles, and fish. There was a packet line
of four boats running at regular intervals to Boston, and the
freight commerce was so immense that it became a prize sought
for by the first railroad across New England. Rates to Boston
averaged $3.00 a ton, including the insurance; the New York
freights ran from $1.50 to $2.00.[67] Nevertheless, like all sailboat
navigation, that of the Hudson was unsatisfactory. Head winds
particularly in the Highlands were often severe and the extended
calms compelled the impatient resort to rowing and kedging.

[65] Arthur J. Weise, *Troy's One Hundred Years, 1789–1889* (Troy: William H.
Young, 1891), pp. 134, 143.
[66] Albany *Argus*, May 10, 1825.
[67] Albany *Advertiser*, October 13, 1824; Report of the Commissioners Appointed
under the Act of April 15, 1828 Relative to the Construction of a Railroad from
Boston to the Hudson River, New York *Senate Documents*, 1829, no. 113, ap-
pendices.

With good luck a round trip to New York might take four days, with bad luck much more. In 1800 a traveler to Albany took four days for the trip; his fare was $2.00 and he spent an additional $4.50 for "board and liquors." [68]

The dramatic introduction of the steamboat upon the Hudson *steam + canal* River needs no repetition; the monopoly grant of the waters of New York State to its successful promoter, Robert R. Livingston, and inventor, Robert Fulton, does. The privileges, first bestowed in 1803, were subsequently altered by the legislature to a monopoly of five years for each boat that the grantees put in service, with the total grant of exclusive privilege not exceeding thirty years. After some hesitation, the monopolists decided to enforce their legal rights against interlopers and they and their heirs succeeded in controlling the Hudson until 1824, the year of Gibbons v. Ogden. In spite of their protected position they made continued advances in the construction of vessels and marine machinery. The original steamboat was practically rebuilt within a year. The *Chancellor Livingston* of 1816, later on the Sound and down-East runs, their pride, was 157 feet long and afforded the luxury of cabins and saloons. Although subsequently the running time of the New York-Albany trip was greatly reduced from the thirty or so hours of the early days, the fares apparently stood level for some years at the $7.00 charged for the original voyage. The passing of the monopoly wrought a change. Opposition lines at once put boats upon the river and, in spite of temporary combinations, spasms of feverish competition shook such arrangements to pieces. By 1827 the fare had been reduced to $2.00. [69]

Meanwhile navigation on Lake Champlain completed its pioneer age. Sloop building began after the Revolution. Fortunately an emigrant from Norwich, Connecticut, a sea-faring man, gave

[68] Balthasar H. Meyer, *History of Transportation in the United States before 1860* (Washington: Carnegie Institution, 1917), p. 76; Weise, *Troy's One Hundred Years*, pp. 87–88.

[69] H. W. Dickinson, *Robert Fulton, Engineer and Artist, His Life and Works* (London: John Lane, 1913), pp. 215–254; Lane, *Commodore Vanderbilt*, pp. 52–60; *Hunt's Merchants' Magazine and Commercial Review*, XXV (1851), 243; *ibid.*, XXXII (1855), 506–507; Morrison, *History of American Steam Navigation*, pp. 19–54.

the first vessels the improved lines of the New London sloops. The most extensive owner and financier was, however, a Burlington merchant, Gideon King, whose operations became so extensive as to win for himself the title, "the admiral of the Lake." When the era of steam arrived, the Hudson was the nursery of steamboat building on Champlain. Inspired by the success of the *Clermont*, two Burlington men in 1808 built and launched the *Vermont:* the next year she began operations. She had the lines of a large canal boat and was powered by a second-hand engine, the connecting rod of which finally tore loose, punctured a hole in the hold, and sank her. In 1813 a group of Vermont enterprisers, in alliance with Albany capitalists, chartered in New York State the Lake Champlain Steamboat Company. They brought from the Hudson the engine of a dismantled vessel that Fulton and Livingston had run off the river and employed Jehaziel Sherman, born in Dartmouth, Massachusetts, and a captain of sailing and steam packets at Troy, to build the hold in which to place it. The *Phoenix*, launched in 1815, was well named, for a few years later she burned to the water's edge in a lake tragedy, the remembrance of which long filled travelers with apprehension. Fittingly enough, her salvaged engine was placed in a second *Phoenix*.[70] These, as well as later vessels, traversed with frequent stops the distance from Whitehall, a "thriving little place," to St. Johns, Quebec, "whose appearance is generally . . . mean, dirty, and disagreeable." Fortunately the traveler did not need to stay there, for stages owned by enterprising Americans whisked him across the miles to the St. Lawrence opposite Montreal.[71] In 1826 Vermonters incorporated the Champlain Transportation Company and employed Sherman to build them a vessel embodying the latest improvements of their Hudson River contemporaries. Within a decade all the steam-driven vessels of the Lake were in the company's possession.[72]

[70] Thomas H. Canfield, "Discovery, Navigation, and Navigators of Lake Champlain," A. M. Hemenway, ed., *The Vermont Historical Gazetteer: A Magazine Embracing a History of Each Town, Civil, Ecclesiastical, Biographical, and Military* (Burlington: A. M. Hemenway, 1867), I, 668–670, 686–693.

[71] Silliman, *Remarks Made, on a Short Tour*, pp. 170–191; Eldridge, "Journal of a Tour," pp. 74–75.

[72] *Badger and Porter's State Register* [1836], p. 29.

Undoubtedly the stimulus to this greater and successful corporation was the completion of the Champlain Canal; but even before this artificial waterway had wedded Champlain with the Hudson, the flow of traffic on the Lake had shifted from its natural northern outlet, the Richelieu River, toward the south. The change, begun during the War of 1812, accelerated when shipbuilders and merchants located their shipyards or agencies at Whitehall. "Admiral" King established a branch house there and, by arrangement with R. P. Hart, a great wagoner of Troy, shipped goods over the roads to the latter city and distributed the return cargoes. Such arrangements, however, could accomplish little against the physical handicaps of the area. Freight shipments from St. Albans at the head of the lake in Vermont to New York City took twenty-five to thirty days and the charge per ton was from $25 to $30.[73] But personal travel was much quickened by the new facilities. Benjamin Silliman, proceeding by private coach and by steamer reached Montreal from Hartford in ten days. He commented, "Such is the expedition of public vehicles, that this distance *may* be travelled in three days." [74]

[73] Canfield, "Discovery, Navigation, and Navigators of Lake Champlain," p. 681; Albany *Argus*, September 9, 1823.
[74] Silliman, *Remarks Made, on a Short Tour*, p. 191.

II

HIGHWAYS AND THEIR HERITAGE

"Facilities to husbandry, commerce, and manufactures are good roads. Most of our great ones are now in such convenient and unalterable directions, as will probably command an increasing travel for centuries to come. Would not a law protecting and encouraging to individuals to border them with trees give ornament to the country, comfort and refreshment to the traveller, fuel to the planters and gratification to all?" Levi Lincoln, Message of Lieutenant-Governor, January 26, 1809, Resolves of the General Court of the Commonwealth of Massachusetts . . . May, 1806 . . . March, 1810. p. 230.

I

Every important port in New England was a ganglia of roads. Take the places served by river navigation. Along the Hudson, Poughkeepsie and Hudson had roads running eastward to tap the commerce of western Connecticut and Massachusetts and at Troy "the liberal enterprise of the inhabitants is in no subject more conspicuous than in their roads." One reached northward toward Lake Champlain; a second led southeast into Massachusetts and by extensions to the cities of Connecticut; a third, the Troy Macadam and Railroad "paved on the Macadams plan," ran northeast over "fine stone bridges" to southwestern Vermont.[1] On the Connecticut, Hartford sat astride three routes between Boston and New York, and from it radiated two routes

[1] Thomas F. Gordon, *Gazetteer of the State of New York . . . . with a Map of the State, and a Map of Each County* (Philadelphia: T. K. and P. G. Collins,

to Albany, one to Hudson, two northward along the Connecticut, three to New Haven, and others to Providence, Norwich, and Danbury.[2] Even Newbury, Vermont, on the upper river was a focus of highways. Finally, to Concord on the Merrimack drained down the commerce of northern New Hampshire and northeastern Vermont to seek further transportation Bostonward by river and canal or by highway.[3] The ports of the seacoast, Portsmouth, Boston, Providence, Norwich, and New Haven, repeated the pattern.

Although roads were thus usually supplements to waterways, they were frequently rivals to them. Steam navigation, for instance, could not compete with the turnpike between Salem and Boston; roads from New Bedford, Taunton, and Newport to Boston encroached upon the sailing commerce around Cape Cod; pikes from Hartford to Norwich and to New Haven shortened routes once involving a journey down the Connecticut and east or west on Long Island Sound; and hill roads connecting Boston and Vermont across New Hampshire were the shortened bowstring of a long curve of water transportation along the Connecticut, Long Island Sound, around Cape Cod into Massachusetts Bay. Furthermore Boston's roads led along the shore to Plymouth and down East as far as Passamaquoddy. Of these independent routes, however, the most important were the three trunk roads connecting Boston and New York. All shared a common route between New York and New Haven; from the latter place the lower post road continued along the shore, then crossed through Providence to Boston, and the middle and upper post roads turned northward to Hartford, whence they proceeded either through northeastern Connecticut or by way of Springfield and Worcester to the Massachusetts capital.[4]

1836), p. 649; Report of Albert Gallatin on Roads and Canals, April 4, 1808, *American State Papers*, Miscellaneous, I, 876.

[2] John C. Pease and John M. Niles, *A Gazetteer of the States of Connecticut and Rhode-Island* (Hartford: William S. Marsh, 1819), p. 41.

[3] Henry McFarland, "Canals, Stage Lines, and Taverns," James O. Lyford, ed., *History of Concord, New Hampshire, from the Original Grant in Seventeen Hundred and Twenty-five to the Opening of the Twentieth Century* (Concord: Rumford Press, 1903), II, 833.

[4] Nathanael Low, *An Astronomical Diary or Almanack . . . 1787* (Boston:

Government built a part of the skeletal system of land transportation. In early days the general court or legislature often planned the inter-town public or common roads and the practice persisted into the nineteenth century on the New England frontier where pioneer conditions perpetuated colonial institutions. Thus the legislatures of Maine and Massachusetts attempted to build roads into the Maine wilderness where the public lands of the two states lay, and those of Vermont and New Hampshire interested themselves in providing roads through their comparatively unsettled northern areas. They authorized committees or individuals to lay out roads, construct them, and raise the necessary funds by town taxes, taxes upon lands, or by lotteries.[5] For less exceptional circumstances, however, state legislation had mixed from different ingredients a statutory recipe for road-making. The construction of new roads and the alteration of old ones was to be effected by petitions, town selectmen, county courts, state courts, and commissions or committees of "disinterested freeholders."

Although in this welter it is difficult to distinguish the place of responsibility for planning a road system or indeed any single road, the judiciary was by and large the core of the process. The reason for this arrangement lies probably in the fact that the construction of roads involved the taking of private property for public purposes, or, as the awed phrase of Governor Levi Lincoln of Massachusetts put it, because the government "can divest the freeholder of his possessions, and create an easement for the public, out of his absolute fee."[6] The first step was a petition to the selectmen if a town way were to be made or altered; to the county court if a highway "over land in two or more towns in the same county or in different counties" were involved or if the selectmen of the town refused to deal with the request for a new

---

T. & J. Fleet, n.d.) ; *Low's Almanack and Astronomical and Agricultural Register for . . . 1818* (Boston: Munroe & Francis, n.d.).

[5] Maine *Annual Report of the Land Agent, 1834,* pp. 11–13; *ibid., 1840,* pp. 39–62; *Laws of New Hampshire Including Public and Private Acts, Resolves, Votes, Etc. Second Constitutional Period, 1801–1811,* VII, 75–76, 596, 892–893.

[6] Levi Lincoln, Governor's Message, January 3, 1827, *Resolves of the General Court of the Commonwealth of Massachusetts . . . May, 1824, to . . . May, 1828,* p. 446.

or improved town road. In New Hampshire and Vermont, roads in two or more counties became a concern of the supreme court. The courts, usually through a committee or commission of disinterested freemen, proceeded to inquire into the "convenience or necessity" of the road, laid out the route, and estimated the damages landowners were entitled to recover. There were ample provisions for appeal to juries or commissions. The towns were to pay these damages, build the roads, providing both the funds and the supervision, in the persons of their superintendents of roads, and keep the roads in repair. Even on paper, it would be hard to imagine a more effective arrangement for accumulating administrative recalcitrancies. The many provisions in the acts for fining the towns because they ignored or grudgingly and tardily fulfilled the obligations imposed upon them reveal the functional weakness of the method.[7]

These difficulties were not due solely to the shortsightedness or indifference of many towns when through roads were at issue. More commonly the inadequacy of tax resources or the unwillingness to press existing resources heavily, in short, economic and political considerations, frustrated advance. In the nineteenth century the starkness of these considerations was most clearly revealed on the New England frontier where a town's highway taxes continued to be thought of in terms of labor. While this equivalence, once universal, had been modified or abandoned in more populous and prosperous regions,[8] Vermont until the middle twenties laid a minimum tax of four days in labor upon all male

[7] *Acts and Resolves of Massachusetts, 1786–1787*, pp. 203–206; *The Public Statute Laws of the State of Connecticut as Revised and Enacted by the General Assembly in May 1821 . . .*, pp. 269–273; *Laws of the State of Maine to Which Are Prefixed the Constitution of the United States* [1830], pp. 406–412; *The Laws of Vermont of a Publick and Permanent Nature: Coming Down to, and Including, the Year 1824*, pp. 427–437, 443–445; *Laws of New Hampshire Including the Public and Private Acts, Resolves, Votes, Etc. First Constitutional Period, 1784–1792*, V, 577–578.

[8] *The Public Statute Laws of the State of Connecticut as Revised and Enacted by the General Assembly in May 1821*, p. 273 note; *Laws of the State of Maine to Which are Prefixed the Constitution of the United States* [1830], pp. 411–412; *Laws of New Hampshire Including the Public and Private Acts, Resolves, Votes, Etc. Second Constitutional Period, 1821–1828*, IX, 248; Jarvis M. Morse, *A Neglected Period of Connecticut's History, 1818–1850* (New Haven: Yale University Press, 1933), p. 258.

inhabitants over twenty-one and under sixty. Ministers of the gospel, the president, professors, tutors and residents of colleges, and schoolmasters did not have to work out the tax; all others with their tools, oxen, teams, and wagons, as the surveyor of roads might direct, were part-time road makers. Successive acts set hourly wage rates for taxes and arranged that their fulfillment in hours of labor should not take place during the haying season. Later Vermont provided for a town highway tax proportioned to the value of property and spurred a transition to a money economy by permitting those, who elected to pay it in cash, a 25 per-cent reduction.[9]

Even if the legal basis for road development had been simple, straitened agricultural communities and local superintendents of roads possessed neither the means nor the information fundamental to the construction of good roads. Workers used shovel, spade, and hoe; taxpayers or contractors provided ox team and wagon; and towns might purchase "an ax-shovel, or scrape, well ironed." [10] Then they went to work. In the mid-thirties on the through road between Albany and Northhampton, Patrick Shirreff, acquainted with the methods of English road-making, saw exemplified the indigenous New England school of "road-mending, or more correctly speaking, road-destroying. A plough drawn by four and occasionally six oxen, with two drivers, one man holding by the stilts, and another standing on the beam, is passed along the margins of the road, turning every fifty yards. The loosened earth is then moved to the centre of the road, by men with shovels, or by a levelling-box drawn by oxen, the stones, great and small, being first carefully removed from the earth, and in many instances more were thrown aside than sufficient to Macadamize the road." [11] Little wonder that the roads were often, in a legal phrase of the day, "miry, foundrous, ruinous,

<hr>

[9] *The Laws of Vermont of a Publick and Permanent Nature . . . 1824*, pp. 429–430, 435–436, 437, 444–445; *The Revised Statutes of the State of Vermont, Passed November 19, 1839*, pp. 135–136.

[10] *The Laws of Vermont of a Publick and Permanent Nature*, p. 437.

[11] Patrick Shirreff, *A Tour through North America; together with a Comprehensive View of the Canadas and United States. As Adapted for Agricultural Emigration* (Edinburgh: Oliver and Boyd, 1835), p. 37.

and unsafe." [12] Little wonder that in many parts of New England winter rather than hampering, expedited land traffic. When a deep blanket of snow buried roughness, sandwallows, and quagmires alike, long lines of sleighs and pungs, loaded with country produce, drove to markets unreachable before and returned with the necessities and luxuries of store goods. Only in the neighborhood of the larger cities were financial resources and community interest sufficient to support the construction and maintenance of adequate public roads.

II

Meanwhile the New England states had turned to another method of road construction and maintenance in the hope that it would overcome the division of authority, the inadequacy of public finance, and the amateurism of road labor and engineering responsible for the region's generally poor roads. The demand for their improvement grew wider and more insistent as interior towns multiplied in number and in population. Apparently Great Britain had shown the way through the dilemma by a series of turnpike acts. That the users of the highways were to furnish the funds for their improvement and maintenance was the fundamental concept of this legislation; it sought this objective by establishing trusts which were to borrow money on the security of future tolls, use the funds to improve and maintain the road, and, after they had recouped their expenditures, to surrender the road to the public. At least such was the theory.[13] New England adopted the conception of user-support; it did not imitate the institution of a trust. Instead the states chartered private corporations to build turnpikes and maintain them; the hope of profit or of indirect financial gain was relied upon to induce private capital to make these investments.

The turnpike era began. The period of most active construc-

---

[12] Asaph Rice et al. *v.* The Commissioners of Highways of Middlesex, 30 *Massachusetts* (13 *Pickering*), 225.

[13] Edwin A. Pratt, *A History of Inland Transport and Communication in England* (New York: E. P. Dutton and Company, 1912), pp. 77–84.

tion, though not of greatest usefulness, was the turn of the century; in the decade, 1797–1806, New England states chartered 135 turnpike corporations with a mileage of 2,547. A few years later the network was virtually complete. In 1838 its mileage approximated 3,764; its conjectured total cost was $6,500,000.[14] It is now impossible to assay the extent to which these turnpikes supplanted the public roads. For the latter no mileage figures exist, and information on their location and history is fragmentary. Clearly, however, a mixed system emerged. On the routes between Boston and New York the traveler could proceed by turnpikes all the way from Boston to New Haven whether he went by way of the Worcester pike and its various extensions through Connecticut or elected the middle post road composed of the Norfolk and Bristol, the Hartford and Dedham, the North Massachusetts, and the Boston turnpikes, the last terminating at Hartford. But considerable portions of the road along the Sound were unvexed by toll gates; from Saybrook to New Haven and from Milford to Fairfield public highways carried the traffic of the old Boston post road. In terms of commerce the public roads often carried more than the turnpikes. Thus the old road — a public one — between Boston and Worcester had three times as much traffic as the Worcester turnpike, a fact esteemed "remarkable since the turnpike is two or three miles shorter."[15]

In northern New England, while Maine was hardly touched by the turnpike craze, Vermont and New Hampshire each had a considerable mileage. In general their pikes were feeders for waterways. In Vermont, in spite of some cross-state lines, the new "artificial roads" generally ran to Lake Champlain or the Connecticut; in New Hampshire, the Connecticut was the magnet that drew them. From these upper roads and the Connecticut River, however, a series of turnpikes cut diagonally, northwest to southeast, across New Hampshire to the Massachusetts state line, where they connected with the thoroughfares of that Com-

---

[14] P. E. Taylor, "The Turnpike Era in New England," Ms., Thesis, Yale University Library, pp. 208, 210, 220.

[15] *Ibid.*, p. 218; *Report of the Directors of the Boston and Worcester Rail-Road Corporation to the Stockholders, with the Report of John M. Fessenden, Esq.* (Boston: W. L. Lewis, 1832), pp. 16–17.

monwealth.[16] Even in Massachusetts the turnpike system was at first auxiliary to waterways. The first eight turnpikes were all located in the western part of the state. With perhaps one exception, they were clearly designed to connect the hill towns of the eastern plateau or the Berkshires with the rivers or to improve transportation for the area in which the Connecticut and the Hudson valleys were the main channels of communication and commerce. At a later period, however, a series of turnpikes, all heavily capitalized and constructed in an improved fashion, were built around Boston. To the north the pikes to Salem and to Newburyport were the most important, the Worcester turnpike led directly westward to a town from which radiated a series of improved roads, and the Norfolk and Bristol applied big business enterprise to the route to Providence.[17] In Connecticut no dominant city like Boston imposed a pattern upon the turnpike network. Instead, a multitude of equal rivals — New Haven, Norwich, New London, Hartford, and Bridgeport — spread their overlapping webs toward each other and toward Providence, Worcester, Boston, Troy, and New York. Not single enterprises but end-to-end routes attained these ultimate destinations. The most important turnpike in the state was the Hartford and New Haven.[18]

Although by twentieth-century standards turnpikes were crude roads, they represented some technical advance over their predecessors. Except in the back country of Vermont, New Hampshire, and Massachusetts, they were two-way thoroughfares. Thomas Dwight, whose experience in the First Massachusetts was the basis of his valuable letter of advice to the incorporators of the Norfolk and Bristol, thought twenty feet a desirable width; Massachusetts by law in 1805 required the "travelled part" to be twenty-four.[19] Most of them were unusually straight. Thus

[16] Frederic J. Wood, *The Turnpikes of New England and Evolution of the Same Through England, Virginia, and Maryland* (Boston: Marshall Jones Company, 1919), p. 211, map opposite p. 215.

[17] *Ibid.*, pp. 63–75, 80–100, 123–127, 160–166.

[18] *Ibid.*, pp. 331 (map), 349–351.

[19] Thomas Dwight to Phillip Ammidon, March 10, 1800, Ms., Norfolk and Bristol Papers, Dedham Historical Society; *Acts and Resolves of the Commonwealth of Massachusetts, 1804–1805*, p. 185.

they shortened the distance between termini and competed successfully with the public roads which had often evolved from mere local meanderings between houses, fields, and villages. In the days of oxen and horseflesh, a mile was a stern measure of effort and time. To locate a road like the Newburyport turnpike which deviated only eighty-three feet from a straight line in thirty-two miles with the surveying instruments then available was an engineering accomplishment of a high order.[20] To charge across a succession of ridges, ignoring villages to the right and left, in order to connect two places between which communication by sea was considerable, was not, however, business prudence. The turnpike era, therefore, has frequently been indicted with making straightness a fetish. The accusation is unjust. The road engineers of the day were also grade-conscious. With great elaboration they calculated the savings in horsepower and gains in loads secured on roads with proper grades. Sometimes they stopped there. The Connecticut correspondent of Secretary Gallatin informed him that in the state "an opinion has prevailed . . . that no ascent greater than five degrees should be allowed. Nothing, however, is more certain than that no such principle has been adhered to." [21]

In general the turnpikes were not hard-surfaced. At the time neither McAdam nor Telford had developed and publicized his system. The road makers of New England were content to avoid muddiness, rutting, scouring, and road erosion by proper drainage. They gave the surface of the road a convex surface to shed the water; on steep hills a succession of low earth ridges across the road, thank-you-marms, diverted the menacing rivulets to the edge; and ditches parallel to the road led the water away. A few artificial roads were more than highways of crowned natural earth. The Salem turnpike, "a bold project" since it crossed a salt marsh four miles wide on an ingenious causeway of branches, earth, and sods, was graveled, the Newburyport turnpike had ten inches of gravel, and the Norfolk and Bristol was hard-sur-

---

[20] Wood, *The Turnpikes of New England*, pp. 15, 38; Taylor, "The Turnpike Era," p. 170.

[21] *American State Papers*, Miscellaneous, I, 869–870.

faced. Some of the larger turnpikes also built the bridges on their routes rather than resorting to toll companies.[22] Under such circumstances the costs of construction were impressive. The Salem cost $14,600 a mile, but William Bentley, the erudite dominie of that city, was still certain "the compensation will be sure." The Newburyport spent $11,730. Probably the average for Massachusetts was $4,500. In Connecticut the expenditures were less. Since most of them simply improved existing roads, they avoided heavy expenditures for rights of way and no Connecticut turnpike was graveled. Even the Hartford and New Haven, Connecticut's lordliest turnpike, which owned its bridges, bought a new right of way, and landscaped its route, cost only $2,280 a mile. In fact the costs in Connecticut were lower than in the back-country of Vermont and New Hampshire.[23]

III

Though as avenues of travel and commerce the day of the turnpikes was soon done, they introduced business innovations of profound influence upon the later railroad history of New England. For, like the railroad, turnpikes were incorporated by the state. In 1805 Massachusetts established a general law under which turnpike concerns secured charters; Maine, when it gained its independence in 1820, passed a similar measure; every other state granted incorporation by special enactment.[24] In each case the English turnpike acts, with the reservation already noted, set the pattern of details.

Although Connecticut under certain conditions exempted turnpike stock from taxation, the most important privilege granted by every state to these corporations was that of taking land for a right of way on the payment of suitable damages. As in the case of public roads this privilege was exercised under the super-

[22] Taylor, "The Turnpike Era," pp. 175–178; William Bentley, *The Diary of William Bentley, D.D., Pastor of the East Church, Salem, Massachusetts* (Salem: The Essex Institute, 1914), III, 31.

[23] Taylor, "The Turnpike Era," pp. 185–190, 210, appendix V; Bentley, *Diary*, III, 46.

[24] *Acts and Resolves of the Commonwealth of Massachusetts, 1804–1805*, pp. 184–190; *Laws of the State of Maine; to Which are Prefixed the Constitution of the United States, . . .* [1830], pp. 477–484.

vision of county courts or committees or commissioners appointed by them. Such restraints, however, did not quiet the popular criticism that for a private corporation to possess the right of eminent domain was tyranny and for the legislature to transfer a public road to a turnpike company for improvement was unjustifiable favoritism. The state legislature customarily decided the issue of public convenience or necessity.[25] The legislature also set the tolls either by charter or by general legislation. The Massachusetts general act of 1805 erased previous variants based upon the length of the road, the cost of construction, and the estimated traffic in favor of a systematized structure common to all roads. The tolls, displayed publicly at each gate, would read, therefore, somewhat as follows:

Coach, chariot, phaeton, or other four-wheel spring carriage
  drawn by two horses (additional horses 2¢ a piece) ...... 25¢
Wagons drawn by two horses (additional horses 2¢ a piece) 10
Cart or wagon drawn by two oxen 10
Curricle 15
Chaise, chair, sulky, or other carriage for pleasure drawn by
  one horse 12½
Cart, wagon, or truck drawn by one horse 6¼
Man and horse 4
Sleigh or sled drawn by two horses or oxen (additional oxen
  or horses 1¢ a piece) 8
Sleigh or sled drawn by one horse 4
Horses, mules, or neat cattle, led or driven, each 1
Sheep or swine by the dozen 3

Carts or waggons having wheels, the fellies [sic] of which shall be Six Inches broad or more, shall be subject to pay only half the toll which carts or waggons otherwise constructed, shall be liable to pay.

Such tolls were collected at gates usually placed at ten-mile intervals along the road.[26] The schedule revealed certain crude principles of rate making. The legislature made little effort to discriminate between commodities unless it be in the matter of livestock; it favored vehicles with broad tires since narrow ones cut the road's

[25] Taylor, "The Turnpike Era," p. 105; *Acts and Resolves . . . of Massachusetts, 1804–1805*, pp. 184-185.
[26] *Acts and Resolves . . . of Massachusetts, 1804–1805*, pp. 185–186.

surface; and it gave a generous preference to commerce over travel. Freight carriers and carts were charged less than passenger vehicles, two-wheeled pleasure vehicles less than coaches, chariots, and phaetons. Exemptions modified these rigidities. The Massachusetts act of 1805 forbade the collection of tolls from persons going to or from a church or a grist mill, on military duty or on journeys within the town where the gate was located, or "on the common and ordinary business of family concerns," [27] — the last proviso, of course, arousing contentious interpretation. Turnpike corporations were also authorized to give rebates by commuting toll payments to a fixed sum.[28] Stagecoach companies often used this arrangement for their vehicles, and individuals did so for their business and pleasure. Occasionally romance as well as calculation tinged such adjustments. A Vermont toll bridge, presumably a soulless corporation, compounded with a certain "Mr. Carlos Coolidge to pass the Bridge one year for $3, pleasure passing only and to have a lady with him if he pleases." [29]

Somewhat doubtful, apparently, whether the balance of privileges and obligations in turnpike charters or general enactments would neatly work out to the public interest, the state asserted its right to repossess such enterprises. In Massachusetts, for instance, the legislature could exercise this power at any time after twenty years "if it shall appear to their satisfaction that the income of said road shall have compensated such Corporation for all money they may have expended in purchasing lands for said road, and in making, repairing, and taking care of the same, together with twelve percentum by the year." [30] Other New England states had similar provisions although Connecticut in 1807 reduced the return to 8 per cent.[31] In order to enforce this right the states required the turnpikes to keep books subject to inspection by state officials and to submit a statement

---

[27] *Ibid.*, pp. 186–187.
[28] *Ibid.*, p. 187; Taylor, "The Turnpike Era," p. 143.
[29] Harold F. Wilson, "The Roads of Windsor," *Geographical Review*, XXI (1931), 382.
[30] *Acts and Resolves . . . of Massachusetts, 1804–1805*, p. 188.
[31] Taylor, "The Turnpike Era," p. 149.

of their costs of construction and annual reports of their receipts and disbursements. These reports, unfortunately for the historian, were not filed but simply "exhibited" to the proper authorities.[32]

Before the turnpike era, banks had been the most important private corporations issuing securities; now the turnpike companies surpassed them. They never utilized bonds and preferred stock; common stock was their only issue. Legislative provisions regulating its issuance occasionally set a value for each share or a limit to the total capitalization of the common stock. The most usual procedure was to state the number of shares and authorize the directors to lay assessments until they collected enough money for the construction of the road.[33] In a day of imperfect engineering estimates, this arrangement gave flexibility. Besides, it introduced the convenient device of installment purchasing. There was considerable debate among turnpike promoters, however, over the relative advantages of a limited stock issue, heavily assessed, or a large issue with moderate assessments. Thomas Dwight felt that the small down payment and small assessments brought into the company "very little men of very little minds." [34] At corporation expense, these came to its meetings and contributed nothing but obstruction. In Massachusetts the greater turnpikes generally avoided this outcome. The Newburyport turnpike issued 995 shares upon each of which the many assessments of $20 eventually totaled $420. In Connecticut, on the other hand, the Hartford and New Haven turnpike was financed by 800 shares of $100 each.[35]

Although the ownership of stock might be considerably dispersed among small capitalists along the route, the largest blocks were generally in a few hands. Of the 800 shares in the Hartford and New Haven, Oliver Ellsworth and James Hillhouse each owned 150 shares. In later years when this road was threatened by the railroad, the incorporators pictured it to the legislature

[32] *Acts and Resolves . . . of Massachusetts, 1804–1805*, pp. 187–188.
[33] Taylor, "The Turnpike Era," pp. 156–157.
[34] Thomas Dwight to Phillip Ammidon, March 10, 1800, Norfolk and Bristol Papers.
[35] Taylor, "The Turnpike Era," pp. 162–163.

as owned by widows and orphans and persons of moderate means; actually 80 per cent of the stock was held by twelve of the forty-two owners. In view of their larger prices — the stock of the Norfolk and Bristol, for example, cost $1,000 and had a down payment of $200 — only wealthy men could afford to invest in the stock of the turnpikes around Boston. The smaller companies and those in the rural regions were more democratically owned and controlled. Where there were large investors, they were merchants, landed grandees or men with inherited wealth. Generally they invested in only one undertaking; interlocking stock ownership and interlocking directors were virtually unknown. In any case private funds were sufficient in New England to build the turnpike network. No state made financial contributions.[36]

Though individual corporations in some cases continued to function into the next century, the turnpike era reached full tide in the twenties and early thirties. After that promoters and investors embarked upon a limited number of new undertakings. Owners of established turnpike corporations petitioned legislatures to release them from their obligations, or negotiated with the county authorities to transform their turnpikes into public roads, or, indifferent to further maintenance and operation, let the court order the gates thrown open. Years later, when the old collector at gate no. 1 of the Salem turnpike received orders to take no more tolls, he set down his last entry in rhyme:

"The last toll is taken, — I've swung wide the gate,
The word has been spoken, — We yield to our fate!" [37]

As for the cause of "fate," it was simple: the turnpikes did not make money. As a whole this was true; as a rule it was clear from the beginning. The Massachusetts correspondent of Albert Gallatin in 1809 wrote that the Neponset made 8 per cent, the Salem turnpike 6 per cent, the Newburyport 2 per cent, and "all the other turnpikes in the State will not, upon an average, yield

---

[36] *Ibid.*, pp. 100–101, 164–166, 312.
[37] Robert S. Rantoul, "Some Notes on Old Modes of Travel," *Historical Collections of the Essex Institute*, XI (1871), 37; Taylor, "The Turnpike Era," pp. 322–324; *The Revised Statutes of the Commonwealth of Massachusetts. Passed November 4, 1835*, pp. 337–338.

more than 3 per cent per annum, net income." [38] From Connecticut the Secretary of the Treasury learned that the Hartford and New Haven had averaged only 1 per cent above the ordinary cost of repairs in the four years since its opening.[39] Granted that population, agriculture, and industry had not at that time matured sufficiently to support the turnpikes with their commerce, this was still the period when turnpikes were new and did not require extensive maintenance. So the tendency to inadequate earnings, thus early marked, continued. In the forties, even the Salem turnpike went poor.[40] As was to be expected these disappointing profits were reflected in falling stock prices. That in the Newburyport turnpike fell to $63 in 1814 and in 1831 it sold for $10.50 a share. Eventually the investment in most turnpikes was a total loss.[41] If they could find any compensation, stockholders were driven either to calculating the indirect benefits which might have accrued to them as landowners whose acres had risen in value or as merchants whose commerce and transactions had been multiplied or stimulated; or they could brood over the more intangible satisfactions flowing from their display of a public spirit. It was an easy step to believe such had been the motives for their investment in the first place.

The calamity which buried the turnpikes was, in part, due to the competition of other means of transportation. Although the railroad finally gave them the *coup de grace*, it was not a rival when the turnpike business first came to a standstill. Nor were the waterways a fatal menace. On paper the latter had a visible superiority in cheaper rates. From Salem to Boston, water-borne goods paid 85 cents a ton, while overland carriage was $3.34; from Providence the comparable sums were $2.00 and $10.[42] Delivery times by sea or river were fairly satisfactory. Land

---

[38] *American State Papers*, Miscellaneous, I, 867.

[39] *Ibid.*, p. 871; Taylor, "The Turnpike Era," pp. 266, 275.

[40] Wood, *Turnpikes of New England*, pp. 82, 84.

[41] Taylor, "The Turnpike Era," pp. 274–275, 280.

[42] Senate Committee on Rail-ways and Canals, Report on an Eastern Rail-road, Massachusetts *Senate Documents*, 1836, no. 77, p. 2; *Report of the Board of Commissioners, of Internal Improvements in Relation to the Examination of Sundry Routes for a Railway from Boston to Providence* (Boston: Dutton & Wentworth, 1828), pp. 40, 44.

carriage, however, had the advantages of safety, regularity, and, above all, convenience. Goods could be carried from the door of the consignor to that of the consignee without the cost and bother of transhipment. When the agent of the Middlesex Canal and the improved navigation upon the Merrimack inquired in 1824 why shippers from the interior of New England sent their goods all the way to Boston by land rather than transhipping to water transport at Concord, New Hampshire, he discovered among other reasons:

> Land carriage is probably preferred:
> *First* — Because the teams take the goods to & fro from the warehouses in Boston without the expense of truckage —
> *Second* — There is almost a certainty as to the time of the teams' arrival. . . .
> *Fifth* — There is so much shifting of the goods necessary when sent by water, that if any damage arise, it is difficult to charge it upon the proper person —
> *Sixth* — The trader prefers paying the expense of land carriage (even if it is a little more) in his way, that is, out of his store, — to paying cash to the Boatsmen — [43]

In brief, published rates were not everything.

A renaissance in public road construction provided, however, a more formidable competitor to the turnpike. Massachusetts took the lead. Between 1808 and 1822, Middlesex county alone established 115 public roads.[44] From 1825 to 1835, the state itself passed a series of sweeping statutes simplifying the cumbersome procedure of road planning and providing a wider financial base for road construction. In every county the voters were to elect a board of three road commissioners to which were assigned most of the functions formerly exercised by county courts, committees, and commissioners in laying out, altering, improving, and repairing highways. Though the towns under the commissioners' order or direction were still to do the road work, the county treasurer was to pay the commissioners' expenses, all the land damages, and, for the construction and repair of the road,

[43] Christopher Roberts, *The Middlesex Canal, 1793–1860* (Cambridge: Harvard University Press, 1938), pp. 149–151.
[44] Taylor, "The Turnpike Era," p. 288.

"a sum not exceeding one half the expense" if the commissioners adjudged the road "to be of general use and importance to the public." [45] In the early thirties New Hampshire diffidently followed suit.[46] The novelty of these arrangements affrighted some persons. Even in Massachusetts, when they were adopted, Governor Lincoln was somewhat stunned. The duties of the county commissioners were "multifarious, arduous, and highly responsible. They present the anomaly of judicial, ministerial, and executive functions, united in the same official character." [47] But the pressure for new methods was irresistible. The popular distaste for turnpikes was partly a matter of democratic principles, partly a dislike of paying tolls, as the illegal detours or shun-pikes about the gates demonstrated, and partly the physical character of the roads. Typical is the petition to the Massachusetts General Court in 1823 which began: "In this age and in this land of liberty turnpike gates are everywhere considered a nuisance and vexatious to travellers, . . . as well as the turnpike roads themselves, which are generally the poorest roads over which the traveller passes from one part of the country to another." [48]

IV

Such an attitude might be understandable in contemporary conditions, but it lacked perspective and failed to acknowledge the contributions of the turnpikes to their day. Their mileage — and that of the improved public roads which were, in a way, their step-children — made possible overland commerce and travel on an enlarging scale. For personal use, horseback gave way to vehicles of varied style and comfort. In Connecticut between 1796 and 1812 the number of conveyances multiplied three

[45] *Laws of the Commonwealth of Massachusetts . . . 1825 to . . . 1828*, pp. 304–305, 718–724; *Laws of the Commonwealth of Massachusetts, . . .* [1835], pp. 545–550.

[46] *Laws of New Hampshire Including the Public and Private Acts, Resolves, Votes, etc. Second Constitutional Period, 1821–1828*, IX, 915–918; *ibid., 1829–1835*, X, 137–138, 276.

[47] Levi Lincoln, Governor's Message, January 3, 1827, *Resolves of the General Court of the Commonwealth of Massachusetts . . . May, 1824 to . . . May, 1828*, p. 445.

[48] Frederick A. Currier, "The Old Turnpike and Turnpike Days," *Proceedings of the Fitchburg Historical Society*, IV (1908), 166.

times, a rate of growth faster than that of the population, and in 1845 coach making was in value of output still the fifth industry in the state. The well-to-do owned four-wheel vehicles — phaetons or light coaches; men of moderate means were content with light two-wheel vehicles, drawn by a single horse, and made more comfortable early in the century by the substitution of an elliptical metal spring for crude springs or the old method of suspension by leather straps.[49] Such private carriages played an unsung part in increasing the mobility of the population. In 1814 the Norfolk and Bristol passed through its Roxbury gate approximately 16,660 one-horse vehicles and 5,330 coaches and chariots.[50] In the early thirties the annual number of travelers in private conveyances between Worcester and Boston was placed at 32,500; and estimates calculated that between 3,000 and 4,000 people used such vehicles between Boston and Providence.[51] Indeed, the railroad had hardly placed its cold hand upon this manner of travel before its devotees began celebrating its virtues. Thus to Samuel Breck, the Philadelphia gentleman exiled from Massachusetts, it seemed: "After all its old-fashioned way of five or six miles an hour, with one's own horses and carriage, with liberty to dine decently in a decent inn, and be master of one's own movements, with the delight of seeing the country and getting along rationally, is the mode to which I cling, and which will be adopted again by the generations of after times."[52]

The public conveyance, the stage coach, was more important. Toward the end of the eighteenth century, stage-coach lines departed from Boston toward nearby cities, and Levi Pease, a Massachusetts man, one of the great stagemen of the country, had established a through route to New York. In the first decade of the nineteenth century stage lines penetrated the New England hinterland. But the heyday of stage business began in the

---

[49] Taylor, "The Turnpike Era," pp. 233–234, 248–249; Morse, *A Neglected Period of Connecticut History*, p. 242.

[50] Taylor, "The Turnpike Era," pp. 260–261.

[51] *Report . . . of the Boston and Worcester Rail-Road. Together with the Report of John M. Fessenden, Esq.*, p. 17; *Report of the Board of Commissioners . . . for a Railway from Boston to Providence*, p. 43.

[52] H. E. Scudder, ed., *Recollections of Samuel Breck with Passages from his Note-Books, 1771–1862* (Philadelphia: Porter & Coates, 1877), p. 277.

1820's, and lasted at least for twenty years. While population growth and road improvements were essential to this flowering of highway transportation, technical and business innovations contributed to it. For one thing the vehicles were improved. The American "stage-waggon," as it was fitly denominated, had been a "clumsy and uncomfortable machine . . . calculated to hold twelve persons, who all sat on benches placed across, with their faces toward the horses. The front seat alone holds three, one of whom is the driver, and as there are no doors at the sides, the passengers get in over the front wheels, and take their seats as they enter. . . . It is covered with leather, and instead of windows, there are flaps of that article, which in bad weather are let down, and secured by buckles and straps. In summer these flaps are folded up, and this is some alleviation from the repeated shocks you receive in going over the roads." [53] At the turn of the century, Levi Pease had designed for the Post Office Department a coach entered by a side door; the interior had three seats, the first one facing backwards, and the driver with additional passengers rode outside. [54] As the years passed, such coaches assumed a graceful oval shape, and soon after the midtwenties their bodies were mounted upon the elliptical metal spring. [55] The Concord coach, however, regarded generally as the perfect flower of stage-coach evolution, continued to rest the body upon through-braces of very heavy leather. As the coach rocked back and forth upon this underpinning, the passengers were buffeted, but the shocks of an uneven road were not felt severely by the racing teams. Such coaches, if equipped with seats on top, carried a large number of passengers; baggage racks fore and aft were capacious; and the Yankee care used in the selection of woods and in the joinery produced a sturdy, enduring vehicle. The first example of this type was completed at Concord, New Hampshire, in 1827. Its designers were Lewis Down-

[53] Charles W. Janson, *The Stranger in America, 1793–1806,* . . . *Reprinted from the London Edition of 1807* (New York: The Press of the Pioneers, 1935), pp. 177–178.

[54] Oliver W. Holmes, "The Stage-Coach Business in the Hudson Valley," *Quarterly Journal of the New York State Historical Association,* XII (1931), 236.

[55] Taylor, "The Turnpike Era," p. 246.

ing, a Concord wheelwright, and J. S. Abbott, a young artisan who had recently come to Concord from Salem, a place famous in its own right for coach making.[56] Clearly, however, the Concord coach arrived too late to explain entirely the coaching era in New England.

Stage-coach business was highly competitive, since entry into it was easy. Funds other than those of the stage owners provided the right of way; roads built by public finance or private finance were open to all users. Nor was the original investment in equipment prohibitive. A Concord coach cost $500, and in the late thirties the Eastern Stage Company, in a sale, which perhaps was somewhat of a forced one, was willing to dispose of a coach, a stage sleigh, and sixteen horses for $875.[57] Rivals were, therefore, always tempted upon profitable routes. The resulting competitive engagements were severe. Fares were slashed, schedules duplicated, and every civility and convenience offered to the traveling public. Usually some reconciliation of "interests" ended these unpleasant procedures. The trustees of the Eastern Stage Company, for instance, bought the teams of a rival between Salem and Portsmouth for $300. The seller signed a paper, "I hereby agree to take my stage from said route — and promise and agree that I will not, in future, either own, Drive, or be interested in any way or manner in any stage or stages to be run" in competition with the Eastern.[58] Another device for harmony was a consultation between committees from the rival concerns or a conference of stage-coach proprietors. The latter was the favorite method for creating a through line. Thus the business conduct of the routes between Boston and Maine termini was determined in conference between the Eastern Stage Company which ran from Boston to Portsmouth and the Maine Stage Company and other "eastern companies" which ran north and east of the

---

[56] Charles R. Corning, "Material Development," J. O. Lyford, ed., *History of Concord*, I, 637–639; William and George H. Banning, *Six Horses* (New York: The Century Co., 1930), pp. 22–26; Rantoul, "Old Modes of Travel," p. 59.

[57] McFarland, "Canals, Stage Lines, and Taverns," J. O. Lyford, ed., *History of Concord*, II, 852; Records of the Trustees of the Eastern Stage Company, 1838–1840, Ms., Essex Institute.

[58] Eastern Stage Company, Miscellaneous Papers, Ms., Essex Institute.

New Hampshire boundary.[59] The line of stages between New York and Boston, commonly regarded as the Pease line of stages, was in reality an alliance of end-to-end routes which functioned through regular consultation and through contracts. They employed common agents, divided the proceeds on a mileage basis except for additional grants to proprietors running stages on less profitable links, and fought off interlopers. At a meeting in 1800 they expressly rejected the idea of making this a "joint concern" with through waybills and quarterly dividends.[60]

The units in such arrangements might be individual drivers; they might be partnerships, which, in fact, were far more common than proprietorships in this business; or they might be corporations. Indeed, with the heyday of stage coaching, its owners frequently assumed this last form of organization. One of the most impressive was the Eastern Stage Company which ran stages from Boston to Newburyport, Portsmouth, Dover, and to Lake Winnepesaukee, on which a steamboat in 1834 supplied transportation "to accommodate." Chartered in New Hampshire for a period of twenty years, the concern was permitted a capitalization of $100,000 divided into not more than 500 shares.[61] At the outset these were owned by 63 stockholders of whom ten held nearly half the total.[62] Later Newburyport banks invested in the concern. When their New Hampshire charter ran out in 1838, the company was unable to secure either a reissue or an extension because of the hostility to corporations in the legislature of the state. Meanwhile the corporation had prospered. It owned over 500 horses, brick stables, and blacksmith shops; through lease or ownership it had an interest in inns or hotels at the principal centers served by its lines; and its sinking fund was invested in real estate and the securities of banks, toll bridges, and the Newburyport turnpike — in which actually it owned 70

[59] Eastern Stage Company, Miscellaneous Papers; Record of the Directors of the Eastern Stage Company, Ms., Essex Institute.

[60] Book of Records Belonging to the Proprietors of the Boston and New York Mail Stages by Way of Worcester, Brookfield, Springfield, Suffield, Hartford, New Haven &c., 1800–1814, Ms., American Antiquarian Society.

[61] Record of the Directors of the Eastern Stage Company.

[62] Eastern Stage Company, Records and Accounts, 1808–1814, Ms., Essex Institute.

shares. In the prosperous early thirties its annual receipts were over $115,000 and the value of its property was $101,060. No wonder the directors' "most sanguine expectations" were realized; their chief irritation was the annual payment of nearly $9,000 in tolls to bridges and turnpikes.[63] When the company was finally liquidated, the president announced that "the holders of stock, during twenty years, [had] received eight and one-third per cent in dividends annually, and after paying all debts, between $66 and $67 on each share." [64]

Neither the partnership nor the corporation, however, gave the final pattern to the stage-coach business; it was personal leadership. The chief instrument by which these leaders forged ahead was the contract for carrying the mails. The returns from such contracts generally paid the expense of operation; such passengers as traveled in the mail coach were pure velvet.[65] Those who secured contracts, therefore, were in a position to weld disparate enterprises into a through route and by threatening to start new lines force their admittance into existing partnerships. The process was profitable. For a mail contract Levi Pease secured from the line between New York and Boston not only his proportion of the mileage but $1,600 as well.[66] The contracts were potentially so dangerous that lines in an area where traffic was stabilized agreed in advance that they would not compete in bidding.[67]

Through the agency of mail contracts, exclusive franchises, and competitive struggle there developed a network of interlocking partnerships, directorates, and personal influence. Thus individuals ruled little stage-coach empires. In the seventeen nineties Levi Pease had spread his interests to the lower route between Boston and New Haven, to the middle Connecticut, and

[63] Eastern Stage Company, Miscellaneous Papers; Record of the Directors of the Eastern Stage Company.

[64] Rantoul, "Old Modes of Travel," p. 64

[65] Thomas P. Kettell, "Travel and Transportation," *Eighty Years' Progress of the United States: A Family Record of American Industry, Energy and Enterprise* (Hartford: L. Stebbins, 1868), p. 178.

[66] Book of Records Belonging to the Proprietors of the Boston and New York Mail Stages.

[67] Record of the Directors of the Eastern Stage Company.

to the Boston-Portsmouth run; later the Paines of Portland dominated the Portland lines and owned stock in the Eastern Stage Company; Chester W. Chapin was the overlord of the lower Connecticut valley; and Ginery Twichell, "a Napoleon among mail contractors," was the coach king of Worcester.[68]

The liaison man with the public was, however, the driver. Saluted universally throughout New England as "captain," the duties of this individual were legion. He looked after the welfare of children and the aged, sold and bought goods, transported express, and carried bank notes for remittance or collection. Because they dreaded the indirect assumption of liability, the Eastern Stage Company sought to prohibit some of these functions. The directors were compelled, however, to permit drivers to conduct a "pocket business" and, with suitable disclaimers of corporation responsibility, to carry "all bills of any Bank or Banks with which any person or persons may intrust to the care of any Driver of our Stages." The fees which drivers thus picked up supplemented their monthly wages of $22.50 to $28.[69] Other regulations sought to ensure employment of competent and responsible "whips." Intemperance was forbidden so successfully that one New England old-timer remarked: "You were saying that passengers in your section were uneasy and often had fears for their safety while riding with your drivers. Here all that is reversed, for in former years the travellers used every precaution to keep the drivers sober, but now the drivers by their example try to keep the passengers sober."[70] This new breed was capable of meeting with punctuality the shortened schedules upon which the developed stage-coach lines ran.

[68] Oliver W. Holmes, "Levi Pease, the Father of New England Stage-Coaching," *Journal of Economic and Business History*, III (1931) 254–256; Eastern Stage Company Stock Book, 1818–1838, Ms., Essex Institute; *Dictionary of American Biography* (New York: Charles Scribner's Sons, 1928–1936), IV, 14–15; Alice M. Earle, *Stage-Coach and Tavern Days* (New York: The Macmillan Company, 1900), pp. 305–306.

[69] Records of the Directors of the Eastern Stage Company; Shirreff, *A Tour through North America*, p. 49.

[70] Rantoul, "Old Modes of Travel," p. 45; Records of the Directors of the Eastern Stage Company.

V

The stage-coach network was extensive. Take Boston alone. In the mid-twenties the city boasted sixty-seven different stage lines. About a quarter of them ran to nearby cities on schedules by which the traveler could come to the metropolis in the morning and return to his home the same day. A few of such routes had a dense business. The Roxbury stages left every other hour both from Roxbury and Boston and charged 12½ cents. Between Boston and Salem there were six trips daily each way; the fifteen miles were covered in two hours, and the fare was $1.00. Another group of lines ran to an intermediate zone of places in Massachusetts and New Hampshire; a visitor to Boston had to spend at least a night there before he could return. The remainder, about half the stages, connected Boston with more distant destinations. Three stage lines ran to Portland. Two of them, "accommodation" stages, broke the journey either at Portsmouth or Dover and charged $6.00; the third, the "Eastern Mail Stage," left Boston at 2 A.M. and without important rest ran through to Portland which it reached at eight the same evening; its fare was $8.00. On the Burlington route, also served by three lines, even the mail stage stopped overnight. South and west of Boston the through traffic to New York City traveled generally by stage to some port in southern New England and transferred there to steam navigation. The only through stage, the Boston and New York Mail Coach, began its journey in the afternoon and completed its uninterrupted progress of 210 miles to New York forty-one hours later at six in the morning. The fare was $11. The traveler could ease his purse and his aching frame by changing to a boat at Hartford or New Haven. The greatest New England route, however, was the one between Boston and Albany. By various roads eight lines connected the two places. Even a mail stage, which broke its journey at Springfield, required two days of sixteen or seventeen hours each for the trip. Its fare was $8.75. One line charged $6.00.[71]

Compared with earlier days the stage coaching of the twenties

[71] *Badger and Porter's Stage Register* [1826], pp. 2–17.

represented rapid transportation. In 1784 the first through stage route, that from Boston to New York, had taken six days; by the twenties the journey required somewhat less than two.[72] Part of the reduction was due to the greater speed of the coaches; part to the willingness of travelers to test their stamina by a continuous passage. As for fares precise averages are difficult. They ranged from .066 cents a mile charged on the Salem coaches to the .037 cents on the cheapest line to Albany, perhaps a competitive interloper, for its fare was unusually low. Mail coaches charged more than the accommodation ones. Stages paying tolls may have taken this extra expense into account. On the Providence run, at least, the Citizen's Mail Coach "over the turn-pike" charged $2.50, while another line charged $1.50. On the whole, in the New England of the twenties 5 cents a mile was an approximate fare.[73] At such rates the annual totals of passengers were occasionally prodigious. In the early thirties stages between Boston and Worcester annually transported 22,360 passengers, between Boston and Newburyport 30,000, Boston and Providence 35,000, and between Boston and Lowell 37,440. The Salem stages carried 77,500.[74] Averaged into daily travel these figures, of course, were not as impressive.

Stage coaching was showy business. The sweating horses, the clouds of dust, the fire-lit taverns, the ark-like stables, the genial hosts and skillful drivers — all aroused contemporary attention and admiration. This color obscured the more drab and the more important movement of freight over the highways. Turnpikes and improved highways had facilitated this commerce. The four wheel "waggon," often drawn by horses, had been introduced. Though a rarity as late as the War of 1812, twenty years later enumerators at toll gates discovered that the number of the new vehicles was somewhat greater than that of the primi-

[72] Holmes, "Levi Pease," p. 245.

[73] *Badger and Porter's Stage Register* [1826], pp. 2–17.

[74] William Lincoln, *History of Worcester, Massachusetts, . . . to September, 1836* (Worcester: Moses D. Phillips and Company, 1837), p. 329; Massachusetts *Senate Documents*, 1836, no. 77, pp. 2–3; *Report of a Committee on the Boston and Lowell Rail Road* (Boston: 1831), p. 7; *Report of the Board of Commissioners, . . . for a Railway from Boston to Providence*, p. 43.

tive two-wheel cart.[75] From every quarter of New England wagoners plied their trade. Of course this was especially true in districts without navigation. The commerce of north-central Massachusetts with Boston aggregated annually 14,600 tons, all carried over highways.[76] In Berkshire county, cut off from the Connecticut and the Hudson, twenty-two towns imported 6,891 and exported 11,584 tons of merchandise and raw materials, all transported over roads. The marble of western Massachusetts and the iron and lime of western Connecticut thus found outside markets.[77] When trade in bulky products was feasible for short distances in rural regions, it flourished naturally where industries and population were both growing. According to the promoters of the Boston and Worcester Railroad, freight tonnage between Worcester and Boston over "the old road" and the turnpike was 9,000 tons a year at rates of $2.50 a ton.[78] Overland traffic was even possible between seaports. Though vessels, including four packet lines, carried 3,400 tons between Providence and Boston, wagons pulled 1,706 tons over the whole distance and picked up an additional 7,720 along the way.[79] Though a continued stream of coasters carried 7,600 tons between Salem and Boston, the merchandise trade by land was still 3,000 tons a year.[80]

The arrival of the railroad made neither stage coach nor freight wagon obsolete. As late as the seventies, when Charles Francis Adams, Jr., chairman of the new Massachusetts railroad com-

[75] Ellery B. Crane, "The Boston and Worcester Turnpike," *Proceedings of the Worcester Society of Antiquity*, XVII (1900–1901), 598; Percy W. Bidwell, "Rural Economy in New England at the Beginning of the Nineteenth Century," *Transactions of the Connecticut Academy of Arts and Sciences*, XX (1916), 314–315.

[76] *Report of the Commissioners of the State of Massachusetts on the Routes of Canals from Boston Harbour, to Connecticut and Hudson Rivers* (Boston: True and Greene, 1826), appendix, pp. 59–60.

[77] *Report of the Board of Directors of Internal Improvements . . . on . . . a Railroad from Boston to the Hudson River*, p. 31; *First Annual Report of the Board of Directors to the Stockholders of the Housatonic Rail-Road Company* (New Haven: Hitchcock & Stafford, 1838), pp. 21–24.

[78] *Report . . . of the Boston and Worcester Rail-Road . . . Together with the Report of John M. Fessenden, Esq.*, pp. 17, 19.

[79] *Report of the Board of Commissioners, . . . for a Railway from Boston to Providence*, pp. 43–44; *Report of the Board of Directors of Internal Improvements, . . . on . . . a Railroad from Boston to the Hudson River*, pp. 66–67.

[80] Massachusetts *Senate Documents*, 1836, no. 77, p. 2.

mission, was berating the railroads for their sins, he lamented their failure to absorb the wagon and express business in the neighborhood of Boston where railroads were densest. Yet by this decade freighting over the highway was generally subsidiary to the railroads. The same destiny touched the stage coach. For two decades or more after 1835 the expanding railroad network still permitted an extensive use of the stage coach, for the continually advancing termini of the through routes from Boston were the stubs around which a new network of stages clustered like a quick growth of saplings. When the Boston and Worcester reached Worcester, the latter became an important nexus of stage coaching and as railroads thrust northward along the Merrimack, Lowell, Nashua, and Concord in turn experienced the same sudden and passing apotheosis.[81] As these main railroads were completed, moreover, they were on the alert to encourage stages as feeders for their own routes and invaders of the tributary territory of their rivals. In the sixties and seventies the new passion for branch railroads severely curtailed the stage-coach era. Still they served in rural and vacation regions until the trolley, the private automobile, and the motor bus did away, once and for all, with the age of horseflesh.

But long before the twentieth century the inferior position of highway commerce had been signalized by a change in the policy of the United States Post Office. As mail contracts had once been transferred from the horseback carrier to the stage coach, they were now awarded to the railroad. There were preliminary hesitations, for railroads at first were neither as dependable nor as rapid as the coaches and the absence of railroad competition prevented the competitive bids specified by Congress. In 1838, however, Congress declared every railroad a post route and authorized the postmaster general to make contracts with the railroad "not paying more than twenty-five per centum over and above what similar transportation would cost in post-coaches." Actually the postmaster general, in order to expedite the mails between Boston and Washington, had earlier made a contract with the steamboats on the Sound and the Boston and Providence

[81] *Badger and Porter's Stage Register* [1836], pp. 15–16, 26–27.

Railroad.[82] Although in the railroad world payments for carrying the mail were not to play a part comparable to that which they had for stage coaching, the change in government policy was a significant tribute to the new mode of transportation.

[82] History of the Railway Mail Service: A Chapter in the History of Postal Affairs in the United States, *Senate Executive Documents*, 48 Cong., 2 Sess., no. 40 (s.n. 1313), pp. 15, 35, 37, 128.

III

IMPROVED WATERWAYS AND CANALS

So the swift sail shall seek thy inland seas,
And swell and whiten in thy purer breeze;
New Paddles dip thy waters, and strange oars
Feather thy waves and touch thy noble shores. —
"On Connecticut River," The Poems of John G. C. Brainard
(1842), p. 5.

I

Since canals were waterways, they offered a means of transportation that profitably could carry heavy products — that is, if they were prudently promoted and cautiously constructed. The topography of New England, however, seemed to foreclose such possibilities. The essential through routes everywhere collided with the most forbidding terrain. Since dreams, however, could vault mountains, New England had its canal eras. The first, that of the seventeen nineties, revealed the region as a leader in appreciating the value of the new means of transportation. Its greatest accomplishment, the Middlesex Canal between Boston and the Merrimack, was one of two pioneer works in the nation; the other, the Santee Canal, was in South Carolina. A second and more important canal era blossomed in the twenties. The stimulus was New York's Erie Canal which even before its successful completion in 1825 stirred the imagination and quickened the zeal of New England communities ambitious for commercial greatness. Almost in a twinkling the whole region was criss-crossed with a network of canals — on paper. Maine dreamed of canal connections with the St. Lawrence and the Connecticut. Of the plethora of projects charted in New Hampshire, the most important was a diagonal cross-state canal uniting the Merrimack and the Connecticut. At the very least Vermont thought canals from the Connecticut to Lake Memphremagog or Lake Champlain or both were desirable. Massachusetts and Connecticut alike planned cross-state projects, some of which actually reached the survey stage, enlisted popular support, and complicated the decision as to whether railroads or artificial waterways were superior.[1] This later era, as we shall see, had major accomplishments. The transportation network which these canals were designed to extend already included extensive works facilitating the navigation of the Merrimack and the Connecticut.

Into the former stream the lock-tender at Middlesex, one Sunday in 1839, let down from the Concord River a small craft with two boatmen. One, Henry D. Thoreau, was soon saluting the river which lay before them: "The Merrimack, or Sturgeon River, is formed by the confluence of the Pemigewasset, which rises near the Notch of the White Mountains, and the Winnipisiogee, which drains the lake of the same name, signifying 'The Smile of the Great Spirit.' From their junction it runs south seventy-eight miles to Massachusetts, and thence east thirty-five miles to the sea. I have traced its stream from where it bubbles out of the rocks of the White Mountains above the clouds, to where it is lost amid the salt billows of the ocean on Plum Island beach. . . . Rising at an equal height with the Connecticut, the Merrimack reaches the sea by a course only half as long, and hence has no leisure to form broad and fertile meadows like the former, but is hurried along rapids and down numerous falls without long delay." Because of its precipitous character, only the last twenty miles were navigable for vessels of burden. At Haverhill, "it first suffers a sea change, and a few masts betray the vicinity of the ocean."[2] From its upper

[1] George Armroyd, *A Connected View of the Whole Internal Navigation of the United States; Natural and Artificial, Present and Prospective* (Philadelphia: Lydia R. Bailey, 1830), pp. 9–45.

[2] Henry D. Thoreau, *A Week on the Concord and Merrimack Rivers* (Boston: Houghton Mifflin Company, 1893), pp. 100, 106, 108, 109–110.

reaches it was also possible to run down lumber and shipbuilding materials. Since these limited traffics had benefited Newburyport, Boston, only a few miles to the south, resented its narrow separation from a river that traversed an agricultural country and that tapped "a living magazine of masts and naval timbers." [3]

To give Boston a better hold upon this inland trade, a group of influential capitalists and investors secured from Massachusetts in 1793 a charter for the Middlesex Canal. Although the more timid and more speculative withdrew as costs mounted, a core of tenacious, public-spirited shareholders clung on, determined to vindicate their judgment and complete a necessary public work. Their faith was justified. On December 31, 1803, the canal was at last completed. A narrow, shallow ditch, nearly twenty-eight miles long, it ran from the mill pond at Charlestown to the Merrimack at Middlesex village, about a mile above the present dam at Lowell. Twenty locks of wood or stone carried boats over its summit level, 107 feet above tidewater at Boston.[4] When the canal was opened, the devoted stockholders had already paid $554,000 in assessments upon their 800 shares of stock.[5] They confronted additional sacrifices. Although the canal diverted the Merrimack traffic toward Boston, the enlargement of that commerce required further improvements. The ever-falling river bristled with rapids and obstructions. Around some of these barriers, canals and locks had already been built. They were inadequate. Elsewhere entirely new works were required.

Fortunately for the efficiency of the system, John Langdon Sullivan became in 1808 secretary, treasurer, and superintendent of the Middlesex Company. A Harvard graduate, an amateur engineer, an innovator and business dreamer, he insisted that the company control the existing improvements on the Merrimack and build the dams and locks required to complete the navigation of the river. This conception he largely brought to suc-

[3] Christopher Roberts, *The Middlesex Canal, 1793–1860* (Cambridge: Harvard University Press, 1938), pp. 17, 26–27.
[4] *Ibid.*, pp. 28–30, 40–43, 191–192.
[5] *Ibid.*, p. 44.

cess. By the mid-twenties the company controlled between its terminus on the Merrimack and Concord, New Hampshire, six enterprises, the most extensive of which were the Union Locks and Canals, avoiding a long series of rapids in New Hampshire, and the nine locks of the Amoskeag Canal. Reinvestment of receipts and additional assessments upon the stockholders, financed this expansion. By 1817 the total assessments amounted to $740 a share. Still the river was navigable as far as Concord and occasionally very small boats pushed thirty-eight miles farther to Plymouth, New Hampshire. All the improvements on the river were under a common management.[6]

Before he withdrew from the Middlesex Company, Sullivan put into practice his early design of a steamboat to tow barges and canal boats along the river and canal. His first experiment in 1812 used a high-pressure engine from the works of Oliver Evans; the boat was propelled by chain floats, a sort of paddle wheel along the side. This was the first steamboat in Massachusetts. In 1818 he launched the *Merrimack*. The vessel was powered with a Morey engine — named after another of the steamboat's inventors — and utilized a stern paddle wheel. Though both vessels performed satisfactorily, their passage at high speed on the canal badly washed the banks and on the river traffic their schedule was not regular enough to compensate for the delays at the frequent lockages.[7] The canal boats, therefore, remained the mainstay on the Merrimack and Middlesex. Not over seventy-five feet long, the length of the locks on the canal, they were built anywhere and by any one. They were cheap — $200 each. On the canal, oxen or horses pulled them. On the river, downward bound, they kept in midstream to catch the current or the breeze. On their upstream journey their methods enchanted Thoreau. If there was no favoring wind, they hugged the shore and the rivermen, taking their fourteen or fifteen-foot poles, set the pointed iron tip in the river's bed and, pushing as they went, walked back about a third of the length of the

[6] *Ibid.*, pp. 125–135, 179, 182; Thoreau, *A Week on the Concord and Merrimack Rivers*, p. 110.
[7] Roberts, *The Middlesex Canal*, pp. 142–147.

boat. With hardly a sound, they were "creeping stealthily up the side of the stream like alligators." And when the breeze blew they loosed their sails. "By and by came several canal-boats, at intervals of a quarter of a mile, standing up to Hooksett with a light breeze, and one by one disappeared round a point above. With their broad sails set, they moved slowly up the stream in the sluggish and fitfull breeze, like one-winged antediluvian birds, and as if impelled by some mysterious counter-current. It was a grand motion, so slow and stately." [8] The little crews which manned them seemed to the Concord sage a different and a better race. He discovered their type at Cromwell's Falls: "A brawny New Hampshire man, leaning on his pole, bareheaded and in shirt and trousers only, a rude Apollo of a man, coming down from that 'vast uplandish country,' to the main; of nameless age, with flaxen hair, and vigorous, weather-bleached countenance, in whose wrinkles the sun still lodged, as little touched by the heats and frosts and withering cares of life as a maple of the mountain; an undressed, unkempt, uncivil man, . . . His humanity was genuine and instinctive, and his rudeness only a manner." [9]

Boatmen like Apollo were certainly entitled to a golden age. That on the Middlesex and Merrimack came in the early thirties. The railroads had not yet paralleled its route and its own improvements had been long completed. The industrialization of the lower valley, symbolized by the new factory town of Lowell, created an additional commerce. Stockholders, more wonted to paying assessments than receiving returns, saw toll receipts amount to $45,500 in 1833, and collected annual dividends from 1834 to 1837 of $30 a share. This belated and temporary success reflected the extensive commerce of the canal-river system. "Transient boats," as they were called, carried the larger share of the cargoes. These were private carriers, running generally on owner's account, and were often seasonal in operation. Boating companies assembled fleets, built warehouses, and collected bulk products — salt, lime, plaster, and wood — to assure themselves

---

[8] Thoreau, *A Week on the Concord and Merrimack Rivers*, pp. 274, 280, 340.
[9] *Ibid.*, pp. 262–263.

full cargoes. Of these larger enterprises the Boston and Concord Boating Company became a notable representative in the mid-twenties. It ran its fleet of twenty or so boats between Boston and Concord. Freights, which in 1815 had been $8.00 per ton from Concord to Boston and $13 for the return voyage, had by 1831–1836 declined to $4.00 and $5.00, respectively.[10]

In the golden age these useful boats carried a varied cargo. Gone were the early days when most traffic was downstream and consisted chiefly of lumber and boards. The Middlesex Canal and cotton manufacturing disrupted this primitive pattern. From Boston to Lowell went mountains of cotton for the factories and heavy burdens of coal — for the Lowell mills used 11,239 tons of anthracite in 1835. Back were carried the finished goods which the canal had finally secured for itself by creating a new classification, "Factory Cotton Cloths," on which the toll was 50 cents a ton rather than the $1.00 customarily charged merchandise. From the ports between Lowell and Concord, river and canal won from the ubiquitous competition of wagoners, the carriage of heavy commodities. They transported the lumber, firewood — 5,723 cords of it in 1818 — stone, shooks and hogsheads, iron from Franconia, copperas from Vermont, and bricks. "From Bedford and Merrimack have been boated the bricks of which Lowell is made. . . . About twenty years before, as they told us, one Moore, of Bedford, having clay on his farm, contracted to furnish eight millions of bricks to the founders of that city within two years. He fulfilled his contract in one year, and since then bricks have been the principal export from these towns. The farmers found thus a market for their wood, and when they had brought a load to the kilns, they could cart a load of bricks to the shore, and so make a profitable day's work of it. Thus all parties were benefitted. It was worth the while to see the place where Lowell was 'dug out'! So likewise Manchester is being built of bricks made still higher up the river at Hooksett." [11] Upstream the boats carried salt, lime, and plaster. The river commerce shared with wagons the downtrade in country

[10] Roberts, *The Middlesex Canal*, pp. 138–141, 170, 183.
[11] Thoreau, *A Week on the Concord and Merrimack Rivers*, pp. 311–312.

produce and the uptrade in groceries, iron and flour, codfish and mackerel, and imported goods.[12]

II

Though many aspired to the rôle and wrote many books many times as long as Thoreau's on the Merrimack, the Connecticut has not yet found its laureate. Perhaps it speaks for itself, this magnificent central river of New England. But in spite of its four-hundred mile course from the small lakes which are its source in the heart of New England's northern wilderness to the lower reaches bordered by rich fields and historic towns, it fell short as a channel of commerce. On the Hudson, for example, navigators sailed inland as far as Troy; on the Connecticut only as far as Hartford. Even here the stretch between Middletown and Hartford was interrupted by sandbars. The Connecticut above Hartford might seem, as Thoreau implied, to meander in long lazy curves through green intervals and to descend so gradually as to be almost imperceptible. In fact such was not the case. In the 219 miles between the Fifteen Mile Falls above Barnet — a natural obstacle beyond which only the most extravagant dreamer spoke of navigation — and Hartford, the river fell 420 feet.[13] Aside from shoals and rapids there were at least six major descents in this distance. Immediately north of Hartford, Enfield Falls, with a drop of 30 feet, put a term to further sloop navigation. At South Hadley the river fell about 50 feet in two miles, and at Miller's Falls, still father north, nearly 70. At Bellows Falls the Connecticut rushed downward 52 feet through a short, rocky, circular channel. These falls "are certainly an interesting natural curiosity; although we did not find the water beneath them so hard, as to be impervious to an iron crow," commented Timothy Dwight in scorn for an earlier tall tale. Finally, before the north-bound traveler reached Wells River he had to detour the Queechee Falls near Hartland, Vermont, a

---

[12] Roberts, *The Middlesex Canal*, pp. 148–154, 165–170.
[13] Henry W. Erving, *The Connecticut River Banking Company, 1825, One Hundred Years of Service, 1925* (Hartford: Henry W. Erving, 1925), p. 60.

descent of only 12 feet, and Olcott's Falls, south of Hanover, where the river fell 36 feet in a mile.[14]

As on the Merrimack, the earlier movement for better waterways had effected considerable improvement. For the lower river, the Connecticut legislature in 1800 chartered the Union Company. This concern spent $45,000 south of Hartford, revetting banks with stone and willows and dredging sandbars to secure a channel of at least 7½ feet. It recouped its expenditures by collecting tolls. Although its activities made Hartford instead of Middletown the great port of the Connecticut River, its charges and corporate privileges aroused intermittent hostility through the six decades of its chartered life.[15] At the same time the upper river had been made navigable. Separate companies, operating under charter from the several states, had built canals and locks around the chief obstructions and had thrown dams or wing dams into the stream to divert the water through these artificial channels. Since for the time these improvements involved large sums of money — the canal at Bellows Falls alone costing approximately $105,000 — their promoters had recourse to foreign capital. Dutch funds were invested in these Massachusetts canals and English capital in that of Bellows Falls.[16] Still by the 1820's the native stockholders were in control. These were merchants from Hartford and Springfield and other river ports, and large landowners and promoters from the upper valley.[17]

In the commerce that utilized this improved channel the most important single item was lumber, gathered in rafts which were floated downstream and warped through the canals. The crews lived on these lumber "boxes," as they were called, broke them up at Hartford, cashed in the proceeds, and rode home in the

[14] W. DeLoss Love, "The Navigation of the Connecticut River," *Proceedings of the American Antiquarian Society, New Series*, XV (1904), 406, 411, 413, 414, 415; Timothy Dwight, *Travels in New-England and New-York* (New Haven: S. Converse, 1821), II, 91.

[15] Love, "Navigation of the Connecticut," pp. 398–400.

[16] *Ibid.*, p. 407; Lyman J. Hayes, "The Navigation of the Connecticut River," *Proceedings of the Vermont Historical Society for the Years, 1915–1916*, p. 74; Erving, *The Connecticut River Banking Company*, pp. 37–38.

[17] Love, "Navigation of the Connecticut," p. 407.

valley stages to repeat perhaps three times a summer their laborious and vexing excursion. But this traffic could last only as long as the lumber lasted; Silliman observed in 1819 that most of the large pines had been cut away from the valley south of Hanover.[18] The general merchandise traffic was carried by flat boats. The larger examples of this type, loaded with fifteen to eighteen tons of cargo, could use the river only at "boating pitch," that is, during the high water of spring and fall. Lighter boats and cargoes, with a draught of only twelve or fifteen inches, could navigate the river during the summer months; but since their expenses did not shrink proportionately to their size, they were not as profitable as the larger flats. In either case these vessels loaded with country produce — ashes, whiskey, butter, cheese, and wool — found the down journey with the current easy enough. The upstream voyage, with West Indian and manufactured goods, took twice as much time and was much more arduous. As on the Merrimack, the crew laboriously poled the boat unless a wind came to the rescue. When the happy moment of a "tidewater breeze" arrived, a fleet of as many as thirty vessels would often hoist sail above Hartford and scurry up the Connecticut. A round trip from Wells River to Hartford often took thirty days; with wages and tolls and other costs included, freight rates for the distance were $10 a ton downstream, twice that on the return.[19]

In the circumstances traffic tended to thicken on that portion of the river south of the Massachusetts line. Here were the larger towns, Springfield, Holyoke, and Northampton; here were fewer locks and the shorter voyages. Flat-boat lines operating with some regularity of schedule developed. Between Springfield and Hartford individual vessels made three trips a week.[20] As for the upper valley, the inhabitants often found it cheaper to trade

---

[18] Benjamin Silliman, *Remarks Made, on a Short Tour between Hartford and Quebec in the Autumn of 1819* (New Haven: S. Converse, 1820), p. 420; Hayes, "Navigation of the Connecticut River," pp. 60, 74.

[19] *Facts Connected with the Application for Power to Improve the Navigation of the Connecticut River* (n.p., n.d.), pp. 2–5; Hartford *Courant*, June 26, 1876.

[20] Margaret E. Martin, *Merchants and Trade of the Connecticut River Valley, 1750–1820* (Northampton: n.d.), p. 197; Hartford *Courant*, June 26, 1876.

with centers other than those on the lower Connecticut. Wagons creaked overland to Boston and Portland. Occasionally counties in northern Vermont sent products forty or fifty miles by cart or wagon to Lake Champlain, and then by boat along the lake, the Champlain Canal, and the Hudson, and by sea to Boston.[21] In the mid-twenties salt was carried from the Champlain Canal across southern Vermont and sold within twenty miles of the banks of the Connecticut more cheaply than if it had come by river from Hartford.[22] Such disquieting performances turned apostles of river transportation to a scrutiny of the Connecticut transportation system.

They did not need to peer deep. The defects were obvious. For one thing no unified system governed the existing canals. To be sure, the two in Massachusetts, those at South Hadley and at Miller's Falls, were owned by related companies, but the others were all separate enterprises. There was no uniformity in tolls or indeed in technical features, for boats that could pass the locks in the lower river could not squeeze through those in Vermont.[23] Nor had the existing enterprises created anything resembling a slackwater navigation. One dam did not back the water to the foot of the next. Six times between Miller's Falls and Bellows Falls, three times between Bellows Falls and Sumner's Falls, and finally again in sight of the haven at Wells River, rapids required the help of extra men or of oxen and occasionally the toilsome expedient of lightening cargo.[24] The most startling lack, however, was any certain means of passing Enfield Falls. A long canal would here have been necessary; and the high estimated cost deterred investors. Meanwhile shippers could get along by transferring their goods from sloop to flat boat or by passing the rapids at times of high water. Whatever the excuse, the river system as a whole certainly deserved the succinct

---

[21] *Facts Connected with the Application for Power*, pp. 5–6.

[22] Bellows Falls *Intelligencer*, March 22, 1824, quoted in Hayes, "The Navigation of the Connecticut River," p. 82.

[23] *Journal of the Convention, Holden at Windsor, Vermont, Sept. 29th & 30th, 1830. For the Purpose of Taking into Consideration Subjects Connected with the Improvement of the Navigation of Connecticut River* (Windsor: Simeon Ide, 1830), pp. 7, 13–15; Love, "Navigation of the Connecticut," pp. 407, 411–412.

[24] *Facts Connected with the Application for Power*, p. 3

strictures passed upon it in 1830 by William Jarvis, once consul at Lisbon, the importer of the merino sheep, and now a sheep fancier at Weathersfield, Vermont: "The present barriers or obstacles to a navigation of the river are the *bars* across the channel; the *imperfect* and decayed state of some of the locks and canals; the *uncertainty* in the arrival and departure of boats." Because of their competition with each other, the changes in fashion and in prices, and the loss of interest on their money, merchants suffered peculiarly from the uncertainties and irregularity of river transportation. "The doubt when goods could be delivered, has deterred more shipments than the price of freight." [25]

III

By the twenties Hartford could no longer dismiss these complaints as the vaporings of perfectionists. The booming steamboat business between Hartford and New York inevitably suggested a means of transportation by which the commercial possibilities of the upper Connecticut could be realized if the river's navigation system could be adapted, through alteration and completion, to the steamboat's use. A spur to this and other energetic measures was provided by the sudden emergence of New Haven as a potential engrosser of the Connecticut Valley trade. Hartford was accustomed to the nagging rivalries of other Connecticut river communities, notably Middletown. But New Haven was not on the Connecticut. Still Boston had not been on the Merrimack. Perhaps no observer would at first blush think of comparing the two — New Haven, a town stagnating industrially and dreamily watching its colonial commerce fade away, and Boston, the metropolis of Massachusetts, one of the great cities and seaports of the nation. Still what Boston had achieved with the Middlesex Canal, New Haven *might* accomplish with a waterway of its own running inland to cut the Connecticut above Hartford. All that was required was the imagination to inaugurate such an enterprise and the means to

[25] *Journal of the Convention, Holden at Windsor . . . 1830*, pp. 10, 14–15.

complete it. At once New Haven demonstrated its civic spirit. In 1822 the Connecticut legislature chartered the Farmington Canal Company to build northward from New Haven to the Massachusetts state line; the next year Massachusetts authorized the Hampshire and Hampden to extend the Farmington by way of Westfield and Northampton to the Connecticut River.[26] As if all this were not grandiose enough, New Haven later proposed to build a canal along the Connecticut, first to Brattleboro, and finally deserting the river, overland to Lake Memphremagog on the Canadian border. For the feasibility of this enterprise they mobilized their authorities. Loammi Baldwin II, son of the engineer for the Middlesex and now the most eminent engineer of Massachusetts, expressed a preference for a canal as a more dependable means of transportation, and DeWitt Clinton, the father of the Erie, who was taken over the route on a junket financed by the New Havenites, requited their hospitality by asserting that a canal parallel to the Connecticut was practicable and would cost less than $10,000 a mile as far as Barnet, one half the sum spent on the Erie.[27] Thus notice was served upon Hartford.

Since both Hartford and New Haven required charters for their projects and since many doubted whether the river contained enough water to serve or the valley was wide enough to contain them both, first Connecticut, then Massachusetts, and finally Vermont and New Hampshire were swept by the clamorous fury of the two schools — "riverites" and "canalites." They raged and boosted in the press and pamphlets, they invaded the legislatures. A canal, the Massachusetts solons were informed, is technically better than river navigation, since it opens earlier in the spring and is unaffected by freshets; it is more democratic than slackwater navigation which utilizes expensive and perhaps monopolistic steamboats; and finally it does not injure the

[26] *Resolves and Private Laws of the State of Connecticut from the Year 1789 to the Year 1836*, I, 301–306; *Private and Special Statutes of the Commonwealth of Massachusetts from May 1822, to March 1830*, VI, 42–49.

[27] *Letters of Governor Clinton and of Colonel L. Baldwin, Civil Engineer of the United States, Improved as Evidence before the Joint Committee of the Legislature of Massachusetts, on the Petition of Samuel Hinkley and Others, for the Extension of the Hampshire and Hampden Canal, February, 1828* (Boston: Dutton and Wentworth, 1828), pp. 3–6, 10–22.

health of the population. On this and other points, a petition from the town of Northampton was peculiarly persuasive. Dams across the Connecticut by flooding and saturating the land, have caused "a pestilential miasma," and by destroying the shad and salmon fisheries, deprived "a passive people of Heaven's bounty to rich and poor." [28] Northampton, be it noted, was the town first projected as the northern terminus of New Haven's canal.

Somewhat more somberly but also buttressed by authorities with an Erie Canal background, the riverites retorted that a river improvement would cost one-third that of the canal and, in view of the smaller number of locks, be much less cumbersome in operation.[29] Most of the states solved the dilemma by clearing the way for both projects. While Connecticut could hardly de-cide between its embattled citizens, Vermont and New Hampshire clutched at any scheme for improvement; and Massachusetts gave a grudging assent. For Boston both plans were harmful. "And while this Legislature is lending its aid to afford accom-modation to the trade of that extensive and fertile part of New-England," reflected a committee of the General Court, "it would seem the part of wisdom to consider how far it may be in their power, to give such direction to it, as to secure some portion of it, at least, to the Capital of Their own State." [30] Meanwhile Hartford and New Haven plunged into the materialization of their visions.

The design of Hartford was heavily indebted to the system of navigation on the Merrimack River. Like that earlier example,

[28] *Remarks of the Hon. James Hillhouse, before the Joint Committee, on the Petition of Samuel Hinkley and Others, for the Extension of the Hampshire and Hampden Canal* (Boston: True and Greene, 1827), pp. 3–7; *George Beach, Esq. and the Northampton Town Meeting* (n.p., n.d.); *Report of Jarvis Hurd, Esq. Civil Engineer Employed by the Hampshire and Hampden Canal Company, to Make a Survey, and Estimate the Expense of a Canal from the Termination of the Hampshire and Hampden Canal, in Northampton, to the North Line of Massa-chusetts, and Thence to Brattleborough, in the State of Vermont* (Boston: True and Greene, 1827), pp. 3–4.

[29] Report of the Joint Committee on Roads and Canals on Extension of Hamp-shire and Hampden Canal, Massachusetts *House Documents*, 1827, no. 45, pp. 4–13; *Facts Relating to the Improvement of the Connecticut River* (n.p., n.d.).

[30] Massachusetts *House Documents*, 1827, no. 45, p. 16; Report of the Joint Committee to Whom was Referred the Petition of Samuel Hinkley, Massachu-setts *House Documents*, 1828, no. 41, pp. 1–13.

the riverites sought to create a single great company ruling the whole stream. Accordingly, in 1824 the Connecticut legislature chartered the Connecticut River Company and endowed it with embracing powers: to remove obstacles to navigation, to dig a canal around Enfield Falls, to hold the stock of other companies owning locks and dams, and to possess steamboats.[31] An amendment to that document eventually contained a clumsy arrangement permitting a maximum return of 6 per cent upon the investment.[32] Apparently those who improved a river, Heaven's bounty, were entitled to less remuneration than those who built a turnpike. Meanwhile the river partisans bent to the task of arousing enthusiasm. Down-river there were meetings of respectable and influential citizens; on the upper river there were conventions which pictured the commerce of Vermont and New Hampshire as a flood held back by inadequate communications; once these were provided the golden tide would flow to Hartford's feet.[33] Such promises did something to soften the stark estimates of the cost of the new system. Early in 1826 Holmes Hutchinson, an engineer of the Erie, reported that the cost of acquiring the existing works and building the additional locks, dams, and canals would amount to $1,500,000.[34]

Since time and showmanship were the essence of competition, the Connecticut River Company, before it commenced the essential improvements at Enfield Falls, decided to demonstrate the seductive utility of the steamboat. The directors authorized the construction at New York of the *Barnet*, on the plan of the flat-bottom, stern paddle-wheel boats successfully employed on the western rivers. Preliminary investigation proved the feasibility of the type.[35] In the fall of 1826 she was taken to Hartford

[31] *Resolves and Private Laws of the State of Connecticut . . . 1789 to . . . 1836*, I, 73–75.
[32] *Ibid.*, pp. 82–83.
[33] *Facts Connected with the Application for Power*, pp. 6-7; Erving, *The Connecticut River Banking Company*, pp. 52–54.
[34] *Report of the President and Directors of the Connecticut River Company, with the Report of H. Hutchinson, Esq. Laid before the Stockholders, at Their Annual Meeting, January 3d, 1826* (Hartford: Philemon Canfield, n.d.), p. 4.
[35] Hartford *Courant*, August 14, 1868; Erving, *The Connecticut River Banking Company*, pp. 75–76, 101–102, 107.

and lifted over the Enfield barrier by heroic efforts. Then began the slow celebrant voyage northward. She finally halted at Bellows Falls, for the locks were too small to pass her and ice was forming in the river. The warmth of her reception atoned for this failure; the fervency of the innumerable toasts promised a glowing future. One: "The Town of Barnet — may She speedily be gratified by the sight of her first-born" expressed the purpose of the riverites. But her trip had proved anew the necessity of river improvements. The following year the company went to work in earnest on the Enfield Canal; in 1829 its six miles and three locks were formally opened. After the official party had traveled its length and exchanged "friendly salutations" with other celebrants, "sixteen boats loaded with merchandise passed through the canal the same day." [36]

Aside from the dubious demonstration of the *Barnet*, this canal was the only achievement of the Connecticut River Company. The attainment of these limited results had, however, involved the most desperate financial expedients. The original capitalization of $500,000 had been increased to $1,000,000; shares had been forever exempted from taxation; and then the subscribers to the River Company were permitted to invest share for share in the newly chartered Connecticut River Banking Company, a rare privilege since bank charters were then sparingly bestowed. The bank, with which the course of river improvement was now entangled, could issue notes to the amount of 50 per cent more than the value of its capital and the monies deposited with it. Eventually its capital was increased; it was authorized to subscribe $60,000 to the stock of the River Company; and its own stock was exempted from taxation until the River Company earned 6 per cent.[37]

All this was not enough. By the thirties the riverites were trying to piece together some substitute from the wreckage of their earlier ambitions. With a charter from the Vermont legislature fortunately giving limited liability, they formed the Con-

[36] Erving, *The Connecticut River Banking Company*, pp. 107–131; Love, "Navigation of the Connecticut," pp. 424–426.

[37] *Resolves and Private Laws . . . of Connecticut . . . 1789 to . . . 1836*, I, 78–82.

necticut River Steam-boat Company. In 1831 under its auspices
the river was divided into sections upon each of which was placed
a small steamboat to tow freight barges from one improvement to
another. The steamboats did not pass through the locks and
canals, which they didn't fit anyway, and avoided the paying of
tolls. In the same year, as a last act of defiance, the *John
Ledyard*, fittingly named after the Dartmouth explorer, actually
wormed its way up the river from Hartford to a sandbar near
Wells River. This was "farthest north." The *John Ledyard* never
repeated the feat. The next year the relay company failed to
resume operations.[38]

Steamboat navigation wilted back to a main stem south of
Miller's Falls. Individuals in the river towns constructed vessels for the short runs north from Hartford. They were small.
The *Vermont* of 1829, "the first steamboat ever built in Springfield," was 75 feet long and 15 feet wide and was carted through
Main Street to its launching.[39] On a stern-wheeler of this type,
Charles Dickens embarked at Springfield in 1842 for the downstream trip to Hartford: "I am afraid to tell how many feet
short this vessel was, or how many feet narrow: to apply the
words length and width to such measurement would be a con-
tradiction in terms. But I may state that we all kept the middle
of the deck, lest the boat should unexpectedly tip over; and that
the machinery, by some surprising process of condensation,
worked between it and the keel: the whole forming a warm sand-
wich, about three feet thick." [40] Most of these tiny vessels acted
as towboats for strings of freight barges. Stage coaches generally
absorbed the passenger traffic north of Hartford. Such were the
fruits of a decade of human effort.

IV

No happier fortune attended New Haven's canal. The charter,
though the state made no financial contribution, provided for an

[38] Love, "Navigation of the Connecticut," pp. 429–430; Martin, *Merchants and
Trade of the Connecticut River Valley*, pp. 197–198.

[39] Boston *Advertiser*, May 16, 1829.

[40] Charles Dickens, *American Notes for General Circulation* (New York: Harper
& Brothers, 1842), p. 30.

extensive state participation in management, at least during the formative period. It appointed six "Commissioners of the Farmington Canal" who were to have no interest in the corporation aside from the receipt of their salaries from it. These commissioners were to lay out the canal, appraise land damages, determine the capitalization so that the number of $100 shares would be sufficient "to effect the entire object of said corporation," see that all the expenses of the corporation were paid, sell or lease the right to run packet boats, set the tolls so they would yield no more than 12 per-cent annual dividends, and inspect the condition of the canal and its works. In other matters the "President, Directors, and Company of the Farmington Canal" could run their corporation.[41] Thus it happened that the two most prominent figures in the early history of the canal were Simeon Baldwin, lawyer, law teacher, and a now unemployed and venerable jurist, who became chairman of the commissioners, and James Hillhouse, revolutionary veteran and treasurer of Yale College, who originally conceived of the canal and held various offices in the canal corporation.[42] Benjamin Wright, a Connecticut man who won fame as the engineer of the central section of the Erie Canal, made the survey as far as the Massachusetts line. He estimated the cost for a canal with wooden locks would be $420,698, a sum which did not include the land damages.[43] The extension to Northampton was surveyed a few years later by the Hurd brothers, one of whom was a lumber merchant and the other a shoe manufacturer who had lived in central New York and had been connected with the Erie. Their

[41] *Resolves and Private Laws . . . of Connecticut . . . 1789 to . . . 1836*, I, 301–306.

[42] *Dictionary of American Biography* (New York: Charles Scribner's Sons, 1928–1936), I, 543; *ibid.*, IX, 52; *An Account of the Farmington Canal Company; of the Hampshire and Hampden Canal Company; and of the New Haven and Northampton Company, till the Suspension of Its Canal in 1847* (New Haven: Thomas J. Stafford, 1850), pp. 8, 10.

[43] Charles R. Harte, "Some Engineering Features of the Old Northampton Canal," *Annual Report of the Connecticut Society of Civil Engineers*, 1932–1933, p. 23; *The Act of Incorporation of the Farmington Canal Company, with the Reports of the Hon. Benjamin Wright and Andrew A. Bartow, Esq. and of the Committee of the Legislature, . . . on that Subject* (New Haven: S. M. Dutton, 1822), pp. 3–5.

estimate for this section, again excluding land damages, was $290,000. For this sum New Haven could have a canal like the Champlain, but it passed through a country with a denser population and a more fertile soil and attained on the Connecticut a more promising terminus than Lake Champlain.[44]

Meanwhile, on July 4, 1825, the first shovel of earth had been turned with an appropriate parade two miles long and with equally long speeches. Perhaps it was a portent that the canal commissioners were drawn to this ceremony in a canal boat mounted on wheels.[45] Four years later the canal reached Westfield — in a fashion. A newspaper account described an excursion in which "after beating and luffing, and puffing, and sweating and waiting for the ebbing and flowing of tides to get over locks, and stones, and shoals, for about nine hours, it was found that one boat had advanced the immense distance of eight miles and the other six."[46] Finally, in 1835, the Massachusetts extension staggered over the difficult terrain of hill and valley into Northampton. The whole canal was 78 miles long. One of the toasts at the resulting banquet was so inappropriate as to be derisive: "Locomotive engines and railroad cars. They give reality to the fable of Phoebus, with his chariot and steeds of fire, and light up the world with the dawn of a new era."[47]

Those in charge of the canal, however, confronted the here-and-now of a financial emergency. After the first hurrah had passed, it was difficult to interest investors. The stock, originally

[44] *Report of Jarvis Hurd, Esq. Civil Engineer Employed by the Executive Committee of the Hampshire and Hampden Canal Company with an Estimate of the Expense to Complete the Canal, from the Termination of the Farmington Canal, on the Line of the State at Southwick, to the Great Bend of Connecticut River at Northampton* (Northampton: Hiram Terry, 1826), pp. 3–12, 36; Harte, "Some Engineering Features of the Old Northampton Canal," pp. 26–28.

[45] Julius Gay, *Farmington Papers* (Hartford: Case, Lockwood & Brainard Co., 1929), pp. 179–181.

[46] New Haven *Register*, July 11, 1829; *An Account of the Farmington Canal Company*, p. 6.

[47] New Haven *Register*, August 6, 1825; *An Account of the Farmington Canal Company*, pp. 9–10; John H. Lockwood, *Westfield and Its Historic Influences, 1669–1919* (Springfield: Springfield Printing and Binding Company, 1922), II, 288–295; *Mitchell's Compendium of the Internal Improvements of the United States: Comprising General Notices of All the Most Important Canals and Rail-Roads* (Philadelphia: Mitchell & Hinman, 1835), p. 16.

tax-free for twenty years, was given a perpetual exemption. Then stronger enterprises were promised life if they would aid the struggling canal. In 1824 the state chartered the Mechanics Bank in New Haven on condition that it subscribe $200,000 to the stock of the canal. In 1831 New Haven again received increased banking facilities in the City Bank of New Haven which as a prelude to operation was to subscribe $100,000 to the canal's stock. Under certain conditions the stock of both banks was free from taxation.[48] All this was not enough. Appeals were twice made to the city of New Haven for financial assistance; the municipality first subscribed $100,000 and later voted a loan and an annual subsidy.[49] Then on the Massachusetts extension the contractors took part of their pay in 1,000 shares of stock.[50] Desperate as these devices were, they did not prevent the accumulation of additional debts. Directors hid the chief engineer from creditors and were alleged "to elude, evade, prevaricate, procrastinate and totally neglect to liquidate, and absolutely refuse to pay any old claims since last December." [51]

In 1836, when the canal underwent the inevitable financial reorganization, the old stock was wiped out. Because of this and other financial mishaps it is extremely difficult to ascertain the cost of the canal. In 1845 it was asserted "the property . . . actually cost, first and last, nearly *two million of dollars*." The chief investors, aside from the institutional ones, were inhabitants of Northampton, Farmington, New York, and New Haven. The stock was fairly widely dispersed.[52] "The monied people in Boston" had not been interested in encouraging a project which brought their city so little benefit.[53]

[48] *Resolves and Private Laws . . . of Connecticut . . . 1789 to 1836*, I, 67–70, 104–107.
[49] *An Account of the Farmington Canal Company*, pp. 6, 12.
[50] *Ibid.*, p. 10.
[51] Stephen Walkly to Samuel J. Hitchcock, November 12, 1828, Ms., Farmington Canal Papers, Yale University Library.
[52] *Annual Report of the Board of Directors, to the Stockholders of the New Haven and Northampton Company. New Haven, January 15, 1845* (New Haven: Hitchcock & Stafford, 1845), p. 5; *An Account of the Farmington Canal Company*, pp. 9–10, 13.
[53] Samuel Hinckley to Simeon Baldwin, June 7, 1822, same to same, January 7, 1827, Ms., Farmington Canal Papers, New Haven Colony Historical Society.

Even in Connecticut the canal had few friends. It was unpopular in the country districts.[54] In New Haven it was condemned as a nuisance and as a violation of sound principles. On the former count old women objected because boys swam naked, and mothers because children fell into it on their way to school, and every user of the streets because its bridges and fences were kept in disrepair.[55] The objection on principle stemmed largely from the city's subscriptions, actual and projected. These expenditures had raised taxes which were paid by the poor and not by the rich and the educated, notably the officers and professors of Yale who were exempt from taxation. "The presiding officer of the city meeting that voted to borrow this 100,000 dollars, and mortgage the taxable property of the city for its payment, was an officer of the College, who is exempt from taxation." Emotional overtones consequently clustered about the issue. The canal quarrel was one between aristocrats and the common man, Whigs and Jacksonians, town and gown.[56]

Commercially the canal was a failure. Reorganized in 1836 as the New Haven and Northampton Company, the new enterprise wiped out the old stock, extinguished claims by the issue of new securities, and bludgeoned ready cash from subscriptions and assessments.[57] There were years when there was some business; in 1844 roughly 15,000 tons were transported down the canal and 9,000 tons found their way back. With a stab of hope it was said that ordinary receipts exceeded ordinary repairs, with despair that "extraordinary repairs were still heavy." [58] Some

[54] Thelma M. Kistler, *The Rise of Railroads in the Connecticut River Valley* (Northampton: 1938), pp. 27–28.

[55] New Haven *Register*, July 11, 1831.

[56] New Haven *Register*, April 26, 1834; *An Argument to the Opponents of the Proposed Loan to the Canal Company* (New Haven: J. L. Sullivan, 1839); *The City of New Haven and the New Haven and Northampton Canal Company* (Broadside, 1839); *Calm Considerations Relative to the Canal, Addressed to the Citizens of New Haven. . . .* (New Haven: 1839).

[57] *Resolves and Private Laws . . . of Connecticut . . . 1789 to 1836*, I, 308–311; New Haven *Register*, October 31, 1835, February 20, 1836; *An Account of the Farmington Canal Company*, pp. 10–12.

[58] *Annual Report . . . of the New Haven and Northampton Company, . . . January 15, 1845*, p. 16; *An Account of the Farmington Canal Company*, pp. 15–16.

years drought or freshet closed the canal entirely. Fundamental was the original niggardliness in construction. The Massachusetts extension was built on a smaller scale than the canal in Connecticut and even this shrunken prism, supposedly thirty-four feet wide at the surface and four feet deep, was not attained in practice. The by-laws of the canal required that when boats approached any place less than twenty-six feet wide on the surface, or where they could not pass, tidewater-bound vessels had the right of way. Again the wooden locks rotted rapidly.[59] With navigation frequently halted or interrupted, even the canal's friends had to admit that a lack of confidence prevented individuals from building boats and warehouses or relying upon the waterway.[60]

The New Haven opposition discovered other infirmities. Between Northampton and Hartford, New Haven's rival, the Connecticut River had a fall of but 90 feet. Its locks numbered only ten; it had steam navigation. Between Northampton and New Haven, the Farmington Canal was longer and canal boats, pulled by horses, had to pass sixty locks with a rise and fall of 520 feet. The canal was simply a subsidy conferred upon New Haven lumber and coal merchants, wood and iron dealers, packet owners and shippers. As soon might the city give vessels to its West India merchants.[61] Though these were sound arguments against the canal, they did not consider the value of its route as a possible right of way for a railroad. In the forties New England's longest canal was to have this worth and nothing more. So Hartford had triumphed not because of its river but because "railroads from Hartford up the Valley of the Conn. had changed the course of trade, and it fell into the laps of Hartford merchants, while those of New Haven were sitting still —

[59] Harte, "Some Engineering Features of the Old Northampton Canal," p. 31; *Report of Jarvis Hurd, Esq. . . . with an Estimate of the Expense to Complete the Canal . . . to . . . the Connecticut River,* pp. 11–13; *By-Laws of the New Haven and Northampton Company* (New Haven: 1836).

[60] *Report and Resolutions in Favor of a Loan of Credit by the City in Aid of the Canal* (New Haven: 1839).

[61] *Calm Considerations Relative to the Canal;* Smeaton, "Farmington and Hampshire and Hamden Canals," *American Railway Journal and Mechanics' Magazine,* XI (1840), 6–8.

sucking their fingers — and whining over the failure of the 'Old Canal.' " [62]

V

While Boston and eastern Massachusetts regarded these remote Connecticut enterprises with disfavor, they felt a positive dread of the Blackstone Canal connecting Providence and Worcester, a project practically on Boston's doorstep. Indeed some of her citizens and promoters had in the seventeen nineties successfully stifled in the Massachusetts legislature a charter for this harmful proposal.[63] By the twenties, however, Worcester was no longer an inconsequential village of the Commonwealth; her wishes carried weight; and the zeal of Providence merchants — Nicholas Brown, Edward Carrington, and Thomas P. Ives — for a connection with the interior was as strong as ever. The canal would make Providence an outlet for a most fertile area; Providence real estate would rise in value; and Providence business would be extended fifty or sixty miles.[64]

Consequently in 1823 charters were secured in Rhode Island and in Massachusetts. They had features in common. The canal was to secure its right-of-way much as highways and turnpikes had; tolls were placed at 6 cents a ton mile; and the shares of $100 each — no limit was placed upon their total — were tax exempt for eight years.[65] The Rhode Island promoters, however, were distressed at the illiberal nature of certain sections in their charter. The Blackstone River, along which the canal was to run, furnished water power for 20,000 spindles in cotton mills alone and the mill owners were alarmed lest the operation of the canal divert and diminish the flow of water to their water wheels.[66] In re-

---

[62] Joseph E. Sheffield, The "Old Canals" — Farmington and Hampshire & Hampden, Ms., Sheffield Papers, Yale University Library.

[63] Robert P. Montague, "The Blackstone Canal and Its Successor," Ms., Thesis in the possession of the author, Southbridge, Massachusetts, pp. 4–7.

[64] *Ibid.*, pp. 8–9.

[65] *Acts and Resolves of Rhode-Island and Providence Plantations, . . . June Session, 1823*, pp. 31–38; *Private and Special Statutes . . . of Massachusetts . . . 1822, . . . 1830*, VI, 16–21.

[66] Stephen H. Smith to John W. Lincoln, December 23, 1822, Same to Same, April 21, 1823, Same to Same, June 11, 1823, Ms., Blackstone Canal Papers, American Antiquarian Society.

sponse to their representations, the Rhode Island legislature prohibited the canal corporation from interfering with the "natural run of the waters" from the sources — ponds, streams, and brooks — of the Blackstone or from drawing these sources lower than low water mark, designated by "monuments" set by commissioners. When the canal corporation drew water from the river itself, it must return an equal amount through the locks within an hour.[67] The clumsiness of such restrictions certainly raised a question whether the canal could be legally operated at all.

For the moment these doubts were adjourned to later settlement. Amidst enthusiasm the subscription books were opened at Providence and Worcester. The leaders had determined that $500,000 was enough, but in Providence $1,130,000 was subscribed in three hours, and when messengers were dispatched to Worcester to obtain a share in the allotment granted in that city, they found that Worcester had already exceeded its quota. As usual installment buying had been authorized.[68] The promoters would have been wiser to have been less optimistic. Even after the canal was opened the directors issued new stock to meet its debts and finally ran to the shelter of a bank. In 1831 Rhode Island incorporated the Blackstone Canal Bank. Half of its capitalization of $250,000 was to be invested in the stock of the canal and the stockholders in the canal were given the privilege of subscribing share for share in the stock of the bank.[69]

Meanwhile construction had proceeded with spirit. The lower portion was opened for celebrant purposes on July 4, 1828, and by October the canal reached Worcester, alas a day too late for the cattle show. A Worcester paper thus gave the glad tidings: "SHIP NEWS FOR THE PORT OF WORCESTER, Oct. 8, 1828. Arrived yesterday the Lady Carrington. *Cargo*, Canal Commissioners, Salt, and Corn." The canal, forty-five miles long, used slackwater navigation for one-tenth of the distance; else-

[67] *Acts and Resolves of Rhode-Island and Providence Plantations . . . June Session, 1823*, pp. 29–31.

[68] Montague, "The Blackstone Canal," pp. 13–14.

[69] *Acts and Resolves of Rhode-Island and Providence Plantations, . . . January Session, 1831*, p. 13.

where an artificial channel closely followed the river until at the southern end it diverged from the Blackstone in order to move overland into the heart of Providence. It was substantially built.[70] Like the Middlesex, the Blackstone had a brief day of glory in the early thirties. Traffic increased, for, under its lowered charges, the average rate per ton between Boston and Worcester of $1.50 was considerably less than that of the earlier wagon trade. Inland it carried cotton, gypsum, salt, flour, molasses, and oil, and brought back cordwood and coal from a mine opened near Worcester. Worcester was the greatest destination of products, but some of the smaller places along the route furnished a heavier tide-bound traffic. The total tonnage in 1834 was: northbound, 12,761; southbound, 4,743.[71] This commerce gave employment to twenty or twenty-five boats. Although some were owned by individuals, corporations predominated. The Union Line had six boats in service with daily departures from Providence to Worcester and way places; the Providence and Worcester Canal Boat Company owned twelve freight boats and one packet, the *Lady Carrington*, which in spite of its luxurious fittings was never a successful competitor to the stage coaches for the passenger business. This second line was owned by the Blackstone Canal Company itself.[72]

In a short history, cramped between its inception and its displacement by a railroad in the forties, the Blackstone, like other canals, confronted the opposition of localities not served by its stream. Boston to the east, Springfield to the west both preferred a cross-state canal and begrudged Providence and Worcester their achievement. But "we struck as they say while the iron was hot," rejoiced a Worcester partisan, "and welded Worcester and Providence together and it will take a stronger arm than that of Samson to break us apart."[73] Much

[70] Montague, "The Blackstone Canal," pp. 17–22.

[71] *Ibid.*, pp. 24–25; William Lincoln, *History of Worcester, Massachusetts, from Its Earliest Settlement to September, 1836: With Various Notices Relating to the History of Worcester County*, p. 372.

[72] Montague, "The Blackstone Canal," pp. 20, 26–27; Anthony Chase to Buffom, October 4, 1830, Ms., Blackstone Canal Papers.

[73] Isaac Davis to J. W. Lincoln, June 9, 1825, Ms., Blackstone Canal Papers.

more vexatious were the quarrels with the mills over the division and regulation of the available water. Though the "canal gentry" made unusual efforts to secure reservoirs for impounding water, most of the ponds and lakes were in Massachusetts at a considerable distance from the mills in Rhode Island. In any case they proved inadequate. Charter provisions were altered, and compromise agreements made — all to no avail. To the canal supporters, the mill owners lacked "honor"; they were fired by a "spirit of speculation." [74] In the eyes of mill owners, the canal did not observe the legal obligations imposed upon it. They pressed a suit for penalties and secured an award of $6,450.[75] Long since, the canal had proved unremunerative. Tolls reached their peak in 1832, $18,907; in 1836, the year after the Boston and Worcester reached Worcester, they were $11,500. Either sum was a trivial return upon the estimated cost of $750,000. For the Blackstone, therefore, the contemporary historian of Worcester wrote a proper epitaph: "The canal has been more useful to the public, than to the owners." [76]

VI

Paradoxically, the most important canals for New England were beyond the borders of the area, the Erie and the Champlain canals. The former, by its example and by its connection with the West, had the wider influence upon the whole history of New England transportation; but the latter, by completing a waterway along New England's west coast, hastened at first hand the economic advance of her northwest. The Champlain Canal was to tap the products of the Champlain basin. Lumber, the most important commodity of this northern area, was to find a new outlet along the Hudson; country produce, including pot and pearl ashes, was to supply the New York City market; and the iron of New York now "unwrought in the mine and the fine

[74] *Acts and Resolves of Rhode-Island and Providence Plantations . . . January Session, 1826*, pp. 37–41; Isaac Davis to J. W. Lincoln, December 12, 1825, Ms., Blackstone Canal Papers; Montague, "The Blackstone Canal," pp. 15–17.

[75] Montague, "The Blackstone Canal," pp. 30–31.

[76] Lincoln, *History of Worcester*, pp. 339–340, 372; Montague, "The Blackstone Canal," p. 29.

marble of Vermont which now lies useless in the quarry" were to be sold in the East or exchanged for salt and gypsum in up-state New York and in the West. In short, the great aim of these inland waterways — the Erie and the Champlain — was to "unite the forty-fifth degree of latitude on Lake Champlain with the farthest verge of Lake Superior." [77]

From the engineering point of view it was easier to reach Lake Champlain than Lake Erie from the Hudson. For one thing the distance was much shorter, only twenty-eight miles separating Whitehall on the lake from Fort Edward on the Hudson; for another, the elevation to be surmounted was trivial. A dam one hundred and fifty feet high thrown across the Hudson at the Highlands would have turned the current of that stream northward through Lake Champlain. At the outset, however, this northern canal was planned on a more puny scale than the Erie. Its prism was to have a surface width of 30 and a bottom width of 20, and a depth of 3 feet; similar dimensions for the Erie were to be 40 x 28 x 3; the locks on the Champlain were 75 feet long and 10 feet wide; those on the Erie 90 x 12 feet. Finally, although New York's earlier experience had convincingly demonstrated to DeWitt Clinton and others the folly of improving a river and the wisdom of a canal paralleling its banks, the long mileage of the upper Hudson between Fort Edward and Troy was to be covered by slack-water navigation. Three dams were to set back the water; the upper two were each passed by canals and two locks; from the third a twelve mile canal with eight locks ran southward to Waterford on the Hudson's west bank. Here it entered the river.[78]

Fortunately modifications were soon made in this original design. The canal commissioners immediately enlarged the dimen-

[77] Report of the Canal Commissioners on the Northern or Champlain Canal, March 19, 1817, *Laws of the State of New York in Relation to the Erie and Champlain Canals, Together with the Annual Reports of the Canal Commissioners, and Other Documents, Requisite for a Complete Official History of Those Works* (Albany: E. and E. Hosford, 1825), I, 287–289; Report of the Canal Commissioners, January 31, 1818, *ibid.*, I, 381.

[78] Report of the Canal Commissioners, February 17, 1817, *Laws . . . in Relation to the Erie and Champlain Canals*, I, 198; Report of the Canal Commissioners on the Northern or Champlain Canal, March 19, 1817, *ibid.*, I, 289–291.

sions of the Champlain Canal to those of the Erie; its prism was
to be 40 x 28 x 4 and its locks were 90 x 14, the new measurements for the Erie.[79] This change made it possible for the same
boats to use the entire system; it also expedited the lumber trade
from Lake Champlain by a more ample channel. The commissioners abandoned slack-water navigation, however, in a series
of partial decisions. As a consequence the canal was officially
completed time and time again. It was completed in 1820 in
accordance with the original design; it was again completed in
1823 when the canal north from Waterford had been extended
far enough to eliminate some of the projected slack-water navigation; and it was finally completed in 1827 when a canal
paralleled the river throughout.[80] By then this improved waterway had cost $1,252,707,[81] a figure obtained by adding costs of
construction and operation and deducting the tolls received. New
York bore this expense. In contrast with the New England canals,
the former's enterprises were not built by private investors but
by state funds.

Meanwhile a war between Albany and Troy was fought over
the canal's southern terminus. The original selection of Waterford, while it did not delight, did not antagonize either rival;
from Waterford canal boats could proceed impartially down river
to either Albany or Troy. The canal commissioners soothingly
announced, "The termination of the northern canal in the Hudson at Waterford, will afford the cities of Albany and Troy, and
the villages of Lansingburgh and Waterford, a full participation
of its benefits." [82] Still Troy was uneasy, for the canal and its
terminus was on the west or Albany side of the river. For the

[79] Annual Report of the Canal Commissioners, January 31, 1818, *Laws . . . in
Relation to the Erie and Champlain Canals*, I, 378–379; Annual Report of the
Canal Commissioners, February 18, 1820, *ibid.*, I, 457.

[80] Annual Report of the Canal Commissioners, March 12, 1821, *Laws . . . in
Relation to the Erie and Champlain Canals*, II, 22; Annual Report of the Canal
Commissioners, February 24, 1823, *ibid.*, II, 112; Report of the Canal Commissioners, March 4, 1825, *ibid.*, II, 253–254; *Annual Report of the Canal Commissioners to the Assembly, February 10, 1827*, pp. 15–17.

[81] Report of the Canal Board on the Cost of the Champlain Canal, New York
Senate Documents, 1836, no. 2, pp. 8–10.

[82] Report of the Canal Commissioners on the Northern or Champlain Canal,
March 19, 1817, *Laws . . . in Relation to the Erie and Champlain Canals*, I, 292.

moment she held her fire. Later, however, the canal commissioners blandly announced that the Champlain Canal was to be continued down the west bank, carried across the mouth of the Mohawk, and joined with the Erie Canal which ran southward to a basin at Albany. They implied that such a connection had always been intended and pointed out that it shortened the route to the north by five miles. A side cut opposite Troy still afforded that city access to the northern trade.[83] This sweet reasonableness was intended to calm the angry Trojans, who had dispatched a thundering petition to the legislature. The northern trade of New York and Vermont had always been Troy's but "now it is passed down on the West or opposite bank of the Hudson in boats and if it reaches them at all, it is after passing both the Mohawk and Hudson which is sometimes impracticable, always difficult and vexatious and producing risk, delay, and expense." The remedy was the extension of the Champlain Canal across the Hudson by an aqueduct to Troy. A committee of the New York Assembly was moved by sympathy. They believed "that a particular branch of trade which has built up and sustained a village, town, or city, should not be transferred to another, unless the public interest imperiously demands it," and granted the prayer of their petitioners.[84] The plan, however, did not materialize. Long since, the quarrels of the two cities had tired the canal commissioners. They "have certainly had to encounter the difficulties arising from local interests, and the disappointments of individual cupidity." [85]

Even as Troy and Albany snarled, traffic had turned to the new waterway. Its first users were lumber rafts and canal boats; the complete demonstration of its value waited upon the autumn of 1823. Then the sloop, *Gleaner*, Vermont-built, sailed down the lake from St. Albans with a thousand bushels of wheat, thirty-five barrels of potash, and berths for ten passengers. After

---

[83] Report of Canal Commissioners under a Resolution of the 18th and 20th of March, 1823, April 3, 1823, *Laws . . . in Relation to the Erie and Champlain Canals*, II, 120–121, 129.

[84] New York *Assembly Journal*, 1824, p. 246; Albany *Argus*, March 21, 28, 1823.

[85] Report of Canal Commissioners, April 3, 1823, *Laws . . . in Relation to the Erie and Champlain Canals*, II, 129.

a passage through the canal and the works on the Hudson, she docked at Troy, where there was a procession and a public dinner. Then, raising her sails, she glided down river to New York City. There the Veteran Corps of Artillery fired a federal salute, a tow of rowboats warped her into Coenties slip, and a local poet hailed her as "The Barque of the Mountains." The time from St. Albans to New York was cut more than half — it was now ten to fourteen days — and freight rates were reduced from $25 or $30 to $10.[86]

The *Gleaner* was in advance of her time. Not until the forties were vessels generally built with a sloop rig to be used on the lake, taken down at Whitehall, and hoisted again at Troy for the voyage down the Hudson. Until that time transhipments were the rule. On Champlain large schooners or sloops, some of them of two hundred tons, carried lumber, iron, and other products to Whitehall and transferred their cargoes to the canal boats, which in turn transferred them to barges on the Hudson. These separate successive steps were under common management. Merchants, lumbermen, and steamboat owners built up lines of lake sloops and schooners, canal boats, and barges and steamers on the Hudson, and established agencies at Troy, Albany, New York, Whitehall, and Burlington. Meanwhile better and larger steamboats were built for the lake traffic.[87]

If it had not been for the collection of tolls, the extent and variety of this commerce would have been unchronicled. As it is, the records of the Champlain Canal give a key. At first the traffic was largely in lumber, gathered in long rafts which, when the water was low, choked the waterway for miles.[88] After the partial abandonment of slack-water navigation in 1823, both the variety and amount of commodities rapidly increased. Within a

[86] Albany *Argus*, September 9, 1823; Thomas H. Canfield, "Discovery, Navigation and Navigators of Lake Champlain," A. M. Hemenway, ed., *The Vermont Historical Gazetteer: A Magazine Embracing a History of Each Town, Civil, Eccelesiastical, Biographical and Military* (Burlington: A. M. Hemenway, 1867), I, 681; Albany *Argus*, October 10, 1823.

[87] Canfield, "Discovery, Navigation and Navigators of Lake Champlain," pp. 682–683.

[88] Annual Report of the Canal Commissioners, February 20, 1824, *Laws . . . in Relation to the Erie and Champlain Canals*, II, 176.

decade the shipments of wool multiplied forty-five times, those of butter and cheese nearly fifty, and those of beef and pork increased from zero to 4,599 barrels. Although the percentages of increase for lumber were less, the totals were staggering. In 1833, 70,347,099 feet of sawed lumber floated down the canal. In fact, in the thirties lumber shipments on the Champlain were greater than on the Erie, the only classification in which the former was superior.[89] The upbound traffic on the canal as far as quantity was concerned was about one-sixth that of the down traffic. Gypsum, coal, flour, and salt furnished the chief tonnage; and merchandise its chief value.[90] In the same decade tolls on the canal increased from $26,986 to well over $100,000.[91]

Since Canada was but a poor third, the source and destination of these products were determined by the two worlds of Lake Champlain. The western world was New York's; its rough terrain, lifting from the lake to the Adirondack mountains, was a region of raw materials — lumber, pig iron, and its derivative,

[89] Report of the Commissioners of the Canal Fund, Relative to the Amount of Tolls Collected and Property Transported on the Canals in 1835, New York *Senate Documents*, 1836, no. 70, Tables C-1, D-1.

[90] Annual Report of the Commissioners of the Canal Fund, Relative to the Amount of Tolls Collected and Property Transported, 1834, New York *Senate Documents*, 1835, no. 58, Tables E, I.

Bound Down at Whitehall	1823	1833
Butter and cheese, lbs.	27,776	1,322,000
Beef and pork, barrels	....	4,599
Glass, boxes	3	13,788
Iron nails, tons	153	2,043
Iron pig, "	....	7
Iron ore, "	101	830
Marble, "	44	708
Stoves, number	21,000	107,000
Wool, lbs.	9,660	432,000
Sawed lumber, feet	22,426,067	70,347,099
Timber, cu. ft.	1,179,515	1,190,908
Wood, cords	....	4,532
Bound Up at Whitehall		
Beef and pork, barrels	1,493	5,526
Coal, tons	40	423
Flour, barrels	5,064	61,247
Plaster { Western } tons	48	115
Plaster { Nova Scotia } tons	34	273
Salt, bushels	138,045	123,337

[91] *Ibid.*, p. 2.

ironware. New England's was a gentler shore. Vermont furnished over half the butter and cheese, four-fifths of the wool, and nearly all the barreled beef. As destination for the flour and salt, the differences between the two worlds was insignificant.[92] Meanwhile, at the lower end of the canal, Troy and Albany continued their vindictive competition. The latter city engrossed the trade in lumber, wheat, corn, and other cereals, and her clearances and arrivals far surpassed those at Troy. Nevertheless the Trojans were content. Their river front was still thriving and they kept their hold on the trade in flour and iron.[93] In 1836 they announced that, in spite of all the favors granted by the legislature to the capital city, "Troy has thus far sustained herself in a competition with Albany." Still the fear of a falling population and of "deserted habitations, wharves, and ware houses" would not down.[94] Perhaps if Troy could become the terminus of the railroad projected westward from Boston, she could dispel that nightmare forever.

VII

With the canals the pre-railroad era in New England came to an end. They were the last step in the long march to improve and supplement the original endowment of the region — its rivers and its seacoast. In part, therefore, all were prelude. Organized in the most diverse fashion, from the individualism of the coastal trade to the turnpike and canal corporations; infused to a varying degree with the conception of government control, they gave to the railroads a comparatively unrestricted choice among the methods of organizing their business. It is, however, a mistake to regard this earlier transportation as a mere preparation for

[92] Annual Report of the Commissioners of the Canal Fund, Relative to the Amount of Tolls Collected and Property Transported, 1836, New York *Senate Documents*, 1837, no. 52, Tables F-1, G-1, G-2.
[93] Annual Report of the Canal Commissioners for 1831, New York *Assembly Documents*, 1832, no. 42, Table B.
[94] *Report of the Committee of the Common Council of the City of Troy, and Adopted by Them Remonstrating Against the Direct Route for the Eastern Termination of the Erie Canal, and an Answer to the Report of Allan Campbell, Civil Engineer, Made by the Authority and under the Direction of the Common Council of the City of Albany* (Troy: Kemble & Hooper, 1836), pp. 32, 34.

the railroad network. In their day coasting trades, highways, and canals were the transportation system of the area. As such, it had accomplishments, though innovations may have failed to return their capital to investors. Even before the railroads, commercial agriculture had begun to replace the self-sufficiency of the farm, manufacturing was organized on a large scale at Waltham and Lowell, and population was so mobile that it had spread throughout New England with the exception of central and northern Maine and had spilled over into a westward migration. These considerable achievements were possible because New England was different. It was a region not of magnificent but of short distances. Within it even the wagon trade was more useful than in states with imperial domains. When Massachusetts farmers opposed the railroad because it would introduce the competition of western agricultural products, they feared because they had something to lose.

IV

"THE RAILROAD SCHEME"

"A happy New Year to you, my beloved husband! May it preserve to you all your blessings, confirm all your virtues, realize all your hopes! May it ripen your peaches, multiply your strawberries, extend your grapes, & build your RAILROAD!" — Susan Sedgwick to Theodore Sedgwick, January 6, 1828. Sedgwick Papers, Massachusetts Historical Society.

I

By the eighteen twenties, New England was in ferment. Unitarianism had shattered the old religious orthodoxy and, while the Dedham case provided a material dowry for the new religion, the sermons of William Ellery Channing furnished a theology and creed. In politics the dogmas of regional Federalism were weakened and soon Daniel Webster was to celebrate the virtues of an embracing nationalism which Pickering and his fellow conspirators of an earlier period would have found incomprehensible. Along the Merrimack were arising the cotton-mill towns, symbols of a new industrialism. An old order was giving way to a new. Once begun, change accelerated and touched one by one the institutions and ideas of the region. Of the economic factors that gave momentum to this transformation, the railroad was the most important. For it was the railroad that after 1830 tied New England into the nation. No longer was it to be a fringe of Hanseatic ports communicating with the rest of the world and with America by sea; it was to become a section in a developing nation. When Emerson wrote of Massachusetts, "From 1790 to

1820, there was not a book, a speech, a conversation, or a thought in the State," [1] he should have added that there was not a railroad. For the railroad, even though it may not have opened wider prospects, at least revealed different ones.

The railroad excited even Boston, too long content with her coasting trade, her Middlesex Canal and her turnpikes. She did not suffer the decline of foreign commerce experienced by the smaller and once prosperous seaports of the New England coast line from Portsmouth to New Haven, and, sufficiently remote from New York, she was not immediately upset by the excitement over the projected Erie Canal. In the twenties she waked suddenly to danger. The restless ambitions of her smaller rivals alarmed her and the completion of the Erie for the potential benefit of her great foe, New York, added more pressing reasons for action. First of all, the "traditional area" tributary to Boston was invaded. This conception was as nebulous, no doubt, as that of "strategic frontiers," but it packed as much passion. Near at hand was Worcester County, the largest in the state and a veritable province in itself, for it stretched from the northern to the southern boundary of the Commonwealth. Now it was tapped by the Blackstone Canal thrust northward from Providence. On its completion Governor Lincoln of Massachusetts sounded a note of alarm: "The most serious diversions of trade are taking place to other markets. Already hundreds of tons of merchandise have been carried from the warehouses of a neighbouring Government, through a new channel, into a central and populous district of the Commonwealth, . . . By this channel also, a direct trade in lumber has commenced with the State of Maine, and in goods with the city of New York, from either of which places water conveyance fifty miles inland into Massachusetts is at half the cost of land carriage from Boston to Worcester only." With overland costs of transportation at $9.00 a ton, the metropolis of Massachusetts was confronted with the possibility of sharing the extensive traffic of Worcester County in manufactured and agricultural goods not only with Providence but with

[1] E. W. Emerson and W. E. Forbes, eds., *Journals of Ralph Waldo Emerson* (Boston and New York: Houghton Mifflin Company, 1909–1914), VIII, 339.

New York, the latter already dominating the southern shore of New England.[2]

Farther west the Connecticut Valley trembled in the balance. The desperate rivalry of Hartford and New Haven had brought to the point of execution schemes for the improvement of river navigation and the construction of the New Haven and Northampton canal. Even before their completion the traffic of central Massachusetts revealed a tendency to float downstream to the benefit of Springfield, Hartford, and New Haven. Nor was Boston so confused by the boastful enterprise of these minor centers as to overlook the fact that behind them loomed the real beneficiary of their ambitions — New York City. When it cost on the average $14 to $20 to haul a ton overland by wagon from the Connecticut Valley to Boston, a price that only light and choice goods could pay, when the more bulky products that had to go all the way by water paid at least a dollar a ton less from Connecticut River points to New York than to Boston, it was not surprising that the latter had only a fifth of the total traffic of the Massachusetts river counties and feared the improvement of river navigation would deprive her of the wagon trade with the upper valley in Vermont and New Hampshire. Finally Berkshire, the westernmost county of Massachusetts, though it still had political relationships with the state of which it was a part, was turned toward the south and west by its remoteness from the state capital, by its proximity to the Hudson River, and by the mountain barrier between it and the Connecticut. Perhaps the trade of this region was not worth bothering about; like its population it was stagnant. But it was galling for Massachusetts men to reflect that Lee and Stockbridge exported and imported by way of the Hudson, that the people of Berkshire and Boston were almost total strangers to one another, and that the region had become for all practical purposes of

[2] Levi Lincoln, Governor's Message, January 7, 1829, *Resolves of the General Court of the Commonwealth of Massachusetts, Passed at the Several Sessions of the General Court, Commencing May, 1828, and Ending June, 1831*, pp. 81–82; Nathan Hale, *Remarks on the Practicability and Expediency of Establishing a Railroad on One or More Routes from Boston to the Connecticut River* (Boston: William L. Lewis, 1827), pp. 59–60.

trade an appendage of the state of New York. With the exception of some commerce with Hartford, Berkshire imported and exported through Troy, Hudson, and Albany.[3]

After the Erie was opened in 1825, goods from up-state New York and the Middle West were laid down on the upper Hudson. They could be carried profitably to New England only by the river and coasting trade. Figures for the importance of this traffic were provided by the water-borne trade between Albany and Troy and the ports of New England and by an additional tonnage of approximately 25 per cent which was transshipped at New York City. The direct trade from Albany alone increased 150 per cent between 1824 and 1827; it gave employment to 123 vessels, one third of which were regular traders making five trips a year to ports ranging from Boston through Taunton and New Bedford to Newport and Providence. East were sent the heavy products of lumber, iron ore, wool, and flour; Boston took in a single year 23,500 barrels of flour and 290,000 bushels of grain. Westbound went the assorted products that were traditional with New England commerce — fish, oil, nails, castings, molasses, New England rum, sugar, glass, rolled iron, and factory goods.[4] The arguments advanced for improved means of transportation for Boston, while they emphasized the local traffics of Massachusetts, muted these western possibilities. Policy, not provincialism, explained this reticence. The opposition, both to a western canal and a western railroad, came from rural Massachusetts. To stress the future importation of whisky, livestock, lumber, and grain from the American West was hardly a way to

[3] Hale, *ibid.*, pp. 56, 59, 62–63; Hale, *Remarks on the Practicability and Expediency of Rail Roads from Boston to the Hudson River and from Boston to Providence* (Boston: Boston Daily Advertiser, 1829), pp. 24–31; *Report of the Board of Directors of Internal Improvements of the State of Massachusetts, on the Practicability and Expediency of a Rail-Road from Boston to the Hudson River, and from Boston to Providence. Submitted to the General Court, January 16, 1829*, pp. 30–35.

[4] Report of the Commissioners, Appointed under the Act of April 15, 1828, Relative to the Construction of a Rail-Road from the City of Boston to the Hudson River, New York *Senate Documents*, 1829, no. 113, pp. 54, 59–62; *Report of the Board of Directors of Internal Improvements of the State of Massachusetts, on the Practicability and Expediency of a Rail-Road from Boston to the Hudson River, and from Boston to Providence*, pp. 27–30.

endear a project to the landowners and farmers of Franklin or Worcester. "The only objection I have heard offered by any one [against the railroad]," wrote a correspondent to James F. Baldwin from Petersham, "is that it will open an avenue for the produce of the West to Boston Market, and thereby injure the farmers here. This is the objection of all."

The transportation enterprises of Massachusetts, moreover, required the good will of New York State if they were to secure a terminus upon the Hudson. Interstate diplomacy obviously required a disavowal of vigorous competition between Boston and New York City. The Massachusetts literature of promotion, therefore, breathed an air of sweet conciliation; Boston did not wish to rival New York but "harmoniously participate" with it in western commerce. Beneath the tact of these early reports, the design to secure the western trade ran strong. Boston dreamed of the commerce on the Great Lakes, appropriately denominated the "Mediterranean Seas of America," of the copper trade of Lake Superior and the lead trade of Missouri, of an all-water route through canals and the Mississippi to the "Gulph," of the fur trade of the "uninhabited regions, extending to the Rocky Mountains." The West was not beyond Boston's business horizon.[5] On this score her editors, politicians, manufacturers, and merchants were as foresighted as those of New York, Pennsylvania, Maryland, and South Carolina.

In the eyes of their advocates, internal improvements involved more than the mere interchange of commodities. They promised the regeneration of Boston, of the Commonwealth, and of all New England. The arguments have the ring of sectional mercantilism. The drain of specie to the voracious market of New York and to the South would cease, the price of lands would rise, and general business would flourish. Above all, the prosperity induced by a quickened transportation would put a stop to the alarming emigration from the region. The population of Massachusetts was increasing less rapidly than that of the rest of the nation; be-

[5] William S. Prentiss to James F. Baldwin, February 16, 1829, Ms., Baldwin Papers, XXXVI, Harvard Business School Library; *Report of the Commissioners of the State of Massachusetts, on the Routes of Canals from Boston Harbour, to Connecticut and Hudson Rivers*, pp. 167–174.

tween 1810 and 1820 Berkshire County declined in numbers. While a few accepted the phenomenon with resignation as drain- *sense of "decay"* ing away the least desirable portion of the population, state patriots feared the westward march as a symptom of decline.

> Between the close of 1825 and the beginning of 1831 gloom and despondency seemed to settle down upon Massachusetts. Her sons left her to build up rival states and cities, and her fairest and richest daughters were courted away to grace more prosperous lands. The grass began to invade the wharves and pavements of her commercial centers and the paint to desert the front of her villages . . . . She seemed to stand at the ancestral tomb, sorrowing that she could not partake of the progress of the age, or to be dropping a tear beside the old hive as it grew yearly darker, or crumbled away while swarm after swarm left it for sunnier skys. . . . Wedded to the systems of the past, she could not realize that men and merchandise were to be whirled through her granite hills and deep ravines, winter and summer, regardless of frost and snow.[6]

Before this vision materialized, a canal was naturally proposed as the first means to redeem for Boston her old position and to conquer a new eminence. Providence, New Haven, and New York were menacing Boston through waterways, and by the device of the Middlesex Canal, Boston had undercut Newburyport and won for herself the trade of the Merrimack Valley. Consequently, in 1825 the legislature, imitating the pattern set by states from New York to South Carolina,[7] appointed three commissioners to conduct a survey of the routes for a canal to the Hudson. The three in turn appointed Loammi Baldwin II as their engineer. On January 11, 1826, Governor Levi Lincoln hastened to transmit the report of their labors to the legislature. The eminence of the engineer gave it the imprint of presumed authority. The son of the Loammi Baldwin who had

---

[6] Elias H. Derby, "Progress of Railroads in Massachusetts," *Hunt's Merchants' Magazine and Commercial Review*, XIV (1846), 30; Hale, *Remarks on the Practicability and Expediency of Rail Roads from Boston to the Hudson River and from Boston to Providence*, p. iv.

[7] "Annual Report of the President and Directors of the Board of Public Works of Virginia," *North American Review*, VIII (1818), 1–26; "Internal Improvements of North Carolina," *ibid.*, XII (1821), pp. 16–33; "Internal Improvements in South Carolina," *ibid.*, XIII (1821), 143–154; "The New York Canals," *ibid.*, XIV (1822), 230–250; "Baltimore," *ibid.*, XX (1825), 99–138.

built the Middlesex Canal, Loammi Baldwin II was a graduate of Harvard and already well on his way to the title of "The Father of Civil Engineering in America." [8] Rejecting the several routes through Worcester, Baldwin led his imaginary waterway north and west from Boston. In this fashion the central portion of the canal used Millers River as an approach to the Connecticut, and the Deerfield River as an avenue into the Berkshires; it crossed the Connecticut above existing dams and locks which, it was hoped, would be a sufficient obstruction to divert down-river traffic into the new waterway. These advantages must have been convincing ones, for to the east the projected canal had to cross a series of valleys and ridges between Boston and the eastern New England plateau and then by a series of interminable locks cross the plateau whose highest point was "1065.84 feet above low water mark, in Boston Harbour." Baldwin thought the cost for this eastern section would be roughly $3,000,000. The section between the Connecticut and the Hudson could hardly have been said to be surveyed; it would be more proper to describe it as viewed. The ascent of the Deerfield required almost as much lockage as the whole Erie Canal. Between the Deerfield's upper reaches and the Hoosic River, leading to the Hudson, the projected route had to conquer the elongated mass of Hoosac Mountain. The latter could be circumvented by a canal requiring 220 locks and two days for their passage or it could be pierced by a four-mile tunnel, costing only $920,832. Once escaped from "the Alpine regions of Massachusetts and Vermont," the canal would run easily to a terminus at Troy. The cost of the western section was estimated at $3,023,172.

The report closes with a calculation of traffic from existing farms and mines and "future Manchesters and Birminghams" and recommends that the state finance the construction through a canal fund collected from various taxes, a state lottery, the sale of public lands, and canal tolls. Without a hint that private capital was inadequate or too timid for so grandiose an enter-

[8] George L. Vose, *A Sketch of the Life and Works of Loammi Baldwin, Civil Engineer. Read before the Boston Society of Civil Engineers. Sept. 16, 1885* (Boston: George H. Ellis, 1885), p. 3.

prise — perhaps such an admission would be an impolitic reflection upon its soundness — the commissioners set their choice of state finance upon the high ground of principle.

> Doubting whether a work of this extensive, permanent and costly character, which is calculated to have such a powerful and lasting influence upon the great mass of the people, and involving so many interests, of a local, private and public nature, should be accomplished by an incorporated company, the Commissioners have, on mature reflection, come to the conclusion, to suggest the expediency of it being undertaken by the State. As the whole object is ultimately to facilitate the intercourse between all parts of the Commonwealth, and extend it to other sections of the Union, not for the purpose of speculation, or pecuniary profit but to subserve the general weal, the controul should ever be kept within the power of the State Authorities.[9]

The sponsors of this report bear a heavy responsibility. The delusion that they inspired, the ease and cheapness of tunneling Hoosac Mountain, bedeviled for fifty years the commercial and railroad policy of Massachusetts. Fortunately it had little immediate effect. In a state with a Treasury balance at the end of 1827 of less than $30,000, the sums mentioned were staggering. The engineering proposals, moreover, affronted many hardheaded Yankees. A correspondent to the Boston *Courier*, selecting differing premises, calculated that to build the canal would take 52 or perhaps 182 years.[10]

II

Meanwhile the Bunker Hill Monument Association had retained Loammi Baldwin to determine the scale of their immense stone obelisk. While the distinguished engineer may have felt this engineering employment less important than the survey of a cross-state canal, Bunker Hill Monument was actually to have more immediate influence upon Massachusetts transportation.

[9] *Report of the Commissioners of the State of Massachusetts on the Routes of Canals from Boston Harbour, passim.*
[10] Charles F. Adams, Jr., "The Canal and Railroad Enterprise of Boston," *The Memorial History of Boston, Including Suffolk County, Massachusetts, 1630–1830* (Boston: James R. Osgood and Company, 1881), IV, 115.

The members of the Association had to solve the problem of carrying granite from the Quincy quarries, selected by their agent as the most suitable source for stone, to the edge of Boston harbor. When a short canal, built through the energy of Quincy citizens, proved a failure, Gridley Bryant proposed the construction of a railroad. A self-taught master builder, Bryant had his own contracting business at the age of twenty-one; no mere artisan, he studied books on mechanics and natural philosophy and sought to master underlying principles. He did not find all his associates enthusiastic for the railroad; in the legislature, when he applied for a charter, he was met with the objections, "What do we know about railroads? Who ever heard of such a thing? Is it right to take people's land for a project that no one knows anything about? We have corporations enough already." But he had the financial and personal support of Thomas H. Perkins, the enlightened merchant prince, and the proposed railroad was a small enterprise. On March 4, 1826, the state incorporated the Granite Railway Company, authorized it to lay out a line from the quarries to tidewater in Milton and Quincy, and set tolls for the carriage of stone and other property. Although the opening of the road in October aroused little excitement, the Granite Railway at once furnished an encouraging example of specific and local success.[11]

With a trunk line a little less than two miles long and with a five-foot gauge, it solved in the most massive fashion the problem of supporting the rails and the heavy loads passing over them and of anchoring this support beneath the frost line. For each rail a dry stone wall was first laid in a deep trench; immense granite sleepers, sometimes weighing a ton apiece, were placed across these bearings at intervals of eight feet; upon these sleepers were laid longitudinally first a pine timber, twelve inches deep and six inches wide, and then a strip of oak three inches wide by two inches thick, to which was attached an iron plate rail, two

[11] Charles B. Stuart, *Lives and Works of Civil and Military Engineers of America* (New York: D. Van Nostrand, 1871), pp. 122–123; *Laws of the Commonwealth of Massachusetts, Passed at the Several Sessions of the General Court, Beginning May, 1825, and Ending March, 1828*, pp. 329–334.

and a half inches wide and three-eighths of an inch thick. When the underlying wooden stringers decayed, granite replaced them in 1828. The steepest ascent, an "inclined plane" as the phrase of the era had it, was sixty-six feet to the mile. A single horse "perhaps about the quality of the Truck Horses used in Boston," usually made four round trips a day, carrying down a load of twelve and a half tons, exclusive of wagons, in thirty-five minutes.[12] Although Bryant regretted his lack of time to make more accurate experiments, he built a turntable, a portable derrick, switches, and cars whose frames or platforms were mounted upon two four-wheeled trucks and attached in such a fashion as to swivel when rounding curves. "When stones of eight or ten tons were to be carried, I took two of these [four-wheeled] trucks and attached them together by a platform and long bolts. This made an eight wheel Car. When more stones were carried, I increased the number of trucks and thus made a sixteen wheel car." Byrant thus anticipated the long wheel base and the four-wheel swiveled trucks of the later American railway car.[13] The Quincy railroad furnished a powerful illustration for the protagonists of further railroad construction in Massachusetts.

In the educational campaign that followed, no horizon limited the field from which material was drawn. The current progress in Great Britain, the successful opening of the Stockton and Darlington Rail-way in September 1825, the famous Rainhill trials of 1829 on the Liverpool and Manchester Rail-way won by George Stephenson's locomotive, *The Rocket*, and the epochal opening of the same railroad to traffic a year later — information of all these events was swiftly carried to the United States by the British press or by articles in British periodicals like their *Quarterly Review*. Then public works in this country, the Baltimore and Ohio and the Delaware and Hudson, exemplified the

[12] Gridley Bryant to James F. Baldwin, January 21, 1828, Baldwin Papers, XXXVI; Hale, *Remarks on the Practicability and Expediency of Establishing a Rail Road on One or More Routes from Boston to the Connecticut River*, pp. 3–8; *Report of Board of Commissioners for the Survey of One or More Routes for a Railway from Boston to Albany* (Boston: Dutton and Wentworth, 1828), pp. 28–29.

[13] Stuart, *Lives and Works of Civil and Military Engineers of America*, pp. 123–127.

new science of transportation. An extensive printed literature on railways and locomotives appeared at once and was continually revised to keep abreast of the rapid changes in the field. Massachusetts controversialists continually repaired to a book by Nicholas Wood, a "colliery viewer," entitled *A Practical Treatise on Rail-Roads and Interior Communication in General*, the first (1825) English edition of which sought in 315 pages to give a systematic knowledge of the subject. The first American edition, that of 1832, was a veritable encyclopedia of railroad lore in nearly 600 pages. Much shorter was *A Practical Treatise on Rail-Roads and Carriages*, by Thomas Tredgold, an eminent English architect and engineer whose investigation of strains in wood was a pioneer work. The book, jammed with calculations on functions and motive powers, appeared in an American edition in 1825, the same year as the first edition in England.[14] So practical and so up-to-date were the details of these volumes that the directors of the Boston and Worcester in ordering an engine in 1833 wanted "the performance to be equal to that specified in page 365 of Wood's treatise on Rail Roads — American edition — ." [15]

Such were the practice and theory that inspired a small group to conceive and promote "the railroad scheme," a railroad network for Massachusetts. Theirs was almost a conspiracy. It was in "the obscure chamber and studied privacy" that "the first measures were concerted to enlighten the community" about the

---

[14] Thomas Tredgold, *A Practical Treatise on Rail-Roads and Carriages, Shewing the Principles of Estimating Their Strength, Proportions, Expense, and Annual Produce, and the Conditions Which Render Them Effective, Economical, and Durable; with the Theory, Effect, and Expense of Steam Carriages, Stationary Engines, and Gas Machines* (London: Printed for Josiah Taylor, 1825); *ibid.* (New York: E. Bliss and E. White, 1825); Nicholas Wood, *A Practical Treatise on Rail-Roads, and Interior Communication in General; with Original Experiments, and Tables of the Comparative Value of Canals and Rail-Roads* (London: Printed for Knight and Lacey, 1825); Wood, *A Practical Treatise on Rail-Roads and Interior Communication in General, Containing an Account of the Performance of the Different Locomotive Engines at and Subsequent to the Liverpool Contest; Upwards of Two Hundred and Sixty Experiments; with Tables of the Comparative Value of Canals and Rail-Roads, and the Power of the Present Locomotive Engines* (Philadelphia: Carey and Lea, 1832).

[15] *Proceedings of the Directors and Stockholders of the Boston and Worcester Railroad*, I, 147, Ms., Harvard Business School Library.

novel method of transportation and its superiority to canals, and to follow instruction with action. These conspirators were a diverse group. Abner Phelps, a Boston physician, railroad en-thusiast and railroad bore; Nathan Hale, editor of the Boston *Daily Advertiser*, who used his paper to transmute the barebones of legislative reports into persuasive journalism; P. P. F. De Grand, a broker and commission merchant of considerable means and prosaic imagination; Josiah Quincy, Jr., eldest son of the President of Harvard University, lawyer, champion after-dinner speaker, and later mayor, railroad official, and humanitarian; and T. H. Perkins, merchant, philanthropist, president of the Quincy railroad and its largest shareholder. From Cambridge came James Hayward, Harvard graduate, who eventually dis-covered that an engineering career did not blend with a pro-fessorship of mathematics and philosophy at his alma mater and chose the former, and Royal Makepeace, merchant and dealer in real estate. From the interior came Emory Washburn of Worcester and Theodore Sedgwick of Stockbridge, lawyer, and obviously a man of "enlarged intellect" since he came from the Berkshires and still advocated railroads.[16]

Luckily this railroad party gradually obtained a sympathetic hearing from Levi Lincoln, the governor. Weaned from an en-thusiasm for canals, in 1829 he whole-heartedly announced his allegiance to the railroad cause in an annual message declaring there was no doubt of the feasibility of railroads in England and this country. In the same year the railroad party established an educational department, the Massachusetts Rail Road Associa-tion, which through membership fees solicited funds for the pub-lication and distribution of documents and which built a model railroad in Faneuil Hall to demonstrate how little power was required to move a railway car. Its corresponding secretary was Nathan Hale.[17] Whatever its activities, the startling feature of

---

[16] Derby, "Progress of Railroads," p. 30; James F. Baldwin to Col. S. M. McKay, December 20, 1827, Baldwin Papers, XXXVI; *The National Cyclopedia of American Biography* (New York: James T. White and Company, 1893–), III, 147, VI, 289.

[17] Boston *American Traveller*, April 14, 1829; *Massachusetts Rail Road Associa-tion, Constitution* (Boston: 1829).

the group was the absence, with the exception of Perkins, of men of wealth and of business prominence. On the whole the railroad partisans were professional men; furthermore they were politicians. Hale, Hayward, Makepeace, Phelps, Sedgwick were members of the Massachusetts General Court where they could make their influence felt through conversation or through their seats on strategic committees.[18]

Their educational campaign sought to demonstrate to Massachusetts the technical feasibility of the railroad. Their task was made easier by the technical simplicity of their proposals. In spite of contemporary English experience, the locomotive was almost always rejected in favor of horsepower. Not only was the horse deemed cheaper but also his employment was "the most simple system" and one that "in practice will be found to comport with the common habits and opinions of the people." In essence therefore the railroad became simply a land canal. A roadway of wood or stone — generally after the model of the Quincy railroad — was to be laid over a terrain through which a waterway was impracticable and over it horses could pull greater loads with greater regularity than along a highway. The science of railroading was therefore the science of the horse. With a vast display of erudition culled largely from Wood and Tredgold, Nathan Hale wrote that the only resistance the horse has to overcome is friction on the level and additional gravity on an uneven road: "The average power of a good horse for continual exertion, day after day, and eight hours in each day, and travelling only at the rate at which he can produce the greatest effect, is generally estimated as equivalent to raising a weight of 150 lbs., suspended by a rope passing over a pulley." If there were no inclined planes, this was the friction a horse would have to overcome in pulling a train of somewhat less than fifteen tons.[19]

[18] Card Catalogue of the Members of the Massachusetts General Court, Massachusetts State Library.

[19] *Report of the Board of Commissioners for the Survey of One or More Routes for a Railway from Boston to Albany*, p. 24; Hale, *Remarks on the Practicability and Expediency of Establishing a Rail Road on One or More Routes to the Connecticut River*, pp. 16–23.

The several conditional items in this calculation multiplied when it came to the financial features of railroads.

III

Finance was the second problem of the railroad party. Publicly they approached the difficulty slowly, for it was more judicious to convince the electorate of the advantages and the necessity of railroads, and to inspire it with a passion for their construction, before revealing that the state was to provide the funds. But in 1829 the Board of Directors of Internal Improvements, appointed by the state, unveiled the true situation. Private capital, at first hand, was to have no part in building the proposed railroads to Providence or Albany. The state was to provide the funds. He who financed, controlled. In arguments reminiscent of those earlier associated with the cross-state canal, the directors declared: "To enlist in such works the enterprise of individuals or corporations, it will be necessary to make a grant of privileges which it will be difficult to define with sufficient limitations, to secure all the interests of the public, while at the same time they are made broad enough to induce a sufficient investment of capital for the enterprise."

State aid was no untrod path: New York, Pennsylvania, and Maryland were following it with advantage. This was no hazardous speculation. A simple calculation showed it would yield returns. First the cost of the roadbed was estimated. This was bound to be much less than in England. Then the requisite number of horses — a variable of the grades, distances, and equine powers — was determined. Detailed estimates of their costs and maintenance, even down to such minor matters as blacksmithing, were made. To meet the total costs were the existent traffic by stage or sloop and the rates it was already paying. Thus for the stage journey from Boston to the Connecticut River, which usually began at 2:00 A.M. and ended at 7:00 or 8:00 in the evening, it required thirty-two horses to carry a maximum of ten passengers. The fares were from $4.50 to $6.00. With a railroad over this distance eight horses could convey twenty passengers in thirteen and a half hours. A fare of $1.35 to $1.70 would give ample profit.[20]

Although such calculations were made with tedious patience, they failed to remove opposition. Even in enlightened Boston derisive voices were occasionally raised against railroads. The editor of the Boston *Courier*, after examining one of Dr. Phelp's lucubrations, declared that a railroad from Boston to the Hudson was not only "impracticable" but also as "every person of common-sense knows would be as useless as a railroad from Boston to the moon." [21] But the center of hostility remained among Massachusetts countrymen. Village dwellers along the line of proposed railways might be enthusiastic, but farmers, apprehensive over the possibility of lost markets, were unwilling to have the state raise taxes to pay for railroads which would primarily benefit the Boston metropolis. Batteries of propaganda could not pulverize their suspicions. Theodore Sedgwick, with an air that his quest was fruitless, instructed Massachusetts agriculturists on the superiority of a cash to a barter economy. The railroad, once introduced, would give value "to all they possess above and under ground; to ore, lime, stone, sand, clay, timber, wood, hay, fruit, vegetables, to the very herbs and weeds that he treads underfoot. . . . But it is said, that these public works are best managed by individuals, that the state can do nothing as *economically* as they. This is a popular cant, very current, and very foolish." The Directors of Internal Improvements chanted of rising prices for farm lands; when the railroad came, acres in the western counties of Massachusetts would approach in value those "of the same quality, situated within a few miles of Boston, or of navigable waters." And a year later Governor Lincoln, while reiterating the argument that the railroads benefited agriculture, came to the defense of Boston's prosperity. If Boston were not prosperous and able to pay taxes, the financial

[20] *Report of the Board of Directors of Internal Improvements of the State of Massachusetts, on the Practicability and Expediency of a Rail-Road from Boston to the Hudson River, and from Boston to Providence*, pp. 72–75; Hale, *Remarks on the Practicability and Expediency of Establishing a Rail Road on One or More Routes from Boston to the Connecticut River*, pp. 42–44.

[21] Boston *Courier*, June 27, 1827, quoted in Adams, "The Canal and Railroad Enterprise of Boston," p. 122.

support of the government would devolve upon the "Yeomanry." [22]

By now the railroad case had indeed left the secrecy of the caucus. Newspapers wrote about it, pamphlets gave instruction, and in country places people were discussing with equal energy and interest "The Rail Road and Orthodoxy." [23] Nor was talk all. Through the agency of the General Court a welter of commissioners and directors came into existence. In 1827 one commission, of which James Hayward was a member and for which he served as engineer, surveyed a route between Boston and Providence; a second commission retained James F. Baldwin, a younger brother of Loammi, for the survey of a western railway. Both groups made reports early in the following year.[24] The General Court promptly authorized a Board of Directors of Internal Improvements. Dalliance with canals ceased. This board was to provide for internal improvements by railroad. Its members were to make more thorough investigations of both routes, to estimate their cost and utility, to enter into arrangements with owners for donations of land and with adjacent states for connecting lines, to receive from individuals or corporations "contributions, either in money or other things," and to present to the legislature a scheme for financing their projected enterprises. The nine members of the board included Royal Makepeace, Levi Lincoln, and Nathan Hale; they sent Hayward and Baldwin back to their labors.

[22] Levi Lincoln, Governor's Address, May 30, 1829, *The Resolves of the General Court of the Commonwealth of Massachusetts Passed at the Second Session of the General Court, Commencing May, 1825, and Ending June, 1831*, pp. 166–173; Theodore Sedgwick, *Brief Remarks on the Rail Roads, Proposed in Massachusetts, by Berkshire* (Stockbridge: Charles Webster, 1828), pp. 11–13; *Report of the Board of Directors of Internal Improvements of the State of Massachusetts, on the Practicability and Expediency of a Rail-Road from Boston to the Hudson River, and from Boston to Providence*, pp. 46–47.

[23] William E. Prentiss to James F. Baldwin, February 16, 1829, Baldwin Papers, XXXVI.

[24] *Resolves of the General Court of the Commonwealth of Massachusetts Passed at the Several Sessions of the General Court, Commencing May, 1824, and Ending March, 1828*, pp. 479–480, 491–492, 589–590; *Report of the Board of Commissioners of Internal Improvements in Relation to the Examination of Sundry Routes for a Railway from Boston to Providence. With a Memoir of the Survey; Report of the Board of Commissioners for the Survey of One or More Routes for a Railway from Boston to Albany*.

Early in 1829 the directors reported to the legislature. The document was a hardheaded, forceful summary of the railroad case. As far as techniques were concerned, it rehearsed the traditional recommendations of granite roads and horsepower. The report was notable rather for its portrayal of the railroad as an essential element in metropolitan greatness. Railroads were required for foreign trade. Although Boston had a harbor, nautical skill, and an extensive navigation, its commerce could not flourish without a hinterland for production and for markets. The railroad was required for the new manufacturing order: "The industry of the people of this state is becoming every year, more and more, diverted to manufacturing employments. It is this exercise of the labour and skill of our population which must hereafter constitute our chief means of wealth." But manufacturing requires a market place. "To have such a market centrally situated, and easily resorted to, will be beneficial to those who buy as well as sell. It is very obvious that it must be important to the interests of the state to have this market seated at our own capital or at least within the limits of our state." Purchasers must come here, manufacturers must make Massachusetts a place of depot and sale. Here as elsewhere the great rival is New York, whose steam navigation is "upon the very borders of the state" and whose facilities for commerce and interchange are so great that already New England manufacturers resort thither for the sale of their goods.[25]

The activities of the Board of Directors of Internal Improvements, however, created an array of new enemies to financial aid from the state. As the officials had staked out the roads, the resulting definiteness of survey had inevitably left aside towns and termini which had once anticipated the blessings of internal improvement. Not principle but local resentment and pride now explained their hostility. Thus Taunton was outraged when Providence was selected as the terminus of the railroad from

[25] *Laws of the Commonwealth of Massachusetts, Passed at the Several Sessions of the General Court, Beginning May, 1825, and Ending March, 1828*, pp. 815–818; *Report of the Board of Directors of Internal Improvements of the State of Massachusetts, on the Practicability and Expediency of a Rail-Road from Boston to the Hudson River, and from Boston to Providence*, pp. 43–51.

Boston. Providence was the terminus of the Blackstone Canal
which Massachusetts partisans wished to checkmate, and had
in Narragansett Bay an easier approach from the sea than the
longer and more difficult navigation of Taunton River.[26] As the
route was longer, the specific survey of the western railroad
aroused more numerous jealousies. When the various commissioners and directors and James F. Baldwin, their engineer,
rejected the route chosen by the latter's brother for a cross-state
canal in favor of a southern location through Worcester, Springfield, and Pittsfield, they antagonized the entire northern edge
of the state as well as an embattled company of neglected towns
along the Connecticut and in the Berkshires.[27] Though New
York State, rising above provinciality, promised to incorporate
the extension from the Massachusetts-New York boundary to
the Hudson, a furious rivalry for the western terminus at once
flared among Hudson, Troy, and Albany. The Massachusetts
authorities selected Albany "as presenting the advantages of a
greater market, a shorter distance from Boston, a less change of
level in the line of the road, and equal facilities for the construction of the road." A spokesman for Troy responded with sullen
reflections upon the impracticability of the whole enterprise.[28]

Under such circumstances the movement for state aid came
to a climax. The legislature gave wide circulation to the report
of the directors, Nathan Hale issued pamphlets, and committees,
headed by Sedgwick and Hale, introduced into both houses of

---

[26] *Report of the Board of Commissioners, of Internal Improvements in Relation
to the Examination of Sundry Routes for a Railway from Boston to Providence*,
pp. 9–16, 51–72; *Report of the Board of Directors of Internal Improvements of
the State of Massachusetts on the Practicability and Expediency of a Rail-Road
from Boston to the Hudson River, and from Boston to Providence*, pp. 60–68.

[27] *Report of the Board of Commissioners for the Survey of One or More Routes
for a Railway from Boston to Albany*, pp. 9–23; *Report of the Board of Directors
of Internal Improvements of the State of Massachusetts, on the Practicability
and Expediency of a Rail-Road from Boston to the Hudson River, and from
Boston to Providence*, pp. 14–18, 50–59.

[28] *Laws of the State of New York, Passed at Fifty-first Session*, pp. 258–259;
Report of the Commissioners to aid the Railroad from Boston to the Hudson
River, New York *Senate Journal*, 1829, pp. 235–241; Report of the Commissioners
Appointed under the Act of April 15, 1828, Relative to the Construction of a
Rail-Road from the City of Boston to the Hudson River, New York *Senate Docu-
ments*, 1829, no. 113, pp. 17–18, 51.

the General Court a series of resolutions declaring it was "expedient for the State to aid and encourage by its funds, the construction" of the proposed roads but postponing a decision until the summer session. In the interim the annual state election might reveal whether the people wished the government to exercise so unusual a power.[29] In spite of the objection that the procedure was contrary to republican principles, many towns instructed their representatives. The governor, however, apparently regarded this referendum as inconclusive. In his address to the new General Court he added a new note of urgency to old arguments. The proposed works in Massachusetts were "inconsiderable" compared to those in sister states, the legislator who waits for more than "a reasonable probability" of success from internal improvements "will be in danger of passing his life in fruitless indecision, and to the end of it, may see his country without progress in improvement." Without government "patronage," exercised to some extent in advancements toward expense, "it is much to be feared they can't be undertaken." For the first time the alternative, uncomplicated by matters of principle, was presented to legislative attention: no state funds, no railroad.[30] So little confident was the railroad crowd, however, that it sponsored a compromise; the state was to subscribe one third of the capitalization, individuals the remainder. A House committee introduced charters for roads to the Hudson and to Providence. Finally in 1830 state aid, even in limited form, was buried under an adversity of votes, 284 to 160. Localism ran rampant. Boston and Boston's suburbs provided an unwavering core of support, but the inland towns, unless the railroad was to run through them, united with ports from Newburyport to Nantucket to sink the

[29] Report of the Committee of the House of Representatives, February 28, 1829, Massachusetts *House Documents*, 1829, no. 42; Report of the Committee of the Senate, February 28, 1829, Massachusetts *Senate Documents*, 1829, no. 24; House Journal, May 1828–March 1829, Ms., Massachusetts State Library, pp. 302, 335, appendix; Senate Journal, May 1828–March 1829, Ms., Massachusetts State Library, p. 454.

[30] Levi Lincoln, Governor's Address, May 31, 1829, *Resolves of the General Court of the Commonwealth of Massachusetts . . . Commencing May, 1826, and Ending June, 1831*, pp. 166–173; Boston *American Traveller*, May 19, 1829; Boston *Advertiser*, May 9, 1829.

proposal. The cause for state aid was weaker than it was a year earlier. By March 1830 when the legislature adjourned, the only sums so far appropriated for Massachusetts railroads were the trivial ones for the surveys already made in the late twenties.[31]

IV

Yet on June 5, 1830, the state incorporated the Boston and Lowell and before the end of the following June issued charters to the Boston and Providence and the Boston and Worcester. These pioneer three were the nucleus of the Massachusetts and the New England railroad system. Interestingly enough, the first followed a route from Boston to Lowell that had not aroused the enthusiasm of the early railroad conspirators. The Middlesex Canal already connected the two places, improved navigation carried traffic to Concord, and surveyors of the national government were traversing divides, viewing ridges, and following valleys in the hopeless and archaic task of discovering a canal route northwestward from the Merrimack to Lake Champlain. Since they were realists, however, the manufacturing capitalists of Lowell did not bother about these remote visions; it was enough for them that the canal connection with Boston was inadequate and provided only seasonal transportation. While others talked or wrote of the West, they petitioned the legislature to authorize and finance a survey, and the ubiquitous Hayward traced a route, with no inclinations greater than 26 to 30 feet to the mile, which was shorter than the highway traveled by stage and which closely followed the line of the canal. Against the proposed railroad the proprietors of the Middlesex plaintively protested in a curious document, which confessed their own failure and pleaded that the legislature restrain the promoters of the railroad from a similar business disaster! Their

[31] *Laws of the Commonwealth of Massachusetts, Passed at the Several Sessions of the General Court, Beginning May, 1828, and Ending March, 1831,* pp. 412–438; An Act to Establish the Massachusetts Rail Road Corporations, Massachusetts *House Documents,* 1829–1830, no. 4; House Journal, May 1828–March 1829, Ms., Massachusetts State Library, p. 285; House Journal, May 1829–March 1830, Ms., Massachusetts State Library, p. 229, appendix.

obstruction was brushed aside when the Lowell capitalists pointed out that the canal was closed five months a year and that the rates were higher than on their proposed railroad.[32] The conception behind that project, in short, was the same as that which underlay the Granite Railway. The Boston and Lowell was simply an adjunct to an existing industrial development. The Proprietors of the Locks and Canals on Merrimack River subscribed largely to the high-priced shares of $500; the "agent" for the construction of the road, P. T. Jackson, was one of the powerful textile capitalists of Lowell; and one of the most cautious and somber prospectuses ever written based the hope of a "small rent" of 6 per cent primarily upon the business between Boston and Lowell.[33]

On the other hand, a route from Boston to either Providence or Taunton had been regarded as a matter of state policy from the outset. The proposed railroad was to speed and cheapen transportation between Boston and the developing industrial regions in southeastern Massachusetts and Rhode Island. Only under antiquated conditions did overland wagon routes or coasting vessels around Cape Cod care for their trade. Once this aim was left behind, however, the objectives of the promoters contained incompatibilities. On the one hand, the Boston and Providence railroad was to checkmate New York by lowering land rates between Boston and Rhode Island points to the level charged by the new steam navigation from New York through Long Island Sound. On the other hand, the railroad aimed to form with the menacing steamboats "a line of regular transportation between New York and Boston." [34] On the whole the final location of

[32] Report of James Hayward, January 7, 1830, on the Survey of a Rail Route between Boston and Lowell, Massachusetts *Senate Documents*, 1829-30, no. 3; Report of the Committee on Railways and Canals on Petition for a Charter of the Boston and Lowell Railroad, Massachusetts *Senate Documents*, no. 21; Remonstrance of the Proprietors of the Middlesex Canal against a Charter to the Boston and Lowell Railroad, Massachusetts *House Documents*, 1829-1830, no. 40.

[33] *Report of a Committee on the Boston and Lowell Rail Road* (Boston: 1831).

[34] *Report of the Board of Commissioners of Internal Improvements in Relation to the Examination of Sundry Routes for a Railway from Boston to Providence*, pp. 10-11, 42-50; *Report of the Board of Directors of Internal Improvements of the State of Massachusetts, on the Practicability and Expediency of a Rail-Road from Boston to the Hudson River, and from Boston to Providence*, pp. 63-67.

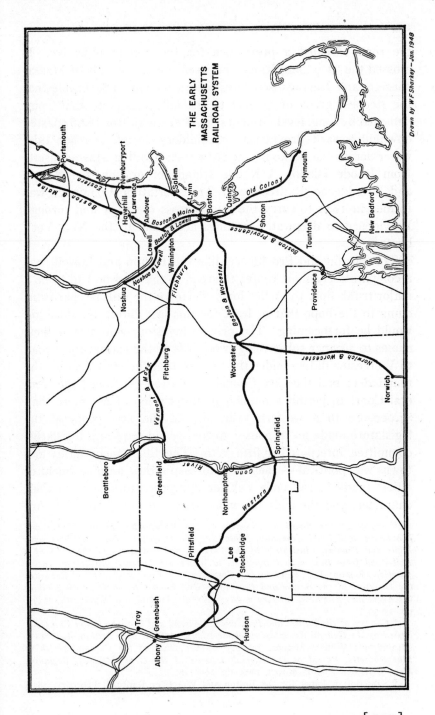

THE EARLY
MASSACHUSETTS
RAILROAD SYSTEM

Drawn by W.F.Sharkey—Jan. 1948

the road revealed a preference for the second objective. It crossed the "Dividing Ridge" between the watersheds of Massachusetts and Narragansett bays over a terrain so favorable that the steepest grade of 37 feet to the mile was more than compensated by long, level stretches.[35] After the railroad had coasted downhill toward Providence, its builders elected to reach tidewater across the Seekonk, the river then dividing Massachusetts from Rhode Island. A Rhode Island corporation, the Boston and Providence Railroad and Transportation Company, was formed in 1834 to carry the route across the river and through Providence to deepwater landings accessible to the New York boats.[36]

The Boston and Providence, like the Boston and Lowell, was a comparatively short route; the road to the Hudson had to be a major trunk line, 198 miles long. Perforce the railroad partisans clung to the hope that at least for this last enterprise state aid would be forthcoming. The private investors who affixed their names to a paper subscribing two-thirds of the capital for a road to Worcester did so under the proviso that the state furnish the remainder; and the City Council of Boston petitioned the General Court to permit a municipal subscription of not more than $1,000,000 to a western railroad. To the first proposal the legislature made no response; to the second request a legislative committee interposed a firm veto. The function of cities and towns was political — they were to keep order; an investment of cities' funds in railroads was for "purposes foreign from their character, and the ends for which they were instituted." [37] Ad-

<hr/>

[35] *Report of the Board of Directors to the Stockholders of the Boston and Providence Rail-Road Company, Submitting the Report of Their Engineer with Plans and Profiles, Illustrative of the Surveys, and Estimates of the Cost of a Rail-Road from Boston to Providence, to Which are Annexed the Acts of Incorporation* (Boston: J. E. Hinckley and Company, 1832), pp. 8–46; *Annual Report of the Directors of the Boston and Providence Rail Road Corporation with That of the Agent and Engineer, January 2, 1833* (Boston: Dutton and Wentworth, 1833), pp. 15–32.

[36] *Charter of the Boston and Providence Railroad and Transportation Company, Passed by the General Assembly of Rhode-Island, at Their May Session, A. D. 1834* (Providence: William Simons, January, 1834); *Laws of the Commonwealth of Massachusetts, Passed at the Several Sessions of the General Court, Beginning May, 1831, and Ending March, 1833*, pp. 109–118.

[37] Subscription Paper for the Boston and Worcester Railroad, February, 1831,

mittedly, also, the proposed railroad to the Hudson was technically an experiment. Deserting the comparative ease of the
narrow coastal plain, the route, before it reached Albany, climbed
and descended a series of formidable highlands: those between
Worcester and the Connecticut had an elevation of 918 feet;
the Berkshires were crossed in Washington at a point 1,440 feet
above the Connecticut; while the ridge between the Housatonic
and the Hudson was 166 feet above the former river. Moving
westward, trains had to ascend twenty-four miles with gradients
that ranged between 52 and 80 feet to the mile; when they were
eastward bound, twenty-seven miles fell within the same limits.
The 80-feet maximum was a convenient round number; the
maximum gradient according to Baldwin's survey was 83 feet to
the mile.[38] Whether steam transportation over such a route was
feasible was still a question to which American development had
given no answer.

Of the forty-four miles between Boston and Worcester, one
third was of grades of 30 feet to the mile. However, investors
were inclined to overlook the forbidding features of this shorter
stretch as they focused upon its immense existing traffic. Over
the two main roads between Worcester and Boston wagons carried at least 9,000 tons of freight, and the stages of the Boston
and Worcester Stage Company annually transported 14,000
passengers. Additional traffic in goods and travelers flowed into
the route at places between Boston and Worcester. The superiority of the railroad was counted on to increase this local commerce as well as the more distant one drawn to Worcester as
an entrepot. So on June 23, 1831, the General Court incorporated
the Boston and Worcester Railroad. In terms of earlier dreams,
this enterprise was a diminished thing. Still it held promise.
"It is however hardly reasonable to suppose that after all the

Baldwin Papers, XXXVII; Report of a Committee on the Petition of the City
Council for Permission to Subscribe to a Railroad from Boston to the Western
States, Massachusetts *House Documents*, 1830–1831, no. 54.
  [38] *Report of the Board of Commissioners, for the Survey of One or More
Routes for a Railway from Boston to Albany*, pp. 16–23; *Report of the Board of
Directors of Internal Improvements of the State of Massachusetts, on the Prac-
ticability and Expediency of a Rail-Road from Boston to the Hudson River, and
from Boston to Providence*, pp. 14–18, 54–56.

proofs which will be given of the advantages of the Rail Road, both to the public at large, and to the stockholders, it will fail to be continued in a very few years to the Connecticut River, and thence to Albany." [39]

The charters of these pioneer three initiated not only Boston's railroad system but also Massachusetts railroad policy. In their verbalism as well as their concepts, many provisions simply distilled the lessons of the turnpike era. Railroads were permitted to establish their own "tolls," to erect toll houses, build toll gates, and appoint toll gatherers. The later troublesome question of connections and railroad relationships was in germ in the provisions that others might use the road on complying with its rules or regulations and that other railroads, with authorization from the state legislature, could enter upon and use the track of the corporation in question. For its right of way the railroad could purchase land, but, if owners and railroad could not agree upon a price, the latter could take land in "the manner provided by law, for the recovery of damages happening by the laying out of highways." In nearly every county special highway commissioners were appointed to determine the amount of damages, and, if objections to their findings were made, the case was heard by a county court with a jury or by a new set of commissioners.

Ostensibly Governor Lincoln and like-minded associates had dreaded the concessions entailed by the surrender of railroad construction and operation to private corporations. In actuality the most important privilege was a thirty-year monopoly of the particular route; within that period no roads could be laid out from Boston and its suburbs to any place within five miles of Lowell, Providence, or Worcester.[40] Although such grants had

[39] *Report of the Directors of the Boston and Worcester Rail-Road Corporation to the Stockholders, together with the Report of John M. Fessenden, Esq., Civil Engineer, and a Plan and Profile of the Location of the Rail Road* (Boston: W. L. Lewis, 1832), pp. 4–5, 9–19, 22.

[40] *Laws of the Commonwealth of Massachusetts, Passed at the Several Sessions of the General Court of Massachusetts, Beginning May, 1828, and Ending March, 1831*, pp. 494–501; *Laws of the Commonwealth of Massachusetts, Passed at the Several Sessions of the General Court of Massachusetts, Beginning May, 1831, and Ending March, 1833*, pp. 109–118, 152–162; *The General Laws of Massachusetts,*

long been a commonplace in corporation history, more specific considerations of time and place were at work. Some special stimulus to private investors was essential. Justice Shaw, of the Massachusetts Supreme Judicial Court, reviewing the Boston and Lowell monopoly years later, thus reconstructed the situation: "After the experience of capitalists, in respect of the turnpikes and canals of the Commonwealth, which had been authorized by the public but built by the application of private capital, but which as investments had proven in most instances to be ruinous, it was probably no easy matter to awaken anew the confidence of moneyed men in enterprises of internal improvement." Contemporaries, particularly those attempting to launch railroad corporations, were more apt to emphasize the disquiet aroused in the minds of "moneyed men" by the failure of the Massachusetts courts to protect the property of the Proprietors of the Charles River Bridge who felt that at least by "implication" they had a monopoly right to their toll bridge between Charlestown and Boston. In 1828 the legislature chartered a rival, the Proprietors of the Warren Bridge; finally in 1829 four Massachusetts judges delivered four lengthy opinions, groaning under the burden of citation and logic. Since in essence two justices felt the charter of the Warren bridge violated provisions of the Massachusetts and the Federal Constitution and two did not, the competitor stood and the Proprietors of the Charles River Bridge in pursuit of redress appealed to the Supreme Court of the United States, where Chief Justice Taney, announcing charters should be narrowly construed, affirmed the decision of the Massachusetts courts.[41] The incorporators of the pioneer

from the Adoption of the Constitution to February, 1822, I, 295–296; *The General Laws of Massachusetts, From June, 1822, to June, 1831*, pp. 138–139.

[41] The Proprietors of Charles River Bridge in Equity *v.* The Proprietors of Warren Bridge et al., 23 *Massachusetts* (6 *Pickering*), 376–377, 392, 399; The Proprietors of Charles River Bridge *v.* The Proprietors of Warren Bridge et al., 24 *Massachusetts* (7 *Pickering*), 344–532; The Proprietors of the Charles River Bridge, Plaintiffs in Error *v.* The Proprietors of the Warren Bridge, and Others, 36 *United States*, 420–469; Boston and Lowell Railroad Corporation *v.* Salem and Lowell Railroad Company, and Others, 68 *Massachusetts* (2 *Grey*), 1–42; *The Contemplated Plan of the Franklin Rail Road Company to Commence with a Route through the Counties of Middlesex, Worcester, and Franklin, to the Line of Vermont; from Thence to Lake Champlain and to Lake Ontario, with Branches Convenient to*

railroads did not await this decision to grasp the necessity of a specific monopoly grant. When the Boston and Lowell, with its privilege of monopoly, paralleled the Middlesex Canal, the charter of which a committee of the General Court discovered did not confer a similar monopoly, final irony was imparted to the issue.

Two provisions, it was hoped, would enable the state to retain tight rein over its corporate creations. For one thing the charters regulated rates. Rejecting the frequent practice of turnpike days, these charters did not enact an elaborate schedule of specific tolls; instead they restrained rates through a limitation upon profits. If for four years the net income should exceed 10 per cent upon the cost of the road, the legislature could reduce "the rate of tolls and other profits in such manner as to take off the overplus for the next four years." Secondly, the whole railroad could be withdrawn from the ambivalent region of a public enterprise financed by private capital to the clearer basis of government ownership. Initially nuclear and diverse, the original charter provisions for this procedure were in the early thirties made uniform and explicit. After twenty years the state could possess itself of the railroad's franchise and property by paying a sum equal to the original cost of the road, its expenses and repairs, and such additional amounts as were required to give the stockholders an income equal to 10 per cent a year on the original cost, if they had not already received it. To enforce such objectives, it was necessary to know what the railroads were doing. Under heavy penalties for failure, they were to report annually to the legislature on "their acts and doings, receipts and expenditures." [42] Such were the more obvious provisions of the contract between the state and the railroads. But on March 11, 1831, nine months after chartering the Boston and Lowell and three months before chartering its two colleagues, a Massachusetts act announced: "All acts of incorporations, which shall be

---

Accommodate the Inhabitants of Massachusetts (Boston: John H. Eastburn, 1830), pp. 3–5; Derby, "Progress of Railroads," pp. 34–35.

[42] *Laws . . . of Massachusetts . . . Beginning May, 1828, and Ending March, 1831*, pp. 494–500; *Laws . . . of Massachusetts . . . Beginning May, 1831, and Ending March, 1833*, pp. 110 ff., 153 ff., 280, 314, 454.

passed after the passage of this act, shall at all times hereafter be liable to be amended, altered, or repealed at the pleasure of the legislature." This assertion of omnipotence — except for the Boston and Lowell — might jeopardize alike the monopoly privileges of the railroad and the provisions more generally esteemed "the precious palladium of the public welfare." Were charters, in fact, anything but a "blank sheet of paper?" [43]

V

Although charters came from the same mold, details of construction varied among the three roads. All were originally planned under the influence of the Massachusetts-English school of railroad engineering. Bryant was its forerunner, Baldwin and Hayward were its prophets. Their gospel was the permanent right of way as revealed on the Quincy and the English railroads. At first the Quincy influence predominated. The continuous bearing of a deep trench filled with stonework, the heavy granite longitudinal stringers, and the thin attached plate met American conditions better, it was claimed, than did the English edge rail supported at intervals upon stone blocks, for the former plan conquered derangement by frost and used granite which was cheaper than iron in the United States. There were, also, absolute advantages. The granite rail did not yield to the passing train and hence the wheels were not continually climbing a grade. The plate rail did not wear a groove in the wheels; roadbed and track were durable. Solidly constructed in the first place, they did not require an expensive piecemeal reconstruction. Repairs, therefore, would average about 1 to 1.5 per cent a year upon the cost. Roadbed and tracks would cost originally about $8,217 a mile. Such were the structures Hayward and Baldwin were recommending in the second half of the twenties.[44]

---

[43] *Laws . . . of Massachusetts . . . Beginning May, 1828, and Ending March, 1831*, p. 613; C. F. Adams, Jr., "Railroad Legislation," *Hunt's Merchants' Magazine and Commercial Review*, LVII (1867), 341–342.

[44] *Report of the Board of Commissioners of Internal Improvements in Relation to the Examination of Sundry Routes for a Railway from Boston to Providance*, pp. 18–31; *Report of the Board of Directors of Internal Improvements of the State of Massachusetts on the Practicability and Expediency of a Rail-Road*

By the time New England construction commenced, further experiment in Great Britain and in this country and the cheapening of rails by a provision of the tariff of 1832, which permitted a refund of duties upon iron actually laid in railroad track, swung the partisans of a permanent right of way to an imitation of the English pattern. The Boston and Lowell was its chief New England example. Here P. T. Jackson, agent, was a devotee of thoroughness, and James F. Baldwin, whom he employed to survey the road, to aid in its construction, and to "give me your advice and your opinions in all cases where you may think it useful to me, whether asked for it or not, even though I should not always adopt them," professed the same devotion.[45] They used the iron edge rail of the Liverpool and Manchester; this was a fish-belly pattern in which the profile sagged down to give extra strength between the supports. Such rails were from twelve to eighteen feet long and weighed thirty-five pounds a yard. They were supported by iron chairs, a sort of elevated clamp, the base of which was spiked to stone blocks set three feet apart; at intervals a transverse stone sleeper was inserted to hold the rails in line. Both blocks and sleepers rested on trench walls, the bottom of which was thirty to thirty-six inches below the surface of the road and two and a half feet wide.[46] In spite of these precautions the New England winter raised havoc. Thus Baldwin reported: "The blocks and sleepers have been lifted by the action of the frozen earth upon them & when a few warm days thaws the ground the blocks sink to their places before the cross sleepers which still keep support in the center & makes the surface of the road undulatory & the line serpentine." The cause, Baldwin thought, was the adhesion of frozen soil to the sides of his stone supports. On the track already laid, he bedded the stone blocks in gravel or sand; for the second track

---

from Boston to the Hudson River, and from Boston to Providence, pp. 4–5, 16–17, 69–70.

[45] Loammi Baldwin II to James F. Baldwin, March 17, 1831, Baldwin Papers, XXXVI; P. T. Jackson to James F. Baldwin, April 1, 1831, Baldwin Papers, XXXVII.

[46] Description of the Boston and Lowell Railroad by James F. Baldwin (?), Baldwin Papers, XXXVII.

in course of construction he dug a trench eight or nine feet wide beneath the track and filled it with crushed stone.[47]

On the Boston and Worcester and Boston and Providence, the West Point-American school of railroad construction had greater influence. Their respective engineers, John M. Fessenden and William Gibbs McNeill, were both graduates of the Military Academy, both had cut their eye-teeth on the Chesapeake and Ohio Canal, and both had served a turn on the Baltimore and Ohio Railroad, which as a training ground for engineers occupied in the history of American railroading a position comparable to that of the Erie for canals.[48] Since the Boston and Providence and Boston and Worcester were also nearly twice as long as the Boston and Lowell, there was a greater spur to economy in their construction. For the Boston and Worcester, Fessenden at the outset advised a form of construction similar to that of the Boston and Lowell.[49] Fifteen months later, when the directors ordered their rails from England, they authorized the superintendent and engineer to "contract for *stone-blocks* for such portions of the first thirteen miles of the Rail Road as they shall think expedient to lay upon *stone* and for *wooden* sleepers for the residue of the said thirteen miles of road." The officials chose the latter form of construction throughout.[50] On the completed road the rails rested in chairs and the chairs were spiked to transverse cedar sleepers; instead of walls or sills a prism of rubble and broken stone was laid in a trench beneath each rail. This gave an elastic roadbed easier on rails and cars alike.[51] In

[47] James F. Baldwin to Thomas I. Lobdell, March 2, 1836, Baldwin Papers, XXXVII.

[48] George W. Cullum, *Biographical Register of the Officers and Graduates of the U. S. Military Academy at West Point, N. Y., from its Establishment in 1802, to 1890 with the Early History of the United States Military Academy* (3d ed.; Boston and New York: Houghton, Mifflin and Company, 1891), III, 161–166, 328–329.

[49] *Report of the Directors of the Boston and Worcester Rail-Road Corporation to the Stockholders, together with the Report of John M. Fessenden, Esq.*, pp. 32–34.

[50] Proceedings of the Directors and Stockholders of the Boston and Worcester Railroad, Ms., Harvard Business School Library, I, 120–121.

[51] H. S. Tanner, *A Description of the Canals and Rail Roads of the United States, Comprehending Notices of All the Works of Internal Improvement throughout the Several States* (New York: T. R. Tanner and J. Disturnell, 1840), p. 38;

his recommendations for the Boston and Providence, McNeill vacillated; perhaps by discussing every possibility, he hoped to maneuver the board of directors into giving him freedom of action. He preferred an iron edge rail laid upon longitudinal stringers of wood instead of granite. It was cheaper, less subject to derangement by frosts, easier to maintain. To the iron rail on continuous wood stringers he preferred the rail set upon stone blocks and stone sleepers; this edge rail can be "of uniform depth, of the T form, as recommended by the late Mr. Tredgold, and so arranged by Mr. Stevens on the Camden and Amboy Rail-Road and others elsewhere, that the necessity of *chairs* is dispensed with." Finally he really preferred to substitute for the stones transverse wooden sleepers and to spike the rails directly to them. The sleepers would be supported by sills or logs and scantlings. Such a track was admirably suited for a "green embankment." It would cost $7,000 a mile. In actuality, the Boston and Providence conformed to McNeill's final preference.[52]

As directors levied assessments upon stockholders, and struggled to secure Boston termini, as contractors opened raw cuts through suburban estates and filled embankments, and as the tracks crept outward from the city, each road definitely abandoned the idea of horses as the motive power except perhaps in winter. Though ritualistic references to "horsepaths" persisted into the thirties, the locomotives won. Like the iron rail, the iron horse came from England. American coach makers or car makers provided the rolling stock. And then at the last minute there was a flurry of almost breathless directors' meetings to find answers to the many novel questions of operation. The directors' records of the Boston and Worcester reflect the excitement. On March 15, 1834, the board appointed a committee "to recommend the measures necessary for the putting of the Passenger-

---

Second Annual Report of the Directors of the Boston and Worcester Railroad to the Massachusetts Legislature, February 5, 1834, pp. 9–10.

[52] *Report of the Board of Directors to the Stockholders of the Boston and Providence Rail-Road Company, Submitting the Report of Their Engineer . . . and Estimates of the Cost of a Rail-Road from Boston to Providence,* pp. 39–42; *Annual Report of the Directors of the Boston and Providence Rail Road Corporation — January 2, 1833,* p. 24; Tanner, *A Description,* p. 41.

Cars into operation, the number and description of agents necessary for superintending them, the time when the running of the
cars shall commence, the price which shall be charged for seats
&& . . ." The superintendent was to take measures to keep
people away from the tracks and the engines and "employ a
sufficient number of efficient men to keep off the boys." [53] Three
weeks later the *Meteor*, built by Robert Stephenson, "a light
engine but of a fine model," ran over a portion of the track with
a director and his wife in the tender, "the first time a lady was
ever carried over a railway by steam power in New England."
On April 12 the directors made their final appointments of the
necessary officials and voted that employees must "wholly ab-
stain from the use of ardent spirits." On April 16, 1834, regular
service began to Newton.[54]

On the experience and emotions of the moment the records of
the Boston and Worcester are silent. The moving film broke at
the very moment of climax. But for the Boston and Lowell,
opened like the others throughout its length in mid-1835, James
F. Baldwin fortunately wrote down his elation:

> Monday Mr. Jackson and I went to Lowell & on that day got our
> Largest Locomotive onto the Track — Tuesday got the Steam up &
> went moderately down the Rail Road 6-½ Miles & back — this was
> its first movement & she went kindly & well Today Mr. G. W.
> Whistler & myself came thro with her & the tender & a passenger
> Car — We left Lowell 24 minutes past seven & got to Boston in
> 1-¾ hours — We then rallied the Directors & a few stockholders
> &c. — to the number of 24 & started for Lowell at nine min past 12 —
> & arrived at Meremack town in 1 hour & 17 minutes — we carried up
> a Salmon & dined & left at between 4 & 5 & came in in 1 hour & 23
> minutes — all were pleased with the travelling & the Engine worked
> well & the country people were out on the bridges & banks & the
> Track labourers swung the hats with huzzars. I am quite weary &
> fatigued with anxiety & care but one nights rest will restore me espe-
> cially as we have proved our road & are satisfied — .[55]

[53] Proceedings of the Directors of the Boston and Worcester Railroad, I, 185–186.
[54] *Report of the Directors of the Boston and Worcester Rail Road, to the
Stockholders, at Their Third Annual Meeting, June 2, 1834*, p. 4; Proceedings of
the Directors and Stockholders of the Boston and Worcester Railroad, I, 190–191.
[55] James F. Baldwin to Loammi Baldwin II, May 27, 1835, Baldwin Papers,
XXXVII.

In a wider sense the last sentence, "we have proved our road & are satisfied," would serve as judgment for the achievement of the decade that ended in 1835. A survey of dates shows that New England was tardy in the adoption of the railroad. South Carolina already had a single line of 136 miles open to traffic; Maryland had embarked upon the construction of the Baltimore and Ohio, the nation's first great rail connection to the West; and engines had run upon two short lines in New York State. But chronology is not everything. Unlike Maryland, Massachusetts had not secured her railway system by a compromise with a canal, a compromise which was to bring financial disaster. Nor had she made the mistake of rejecting the railroad for a state system of canals as did contemporary Pennsylvania. Nor were her railroads, like those of New York, merely auxiliaries or adjuncts to waterways, separate parts of an unco-ordinated whole. Massachusetts had prudently chosen the transportation method of the future. In the strategy of commerce her railroads ran toward the proper destinations and for the right reasons. She entered the new world of the railroad, not handicapped, but on superior terms.

V

THE FIRST TRANSECTIONAL RAILROAD

*"The people of the West, from St. Louis to Albany, are look-
ing with intense interest to the completion of our Western
road. . . . They look to Boston, not merely as the seat of literature and the arts, not merely as a seaport, where capital, in
which they are deficient, has accumulated to a large amount, but
as the best market in America for the produce of the West, and
the great center and depot of American manufactures."* — Report
of the Delegation to Albany, to the Stockholders of the Western
Railroad Corporation, April 12, 1840, pp. 12–13.

I

From the Boston and Worcester grew the Western Railroad
between Worcester and Albany. Such had been the original in-
tention of the Massachusetts railroad schemers who had hoped
that the first enterprise, as a triumphant illustration of railroad
success, would dispel all doubts darkening the far more difficult
project of a railroad to the Hudson. So it was no surprise that
the charter of the Western Railroad, granted in March, 1833,
welded the two enterprises. The incorporators of the new road
were the directors of the Boston and Worcester and the shareholders in the Boston and Worcester were to have a preference
in purchasing the stock of the Western in case the subscription
exceeded the maximum set by the act of incorporation. The
other details of the charter followed the pattern already set by

the pioneer three in Massachusetts. The state reserved the right of recapture and the right to reduce tolls when returns exceeded 10 per cent, and granted a most generous monopoly of the route — for no other railroad, within thirty years, could be chartered from Worcester to Hampden County or from Springfield to Berkshire County. A curious provision in this document, however, was that establishing a maximum capitalization of $2,000,000.[1] Perhaps this extraordinarily inadequate calculation of costs was derived in some fashion from the estimate which James F. Baldwin had made in 1829 for the through route from Boston to Albany. His figure had been $3,254,876.[2] Deductions for the Boston and Worcester, in course of construction, and for the mileage in New York state might explain the capitalization of $2,000,000.

When, on the completion of the Boston and Worcester in 1835, the incorporators of the Western at last moved to open the books for subscriptions and to organize the company, such figures were no longer tenable. A most cursory survey in that year estimated that the road between Worcester and the New York state line would cost $2,400,000.[3] Already the forty-three miles of the Boston and Worcester had cost at the very least $1,160,000; the route to the New York state line was twice as long.[4] Furthermore between Worcester and Springfield it had to penetrate the rugged territory of the eastern highlands, and beyond the Connecticut it had to cross the Berkshires. Whether a locomotive could profitably surmount the grades which at their maximum had been placed at 83 feet to the mile was highly conjectural. Captain Basil Hall had been so depressed by the country in question, "ribbed over by a series of high ridges running north and

[1] *Private and Special Statutes of . . . Massachusetts . . . 1830 to . . . 1837*, pp. 344–349.
[2] *Report of the Board of Directors of Internal Improvements of the State of Massachusetts on the Practicability and Expediency of a Rail-Road from Boston to the Hudson River, and from Boston to Providence. Submitted to the General Court, January 16, 1829* (Boston: Boston Daily Advertiser, 1829), p. 17.
[3] *Report of the Executive Committee of the Subscribers for Procuring a Survey of the Western Rail-Road* (n.p., n.d.), pp. 9, 16.
[4] *Third Annual Report of the Directors of the Boston and Worcester Rail-Road Corporation to the Legislature, February, 1835* (n.p., n.d.), pp. 6–7.

south," across which "the rail-way . . . would have to pass along a sort of gigantic corduroy road," that he felt to execute the project would be "madness." [5] Massachusetts investors, brooding over these topographical barriers, might be pardoned both a suspicion that the stated capitalization was entirely inadequate and a reluctance to subscribe heavily in the enterprise. Still without such a subscription the corporation could not come into being. Amidst the customary salvos, asserting the road was a public necessity and a profitable private speculation, the books were opened in August, 1835. The subscription fell short.[6] To the accompaniment of a mass meeting in Faneuil Hall and a committee of solicitation in each Boston ward and for each major city, a second attack was made. Again it fell short.[7] Finally by the end of the year, the 20,000 shares were taken.[8] The campaign had required an unexampled display of energy; it had been a discouraging business. At the end of a hard day, Josiah Quincy, Jr., wrote in his diary: "November 25th. Went round with Mr. Edmund Dwight to obtain subscribers for the Western railroad, and they all with one accord began to make excuses. Some think the city is large enough and do not want to increase it. Some have no faith in legislative grants of charters since the fate of the Charlestown bridge, and very few say they won't subscribe. It is the most unpleasant business I ever engaged in." [9]

However tedious the solicitation of subscriptions, an analysis of the list is revelatory. In the first place, the Western Railroad was a Massachusetts enterprise; there were few investors from outside the Commonwealth. In the second place, it was a Boston enterprise; purchasers in that city held over three-fourths of the stock and provided nearly three-fifths of the stockholders. Of the places outside the Boston area, only Springfield and Pittsfield were greatly interested, for naturally the final selection of a

[5] Basil Hall, *Travels in North America in the Years 1827 and 1828* (Edinburgh: Cadell and Co., 1829), II, 93.

[6] Boston *Advertiser*, July 16, August 19, 1835.

[7] *Ibid.*, August 25, October 8, November 13, 1835.

[8] *Ibid.*, December 10, 1835.

[9] Charles F. Adams, Jr., "The Canal and Railroad Enterprise of Boston," Justin Winsor, ed., *The Memorial History of Boston, Including Suffolk County, Massachusetts, 1630–1880* (Boston: James R. Osgood & Company, 1881), IV, 131.

route had filled with disaffection the neglected communities and even angered Worcester who risked exchanging her position as a terminus on the Boston and Worcester for that of a station on a through route. In view of the current localism, this parochial sentiment, like a bereavement, excited unusual understanding and sympathy.[10] Among individual holders the stock was widely dispersed. Many subscribers bought a single share merely to placate the zealous canvassers. And yet, though the total number of subscribers was 1,863, the control was concentrated: a ninth of the subscribers held half the stock and the twenty owners of 100 or more shares apiece held 11½ per cent. This last group reads like a directory of the great merchants or mercantile houses of Boston and Springfield.[11] Then and since, it has been the fashion to berate these large holders as lacking in vision and niggardly in their contributions. In a day when $50,000 was wealth, a subscription of 100 shares was a major undertaking.[12]

The promoters of the Western, however, for the moment found it well to emphasize the small holder. The state would hardly be interested in aiding a corporation controlled by large capitalists; its sympathy would be aroused only by a people's road. For it was early decided that the government must be summoned to reverse the policy which it had so decisively rejected in 1828–1830 and grant financial assistance to this essential enterprise. Prominent in the counsels of the Western were the old railroad conspirators of the twenties — Nathan Hale, Josiah Quincy, Jr., Emory Washburn, and P. P. F. De Grand. They gained new recruits, of whom the most able and zealous was E. H. Derby. Until Charles Francis Adams, Jr., appeared in the late sixties, Derby was the most intelligent thinker and voluminous writer

[10] Report of a Special Joint Committee concerning Statistical Information in Relation to the Western and other Rail-Roads, Massachusetts *Senate Documents,* 1838, no. 28, p. 9.

[11] List of Western Subscribers as of February 1, 1836, Ms., Stock Journal, Western Rail Road, Harvard Business School Library.

[12] *Argument of Hon. Daniel Webster on Behalf of the Boston & Lowell R. R. Company, at a Hearing of the Petitions of William Livingston and Others, and Hobart Clark and Others, before the Rail Road Committee of the Massachusetts Legislature, Boston, January XX, MDCCCXLV* (Boston: Dutton and Wentworth, 1845), p. 12.

and speaker on railroad questions in New England. The descendant of Salem merchants, he knew water transportation, and as investor and official in railroads, he mastered the new science of land transportation. Although his legal training and frequent employment as railroad lawyer gave to many of his utterances an *ex parte* character, his enthusiastic appreciation of the railroad's importance was not a matter of a lawyer's retainer.

Even during the subscription campaign, these individuals at judicious intervals dropped hints that the capital of $2,000,000 was inadequate and that the balance should come from the Commonwealth; by December these hints assumed a more determined note [13] and on January 15, 1836, the annual message of Governor Everett, an original subscriber and early public advocate of the Western, blandly anounced: "Should this work, in its progress, stand in need of resources beyond the reach of the enterprise and means of the individual citizens, by whom it is undertaken, it is believed that the public patronage could be safely extended to it, as a project of vast general utility whose successful execution would form an era in the prosperity of the State." [14] This was no accidental clairvoyance. At their second meeting the stockholders of the Western had already instructed the directors to petition for state assistance. [15]

Apparently the task of reversing state policy faced a fair prospect. The proponents of state assistance still had at hand the arguments of the earlier decade; these arguments for the utility and necessity of a great connection with the West had been repeated throughout the state with all the insistence and decoration of which the eloquence of that day was capable. As for earlier objections, they were swept away with the argument that things were now different. The success of railroads had been demonstrated elsewhere and in Massachusetts; and state after

---

[13] Boston *Advertiser*, August 25, November 23, December 11, 1835.

[14] Address of Governor Edward Everett, January 15, 1836, *Resolves of the General Court of the Commonwealth of Massachusetts,* . . . *1835 to,* . . . *1838,* pp. 290–291; Edward Everett, *Orations and Speeches on Various Occasions* (Boston: Charles C. Little and James Brown, 1850), II, 362.

[15] Records of the Western Railroad Corporation, Ms., Harvard Business School Library, I, 18.

state had accepted the feasibility of financing internal improvements.[16] The whole speculative era of the early thirties caught
fire from this exciting policy. To assure a wide body of legislative support, nevertheless, the apostles of state assistance to
the Western joined their proposal with another then current —
an immense state bank. In return for its charter this ten-million-
dollar bank was to subscribe to 10,000 shares in the Western
Railroad.[17] Finally, to escape the tangled antagonisms aroused
by the spectacle of this institutional monster, the General Court
by immense majorities in April, 1836, decided simply to subscribe $1,000,000 to the stock of the Western and, to make this
arrangement possible, increased the capital stock of the road to
$3,000,000. The state was to appoint three of the nine directors.[18]
In the following year, in order to pay for its subscription, the
legislature authorized the issue of state scrip and to liquidate the
debt established a sinking fund, to which the bonus from the
sale of this state scrip, dividends on the 10,000 shares of Western
stock owned by the state, and one half the money from the sale
of public lands, largely in Maine, were appropriated.[19] The
further history of this grant was a happy one. Assessments were
levied so slowly that it was not until 1842 that the final payments were made. The sinking fund grew steadily, through the
sale of land and through unexpected accessions, the chief of
which was a portion of the money from the Federal government
under the terms of the Webster-Ashburton treaty. By 1857 the
scrip was wholly redeemed. Such was the fortunate outcome of
this early land-grant policy.[20]

[16] Boston *Advertiser*, December 11, 1835.

[17] Records of the Board of Directors of the Western Rail Road Corporation, Ms.,
Harvard Business School Library, I, 12; George Bliss, *Historical Memoir of the
Western Railroad* (Springfield: Samuel Bowles & Company, 1863), pp. 31–33;
Petition of the Western Rail-Road for the Establishment of a Bank, Massachu-
setts *House Documents*, 1836, no. 16; Report of Legislative Committee on the
State Bank of Massachusetts, Massachusetts *House Documents*, 1836, no. 43.

[18] *Private and Special Statutes of . . . Massachusetts . . . 1830 to . . . 1837*,
pp. 644–645.

[19] *Ibid.*, pp. 788–789.

[20] Report of Joint Special Committee on the Sale of State's Shares in the
Western Railroad, Massachusetts *Senate Documents*, 1863, no. 133, p. 6; Josiah G.
Holland, *History of Western Massachusetts. The Counties of Hampden, Hamp-*

II

The triumph was in the future. Meanwhile a new financial crisis confronted the promoters of the Western. In 1836–1837, they at last authorized the first serious survey of a route for a modern railway. A tight little trio of West Pointers, William H. Swift, George W. Whistler, and W. G. McNeill, superintended the field work, gave counsel, and compiled estimates. All had been busy surveying railroad routes in southeastern New England; Whistler had been chief engineer of the Proprietors of the Locks and Canals on Merrimack River, had designed the engines manufactured in their machine shop, and had become brother-in-law of Swift by his first marriage and of McNeill by his second.[21] Their appraisals and the initiation of actual construction soon made it clear that the cost of construction would be not three million dollars but four.[22]

This news came at a most unsuitable moment. The panic of 1837 had fallen like a blizzard upon American business, the properties and fortunes of New England merchants melted away, and the payments of the first six assessments already laid upon the Western's stock were foundering. One group of directors and stockholders proposed to stop the work immediately, discharging officers and employees and terminating existing engagements. After an interval of a few years contracts could be made at cheaper prices and the process of assessment profitably resumed. Another group, partisans of the "railroad scheme," determined to seek a state loan, the amount of which they set at $2,400,000. In effect the state was to interpose its superior credit in behalf of the Western; it was expected that this Massachusetts scrip

shire, Franklin, and Berkshire (Springfield: Samuel Bowles and Company, 1855), II, 421–422.

[21] George W. Cullum, *Biographical Register of the Officers and Graduates of the U. S. Military Academy at West Point, N. Y., from Its Establishment, in 1802 to 1890, with the Early History of the United States Military Academy* (3rd ed., Boston and New York: Houghton Mifflin & Company, 1891), I, 162–164, 215–217, 237–239.

[22] *Reports of the Engineers of the Western Rail Road Corporation, Made to the Directors, in 1836–7* (Springfield: Merriam, Wood and Company, 1838); Bliss, *Historical Memoir*, p. 40.

would be sold in the English market not yet shaken by the revulsion against American state securities.[23]

Fortunately for the design, no new principle of state action was involved, since early in 1837 the General Court had in this fashion already come to the aid of three harassed railroads.[24] But the size of the request apparently required a most far-reaching campaign to convert not only the leaders of public opinion but the masses themselves. P. P. F. De Grand stepped forward as the impresario of enthusiasm and organization. Once again in petition, press, memorial, and address, the changes were rung on the state character of the work, the necessity of reaching the West, the profitableness of state works in New York, Pennsylvania, and Maryland, and the common-man character of the Western's stockholders. "The subscribers in making this application do not come as representatives of speculators, who have failed in an enterprise by which they had hoped to enrich themselves or their children, but of deserving citizens who have made, and are willing to make sacrifices for the public good." [25] A state loan would not only build the railroad, it would reduce the length of the militia term, make work for the unemployed, and enable banks to resume specie payments.[26]

In February, 1838, under the skillful leadership of Emory Washburn, luckily chairman of the Joint Select Committee to which the memorial of the Western was referred, the railroad won a grant. The state transferred its own securities in the amount of $2,100,000 to the treasurer of the Western; as a prerequisite to this loan the railroad was to collect from its stockholders, including of course the state, the first six assessments, at $30 a share. The Western was to pay the interest upon the state

[23] *American Railroad Journal,* XXI (1848), 675–676, 705–706; Records of the Western Railroad Corporation, Ms., Harvard Business School Library, I, 40–44.

[24] *Private and Special Statutes of . . . Massachusetts, . . . 1830 to . . . 1837,* pp. 752–753, 776–778, 792–793.

[25] Memorial and Report of the Western Rail-Road Corporation, Massachusetts *Senate Documents,* 1838, no. 8, p. 5; *American Railroad Journal,* XXI (1848), 706–707.

[26] *Proceedings of the Western Rail-Road Corporation, November 23, 1837. Including an Address to the People of the Commonwealth of Massachusetts, on the Application for a Loan of the State Credit* (Boston: Dutton and Wentworth, 1837), pp. 4–11.

securities and, to protect the Commonwealth against loss, was to execute to it a mortgage upon the franchise, income, and property of the road. For the liquidation of this loan the road was to set aside annually from its earnings 1 per cent on the amount of state scrip, to form, with any bonus from its sale, a sinking fund.[27] As it turned out, this loan was but a beginning. While the dreary years went by, the costs of construction were recurrently set at higher figures, and private investors were neither able nor willing to meet them. The state should provide. In 1839 Massachusetts gave a second loan of $1,200,000 and in 1841 a final issue of $700,000 in state securities.[28]

As the loans mounted to a total of $4,000,000, the state tired of the policy. Governor Morton in 1840, when the Democrats won the governorship, delivered a safe and moderately forceful criticism of corporations in general, and the legislature launched a disjointed investigation into the competency of the Western's engineers and the expenses of their propaganda and lobbying campaigns.[29] The next year even Emory Washburn deserted the cause with the statement that the private shareholders should finance the road.[30] In their successive loan measures, the General Court had meanwhile increased the number of state directors to four and insisted upon the collection of additional assessments on the stock. Whether or not the state would have continued its

[27] *Private and Special Statutes of . . . Massachusetts, . . . 1838 to . . . 1848*, pp. 5–7; Report of the Joint Select Committee Relative to the Memorial of the Western Rail-road, Massachusetts *House Documents*, 1838, no. 17; *Speech of Emory Washburn, of Worcester, Delivered in the House of Representatives of Massachusetts, February 14, 1838, on the Bill to Aid the Construction of the Western Rail Road* (Springfield: Merriam, Wood & Co., 1838).

[28] *Private and Special Statutes of . . . Massachusetts, . . . 1838 to . . . 1848*, pp. 103–105, 235–237; *Proceedings of the Western Rail-Road Corporation, December 12, 1838; Including an Address to the People of the Commonwealth of Massachusetts, on the Application for an Additional Loan of the State Credit* (Boston: James Munroe and Company, 1838); *Proceedings of the Western Rail-Road Corporation, January 27, 1841; Including an Address to the People of the Commonwealth of Massachusetts, on the Application for an Additional Loan of the State Credit* (Boston: Dutton and Wentworth, 1841).

[29] Address of Governor Marcus Morton, *Acts and Resolves Passed by the Legislature of Massachusetts in the Years 1839, 1840, 1841, 1842*, pp. 300–301; Report of Joint Special Committee on the Western Rail-road, Massachusetts *House Documents*, 1840, no. 62.

[30] Bliss, *Historical Memoir*, p. 64.

liberality was now an academic question. By 1842 the market
for Massachusetts securities had turned sour. They suffered from
the revulsion English investors felt when the continuing depression compelled certain American states to adjourn the payment
of interest upon their obligations and to consider repudiation. The
last sales of the Massachusetts scrip had been made at a discount.
To finish the road, therefore, and "to protect the State Stock"
there was no other recourse than the renewal of assessments. The
directors and Josiah Quincy, Jr., the masterful treasurer, descended upon the stockholders and collected the last forty dollars
upon each of the 30,000 shares; [31] the last hope of public-spirited
subscribers that they might be spared the full extent of their
sacrifice went glimmering. As events turned out, they had no
cause to bemoan their purchases nor the state to regret its policy.
Though the sinking fund for these Commonwealth loans did not
operate as smoothly as had that for its stock, the issues of state
scrip were paid off in 1871 either through the fund or the action
of the corporation. [32]

These financial arrangements simply carried the railroad to the
western boundary of Massachusetts. The traverse of the area between the state line and the Hudson involved additional financial
exactions and stirred to life the aspirations of the several Hudson
River ports for the western terminus of the road. Luckily the
disappointed Trojans had retired from the competition; rejected
earlier by the Massachusetts men, they turned their efforts to the
construction of a railroad network north and west. Now all they
wanted was a spur line from Troy to Greenbush, the Western's
terminus opposite Albany. On the other hand Hudson had ag-
gressively pushed a railroad to meet the advancing Western. Of
this achievement, however, the promoters of the Western thought
ill. The road was frailly built, it defied both grades and financial
proprieties, and Hudson was not opposite the mouth of the Erie

---

[31] *Eighth Annual Report of the Directors of the Western Rail-Road Corporation
to the Stockholders. Presented February 8, 1843, Comprising a Copy of the Seventh Report to the Legislature* (Boston: Dutton & Wentworth, 1843), p. 25.
[32] Bliss, *Historical Memoir*, pp. 133–145; *Fourth Annual Report of the Directors of the Boston and Albany Railroad Co. to the Stockholders. January, 1872*
(Springfield: Samuel Bowles & Company, 1872), p. 7.

Canal for which, it had been asserted over and over again, the Western was simply an extension. Albany alone fitted the Massachusetts design. In general the Albanians relished the relationship.[33] Against the opposition of a minority, protesting the "undisguised effort, on the part of the citizens of Albany, to divert the Western trade from our commercial metropolis to the city of Boston," [34] they secured a charter for the Albany and West Stockbridge and permission to aid it by a subscription of municipal funds. In 1840 and 1841 the bond was sealed. Albany took a million dollars in the stock of the railroad, tendering in payment its city bonds. There was no doubt of their value, for Albany's "finances are administered with the caution and frugality which have always distinguished the nation who founded it, and to which a large proportion of its inhabitants trace back their origin." [35] As in the case of the Massachusetts loans, the Western was to pay the interest on the city bonds and establish a sinking fund by at once setting aside $100,000 of the municipal grant and by annual payments of 1 per cent. When the bonds were thus discharged, the Western was to become the owner of Albany's stock in the Albany and West Stockbridge; in the meantime, it could lease, operate, manage, and construct the road. The last was no mean obligation, since the Western had to advance over a million dollars above the city's contribution. With a last fling at Troy, the Western was forbidden to run its engines north of Greenbush, the terminus on the east bank of the Hudson, or of Albany without the consent of the Albany government.[36]

III

The Western was opened progressively. In October 1839 it reached the Connecticut River at Springfield, at the close of 1841 it was forced through in a fashion to the Hudson and Albany, and early in the following year the road was pronounced finished. Meanwhile the celebrations had been unloosed. No

---

[33] *Report of the Delegation to Albany, to the Stockholders of the Western Railroad Corporation. April 12, 1840* (n.p., n.d.), pp. 6–11.

[34] Bliss, *Historical Memoir*, p. 155.

[35] *Report of the Delegation to Albany*, p. 15.

[36] Bliss, *Historical Memoir*, pp. 47–53.

mere passage over the road by the directors and their friends, no mere collation with toasts would suffice; an intenser symbolism was required. On December 27, 1841, the Boston city government and other "gentlemen" went by rail to Albany. The New Bedford delegates carried spermaceti candles, molded the morning of departure and used to illuminate the banquet the following evening. The next day the Albanians journeyed to Boston to be wined and dined; they brought with them barrels of flour. Only a few days earlier the barrel had been a tree in a New York forest and the flour had been wheat in a Rochester grist mill. Now it was used to bake bread for the evening's celebration.[37] And from the Berkshire hills, Miss Sedgwick, sister of one of the railroad schemers, indited a poetic appreciation that descended into prosaic anti-climax: "But now the hills are brought low, and the rough places are made smooth. Man has chained to his car a steed fleeter than the rein-deer, and stronger than the elephant, and we glide through our mountain passes with a velocity more like the swiftness of lovers' thoughts than any material thing to which we can liken it. That section of the western railroad which traverses the wild hills of Berkshire is a work of immense labor, and a wonderful achievement of art. The pleasure of our citizens in surveying it is not impaired by the galling consciousness that there is yet a foreign debt to pay for it, or doubtful credit involved in it." [38]

The hills certainly determined the road's character. The Boston and Worcester had seventeen miles of level track, the Western only seven; the maximum gradient on the former was 30 feet to the mile, on the latter the maximum was 83 feet and there were one hundred and seven miles that had grades in excess of any on the Boston and Worcester.[39] The Western was a road of deep cuts, great embankments, sharp curves, and great costs. The summit section at Washington, 1,456 feet above sea

[37] *Ibid.*, p. 66; Adams, "The Canal and Railroad Enterprise of Boston," p. 139.

[38] John Hayward, *A Gazetteer of Massachusetts, Containing Descriptions of All the Counties, Towns and Districts . . . with a Great Variety of other Useful Information* (Boston: John P. Jewett & Co., 1849), p. 34.

[39] Charles L. Hodge, "Economic Beginnings of the Boston and Albany Railroad, 1831–1867," *Facts and Factors in Economic History, Articles by Former Students of Edwin Francis Gay* (Cambridge: Harvard University Press, 1932), p. 458.

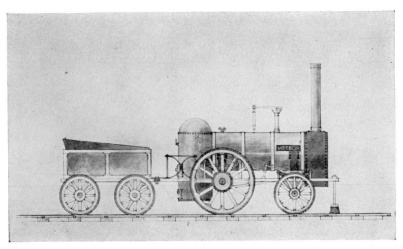

Meteor (1834), Robert Stephenson and Company
Boston and Worcester Railroad

A Train on the Western Railroad (1842)

Josiah Quincy

George W. Whistler

Nathan Hale

P. T. Jackson

A QUARTET OF MASSACHUSETTS RAILROAD BUILDERS

level, was 1.8 miles long and cost $241,311. As late as the mid-
sixties the most powerful engines were carrying over the road
trains of only eight to ten cars averaging ten tons to a car fully
loaded. [40] That such technical difficulties, unprecedented up to
that time in America, were satisfactorily solved was due to the
ability of the Western's engineering corps of whose high salaries
the legislature and even some stockholders were constantly suspicious. Of course the cost of the Western exceeded the most
lavish estimates. Nathan Hale had once calculated the cost of a
railroad to the Connecticut at $1,200,000; the route from
Worcester to Springfield alone cost nearly twice that much; the
Board of Directors of Internal Improvements in 1829 had set
the cost of the granite railroad from Boston to Albany at
$3,254,876; the actual cost by 1842–1843 was well over
$7,000,000. Loammi Baldwin's estimates for his cross-state canal
came nearest to the cost of this transectional thoroughfare. [41]

Boston now had an uninterrupted line of roads as far as Albany. But her Greenbush terminus on the east bank of the
Hudson was not closely articulated with the Erie Canal or with
the railroads paralleling the canal which later formed for the
Western Railroad as well as for Albany an extension to the
American West. Cattle were driven by a long route across
bridges farther up the Hudson; canal boats could cross the
river to the Western's depot; but freight cars and passengers had
to be lightered or ferried. Only a bridge could overcome these
interruptions and inconveniences. Not the river but the rivalry
between Troy and Albany prevented its construction. Whenever
proposals for such a structure were made, rivermen, merchants,
and politicians thronged the legislative hearings and poured forth
opinions as to whether a drawbridge would obstruct navigation. [42]

[40] Bliss, *Historical Memoir*, pp. 71–72; Report of the Joint Special Committee of
the Legislature on the Facilities of the Western Railroad, Massachusetts *House
Documents*, 1866, no. 330, p. 51.

[41] Nathan Hale, *Remarks on the Practicability and Expediency of Establishing a
Rail Road on One or More Routes from Boston to the Connecticut River* (Boston:
William L. Lewis, 1827), p. 38; *Eighth Annual Report . . . of the Western Rail-
Road . . . February 8, 1843*, p. 20; *Supra*, p. 98.

[42] Report of the Committee on Roads and Bridges on a Bridge across the Hudson, New York *Assembly Documents*, 1831, no. 29; *ibid.*, New York *Assembly*

The Trojans, whose city lay above the projected bridge, had no doubts. It would hamstring or destroy their steam and sloop tonnage, and was, in fact, a positive plot against the prosperity of Troy. A memorial of the mayor, recorder, aldermen, and commonalty of that city informed the legislature in 1845 that Troy had had to contend against that "priority of birth [which] has given to Albany all the benefit of the law of primogeniture" and declared "the grasping and monopolizing spirit, which has ever sought to exclude our citizens from a fair participation in the trade and transportation . . . turns, once more, to the erection of a bridge, as the means of consummating our ruin." To appreciate the perils of a bridge is "beyond the reach of human sagacity." [43]

For years these arguments were effective. Troy kept her water-borne commerce unscathed by drawbridges and also kept the terminus of the Western on the same side of the river as herself. In the fifties, however, when the cross-state railroads of New York were consolidated into the New York Central and when the Hudson River Railroad was completed along the east bank of the river, the drive for a bridge proved irresistible. In 1856 a committee of the legislature, prophesying that transportation of freight by railways would ultimately equal if not excel that by water, brushed aside the self-interest of competing cities as trivial in comparison with "the prosperity of the State and the exigencies of commerce." [44] A charter was granted to the Hudson River Bridge Company, in which the Western and the Hudson River Railroad each owned one-quarter of the stock, while the New York Central owned the remainder. Injunctions could not stay the completion of the bridge in 1866. [45]

Documents, 1841, no. 200; *ibid.*, New York *Assembly Documents*, 1845, no. 198; Massachusetts *House Documents*, 1866, no. 330, appendix, pp. 15–18, 84–86.

[43] Memorial of the Mayor, Recorder, Aldermen and Commonalty of the City of Troy concerning a Bridge across the Hudson, New York *Assembly Documents*, 1845, no. 72, pp. 1–3.

[44] Report of the Committee on Roads and Bridges Relative to the Bridge Across the Hudson at Albany, New York *Senate Documents*, 1856, no. 70, pp. 8–13.

[45] *Thirty-second Annual Report of the Directors of the Western Rail Road Corporation, to the Stockholders. January, 1867* (Springfield: Samuel Bowles & Company, 1867), p. 6; Massachusetts *House Documents*, 1866, no. 330, p. 84.

IV

Long since the Western and the Boston and Worcester had begun the administrative task of fulfilling the objectives for which presumably they had come into being. The sponsors of this first transectional railroad had counted upon it to divert the trade of the Connecticut Valley from New York to Boston and to bring the trade of upper New York State and the West, which had once gone by way of the Hudson and the Sound, directly to Massachusetts Bay. Some enthusiasts entertained the conviction that the railroad could haul more cheaply from Albany to Boston than the Hudson could carry from the former place to New York City. Clearly the realization of these aims was a matter of comparative rates. If the Worcester and the Western were to carry Bostonward the travel and trade of the Connecticut Valley, they had to meet the rates charged by the steamers and packets between Springfield or Hartford, on the one hand, and New York, on the other; such passenger fares were $3.00, while the freight rate varied from $3.25 to $4.25 a ton.[46] If the railroad were to win the New England bound traffic at Albany, it would have to meet the through rates down the Hudson and eastward around Cape Cod in the coasting trade. While such sloop freights in the late twenties averaged $3.00 a ton, they were $2.50 on the heavy articles, like marble and granite, $4.00 on lighter merchandise, and 28 to 30 cents a barrel on flour.[47] Such were the figures on the eve of railroad-waterway competition. Later the frenzied steamboat competition on the Hudson and on Long Island Sound brought these rates tumbling. In the mid-forties passengers from Albany to Boston paid $2.00 to $2.50, and flour 15 or 25 cents a barrel. From

[46] *Proceedings of the Annual Meeting of the Western Rail-Road Corporation, Held, by Adjournment, in the City of Boston, March 12, 1840, Including the Report of the Committee of Investigation Appointed by the Stockholders* (Boston: Dutton and Wentworth, 1840), p. 19.

[47] Report of the Commissioners Appointed under the Act of April 15, 1828, Relative to the Construction of a Rail-Road from the City of Boston to the Hudson River, New York *Senate Documents*, 1829, no. 113, pp. 12, 54; *Report . . . of Directors of Internal Improvements . . . of Massachusetts, on . . . a Rail-Road from Boston to the Hudson River*, p. 22.

Albany to New York the rate on flour was 8 cents.[48] Such was the challenge which the railroad had to answer.

When the Western reached the Connecticut in 1839, the debate over principles and the experiment with rates began. For the two roads concerned, the time was unfortunate. The Western, then and for several years, was a raw, young road; its operations raised unsolved technical difficulties of the first order; its financial situation was so desperate that every effort was bent to "retrenchment"; it paid no dividends. Nor was it the master of the through route between Albany and Boston; it shared the line with the Boston and Worcester. The latter was already an established enterprise; it paid dividends of 6 to 8 per cent.[49] The Western was an expensively constructed, long road, the Worcester was a short one; the Western traversed a sparsely settled agricultural area, the Worcester a densely settled industrial one; the Western faced water competition, the Worcester, relatively speaking, did not; through traffic was the life-blood of the Western, local traffic that of the Worcester. If the control of the two roads had remained, as originally, in the same hands, perhaps these penetrating differences would have been reconciled. Instead, in spite of considerable interlocking stockownership, two separate corporations existed, each bound to regard its own peculiar circumstances and to fight for the most favorable possible division of joint rates — for the quarrel over the rate levels was entangled with the quarrel over their division. Eventually the latter issue became the more engrossing.

In the summer of 1839 Elias Hasket Derby fired the first gun; a series of letters from his pen appeared in the Boston *Atlas*. "I do not hesitate to take the ground that the present charges are too high, both for the interests of the stockholders and the

---

[48] *Circular Letter to the Stockholders of the Western Rail Road Corporation, upon the Fares and Income of 1845. By a Committee of Directors* (Springfield: Horace S. Taylor, 1845), pp. 8–9; *An Exposition of the Present Condition and Future Prospects of the Western Rail Road. An Inside View, by an Outsider* (Boston: A. Forbes, n.d.), p. 5.

[49] Joseph G. Martin, *A Century of Finance. Martin's History of the Boston Stock and Money Markets, One Hundred Years. From January, 1798 to January, 1898* (Boston: J. G. Martin, 1898), p. 147.

public. It is a general principle, recognized by all intelligent statesmen, that the demand for luxuries increases more rapidly than the cost declines, when the reduction of price occurs." It remains, therefore, the task of wisdom to make traveling, hitherto a luxury, a commonplace through low fares. Such low fares will give a profit — a moderate return upon a huge amount of business — as the experience of certain Massachu- setts roads, of Belgium, and the calculations of theoreticians all proved. In addition such low fares will further the commerce of the state in its rivalry with New York. "Who are the proprie- tors of the road? They are the enterprising merchants, manu- facturers and artisans of Massachusetts; they took their shares not with a view to profit, but the advancement of commerce, and the development of the resources of the state." Truly the last argument somewhat shadowed the purity of the earlier one, that low fares were profitable, but Derby was not interested in formal consistency; he was advocating action. The passenger rate from Springfield to Boston must be $3.00; such a rate would "conciliate" the trade of the Connecticut from New York to Boston.[50] The directors set freights at $6.00 a ton, passenger fares at $3.75.[51]

A four-year contest ensued. On the Western, directors' meet- ings were convulsed over the fare issues; stockholders held gatherings, official and unofficial, attended by hundreds, and the annual election of directors wore the aspect of a campaign; committees of investigation made recommendations or sought to secure harmony. On the one side were Derby and his sup- porters; on the other those both less sanguine and less doctrinaire. "Nobody," wrote a committee in 1843, "has ever proposed, we think, to put the fares high, *positively*, nor is any one so perverse in theory as to propose, *positively*, to put them low; since in either case the effect must be, to diminish the net income of the road. The true principle, all must admit, is to obtain the largest *net* income. . . . The circumstances to govern a sagacious director,

---

[50] *Proceedings of the Annual Meeting of the Western Rail-Road . . . March 12, 1840*, pp. 43–45, 50–56.
[51] *Ibid.*, p. 19.

will not so much be looked for in Belgium, or France, or Austria, as much nearer home." [52] On the other side, also, stood the Boston and Worcester directorate. Though they partially co-operated in the low fare experimentation, Nathan Hale, their president, expressed the official attitude. Discarding the dreams of commercial greatness he had stirred in the twenties, he sub-stituted calculation. "We directors have a perfect right to estab-lish any rate of fare, not exceeding the rates of stage-coach and wagon transportation charged heretofore, which will afford the greatest amount of income." [53]

For a while Derby was victorious. In 1840 he became a di-rector of the Western, and held office for four years. He charmed the stockholders. At their meeting in 1840 they recommended to the directors the establishment of a $2.50 fare between Spring-fied and Boston even if the Boston and Worcester would not share the reduction, "as we have full confidence that, on trial, our policy of low fares will be so profitable for the stockholders, as to become universal, by the impulse of self interest." [54] Rates for this distance soon became subordinated in importance to those for the crucial distance between Albany and Boston. Though the debate took many forms — winter and summer fares, classifications, quantity shipments, — it focused primarily upon passenger fares and rates for flour. By 1843 Derby had forced reductions from $5.50 to $4.00 for passengers, from 50 to 30 cents for a barrel of flour; by the end of the year the rate for the latter may have been as low as 20 cents.[55] For him this was the end of the trail. Sensing repudiation by the stockholders the following year, he resigned his directorship. But the clamor went on. His opponents declared that the rate levels he had spon-sored had been "disastrous," that the reimposition of higher

[52] *Proceedings of the Western Railroad Corporation. With a Report of the Committee of Investigation, 1843* (Boston: Freeman and Bolles, 1843), pp. 28–29.

[53] Boston *Advertiser*, September 2, 1839; *Report of the Directors of the Boston & Worcester Rail Road, to the Stockholders, at Their Ninth Annual Meeting, June 1, 1840* (Boston: Samuel N. Dickinson, 1840), pp. 5–7.

[54] Records of the Western Railroad Corporation, I, 78, 79.

[55] Records of the Board of Directors of the Western Rail Road Corporation, II, 1–2, 77–78, 82, 219, 221, 240; *American Railroad Journal and Mechanics' Maga-zine*, XVI (1843), 296.

rates had brought prosperity.[56] Derby responded that the rates
he advocated had not been tried for a long enough period and
that reductions, subsequent to his resignation, proved the truth
of his dogmas.[57] Clearly the experiment was somewhat inconclusive. It involved too many extraneous circumstances.

V

At the same time the way had been cleared for the more
energetic struggle between the Boston and Worcester and the
Western over the division of the plunder. The most simple rule,
of course, was to divide the fares and freights in proportion to
the mileage traveled over each road by the passengers or commodities in question. The receipts, in other words, were to be
pro-rated. Historically a division upon this basis rarely satisfied the parties concerned. Both the strong and the weak disliked it; the former were in the position to demand a more
rewarding arrangement, while the latter, because of their dis-
advantageous position, were always pleading for something more
sustaining than a purely proportionate equated division. To this
generalization the claims of the Boston and Worcester and the
Western gave point. While the first was willing to pro-rate on a
mile-for-mile basis, the second demanded a more favorable treatment because of its length, its grades, its terminal costs at the
Hudson, its expensive construction, and because it furnished the
Worcester "passengers and merchandize *in masses.*" The
Western furthermore demanded the right unilaterally to set the
through rates, paying to the Boston and Worcester a fixed sum
per mile for each passenger and ton of merchandise. "The competition which, from time to time, requires a change of price,
is almost wholly on" the Western. "Constant vigilance and
prompt action are necessary, to counteract those opposing influences. The scenes of them are so remote from Boston, where the
officers of the Worcester Company reside, that they cannot al-

---

[56] Records of the Western Railroad Corporation, I, 119–120; *Circular Letter
. . . of the Western . . . upon the Fares and Income of 1845*, p. 6.

[57] Elias H. Derby, "Administration of the Railroads of Massachusetts with
Reference to the Rates of Freight and Fare," *Hunt's Merchants' Magazine and
Commercial Review*, XV (1846), pp. 237–246.

ways have the means of correct judgment on the subject." [58]
For two years a maelstrom of threats, negotiations, and temporary agreements whirled about these rival principles of division. The Western appealed to the General Court to permit it
to enter upon the tracks of the Boston and Worcester at rates
to be determined either by the legislature or by commissioners
appointed by the Supreme Court; the Worcester in retaliation
hired eminent counsel and opened vistas of endless litigation.
There was a temporary settlement by arbitration.[59]

Meanwhile the stockholders, particularly those interested in
both companies, took fright and finally secured from both corporations the appointment of committees to consider the possible
union of the two roads. By the end of 1845 their unanimous
report was ready. Though they did not mention God or Providence in this connection, they announced, "The great Western
route is so clearly marked as a *single distinct and entire route*,
that it must strike every one . . . that the great channel of
Rail Road Communication between these two prominent ports,
should be *one* likewise." Such a union would encourage economies, and "an end will be put forever to all those perplexing
questions, and difficult and expensive controversies which have
already arisen, and are likely continually to arise." A new
company was to exchange its stock for the stock in the two
separate railroads; each share in the Boston and Worcester was
to secure a bonus of 20 per cent.[60] At a special meeting in
January, 1846, the stockholders of the Boston and Worcester
moved to postpone indefinitely the recommendation of their
committee. For this decision a personal interposition of Presi-

---

[58] *Tenth Annual Report of the Directors of the Western Rail-Road Corporation, to the Stockholders, February, 1845* (Boston: Dutton and Wentworth, 1845),
pp. 18–27.

[59] Bliss, *Historical Memoir*, pp. 82–83, 116, 121.

[60] *Report of the Committee of the Boston and Worcester and Western Rail Road
Corporations, on the Subject of Uniting the Two Rail Roads. Also, the Report of
a Committee of the Stockholders of the Boston and Worcester Rail Road In-
structed to Inquire into the Pecuniary Condition and Property of the Boston and
Worcester and Western Rail Roads* (Boston: Eastburn's Press, 1846), pp. 3–10;
Records of the Directors and Stockholders of the Boston and Worcester Railroad,
April 10, 1843 to August 25, 1846, Ms., Harvard Business School Library, V,
184, 214; Records of the Western Railroad Corporation, I, 137.

dent Nathan Hale was responsible. Announcing, of course, his prospective resignation from office, he dissected the Western Railroad as inferior technically and in terms of earning power to his own.[61] The analysis might have been realistic, but it came with a strange irony from the champion, twenty years earlier, of "the practicability and expediency" of a railroad to the Hudson as a means of making Boston great. Experience corrupts. The collapse of this consolidation movement was a disaster for New England. If it had succeeded, not only would the first and greatest transectional railroad have been a more effective transportation instrument, but also the example of union would have shattered the local mold into which the New England roads tended to be cast and have given to New England the promise of an efficient transportation unity.

For the moment the fatal outcome of the quarrel was concealed by the attainment of harmony between the two roads. In 1846 Addison Gilmore, a large stockholder and influential director in the Worcester, became the president of the Western and, immediately after this anticipated palace revolution, suggested the terms of an agreement to the Worcester.[62] They were accepted with alacrity. The resulting contract of 1846 gave to the Western for most joint traffic on passengers and freight a slight bonus over and above a mere pro-rata division.[63] Jubilation ensued. The directors of the Boston and Worcester gave free passes to the newly elected directors of the Western and invited them "to partake of a dinner with the Board and their friends, in honor of the reconciliation between the two corporations." [64]

---

[61] Records of the Directors and Stockholders of the Boston and Worcester Railroad, V, 271–275; *Proceedings of the Stockholders of the Boston and Worcester Rail Road, at Their Adjourned Meeting, January 12, 1846, with the Communication of the President of the Corporation, on the Subject of the Proposed Union with the Western Rail Road Corporation* (Boston: Eastburn's Press, 1846), pp. 5–26.

[62] Records of the Directors and Stockholders of the Boston and Worcester, V, 283–293; Records of the Western Rail Road Corporation, I, 146.

[63] *Contracts &c., between the Boston and Worcester and Western Railroad Corporations with Some Extracts from the Reports of the Former* (n.p., n.d.), pp. 19–20.

[64] Records of the Directors and Stockholders of the Boston and Worcester, V, 294.

The harmony, thus won, continued for nearly a decade. Meanwhile the contrasts between the two roads softened. Though the Western still ran through agricultural Massachusetts, the construction of connections, particularly north and south in the Connecticut Valley, and the growth of population along its route gave new, local traffics. In 1845 the Western declared its first dividend and thenceforth easily matched its earning power with the Worcester.[65] A few years later the two roads faced together the competition of other New England railroad routes to the West, the actual rivalry of the route to Lake Ontario through Vermont, and the threatened construction of the Hoosac tunnel route to the Hudson. Though New England's first transectional road might have had two minds about meeting the rates by water, it was determined not to capitulate to competition from its own kind. Even the annual report of the Boston and Worcester chanted the advantages of mass transportation and low rates. "Many items of expense are the same as they would be if the quantity were doubled. Other items are increased in but a small degree with the increased quantity. It may therefore be good policy to take some freights at very low rates, . . . while a large profit may be fairly charged on goods of high value, where the freight charges bear a trifling proportion to the total valuation." [66]

Then in 1855 the Western shrieked it had been defrauded in the administration of the contract of 1846 and its extensions and renewals. The Worcester felt *that each parcel or ton of freight to each station on the Western Railroad should be divided separately*: the Western, *"that the entire receipts of the joint business should be divided in the proportion to which each Company has performed the work, i.e., that the share of each should be determined by the number of tons carried one mile by each Corporation."* [67] The dispute entered forthwith the realm, if not

[65] Martin, *A Century of Finance*, pp. 147, 149.

[66] *Twenty-second Annual Report of the Directors of the Boston & Worcester Railroad Corporation, for the Year Ending November 30, 1851* (Boston: David Clapp, 1852), pp. 5–7; *Sixteenth Annual Report of the Directors of the Western Rail-Road Corporation to the Stockholders. January, 1851* (Boston: Crocker and Brewster, 1851), pp. 25–26, 30–31.

[67] *Report of the Select Committee of the Board of Trade on the Controversy*

of higher, at least of confused mathematics. The Western retained as expert Benjamin Pierce, Perkins Professor of Astronomy and Mathematics in Harvard College; the Worcester had its own mathematical wizard. The quarrel was continually referred to arbitrators, commissioners, and referees, and meanwhile absorbed the business acumen and intellectual energy of the presidents of both roads.[68] In 1862 a commission from the Boston Board of Trade finally sat in judgment. After ploughing through stacks of evidence, it called down a curse upon both railroads and demanded a union of the two roads as the only solution. "Who does not know that the persons named in the Act of Incorporation of the Western, were the Directors of the Boston and Worcester for the year 1833. And yet, twenty years after the former was opened to the Hudson, this 'single distinct, and entire route' is divided, at variance, and exhibits at every disclosure to Commissioners and to Referees, elements so discordant as to recall the medley fused by the poet's brain, in the cauldron of the three witches in Macbeth." [69]

VI

This debilitating dispute was but one item which Massachusetts men had in mind as they appraised the accomplishments of the first transectional railroad. They could still remember the goals of the twenties and the arguments in the thirties for state loans. Had these been realized? At first there was considerable evidence that the glow of celebrant speeches and the assertions of promoters had not been mere colorful verbiage. The Western both frightened and inspired Boston's urban rivals. From 1835 when New Yorkers refused to subscribe to the stock of the Western lest the road divert trade from their city and "Boston people come Yankee over them," [70] to the mid-forties when they reflected with melancholy upon the decrease from 1841 to 1845 in the value of real and personal property in their own city as

---

between the Boston and Worcester and Western Railroads. *August, 1862* (Boston: Wright & Potter, 1862), pp. 32–33.

[68] *Ibid.*, pp. 32, 39–40, 46.

[69] *Ibid.*, p. 43.

[70] Bliss, *Historical Memoir*, p. 28.

compared with the 22 per-cent increase in Boston, the tone of
alarm and disenchantment was the same. Bostonians were Sam
Slicks who had deceived the New York legislature and the citizens
of Albany into aiding this enterprise dangerous to the metropolis.
New York in self-protection must have its own road to the West.[71]
Philadelphians looking northward were quick to grasp the lesson
and draw a moral. Instructed by New York's unwariness, they,
the Pennsylvanians, must head off the Baltimore and Ohio at all
costs and build the Pennsylvania Railroad. There was even more
to learn. The Boston and Albany set a pattern of technical excellence and financial proprieties. Financially as a city "Boston
did not meddle with any of its numerous railroads." [72]

By the fifties, however, Boston's brief spurt had run out and
from every quarter came evidence of her failure to attain earlier
ambitions. In the twenties a railroad to the West was to make
her the great emporium of the Atlantic seaboard in foreign trade.
Although thirty years later the absolute figures of her total imports and exports had risen astonishingly, her relative achievement was disappointing. In 1811 the foreign commerce of Massachusetts was approximately equal to that of New York State;
in 1859 Boston's exports were only $16,172,120, while New
York City's were $106,478,429; her imports were $41,174,670,
while New York's were $218,231,093. Even a cursory breakdown
of these sums illuminated sharply the extent of Boston's inferiority. To be sure she surpassed New York in the shipment of
some products culled from her immediate hinterland, such as
cotton goods, but in the great staples of the West she made a
poor showing. Judged by value of product, New York exported
in 1859 five times as much pork, eight times as much lard, ten

[71] J. E. Bloomfield, "The Influence of Internal Improvements on the Growth
of Commercial Cities," *Hunt's Merchants' Magazine and Commercial Review*, XIII
(1845), 260–262; John B. Jervis, "New York: and the Railroad Enterprise," *ibid.*,
XV (1846), 459–460.

[72] *Opinion of John M. Read, Esquire, against the Right of the City Councils to
Subscribe for Stock in the Pennsylvania Railroad Company, and to Increase the
City Debt and Taxes for That Purpose* (Philadelphia: 1846), pp. 25, 27; *The
Pennsylvania Railroad. Address of the Committee of Seven to the Citizens of
Philadelphia, and of Pennsylvania, Appointed at a Town Meeting, Held at Phila-
delphia, on the 28th of April, 1846* (Jesper Harding, 1846), pp. 14–17.

times as much beef, and thirteen times as much bacon and ham. Of flour, New York exported nearly six and a half times as much as Boston; of wheat she sent abroad 1,390,828 bushels, but Boston — not a bushel! [73]

In the second place, the Board of Directors of Internal Improvements of Massachusetts had argued in 1829 with persuasion and insight that a railroad to the Hudson was necessary for the import of articles needed by Massachusetts' growing industry and for the distribution of her manufactured products. Boston must become a great domestic market. Here also the first transectional railroad had its triumphs. Flour from the western region, to which the wheat empire was moving, came increasingly to Massachusetts by railroad. Addison Gilmore indeed determined to set so low a rate on this product over the Western as to drive out the "coasters" and to recoup himself from the local traffic.[74] In 1842, the year the Western was opened, it brought 87,853 barrels to Boston, and New York and Albany both made greater water-borne shipments. In 1860, however, the Western set down at Boston 304,462 barrels, while New York and Albany sent by water only 25,641.[75] But success in this single item could not obscure the fact that in 1853, of the 900,000 tons of goods brought to Boston by her railroads, less than 150,000 came from beyond Albany or Ogdensburg.[76]

In Boston's trade to the West, the Western and other railroads had taken over the carriage of manufactured articles. Still Boston did not become a great marketplace. Purchasers from the West and South did not throng her streets or warehouses and by

[73] Robert G. Albion, "New York Port and Its Disappointed Rivals, 1815–1860," *Journal of Economic and Business History*, III (1931), 607; Report of the Secretary of the Treasury on the Commerce and Navigation of the United States, for the Year Ending June 30, 1859, *Senate Executive Documents*, 36 Cong., 1 Sess. XII (s.n. 1034), 304, 316–317, 324–325, 330–331, 344–345.

[74] Zerah Colburn, "The Economy of Railroads, as Affected by the Adaptation of Locomotive Power — Addressed to the Railroad Interests of New England," *American Railroad Journal*, XXVII (1854), 197.

[75] *Hunt's Merchants' Magazine and Commercial Review*, VIII (1843), 279; ibid., X (1844), 288; *Boston Board of Trade. 1861. Seventh Annual Report of the Government . . . on the 16th January, 1861* (Boston: T. R. Marvin & Son, 1861), p. 71.

[76] Colburn, "The Economy of Railroads," p. 211.

their presence stimulate New England enterprise, business be-
getting business. Quite the contrary. Though Boston kept control of the boot and shoe trade, the marketing of India goods,
once associated with Boston, drifted to New York City and,
more important, the sale of domestic cottons did also. About
1846 an over-accumulation of goods led a few Boston commission
houses to establish selling agencies in New York City "con-
ducted by gentlemen well acquainted with that market, and
with strong local attachments to New York, and with little or no
interest in Boston." By the end of the fifties the New York
branch houses were doing a business of $25,000,000; Boston
sales were somewhat less. She therefore lost rents, taxes, wages,
and insurance monies that ought to be hers. The prophets of
gloom declared that Boston, as a distributing center for cottons,
would rule only New England and the British colonies while New
York would engulf the export trade and the rest of the domestic
market.[77]

The mourners admitted that other factors than the defects of
her railroad system accounted for the decline of Boston as
marketplace. The banks of New York had more ample resources;
auction sales, not heavily taxed as in Boston, disposed of immense quantities of imported and domestic merchandise to delighted purchasers; New York's wide-flung foreign and coasting
trade, even before the Erie Canal was opened, assembled in a
single locality the diverse products that country buyers and
jobbers needed for their stores or stock.[78] Some Bostonians, forgetting these economic realities, thought buyers preferred New
York because it was gayer; they proposed to redress the situation. In his classic article on Boston in 1868, Charles Francis

---

[77] *Boston Board of Trade. The Report of a Committee on a Resolution Submitted to the Government of the Board, February 1, 1858, by James C. Converse,
on the Subject of the Branch House System, for the Sale of Goods Manufactured
in Massachusetts, and in the Adjoining States, on Boston Capital* (Boston: A.
Mudge & Son, 1858).

[78] Hamilton A. Hill, *Boston's Trade and Commerce for Forty Years 1844–1884*
(Boston: T. R. Marvin & Son, 1884), p. 9; *Seventeenth Annual Report of the
Boston Board of Trade, for the Year Ending January 11, 1871* (Boston: Barber,
Cotter & Co., 1871), pp. 30–34; Albion, "New York Port and Its Disappointed
Rivals," pp. 608–612.

Adams, Jr., brought them back to earth. "Men buy where they can buy cheapest. They can buy cheapest where goods can be most conveniently laid down, and at centers where transportation is cheapest and best. Could Boston sell or send out the goods of other lands, or her own manufactures, with a fractional saving on prices or freights or time, she might close and keep closed every theatre and bar-room from Roxbury line to East Boston Ferry, and yet her streets would swarm with customers. Until she can do so, she may as well preserve her morality, for its sacrifice will in no way benefit her trade." [79]

So the trail led back to transportation: "a fractional saving on prices or freights or time." Though the indictment was wide enough to cover the coasting trade and other railroads, Bostonians understandably focused upon the Boston and Worcester and the Western, for this route was their first-born and upon its future they had pinned their hopes. What met their gaze? A raucous factionalism and stagnation. While officers quarreled over the division of receipts, the roads stood still. During the fifties the Boston and Worcester added three engines to its roster but the number of merchandise cars did not increase; the Western added a considerable number of freight cars but few engines.[80] As a carrier, Boston's first transectional railroad was pitiful in comparison with the rail routes of her chief foe, New York. In 1854 the Western carried 358,053 tons of freight, the New York Central 549,805, and the New York and Erie 743,250.[81] Or, if these comparisons were unjust, at least the Massachusetts route could be compared with itself. In 1865 the through business between Albany and Boston was a trifle less than in 1847.[82]

There were more specific grievances. One was the tardiness and irregularity in shipments between the West and New Eng-

---

[79] Charles F. Adams, Jr., "Boston," *North American Review*, CVI (1868), 11.

[80] Annual Reports of the Railroad Corporations in the Commonwealth of Massachusetts, 1850, Massachusetts *Senate Documents*, 1851, no. 22, pp. 31, 241; Returns of the Railroad Corporations in Massachusetts, 1860, Massachusetts *Public Documents*, 1861, no. 46, Report of the Boston and Worcester, p. 5, Report of the Western, p. 4.

[81] *Hunt's Merchants' Magazine and Commercial Review*, XXXIII (1855), 241.

[82] Hill, *Boston's Trade and Commerce*, p. 11.

land. "We cannot, as merchants, afford to sell our merchandise to Western customers on credit, any more than they can afford to buy of us, unless they can be sure of receiving their goods at the proper season to sell again. Neither can we purchase produce, nor can it be sent to us, with no certainty of the time when we shall receive it after it is sent." [83] Apparently the roads of Boston's rivals met this difficulty by guaranteeing to deliver goods on time. By the mid-fifties the pressure of the Boston Board of Trade had induced Boston roads to adopt this improved practice. Goods which had once taken thirty days to go to Chicago now required only ten though the guarantee was sixteen. The leadership in this innovation had been taken by the Boston and Worcester and the Western. A decade later the fast freight lines had extended and systematized these arrangements.[84]

Meanwhile at the end of the fifties rates had superseded time as a grievance. It was not so much their levels as their discrimination against Boston. At one time flour from Chicago to Boston not only paid for the greater mileage but an additional 5 cents the barrel, and indeed the rule was stated: "to ascertain the rate of freight from any place West to Boston, add to the tariff price to New York 10 cents the 100 pounds on first class; 8 cents on second class; and five cents on third and fourth classes." [85] Such differentials were calculated to attract trade to the metropolis "to the injury of Boston. . . . Our merchants were compelled to deliver goods in New York at their expense to keep their customers." [86] The Boston Board of Trade which sought to redress these injustices was well enough informed to

---

[83] *Boston Board of Trade, 1855. First Annual Report of the Government* . . . *on the 17th of January, 1855* (Boston: Moore & Crosby, 1855), p. 6.

[84] *Ibid.*, pp. 6–8; *Boston Board of Trade. 1856. Second Annual Report of the Government* . . . *on the 16th of January, 1856* (Boston: Moore & Crosby, 1856), pp. 12–20; *Boston Board of Trade. 1858. Fourth Annual Report of the Government* . . . *on the 20th January, 1858.* (Boston: Geo. C. Rand and Avery, 1858), pp. 22–23; *Thirty-Seventh Annual Report of the Directors of the Boston & Worcester Railroad Corporation, for the Year Ending November 30, 1866* (Boston: David Clapp & Son, 1867), pp. 10–11.

[85] *Boston Board of Trade. 1859. Fifth Annual Report of the Government* . . . *on the 20th January, 1859* (Boston: T. R. Marvin & Son, 1859), pp. 86–88.

[86] *Boston Board of Trade. 1860. Sixth Annual Report of the Government* . . . *on the 20th January, 1860* (Boston: Wright & Potter, 1860), pp. 23–24.

realize that they were not entirely the fault of New England's transectional railroad; that was only the first link in a line which extended from Albany to Buffalo by the New York Central and then moved westward to Chicago either along the southern shore of Lake Erie or across Canada from Suspension Bridge to Detroit. Still the Boston and Worcester and the Western were the railroads upon which New Englanders could bring pressure; the others were outside their jurisdiction.

VII

As they brooded over the unexpected inadequacy of their western routes, Bostonians naturally searched for a cause. Those most interested in foreign commerce tended to emphasize the defective connections in Boston between the railroads and the wharves and the crowded or inadequate facilities for transferring and storing cargoes. At the outset the Boston and Worcester thought it was both foresighted and generous in its plans in these matters. Through a subsidiary or allied organization, the South Cove Company, it controlled an area large enough for yards, depots, and warehouses. On the 150 feet fronting navigable waters, the road erected a wharf.[87] The self-congratulatory note over these arrangements disappeared by the fifties. Vessels reached the railroad's water-front terminal only by the passage of draws; the filling-in of South Cove, which provided the land, at the same time diminished the tidal basin which once stored waters that scoured the channel deep with the ebbing tide; and the Boston and Worcester was compelled to truck grain at heavy expense to wharves other than its own.[88] The obvious remedy was to connect the Boston and Worcester by a

[87] *Report of the Directors of the Boston and Worcester Rail-Road, Presented at a Special Meeting of the Stockholders, on the Eighteenth of January, 1833* (Boston: Stimpson & Clapp, 1833), pp. 10–11.

[88] *Twenty-fourth Annual Report of the Directors of the Boston and Worcester Railroad Corporation, for the Year Ending November 30, 1853* (Boston: David Clapp, 1854), pp. 11–12; Adams, "Boston," pp. 15–16; Report of the Joint Standing Committee on Boston Harbor, for the Year 1852, Boston *City Documents,* 1852, no. 60. pp. 5–6, appendix, pp. 2–3, 10, 19–24; Report of the Commissioners on Mystic River, Boston Harbor, and Dorchester Bay, Massachusetts *Senate Documents,* 1855, no. 63, pp. 16–21.

rather long spur road with the modern docks in East Boston, where there were large warehouses and railroad tracks running to the sides of the vessels, facilities "unequalled in any commercial city" in the United States and, in fact, at that time used by the Cunarders.[89] It is doubtful, however, if these facilities had either the cheapness or flexibility of New York where the canal boats, after their journey down the Hudson, were brought alongside packet or sailing vessel to transfer easily their bulk cargoes. Be that as it may, financial entanglements and litigation prevented, before the Civil War, the utilization of the Union Railroad and the Grand Junction Railroad connecting the Boston and Worcester with East Boston.[90]

To others the trouble was not Boston's water front, but the fact that the Western stopped at Troy and Albany "where the prize lies comparatively in the palms of our rivals. . . . We must reach the Lakes. We must penetrate into the great Valley of the West itself. . . . We should appear among the merchants of the West at their own homes, and not stand upon the banks of the Hudson beckoning them to visit us, and hoping to draw a few customers from the tide that is swinging relentlessly to New York." [91] In other words, the fault lay not so much with the Boston and Worcester and the Western but with their western extensions. For too long, according to these theories, a timid Boston depended upon the Erie Canal. She should earlier have realized the importance of the railroad and bought or contructed one, presumably across New York State, and operated it in her own interest. She had had the opportunity, for her capital had at one time controlled some of the short roads, paralleling the Erie Canal. On occasion during the fifties and sixties it might have been possible to have bought control cheaply

---

[89] William H. Sumner, *A History of East Boston with Biographical Sketches of Its Early Proprietors* (Boston: J. E. Tilton and Company, 1858), pp. 621–625.

[90] *Twenty-fourth Annual Report . . . of the Boston and Worcester Railroad . . . 1853*, pp. 10, 14–15; *Thirty-first Annual Report of the Directors of the Boston and Worcester Railroad Corporation, for the Year Ending November 30, 1860* (Boston: David Clapp, 1861), p. 12; Adams, "Boston," pp. 578–580; Sumner, *History of East Boston*, pp. 629–635.

[91] Minority Report of Erastus Hopkins on the Consolidation of the Boston and Worcester and Western, Massachusetts *House Documents*, 1864, no. 294, pp. 18–20.

of the New York Central, the successor of those smaller enterprises. Instead, New Englanders invested at least $90,000,000 in the more remote railroad companies in the West and elsewhere.[92]

Somewhat inconsistently, even those who cherished this imperial dream asserted that the real fault lay in the system under which the Western had been built and operated. Charles Francis Adams, Jr., came to the conclusion that the real heart of the matter was the charter limitation of profits to 10 per cent. Since the Boston and Worcester early attained this maximum, it had no further incentive to initiative, enterprise, improvement or competition for through business. "At the end of thirty years of successful operation, and a long succession of ten per cent. dividends, these roads found themselves with their stock at forty per cent. premium, and with large reserve funds on hand, waiting to be conveyed, somehow and in some form least likely to attract legislative notice, into the pockets of shareholders. The management of the roads had been in the meanwhile what is commonly called strictly conservative: change had been regarded with jealousy, and but little advantage had been seen to induce a further outlay of money or exertion of enterprise." The result was "a moral and physical corporate calm." [93] Josiah Quincy, Jr., now entering upon his last phase — that of railroad reformer — agreed with Adams in diagnosis, but disagreed on the remedy. Adams preferred to repeal the limitation on profits and let competition rip; Quincy advocated state ownership, apparently in the belief that the Commonwealth would be indifferent to a return upon its investment.[94] Quite the contrary had been the policy of the state directors on the board of the Western. As one of them put it, he did not "think it the duty of a State Director to favor a policy that would injure the

---

[92] Adams, "Boston," pp. 19–20, 22, 24; Adams, "Canal and Railroad Enterprise of Boston," pp. 141–144; Massachusetts *House Documents*, 1864, no. 294, p. 18.

[93] Charles F. Adams, Jr., "Railroad Legislation," *Hunt's Merchants' Magazine and Commercial Review*, LVII (1867), 347–348.

[94] *The Railway System of Massachusetts: An Address Delivered before the Boston Board of Trade, by Hon. Josiah Quincy, November 19, 1866* (Boston: Mudge & Son, 1866), pp. 3–8.

corporation to the extent of depriving the State of its dividends in order to satisfy the public outside." [95]

It is time to leave these fetching surmises and to point out that in reaching the West New England faced a geographical disadvantage. For one thing, the route from Albany to Boston was approximately fifty miles longer than that from Albany to New York; more important, the former lay over the Berkshires and other highlands; the Western had to carry its freight over a total rise and fall of 3,767 feet, while New York had the Hudson.[96] The railroad which paralleled the latter's course was a water-level route, the grades of the river itself tilted down to New York. Freights by boat were but four mills per ton per mile. The Western, to use Adams' phrase, was built upon "the fallacy that steam could run up hill cheaper than water could run down." [97] The peculiar situation of New England or of Boston also accounted for her failure to construct or buy, as did Philadelphia, Baltimore, and New York, a through rail route to the Great West. Each of these Atlantic ports could reach the edge of the West through the territory of a state committed to the prosperity of its metropolis. The Baltimore and Ohio was a partial exception, for the opposition of Pennsylvania and the Pennsylvania Central forced it to traverse a corner of Virginia rather than of Pennsylvania before the Ohio was reached. But Boston could push rail connections to the West only through the British Provinces, whose transportation policy had always been animated by hostility to American rivals and by the ambition to build up Montreal as a great American emporium, or else through New York State. The generosity which New York on the whole exhibited to the Western Railroad might have extended to the more ambitious and dangerous project of a cross-state railroad in the Massachusetts interest. But it is highly improbable. The continuance of burdensome tolls and restrictions upon the railroads that paralleled the Erie Canal until the New York and Erie Railroad was opened from the Hudson to Dun-

[95] *Ibid.*, p. 6.
[96] Colburn, "The Economy of Railroads," p. 228.
[97] Adams, "Boston," pp. 564, 574.

kirk showed that New York was not only protecting her canals but her metropolitan interests.

Whatever policy the Empire State might adopt was of secondary importance. In her rivalry with New York City, Boston stood in a different location than did Baltimore and Philadelphia. The Baltimore and Ohio Railroad in its course from Wheeling to Baltimore did not pass New York City by, nor did the Pennsylvania Central line between Chicago and Philadelphia. If New York wished to utilize the roads of these rivals, she had the task of drawing them on from the ports for whose benefit they were projected. But New York could fatally injure every road built from Boston to the West merely by tapping it. If that route crossed the Hudson at Albany, Albany was nearer to New York than it was to Boston and besides there was the river; if it passed into New England through Troy or Saratoga, it must still cross the Hudson or railroads paralleling "that river so fatal to Boston, which always will flow to the sea"; if Boston's route contented itself only with reaching for Ogdensburg and the lake traffic, it would come down to a port that on an air line was as near New York as it was Boston and by existing railroads a few miles nearer.[98] No railroad in the Boston interest built through New York state under a New York charter could conceivably have refused to interchange traffic with the roads that would have intercepted it from New York City. Such interception, in view of New York's commercial magnetism, would have been decisive.

[98] Adams, "Boston," pp. 563–567, 570, 574–577.

VI

A ROUTE TO THE LAKES

"For I must, in the course of a few weeks, go again to the Concord Bank for money, and for a renewal of my notes already given; & I am accustomed to tell my friend Cheney there, precisely on what expectations I am borrowing. In the winter to be sure, I stop borrowing, & begin paying, — as the winter brings lectures, & other resources. But, until the middle of November, I live mainly by grace. For the "Vermont & Canada" people dry up what should be my daily spending money." R. W. Emerson to Abel Adams, September 21, 1855. Ralph L. Rusk, ed., The Letters of Ralph Waldo Emerson, IV, 529.

I

In the late twenties everything seemed possible to the New England partisans of improved transportation. The Erie Canal across New York had triumphantly demonstrated the success of artificial waterways and the railroad news from Great Britain confirmed at every turn the boundless possibilities of the prepared track and the steam locomotive. Naturally enthusiasts, nourished on such fare, looked at the map and took fire from their discovery that Boston in some fashion could easily reach Lake Champlain. Turning northward, it could then march on to Montreal, to the St. Lawrence, and to the control of the commerce of Upper Canada. Pressing westward across New York State, it could reach the St. Lawrence at Ogdensburg, then the foot of sloop and steam navigation from Lake Ontario, and with the aid of the Welland Canal around the Niagara barrier, it could engross the commerce of all the Great Lakes. To utilize these ordained advantages, some proposed canals. The inhabitants of northern New York, left aside by the Erie, demanded a waterway from Lake Ontario to Lake Champlain,[1] and in New England, army engineers, paid by the national government, diligently explored canal routes from the Merrimack to the Connecticut and from the Connecticut to Champlain.[2]

Others were convinced that railroads were superior. In Vermont a railroad fever ran through the state. Lecturers instructed lyceums about the new science of transportation, a Montpelier convention with delegates from New York and New Hampshire proposed united action, and editorials strove to strike the blinders from Boston's eyes and reveal to her astonished gaze the benefits of this northern route to Canada and to the West.[3] Finally in 1831 the ubiquitous James Hayward reported the results of a survey between Boston and Ontario. Thoroughness was not its characteristic; in particular, the line west of Lake Champlain was based more upon examining maps and digesting "information" than upon field work. Under these circumstances, the physical features were almost bound to be favorable. "It almost surpasses belief that the dividing 'Range' between the valley of the Connecticut and the Champlain Basin can be crossed with scarcely an acclivity perceptible to the eye." The preferred route from Plattsburg to Lake Ontario crossed country which was "either level or very gently inclining." As far as the route's commercial possibilities were concerned, Hayward implied that they were superior to those ascribed to the Western Railroad. When the road was built it would tap Lake Champlain "bordered mostly by a rich and productive country," bring

[1] *To the Honorable the Members of the Senate and Assembly. The Merits of the Ogdensburgh and Champlain Rail-Road, with Interesting Information Relative to the Business and Resources of the Northern Counties, 1838* (n.p., n.d.), pp. 1–2.

[2] Report of the Chief Engineer to the Secretary of War, *Senate Documents*, 21 Cong., 1 Sess., no. 1 (s.n. 192), p. 79; Report of the Corps of Topographical Engineers, *House Executive Documents*, 22 Cong., 2 Sess., no. 116 (s.n. 235), pp. 5–8; *ibid.*, *House Executive Documents*, 23 Cong., 1 Sess., no. 1 (s.n. 254), p. 120.

[3] Montpelier *Vermont Watchman and State Gazette*, December 8, 1829, February 23, March 30, May 18, 25, October 12, 1830.

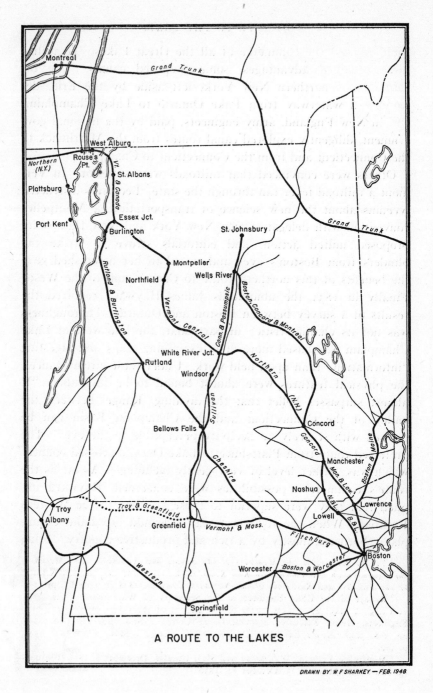

A ROUTE TO THE LAKES

DRAWN BY W. F. SHARKEY — FEB. 1948

B- M,

Montreal in terms of time twice as near Boston as New York and thus encourage the organization of a line of packets to Liverpool, while at Ogdensburg "it strikes boldly for the commerce of the great lakes, a world within itself." Their coastline had "the finest agricultural territory in the United States, and a most inviting climate." [4]

For the moment all this was mirage. In the thirties Boston was more concerned in reaching the West across Massachusetts than across New Hampshire, Vermont, and New York; and the thought of a route to the St. Lawrence and to the Lakes aroused more excitement along the periphery of New England than it did at its center. Local considerations and not distant visions primarily inspired, therefore, the end-to-end roads pushing themselves north and west from Boston. The grantees of the Boston and Lowell did not propose their enterprise as the first link of a great thoroughfare to Montreal and Ogdensburg. A second local road, the Nashua and Lowell, carried the line northward along the Merrimack, and a third, the Concord, opened on September 7, 1842, covered an additional thirty-five miles to a terminus where staging, wagoning, and boating had created an inland center of transportation.[5] Although the promoters of both the Nashua and Lowell and the Concord made obeisance to the larger design of which they might some time form a part, they focused largely on the already developed passenger and commodity trades with that part of New England south of the Canadian border and east of the Green Mountains. They calculated with even greater precision the local traffic likely to be available from the farms and factories of the Merrimack Valley. First there was Nashua, a growing industrial city and, what is more, almost a holy one, since within its confines "for the indolent, the intemperate, and the immoral there is no employment and no room." [6] Then there was Manchester, née Amos-

---

[4] James Hayward, *Report on the Proposed Railroad between Boston and Ogdensburgh* (Boston: Carter, Hendee, & Babcock, 1831).

[5] Henry V. Poor, *History of the Railroads and Canals of the United States of America, Exhibiting Their Progress, Cost, Revenues, Expenditures & Present Condition* (New York: John H. Schultz & Co., 1860), pp. 45, 60, 135.

[6] *Report of the Grantees of the Nashua and Lowell Rail-Road Corporation,*

keag, which with Lowell was already ministering to the great
western markets of America. Finally the almost untouched water
powers of the Winnepesaukee River promised a whole new
series of manufacturing communities. Although uncertain as to
how they would extend their own lines into more remote regions,
these local roads were quite confident that within their tributary
area they could take the existing traffic away from stage and
steamboat and shortly increase it threefold.[7]

In other respects than their ambitions, these three lower
roads, as they came to be called, were similar. On the whole the
provisions of their charters, even when granted by New Hampshire, clearly stemmed from Massachusetts precedents. The
charters of both the Nashua and Lowell and the Concord, enacted
within a few days of each other in 1835, conventionally retained
for the state the right to reduce rates if net annual returns exceeded 10 per cent and to repossess the roads at the end of
twenty years by repaying the stockholders the cost of the railroad and any deficiency in net income below 10 per cent. While
the charter of the Nashua and Lowell gave a monopoly of the
route, that of the Concord did not. By placing the par value
of the shares in the Nashua and Lowell at $25 and in the
Concord at $50, the legislature clearly sought to induce sub-
scriptions from small investors and to give to both enterprises
the cast of people's roads.[8] Like the Lowell, furthermore,
neither of its New Hampshire extensions encountered great
physical difficulties. Before construction began the sponsors of
the Nashua and Lowell were observing, "Nature seems to have
prepared for us a bed for our Rail Road already graded, and
appearing even now almost like the work of art," [9] and in later
years an admirer of the Concord was convinced the road "was

---

with the Report of the Engineer. May 21, 1836 (Nashua: Alfred Beard, 1836),
pp. 8–12, 14–15; *Report of a Committee of the Concord Rail-Road Corporation,
Together with the Estimates of Peter Clark, Esq. and the Act of Incorporation*
(Concord: Asa McFarland, 1841), pp. 3–5.

[7] *Report of a Committee of the Concord Rail-Road*, pp. 6–8.

[8] *Laws of New Hampshire Including Public and Private Acts, Resolves, Votes,
Etc. Second Constitutional Period, 1829–1835*, X, 644–648, 680–686; Concord
New Hampshire Patriot and State Gazette, April 29, 1839.

[9] *Report of the Grantees of the Nashua and Lowell*, p. 7.

built in the place where the creator of this world intended a railroad to be built, assuming that the economic building of railroads was contemplated in the original scheme." [10] Indeed no mile between Concord and Boston had a grade greater than fifteen feet.[11] By 1848, furthermore, the whole route had been double-tracked and the roadbed brought to a high standard.[12] Nor did this achievement involve dangerous financial burdens. The panic of 1837 threatened for a moment both roads. Massachusetts, however, came to the aid of the Nashua and Lowell with the modest tender of $50,000 of state scrip; [13] the Concord, though delayed, weathered the storm through its own resources. Like the Lowell, stock subscriptions financed their construction; like the Lowell both paid dividends.[14] All three were roads of "Egyptian fertility."

II

Although the New Hampshire railroad interests in 1836 induced the national government to assign Colonel S. H. Long, a gifted West Pointer, to a survey of a route from Concord to the Connecticut and then across Vermont to Lake Champlain, the realization of this larger enterprise was still retarded.[15] The depression years after 1837 congealed roads, like the Concord, already under construction; and in 1840 the New Hampshire legislature, in response to the popular hostility to corporations, forbade railroads to acquire a right of way through the exercise of eminent domain. This prohibition did not apply to railroads already chartered. Unhappily the projected connections to the

[10] *Testimony . . . Boston, Concord & Montreal Railroad v. Boston & Maine Railroad . . . 1888* [Consolidated Case], I.

[11] *Seventh Annual Report of the Directors of the Concord Railroad Corporation, May 30, 1848* (Boston: W. W. Clapp, 1848), p. 7.

[12] *Eighth Annual Report of the Directors of the Concord Railroad Corporation, April 30, 1849* (Concord: Asa McFarland, n.d.), p. 4.

[13] Report of the Joint Special Committee on Aid to the Nashua and Lowell Railroad, Massachusetts *Senate Documents*, 1838, no. 57, pp. 5–6.

[14] Joseph G. Martin, *A Century of Finance. Martin's History of the Boston Stock and Money Markets, One Hundred Years. From January, 1798, to January, 1898* (Boston: Joseph G. Martin, 1898), pp. 147–148, 163, 165; Concord *New Hampshire Patriot and State Gazette*, July 22, 1839.

[15] *Thirty-fifth Annual Report of the Railroad Commissioners of the State of New Hampshire, 1879*, pp. 18–20.

Connecticut had not been incorporated; they, therefore, made no move until the era of "extortion" terminated in 1844 with the restoration to enterprises in the public interest of the right to exercise eminent domain.[16]

But neither the reviving investment market nor the victory of railroad sympathizers in New Hampshire explained the final decision to realize the vision of a through route to Montreal and to Ogdensburg. The completion of the Western across Massachusetts to Albany was responsible. By surmounting the Berkshires, New England's first transectional had demonstrated that *"mind* has encountered matter at fearful odds, and gained a glorious victory; — gravitation, the great law of nature, was forced to yield to the greater power of enterprise and skill." [17] Not only did this Massachusetts road show that the locomotive could climb, but its unanticipated success loosened the purse strings of New England investors and speculators. As New Hampshire hills and Green Mountains were made low, the whole enterprise assumed its enlarged and final character. The road was to be pushed to Lake Champlain to seize for Boston the traffic which customarily sought the New York markets by lake, canal, and river; extensions to Montreal were to form an avenue by which the traffic of this growing colony might be carried to Great Britain through the port of Boston; and finally the Erie Canal and Hudson River were to be outwitted, through a connection with Lake Ontario. Once the Welland Canal was large enough, the shipping of the Great Lakes would scornfully sail by Buffalo and Oswego, where New York's canals began, and seek instead Ogdensburg where Boston's railroad stood ready to receive their cargoes.

The first step toward these distant objectives was the Northern Railroad, projected to cross the ranges west of the Merrimack and descend to the Connecticut at a point opposite the mouth of the White River.[18] No Sedgwick was at hand to assuage New Hamp-

only humorous to *superficial* understanding of how much MIND meant in this era.

---

[16] *Ibid.*, pp. 21–24.

[17] *Report of the Directors of the Rutland and the Burlington Railroad Company, at Their Annual Meeting, at Rutland, Held 20th June, 1849* (Burlington: Free Press, 1849), p. 4.

[18] *Laws of the State of New Hampshire, Passed June Session, 1844,* pp. 99–103.

shire farmers, as sensitive to the implications of this project as
those of Worcester and Berkshire had been to the Western, but
C. B. Haddock, Professor of Intellectual Philosophy at Dartmouth College, undertook the task. "If we can't grow wheat,
we can grow corn and potatoes. If we can't export beef and mutton, we can export rock and ice. If we can't maintain our position in the open field of generous and manly conflict, let us
give up the State, and go off in a body to Iowa and Ore-
gon. . . ." [19] When in June, 1844, New Hampshire chartered the
Northern, engineers had already selected the route over the
highlands. For, in contrast with the lower roads, this first of the
upper ones had to surmount heavy grades as it left the Connecticut and the Merrimack Valleys as well as at the summit;
in fact, of the seventy miles nearly a quarter was at the maximum
grade of 52.8 feet to the mile. The costs of construction the
engineer estimated at probably $20,000 a mile.[20] Almost at
once these financial expectations proved too sanguine. As construction crept slowly toward the Connecticut, the capitalization
was from time to time increased from $1,500,000 to $2,600,000;
a portion of these accretions had to be sold at less than par.[21]

By November, 1847, when the road reached Lebanon, just
short of the Connecticut, it was time for celebration. Officers,
stockholders, and guests rolled northward from Boston by special train, and were greeted at Lebanon by assembled thousands.
The immense crowd fell upon refreshments and then listened
to a long oration from Daniel Webster — "one who had been the
steadfast friend of internal improvements, thro' whose farm this
railroad went, connecting the home of his adoption with the
home of his nativity (Boscawen) and his Alma Mater (Dartmouth College, in Hanover.)" The address was a strange amalgam — a panegyric upon national power, a congratulation upon

[19] Charles B. Haddock, *An Address Delivered before the Railroad Convention at
Lebanon, N. H., October 10, 1843* (Hanover: J. E. Hood, 1843), pp. 21, 24.
[20] *Report of the Engineer on the Route Surveyed, for the Northern Railroad,
between Concord, Franklin and the Connecticut River at Lebanon, New-Hampshire, 1844* (Manchester: Wetmore & Wallace, 1844), pp. 3–13.
[21] *Fourth Annual Report of the Directors of the Northern Rail-Road Corporation, to the Stockholders, May, 1849* (Boston: Crocker and Brewster, 1849), pp.
3–4.

the belated awakening of Vermont and New Hampshire to the advantages of the railroad, and an assertion that Boston, if extended as it should be to Newburyport, was as large as New York and did a greater business.[22] For the Northern was a Boston project. The promotion campaign had been directed toward Boston and, though there was intense enthusiasm and generous subscriptions from the towns along the route, Massachusetts investors held, in 1850, one-half the total stock, New Hampshire only 37 per cent.[23]

III

At the Connecticut the Northern touched the Vermont Central already building. This road was chartered on October 12, 1843, to build "from some point on the eastern shore of Lake Champlain, thence up the valley of Onion River, and extending to a point on Connecticut, most convenient to meet a rail road, either from Concord, New Hampshire, or Fitchburgh, Massachusetts." [24] The route here described was certainly a remarkable one. Explored by the canal partisans, publicized by the Vermont railroad frenzy of the thirties, and consecrated by the surveys of both Hayward and Long, it provided the most feasible passage across the state. From the Connecticut the main trunk of the White River ran westward toward the Green Mountains, while its various branches turned abruptly north through gulfs or notches to sources not far from the Onion or Winooski River, which rose east of the central mountain barrier and flowed west through a great dent in the mountains into Lake Champlain. The award of this geographical prize to the Vermont Central and the imminent construction of a railroad along this, the central route, did not, however, satisfy the whole state. It left to one side the lower portion where local ambitions were as intense as those to the north and where projects for diagonal roads across the state from Massachusetts to the southern end of Lake

[22] *American Railroad Journal*, XX (1847), 787–789.
[23] *Report of the Committee of Investigation of the Northern Railroad to the Stockholders, May, 1850* (Concord: Asa McFarland, n.d.), p. 64; *Report of the Engineer . . . for the Northern Railroad, . . . 1844*, pp. 14–15.
[24] *Acts and Resolves Passed by the Legislature of the State of Vermont, at their October Session, 1843*, p. 43.

Champlain had for decades stirred and disappointed the imagination. This region of the state demanded to be heard. The day after approving the charter of the Central, the Vermont governor assented to another for the Champlain and Connecticut. Later re-christened the Rutland and Burlington, it ran south from Burlington to Rutland, crossed the Green Mountain range to Bellows Falls, where it might connect with the Cheshire and the Fitchburg to form a through route to Boston.[25] Thus two railroad enterprises, each over one hundred miles long, competed from the outset for the favor of an undeveloped Vermont and presented Massachusetts with the dilemma as to which road she would back for the unproved route to the Lakes. Their deadly rivalry was to be a decisive factor in the railroad history of Vermont and, to a less extent, of New England.

The solicitation of funds for the two Vermont roads at once revealed their antagonism. Presidents, their subordinates, and the press shouted claims and charges. In the beginning this antiphonal disharmony was confined to Vermont, since the first appeal for subscriptions was necessarily made to localities along the lines; according to the current folklore of railroad promotion, they had to demonstrate their faith in the enterprises. E. P. Walton, clerk of the Vermont Central and editor of the *Vermont Watchman and State Journal*, advised Vermonters to invest in his road their all, "saving something for possible contingencies."[26] Meanwhile a clamor had broken out in Boston. Governor Paine, president of the road, and Walton moved on to Boston as emissaries of the Central, and General DeWitt C. Clark was sent to checkmate them for the Rutland and Burlington. Soon the papers of the metropolis were captured by one interest or the other, and so were the leading investors.[27] As the flood of argument poured forth, both railroads, with the zeal of rival episcopates, claimed the consecration of being the historic or tradi-

---

[25] *Acts and Resolves . . . of Vermont, . . . October Session, 1843,* p. 51; *Acts and Resolves Passed by the Legislature of the State of Vermont, at the October Session, 1847,* p. 93.

[26] Montpelier *Vermont Watchman and State Journal,* June 13, 1845.

[27] *Ibid.,* April 18, July 11, 1845; Boston *Semi-Weekly Atlas,* April 23, 1845; Boston *Semi-Weekly Advertiser,* August 9, 13, 1845.

tional route. Then, forgetting the past, they paraded their technical advantages. The Rutland route to Burlington was twelve miles shorter; the Central had better grades. Though on the calculation of the Rutland's engineer the grades on his road occasionally attained fifty feet, the "maximum" was admitted to be sixty. Where the rails crossed the Green Mountains at Mount Holley, "the rocky ramparts of a mountain that can neither be tunnelled nor rent asunder," they were somewhat more [28] — at least according to the engineer of the Central.

Another controversy flamed over the comparative commercial importance of southern and northern Vermont. Factories, quarries, forests, were all marshaled into competing armies. The Bellows Falls *Gazette*, Rutland protagonist, announced, "No route in the United States can furnish as much way freight as that from Bellows Falls through Rutland to Burlington." [29] Walton from his Montpelier watchtower asserted that the counties in southern Vermont "are old counties that have passed their climax." [30] He went on to point out that the Rutland, before it crossed the mountains, ran southward toward New York, that the counties which it traversed had their marketing habits fixed in New York, and that the railroads, in course of construction north and east from Troy and Albany, would soon connect with the Rutland and drain it to New York. Boston capitalists should beware such an enterprise.[31] So voracious were the Boston investors for securities, both roads secured funds professedly sufficient to justify construction. Actually the Rutland and Burlington came off second-best. Of the original $2,000,000 sought for the Vermont Central, three-quarters was obtained in Boston.[32]

---

[28] Burlington *Free Press*, August 29, 1845; *Report of the Engineer on the Route Surveyed for the Vermont Central Railroad, from Connecticut River, at Hartford, Vt. to Lake Champlain, at Burlington* (Boston: S. N. Dickinson, 1845), p. 9; Zerah Colburn, "The Economy of Railroads, as Affected by the Adaptation of Locomotive Power — Addressed to the Railroad Interests of New England," *American Railroad Journal*, XXVII (1854), 228; *Pathfinder Railway Guide for the New England States, October, 1852* (2d ed., Boston: Geo. K. Snow, n.d.), pp. 64, 84.

[29] Bellows Falls *Gazette*, quoted in Burlington *Free Press*, July 3, 1845.

[30] Montpelier *Vermont Watchman and State Journal*, April 25, 1845.

[31] *Ibid.*, April 11, 1845.

[32] Thelma M. Kistler, *The Rise of Railroads in the Connecticut River Valley*

By the end of 1849 both roads scrambled into Burlington and began racing their trains at excessive speed to demonstrate their superiority to travelers and freighters.[33]

Meanwhile their rivalry had determined the actual route of the Central. On the east it connected not only with the Northern at White River Junction; it had also built down the Connecticut Valley to Windsor where it planned, for a time, a connection with the Fitchburg-Cheshire railroad route to Boston.[34] Much more important was the battle for a Canadian and Western connection. In 1845 the desires of both Vermont roads were apparently harmonized. A group of St. Albans promoters, of whom John Smith, lawyer and politician, and Lawrence Brainerd, merchant and lake shipper, were to become most famous, obtained a charter for the Vermont and Canada Railroad. The provisions of this ingenious document authorized, with all convenient vagueness, a junction in Burlington with the Rutland and "at some point or points in Chittenden County" one with the Vermont Central. The Vermont and Canada was to extend north from St. Albans to the Canadian line and to cross the sandbar above Burlington to the large islands in Lake Champlain. The road was to be completed in thirteen years.[35] When this innocent enterprise was actually organized two years later, Charles Paine, wool manufacturer of Northfield and president and paladin of the Ver-

---

(Northampton: 1938), pp. 255–257; E. P. Walton, Jr., "Montpelier," Abby M. Hemenway, ed., *Vermont Historical Gazetteer. A Local History of All the Towns in the State* (Montpelier: Vermont Watchman and State Journal, 1882), IV, 305–306.

[33] Poor, *History of the Railroads and Canals of the United States*, pp. 74, 78.

[34] Montpelier *Vermont Watchman and State Journal*, July 11, 31, September 4, November 16, 1845, February 11, 1847; Burlington *Free Press*, June 13, 1844; Hemenway, *Vermont Historical Gazetteer*, V, 305; Kistler, *The Rise of Railroads in the Connecticut River Valley*, pp. 137–138, 254–255; Walton, "Montpelier," pp. 304–305.

[35] *Acts and Resolves Passed by the Legislature of the State of Vermont, at Their October Session, 1845*, pp. 65–72; Remonstrance of the Vermont and Canada against the Bill to Incorporate the Champlain Railway Company, Vermont *House Journal*, 1849, p. 349; Report of a Committee on Amendments to the Charter of the Vermont and Canada, Vermont *House Journal*, 1858, p. xxxvi; L. L. Dutcher, "St. Albans," Abby M. Hemenway, ed., *Vermont Historical Gazetteer; A Magazine Embracing a Digest of the History of Each Town* (Burlington: A. M. Hemenway, n.d.), II, 301–302.

mont Central, was discovered to have joined the St. Albans worthies as a director of the Vermont and Canada.[36]

This alliance was firmly cemented in 1849 when the Central leased the Vermont and Canada at an annual rental of 8 per cent upon the latter's cost, and by an additional clause in the following year permitted the Vermont and Canada, if the rent fell into arrears, to take and run the Vermont Central to secure the contracted payments.[37] This last provision hypothecated the entire property of the Vermont Central Railroad as security for the funds invested in the construction of the Vermont and Canada. While the desperate need for subscriptions in part explained these arrangements, the agreements made certain that either the Vermont Central would run the Vermont and Canada or the Vermont and Canada would run the Vermont Central.

Firm in the possession of this critical connection, the Vermont Central located the route of its ally and pushed its construction. A curious dichotomy was at once apparent. The Vermont and Canada joined the Vermont Central at Essex Junction, 6½ miles east of Burlington; it did not join the Rutland and Burlington at Burlington. In answer to the ostensible violation of an explicit clause in the Vermont and Canada's charter, the Central blandly interpreted its own line from Essex Junction to Burlington as meeting the requirements. Whatever may be thought of this sophistry, the connection had a maximum grade of 100 feet to the mile, squirmed circuitously across the main streets of Burlington, and, since it effected no actual fusion of rails with the Rutland, compelled the transfer of passengers and the transhipment of freight between the two roads.[38] The Central, moreover, so

[36] Kistler, *The Rise of Railroads in the Connecticut River Valley*, p. 252; Dutcher, "St. Albans," p. 302.

[37] *Charters of the Vermont Central, Vermont and Canada, and Central Vermont Railroads. The Vermont and Canada Lease. The First and Second Mortgages and Deeds of Surrender of the Vermont Central Railroad Company. Orders and Decrees in the Cause Vermont and Canada R. R. Co. vs. Vermont Central R. R. Co. et al.* (St. Albans: Advertiser Steam Press, 1875), pp. 21–30.

[38] *Report of Special Masters, in the Case of Vermont and Canada R. R. Co. vs. Vermont Central R. R. Co. and Others, Filed April 24, 1877* (St. Albans: Advertiser Print, 1877), p. 9; Vermont *House Journal*, 1849, p. 351; *Charters of the Vermont Central, Vermont and Canada, and Central Vermont Railroads. . . . Lease. . . . Orders and Decrees*, p. 85; *Report of the Directors of the Rutland and Burlington*

artfully arranged the timing of trains over the connection as to
make Essex Junction one of the most vexatious transfer points
in New England. Legislatures passed statutes to eliminate the
nuisance, railroad commissioners pierced subterfuges with analysis, and a popular jingle concluded:

> "I hope in hell, their souls may dwell
> Who first invented Essex Junction." [39]

All was to no avail. Perhaps after thirteen years the Rutland
could bring proceedings to void the charter on the ground that its
provisions were not fulfilled. By then it would be too late. For
the present it clutched at litigation and blackmail.

Satisfactory though this triumph was to the Central, it did
not assure connections with either Montreal or Ogdensburg. As
it turned out both of these lines were eventually built from
Rouse's Point, a location on the western shore of the lake just
below the international boundary. The northern link ran thence
to St. Johns, once head of navigation, from which an existing
railroad covered the distance to Montreal.[40] The route to Ogdensburg was chartered in 1845 by the New York legislature as
the Northern Railroad. While the original impulse to the road
came from the tiny localities in northern New York, it had now
become a through railroad and a Boston enterprise.[41] Its "commissioners," a euphemism for salesmen, repaired to the Boston
investment market in 1845; the Northern of New Hampshire
recommended subscriptions "to the patronage and pecuniary aid

---

Railroad Company, at their Annual Meeting, at Rutland, Held 20th June, 1849
(Burlington: Free Press Office, 1849), pp. 16–18.

[39] Report of a Committee on the Amendment of the Charter of the Vermont
and Canada, Vermont *House Journal*, 1858, pp. xxxviii–xxxix; *Acts and Resolves
Passed by the General Assembly of the State of Vermont, at the October Session,
1858*, pp. 183–184; *ibid.*, 1859, pp. 83–85; *Third Annual Report of the Railroad
Commissioner of the State of Vermont to the General Assembly, 1858*, pp. 10–12;
*Fourth Annual Report of the Railroad Commissioner of the State of Vermont to
the General Assembly, 1859*, pp. 4–7.

[40] George P. de T. Glazebrook, *A History of Transportation in Canada* (New
Haven: Yale University Press, 1938), p. 171.

[41] Report of E. F. Johnson on a Survey of a Railroad from Ogdensburgh to
Lake Champlain, New York *Assembly Documents*, 1839, no. 133; Report of the
Commissioners to Arrange a Survey of a Railroad from Ogdensburgh to Lake
Champlain, New York *Assembly Documents*, 1841, no. 43; Poor, *History of the
Railroads and Canals of the United States*, p. 294.

of such of our stockholders as are able to advance the cause of internal improvement," and the Vermont Central took pleasure in announcing that the road was organized "under highly favorable auspices," probably because on its board of directors sat Charles Paine along with other luminaries from its eastern connections.[42]

Between the Northern or Ogdensburg road and the Vermont and Canada stretched Lake Champlain. From the beginning its broad navigable waters had broken the route to the Great Lakes and had haunted the plans of promoters. In Hayward's report, though its existence was acknowledged, it was treated like a spectre. Only by inference could the reader learn that boats between Port Kent or Plattsburg and Burlington were to connect the proposed New York and Vermont railways.[43] Five years later S. H. Long solved the dilemma by abruptly ending the route at Burlington; the later surveys of the New York Northern copied the stratagem by simply terminating their lines from Ogdensburg at the Champlain ports.[44] Clearly, if the route to the Lakes was to rival the Western, it could not accept such broken solutions. Transhipment across Lake Champlain from railroad to railroad was far more cumbersome than on the Hudson, where canal boats at least easily crossed the river to the Greenbush terminal. Lake Champlain must be bridged. Even in the fevered days of the forties, only a few proposed a structure five miles long over deep water from South Hero. The charter of the Vermont and Canada, therefore, took the rails to the islands and fell silent. But then the answer was found: a bridge between West Alburg, Vermont, and Rouse's Point. Here the distance was only 3,880 feet and the water comparatively

---

[42] *First Annual Report of the Directors of the Vermont Central Railroad Company, to the Stockholders. Submitted July 15, 1846* (Montpelier: E. P. Walton & Sons, 1846), pp. 5–6; *The Second Annual Report of the Directors of the Northern Railroad Corporation, to the Stockholders. Presented May 19, 1847* (n.p., 1847), pp. 15–16; *The Third Annual Report of the Directors of the Northern Railroad Corporation to the Stockholders, Presented May 24, 1848* (Concord: Asa McFarland, 1848), p. 13; *By-Laws and Officers of the Northern Railroad Company, New York, 1847* (Boston: S. N. Dickinson, 1847), p. 2.

[43] Hayward, *Report on the Proposed Railroad Between Boston and Ogdensburgh*, pp. 6-10.

[44] New York *Assembly Documents*, 1839, no. 133; *ibid.*, 1841, no. 43.

shallow.[45] In New York, the Northern appealed to the legislature for permission to bridge the channel; in Vermont, the Vermont and Canada sought an amendment to its charter to a similar effect.[46]

War ensued. In both states the shipping interests on Lake Champlain vehemently opposed a drawbridge as an obstruction to navigation; and traditional ports like Plattsburg, Whitehall, and Burlington, smarting at being left aside, joined this opposition. In both states representatives of the Rutland and Burlington Railroad, angered at the prospect of further favors to the Vermont and Canada, the tool of their rival, came to the legislatures with hearts aching for the immemorial rights of Champlain's navigators.[47] In Albany it was said the bridge would become a means for detaching northern New York from its dependence upon New York City and for winning the western trade away from the Erie Canal. When the supporters of the bridge stressed New York's liberal policy in regard to the Western, the wisdom of multiplying the means of communication, and the inevitable superiority of New York City as a mart, they were met with the reply: "While we admire the intelligent sagacity of the far-seeing capitalists of Boston in their efforts to draw from this state the rich trade of the West and the Canadas and however earnest their perseverance, yet it appears to the undersigned that the Legislature of New York will hesitate long before they will throw away from their own state a trade which is the foundation of their greatness and wealth and give it to their more cautious and calculating rivals." [48] In

[45] *Acts and Resolves . . . of Vermont, . . . 1845*, p. 66; Dutcher, "St. Albans," p. 302; Montpelier *Vermont Watchman and State Journal*, April 29, 1847; James Hayward, *Report of Surveys and Estimates for the Northern Railroad in New York* (Boston: S. N. Dickinson & Co., 1847), pp. 13-17.

[46] J. B. Varnum, "Railroad Legislation of New York in 1849," *Hunt's Merchants' Magazine and Commercial Review*, XXI (1849), 171; E. P. Walton, *A Review of the Proceedings in the Legislature of Vermont, October Session, 1847, on the Bill Granting to the Vermont and Canada Railroad Company the Right to Bridge Lake Champlain, Opposite Rouse's Point* (Montpelier: E. P. Walton & Sons, 1847), p. 5.

[47] Walton, *A Review of the Proceedings*, pp. 20-22; *American Railroad Journal*, XXII (1849), 472.

[48] Report of a Select Committee on the Bridge at Rouse's Point, New York *Senate Documents*, 1849, no. 24, pp. 15-18; Report of Committee on Railroads on

Vermont a solid phalanx of railroad opposition and the popular distaste for the high-handed methods of the Central conditioned the permission to bridge upon so many favors to the Rutland and Burlington that the Central's leaders apparently lost interest in the matter.[49] In February, 1851, the *Vermont Watchman and State Journal* announced: "We have done caring very much about this vexed question for reasons which will develop themselves by and by." [50]

Meanwhile the eastern terminus of the Northern of New York had been shifted to Rouse's Point, and the Vermont and Canada, by a highly constructive interpretation of statutes and under the leadership of their engineer, Henry R. Campbell, "the Hero of the Bridges," built northward from St. Albans, crossed by a pile bridge to the tongue of land which, with the islands, divided Lake Champlain, and carried their rails to water's edge in West Alburg.[51] In winter passengers and freight crossed the ice, and in summer a steamer covered the distance.[52] Then in 1851 the legislature of New York permitted the Northern to extend a pier into the lake provided it stopped 125 feet short of the center of the channel; the Vermont and Canada and the Central, with their customary artifice, built a similar pier from the opposite shore, under the general statute regulating the rights of riparian owners.[53] To close the resulting gap Campbell devised the famous

---

Bridge at Lake Champlain, New York *Senate Documents*, 1851, no. 20, pp. 26–46; Report of a Majority of Committee on Railroads on Bill for a Bridge at Rouse's Point, New York *Assembly Documents*, 1851, no. 154; Report of a Select Committee of the Assembly on the Rouse's Point Bridge, Minority Report, New York *Assembly Documents*, 1851, no. 134; Varnum, "Railroad Legislation of New York in 1849," p. 171.

[49] Walton, *A Review of the Proceedings*, pp. 7–16; Vermont *House Journal*, 1849, pp. 349–351; Vermont *House Journal*, 1858, p. xxxvii; *Acts and Resolves Passed by the Legislature of the State of Vermont, at Their October Session, 1850*, pp. 65–69.

[50] Montpelier *Vermont Watchman and State Journal*, February 6, 1851.

[51] Walton, *A Review of the Proceedings*, pp. 16–17; Report of the Committee on Railroads Relative to the Change in the Location of the Northern Railroad, New York *Senate Documents*, 1847, no. 144.

[52] *Sixth Annual Report of the Directors and Treasurer of the Vermont Central Railroad Company, Prepared for the Stockholders' Meeting, August 27, 1851* (Montpelier: E. P. Walton & Son, 1851), p. 13.

[53] *American Railroad Journal*, XXIV (1851), 421; *Hearing before the Special Masters to Adjust the Accounts of the Receivers and Managers of the Vermont*

floating bridge, of which the boat or ferry was three hundred feet long and laid with track. "The two sections of the bridge lay in reference to each other like two men on their backs with their feet toward each other; and the Boat plies between them as a dog might crawl from between the feet of one of the aforesaid men and then lie down between the feet of the other. At the close of navigation the Boat was placed between the right foot of the New York man and the left foot of the Vermonter and exactly filled the space."[54] Late in 1851 trains crossed this "Sea Serpent." The road between Ogdensburg or Montreal and Boston was done.[55]

IV

By then the jubilation over these competitive stratagems was submerged by financial disaster and internal dissension. As usual the initial error had been the familiar underestimate of construction costs. The engineer of the Vermont Central placed them at $21,000 a mile at a time when the Western, through comparable territory, was known to have cost more than twice that much.[56] Investors and perhaps directors were soon disillusioned. More money was required; more stock had to be marketed. Successive issues brought lower and lower prices. The first $2,000,-000 had sold at par; the second $1,500,000 at $50 a share; and the last $1,500,000 at $30.[57] Attempts to stay this decline were in vain. Foreign investors looked coldly upon the securities; their appearance upon Wall Street brought derisive warning

Central & Vt. & Canada R. R.'s. *Testimony of John Gregory Smith, from the Official Minutes* (St. Albans: Advertiser Steam Printing House, 1875), p. 4; *Laws of the State of New York, Passed at the Seventy-fourth Session of the Legislature . . . 1851*, pp. 681–682.

[54] Montpelier *Vermont Watchman and State Journal*, February 26, 1852.

[55] *American Railroad Journal*, XXIV (1851), 615; *Sixth Annual Report . . . of the Vermont Central Railroad . . . August 27, 1851*, p. 14; *Annual Report of the Directors of the Champlain and St. Lawrence Rail Road Company to the Stockholders. Monday, 17th Jan. 1853* (Montreal: William Salter & Co., 1853), pp. 3–4.

[56] *Report . . . of the Engineer on the Route Surveyed for the Vermont Central Railroad, from Connecticut River, at Hartford, Vt. to Lake Champlain, at Burlington* (Boston: S. N. Dickinson, 1845), pp. 7–9.

[57] *Report of the Investigating Committee of the Vermont Central Railroad Co. to the Stockholders, July 1, 1853* (Boston: George C. Rand, 1853), pp. 55–56.

from the *American Railroad Journal* that New Yorkers should not be humbugged by the blarney that had succeeded in Boston.[58] Then the Central resorted to short-term bonds in the desperate hope of getting its road completed and earning a return before their maturity.[59] This was only a financial façade.

As a matter of fact, the Vermont Central, as well as the Vermont and Canada, was built by a floating debt. Capitalists, like Charles Paine, John Smith, Lawrence Brainerd, endorsed the notes of the companies and took the securities of the concerns as collateral.[60] In 1849 they had come to the end of their efforts. The directors, the Massachusetts majority as well as the Vermonters, appealed to Josiah Quincy, Jr., to save them. He had been the architect of success on the Western; he had come to the rescue of the Old Colony, later the dominant system in southeastern Massachusetts, at a moment of need; he had a considerable personal fortune and knew how to command money from others; he was a champion of railroad expansion, a magnetic and voluble civic figure, and a magician.[61] Addressing the friends of the northern routes, he declared, "It had always been his luck to take care of very sick children in the form of railroad corporations, but that they generally grew up to be stout." [62] He was made treasurer, first of the Vermont Central and then of the Vermont and Canada. The directors of the former enterprise, though they later denied the intent of their actions, passed a series of resolutions surrendering the financial affairs of the concern to him and permitting him to use its securities as he saw fit.[63]

[58] Kistler, *Rise of Railroads in the Connecticut River Valley*, p. 161; *American Railroad Journal*, XXIII (1850), 665.

[59] *Report of the Investigating Committee of the Vermont Central . . . 1853*, pp. 58, 61–62.

[60] *Ibid.*, pp. 116–117.

[61] *Report of the Committee for Investigating the Affairs of the Old Colony Railroad Company, Appointed by the Stockholders, December 26, 1849* (Boston: Eastburn's Press), pp. 95–99.

[62] Boston *Evening Traveller*, January 30, 1850, quoted in Kistler, *Rise of Railroads in the Connecticut River Valley*, p. 103.

[63] *Report of the Investigating Committee of the Vermont Central . . . 1853*, pp. 87–93; *Letter to the Shareholders of the Vermont Central Railroad from Josiah Quincy, Jr., March, 1852* (Boston: Eastburn's Press, 1852), pp. 12–16; Kistler, *Rise of Railroads in Connecticut River Valley*, pp. 222–223.

Since the stock was languishing, Quincy at once made a large subscription, paying for it by his own note; then he raised money on notes, some endorsed as treasurer of the railroad and some on his name alone; to provide security for both, he utilized the stock and bonds of the corporation as collateral. His labors were Herculean. His successive borrowings, borrowings to pay borrowings, ran to $1,000,000; interest charges were frequently 12 per cent and occasionally twice that.[64] Then in 1851, with the road at last completed, the directors withdrew the financial affairs of the corporation from Quincy's care on the ground that he had exceeded his powers and committed other irregularities. In the resulting difficulties, Quincy went bankrupt.[65] Both parties now sought to justify their performances in speech and in pamphlet. There was a battle over motives. Quincy asserted that civic pride had moved him to undertake the arduous task of completing the line; the directors of the Vermont Central implied that his interest was speculative merely and that he had used the funds of the corporation for his private debts and to support his private credit and not "for the use and benefit of the corporation." Nor could either controversialist quote accurately from the records of directors' meetings or contracts.[66] Eventually under a compromise Quincy assigned certain property to the railroad and the railroad paid the balance of Quincy's indebtedness.[67] To extricate itself from its liabilities, particularly its short-term bonds and floating debt, the railroad proceeded to authorize in 1851 $2,000,000 worth of first mortgage bonds bearing 7 per cent and due in ten years and in 1852 second mortgage bonds totaling $1,500,000.[68]

[64] *Letter to the Shareholders . . . from Josiah Quincy, Jr.*, pp. 5, 18; *Report of the Investigating Committee of the Vermont Central . . . 1853*, pp. 93–100, 142–156.

[65] *Report of the Investigating Committee of the Vermont Central . . . 1853*, pp. 93–94; *Letter to the Shareholders . . . from Josiah Quincy, Jr.*, pp. 9–10, 19–21; *Reply of the Directors to the Letter of Josiah Quincy, Jr., to the Stockholders of the Vermont Central Railroad* (Montpelier: E. P. Walton and Son, 1852), pp. 30–35.

[66] *Letter to the Shareholders . . . from Josiah Quincy, Jr.*, pp. 12–16, 21; *Reply of the Directors to . . . Josiah Quincy, Jr.*, pp. 12–28, 37; *American Railroad Journal*, XXV (1852), 225.

[67] *Report of the Investigating Committee of the Vermont Central . . . 1853*, p. 100.   [68] *Ibid.*, pp. 55, 58.

The earthquake of the Quincy affair, followed by a most damaging "impeachment" of other officers, including President Paine, shook the stockholders into an investigation of their corporation.[69] For months their three appointees, with the assistance of experts, labored to reduce the tangled confusion to a comprehensible and ordered picture of what had actually occurred. Their report, while it rejected "imputations" against the officers and exonerated their "personal integrity," was a candid and convincing arraignment of extensive mismanagement. The investigators discovered that the Vermont Central, instead of costing somewhat over the estimated $2,000,000, had by 1853 actually cost $8,072,281.[70] A large share of this sum was the result of preventable waste. Paine, who united to the presidency of the Vermont Central duties as construction agent for both railroads, disbursing agent at Northfield, contract negotiator, and charter procurer, had no time for system. Directors were negligent.[71] So losses accumulated. The Quincy debacle cost the road $295,205; the alliance with the Vermont and Canada had cost almost as much; and the contract for the construction of the road made with S. F. Belknap, a prominent builder of these northern railroads, involved losses of $500,000. When the latter went bankrupt, it was discovered that the directors of the road had allowed him to fall behind in payments to his stock subscription, had loaned him bonds, and paid him a part of the price they were supposed to retain until the road was completed. When certain unavoidable losses, such as discounts on bonds and on forfeited stock, were added to those arising from negligence, almost one-quarter of the book cost of construction was accounted for.[72]

Events did not wait upon this impartial distribution of cen-

[69] *Statement to the Stockholders of the Vermont Central Railroad Company, as Read at Cochituate Hall, Boston, April 20, 1852 by John W. Seymour* (Boston: John W. Seymour, 1852); *Proceedings of the Stockholders of the Vermont Central Railroad, at a Special Meeting Holden at Northfield, Vermont, May 4, 5, 1852* (Montpelier: E. P. Walton & Son, 1852), pp. 3–5.

[70] *Report of the Investigating Committee of the Vermont Central . . . 1853,* p. 77.

[71] *Ibid.,* pp. 108–112.

[72] *Ibid.,* pp. 76–81, 86–100.

sure and exoneration, or even upon the resulting changes of management and the downfall of Paine. In 1852 when the road failed to meet interest charges upon the first mortgage bonds, it was surrendered to the trustees of that security.[73] Two years later, when the road failed to pay the rent guaranteed the Vermont and Canada, the latter demanded the former's surrender; under the agreement of 1850, the lease was an obligation prior to all bond issues.[74] Every interest involved now rushed into the courts — the trustees of the second mortgage, some holders of the first mortgage who disliked the policy of their trustees, the directors of the Vermont Central who wished to repossess their property, and the directors of the Vermont and Canada whose policy and wishes vacillated as the "Vermont wing" or the "Boston wing" secured the ascendancy. There were cases in the county courts, cases in the Federal courts, a veritable Donnybrook Fair of cases and legal complications.[75]

Ultimately in 1861 the Court of Chancery, after years of taking testimony and brooding, issued a "final decree." Since the lease of the Vermont and Canada by the Central was valid, the court asserted that the rent was a first obligation upon the Vermont Central and set the cost of construction upon which the rent was to be paid. As the Vermont and Canada had prayed, both roads were henceforward to be run, under the supervision of the court, by a board of receivers and managers; its three members — as appointed by the court — were Lawrence Brainerd, Joseph Clark, and J. Gregory Smith.[76] The first two had long been associated with the Vermont and Canada; the newcomer, J. Gregory Smith, was the son-in-law of Brainerd and the son of John Smith, once president of that road. All three were

[73] *Vermont Central Railroad. Eighth Annual Report of the Directors and Treasurer to the Stockholders, Presented at the Annual Meeting, July 27, 1853* (Montpelier: E. P. Walton & Son, 1853), pp. 3–5.

[74] *Tenth Annual Report of the Directors of the Vermont Central Railroad Co. to the Stockholders, Presented at the Annual Meeting, October 13, 1855* (Montpelier: E. P. Walton, Jr., 1855), pp. 19–39.

[75] *Report of the Special Masters, . . . Vermont and Canada R. R. Co. vs. Vermont Central R. R. Co. . . . 1877*, pp. 11–13, 16–18; *Hearing before the Special Masters . . . Testimony of John Gregory Smith*, pp. 6–10.

[76] *Charters of the Vermont Central, Vermont and Canada, and Central Vermont Railroads . . . Lease. . . . Orders and Decrees*, pp. 164–166.

also trustees of the first mortgage bonds of the Vermont Central Railroad, and in 1855 J. Gregory Smith had become the latter's president. He was also its largest stockholder. Thus began the first major railroad receivership in the country, which years later the Vermont railroad commissioner acclaimed as doing "more to settle and fix the railroad law of the country than any other railroad company or State in the United States." [77] Thus was consummated an evolution through which J. Gregory Smith became the Vermont Central and the Vermont Central J. Gregory Smith.

While the maneuver of attack and agreement slowly worked out the result which the court had validated, the stock of the Vermont Central coasted toward oblivion — from a high of 25⅞ in 1852 to a low of 1¼ in 1854. Within ten years of their issue the first mortgage bonds had declined to a low of $10 on the hundred and the second mortgage to one of 50 cents. [78] It was cold comfort to genuine investors to perceive that the Vermont Central was not alone, that west of the Connecticut River universal ruin met the eye. The Rutland and Burlington, the Central's rival, was burdened not with two but with three mortgages; after the inescapable collapse, the second mortgage bondholders ran the road. [79] The Northern of New York, the Central's ally, talked bravely of mounting business, borrowed money to pay the interest on its bonds, and then in 1854 capitulated. "A very careful examination of the traffic statistics had disclosed the fact, that the net income of the most productive year in the history of the road, had not nearly paid the annual interest on the debt, even without any appropriation from earnings, for depreciation of rails, cross ties, bridges and equipment." [80]

---

[77] Kistler, *Rise of Railroads in the Connecticut River Valley*, pp. 252–254; Biennial Report of the Railroad Commissioner of the State of Vermont for 1873–1874, Vermont *Legislative Documents, State Officers' Reports, 1874*, p. 5.

[78] Martin, *A Century of Finance*, pp. 146, 163, 165.

[79] *Cheever & Hart, Trustees, et al. v. The Rutland & Burlington R. R. Co. Birchard & Stewart, Trustees, et al. Opinion of Chancellor Barrett, upon the Motion of Orators for Injunction or Receiver* (Rutland: Tuttle & Gay, 1863), pp. 3–4.

[80] *Report of the Directors of the Northern Rail Road Company, from Odgensburgh to Rouse's Point, New York. Submitted to the Stockholders July 25, 1855* (Boston: Brown, Bazin & Co., 1855), p. 3.

V

The prospective inauguration of the Great Northern Route from Boston to Montreal and Ogdensburg was the occasion, as it had been on the Western, for a systematic debate over the proper principles of rate-making. The forum, however, was a different one. Instead of articles, letters to the newspapers, and resolutions of stockholders, a railroad convention attended by delegates of the northern lines met in Boston late in 1850. It was at once clear that the issue had shifted since 1841. Although an occasional spokesman sounded like Nathan Hale, the real dispute was between the advocates of low and of lower fares, for a large committee agreed that on the freight from the West at Ogdensburg, "it may be advisable to adopt a somewhat lower tariff in regard to some articles, because it is supposed that the quantity will be very great both ways, and thus, although the *per centage* of profit may be small, the aggregate will be large." [81] But days of deliberation led at the end only to frustration. Not general principles but a concrete situation confronted the convention. Speaker after speaker reiterated the stark necessity of "getting the freight" and of "diverting the business." [82] Not the example of Belgium or France or even the Philadelphia and Reading Railroad, but the competitive situation of 1850 was the decisive factor. Like the Western, the Great Northern Route confronted railroad competition. To Canada, the Grand Trunk from Portland was a potential rival. In the more important struggle for the American West, the Western itself was the enemy. In such a setting the character of this new contestant did not promise success.

It was a route divided. To be sure one division, that between the upper and lower roads at Concord, resembled the one on the Massachusetts line at Worcester. As in the case of the Boston and Worcester, a profitable local traffic gave an ample living to the Boston and Lowell, Nashua and Lowell, and Con-

[81] *Proceedings of the Convention of the Northern Lines of Railway. Held at Boston, in December, 1850, and January, 1851* (Boston: J. B. Yerrinton & Son, 1851), pp. 18, 51, 67, 70.
[82] *Ibid.*, pp. 52–55, 72–73, 88–97, 102–106.

cord and enabled them to question the value of a through traffic at low or unremunerative rates. On the whole the Boston and Lowell kept its doubts to itself and sought to redress unfavorable rates by negotiation or maneuver. The Concord was more outspoken. Its president at the Boston convention felt "everything went well, so long as the roads only extended to the Green Mountains, and the Vermont Central road was open only to Montpelier. The lower roads were better off until then." [83] And a few years later some of his stockholders calculated the Concord did the through business for the Vermont Central at a loss and had better abandon sizable portions of it.[84] On the contrary, the Northern of New York, the most vulnerable of the upper roads, dependent upon through freight rather than passengers, declared with desperation, "The Directors have been able to see no way of inducing foreign freight to take this route, at rates of transportation essentially higher than at present charged, and they have had but one alternative, to take this business at such rates as it could be done for on other routes, or abandon it altogether." [85] But more significant than this cleavage, already made familiar by the factionalism on the route to Albany, was the division of the route to the Lakes not into two but into seven separate corporations, five of which could become independent of each other. At least on the route to Albany, the Boston and Worcester had no other route to the West than the Western and the Western no other outlet to Boston than the Boston and Worcester.

On the route to the Lakes, although the Boston and Lowell had a charter monopoly of its route, the Boston and Maine was a parallel road only a few miles to the east, and at one point was a mere nine miles from Lowell. Only by incessant vigilance in the legislature and in the courts did the Boston and Lowell

[83] *Ibid.*, p. 99.

[84] *Report of the Investigating Committee of the Concord Railroad to the Stockholders, December, 1857* (Concord: McFarland & Jenks, 1857), pp. 30–33.

[85] *Report of the Directors of the Northern Rail Road Company (Ogdensburgh to Rouse's Point, New York), Submitted to the Stockholders, June 16, 1852* (Boston: T. R. Marvin, 1852), pp. 13–16; *Report of . . . the Northern Rail Road Company, from Ogdensburgh to Rouse's Point, New York, . . . July 25, 1855,* pp. 11–12.

prevent the Boston and Maine and others from forming a circuitous competing line capable of seizing or dividing the northern traffic.[86] The Concord lived in dread of some new route from the Connecticut to Manchester, Nashua or Lowell or of some sly encroachment from the east likely to siphon traffic away from its line to Portsmouth or to a station on the Boston and Maine. A portion of its fears materialized when a single-track road climbed over the hills to connect Manchester on the Concord with Lawrence on the Boston and Maine and at a single stroke diverted traffic from the lower half of the former's route.[87] This new route by the Boston and Maine also seemed to supersede the Nashua and Lowell and the Boston and Lowell as the first link in the route to Canada and the Lakes.[88] On its part the Northern Railroad with good reason constantly imagined itself by-passed. Freight from the Vermont Central and beyond could turn down the Connecticut at White River and proceed via Bellows Falls to Boston; freight from the upper Connecticut could be intercepted at Wells River by the Boston, Concord and Montreal and seek Concord and Boston without ever touching the Northern's rails. Although the Vermont and Canada was unlikely to revolt against the Vermont Central, the traffic from the Northern of New York during the summer could take boat at Rouse's Point for shipment by Lake Champlain, the canal, and the Hudson to New York, or, even worse, by the lake to Burlington for transfer to the Rutland and Burlington.

The roads to whom this traffic was important bent every

[86] *Infra*, I, 270–271.

[87] *Eleventh Annual Report of the Directors of the Concord Railroad Corporation, May, 1852* (Concord: McFarland & Jenks, n.d.), pp. 9–11; *Twenty-first Annual Report of the Directors of the Concord Railroad Corporation, March 31, 1862* (Concord: McFarland & Jenks, 1862), pp. 10–12.

[88] *Arguments of Hon. J. G. Abbott, before the Committee on Railways and Canals, February 18, 1864, on the Petition of the Boston and Lowell Railroad for a Union with Certain Railroads in Massachusetts and New Hampshire. With the Evidence for the Petitioners* (Boston: Wright and Potter, 1864), pp. 25–28; *Report to be Presented to the Stockholders of the Boston and Maine Railroad, at Their Annual Meeting, at Exeter, N. H., Wednesday, September 8, 1852* (Boston: Dutton and Wentworth, 1852), pp. 6–7; *Report of the Directors of the Boston and Maine Railroad to the Stockholders, September 8, 1858* (Boston: Henry W. Dutton & Son, 1858), p. 19.

effort to make sure it continued to flow over their rails. The Boston and Lowell and Nashua and Lowell drew together in self-protection. In 1857 an agreement divided their combined net income on a percentage basis and gave them a joint president, F. B. Crowninshield, and a joint agent, George Stark, two of the first railroad men in New England trained on the railroads themselves.[89] With a none too careful attention to legal niceties, the Concord leased the Manchester and Lawrence by a move "whose audacity . . . was for a time thought unparalleled." [90] Or they paid the price in traffic agreements. In 1854 the Northern of New York guaranteed to send its passengers and freight over the Vermont Central, the Vermont Central guaranteed to send its passengers and freight over the Northern of New Hampshire, and these exclusive exchanges were reciprocated on the up-traffic; the contract arranged a pro-rata division of receipts with certain deductions for loading and unloading. The Northern of New Hampshire paid the price — an annual subsidy to a rival for withdrawing from the through business and the purchase at par of $180,000 in second mortgage bonds of the Ogdensburg road.[91]

Apparently the Northern hoped to induce the lower roads to share the philanthropies bestowed upon its colleagues in the contract of 1854. The Boston and Lowell refused.[92] Over the years it had been a signer of contracts designed to prevent the lower roads from competing so wildly for the through traffic as

---

[89] *Report of the Directors of the Boston and Lowell Railroad, for the Ten Months Ending September 30, 1857* (Boston: J. H. Eastburn, 1857), pp. 12–19; *Argument of Hon. J. G. Abbott, . . . February 18, 1684,* pp. 30–31, 59–61.

[90] *Reply of the Directors of the Concord Railroad to the Report of the Committee of Investigation, December, 1857* (Concord: McFarland & Jenks, 1857), pp. 22–23; *Report of a Committee of Stockholders of the Concord Railroad, May, 1851* (Concord: McFarland & Jenks, n.d.), pp. 79–81; *Sixteenth Annual Report of the Directors of the Concord Railroad Corporation, May, 1857* (Concord: McFarland & Jenks, 1857), pp. 14–19.

[91] *Contracts between the Northern (New-Hampshire) and the Vermont Central, Vermont and Canada, Northern (New York) and the Sullivan Railroads, and between the Northern (New-Hampshire) and Lower Railroads.* (Concord: McFarland & Jenks, 1862), pp. 3–26.

[92] *Ibid.,* pp. 27–40; *Eleventh Annual Report of the Directors of the Northern Rail-Road, to the Stockholders, May, 1856* (Boston: Crocker and Brewster, 1856), p. 8; *Argument of Hon. J. G. Abbott, . . . February 18, 1864,* p. 69.

to offer the upper roads unprincipled concessions in rates or divisions. In its eyes remunerative specific mileage payments for passengers and freights were especially desirable; then, if the runners and agents of the Vermont Central route solicited business in the West at ruinous rates, the upper roads would bear the sacrifice. In 1859 the Boston and Lowell, the Nashua and Lowell, and the Boston and Maine arranged things in accordance with this formula. All the through business of the Northern, the Vermont Central, and the Ogdensburg was to go over the Boston and Lowell and the Nashua and Lowell; all that of the roads in northern New Hampshire, over the Boston and Maine. The through rates to be charged for passengers and for various classes of freight were set. Though some of the upper roads held their peace, the Concord which had hitherto participated in the contracts of the lower roads shrieked it was now "bottled up." [93]

The solution for such intercorporate warfare was, of course, unified control. But that proved impossible. Though conferences of representatives from all the roads sometimes arranged rates, though the Boston Convention proposed a "Central Board" for each of the great lines between Boston and Lake Champlain to consult and adopt regulations for the joint business, the making of partial contracts and the operation upon the basis of unwritten agreements persisted. [94] Nor did plans to effect a more thorough consolidation bear fruit. In the mid-fifties, W. R. Lee, a Boston railroad promoter, was for a single year president of the Northern, the Rutland and Burlington, and the Vermont Central, but the Vermont legislature refused to pass enabling legislation for a closer union of the Vermont and Canada and

---

[93] *Railroad Controversy: Containing a Copy of the Contract between the Boston & Maine, and Boston & Lowell, and Nashua and Lowell Railroads, with Correspondence and Documents Relating Thereto* (Concord: McFarland & Jenks, 1859), pp. 5–8, 14–18, 56–58; *Agreement between the Concord, Nashua and Lowell, Manchester and Lawrence, Boston and Lowell, and Boston and Maine Railroads* [February 19, 1852] (n.p., n.d.).

[94] *Proceedings of the Convention of the Northern Lines*, pp. 28–29, 49–50, 59–62, 72; *Twelfth Annual Report of the Directors of the Northern Rail-Road, to the Stockholders. May, 1857* (Boston: Crocker and Brewster, 1857), pp. 6–7; *Argument of Hon. J. G. Abbott, . . . February 18, 1864*, p. 41.

the Vermont Central.[95] In 1864 when the Boston and Lowell proposed the consolidation of the three lower roads, not even Massachusetts gave permission.[96] Popular hostility to a possible monopoly, the suspicion that projectors were interested in speculation or a squeeze preparatory to an agreement, and an ingrained localism prevented the first steps toward consolidation.

VI

As a transportation agency, the Great Northern Route had certain advantages over the Western. Its terminal facilities in Boston harbor were outside the crowded city and, though the water-front property of the Boston and Lowell was congested, the construction of a short connection gave it access to other docks and to areas blessed with the liberating possibilities of expansion.[97] Both the Western and the Great Northern crossed highlands and ranges. Of its 157 miles from Worcester to Albany, the former had 57 per cent at an inclination of more than 30 feet a mile; of the 172 miles between Concord and Burlington, the Northern and the Vermont Central had only 29 per cent above the same minimum. The Western's maximum grade was 83 feet; the Great Northern Route's 52.8.[98] But here the superiority of facilities stopped. Though the lower roads maintained their equipment and roadbed at a level of technical proficiency equal to the Western's, decline set in at the Connecticut River. Two years after its official completion, a good share of the track on the Vermont Central was still laid at subgrade; the bridges, originally weak, had had to be retrussed; several miles of second-hand rails had worn out; and the ties, since they were hemlock and spruce, had naturally decayed.[99] "It must be ap-

[95] Montpelier *Vermont Watchman and State Journal*, June 16, 23, July 7, 1853, October 6, 1854, December 14, 1855.

[96] *Argument of Hon. J. G. Abbott*, . . . *February 18, 1864*, pp. 3–29.

[97] *Ibid.*, pp. 46–47, 64; *Opening Argument of John H. George, Esq., in Behalf of the Petition of the Boston & Lowell Railroad for Leave to Consolidate and Unite with the Fitchburg Railroad, and Other Connecting Roads, before the Railroad Committee of the Massachusetts Legislature, Tuesday, Feb. 11, 1873* (Boston: Wright and Potter, 1873), pp. 17–24.

[98] Colburn, "The Economy of Railroads," p. 228; *Report of the Engineer on the Route Surveyed, for the Northern Railroad*, p. 13

[99] *Vermont Central Railroad. Eighth Annual Report . . . 1853*, pp. 13–15;

parent to the most casual observer," wrote the trustees, "that
the rails and freight cars are depreciated and depreciating. The
degree and rapidity is not only unexampled in railroad statistics,
but is alarming."[100] A similar discovery was made on the
Northern Railroad of New York.[101]

But it was the original assumptions concerning the superiority
of this route which soon proved fallacious — an outcome which
might in part have been anticipated. Though the line secured
a connection with Montreal, it did not control that city or its
trade. Canadian loyalties and the commercial ambitions of
Montreal were not served by dependence upon Boston, and, with
the construction of the road to Portland and the formation of
the Grand Trunk, an important and powerful interest committed
to Portland as Montreal's winter port successfully bestirred itself
to keep the other American routes at arm's length. As for the
trade of the West, the Great Northern Route, compared with
the Western Railroad, had a longer rail trip and a shorter water
link, to Lake Erie.[102] In other words it lengthened the comparatively expensive transit by railroad and shortened the cheaper
transit by water. Conceivably the savings in transhipments, in
propellers rather than canal boats, and in canal tolls might compensate, if Ontario had been a genuine link in the Great Lakes
thoroughfare.[103] It was not. The bulk of shipping stopped at
the eastern end of Lake Erie. For one thing, the prism of the
Welland Canal, though enlarged between the years 1842 and
1845, with locks 150 feet long and 9 feet deep, did not catch up
with the size of the larger vessels on the lakes above Ontario,
and such larger vessels were the most efficient bulk carriers.
Even when vessels proceeded beyond Buffalo and Niagara, they

Report of the Investigating Committee of the Vermont Central . . . 1853, pp. 140–
144.
[100] Ninth Annual Report of the Directors of the Vermont Central Railroad Company, to the Stockholders, Presented at the Annual Meeting, Sept. 12, 1854 (Montpelier: E. P. Walton, Jr., 1854), p. 20.
[101] Report of the Directors of the Northern Rail Road Company, Ogdensburgh
to Rouse's Point, New York, Submitted to the Stockholders, July 26, 1854 (Ogdensburgh: Hitchcock and Tillotson, 1854), pp. 22–23.
[102] Pathfinder Railway Guide, 1852, pp. 84, 88.
[103] The Northern Railroad in New York, with Remarks on the Western Trade
(Boston: S. N. Dickinson & Co., 1847), pp. 3–4, 6–9.

might put into Oswego with its canal and railroad thoroughfares to Albany or they might sail on to Montreal.[104] As soon as the Northern reached Ogdensburg, its sponsors experienced these handicaps. In 1850 the road, to tempt vessels thither, agreed to pay the Welland Canal tolls for vessels bringing their freight to it.[105] Such temporary arrangements were soon succeeded by contracts with various lines, one of which, a line of propellers through the Welland to the western lakes, was actually created by this device. Absolutely essential, it had the Great Northern Route almost at its mercy.[106]

Such details, however, were only part of a larger handicap. Essentially the Great Northern Route was attempting to do for Boston what Montreal had sought for decades to do for itself — divert the commerce of the West from the New York canal system. Boston used the railroads to Ontario; Montreal used canals along the St. Lawrence. Montreal had failed. It completed its system too late; when it threatened, New York reduced the canal tolls.[107] Boston's route faced the same fate. But perhaps things would be better when the westward extension of the railroads gave both Boston and Montreal a chance for an all-year route to the American West.[108] By 1856 the Grand Trunk along the northern shore of Ontario connected

[104] *Ibid.*, pp. 6, 9–11; Glazebrook, *A History of Transportation in Canada*, pp. 85–87, 417–418; Report of Israel D. Andrews, on the Trade and Commerce of the British North American Colonies, and upon the Trade of the Great Lakes and Rivers, *Senate Executive Documents*, 32 Cong., 1 Sess., no. 112 (s.n. 622), pp. 50–52, 437.

[105] *Proceedings of the Convention of the Northern Lines*, p. 119; *Senate Executive Documents*, 32 Cong., 1 Sess., no. 112 (s.n. 622), pp. 75–78.

[106] *Report of the Northern Rail Road Company (From Ogdensburgh to Rouse's Point,)* . . . *1852*, pp. 12, 16; *Report of the Directors of the Northern Rail Road Company (From Ogdensburgh to Rouse's Point,) New York. Submitted June 6, 1853* (Boston: T. R. Marvin, 1853), pp. 14–15; *Twelfth Annual Report . . . of the Northern Rail-Road, . . . May, 1857*, p. 7; *Argument of Hon. J. G. Abbott, . . . February 18, 1864*, p. 68; Montpelier *Vermont Watchman and State Journal*, September 9, 1851.

[107] *Boston Board of Trade. 1859. Fifth Annual Report of the Government, Presented to the Board at the Annual Meeting, on the 20th January, 1859* (Boston: T. R. Marvin & Son, 1859), pp. 65–69; Glazebrook, *A History of Transportation in Canada*, pp. 89–97; *Senate Executive Documents*, 32 Cong., 1 Sess., no. 112 (s.n. 622), pp. 441–443.

[108] *Twelfth Annual Report . . . of the Northern Rail-Road, . . . May, 1857*, p. 7.

with the Great Western, which led westward to Detroit; three
years later the Grand Trunk had its own route to Sarnia on
the straits above Lake Huron. But the New York Central also
connected with the Great Western; the Great Western — hence
the New York Central — and the Grand Trunk alike depended
upon the Michigan Central to reach Chicago.[109] The railroad
no more than the lakes conferred upon the Great Northern Route
benefits that the Western of Massachusetts did not possess in
equal measure.

Nor was the route to the Lakes in a position to charge lower
rates than the Western. Through rates could be cut to the bone
only if local rates gave the road a compensatory return. The
Boston and Worcester and the Western had this recourse. They
traversed a thickly settled industrial region; tributary roads
poured an additional stream of commerce upon their lines. They
connected Boston with Albany and Troy, cities with a combined population of 100,000.[110] As soon as it left Concord, however, the Great Northern Route traversed a thinly settled agricultural region; in Vermont, the passion for throughness, combined
with the self-interest of the railroad promoters, led the Vermont
Central and the Vermont and Canada along a route which left
to one side of the main line Montpelier, Burlington, and St. Albans Bay; the Northern of New York, according to its directors,
was located "through a comparative wilderness" and terminated
at Ogdensburg, a country town.[111] No wonder the mire of financial insolvency sucked them down. "The Vermont Central like
the Western Railroad! 'Hyperion to a satyr' !! " commented
the *American Railroad Journal*.[112]

Nonetheless the Great Northern Route had accomplishments.
As commercial relationships with Canada were liberalized, first
through the practice of permitting the transit of goods in bond

[109] Glazebrook, *A History of Transportation in Canada*, pp. 164–171.
[110] *American Railroad Journal*, XXIII (1850), 665.
[111] *Report . . . of the Northern Rail Road Company, from Ogdensburg to
Rouse's Point, . . . July 25, 1855*, p. 11; *The Boston Committee in Canada. A
Series of Eight Letters Reprinted from the Boston Atlas* (Boston: Eastburn's
Press, 1851), p. 9; Kistler, *The Rise of Railroads in the Connecticut River Valley*,
pp. 127–220.
[112] *American Railroad Journal*, XXIII (1850), 665.

and then through the Reciprocity Act of 1854, these railroads gave Boston a share in this expanding commerce. The value of goods in bond for Canada transported from Charlestown and Boston rose from $21,715 in 1847 to a high point of $5,178,911 in 1854.[113] There was also trade to and from the West. It was at its best in the mid-fifties; then it broke sharply. That invaluable barometer, flour receipts at Boston, sank from 110,232 barrels in 1857 to 60,587 in 1860. The latter figure was only a fifth of that received by way of the Western; it was smaller than the receipts by the Boston and Providence — New York was their source — or by boat from Portland — the Grand Trunk was its railroad connection.[114] Nor must it be forgotten that these routes transformed the economic life of the areas through which they passed. With the arrival of the Nashua and Lowell at its northern terminus, "Every man steps quicker, and life seems about to infuse itself into things inanimate."[115] When the Vermont Central reached the interior of the state, it shattered the old self-sufficiency and the circumscribed local traffics. New products like potatoes, grain, and cereals found a market; livestock leaving Montpelier one day was only a few miles from the yards at Cambridge or Brighton the next. The area of barter sank as a cash economy pushed in.[116] Even the hapless upper roads gave to the upper half of New Hampshire and to the whole of Vermont their railroad systems.

It was not for accomplishments so limited that some of the

[113] *Boston Board of Trade. 1855. First Annual Report of the Government, Presented to the Board at the Annual Meeting, on the 17th of January, 1855* (Boston: Moore & Crosby, 1855), p. 12; *Boston Board of Trade. 1861. Seventh Annual Report of the Government, Presented to the Board at the Annual Meeting, on the 16th January, 1861* (Boston: T. R. Marvin & Son, 1861), p. 121; *Senate Executive Documents*, 32 Cong., 1 Sess., no. 112 (s.n. 622), pp. 432–433.

[114] *Boston Board of Trade. 1858. Fourth Annual Report of the Government, Presented to the Board at the Annual Meeting, on the 20th January, 1858* (Boston: Geo. C. Rand & Avery, 1858), p. 134; *Boston Board of Trade. 1861. Seventh Annual Report*, p. 71; *Fourteenth Annual Report of the Directors of the Concord Railroad Corporation. May, 1855* (Concord: McFarland & Jenks, 1855), p. 10; *Nineteenth Annual Report of the Directors of the Concord Railroad Corporation. May, 1860* (Concord: McFarland & Jenks, 1860), p. 8.

[115] Concord *New Hampshire Patriot and State Gazette*, April 29, 1839.

[116] Montpelier *Vermont Watchman and State Journal*, September 27, 1849, April 21, 1853, February 6, 1857; *First Annual Report of the Railroad Commissioner of the State of Vermont to the General Assembly, 1856*, pp. 3–4.

shrewdest among Boston investors had risked a portion of their fortunes. In their minds this route was to redress the inability of the Western successfully to challenge New York. Unlike the Western, it was to reach the Lakes; unlike the Western, it was to pass so far to the north that the Hudson or the New York railroads would not cast their spell upon it, drawing its commerce down to Manhattan.[117] Theirs was a delusion. Though it arose from a perhaps accurate enough examination of the map, it ignored political and commercial actualities. Trade had worn its channels to New York. When the Rutland and the Vermont Central reached Burlington, only a handful, as the Boston Railroad Convention of 1850 demonstrated, believed it was possible or desirable to divert the trade of Lake Champlain and western Vermont to Boston from New York. The latter was its "normal" course.[118] Nor was New York's government likely to sit passively by as Boston made inroads upon the mercantile welfare of her chief city. Similar fanatics of the map and of foreign trade saw that Boston was a day nearer to Liverpool than was New York. They did not realize that, owing to the immense commerce of New York, grain sent thither had "the advantage to the last moment of sale for consumption in the Eastern States, and was sure, in any case, of carriage to Liverpool at so low a rate as nearly to counterbalance the higher charge for inland transportation."[119] Bostonians knew these things at the end of the fifties; they would have saved money if they had realized them a decade earlier.

[117] *Argument of Hon. J. G. Abbott,* . . . *February 18, 1864,* pp. 12–13, 41–42.
[118] *Proceedings of the Convention of the Northern Lines,* pp. 50–55, 88–95, 97–113.
[119] *Boston Board of Trade. 1859. Fifth Annual Report,* p. 67.

VII

PORTLAND: RIVAL OR SATELLITE

"You know something of Maine. What are the first steps which a young and flourishing State should take who intends to embark upon a liberal and effective system of Internal Improvements?" George W. Pierce to James Baldwin, January 20, 1834. Baldwin Papers, Harvard Business School Library, XLVIII.

I

Boston enthusiasm for railroads in the early thirties was so boundless that projects of lines to the "Great American West" could not contain it. As some of its railroad leaders chartered the Western and imprudently explored the possibilities of a route to the Lakes, others were fascinated by the design of expediting and enlarging the trade between Boston and eastern New Hampshire and Maine. In engineering terms the proposals to cross the interior mountains to the Hudson or Lake Champlain were the more audacious; in commercial terms a railroad down East was the more daring project. The Western and the Vermont Central at worst confronted only indirect water competition by lake, canal, river, and sound; the roads to the State of Maine undertook the dangerous experiment of paralleling a coastal trade already well served by sailing packet and steamboat. As it turned out, however, not one but two railroads embarked upon the adventure.

The Boston and Maine had a three-year head start. Ostensibly it began as a local project for in 1833 the Massachusetts General Court chartered a seven-mile road, the Andover and Wilmington, to run from the latter place on the Boston and Lowell "so as to form a branch thereof, . . . and to enter . . . on the Boston and Lowell, . . . paying . . . such a rate of toll as the legislature may from time to time prescribe"; [1] and soon thereafter the directors induced Loammi Baldwin to lend his prestige to their little enterprise by viewing and selecting the most favorable route for it.[2] Actually they had from the beginning a far larger objective than a mere local connection: their company was but "the beginning of a long line of travel." They proposed to extend their road to Haverhill on the Merrimack, bridge the river to a connection with the Boston and Maine, chartered in New Hampshire simply to build across that state to its eastern edge, and thus attain their object — "the accommodation of the general travel from eastern New Hampshire and the State of Maine." [3] In this fashion also, a New Hampshire corporation introduced into New England railroad designations the famous "Boston and Maine."

On the whole all moved with celerity. James Hayward, fresh from his triumphs on the Boston and Providence, superintended the construction, and the Cranes of Haverhill, one of whom, Edward Crane, later became one of the most spectacular promoters and operators of dubious railroad enterprises in New England, secured the contract.[4] When the panic of 1837 caught their enterprise unfinished and retarded the sale of securities and the collection of assessments, the corporation turned to the state for assistance. The General Court responded in 1837 and 1839 with

[1] *Laws of the Commonwealth of Massachusetts, Passed at the Several Sessions of the General Court, Beginning May, 1831, and Ending March, 1833,* pp. 645–652.

[2] *First Report of the Directors of the Andover and Wilmington Rail Road Corporation with That of the Engineer. Oct. 21, 1834* (Andover: Gould and Newman, 1834), pp. 3–4.

[3] *Report of the Engineer to the Directors of the Andover and Haverhill Rail Road Corporation, on the Subject of the Location of the Proposed Bridge over the Merrimack at Haverhill. December 15, 1838* (Andover: Gould and Newman, 1838), pp. 14–15; First Annual Report of the Andover and Wilmington, Massachusetts *Senate Documents,* 1836, no. 49, pp. 10–11; Loammi Baldwin to J. P. H. Odiorne, December 10, 1835, Ms., Baldwin Papers, Harvard Business School Library, XXXVII.

[4] Massachusetts *Senate Documents,* 1836, no. 49, p. 9; Report of Testimony upon the Petition of the Boston, Hartford and Erie Railroad Co., Massachusetts *Senate Documents,* 1870, no. 133, p. 537.

the loan of state securities aggregating $150,000. To protect its advances, the state took a mortgage on the road and $100,000 of its stock.[5] Thus aided, the tracks were driven forward until in 1843 they connected at South Berwick with those of the Portland, Saco and Portsmouth, a corporation chartered by Maine to provide the final link to Portland.[6] By this time also legislation in Massachusetts, New Hampshire, and Maine had permitted the various little roads to blend and blend again into a single corporation, the Boston and Maine, the earliest and most conspicuous railroad consolidation in New England history.[7] In later years when the Boston and Maine, incidental to its railroad tactics, attacked railroad mergers it did not favor, opposing counsel with fine irony adduced the early history of the protesting railroad.

So powerful an enterprise was not content to remain as a mere "branch" to the Boston and Lowell or forego the obvious convenience and advantage of a direct connection with Boston. Consequently, as soon as its route to Maine had been built and consolidated, the Boston and Maine petitioned the legislature to charter the Boston and Maine Extension Company and aroused thereby screams of protest from the Boston and Lowell. The latter corporation rehearsed the benefits which the Boston and Maine had drawn from their mutual relationship and stood immovable upon the provisions of a charter prohibiting a parallel railroad between Boston and Lowell.[8] To the latter argument the legislature harkened to the extent of inserting in the charter of the Extension Company a clause forbidding the establish-

[5] Laws of the Commonwealth of Massachusetts, Passed by the General Court, in the Years 1837 and 1838, pp. 196–198; Acts and Resolves Passed by the Legislature of Massachusetts, in the Years 1839, 1840, 1841, 1842, pp. 75–76; Petition for Aid to the Andover and Wilmington, Massachusetts Senate Documents, 1837, no. 82, pp. 7–11.

[6] Fifth Annual Report of the Boston and Portland Railroad, Massachusetts Senate Documents, 1840, no. 18, p. 8; Ninth Annual Report of the Boston and Maine, Massachusetts Senate Documents, 1844, no. 19, pp. 46, 50.

[7] Constitution and Charters of the Boston and Maine Rail Road Corporation, With Other Laws Relating Thereto, in the States of Massachusetts, New Hampshire and Maine (Boston: Samuel N. Dickinson, 1843), pp. 7–11, 12, 13–20, 24–25; Seventh Annual Report of the Boston and Portland Railroad, Massachusetts Senate Documents, 1842, no. 26, pp. 13–14.

[8] The Boston and Maine Rail-Road Extension; A Brief Statement of the Prin-

ment of any station between Andover and Reading without previous assent from the Boston and Lowell.[9] In 1845 the Boston and Maine reached Boston over its own rails.[10] This achievement not only freed the Boston and Maine from the asserted extortions of the Boston and Lowell; it gave the former road a strategic position in its competition for down-East trade and travel.

This competition, at least on land, came primarily from the Eastern Railroad. Originally this line, too, was a local enterprise, designed to connect Boston and Salem, places already more closely and effectively united than any others in the Commonwealth by a modern turnpike, organized stage lines, freight wagons, and coastal packets. Under such circumstances it is probably just to regard the railroad as largely accessory to the ambitions of rival land speculators. Those, headed by General W. H. Sumner, who were profitably transforming Noddle's Island into East Boston, insisted the Eastern should make their holdings the site of its eastern terminus; those who had purchased lands in Chelsea thought the Eastern should locate its terminus in their area.[11] For the road this rivalry was unfortunate. In 1833 a legislative committee dismissed petitions for its charter with the ironic comment, "Though the Committee highly appreciate the enterprise of those gentlemen who are desirous of bringing the lands of Chelsea and Noddle's Island into the market, and thereby enlarging the bounds of the city, they think that this enterprise ought not to be confused with the necessity of a rail road to Salem." [12]

---

cipal Points for the Extension, Made before the Committee on Rail-Roads and Canals (n.p., n.d.) ; *The Boston and Maine Rail-Road Extension Company. Statement of Principal Facts and Points Relied upon by the Remonstrants, at the Hearing before the Committee* (Boston: Samuel N. Dickinson, 1844).

[9] *Acts and Resolves Passed by the General Court of Massachusetts, in the Years 1843, 1844, 1845*, pp. 279–281.

[10] Eleventh Annual Report of the Boston and Maine Railroad, Massachusetts *Senate Documents*, 1846, no. 21, pp. 16–17.

[11] George Peabody, *Address at the Opening of the Eastern Rail Road, between Boston and Salem. August 27, 1838* (Salem: Gazette Office, 1838), p. 12; *Laws . . . of Massachusetts, . . . 1831, . . . 1833*, pp. 803–805; Report of the Joint Committee on Railways and Canals on a Railroad from Boston to Salem, Massachusetts *Senate Documents*, 1833, no. 52, pp. 3–13; William H. Sumner, *A History of East Boston with Biographical Sketches of the Early Proprietors* (Boston: J. E. Tilton and Company, 1858), pp. 605–609.

[12] Massachusetts *Senate Documents*, 1833, no. 52, p. 13.

To convince doubting legislators of the public need for such a road the Eastern was now given a new tone and larger objectives. Any ostensible association with land speculation was buried beneath a tide of petitions signed by thousands and led by George Peabody, the rising merchant and banker of Salem and Baltimore. Not East Boston, but Salem craved the route. To refute the charge that the road was too short to be profitable, as well as to attach more localities to its chariot, the petitioners engaged to extend the route to Newburyport and then across New Hampshire to a railroad connection with Portland.[13] Engineering talent of the highest caliber certified its success for John M. Fessenden, surveyor of the Boston and Worcester, laid out the line in Massachusetts with no grades of over thirty-five feet to the mile. Somewhat less successfully he attempted to settle the contentious issue of an eastern terminus by selecting East Boston. To his mind the ferry ride and the train ride were both somewhat shorter by that route.[14] Furthermore the East Boston Company obligingly surrendered the management of its ferry connection to the Eastern and donated a right of way, extensive station grounds, and an area of flats.[15] Though a new remonstrant, the "upper road" — as the vernacular of the day christened the Boston and Maine — challenged the proposed route as "unwise and inexpedient," [16] the legislature, otherwise minded, granted a charter in 1836. One quarter of the shares could be subscribed by the Salem Turnpike and Chelsea Bridge Corporation, which the new road would put out of business.[17]

Before the panic of 1837 the Eastern had barely a year of financial grace. When subscriptions, obtained largely in Boston and Salem, were inadequate to complete construction even to the latter place, the road appealed to the bounty of the state. The response was lavish. In 1837 the legislature appropriated $500,-

[13] Report of the Committee on Railways and Canals on the Eastern Railway, Massachusetts *Senate Documents*, 1836, no. 77.

[14] John M. Fessenden, *Report on the Surveys and Definite Location of the Eastern Rail Road* (Boston: Freeman & Bolles, 1836), pp. 4–6, 9.

[15] Sumner, *A History of East Boston*, pp. 612–618.

[16] Massachusetts *Senate Documents*, 1836, no. 77, pp. 4–5.

[17] *Laws of the Commonwealth of Massachusetts, Passed at the Several Sessions of the General Court, Beginning Jan., 1834, and Ending April, 1836*, pp. 925–933.

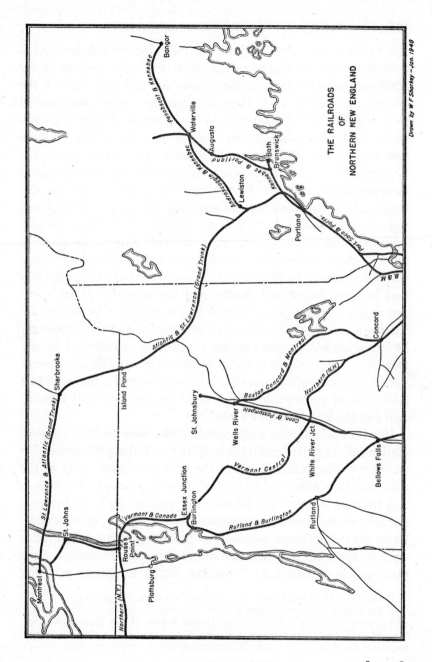

THE RAILROADS
OF
NORTHERN NEW ENGLAND

Drawn by W. F. Sharkey – Jan. 1948

ooo in state securities, and in the following year it granted a
temporary loan of $90,000, seeking at the same time to throw
additional safeguards of sinking funds and collateral around the
advances earlier made.[18] Thus succored, the Eastern was opened
to Salem, reached Portsmouth in 1840, where it leased a like-
named New Hampshire corporation laying track across the state
toward Maine, and finally in November, 1842, joined with the
Portland, Saco and Portsmouth to complete an uninterrupted
communication between Boston and Portland.[19] Thus at the
very moment the Western was attaining Albany on the Hudson,
Boston also reached down East by rail. Though no comparable
celebration occurred, George Peabody had grasped the implications of the new era when the Eastern reached Salem. With a
glance backward, he reviewed the historic methods of transportation between Salem and Boston and the necessity of their improvement. With a look forward he prophesied, "As we are accustomed to regard the discovery of America and the Protestant
Reformation as two great events which have contributed largely
to advance the interests of the human race; so [future genera-
tions], with perhaps a more clear conception and a more evident
deduction of consequences, will point to the American Revolution and the Era of Steam Travel." [20]

However stimulating such cosmic views were to "the contem-
plations of the patriot and speculations of the philosopher," [21]
the shareholders and officials of the road were soon aware of the
unsatisfactory nature of their East Boston terminal. Passengers
had to leave the cars and take a ferry ride to reach the business
section and the transfer of merchandise was equally inconvenient.
Upon these handicaps counsel for the Boston and Maine were
wont to dilate with an amalgam of mockery and sympathy. They
pictured the Eastern as "creeping across a desert, plunging

---

[18] *Laws . . . of Massachusetts, . . . 1837 and 1838,* pp. 200–202, 509–513.
[19] Third Annual Report of the Eastern Railroad, Massachusetts *Senate Documents,* 1839, no. 31, pp. 25–26; Fifth Annual Report of the Eastern Railroad,
Massachusetts *Senate Documents,* 1841, no. 17, pp. 21, 23–29; Seventh Annual
Report of the Eastern Railroad, Massachusetts *Senate Documents,* 1843, no. 31,
p. 72.
[20] Peabody, *Address . . . August 27, 1838,* p. 19.
[21] *Ibid.,* p. 3.

through a marsh, arriving at deep water at East Boston, where the ferry boat was exposed to all the detention of fog, ice and other impediments, and leaving at last the disconsolate passengers in an inconvenient terminus. . . . The necessity of steering by compass and the sound of the fog-bell is upon them, and they cannot avoid it or get rid of it." [22] After a decade of trying to answer such arguments and erase such handicaps, the Eastern, over the opposition of the Boston and Maine, secured a succession of legislative enactments authorizing its extension into the city.[23] In 1854 it finally secured an all-rail connection to a Boston terminal of its own.[24] Whether Fessenden's engineering judgment had been at fault or the land speculators too powerful, the original termination at East Boston was unfortunate.

II

Competition between the Eastern and the Boston and Maine was inevitable. Fortunately for their welfare, the two forswore a cutthroat rivalry in Maine by negotiating in 1843 and again in 1847 common agreements with the Portland, Saco and Portsmouth for a joint connection, by guaranteeing the latter's dividends, and by joining in the ownership and operation of the steamboats which afforded connections at Portland to ports

[22] *Abstract of the Arguments of Hon. Rufus Choate and Charles Theo. Russell, Esq. for the Petitioners, on the Petitions of David Pingree, and over 3,000 Other Legal Voters, for a Rail-Road from Salem to Malden, before the Committee on Railways and Canals, of the Massachusetts Legislature . . . Session 1846* (Boston: Hewes & Watson, 1846), pp. 9–10, 25–30, 47.

[23] *Argument of Charles G. Loring, Esq. on Behalf of the Eastern Rail-Road Company, at a Hearing on the Petitions of David Pingree and Others, and W. J. Valentine and Others, before the Rail-Road Committee of the Massachusetts Legislature, Boston, March 7, 1845* (Boston: Dutton and Wentworth, 1845), pp. 22–30; *Argument of E. H. Derby, Esq. on Behalf of the Eastern Rail-Road Company, at a Hearing of the Petition of David Pingree and Others, before the Rail-Road Committee of the Massachusetts Legislature, Boston, February 20, 1846* (Boston: White & Potter, 1846), pp. 6–11, 35, 37; *Annual Report of the Directors of the Eastern Rail Road Company, to the Stockholders, for the Year Ending June 30, 1851* (Salem: Observer Office, 1851), pp. 7–9; *Annual Report of the Directors of the Eastern Railroad Company, to the Stockholders, for the Year Ending June 30, 1852* (Salem: Observer Office, 1852), pp. 6–8.

[24] *Nineteenth Annual Report of the Eastern Railroad Company, for the Year Ending June 30th, 1854* (Salem: Observer Office, 1854), p. 9.

farther east.[25] Thus there were no parallel rail lines in Maine. A far different condition prevailed in New Hampshire and northeastern Massachusetts. Here the Boston and Maine and the Eastern ran within twelve miles of each other and here each sought to encroach upon the territory of the other by branches and connections. It was riposte and counter-riposte; blow and counter-blow. The Eastern thrust lines westward to Lawrence, Haverhill, and other strategic points on the Boston and Maine; the latter pushed connections eastward to Lynn, Salem and Newburyport.[26] Nor did the initiative for these enterprises always come from either company. Every ambitious town in the area wanted a railroad connection or railroad competition and, after convincing the legislature that public exigency demanded the granting of its request, secured a charter and blackmailed one rival or the other into assisting the construction of the road and into operating it. Rival directorates driven "by that first law of our nature, self preservation and defence" were in no position to resist. Occasionally attempts were made to raise these squabbles to the level of high policy. David A. Neal, elected to the presidency of the Eastern as Peabody's successor, and his allies fought for months to convince the legislature of the folly, if not downright illegality, of parallels and universal competition.[27] The attempt was a failure.

As the struggle continued, both the major contestants occasionally tired of exactions and soothed themselves with self-pity. The Boston and Maine was peculiarly vexed with the necessity of dealing with the legislatures of three states: "Composed as the legislatures usually are, of so much new and mixed material, it is not a little perplexing to your directors to guard properly the

[25] *Report of the Investigating Committee of the Stockholders of the Eastern Railroad Company, July 30th, 1855* (Boston: C. C. P. Moody, 1855), pp. 5–7; *Annual Report of the Directors of the Eastern Rail-Road Company July 10th, 1848* (Boston: William Chadwick, 1848), p. 8.

[26] George P. Baker, *The Formation of the New England Railroad Systems. A Study of Railroad Combination in the Nineteenth Century* (Cambridge: Harvard University Press, 1937), pp. 148–156.

[27] *Salem and Malden Rail Road* (n.p., n.d.), pp. 4–10, 13–14; *Argument of Charles G. Loring . . . March 7, 1845*, pp. 13–17, 32–39, 62–65; *Argument of E. H. Derby, Esq. . . . February 20, 1846*, pp. 25–29; David A. Neal, Autobiography of David Augustus Neal, p. 81, Ms., Typewritten Copy, Essex Institute.

rights of the road from encroachment." [28] On their part the officials of the Eastern bewailed the ingratitude of the Commonwealth and of the public. The "patriots" who built the road "became monopolists. . . . Men who refuse the first dollar to aid in the project while the slightest risk remains will spend hundreds to pull down the structure . . . if . . . they can save a sixpence in their fare, or put a shilling in their pockets. . . . The treasury of a Rail Road seems to be considered like a city, carried by assault, the proper arena and admitted apology for plunder." [29] Harassed and chastened by their own and others' excesses, the Boston and Maine and the Eastern at last formed an agreement in 1855. Neither was to carry the business of the stations on the other's main line or to cross it into the territory beyond; the area between the two roads was carefully apportioned, some to the Boston and Maine, some to the Eastern, and some on a half-and-half basis. If either road did business belonging to the other, it was to refund all receipts after deducting the expense of doing the business. But this provisional settlement — to last ten years — could not erase the millions in losses already incurred.[30]

In its campaigns against the Eastern, the Boston and Maine had always the advantage of a superior location. Though it met water competition between Portland and Boston, it was on the whole an interior road, drawing traffic from both sides. With unusual sagacity it adopted a policy of low fares, particularly on season tickets, and thus built up a populous and dependent suburban territory. The Boston and Maine carried more passengers than any other railroad in New England and occasionally more than any in the nation.[31] Furthermore it traversed a de-

[28] *Report to be Presented to the Stockholders of the Boston and Maine Railroad, at Their Annual Meeting, at Exeter, N. H., Wednesday, September 8, 1852* (Boston: Dutton and Wentworth, 1852), p. 6.

[29] *Annual Report . . . of the Eastern Rail Road . . . June 30, 1851*, pp. 6–7.

[30] *Report of the Investigating Committee of the Boston and Maine Railroad, to the Stockholders. September 29th, 1855* (Boston: Dutton and Wentworth, 1855), pp. 60–62; *Report of the Directors of the Boston and Maine Railroad, to the Stockholders. September 12th, 1855* (Boston: Dutton and Wentworth, 1855), pp. 14–15.

[31] *Report of the Investigating Committee of the Boston and Maine . . . September 29th, 1855*, pp. 41–43; *Report of the Boston and Maine . . . September 12th,*

veloping industrial area and with thoughtful timeliness relocated
its main track through the new manufacturing center of Lawrence
and secured there, over the Manchester and Lawrence, a connection with the route to the Lakes and a share in its traffic.[32]
On the other hand the Eastern throughout its length confronted
water competition. Its industrial area, Lynn in particular, was
so near Boston that wagons and carts continued to transport a
large share of the freight traffic. It was a universal observation
during the forties that, except in the carriage of ice, railroads
could not displace teaming within fifteen miles of Boston; the
latter was more flexible, teams picked up and delivered. The
Eastern also earlier experienced the competition of interurban
horse railroads.[33] Figures talked. In the twelvemonth ending
November 30, 1860, the Boston and Maine carried 1,893,185
passengers and 293,749 tons of freight; the Eastern's totals were
respectively 1,460,653 and 128,566.[34]

Inevitably finances reflected the disparity. The Boston and
Maine was able to finance its construction by stock issues, even
the construction of its intemperate extensions.[35] This was the
approved conservative practice of the day. Though the Eastern's
financial expedients were discreetly concealed, its expenditures in
the fifties and the general railroad prostration of that decade
forced the sale of bonds at sacrificial discounts.[36] Years later a
thorough investigation revealed that the corporation from the
date of its completion had recurrently increased its capital stock
to pay dividends, interest, and even current expenses and had
continually accumulated a floating debt which it recurrently

1855, p. 10; E. B. Grant, *Boston Railways: Their Condition and Prospects*
(Boston: Little, Brown, and Company, 1856), pp. 14–17.

[32] *Report to the Stockholders of the Boston and Maine Railroad at Their
Annual Meeting on September 8, 1847* (Boston: Damrell & Moore, 1847), pp. 4–6.

[33] *Report of a Committee of the Stockholders on the Eastern Rail Road* (n.p.,
1849?), p. 3; *The Twenty-fourth Annual Report of the Eastern Railroad Company,
for the Year Ending May 31st, 1859* (Boston: Henry W. Dutton, 1859), pp. 10-11;
Argument of E. H. Derby, Esq. . . . February 20, 1846, pp. 18–24.

[34] Returns of the Railroad Corporations in Massachusetts, 1860, Massachusetts
Public Documents, 1861, no. 46, attached table.

[35] *Ibid.*, attached table.

[36] *Twentieth Annual Report of the Eastern Railroad Company, for Eleven
Months . . . Ending May 31st, 1855* (Salem: Observer Office, 1855), pp. 5–6.

funded.[37] Nothing exhibited better the extent of its financial malaise than the comparative fate of the state loans to it and to the Boston and Maine. From its earnings the latter repaid the Commonwealth's advances of $150,000 somewhat before the due date.[38] The Eastern cut corners on its sinking fund, requested and secured a postponement of repayments, and during the Civil War sought to discharge its obligations, in the hands of private investors as well as those held by Massachusetts, in legal-tender greenbacks rather than in gold.[39] Any other procedure was "not quite fair"; any other procedure was a sinister discrimination, since the state should not provide "gold for the rich, paper for the poor; gold for the capitalist, paper for the laborer." [40]

III

At the Piscataqua or Salmon Falls rivers the probing railroads from Massachusetts touched the boundary of Maine and encountered the policy of a state determined upon railroad independence. Such an ambition was not entirely presumptuous. Maine had an area larger than that of the five other New England states, and her strategic location as a northeastern extrusion from the United States placed her squarely across the path of communication and commerce between Great Britain and the interior of Canada when the St. Lawrence was closed. Though

[37] *The Forty-first Annual Report of the Eastern Railroad Company, for the Year Ending Nov. 30, 1875* (Boston: Rand, Avery & Company, 1876), pp. 37–40.

[38] *Report of the Directors of the Boston and Maine Railroad, to the Stockholders. September 9, 1857* (Boston: Henry W. Dutton & Son, 1857), p. 9; *Report of the Directors of the Boston and Maine Railroad to the Stockholders. Wednesday, Sept. 14, 1859* (Boston: Henry W. Dutton & Son, 1859), p. 3.

[39] *Speech of Honorable Charles W. Upham, President of the Senate, on the Bill for Extension of the Credit of the Eastern Railroad Corporation. April 11, 1857* (n.p., n.d.); Report of the Treasurer on the Eastern's Failure to Establish a Sinking Fund, Massachusetts *Senate Documents*, 1843, no. 5; Report of Joint Committee on Railways and Canals on the Loan to the Eastern, Massachusetts *Senate Documents*, 1857, no. 120; *To the Stockholders of the Eastern Railroad Company,* Letter of George M. Brown. January 15, 1863; Report of the Treasurer of the Commonwealth on the Eastern Loan, Massachusetts *House Documents*, 1864, no. 151.

[40] *The Twenty-ninth Report of the Eastern Railroad Company, for the Year Ending November 30, 1863* (Boston: Henry W. Dutton & Son, 1864), pp. 8–9; *A Brief Statement Relative to the Claim Made on the Eastern Railroad Company to Pay Its Indebtedness to the Commonwealth in Gold* (n.p., n.d.), p. 3.

in Maine an array of seacoast places aspired to capitalize these advantages, Portland was the pace setter. She was the state's largest city, her magnificent harbor was ice-free the year round, and, if Boston could dream of supplanting New York because she was nearer Liverpool, the same reasoning justified Portland's supplanting Boston. In truth there was soundness in these calculations. And for one brief, crowded, glorious interlude it seemed that, of all the cities of New England, Portland might be a rival, and not a satellite of either Boston or New York. As well as independence, the state's railroad policy for the moment promised system, for Maine, clearly imitating Massachusetts, established in 1834 a Board of Internal Improvements to conduct and finance surveys for canals, roads, and railroads. A policy of state aid was evidently envisaged, for the act specified that no funds were to be appropriated until the Board had determined the necessity and cost of the proposal.[41] In the end this noble conception accomplished less in Maine than it had in Massachusetts. Although the engineers from the Board or the Army surveyed a number of routes from the seacoast toward Quebec in order to get "the immense trade of the two Canadas," each project incited the stubborn opposition of ports and communities left aside.[42]

The appropriation of state funds, even the bonanza promised by the distribution of the national surplus, was prevented by a deep division of opinion within the state.[43] Some felt that the Atlantic had already given Maine "a canal as broad as we can desire" and the state should remain a purely "commercial" and not a "producing" area. Others argued that Maine already was a "producing" state, that its agricultural products would increase

[41] *Resolves of the State of Maine, from 1829 to 1835 Inclusive*, II, 621–623, 773–774.

[42] Report of Maine Commissioners, Maine *Legislative Documents*, 1836, no. 1; Stephen H. Long, Report on a Reconnaisance for a Rail Road from the Coast of Maine to Quebec, Maine *Legislative Documents*, 1836, no. 9; S. H. Long, Report on the Preliminary Survey of the Belfast and Quebec Rail Road, 1836, Maine *Legislative Documents*, 1837, no. 1; W. L. Dearborn, A Report on the Survey of a Rail Road Route from Portland to Lake Champlain, Maine *Legislative Documents*, 1840, no. 1; *Resolves . . . of Maine, from 1829 to 1835*, II, 701–702, 715–720.

[43] Memorial for State Aid to the Belfast and Quebec Railroad, Maine *Legislative Documents*, 1837, no. 8, pp. 4–16.

in value if given a market, and internal improvements were necessary to halt both the damaging emigration to the West and the movement into the Maine wilderness.[44] While the surveys and the controversy continued, the legislature incorporated the Portland, Saco and Portsmouth. The provisions of its charter, forecast by two general acts of the previous year,[45] granted the corporation the conventional powers, including that of eminent domain, and permitted the legislature, if the tolls yielded a revenue greater than 12 per cent on the cost of the road, either to reduce the rates or appropriate the surplus for the public schools of the state.[46]

Unhappily this first important railroad in the state was foreign in ownership and alien to the aims of Maine policy. Bostonians owned over 5,000 shares; Portland only 100 or more; the capitalists and places interested in the Eastern road were its real promoters.[47] When the road was completed in 1842, though the editors of the Portland papers were given free passes for the opening-day excursion, they indulged in few superlatives. A month earlier a Boston correspondent had informed Maineites that the opening of the road would transfer the business of Portland to Boston. "It has been the fate of the small generally, from time immemorial, to be devoured by the large, and you must bear up as well as you can under the affliction." [48] The disturbing purposes of this Massachusetts enterprise did something to cool the ardor of the state for railroads. A general hostility to all railroads, aroused as in New Hampshire by questions of land damages, tax favors, and other corporation privileges, did more.[49] In addition, instructed by the unhappy experience of other states with internal improvements at government expense, Maine

[44] *Resolves . . . of Maine, from 1829 to 1835*, II, 717–720.

[45] *Public Acts of the State of Maine, Passed by the Sixteenth Legislature, January Session, 1836*, pp. 327–334.

[46] *Private and Special Acts of the State of Maine, Passed by the Seventeenth Legislature, January Session, 1837*, pp. 365–374.

[47] Abstract of the Returns of Corporations, 1843, Maine *Legislative Documents*, 1844, pp. 17–23.

[48] Portland *Eastern Argus*, October 21, 1842.

[49] John A. Poor, *Memoir of Hon. Reuel Williams, Prepared for the Maine Historical Society* (Cambridge: H. O. Houghton & Company, 1864), pp. 44–45; Portland *Eastern Argus*, November 28, 1842, March 3, 1843.

enacted in 1847 a constitutional amendment prohibiting the loan of its credit to private enterprise and limiting the size of the state debt.[50]

IV

Though the setting was thus inhospitable, a group of Portland merchants and other civic leaders was gradually maturing the project of a railroad from their city to Canada. This new thoroughfare, probably terminating at Montreal, was to be the land link between interior Canada and Great Britain and western Europe. Portland was to blossom as an entrepôt and the merchant marines of the Atlantic were to throng her harbor. Though not yet a resident of Portland, John A. Poor of Bangor became the flaming evangel of her railroad greatness. Others connected with the Montreal railroad sank into obscurity and Poor acted and spoke as if a unique personal vision had moved him to originate the project. No doubt he was its colorful advocate and advertiser.[51]

A lawyer, railway official, and journalist,[52] Poor went on to become in the vernacular of the era the "philosopher" of the railroad and a self-appointed sovereign over the whole Maine system. In his native state he played the rôle that Quincy, Derby, and De Grand had in Massachusetts. With variations appropriate to his locale he saw in this new means of transportation an instrument for redeeming his native state from economic stagnation and for staying the emigration to Massachusetts and to the American West. For Maine agriculture it would give a market for bulky products. More important was the commercial prosperity with which it would bless her seaboard. "Maine will present at some future day, along our bays and harbors, a line of

[50] *The Revised Statutes of the State of Maine, Passed April 17, 1857; to Which Are Affixed the Constitutions of the United States and of the State of Maine*, p. 49.

[51] Laura E. Poor, ed., *The First International Railway and the Colonization of New England. Life and Writings of John Alfred Poor* (New York: G. P. Putnam's Sons, 1892), pp. 25–32; William A. Goodwin, "An Essay Read Before the Fraternity Club of Portland," Feb. 5, 1883, Ms., Bowdoin College Library, pp. 2–3, 7.

[52] *Dictionary of American Biography* (New York: Charles Scribner's Sons, 1928–1936), XV, 71–73.

cities, surpassing those which are now found upon the shores of the English channel or the Baltic Sea." It would spur manufacturing enterprises. Maine had water power (and Poor was responsible for its first accurate appraisal); it had natural resources, stone and lumber, and would have more after a geological survey had unearthed them; and finally it had the climate. "The capacity of the human frame for labor is found to be greater in Maine, than in Massachusetts or any State, south or west of it. . . . The higher branches of industry, to be carried on with profit, must seek those regions of the earth where physical exertion is a pleasure, and continuous labor invigorates rather than exhausts the human frame." Incidentally Maine had a "low rate of wages." [53] The attainment of this millennium depended upon the railroad, a Maine railroad system. Its construction was, like Maine's greatness, inexorable. As did most lawyers of the day, Poor inserted into his prophecies frequent references to laws, "natural" and "commercial."

Perhaps Bostonian energy might reverse nature. Already the citizens of that dreaded rival had turned their eyes northward to the fruitful Canadas, already they had projected not one but two routes to the St. Lawrence, already they had enchained Vermont and New Hampshire to their "interest," and already they had almost persuaded Montreal to an alliance. Defying this formidable phalanx, Poor and his fellow promoters launched a campaign to turn Montreal from Boston to Portland. They financed a survey which discerned a feasible route through Dixville Notch with grades of 80 to 90 feet a mile, heavy embankments and sidewalling, and a tunnel 1,500 feet long, to a triumphant union with a projected Canadian connection,[54] and they sought a charter from the Maine legislature.[55] As affairs marched to climax, Poor in the winter of 1845 took off for Montreal by sleigh and, in spite of blizzard and sub-zero weather,

[53] Memorial of John A. Poor in Behalf of the European & North American Railway Co., Maine *Miscellaneous Legislative Documents*, 1861, Part 1, pp. 8–11, 16, 19–20, 47–48.

[54] James Hall, *Report of a Reconnaissance of a Route for a Railroad from Portland to Montreal* (Portland: A Shirely & Son. 1844), pp. 10–11.

[55] Memorial of William P. Preble and Others for a Charter, Maine *Legislative Documents*, 1845, no. 1.

reached it in five days, just in time to prevent the merchants there from committing themselves to the Boston route.[56] A week later one of his associates, Judge William P. Preble, arrived with the charter which the Maine legislature had granted on February 10, 1845, to the Atlantic and St. Lawrence Railway.[57]

Portland won the favor of Montreal. Whether the arguments of Preble and Poor mesmerized Canadian promoters, capitalists, and railroad statesmen or not, there were solid reasons for the decision. By ocean transport of that era Portland was two days nearer Europe than New York, a half day nearer than Boston, and the distance by railroad from Montreal to Portland was estimated to be at least a hundred miles less than to Boston. Since the Canadian portion of the line was also designed as a local route to serve the areas east of Montreal — the seigniories and the Eastern Townships — it traversed a wider Canadian territory if it connected with the Atlantic and St. Lawrence rather than with the Vermont and Canada or its alternates. Finally, in an alliance with Montreal, Portland was less apt to be master than was Boston. The latter was a rival to Montreal; it possessed routes to the West and to Canada, independent of her. Portland could achieve no higher destiny than serving as her winter port. So the Montrealers secured a charter for the St. Lawrence and Atlantic, the Canadian link in this Poor-christened "first international railroad of the world." [58]

The whole project faced immense difficulties. For one thing it traversed a comparatively unproductive region. Years later a Maine man acquainted with the project recalled with a combination of lyricism and ruefulness the "sparsely-settled country and farther on a vast wilderness enclosing the hard-won farms which lay in the intervals along the streams, with pastures and tilled

[56] Poor, *The First International Railway*, pp. 33–41; John A. to Henry V. Poor, February 17, 1845, March 21, 1845, Ms., Poor Papers, Maine Historical Society.

[57] *Private and Special Laws of the State of Maine, 1845*, pp. 247–254.

[58] *Montreal in 1856. A Sketch Prepared for the Celebration of the Opening of the Grand Trunk Railway of Canada* (Montreal: John Lovell, 1856), pp. 22–23, 25–26; A. T. Galt, *The Saint Lawrence and Atlantic Railroad. A Letter to the Chairman and Deputy Chairman of the North American Colonial Association* (London: J. Unwin, 1847); George P. de T. Glazebrook, *A History of Transportation in Canada* (New Haven: Yale University Press, 1938), pp. 161–164.

John A. Poor

David A. Neal

Richard D. Rice

CAPTAINS OF THE DOWN-EAST ROADS

Great Eastern

The Celebration of the Opening of the Victoria Bridge
and the Visit of the Prince of Wales

PORTENTS OF PORTLAND'S TRIUMPHS

fields struggling up the sides of the hills, cleared from the adjoining forests, otherwise unbroken except by the inroads of the lumberman. Beyond these the forest primeval. . . . A line of stages . . . led in the general direction of the desired railroad line, and was amply sufficient for the necessities of the public travel in that direction." [59] In addition to its frontier aspect, the terrain was forbidding in the extreme since the Atlantic and St. Lawrence had to pierce, if not the heart, at least the rough outposts of the White Mountains. The charter wisely contented itself with the declaration that the road should run northwest from Portland "in the general direction of Sherbrooke and Montreal" [60] and forthwith one surveying party after another tried to discover a feasible route. Eventually the road crossed from Portland to the valley of the Androscoggin, followed its valley into northern New Hampshire, crossed a divide to the Connecticut River, and finally joined with the Canadian connection at Island Pond in northeastern Vermont. Because of topographical difficulties and the decision of the Canadians to serve as large an area of their country as possible, the route was fifty miles longer than originally intended. "No grades above 45 feet to the mile were tolerated except for nearly three and a half miles of sixty feet." [61]

More critical than the battle with geography was the ceaseless struggle against the wiles of Boston. The minions of Massachusetts had fought the charter of the St. Lawrence and Atlantic in Canada; with their allies they had almost persuaded New Hampshire and Vermont to forbid passage to the Portland road.[62] The newspaper spokesman of the Vermont Central had declared of the enterprise, "The stock if subscribed for in America, would have to be taken by the Esquimaux, and the wolves and bears of

[59] Goodwin, "An Essay Before the Fraternity Club," p. 2.

[60] *Private and Special Laws of the State of Maine, 1845*, p. 247.

[61] *Report of the Directors to the Stockholders of the Atlantic and St. Lawrence Rail Road Co. Presented August 5, 1851* (Portland: Harmon & Williams, 1851), pp. 13–15.

[62] Poor, *The First International Railway*, p. 58; Portland *Advertiser*, March 14, 15, 1845; Sherbrooke *Gazette*, March 20, 1845; J. A. Poor to J. S. Little, November 6, 1848. Ms., Poor Papers..

these hyperboreal regions. The fox and beaver will cast their
influence against the project; but the catamount and panther
will come into the measure provided they can be made to believe
that mutton and poultry will thereby become cheaper."[63] But
Poor and his cohorts had triumphed everywhere. To preserve
the purity of their aim, an independent Maine system, they had
carefully inserted in the charter a provision allowing connections
with their railroad "but only on the easterly side thereof."[64]
Thus Boston was forestalled from tapping their river of commerce. In construction they took further precautions by giving
their road a "medium gauge" of 5′6″ rather than the standard
one. The arguments of A. C. Morton, the engineer they imported from the Erie, itself a road with a peculiar gauge, gave the
impression that their preference was dictated by considerations
merely technological. Engines could have large drivers and still
a low center of gravity, the multiplication of boiler tubes rather
than their inefficient lengthening gave additional power, freight
cars had a larger proportion of cargo space to their weight, and
passenger cars would be more commodious.[65] The real reason
for the broad gauge, however, was to inconvenience the interchange of goods and passengers with the Boston roads.[66] This
difficulty was enlarged when the Canadian roads west from
Montreal, in spite of Boston's efforts, were built to conform to the
Portland connection.[67] Provincialism, Maine and Canadian, won
the victory.

On July 4, 1846 at Portland, the governor of the state, President Preble, and a squad of distinguished spademen turned the
first shovelfuls of earth.[68] Soon thereafter the road was in financial straits. It proved impossible to collect enough subscriptions

[63] Montpelier *Vermont Watchman and State Journal*, December 21, 1848.

[64] *Private and Special Laws of the State of Maine, 1845*, p. 250.

[65] A. C. Morton, *Report on the Gauge for the St. Lawrence and Atlantic Railroad* (Portland: Thurston & Company, 1847), pp. 6–14; *Report of the President
and Directors to the Stockholders of the Atlantic & St. Lawrence R.R. Co.
August 3, 1847* (Portland: Harmon & Williams, 1847), p. 10.

[66] Morton, *Report on the Gauge*, pp. 5, 18–20.

[67] John A. Poor, *No Restrictions on Railway Transit. Argument of John A.
Poor Before the Joint Standing Committee on Railroads, Ways and Bridges*
(Bangor: David Bugbee & Co., 1865), pp. 23–25.

[68] Portland *Tri-Weekly Argus*, July 8, 1846.

to meet even the modest estimates of $2,500,000 to $3,000,000 for a road only as far as the international boundary.[69] Bostonians naturally did not invest; the bursting of a railroad bubble in Great Britain in 1846 blighted expectations of English assistance; and the first million, collected largely in Portland, apparently carried the road only eleven miles and partially built the Portland terminal.[70] Recourse was now had to municipal credit. In 1848 Portland, permitted by the state to extend its credit to the road if two-thirds of the voters consented, granted $1,000,-000; in later years the city loaned two additional sums of $500,000 each, and finally authorized $350,000 which, however, was not utilized. Though the protection given the city varied in different enactments, Portland eventually received a guarantee that the road would repay principal and interest of the municipal advance and, as collateral for its loans, $500,000 in the railroad's bonds and $1,500,000 in its stock; it could sell the latter only when annual contributions to the sinking funds fell behind schedule.[71] More significant than these details, however, was the inauguration of municipal assistance to railroads. This policy was the means, then and later, by which the state secured "a liberal and effective system of internal improvements." [72] Meanwhile, on the Atlantic and St. Lawrence, even municipal credit was not enough. When Poor in 1849 jammed through a construction

[69] Hall, *Report . . . for a Railroad from Portland to Montreal*, p. 16; Statement of Facts Accompanying a Bill for Municipal Aid to the Atlantic & St. Lawrence Railroad, Maine *Legislative Documents*, 1848, no. 15, p. 5.

[70] *Report of the President and Directors to the Stockholders of the Atlantic & St. Lawrence R.R. Company, July 22, 1848* (Portland: Charles Day & Co., 1848), pp. 3, 5; *Report of the President and Directors to the Stockholders of the Atlantic & St. Lawrence R.R. Company, July 22, 1849* (Portland: Thurston & Co., 1849), pp. 3, 9; Maine *Legislative Documents*, 1848, no. 15, p. 4.

[71] *Report of the Directors to the Stockholders of the Atlantic and St. Lawrence Rail Road Company. Presented August 2, 1853* (Portland: Foster, Gerrish & Company, 1853), p. 4; *Annual Report of the Directors to the Stockholders of the Atlantic & St. Lawrence Railroad Company, Presented August 7, 1855* (n.p., n.d.), pp. 5, 6; *Acts and Resolves Passed by the Twenty-eighth Legislature of the State of Maine, A.D. 1848*, pp. 198–203; *Acts and Resolves Passed by the Thirtieth Legislature of the State of Maine, A.D. 1850*, pp. 461–469; *Acts and Resolves Passed by the Thirty-first Legislature of the State of Maine, A.D. 1852*, pp. 474–476; *Acts and Resolves Passed by the Thirty-second Legislature of the State of Maine, A.D. 1853*, Part II, pp. 5–6.

[72] George W. Pierce to James Baldwin, January 20, 1834, Ms., Baldwin Papers, Harvard Business School Library, XLVIII.

contract with Black, Wood, and Company, a Portland firm which he admired, the contractors agreed to accept their payment of $26,200 a mile one-half in cash, one-quarter in bonds, and one-quarter in stock.[73] The road was opened on July 18, 1853. It had cost nearly twice the estimates.[74]

Three weeks later the Atlantic and St. Lawrence was leased for 999 years to the Grand Trunk Railway Company of Canada.[75] Under the aegis of the latter, a monster corporation, Peto, Brassey, Jackson and Betts, the most famous English contracting firm of its day, had undertaken to construct and finance a Canadian rail network. They acquired the roads between Portland and Montreal as an outlet for their more extensive enterprises in the interior.[76] For the Portland line their arrival was an unmixed blessing. They took over a partially unballasted road, with uncovered bridges and defective railroad furniture, and proceeded at great expense to put it into usable condition.[77] Upon their association with the road the stock rose from $30 to $96 a share and the prudent Maineites gradually transferred their holdings to British purchasers.[78] Consequently in the sixties when the Grand Trunk reduced the guaranteed rental from 6 to 4 per cent, momentarily omitted payments to the sinking funds for Portland loans, and funded rent arrears by an issue of scrip, the promoters, merchants, and capitalists of that city were not the chief sufferers.[79]

[73] *Report of the Directors, to the Stockholders of the Atlantic & St. Lawrence Rail Road Company. Presented August 6, 1850* (Portland: Thurston & Co., 1850), p. 6; Poor, *The First International Railway*, p. 59.

[74] *Report . . . of the Atlantic and St. Lawrence . . . 1853*, pp. 1, 9.

[75] *Ibid.*, p. 3; *Charter and By-Laws of the Atlantic & St. Lawrence Railroad Company: Lease to the Grand Trunk Railway Company of Canada, and Other Documents* (Portland: Bearce, Starbird, Rich & Co., 1855), pp. 44–69.

[76] Glazebrook, *A History of Transportation in Canada*, pp. 167–170.

[77] *Proceedings of the First Meeting of the Shareholders of the Grand Trunk Railway Company of Canada, Held at Quebec, the 27th July, 1854. With the Reports of the Board of Directors, the Engineer in Chief, and the General Manager* (Montreal: James Potts, 1854), pp. 5–6, 14–15.

[78] *Annual Report of the Directors to the Stockholders of the Atlantic & St. Lawrence Railroad Company, Presented August 1, 1861* (n.p., n.d.), pp. 3–4; Poor, *No Restrictions on Railway Transit*, pp. 12, 32–33.

[79] *Annual Report of the Directors to the Stockholders of the Atlantic and St. Lawrence Railroad Company. Presented August, 1862* (n.p., n.d.), pp. 3–4, 8; *A Deed Modifying the Lease of the Atlantic and St. Lawrence Railroad to the*

Portland, alone among New England cities, had meanwhile gained a through route to the distant West. At Montreal, its line crossed the St. Lawrence by the Victoria Bridge. A tubular structure, over a mile long, with twenty-four piers, it was to Portlanders one of the wonders of the world, greater even than "the Pyramids of Egypt, the Parthenon of Athens, or the Roman Coliseum." [80] West from Montreal the broad gauge carried its route to Sarnia on the St. Clair River and thence to Detroit, where it had "a complete and independent connection with the Western States." [81] Boston had nothing like it. Nor was she likely to have the *Great Eastern* or *Leviathan*, building in Great Britian and promised on her maiden trip to Portland. Properly to receive this fabulous steamship, with its 18,914 gross tonnage and length of 692 feet, with its 112 furnaces raising steam for a double set of engines and driving both paddle wheels and screw propellers, and with its capacity for 4,000 passengers,[82] Portland built a special wharf and began the erection of a marble hotel "of chaste architecture." [83] Though the London *Times* sneered, "The steam monster, when it arrives, will dwarf hotel, landing place, and the town itself into utter insignificance," [84] it was the moment of Portland's apotheosis.

> Portland is looking up, and all her spunk
> Is centered in those noble words — *"Grand Trunk:"*
> That iron arm that links Atlantic *"Maine"*
> With Huron's waters, in a single chain;
> On whose smooth rail the swift, careering steed
> Shall cross Victoria Bridge, and onward speed,
> Defying time and space, — its journey o'er:
> Shall slake its thirst on the Pacific shore;
> While o'er our waters busy steamers ply
> With flags of every hue, in peaceful harmony;

Grand Trunk Railway Company of Canada, March 31, 1863 (Portland: Stephen Berry, 1863).

[80] Portland *State of Maine*, November 7, 1854.

[81] *Annual Report . . . of the Atlantic & St. Lawrence . . . August 1, 1861*, pp. 2–3.

[82] W. S. Lindsay, *History of Merchant Shipping from 1816–1874* (London: Sampson, Low, Marston & Company, n.d.), II, 491–513.

[83] Portland *State of Maine*, January 22, February 12, June 24, 1856, October 6, 1857.   [84] *Ibid.*, January 20, 1857.

A neutral port with every flag unfurled
That floats on merchant ships throughout the world.[85]

Though some colorful anticipations, like the *Great Eastern*, did not materialize, the Grand Trunk benefited Portland in solid fashion. Clearances and entrances, imports and exports, population and property values, all increased remarkably.[86] Portland became a Canadian city, at least part-time, for weekly steamship service to Liverpool, subsidized by the Canadian government, made Portland its terminus during the winter months.[87] Through bills of lading from Liverpool to British Canada diverted the business in bond from Boston to Portland,[88] and through Portland the products of the West even found their way to Boston. Its flour shipments Bostonward in 1860, 217,897 barrels, were greater than those from any other port and by any other railroad, except the Western with a total of 302,462.[89] Confronted by this series of disquieting events, Boston had sulked and blustered. She pressed invitations upon the *Great Eastern*, chided Portland for cherishing "extravagant anticipations," and advised the Grand Trunk to extend by a third rail along existing roads to Boston, a metropolis and not a "ninth-rate town." [90] Threats of this sort induced the Maine legislature in 1860 to pass an "act to promote safety of travel on railroads." Its only section forbade any road

[85] *Ibid.*, January 5, 1858.

[86] Statistics of Maine, Furnished by John A. Poor, Maine *Senate Documents*, 1869, no. 1, pp. 14–15.

[87] *Annual Report of the Directors to the Stockholders of the Atlantic & St. Lawrence Railroad Company. Presented August 3, 1858* (n.p., n.d.), p. 3; *Annual Report of the Directors to the Stockholders of the Atlantic and St. Lawrence Railroad Co., Presented August 1863* (n.p., n.d.), pp. 3–4.

[88] *Professional and Industrial History of Suffolk County, Massachusetts* (Boston: The Boston History Company, 1894), II, 150.

[89] *Boston Board of Trade. 1861. Seventh Annual Report of the Government, Presented to the Board at the Annual Meeting, on the 16th of January, 1861* (Boston: T. R. Marvin & Son, 1861), p. 71.

[90] Pliny Miles, *The Advantages of Ocean Steam Navigation, Foreign and Coastwise, to the Commerce of Boston and the Manufactures of New England* (Boston: Emory N. Moore & Co., 1857), pp. 83–92; *Boston Board of Trade. 1857. Third Annual Report of the Government, Presented to the Board at the Annual Meeting, on the 21st of January, 1857* (Boston: George C. Rand & Avery, 1857), p. 45; *Boston Board of Trade. 1860. Sixth Annual Report of the Government, Presented to the Board at the Annual Meeting, on the 20th of January, 1860* (Boston: Wright & Potter, 1860), p. 33.

in the state to change its gauge or lay an extra rail without the consent of the legislature. This prohibition did not apply to the roads east of Portland.[91]

V

For the area between the Grand Trunk on the west and the Penobscot Valley on the east, Maine promoters and planners had no railroad design of an imperial scale. In an almost offhand fashion the ruling railroad clique of Portland planned that a branch should diverge from the Atlantic and St. Lawrence at some point north of their city and move eastward to Lewiston and Bangor. If a road consecrated by Poor might be so regarded, this was the canon. To conform with it, the legislature in 1845 chartered two roads, the Androscoggin and Kennebec and the Penobscot and Kennebec; as their names imply they were to connect somewhere in the Kennebec Valley.[92] When this project ran afoul of Augusta's unwillingness to be a way station and her preference for an exclusive and standard gauge connection with Portland, the Poor crowd located its roads farther inland along the "back route" and planned to connect them at Waterville.[93]

Their rival, the Kennebec and Portland, appealed not only to Augusta, "a specimen of that profound selfishness for which *one portion* of the State is remarkable," [94] but to a series of towns nearer the sea, of which Bath was the most important. Since it was to be a "narrow gauge" road — thus sneeringly christened by Poor and his associates — it connected easily with the Portland, Saco and Portsmouth and appealed to Boston investors. Boston merchants subscribed $100,000 to its stock; the Portland, Saco and Portsmouth contributed another $100,000; private capitalists in Bath, Brunswick, and Augusta furnished additional funds; and in 1850 the towns along the route were

[91] *Acts and Resolves Passed by the Thirty-ninth Legislature of the State of Maine. 1860*, p. 135.

[92] Poor, *Memoir of Hon. Reuel Williams*, p. 45; *Private and Special Laws of the State of Maine, 1845*, pp. 314–322, 330–337.

[93] Edwin Noyes to John A. Poor, December 22, 1846, Ms., Poor Papers.

[94] John A. Poor to John Mussey, July 17, 1845, Ms., Mussey Papers, Maine Historical Society.

authorized to advance $800,000 to the enterprise.[95] In 1855 a second corporation extended the route northward along the Kennebec to a junction with the two official roads near Waterville. In 1855 these likewise had been completed.[96] Bangor had contributed $800,000 in scrip to the Penobscot and Kennebec and, though it had cost 75 per cent over the estimates, the Bangor papers looked forward with delight to the time when "lecturers from abroad" could be brought over the rails, and celebrated with enthusiasm the first arrival of flour brought all the way by rail from Montreal.[97]

Discord soon drowned such congratulations. A battle of gauges began. The Kennebec valley and coastal route, the standard gauge, insisted that the broad gauge must interchange through passengers at the junction near Waterville; the Androscoggin and Kennebec and Penobscot and Kennebec, the broad gauge, united to hamper such an arrangement. When the former summoned as allies the Massachusetts roads, which now refused to sell through tickets to Waterville and Bangor via the broad gauge route or to accept them from the same stations, the latter retaliated by connecting with the Boston boats rather than the Boston railroads.[98] Of course the legislature was drawn into the

---

[95] *Report of the President and Directors of the Kennebec and Portland Railroad Company, to the Stockholders, October 5, 1848* (Brunswick: J. Griffin, 1848), p. 7; *Report of the Directors and Treasurer of the Kennebec and Portland Railroad Company, to the Stockholders. Presented October, 1853* (Augusta: William T. Johnson, 1853), p. 7; Poor, *No Restrictions on Railway Transit*, pp. 19–21; Poor, *Memoir of Hon. Reuel Williams*, pp. 45–46.

[96] Henry V. Poor, *History of the Railroads and Canals of the United States of America, Exhibiting Their Progress, Cost, Revenues, Expenditures & Present Condition* (New York: John H. Schultz & Co., 1860), pp. 27, 31.

[97] Portland *State of Maine*, November 14, 1854, November 13, 1855; *Acts and Resolves Passed by the Extra Session of the Thirty-second Legislature, 1853, and the Thirty-third Legislature of the State of Maine, 1854*, pp. 207–212; *Acts and Resolves Passed by the Thirty-fourth Legislature of the State of Maine, 1855*, pp. 477–482; Annual Report to Stockholders of Penobscot and Kennebec Railroad Company, July 12, 1853, Ms., Harvard Business School Library; *Penobscot and Kennebec Railroad Company. Directors' Report* (n.p., 1854?), p. 2; Annual Report to Stockholders of Penobscot and Kennebec Railroad Company, July 9, 1855, Ms., Harvard Business School Library; Treasurer's Report to Stockholders of Penobscot and Kennebec Railroad Company, July 9, 1855, Ms., Harvard Business School Library.

[98] *Report of the Directors to the Stockholders of the Androscoggin and Kennebec Railroad Company. Presented at the Annual Meeting in Waterville, June 24,*

quarrel. In 1856 it conditioned its assent to a merger of the Androscoggin and Kennebec and the Penobscot and Kennebec upon their giving "to all passengers their choice of routes at same rates of fare," [99] and two years later, when the roads refused to accept this injunction, it established a Board of Railroad Commissioners to determine the terms of connection and the rates at which one railroad should carry the goods and passengers of another.[100] This step the directors of the Androscoggin and Kennebec deplored: "The Railroad Corporations of this State are *private* corporations — *not public* — and whenever it is settled judicially that this act is the law of the land, you will have no future need of Directors to manage your affairs, except perhaps, to raise money to pay your debts." [101]

This exception was no small one for the roads in question. Built at excessive costs, overlaid with bond issues, some kept from bankruptcy by the narrowest of margins, and the Kennebec and Portland did go into receivership. Although the investments by town and city were saved, private stockholders lost the whole or a large part of their holdings.[102] All, however, was not dark. After the legislature in 1862 had withdrawn its conditions to consolidation, the broad gauge roads between the Grand Trunk and Bangor became the Maine Central Railroad Company.[103] The rival Kennebec and Portland in the hands of trustees participated

---

1857 (Bangor: Samuel S. Smith, 1857), pp. 6–7, 8; *Report of the Directors to the Stockholders of the Androscoggin and Kennebec Railroad Company. Presented at the Annual Meeting in Waterville, June 29, 1859* (Bangor: Samuel S. Smith, 1850), pp. 5, 6–10, 12; Portland *State of Maine*, June 3, 16, 23, 30, 1857.

[99] *Acts and Resolves Passed by the Thirty-fifth Legislature of the State of Maine, A. D. 1856*, pp. 730–734.

[100] Directors' Report to Stockholders of Penobscot and Kennebec Railroad Company at Special Meeting. Nov. 25, 1856, Ms., Harvard Business School Library; *Report of the Directors to the Stockholders of the Penobscot and Kennebec Railroad Company. Presented at the Annual Meeting in Bangor, July 14, 1857* (Bangor: Samuel S. Smith, 1857), p. 6.

[101] *Report . . . of the Androscoggin and Kennebec . . . June 29, 1859*, pp. 10–11.

[102] Edward E. Chase, *Maine Railroads* (Portland: A. J. Huston, 1926), pp. 34–36.

[103] *Acts and Resolves Passed by the Forty-first Legislature of the State of Maine. 1862*, p. 170; Edmund F. Webb, *The Railroad Laws of Maine, Containing All Public and Private Acts and Resolves Relating to Railroads in Said State* (Portland: Dresser, McLellan & Co., 1875), pp. 306–309.

in the prosperity of the Civil War years.[104] With the steamboat interests of Portland it steadfastly supported the state law prohibiting the laying of a third rail from Portland to Boston.[105] Both were bent upon imprisoning the broad gauge within the state of Maine. The broad gauge sought to escape. Such was the ironic outcome of Maine's effort to create an independent railway system. In order to prosper it had to lose its independence.

VI

During the years of construction, squabbles, and merging in this middle region, Poor had suffered many humiliations. His advice had not been taken, his favorite contracting firm had been squeezed out of one of the corporations, and he himself was caught in contradictions of argument and attitude impossible to conceal.[106] Meanwhile he had turned to happier pastures, eastern Maine, and larger prospects, the European and North American Railway. The latter was a railroad dream of inter-continental stature. In a petition of 1850 to the Maine legislature, Poor, other Portlanders, and Grand Trunkers revealed their plan for a railroad east from Bangor through New Brunswick and Nova Scotia to White Haven on Cape Canso and, if feasible, across the Gut of Canso to Louisburgh. Hence fast steamers were to cross the narrowed Atlantic to Galway. With the "Atlantic ferry" behind them, passengers would proceed by the Great Midland Railroad to Dublin, cross the Irish Sea to Holy Head, and speed thence by railroad to London. The journey between New York and London would shrink from ten days to seven or perhaps six. The European and North American would thus become the great avenue for passengers, mails, and freight between the United States and the continent. It also served local purposes. It would prevent the emigration of men and capital from Maine, increase

---

[104] *Sixth Annual Report of the Trustees, Manager and Superintendent and Treasurer, to the Mortgage Bondholders of the Kennebec and Portland R. R. Company. Presented October 28, 1863 at Brunswick* (Augusta: Pike & Chick, 1863), pp. 3–4.

[105] Poor, *No Restrictions on Railway Transit*, pp. 10–13.

[106] Portland *State of Maine*, February 6, 1855; Poor, *No Restrictions on Railway Transit*.

the valuation of property and develop the eastern part of the state, and, taken in conjunction with the Grand Trunk, furnish the best connection between Montreal and Quebec and the Maritime Provinces.[107] Though minor, this last objective was an urgent one, for already promoters and politicians were planning "the Intercolonial," a circuitous connection between the Canadas and the Maritimes entirely within British territory. Fortunately a lack of capital and local rivalries were for the moment retarding its construction.

As a prelude to the European and North American, Poor assembled in midsummer, 1850, the great Portland convention. It made a vivid impression upon its audience of legislators, judges, governors, businessmen, clergy, and delegates. The Star Spangled Banner, the Cross of St. George, and a huge map of the route decorated the hall. Solicited endorsements poured in from railroad and college presidents, professors, and statesmen. The speaking was a long oratorical marathon; a resolution declared "that the spirit of the Age and the progress of modern improvement" demanded the construction of the line; and the orgy of "repeated and prolonged cheers," "hearty cheers," "enthusiastic cheers," "rapturous cheers" and "ardent cheers" reached its climax on the last day, when three cheers were given for Queen Victoria, three cheers for the President of the United States, three cheers for the "Mother Country," three cheers for "her American Children," and finally "three notable and astounding cheers for the success of 'THE EUROPEAN AND NORTH AMERICAN RAILWAY.' " [108]

Twenty days later the Maine legislature granted a charter for a line beginning at Bangor, crossing the river above it, and thence proceeding "over the most practicable route, in a line to the city of St. John, in New Brunswick, to the eastern boundary

---

[107] *Plan for Shortening the Time of Passage between New York and London, with Documents Relating Thereto, Including the Proceedings of the Railway Convention at Portland, Maine, and the Charter of the European and North American Railway* (Portland: Harmon and Williams, 1850), pp. 4–11; J. A. Poor to Henry V. Poor, December 7, 1847. Ms., Poor Papers.

[108] *Plan for Shortening the Time of Passage between New York and London,* pp. 15–136.

of the state." [109] When the state also decided to finance the
survey, A. C. Morton, engineer of the Grand Trunk, was detailed
to make what he could of these specifications.[110] His researches,
published in 1851, were not entirely conclusive. Although he set
the junction with the New Brunswick connections at Calais and
St. Stephen, he rejected the approach by the coast as too precipitous and a direct overland route from Bangor as impossible because of mountains. Consequently the chosen route ran north
along the Penobscot and then curved eastward through a lake
region to tributaries of the St. Croix, which it followed to Calais.
Although the country traversed was "unknown," the maximum
grades and the cost were not — fifty-three feet to the mile and
$2,266,577.[111]

For nearly fifteen years the company in its own right never laid
a rail. The difficulty was finance. Obviously it was a task for
public rather than private capital, since no existing traffic could
support a project of such magnitude, and the possibility of
sluicing the trade between the United States and Europe along
the coast of Maine and the Maritime Provinces, though it might
dazzle talkers, did not convert investors. So Poor and his associates on "the Executive Committee of Maine for the European
and North American Railway" tried to induce the state to give
them a generous donation from its public domain or from the
sale of its land in northern and eastern Maine. The people were
not in the mood for such assistance.[112] A similar appeal was directed upon Massachusetts, also the owner of lands in Maine.
The European and North American, it was said, would enhance
their value and also develop down East a manufacturing region
and a market to compensate Massachusetts for the loss of western
New England to New York.[113] The Massachusetts General

[109] *Acts and Resolves . . . of Maine, . . . 1850*, Part I, pp. 521–530.
[110] *Ibid.*, Part II, p. 241.
[111] A. C. Morton, *Report on the Survey of the European and North American
Railway: Made Under the Authority of the State of Maine* (Portland: Harmon
and Williams, 1851), pp. 3–37.
[112] *Acts and Resolves Passed by the Thirty-eighth Legislature of the State of
Maine. 1850*, pp. 107–111; Memorial of John A. Poor and Others for State Assistance to Railroads, Maine *House Documents*, 1857, no. 42, pp. 8–11.
[113] Petition of the Executive Committee of the European and North American,

Court was deaf to the plea.[114] Simultaneously the batteries were turned upon the national government, which had just granted lands to the Illinois Central and had paid $10,000,000 to Texas for an old land claim. Maine which had, under the Webster-Ashburton Treaty in 1842, surrendered her lands for a "merely nominal consideration," deserved federal funds as much as these western regions.[115] When these claims produced no cash, Poor turned to those financial angels from overseas — Peto, Brassey, Jackson and Betts. They were willing to provide 80 per cent of the capital if they could have the whole line from Augusta to the border. Even if Maine interests could have been led to this surrender, the outbreak of the Crimean War definitely removed the further possibility of European assistance.[116] The hopelessness of urban assistance was revealed when Bangor citizens refused to appropriate $500,000 in aid of one of the partial projects to which, during the fifties, Poor's grandiose conception had been whittled down.[117]

The Civil War years, however, gave Poor an opportunity to revive the European and North American Railway. Though he was unable to coax any assistance from the Federal government with the plea that the railway was a necessary military measure for the defense of Maine against British invasion,[118] the hitherto

---

Massachusetts *House Documents*, 1851, no. 87; Report of the Joint Select Committee on the Petition of the European and North American, Massachusetts *House Documents*, 1851, no. 197.

[114] Report of the Joint Select Committee on the Petition of the European and North American, Massachusetts *Senate Documents*, 1852, no. 123.

[115] Report of the Committee on Railroads and Bridges Requesting the National Government to Assist the European and North American, Maine *Legislative Documents*, 1851–1852, no. 12, pp. 3–4.

[116] Petition of the Executive Committee of the European and North American Railway, Maine *House Documents*, no. 1, pp. 4–5, 19–24; Report of the Committee of Railroads on a Memorial of the European and North American Railway Company, Maine *Legislative Documents*, 1854, no. 34, pp. 2, 3; Poor, *No Restrictions on Railway Transit*, pp. 53–54.

[117] *Acts and Resolves . . . of Maine, 1859*, pp. 333–337; Message of Governor Coburn to the Legislature, January 8, 1863, Maine *Miscellaneous Legislative Documents*, 1863, p. 11.

[118] Report of Edwin F. Johnson on the Defence of Maine, *Senate Executive Documents*, 37 Cong., 2 Sess., no. 41 (s.n. 1122), pp. 2–5; Resolution of the Maine Legislature on the Defence of the State, *House Miscellaneous Documents*, 37 Cong., 3 Sess., no. 17 (s.n. 1171).

hostile Bangorians summoned him to harmonize and promote their railroad interests.[119] The following year, 1864, the Maine legislature authorized Bangor to loan $500,000 to the European and North American. Both the city government and the voters had to approve the grant. If it were made, the city would elect one director and receive a mortgage on the road as security.[120] On behalf of the state the legislature granted to the railroad the proceeds from the sale of timber on ten townships, certain claims which she was still pressing upon the United States in connection with the losses of timber, and payments of money in the northeastern territory, once in dispute with Great Britain. Furthermore, if Massachusetts would assign to Maine certain joint claims against the national government and release Maine from further payments for the lands she had purchased from Massachusetts in 1853, the railroad could have all the public lands lying on the waters of the Penobscot and St. John Rivers with the exception of lands and timber set aside for public schools and "settlement." The railroad was to promote immigration by an agent and a campaign of education in Europe and America.[121] Nearly all this was conditional. Incredibly, it nearly all came true.

[119] Poor, *No Restrictions on Railway Transit*, pp. 65–66.
[120] *Acts and Resolves Passed by the Forty-third Legislature of the State of Maine. 1864*, pp. 411–415.
[121] *Ibid.*, pp. 387–390.

VIII

NEW YORK CITY AND THE NEW ENGLAND RAILROADS

"Why would not a Rail Road from Worcester to Norwich be good property? The trade of Worcester Co is going more & more to N. York — . . . it is rather against the rail way from Boston to Albany, that the rivers of Massachusetts run from North to South" — W. S. Prentiss to James F. Baldwin, January 12, 1831, Baldwin Papers, Harvard Business School Library.

I

To preserve her commercial realm in New England, New York City had relied upon waterways. Long Island Sound gave her access to the trade poured down by river or by road to the southern ports of New England, the Hudson drew to her the travel and commodities of western Connecticut and Massachusetts, and the Champlain Canal kept the great Champlain Basin dependent upon New York City or her up-river satellites, Albany and Troy. Finally the Hudson and the Erie Canal gave the city so effective a connection with the West that no other Atlantic port could aspire to equal it. But the railroad age threatened to destroy these advantages, for Boston's belligerent use of the new mechanism at once aimed a single blow at the heart of New York's system, the junction of the Hudson River and the Erie Canal; the rails of the Western were to annex this commerce to Boston. The disturbed New Yorkers had sense enough to realize that this artificial Hudson River could not rival the real Hudson were it ice-free; they were equally sure that it could supplant the Hudson when the latter was frozen. A Joint Committee of Aldermen of New York City on January 10, 1842, thus appraised the disastrous prospect occasioned by the opening of the Western:

> Five years ago a prediction that flour would be transported from Albany to Boston at fifty cents per barrel, would have been deemed an idle phantasy, yet the dream of the visionary has been realized; and we can now find an eastern city competing successfully with us for the commerce of that grand canal, which we have been accustomed to regard as exclusively our own, beyond the reach of possible contingency. We cannot shut our eyes to the fact, that during four months of the year our enterprising rival neighbors enjoy these new advantages, while we are entirely excluded from them. A continuous line of railroad running parallel with the canal and terminating at its two extremities, will enable our eastern competitors to carry to her favoured port, the rich agricultural productions of the west, and to return in exchange for them, the produce of every clime, whilst we are waiting for the opening of spring to gather up the gleanings of that rich harvest-field of trade which formerly poured its treasures exclusively into our lap.[1]

New York struck back. Some thought the best defence a railroad to Lake Erie from some other Hudson River terminus than Albany; others advocated a railroad north from New York City to Albany itself. Both projects had been chartered in the early thirties. The one, the New York and Erie, was to run from Piermont on the Hudson to Dunkirk on Lake Erie; the other, the New York and Harlem, was to extend northward from New York City to Troy and Albany.[2] Only the second is of proximate concern for a narrative of New England transportation. The nucleus of this line was a seven-mile railroad on Manhattan Island from Prince Street to the village of Harlem. The northern extension, the New York and Albany Railroad, was to bisect Westchester County, proceed through Putnam and Dutchess counties so near to their eastern boundaries as to be almost in Connecticut, and then cross diagonally through Columbia and Rensselaer counties to a point on the Hudson opposite Albany. By design it was a circuitous route, for those who followed and those who

---

[1] Report of the President of the New-York and Albany Railroad Company, New York *Senate Documents*, 1842, no. 28, p. 18.

[2] Henry V. Poor, *History of the Railroads and Canals of the United States of America, Exhibiting Their Progress, Cost, Revenues, Expenditures & Present Condition* (New York: John H. Schultz & Co., 1860), pp. 278, 287.

led public opinion alike believed that no road closely paralleling the Hudson River could compete during the summer with the Hudson River steamboats; an interior rail route, drawing traffic from both sides, was the only one which would be profitable.[3] Although the New York and Albany was projected in part for local trade, its main purpose was to frustrate New England's attempts to reach Albany by rail. Winter must not interrupt communication between New York and her hinterland and in the pursuit of that *de luxe* prize, the spring trade, Boston must be given no advantages. The city government of New York and the state encouraged these protective measures, but not by stock subscriptions; the road had to rely upon private enterprise.[4] When the first engine reached its northern terminus in 1852, ironically it ran the last part of its journey on the tracks of the Western between Chatham and Greenbush.[5]

Albany chroniclers admitted that the completion of the Harlem aroused little celebration. For one thing, the connection it at last achieved had in 1851 already been forged by a much shorter and more efficiently located line, the Hudson River Railroad. A few New Yorkers, refusing to be frightened by the chimera of river competition, had sponsored in the early forties a survey of the route along the Hudson, but the engineer, deterred by the formidable natural obstacles on the river route, had run the line for the larger share of the distance on the tableland away from its eastern shore. In 1845 the project was taken in hand by capitalists from New York City, and John B. Jervis, an eminent railroad surveyor and inventor of the state, was retained

---

[3] *Facts and Suggestions Relating to the New-York and Albany Rail-Road, with the Proceedings of the Rail-Road Meeting in Canaan, N. Y. February 3, 1835: Including the Reports of the Berkshire Delegation, and of Richard P. Morgan, Esq.* (Albany: E. W. & C. Skinner, 1835), pp. 3–14; J. W. Greene, "New York City's First Railroad, the New York and Harlem, 1832 to 1867," *New York Historical Society Quarterly Bulletin*, IX (1926), pp. 107–123.

[4] Report of the Joint Special Committee on the Communication from the Mayor Relative to the New York and Albany Railroad. July 24, 1840, New York City *Board of Aldermen Documents*, 1840, no. 10; New York *Senate Documents*, 1842, no. 28; Report of the Select Committee to Whom Was Referred the Resolution Accepting the Invitation of the Directors of the New-York and Albany Railroad, To Be Present at the Opening of Said Road, New York City *Board of Aldermen Documents*, 1842, no. 42.

[5] Joel Munsell, *The Annals of Albany* (Albany: Joel Munsell, 1853), IV, 347.

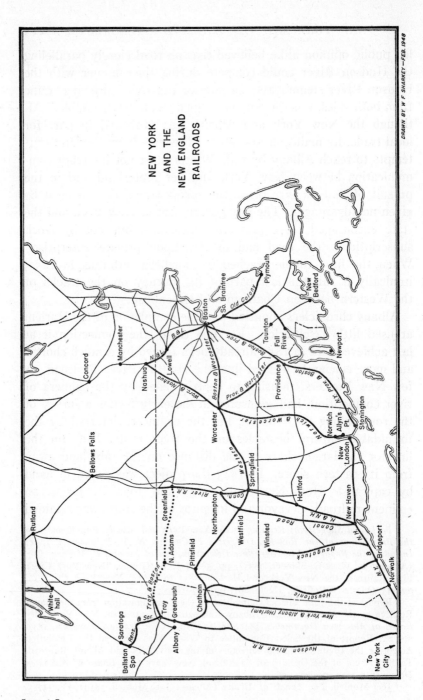

NEW YORK
AND THE
NEW ENGLAND
RAILROADS

DRAWN BY W. F. SHARKEY—FEB. 1948

to explore a shore-line route. He pronounced it favorable. An application for a charter aroused the intense opposition of the Harlem route and legislators were asked how the finances for two routes could be found when subscriptions for one were insufficient. A charter was, however, granted in 1846 and in the following year the road was organized. Actual construction again demonstrated the fallibility of engineering estimates. To secure a relatively straight road bays, whose mud seemed bottomless, had to be crossed by fills, and stony headlands had to be pierced by deep cuts or tunnels. Though contractors were not used to these novel conditions and cholera interrupted the work, it was at last completed in 1851. As the road progressed northward, it proved its ability to compete with steamboats at a price, and its engineer calculated to his satisfaction that it could carry passengers from Albany to New York at a profit.[6] Like the Harlem, it secured a business. As investments, however, both roads were far inferior to the Massachusetts lines they were built to combat. But with the Erie Railroad they checkmated Boston's seasonal superiority in the western trade.

When the Hudson and the Harlem reached Greenbush, Albany, and Troy, they touched the most extensive railroad system of New York State. A series of roads already paralleled the Erie Canal to Buffalo and others were about to connect the Hudson by rail with Lake Champlain or with the Vermont railroad system projected from Boston and designed to bring western Vermont into the commercial orbit of that city. Thus these northern and eastern lines were timely reinforcements in the fight to preserve for New York the trade of northwestern New England. Hostility to Boston was not, however, the reason for their construction; the commercial ambitions of Troy and Albany built them. In the thirties both places had struck out for Whitehall, the southern terminus of navigation on Lake Champlain. In a decade still thinking in terms of water transportation, the choice was logical. The routes, however, were indirect.

The Albanians, utilizing the Mohawk and Hudson from Al-

[6] John B. Jervis, "The Hudson River Railroad: A Sketch of Its History, and Prospective Influence on the Railway Movement," *Hunt's Merchants' Magazine and Commercial Review*, XXII (1850), 278–288.

bany to Schenectady, built northeastward from the latter place through Saratoga Springs to Whitehall. For their part the Trojans in 1832 secured a charter for the Rensselaer and Saratoga Railroad. Like a lance, this was driven north to Ballston Spa on Albany's Schenectady-Whitehall line, to intercept the flow of commerce for Troy's benefit.[7] The Albanians were apparently caught nodding. Now thoroughly awakened to the menace, they detected possibilities of obstruction; the Rensselaer and Saratoga had to bridge the Hudson on its course to Ballston Spa; such a bridge would interfere with the navigation of the river and could be authorized only by the Federal government. These objections the Supreme Court of New York in 1836 swept aside by finding that the bridge was not an obstruction like a dam; it was only a "partial obstacle" which "the best interests of society may render necessary." Furthermore the state had never expressly surrendered to the central government the responsibility for determining the expediency of bridges over navigable rivers.[8]

Though this decision, People v. The Rensselaer and Saratoga Railroad Company, furnished a precedent quoted for three decades in every controversial bridge case in New England and New York, its more immediate importance was to make the Rensselaer and Saratoga an effective railroad instrument for Troy. When a portion of Albany's line fell upon evil times, the champions of Troy purchased it. At the northern extremity they had already built eastward from Whitehall to Rutland, where over the Rutland and Burlington they obtained by 1851 an all-rail route to northern Vermont, northern New York, and Montreal.[9] The New York legislature was determined that neither its traditional water communications nor the railroad newcomer should be at a disadvantage with Boston's Great Northern Route. When the Northern of New York secured permission to extend its piers at Rouse's Point, the bill stipulated that "the corporation

[7] Poor, History of the Railroads and Canals of the United States, pp. 218–219, 303, 308–310.
[8] The People v. The Rensselaer and Saratoga Railroad Company, 15 Wendell, 113.
[9] Poor, History of the Railroads and Canals of the United States, pp. 76–77; F. W. Powell, "Two Experiments in Public Ownership of Steam Railroads," Quarterly Journal of Economics, XXIII (1909), 139.

shall charge no more for transportation of property of the same class over their railroad, when the same is going to or from the city of New York, or other city on the Hudson river, than when going to or from the city of Boston." [10]

Although Troy thus continued to possess her traditional northern commerce, there were several disadvantages to the route by which she did so. The line, swinging westward in an arc, was hardly a direct one to Rutland. The link between Saratoga and Whitehall, since it was a competitor of the state-controlled and operated Champlain Canal, had for a time been forbidden to carry any freight at all, and later only on the condition of paying to the state tolls equivalent to those levied by the canal.[11] One route to Vermont and Canada, particularly a shared one, did not satisfy either Albany or Troy. In finding remedies Troy was in the van. Disgruntled at her earlier failure to become the terminus for Massachusetts' Western, she had been busy for a decade with various abortive projects to improve transportation along the Hoosic Valley.[12] In the mid-forties these projects were given a more extensive character, as the Massachusetts promoters of the Hoosac Tunnel and the Hoosac route promised Troy that at last she should realize her ambition of becoming a railroad junction on a great through route between Boston and the West. The railroad oligarchy of Troy was stirred to enthusiasm. In 1849 they organized the Troy and Boston Railroad and raised $500,000 to invest in its securities. Though the project waited long for the promised tunneling of Hoosac Mountain, two roads, from different junction points on the Troy and Boston, ran northward to Rutland. They traversed the marble and slate districts of Vermont, tapped the extensive wool-growing areas north of Rutland, and by way of Rutland opened a

[10] *Laws of the State of New York, Passed at the Seventy-fourth Session of the Legislature . . . 1851*, pp. 681–682.

[11] *Laws of the State of New York Passed at the Fifty-seventh Session of the Legislature, . . . 1834*, p. 442; *Laws of the State of New York Passed at the Seventy-first Session of the Legislature, . . . 1848*, p. 84; *Laws of the State of New York Passed at the Seventy-fourth Session of the Legislature, . . . 1851*, p. 927; Vermont *House Journal, 1852*, pp. 348–352.

[12] Report on Petition for a McAdam Turnpike and Railroad from Troy, New York *Assembly Documents*, 1831, no. 186; *Laws of the State of New York Passed at the Fifty-fourth Session of the Legislature, . . . 1831*, pp. 225–232.

route 249 miles long to Boston.[13] An alarmed Albany built a parallel to the Troy and Boston, sought to buy northern connections, and loaned $300,000 in city bonds to one of the resulting misbegotten enterprises to keep it out of the hands of the Trojans. Otherwise Troy would control all three routes to Vermont and Canada and "we should have been effectively cut off from all communication with the North and East." [14] At least that was the assumption of the Albanians.

The construction of these many routes was business folly. Retribution was not long in coming. Although roadbeds, bridges, and rails were flimsy and cheap, nearly every road had cost too much to wring a return from available traffic. While main stems like the Rensselaer and Saratoga and the Troy and Boston succeeded in keeping out of bankruptcy and certain leased short lines continued to pay rent to their owners, the rest fell into receiverships or outright bankruptcies. They emerged renamed and often with capital structures still unsound. It was even possible for a road to cease running trains for months with extraordinarily little protest.[15] But this tornado of insolvency cleared the ground for a consolidation of these petty competitors. The process gave Jay Gould, a former hardware merchant, surveyor, and tanner, his first training in the profits and pleasures of railroad speculation.[16] It also marked the final victory of Troy. The Rensselaer and Saratoga leased connections into southwestern Vermont, in-

---

[13] Poor, *History of the Railroads and Canals of the United States*, pp. 76, 81–82, 317–318, 320; Vermont *House Journal*, 1855, pp. 701–742; *Pathfinder Railway Guide. New England States, October 1852-2d Edition* (Boston: Geo. K. Snow, n.d.), pp. 64, 67; *Second Annual Report of the Directors of the Troy and Boston Rail-Road Company, Made January 13, 1852* (Troy: C. L. MacArthur's Steam Press, 1852), pp. 5–8, 10.

[14] *Report of the Commissioners of the Albany Northern Rail Road Loan, Made to the Common Council of the City of Albany, April 14, 1856* (Albany: J. Munsell, 1856), pp. 3, 5–6.

[15] *Report of the Trustees of the Rutland & Washington R.R. April 1, 1859* (Rutland: Cain & McLean, 1859), pp. 7–9; *Copy of a Memorial to the Legislature of the Managers and Trustees of the Rutland & Burlington Rail Road* (Rutland: Tuttle, Gay & Co., 1865), pp. 4–8; *First Annual Report of the Railroad Commissioner of the State of Vermont to the General Assembly*, 1856, p. 9.

[16] Murat Halstead and J. Frank Beale, *Life of Jay Gould. How He Made His Millions. The Marvellous Career of the Man Who, in Thirty Years, Accumulated the Colossal Fortune of $100,000,000, By Far Exceeding in Rapidity and Volume That of Any Other Man in the History of the World* (Philadelphia: Edgewood

cluding Albany's last effort, and the Troy and Boston took the rest. As if to flaunt her railroad supremacy, Troy had already built a magnificent union depot 400 feet long with eight tracks, the largest in the world it was said, with the possible exception of one in Russia.[17] The glory was not for long. The completion of the Harlem and the Hudson River Railroads meant the intrusion of New York City into the competitive nexus of the upper Hudson; that metropolis had little interest in the tiny rivalries between Albany and Troy. The successful chartering of a bridge across the Hudson at Albany, as we saw in an earlier chapter, foreshadowed the identification of these upstate roads with the destiny of New York City. After the Civil War, as Vanderbilt displaced or diminished local control and the Delaware and Hudson consolidated its northern system, the process was complete.

II

Almost on New York's threshold stood Connecticut, New England's second state in wealth and population, and one ripe for railroad invasion. Curiously enough, as a state it had displayed for years neither feeling nor policy about the new means of transportation. While Massachusetts through boards and commissioners was systematically exploring the possibilities of the railroad and surveying desirable routes, Connecticut was passive. While frontier communities like Vermont and Maine were organizing a railroad excitement, Connecticut was still passive. As late as 1838, three years after the pioneer three of Massachusetts were in operation, a committee of the Connecticut legislature pointed out that the state did not have a single important railroad line completed. "The ocean and the Stonington Rail Road on the east, the Western Rail Road on the north, the Hudson River on the west, and Long Island Sound on the south,

Publishing Company, 1892), pp. 55–56; Gustavus Myers, *History of the Great American Fortunes* (Chicago: Charles H. Kerr & Company, 1910), II, 265.

[17] *Hunt's Merchants' Magazine and Commercial Review*, XXXII (1855), 769–770; *Memorial to the Legislature of the . . . Rutland & Burlington Rail Road*, pp. 4–8; *Corporate History of Delaware and Hudson Company and Subsidiary Companies*, IV, 284–289, 306–308, 324–329, 520–533, 541–543, 566–585, 589–594.

leave Connecticut entirely insulated." [18]   Perhaps a partial explanation for her tardiness and indifference was the nature of Connecticut manufacturing, small products, or the conservatism of her inhabitants.[19] More important was the apparent adequacy of existing means of transportation. Connecticut had Long Island Sound, New England's greatest river, the Connecticut, New England's longest and feeblest canal, the Farmington, and on the Sound and on the rivers she had an enlarging steam navigation. An elaborate system of turnpikes covered the comparatively short distances of the state and created a powerful vested interest to ally with the steamboat owners against the railroad and the locomotive.

Finally in 1838 the state legislature directed a belated attention to the importance of a railroad system. Connecticut should no longer be "unmindful of her honor and real interest." Railroads would first of all stay the course of emigration from the state and keep within its borders the "enterprise, energy, and indomitable perseverance" with which her sons were now dowering upper New York and the states of the West. Furthermore "the benefit to the community at large, by diminishing the cost of transportation, is very great and very general. It will greatly diminish the expense of the manufacturer of carrying forward his business, and every barrel of flour carried on the Rail Road can be afforded to the consumer at a diminished price. Besides increasing the taxable property of the State, the benefits of these enterprises, in one form or another, is felt in the most remote and humble dwelling in the State." It required an emergency to shake Connecticut as a state into an appreciation of these truisms. The panic of 1837 had fallen like a blight upon the few railroads private enterprise had undertaken. Now only state credit could save them. The committee advocated, therefore, state loans to roads, already graded, for the purchase and con-

---

[18] Connecticut General Assembly *Report of the Joint Committee on Internal Improvements* (New Haven: Hitchcock & Stafford, 1838), p. 19.

[19] Jarvis M. Morse, *A Neglected Period of Connecticut's History, 1818–1850* (New Haven: Yale University Press, 1933), pp. 270–273, 276–277; Sidney Withington, *The First Twenty Years of Railroads in Connecticut* (New Haven: Yale University Press, 1935), p. 2.

struction of rails, depots, cars, and engines; in no case, was the grant by the state to exceed one-third the total expenditure on the road. Throughout their report, which the legislature failed to follow, the committee relied upon the experience of "noble Massachusetts." She had loaned her credit to railroads; she was building the Western, which would confer immense benefits upon the Connecticut roads once they made connections with it.[20] Yet there was no hint that Connecticut should rival Massachusetts; it should simply imitate her. This dependent relationship, easily formed, persisted through the century. In railroad matters Connecticut was no pioneer.

However laggard state policy might be, urban rivalries operated in Connecticut as elsewhere, and such rivalries naturally centered in the ports of southern Connecticut, which aspired to exploit the resources and enlarge the areas of their hinterlands. There also were the rich men with the money to invest in railroads, and, if their wealth were not forthcoming, perhaps the communities would be willing to place their credit at the disposal of transportation enterprises. The Farmington Canal had pointed the way. The other problem was one of geography. But the location of the ports and the topographical conformation of the state clearly delineated the routes Connecticut's earliest railroads should follow. They were to run inland along her valleys: until a later era they were, with few exceptions, north and south railroads. They did not encounter, therefore, the topographical obstacles that those in Massachusetts and northern New England had met.

Although the state's first charters did little more than fray her eastern border with railroads, her equivalent to the pioneer three in Massachusetts, her Concord, Vermont Central, and Portland, Saco and Portsmouth was the Hartford and New Haven. Between these two largest cities of Connecticut a railroad seemed necessary and desirable; the stage coach or a circuitous water navigation was their only connection and between them lay a multitude of towns eager for improved transportation. Yet Hartford had reservations. While it was doubtless advantageous to

[20] *Report of the Joint Committee on Internal Improvements*, pp. 17, 18, 19, 20–21.

carry the local business between Hartford and New Haven more
expeditiously and to have New Haven as a winter port when
the river was frozen, the prospect that the through business, particularly in passengers, would embark at New Haven for New
York the year round was disturbing. It threatened Hartford's
position as entrepôt of the Connecticut Valley. New Haven
likewise had objections. On paper the road did not seem as
serviceable an instrument of competition with Hartford as the
Farmington Canal. It did not tap the down-river commerce
above the latter city; if it were extended, it would still drain the
Connecticut traffic through Hartford. Still another interest was
opposed. The Hartford and New Haven Turnpike, though pro-
fessing a desire not "to stay the rise of improvement so characteristic of the Republic," disliked losing its investment of
$100,000 and opposed a charter "to foreigners who have no in-
terest in the proposed railroad but speculation." [21]

Dismissing these petty fears, the legislature in 1833 granted
a charter for a road to run by "the most direct and feasible
route" from Hartford to the "navigable waters" of New Haven
harbor. In some respects this document contrasted interestingly
with contemporaneous charters in the other New England states.
While provisions for a fixed capitalization of $100 shares, in-
stallment buying, taking of land, and charging "tolls" were un-
exceptional, it granted no monopoly of the route, contained no
limitation upon profits or threats of recapture by the state, and,
expressing no suspicion of concentrated control, authorized a
vote for each share and proxy voting. Its only significant limitation upon rates was that the directors should fix them in March,
publish them in the press, and not raise them for a year thereafter.[22] Two years later the company had been organized and
the line had been surveyed. The latter task was entrusted to
Alexander C. Twining, the Connecticut equivalent of Hayward,
James Baldwin, or McNeill. His background resembled Hayward's. After graduation from Yale, Twining had had academic

[21] Petition of the Hartford and New Haven Turnpike, 1832, Ms., Connecticut
Archives, State Capitol, Hartford.

[22] *Resolves and Private Laws of the State of Connecticut, from the Year 1789
to the Year 1836*, II, 1002–1005.

interludes as a teacher of mathematics and natural philosophy, a career which he ultimately discarded for one in engineering. He had studied the subject at West Point.[23]

In fulfilling one of his duties on the Hartford and New Haven, the adjudication of the controversial claims of the villages along the line, Twining swung away from the Connecticut and ran the road directly overland, some thirty-six miles, to New Haven. As engineer, he also had to serve as promoter and prophet. Hesitant in the face of effective water transportation, he relied upon passenger travel for the bulk of the returns and assigned the heaviest freight carriage to the winter months. The road, of course, was to be no local enterprise. When the proposed extensions to Springfield and to Worcester were completed, the Hartford and New Haven would participate in the "long travel" between Boston and New York. It would invade the manufacturing traffics of northern Connecticut and southern Massachusetts. "Their raw material is now received by way of Providence and of Boston, and their manufactured articles returned to a southern market by the same route; but if an opening to New-Haven were created, this tonnage would fall into that new channel, both because its market is south, (at New-York and Philadelphia,) and because the saving of insurance from Boston to those cities, would pay a large proportion of the entire freight to New-Haven." [24]

Since Boston could hardly approve the road, books for subscriptions were not opened there. This privilege was confined to Hartford, New Haven, and New York; the response in each revealed significant gradations of enthusiasm. Though Hartford capitalists invested $227,000 and New Haven and New York $1,200,000, the subscriptions of New York alone were enough to build the road at the cost — $830,000 — estimated by Twining.[25]

[23] *Dictionary of American Biography* (New York: Charles Scribner's Sons, 1928–1936), XIX, 83–84.

[24] *Report of the Engineer, Upon the Preliminary Surveys for the Hartford and New-Haven Rail-Road* (New Haven: J. Peck, 1835), pp. 25–30.

[25] Morse, *A Neglected Period*, p. 273; *Report of the Engineer . . . for the Hartford and New-Haven*, pp. 29–30; *American Railroad Journal*, IV (1835), 481.

Almost immediately these happy auspices turned unfavorable. New York's great fire of 1835 resulted in the cancellation of subscriptions, the depression of 1837 slowed the payment of assessments. The chief financial burden then descended upon James Brewster of New Haven, a carriage manufacturer with a fortune and a zeal for railroads, who retired from his business to raise the funds for the Hartford and New Haven.[26] The legislature refused state aid. "Failing in this resource, the Directors turned their attention to capitalists, who lend as a matter of business, and not from benevolence or patriotism." [27] Within this category, unhappily the Bank of the United States at Philadelphia was not interested. In New York the directors induced the American Life Insurance and Trust Company to take $150,000 of its bonds; the Insurance Company was to pay through the sale of its own securities in London. The arrangement broke down when the latter possibility evaporated. Finally the road was completed in 1839 by short-time loans at 9 to 10½ per cent per annum secured from the Hartford banks.[28] Added to its financial difficulties was a quarrel with the Connecticut River Steamboat Company which, as the master of the all-water route between Hartford and New Haven, bought up the steamboat connections between New Haven and New York to prevent the railroad from participating in the through travel. In retaliation the Hartford and New Haven obtained from the legislature the right to own its own vessels.[29]

Though for a time the road did not live up to its early promise as a money maker, in the fifties it entered a decade of uninterrupted prosperity. By then extensions had made it a part of a

[26] George D. Watrous, "Travel and Transportation," Edward E. Atwater, ed., *History of the City of New Haven to the Present Time* (New York: W. W. Munsell & Co., 1887), pp. 360–362, 558–560.

[27] *Third Annual Report of the Board of Directors, to the Stockholders of the Hartford and New-Haven Rail-Road Company* (New Haven: Hitchcock & Stafford, 1838), p. 6.

[28] *Fifth Annual Report of the Board of Directors, to the Stockholders of the Hartford and New Haven Railroad Co.* (New Haven: Hitchcock & Stafford, 1840), pp. 4–8.

[29] *Fourth Annual Report of the Board of Directors, to the Stockholders of the Hartford and New Haven Railroad Company* (New Haven: Hitchcock & Stafford, 1839), pp. 7–9.

great through route. It had reached Springfield on the Western in 1844 and then moved northward by the Connecticut River Railroad and by others until it joined in 1851 with the diagonal roads across Vermont.[30] The route to Canada, which had bemused dreamers in the canal era, was at last secured. The line, moreover, mirrored the expansion of New York capitalist control. On the Hartford and New Haven by the late forties, though Connecticut still had the majority representation, the New York interest was represented, among others by Cornelius Vanderbilt and Elisha Peck, the latter a Hartford product who became a New York shipowner, industrialist, and investor. The directorate of the Connecticut River Railroad, however, included no New Yorkers. Hartford, Northampton, and Springfield were represented; the largest group was from Boston and their connection with the Western was close.[31]

Though the Farmington Canal route had apparently been superseded by the Hartford and New Haven, the former still captured the imagination and loyalties of some New Haven men. The chief was Joseph E. Sheffield, who had as a Connecticut youth gone South and ultimately acquired a fortune from the trade in naval stores and cotton. Solicitude for his wife's health and a dislike for slavery moved him to leave the South in 1835 and settle in New Haven. In philanthropy and in business he became its leading citizen. The old canal first attracted his interest. He became its largest stockholder and supporter, and he was the first to suggest its replacement by a railroad.[32] At this point Connecticut's Alexander C. Twining made the essential survey. His resulting report was devoted to the demonstration, quite understandable under the circumstances, that a railroad

[30] Joseph G. Martin, *A Century of Finance. Martin's History of the Boston Stock and Money Markets, One Hundred Years. From January, 1798 to January, 1898* (Boston: J. G. Martin, 1898), pp. 147, 149; Poor, *History of the Railroads and Canals of the United States*, pp. 80, 108, 127.

[31] *Eleventh Annual Report of the Board of Directors, to the Stockholders of the Hartford and New Haven Rail Road Company* (Hartford: Case, Tiffany & Burnham, 1846), p. 4; Annual Report of the Railroad Corporations in the State of Massachusetts, Massachusetts *Senate Documents*, 1850, no. 30, p. 52.

[32] Joseph E. Sheffield, Memoranda, Dresden, Saxony, Nov. 1856, pp. 3–8; Dresden, January, 1857, pp. 9–10, Ms., Sheffield Papers, Yale University Library.

could succeed where a canal had failed; both particular instances, like the Boston and Lowell, and generalized reasoning proved it. Such comfort, however, could not conceal the fact that the projected enterprise had no certain northern terminus.[33] Whether it should continue into Massachusetts to Westfield and Northampton as had the canal or move westward to Pittsfield and toward the American West depended upon charters from the Massachusetts legislature and its preliminary success as a local Connecticut railroad. Nonetheless, Sheffield was challenged. Inspired, at least according to later recollection, by civic spirit he invested heavily in the new enterprise.[34] In 1846 construction commenced.[35]

A decade of vexation ensued. Engineering difficulties were easily surmounted; but the financial burden seemed unbearable. When the men of vision among her politicians and intellectuals sought to excite private subscriptions or to commit New Haven to a municipal loan of $200,000, they met with rebuff. A committee, headed by Benjamin Silliman, dangling the vision of Vermont and Canada before the incredulous eyes of their fellow citizens, announced, "This is a crisis in the history of our city. By prompt action, we can secure a prosperity such as we have never had, and open resources of trade such as we have never possessed: by supineness we lose the whole." Private investors hung back. To the arguments for municipal aid the opponents simply countered the unhappy history of New Haven's aid to the Farmington. The recital sufficed.[36] Meanwhile the decision of the road's sponsors to build their line to some point on the Connecticut River angered the Hartford and New Haven. The activities of that latter corporation prevented Massachusetts from

[33] *Engineer's Report on the Survey from New Haven City up the Canal to Plainville, and Thence to Collinsville, in the Farmington Valley* (New Haven: Hitchcock & Stafford, 1845), pp. 3–11.

[34] Sheffield, Memoranda, Dresden, January, 1857; Retrospective March 1876, Ms., Sheffield Papers.

[35] *Eleventh Annual Report of the New Haven and Northampton Company. January 20, 1847* (New Haven: Peck & Stafford, 1847), pp. 3–4.

[36] Committee of 23, Appeals in Favor of Subscriptions to the New Haven and Northampton Railroad, Broadside; Circular, The New Haven Railroad, Broadside; To Our Fellow Citizens, Canal Road and Taxation, Broadside.

granting the necessary charter and persuaded the New York and New Haven, to which Sheffield had leased as much of the New Haven and Northampton, or the Canal Road, as had been built, to oppose its completion. Distracted by these petty frustrations, Sheffield turned to the construction of railroads in the Middle West.[37]

When he returned to New Haven a few years later affairs wore a happier prospect. Sheffield financed the completion of the route to Northampton in 1856 [38] and leased this last link forthwith to the New Haven and Northampton, itself already under lease to the New York and New Haven.[39] Apparently New Haven at last had its own line to the interior. But only for a moment. Agreements between the Hartford and New Haven and the New York and New Haven closed the route, from time to time, to through traffic. In retrospect Sheffield saw only personal loss and civic dishonor. He regretted that the sneers of his fellow citizens and the taunts from Hartford rivals — "Sheffield has got to the end of his tether" — had driven him to a costly participation in the Canal Road.[40] Those who did not have access to his private despondencies felt Sheffield was hardly the philanthropist. His successive leases to the New York and New Haven gave the Canal Road an annual rental of $3600 for its tracks in New Haven, an actual return of 9 per cent upon the cost of the road to Plainville, and an attractive rental upon the rest of its trackage in Connecticut.[41] Though the New Haven and

[37] Sheffield, Memoranda, Dresden, January, 1857, pp. 12–14; Recollections of My Early Connection with the New York and New Haven Railroad Co., April, 1880, Ms., Sheffield Papers, pp. 7–9; *Twelfth Annual Report (Second under the New Charter) of the New Haven and Northampton Company. (Canal and Railroad.) January 19, 1848* (New Haven: Peck & Stafford, 1848), pp. 4–5; *Fourteenth Annual Report (Fourth under the Railroad Charter) of the New Haven and Northampton Company, June 4, 1850* (New Haven: T. J. Stafford, 1850), pp. 3–5, 9–11.

[38] Joseph E. Sheffield, Continuation of Memoranda, New Haven, March, 1875, Ms., Sheffield Papers.

[39] Poor, *History of Canals and Railroads in the United States*, p. 126.

[40] Sheffield, Continuation of Memoranda, New Haven, March, 1875.

[41] *The Report of the Board of Directors to the Stockholders of the New-York and New-Haven Rail Road Co., 22 August, 1849* (New York: H. Cogswell & Co., 1849), pp. 11–13; *To the President and Directors of the New York and New Haven Railroad by a Stockholder of the New York and New Haven Railroad, Boston,*

Northampton had been a one-man enterprise, its lease to the New York and New Haven placed its management in the New York interest.

III

When Silliman and his civic-minded colleagues were attempting to convince their indifferent fellow citizens to rescue the Canal Road, they referred often to the example of New London and of Bridgeport. The latter city, though not at the mouth of the Housatonic, had easy access to that river which, running first northwestward and then north, drained the western portion of the state and continued into Massachusetts. The tributary territory was rich in water powers and raw materials. The marble belt of Massachusetts had furnished the building material for Girard College and the New York City Hall; the furnaces and forges of the unique specialized iron region of northwestern Connecticut-southwestern Massachusetts generated "a whole transportation, connected with and growing out of the iron trade" of 20,000 tons annually and paid rates of five to seven dollars a ton for carrying its product to navigable waters; the lime kilns of the valley turned out a product so fine that it could carry twice as much sand in plaster as ordinary lime. Finally, over Massachusetts roads a connection could be secured with the Western Railway.[42] In 1836 the state chartered the Housatonic Railroad: it was to run southward from the Connecticut-Massachusetts line and of three specified southern terminals or connections Bridgeport was one.[43]

Frantic to win the prize, Bridgeport secured a city charter and immediately subscribed $100,000 to the railroad; this sum was increased by $50,000 in 1838. Bridgeport transferred its bonds

---

Feb. 3, 1848; William Johnson, *To the Stockholders of the New York and New Haven Railroad by William Johnson, President of the New Haven and Northampton, 1855.*

[42] *First Annual Report of the Board of Directors, to the Stockholders of the Housatonic Rail-Road Company* (New Haven: Hitchcock & Stafford, 1838), pp. 21–27.

[43] *Resolves and Private Laws of the State of Connecticut, from the Year 1789 to the Year 1836,* II, 1025–1033.

to the railroad; the railroad its stock to Bridgeport. At the outset, also, the firm that secured the construction contract subscribed in work and materials to $300,000 worth of stock — and this firm contained Alfred Bishop.[44] Bishop was the Sheffield of Bridgeport. In the words of his associates, he was a man of "clear perception, strong judgment, never-failing energy, great experience and unstained integrity." Not trade nor manufacturing but agriculture was his background. As a farmer in New Jersey, he made "personal experiments with his pick-axe, shovel, and wheelbarrow, by which he accurately estimated the cost of removing various masses of earth to different distances" and, with this basic knowledge, he developed into a contractor for canals and railroads. Among the latter were the Housatonic and the Naugatuck.[45] The Naugatuck, for which Bishop furnished three-quarters of the means, was Bridgeport's second avenue into the interior. Built after 1845 along the Housatonic and its affluent, the Naugatuck, it, too, sought raw materials but found its greatest traffic in the prosperous brass industry of the valley which it followed.[46]

In December 1842 the cars of the Housatonic Railroad passed over connecting lines to a junction with Massachusetts' Western. Seven years later the Naugatuck was completed to a dead end in northern Connecticut.[47] The financial history of the two roads was as different as their charters. The local road prospered.[48] The Housatonic, the through route, was in trouble from the first; and consequently Bridgeport learned earlier than most American cities the ultimate costs of railroad promotion. Convinced she

---

[44] *First Annual Report . . . of the Housatonic Rail-Road*, pp. 4–5, 10–12; Samuel Orcutt, *A History of the Old Town of Stratford and the City of Bridgeport, Connecticut* (New Haven: Tuttle, Morehouse & Taylor, 1886), II, 696; The City of Bridgeport *v*. The Housatonic Rail-Road Company, 15, *Connecticut*, 475.

[45] Orcutt, *A History . . . of Bridgeport*, II, 697–698; *The Report of the Board of Directors to the Stockholders of the New-York and New-Haven Rail Road Co., 22 August, 1849*, p. 7.

[46] *Second Annual Report of the Board of Directors to the Stockholders of the Naugatuck Railroad Company, February 18, 1850* (New Haven: J. H. Benham, 1850), pp. 5, 8–10.

[47] Poor, *History of the Canals and Railroads of the United States*, pp. 201, 203.

[48] *Annual Report of the President and Directors of the Naugatuck Railroad Company, to the Stockholders, at their Annual Meeting, February, 1861* (Bridgeport: Pomeroy and Morse, 1861), p. 5.

was starting on an adventure whose outcome must be favorable, she made no provision for paying either the interest or the principal of her railroad advances; after the panic of 1837 she defaulted. City officials shrugged the situation aside, until a creditor of the city put an execution in the hands of the sheriff. That powerful financier broke into the stores of private citizens and sold groceries and dry goods to meet the bill. When the Supreme Court of Connecticut declared this levy upon private property legal, the city government imposed taxes and set aside a sinking fund to liquidate its railroad experiment.[49]

Such local lessons did not conceal the fact that Bridgeport's railroads were New York's railroads. New Yorkers filtered into their directorates. The Naugatuck ran out of Bridgeport on the tracks of the New York and New Haven.[50] Along with the Housatonic, the former directed its traffic toward New York and received its commerce from the same source. The Housatonic indeed played a more intimate rôle in New York's prosperity. In 1840 a committee of Bridgeport citizens, appealing to New Yorkers for help, promised the Housatonic, by steamboat and rail, as a year-round connection between New York and Albany. Though the Harlem, a road with prior demands on New York's loyalty, was at the moment presenting similar claims, a committee from the Board of Aldermen could scarcely imagine "a more eligible route for a railroad" than the one proposed for the Housatonic. It was also "the means of a perfect temporary communication between our two principal cities, in ample time to preserve our domestic trade from encroachment by the Boston capitalists, should it become apparent that that object cannot be fully accomplished by the immediate completion of the New York and Albany."[51] Since no direct all-rail route reached Albany until 1851, the Housatonic was New York's winter link with the Hudson River capital until that date. The through freight, however,

[49] Orcutt, A History . . . of Bridgeport, II, 696; Beardsley v. Smith, 16 Connecticut, 368.

[50] Poor, History of Canals and Railroads of the United States, pp. 201, 203.

[51] Report of the Joint Special Committee of the Boards of the Common Council, on a Communication from a Committee of Citizens of Bridgeport, New York City Board of Aldermen Documents, 1849, no. 11, pp. 160, 164–165.

was not as large as that on the Western nor did it perceptibly ease the acute financial agonies of the Housatonic itself.[52]

IV

Beyond the estuary of the Thames and the valleys which continued it inland, New York invaded an area where Boston was both resolved and able to meet her challenge. Here lay, first of all, the two eastern counties of Connecticut, a center of manufacturing. Norwich and New London were their ports; and the growing industrial and railroad city of Worcester, just to the north, was the natural terminus of projected railways. Then came Rhode Island, slightly larger than the Connecticut counties bordering her on the west. In spite of the wealth and ambition of Providence, Rhode Island was a state almost without a railroad history, a mute, inglorious, no-man's land over which the titans of New York and Boston fought for railroad control. Finally there was southeastern Massachusetts. Together its three counties — Norfolk, Plymouth, and Bristol — far exceeded the area of Rhode Island; when crooked Barnstable, the county of the Cape, was added, this Massachusetts region had more than twice as many square miles as Little Rhody. All formed an industrialized district. From the first Boston had served notice of her intent to keep a commercial hold upon these prizes to her south. Of the pioneer three, the Boston and Providence had been the instrument forged for the purpose, one which had at the same time to be reconciled with the aim of forming with the steamboats an improved avenue for the New York-Boston travel and traffic.

In the early days this second objective moved to the forefront of the enterprise. The Boston and Providence extended in Massachusetts only to the eastern shore of the Seekonk River; a Rhode Island corporation, the Boston and Providence Railroad and

[52] *Disturnell's Guide Through the Middle, Northern, and Eastern States; Containing a Description of the Principal Places; Canal, Railroad, and Steamboat Routes; Tables of Distances, Etc.* (New York: J. Disturnell, 1848), p. 39; *Annual Report of the Directors of the Housatonic Rail Road Company, to the Stockholders, at Their Annual Meeting in November, 1847* (New York: H. Cogswell, 1848), pp. 11–12.

Transportation Company, provided a bridge across the river, tracks through the city, and a depot with wharves on deep water at India Point; the Boston and New York Transportation Company built or purchased and operated the connecting vessels to New York. This steamboat concern leased the wharves of the Rhode Island corporation and entered into an exclusive agreement with the Boston and Providence by which the latter agreed to run its steamboat trains solely in connection with the Boston and New York Transportation Company.[53] Interlocking directorates sealed the alliance. Moses Brown Ives and Charles Potter of Providence were directors in both the steamboat company and the Rhode Island railroad. Potter was also on the directorate of the Boston and Providence of Massachusetts. Charles H. Russell and William W. Woolsey, both of New York, were in the steamboat company and also directors of the Boston and Providence Railroad. In 1835 and 1836, of the seven directors of the Boston and Providence Railroad, four were New Yorkers; of the 15,000 shares in the concern, less than 500 were enrolled in the Boston stock books, though the president of the line asserted this was not a true measure of the Boston stock interest. Incidentally the contract between the steamboats and the Boston and Providence was signed by the presidents of both concerns, Charles H. Russell of New York for the former and William W. Woolsey of New York for the latter.[54]

No wonder the road distressed true Bostonians. In 1840 E. H. Derby, incident to his campaign for low fares on the Western, rapped it over the knuckles. The Boston and Providence was prosperous because it had derived "an immense patronage from the steamboat competition on the Sound." It had not, however, won southeastern New England for Boston. "When the Providence trader can come to Boston and buy his goods at less expense of time and money than at New York, he will come often, will buy large quantities of merchandise here, and send it home

---

[53] Report of the Committee on Railways and Canals Relative to the Seekonk Railroad, Massachusetts *Senate Documents*, 1836, no. 89, pp. 34–47.

[54] *Ibid.*, p. 47; Report of the Joint Special Committee Appointed to Investigate the Doings of the Boston and Providence Railroad Corporation, Massachusetts *Senate Documents*, 1840, no. 50, pp. 18–19.

over the road, which he is deterred from doing now by the high rate of charges. At present he can send his goods from New York to Providence, 180 miles, for less than one-half the price charged for 43 miles only on the Boston road; and who sees a Providence customer in Boston? This road, for the purposes of commerce, has thus far been of little or no service to Boston, and one might almost imagine he can see a New York influence in its management." [55] However true the facts, the explanation was too narrow a one; it ignored the relative costs of water and land transportation and the whole nexus of railroad-steamboat competition on the Sound.

Even as Derby was making the charge, the control of the Boston and Providence was returning to the state of its birth. Josiah Quincy, Jr., became its president; Bostonians formed a majority of its directorate; and the shareholders and shares connected with Boston increased. Eventually the New York transfer office was closed for lack of business.[56] Meanwhile the road acquired important extensions. Taunton, once rejected as a terminus for the south-bound road from Boston, almost at once secured a "Branch" from the Boston and Providence at Mansfield. From Taunton the road was completed to New Bedford in 1840. "Among the items of freight, oil is a large one," commented an investigating committee years later.[57] For an extension to the southwest, the Rhode Island legislature incorporated in 1832 the New York, Providence and Boston. This company, the first important one chartered in Rhode Island, ran from Providence to

---

[55] *Proceedings of the Annual Meeting of the Western Rail-Road Corporation, Held, by Adjournment, in the City of Boston, March 12, 1840, Including the Report of the Committee of Investigation Appointed by the Stockholders* (Boston: Dutton and Wentworth, 1840), pp. 46-47.

[56] Massachusetts *Senate Documents*, 1840, no. 50, pp. 18-19; *Statement by the Boston and Providence Rail Road Corporation, in Explanation of Their Proceedings in Relation to the Steam Boats* (Boston: John H. Eastburn, 1838), p. 5; Eleventh Annual Report of the Boston and Providence Railroad, Massachusetts *Senate Documents*, 1843, no. 31, p. 60.

[57] Poor, *History of the Railroads and Canals of the United States*, pp. 138, 154; *Report of the Committee for Investigating the Affairs of the Boston and Providence Railroad Corporation, Appointed by the Stockholders, January 9, 1856* (Boston: J. H. Eastburn, 1856), pp. 12-14; *Annual Report of the Directors of the Boston and Providence Rail Road Corporation with That of the Agent and Engineer. January 2, 1833* (Boston: Dutton and Wentworth, 1833), pp. 9-10.

the southwest corner of the state; a company in Connecticut, temporarily separate, extended the line a few miles to Stonington, Connecticut. To the Stonington road, as it was usually called, was given a thirty-year monopoly of the route. Although the state made no provision for recapturing the road, the General Assembly could reduce the tolls if profits exceeded 12 per cent for four years, and the state might subscribe to 1,000 shares of stock. No stockowner could vote more than one-quarter of the stock unless as a proxy for other members.[58] The provisions were in the pattern of the thirties.

The Stonington road had two great advantages. By placing its southern terminus on Long Island Sound, it avoided the circuitous navigation of Narragansett Bay and the dreaded rounding of Point Judith. Thus for its whole journey it had the comparatively sheltered navigation of the Sound.[59] In the second place, the Stonington water and rail line between Boston and New York was by eighteen or twenty miles the shortest between the two places.[60] With speeds what they were then, this figure represented a saving of at least an hour in time. Consequently the railroad troubadours had early been singing the route's praises. Among the most gifted of the tribe was W. G. McNeill, engineer of the Boston and Providence and later engineer and agent of the New York, Providence and Boston. In the former capacity he had prophesied that the "prolongation" from Providence to the Sound would "facilitate the intercourse between Boston and New York, (and this surely will be with capitalists the paramount object, rather than any reliance on the trade from collateral sources)."[61] For an interval some of the capitalists in the road

---

[58] Laws of Rhode Island Passed by the General Assembly at the June Session, 1832, pp. 67–77.

[59] Annual Report, Submitted at the Meeting of the Stockholders of the New York, Providence and Boston Rail Road Company. Convened in the City of Providence, R. I., September 29th, 1840. By Wm. Gibbs McNeil, Engineer and Agent (New York: W. H. Thompson, 1840), pp. 5–8.

[60] Disturnell's Railroad, Steamboat, and Telegraph Book; Being a Guide through the Middle, Northern, and Eastern States, and Canada: . . . Containing Tables of Distances, &c. (New York: J. Disturnell, 1850), pp. 32–37.

[61] Annual Report . . . of the Boston and Providence Rail Road . . . January 2, 1833, pp. 30–31.

were also interested in the rails between Boston and Providence.[62]

By the time the Stonington was completed in 1837, the two enterprises were distinct. They were connected in Providence by a ferry across the Providence River and the Boston and Providence was still so convinced that its interest might be better served by a direct steamboat line to New York that it held back a whole-hearted committal to the Stonington road. The two roads contrasted. The Boston and Providence, a dowager road, was "unencumbered with debt, and always producing adequate returns to the stockholders." [63] The expenses of constructing the New York, Providence and Boston were a scandal. Its fifty miles, through a far from forbidding territory, had taken $1,300,000 in stock and $1,300,000 in bonds. A few years later its debt was even greater.[64] By the mid-forties, however, the two roads became reconciled. Passenger steamboats which had once stopped at Stonington and then gone on to Providence in 1840 made the former their final destination. In 1847 the Boston and Providence and the New York, Providence and Boston secured a rail connection through the streets of Providence.[65] Though the financial history of the latter became more profitable, one contrast still remained. The Boston and Providence was primarily a Boston enterprise; on the New York, Providence and Boston, in spite of a local flavor imparted by the election of a Stonington man as president, the directorate was one of New Yorkers, including at one time or another such famous representatives as Elisha Peck, Daniel Drew, and Cornelius Vanderbilt.[66] Thus after as well as before the railroad, New York influence crossed the threshold of southern New England.

[62] Report of the Joint Special Committee to Investigate the Doings of the Boston and Providence Railroad, Massachusetts *Senate Documents*, 1840, no. 50, p. 18; *Annual Reports of the New York, Providence & Boston R.R, Co., 1833 to 1874. Published by Order of the Directors* (Westerly: G. B. & J. H. Utter, 1874), pp. 3, 4.

[63] *Annual Report, . . . of the New York, Providence and Boston Rail Road . . . September 29th, 1840*, pp. 10–12, 17.

[64] Poor, *History of the Railroads and Canals of the United States*, p. 187.

[65] *Report of the Directors of the Boston & Providence Railroad. Presented at the Annual Meeting of the Stockholders, June 6, 1849* (Boston: Eastburn's Press, 1849), pp. 4–6.

[66] *Report of the Directors of the New-York, Providence & Boston Railroad*

V

The self-assurance of the Boston and Providence and the Stonington that together they formed the ordained central artery for the New York-Boston trade and that nothing could challenge them was seriously upset by the chartering of the Norwich and Worcester in 1833.[67] The route was so natural a one that in an earlier decade James F. Baldwin, after a survey, had pronounced it practicable for a canal. By the thirties, its promise was even greater. The two eastern counties of Connecticut, which the project traversed, were populous — and their population was a "travelling" one; they were also industrialized. Their iron and paper mills, their lumber mills and quarries had been supplemented by the cotton industry encroaching from Rhode Island. There were seventy-five cotton mills and twenty-seven woolen mills within four miles of the route; in the two counties the number of cotton spindles was 106,220. All this meant local traffic. "Experience has freely proved, that the local business of any long line of communication is its main source of income. It always exceeds the estimates made of it, and is often overlooked, but is by far the most important." [68]

The Norwich and Worcester was also to be a through route. With the assistance of the Boston and Worcester, it was to share in the freight business between Boston and New York, a freight business to be taken away from the packets not by lower rates but by superior certainty, celerity, and savings in insurance. It was also to share in the travel. To be sure, the Stonington was a few miles shorter, but "if one route or the other were to be selected, it would not be on account of the difference of one or two miles in a distance of more than two hundred miles, but other considerations — the accommodations on the route — the su-

Company to the Stockholders, at Their Annual Meeting, at Providence, R. I., September 24th, 1850 (New York: Francis Hart, 1850); Wheaton J. Lane, Commodore Vanderbilt. An Epic of the Steam Age (New York: Alfred A. Knopf, 1942), p. 75.

[67] Private and Special Statutes of the Commonwealth of Massachusetts, from May 1830, to April 1837, VII, 350–354, 679–680.

[68] Worcester & Norwich Rail-Road Company, 1835 (n.p., n.d.), pp. 21–26, 31, 35–36.

perior scenery or pleasantness of the country, &c. would be the
operating motives in the selection of one or the other route." [69]
To boasts and calculations of this sort Bostonians were wonted.
The proposed road, however, really threatened to turn a considerable portion of New England away from its natural dependence
upon Boston. Proposed extensions would reach out to Nashua
and Lowell and put them in direct touch with New York; with
the assistance of the Boston and Worcester, it would supply
leather to the shoe towns of Worcester County and carry away
their product for New York and a southern market; it would
bring in anthracite coal for the factories along its route, and
further fasten the Connecticut area and even Worcester County
to New York. "However extensive the business of Boston may
be, and it certainly would increase very much from the towns in
Connecticut on the borders of this route, it is quite apparent that
everything now tends in the most direct line to New York, as
the great commercial mart. The desire is increasing continually
to facilitate the communication with that emporium of commerce. The manufacturer there purchases his raw material and
there sends his goods, and the merchant would there obtain his
supplies." [70]

Completed in 1840, three years after the New York, Providence
and Boston, the Norwich and Worcester did not as long remain
an orphan. In co-operation with the Boston and Worcester steamboat trains were run through to Boston where, on their arrival, a
signal was raised on the flagpole of the station and another on
the old State House. Nor did the partnership stop there. The
Boston and Worcester paid a commission to agents soliciting
freight for the joint route, accepted stock in the Norwich and
Worcester in settlement of the debts owed by the latter, subscribed to bonds financing the extension of the Norwich road to
a better terminal, Allyn's Point, farther down on the east shore
of the Thames, and loaned it money for the construction of a
steamboat.[71] But it did not take a lease. In truth, the new road

---

[69] *Ibid.*, pp. 28–30, 32–33.   [70] *Ibid.*, pp. 27–28, 34–35.
[71] Records of the Directors and Stockholders of the Boston and Worcester Railroad, Ms., Harvard Business School Library, III, 243, IV, 43, 81, 94, 266–267,
272–273, V, 262–265.

was not a desirable property. Its length, due to the "sinuosity" which McNeill had scorned, prevented it from setting a competitive pace for the through travel. Its financial history had been desperate. Massachusetts came to the rescue with a loan of $400,000, for which she first took stock and later bonds as security; and the city of Norwich lent its aid to the tune of $200,000, receiving in return both stock and mortgage bonds in the road.[72] There were many changes of management. The directors who took office in 1848 found the road had an indebtedness of $1,354,510, payrolls were three months and a half in arrears, and the "property and machinery much dilapidated."[73] It had never paid a dividend. In the fifties a rearrangement of the capital structure provided preferred stock with a modest return.[74] Although a New Yorker or so sat on the board, the control remained in the hands of Norwich and Worcester men. The road at least contributed toward making the latter city a great inland railroad center.

So did the Providence and Worcester, chartered in 1844 and completed three years later.[75] Originally its ambitions were modest. It was projected to replace the canal which ran northward along the Blackstone Valley from Narragansett Bay to the city of Worcester — replace it and no more. The prospectus dilated primarily upon the local traffic. The textile villages of the valley had cotton mills with over 300,000 spindles and 7,000 looms, and Worcester, a great metal working center, consumed annually 120,000 bushels of southern corn, 4,000 tons of coal, 50,000 bushels of salt, and 1,000 tons of lime.[76] Rhode Island capitalists provided the funds for this modest road and the di-

---

[72] *Report of a Committee of the Stockholders of the Norwich and Worcester Rail Road Company, July 8, 1842* (Worcester: Henry J. Howland, 1842), pp. 3–5; Poor, *History of the Railroads and Canals of the United States*, p. 213.

[73] *Report of Directors to the Stockholders of the Norwich and Worcester Rail Road Company. July 1849* (Norwich: John W. Stedman, 1849), pp. 3, 6.

[74] Martin, *A Century of Finance*, pp. 147, 149.

[75] Laws of Rhode Island Passed by the General Assembly at the May Session, 1844, pp. 34–42; Poor, *History of the Railroads and Canals of the United States*, p. 146.

[76] *Facts and Estimates Relative to the Business of the Route of the Contemplated Providence and Worcester Rail Road* (Providence: Knowles & Vose, 1844), pp. 4–18.

rectorate was heavy with local names, many of which are perpetuated in the little textile centers through which the road
passed.[77]

Nevertheless the road became involved in the through business between New York on the one hand and Worcester and the
textile centers beyond — Nashua, Lowell, and Manchester — to
which railroads were extended. Since this was also Norwich and
Worcester territory, a fierce competition ensued. As through
rates tumbled and local rates remained untouched, cries of dis-
content arose from the textile producers of the Blackstone Valley,
especially if they did not enjoy rebates from the railroad. Providence merchants who lost a forwarding business and steamboat
interests outside the exclusive contract between the railroad and
the Commercial Steamboat Company of Providence also complained.[78] These dissidents claimed the original purpose of the
railroad's charter, the welfare of local enterprise, was sacrificed
by the railroad. "It would seem, however, that we were only
granting to the merchants, mechanics and manufacturers of New
York and Philadelphia on one side, and of Massachusetts and
New Hampshire on the other, a *right of way* through Rhode
Island." [79]

VI

In spite of newcomers, the position of the Boston and Providence remained on the whole unharmed. Suddenly in the mid-
forties, it was challenged from a new direction — the east. True
to the conventional pattern, the challenger was a consolidation
of local roads originally projected for quite different purposes
from those served by the united line. One constituent was the
Old Colony Railroad. By charter of March 16, 1844, it was
authorized to build from South Boston to Plymouth.[80] Though

[77] First Annual Report of the Providence and Worcester Railroad Company,
Massachusetts *Senate Documents*, 1846, no. 21, pp. 98, 100.

[78] Edward Harris, *Considerations for the Stockholders of the Providence &
Worcester Railroad Co.* (Woonsocket: S. S. Foss, 1861), pp. 3–13.

[79] *Mr. Harris Reviewed. Being an Examination of His "Further Considerations
for the Stockholders of the Providence and Worcester Railroad." By a Rhode
Islander* (Providence: Alfred Anthony, 1864), pp. 13–14.

[80] *Private and Special Statutes of the Commonwealth of Massachusetts from
January 1838, to May 1848*, VIII, 389–392.

the road was not even directed toward New York, it might as well have been: any other reason for incorporating it was equally incomprehensible. The southern destination, — Plymouth and Cape Cod, — was already adequately supplied with water transportation to Boston. The prospectus of the Old Colony, however, affected to believe that there was traffic enough for a land route. The shoe towns south of Boston provided barrels and boxes of footwear, and passengers, for shoe and leather dealers went to Boston on their "regular business days" of Wednesday and Saturday. Iron manufactures bordered the route and Plymouth produced nails, anchors, and rivets as well as 1,000 tons of cordage a year. When the road was actually constructed, it elected a route which left aside some of the larger shoe centers, and located the track so that no part was more than twelve miles from the ocean. This challenge to the coastal trade distressed many influential stockholders, and the statement in the prospectus that "this road is liable to no competition other than that with which it starts" afforded little reassurance.[81]

The road, completed by the end of 1845, was at once seized with a mania for branches to bring traffic upon the main line.[82] Since nothing could conceal the original weakness of the enterprise, ultimately the barometer of finance revealed a deplorable situation. A floating debt of $640,000, hanging over the enterprise, could be converted into securities on no better terms than by issuing five-year bonds at ninety cents on the dollar and by selling stock at seventy-five.[83] Business depression, water competition, disadvantageous agreements, and irregularities on the part of the officers accounted for this sad state of affairs, thought the analysts. Certainly the Old Colony had trod the road to ruin

[81] *Brief Statement of Facts in Relation to the Proposed Rail-Road from Boston to Plymouth* (Plymouth: James Thurber, 1844), pp. 4–15; *Report of the Committee for Investigating the Affairs of the Old Colony Railroad Company, Appointed by the Stockholders, December 26, 1849* (Boston: Eastburn's Press, 1850), appendix, p. 31.

[82] *A Brief Reply to the Report of the Investigating Committee of the Old Colony Railroad Corporation. By the President of the Company. April 12, 1850* (Boston: Damrell & Moore, 1850), p. 7.

[83] *Sixth Annual Report of the Directors of the Old Colony Rail-Road Corporation, to the Stockholders, December, 1849* (Boston: Crocker & Brewster, 1849), pp. 8–9.

under the best auspices, for many of the greatest railroad names of this early era paraded through the road's offices and directorate. Addison Gilmore was treasurer on his way from the Concord to the Western; Josiah Quincy, Jr., had a brief interlude as financial dictator before incurring final misfortune in Vermont; P. P. F. De Grand moved as usual behind the scenes; and E. H. Derby left the study and the bar for the practical work of a railroad presidency. But whether the talent was disinterestedly employed for the good of the corporation was a matter of dispute. The individuals involved naturally regarded themselves as healers, their opponents thought them speculators with an eye for the main chance.[84] Not till the mid-fifties did the road become a consistent though modest dividend payer.[85] By then it had lost its original character.

Two days before the Old Colony received its charter in 1844, the Fall River Branch Railroad Company was incorporated.[86] Like so many of the early roads, this later one was distinctly subordinate to manfacturing enterprises. The Bordens and the Durfees, who formed the powerful textile and iron dynasty of Fall River, conceived and financed it as a link in improved transportation to Boston and, after dallying with a connection over the Boston and Providence or an independent route of their own, agreed with the Old Colony in 1847 to a junction with the latter at South Braintree. From that point the Old Colony was to lay a double track into Boston and enlarge its facilities to accommodate the expected business from the Fall River Railroad, for such it had become, and from the line of steamers which the Bordens had placed, under the aegis of the Bay State Steamboat Company, upon the run between Fall River and New York.[87]

[84] *Report of the Committee for Investigating . . . the Old Colony Railroad . . . December 26, 1840; Brief Reply to . . . the Investigating Committee of the Old Colony Railroad; Sixth Annual Report . . . of the Old Colony Rail-Road . . . December, 1849,* p. 12.

[85] Martin, *A Century of Finance,* p. 147.

[86] *Private and Special Statutes . . . of Massachusetts, . . . 1838, . . . 1848,* VIII, 356–358.

[87] *Second Annual Report of the Directors of the Fall River Rail Road Company, to the Stockholders, January, 1848* (Fall River: Henry Pratt, 1848), pp. 4–6; *Private and Special Statutes . . . of Massachusetts, . . . 1838, . . . 1848,* VIII, 669–670.

The two roads divided the freight and passenger receipts on a pro-rata mileage basis, but for the use of equipment and "for the benefits to be derived from the connection" the Old Colony paid the Fall River for each passenger and each ton of freight from the latter road "one half a cent per mile, . . . when upon the Old Colony Railroad." Neither was to divert business from the other or charter and promote new roads to the other's hurt. This was the cost of sharing the business of steamboat trains and of the "Express Freight Train . . . established especially for the New York business." [88] The interest of the Old Colony began to turn to the south and west.

The agreement of 1847 was to expire in 1856. Years before that date both parties complained bitterly of its disadvantages and began to canvass alternatives carefully and with full publicity. The solution for each was an extension. The Fall River was bent upon pushing its road from South Braintree into Boston; the Old Colony, with passing attention to the folly of such an expense by the Fall River, surveyed a prolongation of its own tracks south to Newport and threatened to run its own line of steamers to New York.[89] Meanwhile negotiations continued. In 1854 they resulted in the passage of an act of the Massachusetts legislature authorizing the union of the two quarrelers into the Old Colony and Fall River Railroad; the companies were to agree upon the terms.[90] When the corporation was organized, the larger share of its increased capitalization went to the Old Colony.[91]

The merger naturally stilled most of the rivalries between the two interests. For instance, both had contended for the exclusive

[88] *Report of the Committee for Investigating . . . the Old Colony Railroad . . .* December 26, 1849, appendix, pp. 145–148.

[89] *Tenth Annual Report of the Directors of the Old Colony Rail-Road Corporation, to the Stockholders. January, 1854* (Boston: Crocker and Brewster, 1854), pp. 6–12, 23–38; *Seventh Annual Report of the Directors of the Fall River Railroad Co. to the Stockholders, January, 1853* (Fall River: Henry Pratt, 1853), pp. 16–21.

[90] *Private and Special Statutes of the Commonwealth of Massachusetts, for the Years 1854, . . . '59,* X, 60.

[91] *Annual Report of the Directors of the Old Colony and Fall River Rail Road Company, to the Stockholders. January, 1855* (Boston: Crocker and Brewster, 1855), p. 9.

control of the Cape Cod Branch Railroad, a tardy enterprise being driven eastward along Cape Cod; the Fall River had won.[92] Now directors of the combined board watched with comparative calm its completion to Hyannis, which it reached before the Civil War.[93] Whether the rails should be extended to Provincetown seemed now to be a responsibility of the Federal government; at least an effort was made to picture a road to the tip of the Cape as an essential military protection of the Massachusetts coast against some enemy, not precisely identified.[94] On the other hand, when a majority of the board proposed to continue the Old Colony and Fall River to Newport and operate steamboats thence to New York, convulsions followed. Such a measure struck at one of the most profitable of Borden investments, the Bay State Steamboat Company, and at once, undeterred by arguments from tradition or efficiency, they drenched the Massachusetts legislature with fearful estimates of the damage likely to be inflicted by the proposed extension upon factory property and public health. Their opponents interpreted this general solicitude of the Bordens as really an attempt to blackmail a high price for their vessels and their railroad stock.[95] The Bordens lost. The General Court authorized the extension with

[92] Report of the Joint Standing Committee on Railways and Canals Relative to the Proposed Cape Cod Railway, Massachusetts *House Documents*, 1846, no. 70, pp. 1–8; *Second Annual Report of the Directors of the Fall River Rail Road Company, to the Stockholders, January, 1848* (Fall River: Henry Pratt, 1848), pp. 13–14.

[93] *Ninth Annual Report of the Directors of the Cape Cod Railroad Company to the Stockholders, for the Year Ending May 31, 1855* (Boston: William White, 1855), pp. 9–10.

[94] Report of a Committee on Coast Defenses, Massachusetts *Senate Documents*, 1865, no. 230, pp. 4–6; Report of a Joint Special Committee on the Cape Cod Railroad, Massachusetts *House Documents*, 1866, no. 433.

[95] *Sixth Annual Report of the Directors of the Old Colony and Fall River Railroad Company. To the Stockholders. January, 1860* (Boston: Crocker and Brewster, 1860), pp. 8–11; *Argument of Hon. Josiah G. Abbott, Before the Joint Committee of the Legislature of Massachusetts on Railways and Canals in Favor of the Extension of the Old Colony and Fall River Railroad to Newport, R. I., March 13, 1861* (Boston: Geo. C. Rand & Avery, 1861), pp. 13–17, 28–34; Report of the Joint Committee on Railways and Canals Relative to the Extension of the Old Colony and Fall River Railroad, Massachusetts *Senate Documents*, 1860, no. 130, pp. 7–8; Report of the Committee on Railways and Canals Relative to the Extension of the Old Colony and Fall River Railroad, Massachusetts *Senate Documents*, 1861, no. 118.

the proviso, "The Old Colony and Fall River Railroad Company shall, if required by the Bay State Steam-boat Company, deliver to said last named corporation, at Fall River, all articles of freight received by said railroad corporation for transport and to be sent to New York by said Steam-boat Company." [96] That an amendment to a charter should concede to a steamboat company the right to transport the freight consigned over it, was a curious commentary upon the railroad practices of the day. Though the road was now christened the Old Colony and Newport, Newport was actually the steamboat terminus only between 1864 and 1869. [97]

On these roads of southeastern Massachusetts, New York capitalists played an infinitesimal part; Massachusetts and Rhode Island men, or, at the very least, New Englanders held their presidencies and sat on their directorates. [98] Still financial representation was not necessarily synonomous with the course of trade, and the debate over the extension to Newport revealed how far New York threw its influence. Cheap and convenient water transportation with New York turned the trade of Rhode Island toward New York. Even Fall River, still nearer to Boston and allied to it by social and political relations, looked to New York; four-fifths of its flour and groceries were purchased there. [99] But it would be a grave distortion to regard these roads and those in southern Connecticut solely as pawns in the commercial struggle between New York and Boston or as a means for the through communication between them. Places like New Haven, Bridgeport, Norwich, New London, Providence, and Fall River, and a host of lesser communities were not passive. They had ambitions and needs of their own. Like their bigger brethren,

[96] *Private and Special Statutes of the Commonwealth of Massachusetts, for the Years 1860, . . . '65,* XI, 211–212, 299–300.

[97] *Second Annual Report of the Directors of the Old Colony and Newport Railway Company to the Stockholders, July, 1865* (Boston: Geo. C. Rand & Avery, 1865), pp. 6–7; *Sixth Annual Report of the Directors of the Old Colony and Newport Railway Company to the Stockholders, July, 1869* (Boston: Rand, Avery, & Frye, 1869), p. 8.

[98] *Report of the Committee for Investigating . . . the Old Colony Railroad . . . December 26, 1849,* appendix, pp. 155–156.

[99] Massachusetts *Senate Documents,* 1861, no. 118, pp. 9, 14–15.

Joseph E. Sheffield   James Brewster

CONNECTICUT RAILROAD BUILDERS

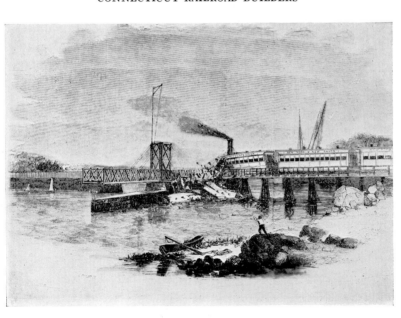

The Norwalk Disaster

End Elevations

Front Elevation

HENRY AUSTIN'S DESIGN FOR THE
NEW HAVEN RAILROAD STATION

they dreamed of a route to the West. Though they could not, like Boston, hope to be an "emporium" where the products of the prairies were exchanged for imports of foreign merchandise, the West was, for them, a market for their products and a source of raw materials.

With the exception of Providence and, perhaps, of Hartford, no one of these southern New England centers had the financial stamina to project and build a railroad of its own to the Hudson. So they were compelled to rest content with connections. The Housatonic, the Hartford and New Haven, the Norwich and Worcester, the Providence and Worcester, and the Old Colony at first relied upon the Boston and Worcester and the Western to fulfill this purpose.[100] By 1860 in the Worcester and Nashua, to mention no other route, the southern New England roads had a link with the Fitchburg and the Boston and Lowell, members of the lines to the St. Lawrence and Lake Ontario.[101] The roads of southern New England, therefore, had quite a different character than those earlier discussed. They were terminal roads; they were local roads. They distributed through the region they served products from the West, northern New England, Boston, and New York; they collected a return traffic. The through business in which they participated was that between New York and Boston. They shared this traffic on terms of inferiority with water transportation. The construction of the New York and New Haven, though few realized it, was to shatter this familiar mold.

VII

Consolidated as it later was with the Hartford and New Haven, the New York and New Haven formed the nucleus of one of the

[100] *First Annual Report . . . of the Housatonic Rail-Road*, pp. 16–17, 26–27; *Statement of Facts in Relation to the Norwich and Worcester Rail-Road Company. June, 1841* (New York: R. Craighead, 1841), p. 9; *Facts and Estimates Relative to the Business of the . . . Providence and Worcester*, p. 19; Report of the Joint Special Committee on Railways and Canals Relative to an Extension of the Old Colony Railroad, Massachusetts *Senate Documents*, 1845, no. 51, pp. 2–4.

[101] *Statement of Facts Concerning the Sources of Business of the Intended Rail-Road from Worcester, Mass. to Nashua, N. H. and an Estimate of Its Probable Cost* (Worcester: Henry J. Howland, n.d.), pp. 5–6, 15–19.

two great railroad systems that dominated New England at the close of the nineteenth century. It was not, however, one of the pioneer roads of the section, for any railroad along Long Island Sound faced a vigorous and uninterrupted water competition. By the forties, nevertheless, enough lines parallel to waterways were in course of promotion or construction to assure the promoters of the New York and New Haven that they would not be alone in their folly. And certainly their route promised greater profits than the Eastern, the Old Colony, or the Portland, Saco and Portsmouth. One destination, New York City, was the acknowledged commercial metropolis of the nation; in Connecticut the Housatonic and the Hartford and New Haven, already constructed, guaranteed railroad connections into New York's New England hinterland. Furthermore the New York and New Haven would complete the first all-rail route between Boston and New York City. Finally, the committee of the Connecticut legislature, which in 1844 recommended the granting of the charter, hailed the proposed road as "the only link which now remains to complete the great chain of internal communication by Rail Road uniting Maine on the North with Georgia on the South." While remonstrances from menaced turnpikes poured into the legislature, other petitions favoring the road disclosed how wide was the regional appreciation of the new enterprise. Though citizens of Derby and of New Haven signed appeals in its behalf, it was not merely a Connecticut project; New Yorkers and Bostonians, the latter headed by the galvanic P. P. F. De Grand, were also petitioners.[102] Connecticut responded with a charter authorizing the road to extend from New Haven to Bridgeport and "thence westerly to the west line of this state towards the city of New York." Another provision declared that "a uniform rate per mile shall be charged for the transportation of such passengers and freight as shall be received from or delivered to the several Railroads in this State with which this Railroad may be connected." [103]

[102] Petitions and Reports Relative to the New York and New Haven Railroad, Ms., Connecticut Archives, State Capitol, Hartford.
[103] *Resolves and Private Laws of the State of Connecticut, from the Year 1836 to the Year 1857*, IV, 1020–1025.

Among the original incorporators were P. P. F. De Grand; Samuel J. Hitchcock, president of the Hartford and New Haven; Anson G. Phelps, a Connecticut man who became a New York merchant, shipper, metal dealer, and finally one of the creators of the copper and brass industry of the Naugatuck Valley; Elihu Townsend, "of the highly respectable and rich Wall Street broker firm"; and Joseph E. Sheffield, at this moment president of the New Haven and Northampton Company. Sheffield assumed the chief financial burden. He subscribed to 12,000 shares, made the required down payments, and forthwith attempted to peddle the securities to others. In New Haven enthusiasm was low — the "prophets in Israel" whom Sheffield always bemoaned hung back — nor did New Yorkers rush forward to contribute. So Sheffield, turning to the Barings with whom he had had previous mercantile relations, offered them a majority control and the right to select the board of directors if they would underwrite. They refused. Discouraged, he returned to this country for another effort. Though John E. Thayer, the banker, secured some subscriptions in Boston, though New Haven investors took $100,000, New York capitalists really financed the project.[104] First of all there were the brothers Robert and George L. Schuyler, brokers, railroad contractors, and promoters. Robert Schuyler was the president of a dozen roads from Illinois to New Jersey and Vermont. Others in the group of New York associates, besides Phelps and Townsend, were Morris Ketchum, an investor in the Housatonic and the Hartford and a member of the brokerage firm of Rogers, Ketchum, and Bement; Jonathan Sturgis, another Connecticut émigré and New York merchant; and Sidney J. Miller, brother-in-law of Ketchum and a railroad contractor.[105]

Meanwhile the road had been surveyed, of course with Alexander C. Twining in charge. Though his report was far from precise about terminals in New Haven or on the Harlem, he

---

[104] Joseph A. Scoville, *The Old Merchants of New York City* (New York: Carleton, 1863), p. 85; Sheffield, Memoranda, Dresden, January, 1857, p. 11; Letter of Joseph E. Sheffield, in New Haven *Journal and Courier*, July, 1868, Sheffield Papers, Recollections, pp. 1-5.

[105] Sheffield, Letter, New Haven *Journal and Courier*, July, 1868; *Portrait*

rejected an inland route in favor of one following the coastline of the Sound. This choice meant frequent bridges with draws and in the extreme southwestern part of the state several "inclinations" between 35 and 40 feet to the mile, for in this "rude region" the ledges and hills of the interior came close to the water's edge. Actually there were some grades between 40 and 50 feet. The engineers planned a heavy superstructure comparable to that of the Western. Estimates of construction costs, including equipment, were $2,233,340 for the 69 miles.[106] Since the funds already raised or promised were not sufficient to meet this sum, the contractors agreed to take their pay in stock to the amount of $900,000, and the remainder, $1,350,000, in cash. The contractors were George L. Schuyler, Sidney J. Miller, and Alfred Bishop. None needs introduction. Bishop was the railroad genius of Bridgeport and already an investor in the New Haven road; Miller and Schuyler were connected with the enterprise before they became its builders. In justice to Schuyler, it must be noted that he soon assigned his interest in the contract to Bishop. Still he was of use in other capacities. The cost of the road, of course, exceeded estimates; and the additional expenses were met by the issue of bonds to various houses, including the Schuylers, and by short-term loans, also from the Schuylers.[107]

On Christmas Day, 1848, a train started over the single track from New Haven to New York but had to return when it was discovered that the route was not completed. The official opening of the road was thus postponed until early in the following year. Adequate freight transportation came two years later.[108]

Gallery of the Chamber of Commerce of the State of New York (New York: Chamber of Commerce, 1890), pp. 59–60, 116–117.

[106] *Engineer's Report on the Survey and Primary Location of the New York and New Haven Railroad. February, 1845* (New Haven: Hitchcock & Stafford, 1845); Zerah Colburn, "Safety System of the New York and New Haven Railroad," *American Railroad Journal,* XXVII (1854), 37.

[107] *Report . . . of the New-York and New-Haven . . . 22 August, 1849,* pp. 7–9, 26–27, 30–31.

[108] *Report of the Directors of the New York and New Haven Railroad Company, Made to the Stockholders at Their Annual Meeting, at New Haven, May 10, 1855* (New York: Baker, Godwin & Co., 1855), p. 7; *Report . . . of the New-York and New-Haven . . . 22 August, 1849.* p. 18; *The Annual Report of the Board of Directors to the Stockholders of the New York & New Haven Railroad Company, May 9, 1850* (New Haven: T. J. Stafford, 1850), pp. 5–6.

Meanwhile it must have been very difficult for those managing the railroad to keep their interests as managers and investors separate from their interests in other and related capacities. The construction contract, for one thing, posed the problem. The extension toward New York City raised even more bewildering complexities. When the New Haven sought a permissive charter from the New York legislature, the successful opponents were the Westchester Turnpike Company and the New York and Harlem Railroad. The task of removing legislative opposition, the New Haven entrusted to negotiators, one of whom was George L. Schuyler. Their statesmanship bought out the turn- *power of impedence.* pike through the payment of damages. Arrangements with the Harlem were somewhat more costly. The New Haven abandoned the project of an independent line to the Harlem River and agreed to connect with the New York and Harlem at Williams' Bridge. Eventually the New Haven had to loan money to the Harlem for the double tracking of the latter's line south of this junction point; the corporation, as well as the directors, had to subscribe to the preferred stock of the Harlem, and had to sign an agreement by which the Harlem was given a varying payment for every passenger from the New Haven carried into New York. For the first 1,000 passengers a day the rate was 14 cents apiece; a sliding scale then operated until the rate was 6 cents. For hauling loaded or empty freight cars in New York City the Harlem also received ample remuneration. Schuyler, forthwith, became president of the Harlem. For decades outsiders frequently referred to the payments to the Harlem as "tribute"; and even the New Haven directorates called them "onerous" and "burthensome," and admitted their aid to the Harlem was a transfusion for a very feeble enterprise.[109] High as they came, however, the New York terminal rights which the New Haven thus obtained were to prove invaluable in railroad warfare.

[109] *Report . . . of the New-York and New-Haven . . . 22 August, 1849,* pp. 5–6, 15–18; *Report of the Board of Directors to the Stockholders of the New York and New Haven Railroad Company. May 8, 1862* (New Haven: T. J. Stafford, 1862), p. 16; Report of the Joint Standing Committee on Railroads Relative to Passenger Fares and Freights and Contracts and Leases of the New York and New Haven, Connecticut *Legislative Documents,* 1871, no. 26, p. 23; Papers

Along the route in Connecticut there was a blurring of interests. The New Haven managers at once came to an agreement with the steamboat lines handling the business of the Housatonic between Bridgeport and New York. Both steamboat and railroad were to charge the same fare and the joint receipts were to be divided 45 per cent to the boats and 55 per cent to the New Haven. The president of the New Haven was Robert Schuyler; the owner of the boats was his brother, George L. Schuyler; and George L. Schuyler also sat on the directorate of the Housatonic. In 1849 the annual report of the New Haven commented, "Whether a similar arrangement would now be made, when the strength of the New-Haven Rail Road has been tested and more justly appreciated, may be questionable." [110] Then came the Naugatuck. Traffic arrangements were easily made, since Bishop had been its contractor as well as the contractor for the New Haven.[111] Finally at New Haven there were both the Hartford and New Haven and the Canal Road. The former could act with displeasing independence, for it could carry passengers and freight to New York by its own line of boats. A lease of the Canal Road, always threatening to tap the Connecticut Valley above Hartford, might check these dangerous tendencies and at the same time offer incidental advantages. The dry bed of the old canal enabled the New Haven to cross the city at sub-grade; its land holdings and old basins near the waterfront, if filled in, were an admirable site for yards, shops, and terminals. Moreover, Sheffield, the overlord of the Canal and the Canal Road, was a director of the New Haven. The leases were negotiated.[112]

Though they drained the earnings of the New Haven by uninterrupted losses, these leases served the purpose of chastening the Hartford.[113] In 1849 the latter agreed to abandon its line of

---

Relative to the Reduction of Railroad Fares, Connecticut *Legislative Documents,* 1872, no. 25.

[110] *Report . . . of the New-York and New-Haven . . . 22 August, 1849,* pp. 18–19.

[111] *Ibid.,* pp. 19–20.

[112] *Ibid.,* pp. 10–13.

[113] *Report . . . of the New York and New Haven . . . May 10, 1855,* pp. 23–25; *Report of the Board of Directors to the Stockholders of the New-York &*

day steamers to New Haven, limit the reduction of fares on the night line of boats, and run more of its trains to the New Haven's station. The New Haven made some sacrifices. In addition, "There are many other arrangements provided for in this agreement which it might be injurious to set forth in detail, from the liability to misconstruction and erroneous inferences." [114] Subsequently the Hartford bought off the threatened extension of the Canal Road by withdrawing its night boats and by paying $12,000 a year to the New Haven.[115] These "iniquitous contracts," [116] as Sheffield called them, did not save the Hartford, for the Canal Road was completed and utilized by the New Haven to divert the down-river traffic at Northampton. The Hartford retaliated with litigation and with the revival of its boat connections between New Haven and New York.[117] These maneuvers were a prelude to a later consolidation.

Meanwhile spectacular events brought the New Haven and New York to the verge of ruin. Conceivably one event was an act of God. In 1853 a passenger train ran through the open draw of the bridge across the Norwalk River and forty-five people lost their lives. Two years later the New Haven had paid nearly $300,000 in damages, a sum one-tenth of its capitalization.[118] The coroner's jury found "the immediate cause . . . to be the negligence and recklessness of the engineer." The

New-Haven Railroad Company, May 8, 1856 (New York: George S. Roe, 1856), pp. 17–18; *Report of the Board of Directors to the Stockholders of the New York & New Haven Railroad Company. May 12, 1859* (New York: Wynkoop, Hallenbeck and Thomas, 1859), pp. 10–11.

[114] *Report . . . of the New-York and New-Haven . . . 22 August, 1849,* pp. 20–22.

[115] *Twenty-second Annual Report of the Board of Directors to the Stockholders of the Hartford & New Haven R. R. Co.* (Hartford: Case, Lockwood and Company, 1857), p. 5.

[116] Sheffield, Letter, New Haven *Journal and Courier,* July, 1868.

[117] *Twenty-second Annual Report . . . of the Hartford & New Haven,* pp. 5–7; *Twenty-seventh Annual Report of the Board of Directors, to the Stockholders of the Hartford and New Haven R. R. Co.* (Hartford: Case, Lockwood & Company, 1862), pp. 7–8; *Thirtieth Annual Report of the Board of Directors to the Stockholders of the Hartford and New Haven R. R. Co.* (Hartford: Case, Lockwood & Company, 1865), pp. 8–9.

[118] *The Report of the Board of Directors to the Stockholders of the New-York & New-Haven Rail-Road Co., 11 May, 1854* (New York: G. S. Roe, 1854), pp. 8–9; *Report . . . of the New York and New Haven . . . May 10, 1855,* p. 19.

American Railroad Journal censured "the general negligence and want of proper system" on the New Haven and asserted that the officers, particularly President Robert Schuyler, were too busy with their private affairs to give proper attention to the road.[119] This and other reflections that all might not be well with the New Haven fell far short, however, of the dramatic reality. Late in June, 1854, a director of the New Haven, mystified by the large sales of its stock on the exchange, began an investigation of the office of the transfer agent. Robert Schuyler held this position as well as that of president. On July 1st Schuyler announced the failure of his brokerage concern, on July 3rd he resigned his positions on the New Haven, on Independence Day the officials of the road tried to decipher the array of false entries, additions, and erasures on the stock books of the company, and on July 5th the news was broken to the world that Schuyler, a paladin of New York finance, had effected an immense over-issue of New Haven stock. Panic ensued.[120] Railroad officers all over the United States were suspected of defalcations, and conservative business men meditated with distress upon the secrecy and selfishness of "stock-jobbing cliques." [121]

The excitement lasted for weeks, since only gradually were the details of the gigantic fraud disclosed. Pressed for money to underwrite his construction of railroads in Vermont and New York, Schuyler had issued to himself, his associates, employees, and to persons unknown approximately 20,000 shares of stock beyond the 30,000 maximum allowed by the charter and had borrowed money upon these additional securities. Other minor peculations, concealed adroitly in a labyrinth of bookkeeping, amounted to $137,527.[122] Long before this total indictment was completed, Schuyler fled the country and the whole board of di-

---

[119] *American Railroad Journal*, XXVI (1853), 328–329.

[120] *The Report of the Directors of the New York & New Haven R. R. Co. to the Stockholders, at Their Special Meeting, October 3d, 1854* (New Haven: T. J. Stafford, 1854), pp. 4–6; *Hunt's Merchants' Magazine and Commercial Review*, XXXI (1854), 207.

[121] *Hunt's Merchants' Magazine and Commercial Review*, XXXI (1854), 208–209.

[122] *Report . . . of the New York and New Haven . . . May 10, 1855*, pp. 4–5, 26–30.

rectors of the New Haven had resigned at the request of the stockholders.[123] Of course a prolonged litigation beset the new board. To them it seemed clear that the New Haven had incurred no liability for Schuyler's over-issue; the charter permitted 30,000 shares and no act of transfer agent, treasurer, or board of directors could legally violate this provision.[124] But the purchasers of the fraudulent stock thought otherwise. They brought suit in the Federal courts and in the state courts of Connecticut and New York, and enjoined the payment of dividends until settlement was made.[125] By 1863 the company, to stop the ceaseless litigation, utilized Connecticut's permission to increase its capital stock and began to exchange the new securities for the "spurious stock" at the ratio of one share to two.[126] A few years later a decision by the New York Court of Appeals compelled the exchange of share for share. Though the stock was spurious, the corporation was liable for the wrongdoing of its agents.[127]

After years of "suffering" the New York and New Haven became in the later sixties one of the most prosperous of New England enterprises. The annual dividends were often 10 per cent, and its 50,000 shares sold well above par.[128] By way of the Hartford and New Haven and the roads east from Springfield it was part of the most important through land route to Boston

[123] *Ibid.*, pp. 3, 32.

[124] *Ibid.*, p. 4.

[125] *To the Stockholders of the New-York & New-Haven Railroad Co.* (n.p., 1855); *Report of the Board of Directors to the Stockholders of the New-York & New-Haven Railroad Company, May 14, 1857* (New York: G. S. Roe, 1857), pp. 5–7; *Report of the Board of Directors to the Stockholders of the New York and New Haven Railroad Company, May 9th, 1861* (New Haven: T. J. Stafford, 1861), p. 6.

[126] *Report of the Board of Directors to the Stockholders of the New York and New Haven Railroad Company, to Be Submitted at the Annual Meeting in the City of New Haven, on Thursday, May 19th, 1864* (New Haven: T. J. Stafford, 1864), pp. 5–6; *Resolves and Private Laws of the State of Connecticut, from the Year 1836 to the Year 1857*, IV, 1031–1032.

[127] *Report of the Board of Directors to the Stockholders of the New York and New Haven Railroad Company, to Be Submitted at the Annual Meeting in the City of New Haven, on Thursday, May 17th, 1866* (New Haven: T. J. Stafford, 1866), pp. 5–7; The New York and New Haven Railroad Company *v.* Robert Schuyler, Morris Ketchum, Edward Bement, et al. 34 *New York*, 30.

[128] Martin, *A Century of Finance*, pp. 148–149.

— for the shaky railroads built along the shore from New Haven to Stonington crossed inlets and bays on insecure piling, were interrupted by ferries at the Connecticut and the Thames, and made little headway against either financial difficulties or steamboat rivalry.[129] Still the foundations of the New Haven's later success were little sounder than those of the earlier failure. Unless travelers and shippers had contributed earnings which could be ploughed back into the business, 40 per cent of the stock represented capitalized corruption. Thus the heritage of the fifties persisted. It was not a creditable one. Henry Varnum Poor, editor of the *American Railroad Journal*, railroad analyst, and partisan of New York railroad expansion, was depressed by the contrast of what the New Haven and New York might have been, with its advantageous location and its generous through and local traffic, and what it had become under the criminal ministrations of Schuyler and the incompetence of other directors. "It is not to be denied," he concluded, "that the tone of railroad management in New York City has been very low." [130]

[129] *Report of the Board of Directors of the New Haven and New London Rail Road Co., to the Stockholders, April 18, 1854* (New Haven: W. H. Stanley, 1854), pp. 3–7; *Annual Report of the Board of Directors of the New Haven, New London & Stonington Railroad Company, to the Stockholders, February 15th, 1860* (New Haven: T. J. Stafford, 1860), pp. 5–7.

[130] *American Railroad Journal*, XXVII (1854), 433–434.

IX

REGULATION: TECHNOLOGICAL CHANGE

"The Locomotive: The only good motive for riding a man upon a rail." — Toast of Philip Hone. Office of the New-York and Harlem Rail-road Company, p. 13.

I

He who finances, controls. Such had been the truism repeated by the Massachusetts railroad protagonists of the eighteen twenties. Since this group and their later imitators in Maine had in view financial assistance to the railroad from the state, it followed that the state was to be the promoter and planner of the railroad system; not private enterprise but the state was to shape the transportation design. But the failure either of Massachusetts, in the decisive early years of the railroad, or of Maine to adopt the policy of state finance entailed the collapse of the whole structure of planning in so far as it was based upon the premises here set forth. There were, however, other approaches to the goal. Charters gave railroad enterprises their life; charters were the gift of the state. Private citizens did not possess a natural right to the receipt of charters; railroad charters with the grant of eminent domain were given not for the asking but to serve a public exigency or need. Theoretically it was, therefore, possible for every New England state to dictate with vigor and in detail the pattern of the railroad system. The legislature had only to adopt clear and unbending criteria of the public welfare.

The task proved no routine sinecure as the deluge of petitions praying for incorporation poured in. Indeed the Massachusetts

General Court felt its own administrative response so inadequate that in 1845 it substituted for a legislative committee a board of five railroad commissioners, appointed by the governor and council, to receive the petitions for railroad charters, accumulate relevant facts, and report to the legislature — an arrangement which lasted only a year.[1] Whether committee or commission did the work, the determination of public exigency in important cases demonstrated that petitions were not a calm request for the application of abstract principles but storm centers of special interests — communities crazy for railroads, shippers insistent upon lower fares and more convenient facilities, investors and promoters hopeful of making money, and railroads alert to use charters for branches and connections to despoil each other in competitive warfare. Many of these pressures were at work in the early thirties when the Eastern first attempted to secure a charter for a line from East Boston to Salem. The legislature detected no public necessity served by incorporating the proposed road, for transportation between the two places was already adequately served by other agencies, whose vested rights were now to be put in jeopardy. For various reasons also, the railroad, it was said, was likely to be unprofitable and besides it was too closely integrated with the real estate speculations of its petitioners.[2] Three years later, nevertheless, the persistence of promoters and their ingenuity — the proposed line was to extend to Newburyport — won a charter. Enough towns were now interested, enough petitioners signed papers, to create a public exigency in the minds of legislators.[3]

As the years went by, the same criteria were advanced again and again with variations. The new road must give more convenient, safer, quicker, cheaper transportation than that already

[1] *Acts and Resolves Passed by the General Court of Massachusetts, in the Years 1843, 1844, 1845,* pp. 582–583; *Acts and Resolves Passed by the General Court of Massachusetts, in the Years 1846, 1847, 1848,* p. 130.

[2] Report of the Joint Committee on Railways and Canals Relative to a Charter for a Railroad from Boston to Salem, Massachusetts *Senate Documents,* 1833, no. 52.

[3] Report of the Committee on Railways and Canals Relative to a Charter for the Eastern Railway, Massachusetts *Senate Documents,* 1836, no. 77; *Report of the Directors of the Eastern Rail-Road to the Stockholders, at the Meeting Held Sept. 22, 1838* (Boston: Henry P. Lewis, 1838), pp. 3–5.

available; it must give promise of being a profitable enterprise. The proof for the first criterion was easy to obtain. Massive petitions with signatures into the hundreds pointed out the defects of existing agencies or simply testified to a faith in a new enterprise. Here was an arithmetic lawmakers could understand. The proof of profitableness was almost as easy, for engineers and learned counsel were adept in formulating costs of construction lower than those of other roads and calculating potential traffics on the experience of the most lucrative railways in the state.[4]

Formless as these criteria were, they were subsequently displaced by ones more meaningless. In 1861 when the Old Colony sought an extension to Newport, its counsel informed the legislature: "The public exigency requires the building of a railroad wherever, upon the whole, that railroad will pay," — and as long as their virtue was not warped by speculation, the best judges of that profitableness were the stockholders of the corporation. "I ask you to try this petition upon the question whether the Old Colony Railroad and the interest of the public through the Old Colony Railroad, demand this extension." In other words, charters were to be granted largely because petitioners requested them.[5] In truth the determination of public exigency had degenerated into the automatic ritual of getting a charter. Railroad officials, lawyers, petitioners, and lobbyists swarmed the capitol corridors; special enactments — for such charters were statutes of this character — congested committee and legislative dockets. At the worst the outcome of this procedure was corruption; at the best, unprincipled log-rolling — unprincipled because no settled principles existed upon which charters were to be granted or denied. Persistence and pressure, not wisdom, were the touchstones of public exigency.

As the number of railroads multiplied, the determination of

---

[4] *Argument of Charles G. Loring, Esq. on Behalf of the Eastern Rail-Road Company, at a Hearing on the Petitions of David Pingree and Others, and W. J. Valentine and Others, before the Rail-Road Committee of the Massachusetts Legislature, Boston, March 7, 1845* (Boston: Dutton & Wentworth, 1845).

[5] *Argument of Hon. Josiah G. Abbott, Before the Joint Committee of the Legislature of Massachusetts on Railways and Canals, in Favor of the Extension of the Old Colony and Fall River Railroad to Newport, R. I. March 13, 1861* (Boston: Geo. C. Rand & Avery, 1861), pp. 13–17.

public necessity had grown into a larger issue than whether communities wanted transportation or whether the projected road promised profits. "It is an obvious, and, we suppose, an established principle of railroad legislation, that, in determining whether an exigency exists for any *particular* road, the consequences of it upon *other roads* and *other property*, is one great element of consideration." [6] In brief, the determination of public exigency raised fundamental questions of monopoly and competition in the railroad world. In the early thirties Massachusetts had elected monopoly; the pioneer three and the Western all had thirty-year monopolies of their routes. To a limited extent, Rhode Island and New Hampshire imitated the Massachusetts pattern. Though the express bestowal of monopoly grants soon disappeared, the conceptions underlying them did not. They came to the surface in Massachusetts when persistent attempts were made in the mid-forties to open, by way of the Boston and Maine, a channel of transportation between Boston and Lowell other than by way of the Boston and Lowell Railroad. In this quarrel, the specific monopoly grant in the charter of the Boston and Lowell was regarded by many railroad men and statesmen as a secondary line of defence, to be fallen back upon only when the more general case — that all roads had or should have a monopoly of their routes — was lost. For this general case was naturally of wider usefulness; it could be utilized, if established, to scotch all "competing parallel roads," as they were always called.

In support of this more embracing case, the economic arguments were more impressive than the constitutional ones. If two roads divided the existing business, it was said, neither would possess the required means for technical improvements. Depreciation would operate unchecked; service would decline. Nor would the railroad·owners have the means for double-tracking and extensions, or, if they had the means, the inclination to invest them in an "insecure" property. Competition, further-

[6] *Argument of Charles G. Loring, Esq. on Behalf of the Remonstrance of the Boston and Lowell Railroad Co. against the Petition of J. S. Cabot and Others, for a Railroad from Salem to Lowell, Delivered before the Joint Committee on Railroads and Canals, February, 1848* (n.p., n.d.), p. 18.

more, prevented just rate-making. Places with two roads had low rates; those with one road high rates. Finally, competition was impossible, for it was "destructive." Roads would reduce their fares again and again, "and so they will proceed until one breaks down, and the strongest will swallow up the weakest. Or a combination between the two will take place, and then, having the possession of both roads, and the public in its power, the fares will be raised high enough to pay a high profit on the cost of both — or to indemnify the victor for the losses sustained in the contest. And all of which will come out of the people for whose especial benefit it was instituted." The true policy of the state was, therefore, to charter a series of through or trunk lines and supply them with branches or feeders. Within its area each system was to be free from competition.[7] Though legislative committees never adopted this artificial structure, they effectively protected the Boston and Lowell in its specific rights and on occasion showed they were impressed by the arguments against unrestricted competition.[8]

Nevertheless the general theory hardly appealed to a generation accustomed to regard monopoly as a monster and a danger. In the eyes of the moderates, if universal competition were neither feasible nor possible, at least state policy should seek a "proper competition" which would reduce fares and freights and yet yield a "fair return" to railroad proprietors. "Competing parallel roads" within a few miles of each other were anathema; indirect or incidental competition was permissible and desirable.[9]

[7] Argument of Charles G. Loring, Esq. on Behalf of the Eastern Rail-Road Company, pp. 13–16, 31–36, 62–65; Argument of Hon. Daniel Webster, on Behalf of the Boston & Lowell R. R. Company, at a Hearing of the Petitions of William Livingston and Others, and Hobart Clark and Others, Before the Rail Road Committee of the Massachusetts Legislature (Boston: Dutton and Wentworth, 1845), pp. 19–21, 24; Argument of Charles G. Loring, Esq. on Behalf . . . of the Boston and Lowell Railroad Co.

[8] Report of the Joint Standing Committee on Railways and Canals Relative to the Petition of William Livingston, Massachusetts Senate Documents, 1845, no. 30; Report of the Second Joint Committee on Railroads and Canals on Various Petitions, Massachusetts Senate Documents, 1847, no. 104, pp. 9–10.

[9] Massachusetts Senate Documents, 1847, no. 104, pp. 25-28; The Case of William Livingston and Fifteen Hundred Other Citizens of Lowell, Petitioners for a Cross Rail Road from Lowell to Andover. Argued Before a Joint Committee of the Legislature of Massachusetts — January, 1845. Argument of E. H. Derby, Esq.

As for the commonalty, it thought the more railroads the better. After the early forties its simpler notions were in the ascendant. "Competition, we are told, is the secret and soul of all enterprise and progress; that wherever it exists, we behold the greatest advancement in economy, safety and comfort; that monopoly begets annoyance, cupidity and disregard of public safety and convenience; in short, that the history of competition is but the history of improvement, and that we have only to establish competition, and we at once attain perfection, or at least, are travelling with railroad velocity toward it," sneered one of the opponents of the vulgar doctrine.[10] It was to no avail. As the influence of the new beliefs accelerated, legislation restricting leases and business contracts between railroads reflected the trend. Massachusetts, which in 1838 permitted connecting railroads, on the most generous terms, to contract with each other for one "to do and perform, all the transportation of persons and freight," in 1867 abruptly declared the exercise of this power was dependent upon permission of the legislature.[11] Maine had taken the step fifteen years earlier.[12] In New Hampshire, where dread of monopolies was a phobia, a series of enactments constantly changed the contours of constraint. Operating contracts, once without restriction, were in 1850 limited to five years and had to have the approval of the railroad commissioners and the governor and council. By an act of 1867, fetchingly titled "An Act to Prevent Railroad Monopolies," the legislature and governor and council had to assent to all contracts, leases or consolidations of competing roads; the acts of 1850 still applied in the case of extensions, branches, and short-time contracts.[13] Permission for one road to

(Boston: Dutton and Wentworth, 1845), pp. 11–14; Boston and Lowell Railroad Corporation *v.* Salem and Lowell Railroad Company and Others, 2 *Gray,* 37.

[10] *Argument of Charles G. Loring, Esq. on Behalf of the Eastern . . . March 7, 1845,* p. 62.

[11] *Laws of the Commonwealth of Massachusetts, Passed by the General Court, at the Session . . . 1838,* pp. 383–384; *Acts and Resolves Passed by the General Court of Massachusetts in the Year 1867,* p. 694.

[12] Edmund F. Webb, *The Railroad Laws of Maine, Containing All Public and Private Acts and Resolves, Relating to Railroads in Said State, with References to Decisions of Supreme Judicial Court* (Portland: Dresser, McLellan & Co., 1875), pp. 596–597.

[13] *The Revised Statutes of the State of New Hampshire, Passed December 23,*

own the securities of another generally required specific permission. Sometimes states ignored these related issues, dealt with them by special enactment, or like Vermont, let the railroads do what they wanted.

II

Meanwhile the development of the railroad system had turned legislative attention to other regulatory issues for which the charters had first raised the questions and first formulated the answers. One such detail had been the exercise of eminent domain. Under its power the earliest railroads in Massachusetts had been authorized to secure a right of way four rods wide and "for the purpose of cuttings, embankments and obtaining stone and gravel, may take as much more land as may be necessary." Nor did the first charters describe with any precision the route to be followed. When railroads and individuals could not agree upon purchase prices for this private property, an appeal was made to the county commissioners to fix damages.[14] Such arrangements, long customary for canals and turnpikes, aroused reactions as varied as human nature. Though some landowners, "with a liberal desire of promoting so great a public improvement," gave a right of way to the railroad, surprise that legislators should bestow the power of eminent domain upon a corporation and hostility to its utilization were more frequent reactions. Sometimes a ruthless incident explained this feeling. The Boston and Providence laid its tracks through a graveyard and the Boston and Maine in southeastern New Hampshire postponed paying land settlements but proceeded untroubled upon construction. Landowners as unsatisfied creditors grew red with anger.[15]

1842 . . . New Edition. Comprising All the Laws Passed to June, 1850, p. 277; *Laws of the State of New Hampshire, Passed June Session, 1850*, p. 432; *Laws of the State of New Hampshire, Passed June Session, 1867*, pp. 5–6.

[14] *Laws of the Commonwealth of Massachusetts, Passed at the Several Sessions of the General Court, Beginning May, 1828, and Ending March, 1831*, pp. 494, 497.

[15] *Report of the Directors of the Boston and Worcester Rail-Road Corporation to the Stockholders, Together with the Report of John M. Fessenden, Esq. Civil Engineer, and a Plan and Profile of the Location of the Rail Road* (Boston: W. L. Lewis, 1832), p. 8; John Daggett, *Remarks and Documents Concerning the Location of the Boston and Providence Rail-Road through the Burying Ground in East*

Gradually a generalized case emerged. Its formulators, if they had realized the eventual implications of what they were doing, would have been chary in basing it upon the premise that "Railroads are *private* corporations, established for *private* purposes and intended to subserve *private* interests." [16] Once this character was established, it was logical to believe the state had no right to allow railroad corporations to take a man's property — the very basis of his freedom and his natural rights. "When I find that corporations are vested with power to take our property without our consent, and to pay what, and when they please, it is time to inquire if we have the right of possession secured to us by the constitution; and I think that I have a right to inquire if corporations can have power by law to do or practice things which it is unlawful for individuals to do or practice." [17] From this point the argument took on greater heat, until the apostles of private property were shedding tears for tavern owners and stage drivers, denying the most obvious advantages of the railroads, and asserting the good society derived from them was "secondary, remote, and incidental." Railroads were "soulless" or "alien" corporations, "trampling" upon our "dearest rights." [18]

This agitation often resulted in a salutary re-examination of the methods of taking land and a more precise formulation of safeguards for the process. The first general railroad statute of Massachusetts in 1833 focused upon the problem. Henceforth railroads were to describe their routes with precision; present maps, profiles and diagrams of their right of way; and give surety that they would pay the awarded damages. [19] In New

---

Attleborough to Which Are Added, the Statutes for the Protection of the Sepulchres of the Dead, with Remarks on Some of the Powers and Rights of Corporations in This State. By a Freeman of Massachusetts (Boston: Light and Horton, 1834), pp. 25–28; Concord *New Hampshire Patriot and State Gazette*, January 8, 1841.

[16] Concord *New Hampshire Patriot and State Gazette*, December 23, 1841.

[17] *Ibid.*, March 30, 1840.

[18] *Ibid.*, May 4, June 8, 1840, December 9, 1841; *A Letter to a New-Hampshire Land Owner, upon the Constitutionality of Granting the Power of Taking Private Property to Railroad Corporations* (n.p., 1840).

[19] *The General Laws of Massachusetts, Passed January Session, 1833*, pp. 97–101; *Laws of the Commonwealth Passed by the General Court, . . . 1835*, p. 535;

Hampshire the popular hostility to corporations, coupled with the ambitions of politicians, unloosed the four-year "railroad war." It began with an act of 1840 for securing landowners the quiet and peaceable possession of their property; henceforth railroads had to purchase their right of way without the assistance of the state. Though, this chilling provision did not effect enterprises already chartered, it fell upon New Hampshire just as the railroad age was gathering momentum. Partisans of progress were aghast. For years they fought to repeal the measure, to emancipate railroad promoters and builders from "extortion." At last in 1844 they succeeded. A statute of that year with the verbal artistry required for the occasion declared, "All railroad corporations which now are, or shall hereafter be, chartered by the authority of the State, and which shall be unable to purchase the lands for their roads of the owners on their respective routes, at rates agreed upon by the parties, are hereby made and declared to be public corporations." Railroads, thus denominated, could appeal to a board of three railroad commissioners to assess land damages; when these damages were paid the state was to "lease" the road a right of way for at least 100 years "for the public use and benefit." [20]

The quarrel over eminent domain led incidentally to the establishment of the second railroad commission in New England, that of New Hampshire. The Rhode Island Railroad Commission, the first in the region, grew from a controversy over a second common charter provision authorizing railroads "to enter upon and use" one another. More specifically, since the quarrel arose on the Boston and Providence, its charter provided "said road may be used by any person who may comply" with its rules and regulations, and "the state may authorize any company to enter with another rail-road at any point of said Boston and Providence

Report of the Committee on Railways and Canals on the Incorporation of Transportation Companies, Massachusetts *Senate Documents*, 1835, no. 64.

[20] *Thirty-fifth Annual Report of the Railroad Commissioners of the State of New Hampshire, 1879*, pp. 20–24; *Laws of the State of New Hampshire, Passed June Session, 1840*, pp. 433–434; *Laws of the State of New Hampshire, Passed November Session, 1840*, pp. 504–506; *Laws of the State of New Hampshire, Passed November Session, 1844*, pp. 83–88.

Railroad, paying for the right to use the same, or any part thereof, such a rate of toll as the Legislature may, from time to time, prescribe." [21]

Perhaps these inheritances from the turnpike era would have rusted away unnoticed, if it had not been for the competition between the railroad or "monopoly" line of boats on the Providence-New York run and an "independent" line under an obstinate Providence boat owner, John W. Richmond. Naturally the Boston and Providence, favoring the boats with which it had a contract, prevented Richmond's vessels from docking at the railroad wharves in Providence or refused to provide a boat train to meet them.[22] Richmond and his colleagues decided to have a boat train of their own. Since they did not possess resources for building another route to Boston and such a route violated the monopoly grant anyway, it was decided to turn the charter of the Boston and Providence against its beneficiaries. Richmond induced the Massachusetts legislature to charter the Seekonk Branch Rail-Road Company. Its track was to run for a half-mile or less from a depot and wharf on deep water opposite Providence, where the independent steamers could dock, to a junction on the Boston and Providence, and thence trains of the Seekonk Branch Rail-Road were to proceed over the whole line of the Boston and Providence to Boston.[23] To rivet the arrangements doubly tight, the Seekonk's charter authorized it "to enter . . . on . . . the Boston and Providence Rail-Road, . . . paying therefor such a rate of toll as the legislature may, from time to time, prescribe; complying with such rules and regulations as may be established by the Boston and Providence Railroad Corporation." [24] Finally the Seekonk, to pile confusion on confusion,

[21] *Laws of the Commonwealth of Massachusetts, Passed at the Several Sessions of the General Court, Beginning May, 1831, and Ending March, 1833*, pp. 112–113, 116–117.

[22] Reports on the Petition of Tristram Burgess and Others for a Branch Railroad in Seekonk, Massachusetts *Senate Documents*, 1836, no. 89, pp. 12–13, 15–16, 17–19.

[23] Massachusetts *Senate Documents*, 1836, no. 89, pp. 8–9, 23–27.

[24] *Laws of the Commonwealth of Massachusetts, Passed at the Several Sessions of the General Court, Beginning Jan., 1834, and Ending April, 1836*, pp. 988–991.

decided to use the tracks of the Boston and Worcester to reach its own station in Boston.[25]

The nub of the resultant clash of interest and argument was the exact meaning of the phrases "to enter" and "to use," so universally and glibly parroted in railroad charters. The Boston and Providence insisted upon the continuation of a railroad practice already customary: the cars of the connecting railroad, the Seekonk, could pass over the Boston and Providence, but the power, the locomotive, must come from the Boston and Providence. The Seekonk Branch Railroad, on the other hand, appealed to remote precedents. In turnpike charters the right of any one to place his motive power upon the road was taken for granted and, in the provisions of the earliest Massachusetts railroad charters, the General Court apparently had in mind distinctions between those carrying goods at a toll for others, as in the case of the Quincy Granite Railway, and those laying a track for others to use, as in the case of the Franklin Railway. The Boston and Providence charter, they asserted, was in the latter tradition.[26]

Aside from right, a practical matter of operation was involved. The Boston and Providence justly feared the presence of other locomotives than its own upon its track; matters were already complicated enough with one "uncertain train," the boat train, on the line. The Seekonk dismissed these fears, since engineers who were in a post of danger would always avoid "coming in contact with any other train." [27] But such fantasies could not withstand any realistic analysis of human nature nor the massive array of evidence from railroad presidents, engineers, and superintendents all over the country in favor of an opposite practice.[28] There were the usual irrelevant arguments. The Boston

[25] *A Brief of the Remarks Made before the Committee on Rail-ways and Canals on the Petition of the Seekonk Branch Rail-Road Co. By Tristram Burgess* (n.p., n.d.), pp. 24, 26–33.

[26] *On the Petition of the Seekonk Branch Rail-Road Co. A Brief Explained by a Statement of the Case* (n.p., n.d.), pp. 1, 11–14; Report of the Committee on Railways and Canals, on Petition of Seekonk Branch Railroad Company, Massachusetts *Senate Documents*, 1838, no. 98, pp. 54–57.

[27] Massachusetts *Senate Documents*, 1838, no. 98, p. 33; *On the Petition of the Seekonk Branch Rail-Road*, pp. 14–19.

[28] Massachusetts *Senate Documents*, 1838, no. 98, pp. 32–40; *Substance of Argu-*

and Providence asserted the Seekonk was not a genuine "branch" railroad, entitled by charter terms to connection; it brought no new traffic; it was simply another depot. The Seekonk said of its rival that it had fallen into the hands of "Wall Street" and Providence capitalists bent upon crushing Massachusetts. And there was the usual name calling. One of the incorporators of the Seekonk announced, "Our adversaries say we are the bird, which, for procreation, invades and expels others from the nest of their own labors. It is not so. We are the carrier Pelican, who, building in the sands of the desert, does in that reservoir placed by nature between her beak and her bosom, supply her young from distant streams; and sits quietly by while . . . the traveler stops and drinks and lives, and blesses the carrier bird for the precious beverage." [29]

While the rivals were matching comparisons from ornithology, the Seekonk was falling upon hard times. It had difficulty in raising funds, and petitioned for an even shorter line; representatives of the "monopoly" bought two of the boats which would have used the former's terminus and the owners of which had offered to subscribe to its stock; the Massachusetts legislature was unwilling to take decisive measures against the Boston and Providence.[30] At this point the Boston and Providence made conciliatory gestures. After the Massachusetts interest was increased on its board of directors and Josiah Quincy, Jr., became president, the railroad annulled its contract with the boat company and the Massachusetts legislature authorized the sale of the Seekonk to the Boston and Providence.[31] Thus the Seekonk

ments of Respondents' Counsel on the Application of the Seekonk Branch Rail Road Company to the Committee of the Legislature to Run Locomotive Engines on the Providence and Worcester Rail Roads and through the Worcester Merchandize Depot (Boston: J. H. Eastburn, 1838), pp. 5–11; *Evidence Showing the Manner in Which Locomotive Engines are Used upon Rail-Roads: and the Danger and Inexpediency of Permitting Rival Companies Using Them on the Same Road* (Boston: Centinel & Gazette Press, 1838).

[29] *A Brief . . . by Tristram Burgess*, p. 37; *On the Petition of the Seekonk Branch Rail-Road Co.*, pp. 7–8; Massachusetts *Senate Documents*, 1838, no. 98, pp. 24–29.

[30] *On the Petition of the Seekonk Branch Rail-Road Co.*, p. 5; Massachusetts *Senate Documents*, 1838, no. 98, pp. 3–5, 42–43.

[31] Report of the Joint Special Committee Appointed to Investigate the Doings of the Boston and Providence Rail-Road Corporation, Massachusetts *Senate Docu-*

Branch Railroad passed from the scene. It had spent $21,235, it sold out for $31,955. It had never run a train. Crusading certainly paid.[32] Meanwhile in 1839 Rhode Island established a railroad commission of five, among whose duties was "to enquire into any contract, understanding, or agreement by which any railroad shall attempt to transfer, or give to any steamboat company or any steamboat, any favor or preference over any other such company or boat." [33]

Although legislative committees in the Seekonk embroglio scornfully rejected the idea that the right to "enter upon and use" authorized a helter-skelter competition over the tracks of a single company,[34] the concept promised to be useful in another context. Under its provisions, when connecting railroads would not or could not agree upon terms for the effective interchange of passengers and traffic, an appeal could be taken to the state. Unhappily neither legislative nor judicial decision had defined the right with precision or arranged for its effective application. In the early forties the mounting quarrel between the Boston and Worcester and Western over the division of through receipts soon gave opportunity for action. The Western besought the General Court to set the terms under which it could enter upon and use the tracks of the Boston and Worcester.[35] The response was a general enactment. First it ratified the result of the See-

---

ments, 1840, no. 50, pp. 11, 18–20; Seventh Annual Report of the Boston and Providence Rail-Road Corporation, Massachusetts *Senate Documents*, 1839, no. 31, p. 17; *Acts and Resolves Passed by the Legislature of Massachusetts, in the Year 1839*, pp. 81–82.

[32] Eighth Annual Report of the Boston and Providence Rail-Road Corporation, Massachusetts *Senate Documents*, 1840, no. 18, p. 10; Third Annual Report of the Seekonk Branch Rail-Road Company, Massachusetts *Senate Documents*, 1839, no. 31, p. 41.

[33] *Public Laws of the State of Rhode Island and Providence Plantations Passed Since the Session of the General Assembly in January, 1839*, pp. 1087–1088.

[34] Report of the Committee on Railways and Canals on the Right of the Public to Use Railroads, Massachusetts *Senate Documents*, 1837, no. 92, pp. 3–6, 13–20; Report of the Joint Standing Committee on Railways and Canals, Massachusetts *Senate Documents*, 1839, no. 19, pp. 9–10.

[35] *Tenth Annual Report of the Directors of the Western Rail-Road Corporation, to the Stockholders, February, 1845* (Boston: Dutton and Wentworth, 1845), pp. 18–20, 23–25, 27; *Report of the Directors of the Boston and Worcester Railroad, to the Stockholders at Their Fourteenth Annual Meeting, June 2, 1845* (Boston: I. R. Butts, 1845), pp. 10–15.

konk case — no locomotive of any company could use the tracks of another railroad without its consent — and then it declared, "Every Rail-road Corporation, . . . is hereby required, at reasonable terms, and for a reasonable compensation, to draw over their road the passengers, merchandize, and cars of any other Rail-road Corporation, . . . authorized by the legislature to enter with their Railroad upon, or to unite the same with, the road of such Corporation, and use such last named road." If the two roads could not agree, the Supreme Judicial Court was to appoint three commissioners to determine the terms of connection.[36]

The arrangement was a cumbersome one. Hearings took time and cost money. After the decisions were made, their final operation was further delayed by threats of litigation and appeals to the courts. Finally they involved an interference by the state in the affairs of the railroad, an interference exceedingly unwelcome to administrators who desired to run their own business as they chose.[37] Nor were state officials enchanted at the prospect of participating in railroad management; they preferred the railroads should settle their quarrels among themselves.[38] So unpopular a device became, therefore, a form of blackmail in railroad negotiations; one party threatened to resort to it unless concessions were made by the other. Perhaps the state could avoid this administrative degeneration by the appointment of permanent railroad commissioners operating on their own initiative to enforce reasonable connections between recalcitrant or competing enterprises. The Seekonk affair had been a stimulus

[36] *Eleventh Annual Report of the Directors of the Western Rail-Road Corporation, to the Stockholders, February, 1846* (Boston: Crocker and Brewster, 1846), pp. 21–22; *Acts and Resolves Passed by the General Court of Massachusetts, in the Year 1845*, pp. 513–514.

[37] *Twenty-sixth Annual Report of the Directors of the Western Rail Road Corporation, to the Stockholders, January, 1861* (Springfield: J. F. Tannatt & Company, 1861), pp. 13–15; *Points Submitted at the Hearings by E. H. Derby, Esq., in Behalf of the Lexington and Arlington Railroad Company vs. the Petition of the Horn Pond Railroad Company to Enter and Use the Lexington and Arlington, Fitchburg, Boston and Maine, Eastern and Grand Junction Railways at Tolls and Hours to be Fixed by Commissioners* (n.p., n.d.), p. 2.

[38] Report of the Joint Special Committee on Railways and Canals on a Petition of the Western Railroad, Massachusetts *Senate Documents*, 1845, no. 105, pp. 1–2.

to the creation of the Rhode Island Railroad Commission. In the fifties a concern with connections explained the establishment of the Maine commission and the array of duties expected from the Vermont commissioner.

III

Although every New England state but Massachusetts had established a railroad commission or its equivalent by the sixties, the regulation of railroads remained primarily the obligation of other agencies. The state still relied upon the complaints of individuals and the alertness of its officials to unearth violations of charters or of particular and general railroad laws or of the "common law of carriers" and to bring such practices before the courts. The legislature, however, was the active instrument of control, the focus of petitions, pressures, and appeals from the public and from railroad corporations. In turn the legislature devolved its duties upon a committee, whose functions were to hold hearings, conduct investigations, and prepare legislation. At least such was the rôle of the Joint Committee on Railways and Canals in Massachusetts. The field of regulation was large; the powers of the regulators embracing. The railroads were public corporations, and charters which might have placed their operations beyond the pale of governmental tinkering were reduced for all practical purposes to the level of ordinary enactments since, sooner or later, every New England state had declared that railroad charters could be altered and amended by legislative action.[39] The few railroads whose charters antedated such declarations, whose charters were "privileged" and not "open," were either chary in standing upon their rights, or lost them when legislatures insisted upon their surrender as a prerequisite to later legislative assistance or favor.[40] When learned counsel

[39] *The General Statutes of the State of Connecticut, 1866*, p. 140; *The Revised Statutes of the State of Maine, Passed October 22, 1840 and to Which are Prefixed . . . the Other Public Laws of 1840 and 1841 with an Appendix*, p. 329; *The Revised Statutes . . . of New Hampshire . . . 1850*, p. 290; *Public Laws of the State of Rhode Island and Providence Plantations, as Revised . . . and Finally Enacted . . . 1844*, p. 65; *The Acts and Resolves Passed by the General Assembly of the State of Vermont, at the October Session, 1851*, pp. 40-41.

[40] *Resolves and Private Laws of the State of Connecticut from the Year 1836 to*

pleaded for respect for chartered rights, they were, therefore, reduced to asking for carefulness in deliberation and reasonableness in action.[41]

Preliminary to intelligent action of any sort was correct information. Pioneer charters in Massachusetts, therefore, had demanded of their railroad corporations annual reports of "acts and doings, receipts and expenditures." Massachusetts, too, led the way in transforming this generalized requirement into more complete, uniform, and detailed accounts. The first statute in 1837 specified only some eleven items; twelve years later the entries numbered over 150 and were grouped under the rubrics of capital and debt, cost of road and equipment, characteristics of the road, doings during the year, expenditures for working the road, motive power and cars, income, dividends, depreciation, and miscellaneous.[42] The Massachusetts enactments were clearly the pattern followed by New Hampshire in 1850 and Connecticut in 1853.[43] Two years later, when Vermont established the office of railroad commissioner, the officials of the railroads were instructed to make annually "to said commissioner, under oath, such returns and in such form and at such time, as he shall prescribe and make known to them."[44] This provision hit upon the correct principle for returns; it avoided rigidity and made it possible to adapt the schedules to a rapidly changing science of railroading.

Chevalier de Gerstner thought, "There can be no doubt of the accuracy of these reports, as they are certified by oath by the directors when made to the state."[45] Chevalier was naive or

the Year 1857, pp. 902–903, 1045; Report of the Senate Select Committee on Interstate Commerce (Testimony), Senate Reports, 49 Cong., 1 Sess., no. 46, pt. 2 (s.n. 2357), pp. 300–301.

[41] Argument of Hon. Daniel Webster on Behalf of the Boston & Lowell, p. 10.

[42] Laws of the Commonwealth of Massachusetts, Passed by the General Court, in the Years 1837 and 1838, p. 255; Acts and Resolves Passed by the General Court of Massachusetts, in the Year 1849, pp. 124–129.

[43] Laws of the State of New Hampshire, Passed June Session, 1850, pp. 433–437; Public Acts, Passed by the General Assembly of the State of Connecticut, May Session, 1853, pp. 140–145.

[44] The Acts and Resolves Passed by the General Assembly of the State of Vermont, at the October Session, 1855, p. 27.

[45] Francis A. Chevalier de Gerstner, "Letters from the United States of North

ironic. In state after state the railroads made excuses for not providing the information sought, and when they did answer left whole segments of the schedules blank, wrote in totals without details, and for these and other lacunae and malformations advanced as justification the fact that they kept their books in a fashion which did not enable them to make reply. In some states there were no penalties for failure to make the reports; in all, no audit was contemplated. Even in Massachusetts the Joint Committee on Railways and Canals and then the secretary of state, to whom the reports were submitted, had neither the time nor the means for a thorough examination of them.[46] In Rhode Island, although railroad accounts were subject to the right of legislative visit and scrutiny, only rudimentary returns were made to the legislature,[47] and returns in New Hampshire, submitted under the reformed schedule of 1850, were not published after 1858 but were consigned to the lumber rooms of the State House at Concord, "contributing nothing whatever to the public intelligence," as a New Hampshire railroad commissioner sarcastically commented.[48]

The greatest defect of the returns, however, was that data provided by one railroad could not be compared with those from another since classifications were not defined with precision and the directions for assembling data were not stated. The rudimentary state of statistical science, the indifference of legislators, the carelessness and calculated secrecy of railroad officials — all these contributed to the discrepancies and errors of reports. Even in the railroad world, however, there were groups pressing for reform. Railroad investors were partisans of publicity and accuracy, for returns with these qualities protected their interest. Railroad superintendents urged detailed schedules and

America on Internal Improvements, Steam Navigation, Banking, etc.," *Journal of the Franklin Institute*, XXVI (1840), 218.

[46] *First Annual Report of the Railroad Commissioner . . . of Vermont . . . 1856*, p. 8; *Fifth Annual Report of the Railroad Commissioner of the State of Vermont, . . . 1860*, pp. 24–25; Massachusetts *Third Annual Report of the Board of Railroad Commissioners. January, 1872*, pp. lxxxvii–lxxxviii.

[47] *Acts of Rhode Island, January 1838*, pp. 55–56.

[48] *Thirty-third Annual Report of the Railroad Commissioners of the State of New Hampshire*, pp. 8–9.

honest reporting, for such aided the transformation of railroad operation into a science.[49]

IV

Years later, when Charles F. Adams, Jr. undertook to improve the Massachusetts returns, he commented, "It is quite out of the question to ascertain from them even how many miles of railroad there were in Massachusetts at any given time; an item of information, perhaps, as important as any, and one in respect to which accuracy would seem not very difficult of attainment." [50] This caveat, however, does not dispel the necessity of using such figures as there are, for a description of New England's technical railroad achievement.[51] They reveal that construction got slowly under way. Five years after the pioneer three of Massachusetts were completed, the mileage of the New England railroad network was less than that of the Southern states and only 40 per cent of that in the Middle Atlantic area. The decade of the forties brought revolution. As New England's mileage multiplied by five, her construction surpassed that of any other region in the Union. By 1850 the length of her roads was far greater than that of the South and was only a little less than that of the

---

[49] Recommendations of the Committee Appointed to Procure Changes in the Railroad Returns, 1849, *Reports and Other Papers of the New-England Association of Railroad Superintendents from the Commencement of the Society to January 1st, 1850* (Boston: Stacy, Richardson & Co., 1850), p. 33.

[50] Massachusetts *Seventh Annual Report of the Board of Railroad Commissioners. January, 1876*, p. 26.

[51]   Railroad Mileage in the New England States, 1835–1860
                        (Fractional miles omitted)

State	1835	1840	1845	1850	1855	1860
Maine	11	11	62	245	415	472
New Hampshire	—	35	92	467	657	661
Vermont	—	—	—	290	529	554
Massachusetts	113	318	567	1,035	1,264	1,264
Rhode Island	—	46	50	68	108	108
Connecticut	—	102	202	402	496	601
Total	124	512	973	2,507	3,469	3,660

Henry V. Poor, *Manual of the Railroads of the United States for 1873–74* (New York: H. V. & H. W. Poor, 1873), pp. xxvii–xxix; Henry V. Poor, *History of the Railroads and Canals of the United States of America* (New York: John H. Schultz & Co., 1860), pp. 12, 20, 53, 60, 93, 194.

states from New York to Maryland. With 1850 the spurt was over. As the financial pressures of the next ten years slowed railroad construction more gravely in New England than elsewhere, students of railroad affairs wondered whether the region's network was not overbuilt.[52]

Clearly on the fringes of New England there were too many railroads. Vermont's systems were in bankruptcy, the western regions of Connecticut and Massachusetts could hardly support the roads that traversed them. In the center of New England, Massachusetts had a railroad situation unique in America. In the early fifties every one of her towns of 5,000 inhabitants or over was reached by a railroad with a single exception, insular Nantucket, to which even to-day no causeway has been constructed! Of ninety-eight places with 2,000 to 5,000 inhabitants, all but twenty-five were reached by railway and one-half of these exceptions were seaport towns. Massachusetts had one mile of railroad for every seven square miles of her area; New York only one for every twenty-eight, Ohio one for fifty-eight.[53] Connecticut's railroad commissioners, brooding over figures only somewhat less impressive than Massachusetts', observed, "Rail roads are fast becoming the general, if not almost exclusive highways for the transportation of the products of our soil, the enterprise and labor of our mechanics and manufacturers." [54] In short, relative to her size, New England's railroad mileage surpassed that of the rest of the country.

Thirty years also had effected a considerable standardization of construction. They attained that result slowly, for, as a new enterprise, the railroad had to pass through its experimental period; the wonder is, it was so brief. The starting line of this development was the "permanent" construction exemplified by some of the Massachusetts railroads, particularly the Boston and Lowell. "The most solid railroads, and which compare best with European structures, are those constructed in the State of Massa-

[52] J. L. Ringwalt, *Development of Transportation Systems in the United States* (Philadelphia: Railway World Office, 1888), pp. 75–76, 115–116, 142–145.
[53] *Hunt's Merchants' Magazine and Commercial Review*, XXV (1851), 115, 639.
[54] *Fourth Annual Report of the General Railroad Commissioners of Connecticut, for 1856–7*, p. 3.

chusetts," observed Chevalier de Gerstner in the later thirties.[55] One of the pioneer three, the Boston and Providence, had already completely departed from these standards and the retreat continued elsewhere. Technical disadvantages were one explanation. A solid road was too rigid; the passage of trains over it pounded both rails and rolling stock to pieces. A decade after both began operation, per-mile expenses for renewals and repairs of iron and for depreciation of engines and cars on the Boston and Lowell were three times those on the Boston and Providence.[56] Promoters and subscribers, furthermore, wished to avoid the large original investment required for solid roads.

So precipitate was the trend toward lightness that even so eminent a railroad as the Hartford and New Haven, against the advice of Twining, decided upon a superstructure of bed-sills imported from Maine, cross ties from Connecticut, yellow pine timber rails imported from Georgia, and a plate rail 13/16 of an inch thick imported from Great Britain.[57] The Housatonic, built about the same time, also chose for its track a "hoop tacked to a lath," as the president of the Western derisively described this type of construction.[58] Such roads immediately demonstrated their unsuitability. They wore out with disconcerting rapidity. Within seven years of its opening, the directors of the Hartford and New Haven were reporting, "The board cannot conceal the fact, that the interest of the stockholders will be greatly jeopardized, if the present superstructure is not speedily replaced by one of a more substantial kind, and adequate to sustain the increasing business of the road. A conclusive reason for the immediate commencement of this work, is the greatly increased economy of maintaining the track, when relaid with heavy rail."[59] The di-

[55] Chevalier de Gerstner, "Letters from the United States," p. 222.

[56] Hunt's Merchants' Magazine and Commercial Review, XXII (1850), 242–243.

[57] Third Annual Report of the Board of Directors to the Stockholders of the Hartford and New Haven Rail-Road Company (New Haven: Hitchcock & Stafford, 1838), pp. 4, 13.

[58] Report of Engineers and Statement of Commissioners, Relative to the Housatonic Rail Road (n.p., 1836), pp. 8–9; Hunt's Merchants' Magazine and Commercial Review, XIV (1846), 32.

[59] Eleventh Annual Report of the Board of Directors to the Stockholders of the Hartford and New Haven Rail Road Company (Hartford: Case, Tiffany & Burnham, 1846), pp. 9–10.

rectors of the Housatonic did not take so long to come to the same conclusion. Two years after the road was opened, they informed the stockholders, "No sacrifice of a part of the Capital of the Company would be too heavy, by which an adequate edge rail should be placed upon your track."[60] Flimsiness had gone too far.

By the mid-forties, therefore, New England railroads had settled upon the edge rail. They used one pattern or another of the T or H rail, as it came to be called in America. Essentially iron beams with larger head and base and with shrunken waist, they were strong enough to displace the fish-bellied rails and other varieties of an earlier day. At first the new edge rails were held to and above the ties by chairs. By 1860, though chairs were often used at the joining of rails, elsewhere on the track they had generally shrunk to a thin plate and the same spike held both the rail and chair to the tie.[61] Over the years rails were made heavier and heavier. The Boston and Worcester had first been laid with rails of 40 pounds to the lineal yard; the second track put down in the forties weighed 60 pounds, "the stiffest rail used on any Road, with one exception in America," and by 1860 the road had some rails weighing 66 pounds, the maximum for Massachusetts. By then, for most main lines in the state, the minimum weight was 56.[62] These heavier rails were counted upon to solve several problems. They were so rigid that they could overcome many of the defects of grading and ballasting; they could

[60] *Report of Directors of Housatonic Rail Road Company, to the Stockholders. 20th June, 1844* (New York: H. Coggswell, 1844), p. 14.

[61] George L. Vose, *Handbook of Railroad Construction; for the Use of American Engineers. Containing the Necessary Rules, Tables, and Formulae for the Location, Construction, Equipment, and Management of Railroads, as Built in the United States* (Boston and Cambridge: James Monroe and Company, 1857), p. 282; Zerah Colburn and Alexander L. Holley, *The Permanent Way and Coal Burning Locomotive Boilers of European Railways; with a Comparison of the Working Economy of European and American Lines, and the Principles upon Which Improvement Must Proceed* (New York: Holley & Colburn, 1858), Plate 12.

[62] Proceedings of the Directors and Stockholders of the Boston and Worcester Railroad, Ms., Harvard Business School Library, I, 120; *Report of the Directors of the Boston and Worcester Rail-Road Corporation to the Stockholders, at Their Eleventh Annual Meeting, June 6, 1842* (Boston: I. R. Butts, 1842), p. 9; Returns of the Railroad Corporations in Massachusetts, 1860. Together with Abstracts of the Same, Massachusetts *Public Documents*, 1861, no. 46, *passim*.

easily support heavier rolling stock and hence the more advantageous application of steam power; they ought not to wear rapidly.

Railroad men gradually learned, however, that heavy rails were not a substitute for the careful preparation of the roadbed; frost was no respecter of weight. With heavy as with light rails the problem of joining them remained, for at the joints the wear was most noticeable. Should they be "staggered" or "squared"? Should they be "supported" by ties or "suspended" between them? Should they be held together by chairs or by "fishing," a method invented in the forties whereby iron plates were placed on each side of a rail joint and bolted through? [63] There were partisans of all methods. Nor did mere weight mean endurance. Quite the contrary. The rate of wear was capricious. The last of the original iron taken up on the Boston and Providence in 1860 was still in good condition after a quarter-century of service; on the other hand, in the fifties the Fitchburg had to re-lay some of its rails near Boston twice within three years; some new rails had not lasted a twelvemonth. [64] Under the circumstances the average life of a rail — seven or eight years — was meaningless. [65] In truth the iron industry of the United States was not equipped to work a heavy rail into as fine a quality as a light one. Still New England purchasers continued to insist upon heaviness. The same fetish bedeviled them when they repaired to the English and Welsh ironmakers. While English railroad men were imposing exact specifications and carefully inspecting the product, American purchasers were not exacting, often because of their pecuniary necessities. [66] Thus it happened that the quality of rails on New England roads was in the fifties inferior to what it had been earlier in the railroad age.

[63] Colburn and Holley, *The Permanent Way*, pp. 95–101, 106–108.

[64] Charles F. Adams, Jr., *Railroads: Their Origin and Problems* (New York: G. P. Putnam's Sons, 1878), p. 76; E. B. Grant, *Boston Railways: Their Condition and Prospects* (Boston: Little, Brown and Company, 1856), pp. 53, 55–56, 57.

[65] *Twenty-sixth Annual Report of the Directors of the Boston and Worcester Railroad Corporation, for the Year Ending November 30, 1855* (Boston: David Clapp, 1856), p. 12.

[66] Grant, *Boston Railways*, pp. 53, 57–58; Colburn and Holley, *The Permanent Way*, pp. 78–81, 91.

Wooden Truss at Fair Haven, Connecticut

Covered Bridge at Augusta, Maine

WOODEN BRIDGES

The Eastern's Station at Salem

The Fitchburg Station at Boston

On the whole Great Britain supplied the major portion of New England's railroad iron. Her iron-working industry was more advanced than that of the United States, and Congressional action in 1832 exempted imports of rail from the payment of duties. For years, therefore, the first step of any directorate was to dispatch an agent to Wales or England or to order through an English financial house, like the Barings. The delays of Atlantic transportation and the loss of vessels at sea with their cargoes of iron were often the explanation, according to directors, for the retarded construction or postponed opening of roads.[67] In the forties the situation changed somewhat. The tariff of 1842 levied a specific duty of $25 a ton upon imported rails and that of 1846 an *ad valorem* duty of 30 per cent. All the wails of the railroad lobby were of no avail.[68] At the same time the American iron industry undertook the rolling of heavy iron rails.[69]

Although New England tried the business,[70] New England railroads relied for their supplies upon the Middle Atlantic states. Their resort thither was occasionally given a patriotic explanation above tariffs. Thus when the Northern of New Hampshire in 1846 awarded rail contracts to the Mount Savage Works in Maryland and the Tremont Iron Company of Wareham, the directors declared, "It is now, we believe, a well settled fact, that Yankee enterprize and skill can work out a better, and we believe, cheaper article from the Bog ores of the middle States, than Wales, or any other foreign country usually furnishes for export. And if our position be correct, we consider it a duty, as well as pleasure, to employ and reward American labor and skill first and always."

[67] *Third Annual Report of the Board of Directors to the Stockholders of the Hartford and New Haven Rail-Road Company* (New Haven: Hitchcock & Stafford, 1838), p. 5; Records of the Directors and Stockholders of the Boston and Worcester Railroad, I, 87, III, 274; *Report of the Committee for Investigating the Affairs of the Old Colony Railroad Company. Appointed by the Stockholders, December 26, 1849* (Boston: Eastburn, 1850), appendix, p. 40.

[68] Lewis H. Haney, *A Congressional History of Railways in the United States* (Madison: Democrat Printing Company, 1908), I, 144–148.

[69] *Thirty-fifth Annual Report of the Railroad Commissioners of the State of New Hampshire, 1879*, pp. 11–12.

[70] *Boston Board of Trade. 1860. Sixth Annual Report of the Government Presented to the Board at the Annual Meeting, on the 20th January, 1860* (Boston: Wright & Potter, 1860), p. 145.

Its rails cost $85 a ton.[71] But the very next year the siren call of lower prices lured the Northern to place a large order in England at £10 the ton, which even with the addition of the American tariff made a price of only $68.70.[72] In brief, the demand for rails was so heavy and the American mills so inadequate, that importations continued over the tariff. In 1848 fourteen New England railroads had contracted for 51,500 tons in England. With the demand what it was, the average price of American rails at Philadelphia rose from $47.88 in 1850 to $80.13 in 1854. There was then a gradual decline to $48.00 in 1860.[73]

V

Of the railroad structures, bridges had to be built at once. In New England this was no requirement lightly to be brushed aside, for water courses were numerous and New England rivers, particularly when they neared the sea, required spans of great length. Also navigators were always on the alert to prevent the erection of "obstructions." Neither the mouth of the Connecticut nor the Thames was bridged until after the Civil War. On European roads bridges were at the outset built of stone — permanent "works of art" which sent commentators into raptures. Though New England railroads adopted the stone arch, particularly when they had to, masonry was expensive.[74] Builders, therefore, turned to wood. Its supply was unlimited and ordinary carpenters could handle it. Fortunately New England at this moment produced and, to a large extent, nurtured the most remarkable group of bridge designers in the nation. They invented a series of novel wooden trusses which distributed the heavy vertical strains of the train to the whole bridge and its abutments. In the group was S. H. Long, government engineer, locomotive

---

[71] Report of the Directors of the Northern Rail Road (n.p., 1846), p. 7.

[72] The Second Annual Report of the Directors of the Northern Railroad Corporation, to the Stockholders. Presented May 19, 1847 (n.p., 1847), p. 9.

[73] Hunt's Merchants' Magazine and Commercial Review, XIX (1848), 659; Annual Report of the Secretary of the American Iron and Steel Association to December 31, 1874 (Philadelphia: Chandler, 1875), p. 42.

[74] Fourth Annual Report of the Western Railroad Corporation, Massachusetts Senate Documents, 1839, no. 18, p. 56.

builder, railroad surveyor, and explorer, who used arch braces to strengthen his truss; Ithiel Town, one of the most eminent archi- tects of his time, who designed a lattice wooden truss the construc- tion of which was so easy that "it might well be made by the mile, and cut off to order according to the span"; and William Howe, by origin a Massachusetts farm boy, who between the upper and lower chords of his truss arranged wooden diagonals to stand the compression and vertical iron tie rods to maintain the necessary tension. The Howe truss became immensely popular.[75] The second bridge of this type erected in the country was for the Western Railroad across the Connecticut at Springfield. Its seven spans, set on heavy granite piers, were each 180 feet long.[76] Long, Town, and Howe all took out patents on their creations and the first two promoted their use by descriptive pamphlets.[77]

Wooden bridges were universal. Massachusetts roads of the highest finish built them. Roads in northern New England, like the Vermont Central, scrambling to completion before the deluge of financial disaster, threw them across streams without provid- ing for covering and without proper trussing.[78] But their cheap- ness — $50 a foot as compared to $81 for iron in 1860 [79] — did not conquer their disadvantages. Though, like all bridges, flood and freshet menaced them, they had their peculiar perils. A high wind

[75] *Dictionary of American Biography* (New York: Charles Scribner's Sons, 1928– 1936), IX, 298, XI, 380, XVIII, 610–611; Vose, *Handbook of Railroad Construc- tion,* pp. 147, 153, 158; Theodore Cooper, *American Railroad Bridges* (New York: Engineering News Publishing Company, 1889), pp. 10–13; Henry G. Tyrrell, *His- tory of Bridge Engineering* (Chicago: Henry G. Tyrrell, 1911), pp. 137–142.

[76] *Eighth Annual Report of the Directors of the Western Rail-Road Corporation to the Stockholders, Presented February 8, 1843, Comprising a Copy of the Seventh Report to the Legislature* (Boston: Dutton and Wentworth, 1843), p. 14.

[77] Stephen H. Long, *Specifications of a Brace Bridge, and of a Suspension Bridge, Patented by Col. Stephen H. Long. Nov. 7th, 1839* (Philadelphia: 1839); *A De- scription of Ithiel Town's Improvement in the Principle, Construction, and Prac- tical Execution of Bridges for Roads, Railroads, and Aqueducts, Whether Built Entirely of Wood, or of Cast or Wrought Iron* (New York: Ithiel Town, 1839).

[78] *Fifth Annual Report of the Directors of the Vermont Central Railroad Com- pany to the Stockholders. November, 1850* (Montpelier, E. P. Walton & Son, 1850), p. 17; *Sixth Annual Report of the Directors and Treasurer of the Vermont Central Railroad Company, Prepared for the Stockholders' Meeting, August 27, 1851* (Montpelier: E. P. Walton & Son, n.d.), p. 15.

[79] Zerah Colburn, "American Iron Bridges. Abstract of the Discussion upon a Paper Submitted by Zerah Colburn," *Minutes of the Proceedings of Civil Engineers, London, Session of 1862–1863,* p. 3.

lifted off its piers the great wooden bridge, built, according to
Howe's patent, across the Connecticut above Hartford. Train
service was interrupted for forty-five days.[80] More customary
and just as spectacular was fire. Provident corporations provided
fire-fighting apparatus, kept adequate material for replacements
at hand, and even considered the construction of parallel bridges
far enough apart not to catch fire from one another.[81] A more
familiar precaution was to cover the floor way with tin.[82] Apparently the directors of the Boston and Worcester had experi-
mented with a cheaper material, for in 1834 they were ordering
the superintendent "to cause the earth spread on the wooden
bridges of the Rail Road for the purpose of protecting the same
from fire, to be removed and to cause to be put on the said
bridges one or more coats of a certain composition, consisting of
paint, black lead and other ingredients, in order to protect said
Bridges, from fire and to preserve the materials of the same from
injury by the water &c." [83] For the other great enemy of wooden
bridges was decay. Even when they were roofed, they rotted at
the piers and at the junction of the vertical and diagonal members
with the chords. They weakened invisibly. Their life expectancy
was capricious. Uncovered bridges of inferior pine fell within
five years; well designed and built bridges, properly repaired,
lasted eight times as long.[84]

Most designing of wooden bridges was empirical. Practice
determined the necessary strength of their members and doubts
were met simply by increasing the size of the timbers. But by
mid-century Americans were making calculations of strains and

[80] Theodore G. Ellis, *Description of the Iron Bridge Over the Connecticut River,
on the Hartford & New Haven R. R. with a Brief History of Iron Bridges* (Hartford: Brown & Gross, 1866), p. 12.

[81] *Eighth Annual Report of the Directors of the Concord Railroad Corporation,
April 30, 1849* (Concord: Asa McFarland, n.d.), pp. 11–12; *Report of the Directors
of the Boston & Maine Railroad to the Stockholders. Wednesday, Dec. 9, 1874*
(Boston: Alfred Mudge & Son, 1874), p. 11.

[82] *Eighth Annual Report . . . of the Western . . . 1843*, p. 14.

[83] Records of the Directors and Stockholders of the Boston and Worcester Railroad, I, 238.

[84] Vose, *Handbook of Railroad Construction*, p. 173; Tyrrell, *History of Bridge
Engineering*, p. 121; *Report of the Railroad Commissioners of the State of New
Hampshire, June Session, 1861*, p. 56.

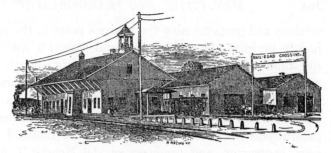

Framingham Station

Worcester Station

Chester Station

Westfield Station

A QUARTET OF STATIONS ON THE ROAD TO ALBANY

tensions and proportioning the bridge's parts to the services they had to perform. Here New England played a somewhat lesser rôle than earlier, for scientific bridge design began in America with Squire Whipple and Herman Haupt. The former, a New England product, did most of his building outside the region. Haupt was a Pennsylvanian, but some of the most important and painful years of his life were spent in New England as the engineer, contractor, and promoter of the Hoosac Tunnel and its attendant railroads.[85] Both Haupt and Whipple did much to popularize at least the partial use of iron in bridges, although the significant experiments in determining its strength were made in Great Britain with its more advanced metallurgical industry. All-iron bridges, however, were a rarity in New England until the late sixties.

Somewhat more slowly railroads realized they would also have to construct freight sheds, warehouses, and passenger depots. Though, in the days of highways, stage-coach corporations had on occasion built or purchased taverns, barns, and stables, they often used buildings owned by others. Perhaps the earliest railroads had some such arrangement in mind, for often their estimated costs of construction contained no appropriations for equivalent structures. Dependence upon others, however, proved unfeasible; the railroads had to provide their own structures. At most stops a small shed or barn served for freight, and depots were small frame buildings from which the roof extended as a shelter for passengers. As the various architectural revivals swept the country, however, their distinctive orders were introduced into railroad architecture, often sheerly for decorative purposes. At other times Gothic piazzas or Greek porticoes were ingeniously and tastefully used to cover the station plaforms. Whatever their style, most stations were of wood and inexpensive. In larger places the train often passed between Doric columns or beneath pointed arches into the station, which thus served as a partial and grimy train shed.[86]

[85] *Dictionary of American Biography*, VIII, 400–401, XX, 70–71; Cooper, *American Railroad Bridges*, pp. 13–15, 22; Tyrrell, *History of Bridge Engineering*, pp. 151, 166.

[86] William Guild, *A Chart and Description of the Boston and Worcester and*

At termini, the largest and most magnificent structures were required. Freight sheds enclosed acres and the gifted builders of wooden bridges were called in to design their roof trusses.[87] Passenger depots were supposed to provide a wide variety of conveniences and comforts from restaurant concessions and "ladies apartments" to railroad offices and public halls; [88] their exterior, moreover, was by its magnificence to be a monumental tribute to the railroad corporation and to the community. Thus Troy's union station, designed by a French architect, had an immense train shed entered by Gothic arches, three towers occupied by the officers of the various companies, the whole in a "style resembling or nearly approaching the Gothic."[89] At New Haven, the station of the New York and New Haven was in the Moorish style; its architect, however, anticipated modern practice by sinking the tracks beneath the building, an arrangement which gave Oliver Wendell Holmes a touch of claustrophobia.[90] Boston by the late forties had five railroad stations, but a somewhat partisan critic thought their brick severity far from suitable. "Barnyard architecture properly belongs to a farm and not to the Athens of America." [91] To the rescue came the Fitchburg. In 1848 it opened an immense station 316 feet long, 96 feet wide; on the first floor were the customary conveniences and two tracks; on the second, a large hall leased for social affairs and concerts. The building material was Fitchburg granite; the style, railroad

---

Western Railroads; in Which Is Noted the Towns, Villages, Stations, Bridges, Viaducts, Tunnels, Cuttings, Embankments, Gradients, &c., the Scenery and Its Natural History, and other Objects Passed by This Line of Railway. With Numerous Illustrations (Boston: Bradbury & Guild, 1847), pp. 21, 25, 29, 39, 53, 57, 67, 79; Records of the Directors and Stockholders of the Boston and Worcester Railroad, I, 201, 231.

[87] Guild, *A Chart and Description*, pp. 10–11; Records of the Directors and Stockholders of the Boston and Worcester Railroad, IV, 77.

[88] Records of the Directors and Stockholders of the Boston and Worcester Railroad, II, 197, III, 72.

[89] *Hunt's Merchants' Magazine and Commercial Review*, XXXII (1855), 769–771.

[90] Talbot F. Hamlin, *Greek Revival Architecture in America* (London, New York, Toronto: Oxford University Press, 1944) pp. 161–162; Oliver W. Holmes, *Favorite Poems and My Hunt After the Captain* (Boston: Houghton Mifflin & Co., n.d.), p. 305.

[91] Boston *Evening Transcript*, July 9, 1847.

or castellated Gothic. At each corner of the massive building rose a huge tower; there were pillars and arches.[92] As usual when such "magnitude and elegance" were involved, directors had to justify the extravagant expenditure.[93]

VI

Although, as Derby observed, "the art of constructing railroads has been and still is progressive," the alignment of roads and the formation of the roadbeds exhibited the least advance of any branch of railroad engineering. Grades and curves which would not have been tolerated in Europe were regarded as a matter of course in New England. Here heavier and more powerful engines were saluted as a substitute for the embankments, cuttings, viaducts, and tunnels required for a level road, and the desire to avoid grades of over thirty feet to the mile was regarded as old-fashioned.[94] Nor were cuts and embankments made on a sufficiently generous scale. Roadbeds were so narrow that the short ties gave an insufficient bearing to the rails and the track rocked from side to side. Slopes were so abrupt and unsodded that erosion, scouring, and slipping were commonplaces. Finally, it was years before builders realized that, if they had enough ballast of sand or gravel or broken stone, and so disposed it that water and moisture would quickly pass through and be carried away in the drains, the phenomena of heaving or sinking rails and of an unequal track in wet or in winter weather would disappear.[95] To prevent such irregularities and also to support their iron rails, the first roads, like the Granite Railroad and the Boston and Lowell, had resorted to stone trench walls built below the frost line. The Boston and Providence, to avoid the expense and the dangerous solidity of such construction, had used longitudinal

[92] R. L. Midgley, *Sights in Boston and Suburbs, or Guide to the Stranger* (Boston: John P. Jewett & Company, 1856), p. 116; Warren Jacobs, "Boston's Old Depots," *Bulletin of the Railway and Locomotive Historical Society*, IV (1923), 4–5.

[93] *Annual Report of the Directors of the Fitchburg Rail-Road, to the Stockholders, at Their Meeting January 10, 1848* (Charlestown: W. W. Wheildon, 1848), pp. 6–7; *The Report of the Board of Directors to the Stockholders of the New-York and New-Haven Rail Road Co., 22 August, 1849* (New York: H. Cogswell & Co., 1849), p. 13.

[94] Derby, "Progress of Railroads in Massachusetts," pp. 31–32.

[95] Colburn and Holley, *The Permanent Way*, pp. 36–59.

wooden subsills. For over ten years the latter practice was standard on all New England railroads. These subsills were planks, usually of hemlock 3 inches thick and 8 inches wide; additional subsills were placed where the rails joined; then chestnut sleepers were placed across this partial flooring.[96] Stronger rails and sufficient ballasting generally enabled builders to dispense with this portion of the superstructure. Better ballasting and better drainage also slowed the decay of ties, an end which more advanced railroads were also seeking through the use of preservatives. The life of ties, it was calculated, was doubled by "Burnettizing," which impregnated the wood with chloride of zinc, or "Kyanizing," which used corrosive sublimate.[97]

Even on the better roads the process of improvement in earthwork and drainage was slow. Deficiencies on this count undoubtedly explained the peremptory vote of the directors of the Boston and Worcester in 1837: "That the superintendent be instructed to require the enginemen to run the Engines at a moderate rate over the road until the rails shall have been adjusted & the road put in order — & to prohibit said Enginemen from passing over the whole road in a shorter time than three hours under any circumstances." [98] The necessity for such instructions was understandable when railroads were new. Twenty years later, however, an investigating committtee of the Boston and Providence was still chronicling the wasteful results of improper practices. "As soon as the severe frost of autumn has set in, the road-bed is more or less deranged by it. The track becomes uneven, the sleepers are disturbed by the alternate freezing and thawing of the ground, the rails get out of level, and the joints imperfect. As winter advances, these defects in the track

[96] Derby, "Progress of Railroads in Massachusetts," p. 32; Fifth Annual Report of the Directors of the Western Railroad, Massachusetts *Senate Documents*, 1841, no. 17, p. 55; *Report of the Directors of the Boston & Worcester Rail-Road Corporation, to the Stockholders, at Their Twelfth Annual Meeting, June 5, 1843* (Boston: A. J. Wright, 1843), p. 10; Third Annual Report of the Fitchburg Railroad Company, Massachusetts *House Documents, 1845*, no. 46, pp. 57–58.

[97] Colburn and Holley, *The Permanent Way*, pp. 67–68; Grant, *Boston Railways*, pp. 58–59.

[98] Records of the Directors and Stockholders of the Boston and Worcester Railroad, II, 207–208.

become as fixed as if the road were converted into cast iron, and the re-adjustment of the track becomes often impossible until the following spring. The cars and engines no longer roll over a smooth road, but are jumped and tossed from one inequality to another, severely jarring all the machinery of the train and rapidly destroying the rail. . . . The whole road becomes, in continued severe weather, crippled and disorganized." [99]

Undoubtedly one explanation for the comparative inferiority of New England railroads to those of Great Britain was technical ignorance. Even when trained engineers were available, American railroad builders groaned over their fees, disregarded their advice, and exalted the abilities of the common man.[100] If selectmen were competent to lay out and construct common roads, surely Charles Paine, a Harvard graduate and a successful manufacturer of woolens, could build a railroad bridge. Comparative costs provided, however, a more fundamental explanation. Legislative expenses, land prices, some material costs were much lower in New England than in Great Britain; the wages of unskilled labor were not. The costs of cuttings, embankments, tunnels, and fills were largely direct labor costs; though Chevalier de Gerstner saw as early as the thirties a steam excavator at work upon the Western, machinery did not play a significant part in the fundamental processes of railroad construction.[101] So New England railroad builders, usually hard pressed to raise investment funds, turned to the items where extensive economies were possible. The greater maintenance costs incurred for an imper-

[handwritten margin note: reversal of cost-ratio Eng / Am.]

---

[99] *Report of the Committee for Investigating the Affairs of the Boston and Providence Railroad Corporation, Appointed by the Stockholders, January 9, 1856* (Boston: J. H. Eastburn, 1856), pp. 25–26.

[100] *Proceedings of the Annual Meeting of the Western Rail-Road Corporation, Held, By Adjournment, in the City of Boston, March 12, 1840, Including the Report of the Committee of Investigation Appointed by the Stockholders* (Boston: Dutton and Wentworth, 1840), p. 11; *Proceedings of the Western Railroad Corporation. With a Report of the Committee of Investigation. 1843* (Boston: Freeman and Bolles, 1843), pp. 13–14; The Records of the Board of Directors of the Western Rail Road Corporation, Ms., Harvard Business School Library, I, 17–20.

[101] E. H. Derby, "American *vs.* English Railroad Management," *Hunt's Merchants' Magazine and Commercial Review*, XXIII (1850), 237; Chevalier de Gerstner, "Letters from the United States," p. 297; Colburn and Holley, *The Permanent Way*, pp. 22–31.

fectly constructed railroad did not bother them — at least in anticipation. The railroad, once built, would create prosperity; then profits and further investments could replace on a nobler scale the original light construction.

VII

Comparatively little is known about the first passenger cars on New England railroads. Those on the Boston and Providence, as on some other roads outside New England, transferred the equipment of the highway to the rails. Their cars were stagecoach bodies mounted on four wheels and suspended from leather springs; their capacity was 25 to 30 passengers. The Boston and Providence also adopted a distinction between first and second-class passengers,[102] for the first railroad managers were far from certain that it was either possible or profitable to treat all passengers alike. Ladies, in an era that deified feminine fragility and gentility, required special comforts and privacy. Gentlemen of the old school, like Samuel Breck, found traveling in crowds extremely distasteful. His strictures on a journey over the Boston and Providence in 1835 have become a classic.

"Two poor fellows, who were not much in the habit of making their toilet, squeezed me into a corner, while the hot sun drew from their garments a villainous compound of smells made up of salt fish, tar, and molasses. By and by, just twelve — only twelve — bouncing factory-girls were introduced. . . . 'Make room for the ladies!' bawled out the superintendent. "Come gentlemen, jump up on the top; plenty of room there.' . . . The whole twelve, were, however, introduced, and soon made themselves at home, sucking lemons and eating green apples. There is certainly a growing neglect of manners and insubordination to the laws, a democratic familiarity and a tendency to level all distinctions. The rich and the poor, the educated and the ignorant, the polite and the vulgar, all herd together in this modern improvement in travelling. The consequence is complete amalgamation. . . . Talk of ladies on board a steamboat or in a rail-

[102] E. G. Young, "The Development of the American Railway Passenger Car," *Bulletin of the Railway and Locomotive Historical Society*, XXXII (1933), 46, 54; J. Knight and B. H. Latrobe, *Report upon the Locomotive Engines and the Police and Management of Several of the Principal Rail Roads in the Northern and Middle States, Being a Sequel to the Report of the 8th of January, 1838, upon Railway Structures* (Baltimore: Lucas and Deaver, 1838), pp. 8, 10.

road car! There are none. I never feel like a gentleman there, and I
cannot perceive a semblance of gentility in any one who makes part
of the travelling mob." [103]

At the other extreme from first class, railroads planned or provided special cars or treatment for, "*colored* or *insane* persons,"
whom the directors of the Boston and Worcester lumped together,
for workmen and for immigrants.[104] For the last group, parties of
twenty on the Western were charged $3.oo each and of one hun-
dred, $2.oo each "for conveyance in the freight train in the second
class or merchandize cars." [105]

In New England, as in the rest of the country, it usually proved
hard to adapt car construction to the distinctions of travelers.[106]
By 1860 only four roads publicly advertised first and second-
class rates.[107] Probably, however, this figure under-estimated the
gradations of passenger accommodations. There were "paddy
cars," "Irish cars," "Jim-Crow cars," — either second-class
coaches or old equipment to which Negroes were, for instance,
often consigned. For the upper classes some roads provided
parlor cars. In the latter classification, the Eastern in 1846 had
the honor of putting into service a car with swivel seats, silk curtains, red plush carpets, and silver-plated spittoons.[108]

All cars had meanwhile become "long" cars, enabled to round
the short curves of the New England lines by a mounting upon
two swivel trucks of four wheels each. Gridley Bryant, or the
railroads which made use of him, successfully proved in an historic patent case that he had invented and used this device for the

[103] H. E. Scudder, ed., *Recollections of Samuel Breck with Passages from His
Note-Books, 1771–1862* (Philadelphia: Porter & Coates, 1877), pp. 275–276.
[104] Records of the Directors and Stockholders of the Boston and Worcester
Railroad, II, 4, III, 79.
[105] Records of the Proceedings of the Board of Directors of the Western Rail
Road Corporation, Ms., Harvard Business School Library, II, 29.
[106] Dionysius Lardner, *Railway Economy; A Treatise on the New Art of Transport, Its Management, Prospects, and Relations, Commercial, Financial, and Social, with an Exposition of the Practical Results of the Railway in Operation in
the United Kingdom, on the Continent, and in America* (New York: Harper &
Brothers, 1850), p. 346.
[107] *Snow's Pathfinder Railway Guide, for the New England States and Part of
Canada . . . January, 1860* (Boston: Geo. K. Snow, n.d.), pp. 11, 13, 14.
[108] Lardner, *Railway Economy*, p. 346; Young, "The American Railway Passenger Car," p. 61; *Liberator*, November 12, 1841, March 4, April 29, 1842.

Granite Railway; John B. Jervis of the Mohawk and Hudson or Ross Winans of the Baltimore and Ohio, however, had first applied it to passenger transportation.[109] The ordinary long coach had reversible seats and a center aisle. With their capacity of sixty passengers,[110] the proportion of dead-weight per passenger was lower than on European railroads; such cars were, therefore, more profitable to operate. But they were graceless and uncomfortable. The center aisle was one long spittoon; they lacked toilet facilities, ventilation, light, and heat. By the early forties, however, the first steps had been taken to furnish luxury to the sovereign people. At the end of the cars builders provided "saloons" for men and women. Stacks through the roof gave crude ventilation, and lamps or candles furnished illumination. Stage-coach precedents for warmth had been discarded — for example, the directors of the Boston and Worcester in November, 1834, had instructed a committee "to procure a suitable quantity of bear, buffalo, or sheep skins . . . to be spread on the floors of the passenger cars," — in favor of a stove.[111] Meanwhile, though the practice of numbering cars had displaced that of naming them, romance was perpetuated in the gay reds and yellows with which the outside of the cars were painted or the pictures with which they were occasionally adorned.[112] Some trains were mobile art museums.

For lack of data the evolution of the prosaic freight car cannot be chronicled. At first there were flat cars upon which some proposed to carry loaded wagons and their drivers, there were open cars in which the goods themselves were covered, and there were

[109] J. S. Bell, "The Genesis of the Locomotive Truck," *Bulletin of the Railway and Locomotive Historical Society*, XV (1927), 72–78; Lardner, *Railway Economy*, p. 338; *Argument of William Whiting, Esq., in the Case of Ross Winans v. Orasmus Eaton, et al., for an Alleged Infringement of His Patent for the Eight-Wheel Railroad Car. Before Hon. Samuel Nelson, Justice of the United States, for the Northern District of New York* (Boston: J. M. Hawes & Co., 1853), pp. 66–68, 99–104.

[110] H. E. Scudder, ed., *Recollections of Samuel Breck*, p. 277.

[111] Records of the Directors and Stockholders of the Boston and Worcester Railroad, I, 248; *American Railroad Journal*, XIV (1842), 380–381; Lardner, *Railway Economy*, pp. 337–338.

[112] Records of the Directors and Stockholders of the Boston and Worcester Railroad, III, 110; C. E. Fisher, "The Famous Color Trains of America," *Bulletin of the Railway and Locomotive Historical Society*, IV (1923), 24.

enclosed cars.[113] On these last the canvas tops gave way to those of wood and tin, and the hinged doors, a menace on a double track, to those that slid.[114] Though the change was somewhat slower for freight than for passenger cars, the four wheels quickly gave way to the eight wheels on two swivel trucks. As early as 1836 the directorate of the Boston and Worcester instructed the superintendent always to buy long merchandise cars when purchases were authorized by the board.[115] By the fifties the ordinary box car was 28 feet x 8½ feet x 6½ feet or 7 feet high; its usual load, eight tons. For the freight as well as the passenger cars the running gear was simple. As early as 1840 the first couplings, chain links and hooks, had given way to the link and pin, and the brakes, once set directly by a lever, were now applied by a chain wound about a shaft turned by a brake wheel.[116]

New Englanders, it is clear, were not the pioneers in the improvement of rolling stock. That did not prevent the development within the area of car manufactories. Even here the railroads had to give some impulse. After purchasing their first cars in the Middle Atlantic states, the directors of the Boston and Worcester were instructing the president "to ascertain whether passenger-cars may be procured to be built at Boston or the vicinity on more favourable terms than can be done at the South, and also to ascertain how soon four passenger cars may be procured to be built by any mechanic or mechanics in this vicinity, — also to examine, & consider, the expediency of establishing on the present depot near Washington Street — without delay, a workshop in which cars may be built & repaired." [117] Within three weeks the road had contracted with Davenport and Kimball of Boston, later Davenport and Bridges of Cambridge, and with

[113] Records of the Directors and Stockholders of the Boston and Worcester Railroad, I, 251.

[114] Eighth Annual Report . . . of the Concord Railroad . . . 1849, p. 5; Ninth Annual Report of the Directors of the Western Rail-Road Corporation to the Stockholders: and the Eighth Report to the Legislature; January, 1844 (Boston: Dutton and Wentworth, 1844), p. 15.

[115] Records of the Directors and Stockholders of the Boston and Worcester Railroad, II, 185.

[116] Young, "The American Railway Passenger Car," pp. 58–59.

[117] Records of the Directors and Stockholders of the Boston and Worcester Railroad, I, 195; American Railroad Journal, XXVI (1853), 403–404.

Osgood Bradley of Worcester for passenger cars. Both were
makers of carriages. Both came to be among the leading car-
building firms of New England. By the next decade individuals
like the Wasons of Springfield, with some mechanical ability
started car works without the apprenticeship of gigs, coaches,
and carriages. The largest of these works made the wheels, axles,
springs, journals, and other iron-ware as well as assembled the
cars.[118] Like the English ironmasters and New England railroad
contractors, they often took their pay in railroad securities.[119]
Meanwhile, as the Boston and Worcester had foreshadowed, the
railroads built cars in their own shops with an efficiency often in
dispute between the directors and investigating committees.[120]

VIII

Since New England at the outset of the railroad age lacked
locomotive works, her railroads were compelled to import their
engines. Like their contemporaries elsewhere in America, they
turned to English makers, among whom the Stephensons were the
most prominent. Stephenson locomotives ran in Maine upon the
Bangor and Piscataquis, and in Massachusetts they were the first
engines upon each of the pioneer three.[121] New Englanders purchased also from American producers, for by 1835, as the region's
first lines were opening, two of the most famous builders in
America, M. W. Baldwin and William Norris, had erected their
works in the Middle Atlantic states. By the end of the following
year, the last of the big three, Rogers, Ketchum, and Grosvenor,

---

[118] Records of the Directors and Stockholders of the Boston and Worcester
Rairoad, II, 196, 199; *American Railroad Journal*, XX (1847), 683, XXII (1849),
120; James L. Bishop, *A History of American Manufactures from 1608 to 1860*
(Philadelphia: Edward Young & Co., 1868), III, 334–336; D. H. Hurd, Com-
piler, *History of Worcester County, Massachusetts, with Biographical Sketches of
Many of Its Pioneers and Prominent Men* (Philadelphia: J. W. Lewis & Co., 1889),
II, 1632–1633.

[119] *Report of the Committee for Investigating . . . the Old Colony Railroad . . .
1849*, appendix, pp. 137–138.

[120] *Report of the Directors of the Boston and Maine Railroad, to the Stockholders, at Their Annual Meeting, September 12, 1849* (Boston: Eastburn's Press,
1849), pp. 7–8.

[121] A Letter from the Secretary of the Treasury Transmitting Information in Relation to Steam Engines, *House Executive Documents*, 25 Cong., 3 Sess., no. 21
(s.n. 345), pp. 30, 45.

announced themselves ready to build locomotives and tenders at their shops in Paterson, New Jersey.[122] Luckily, at this moment the Secretary of the United States Treasury made a careful enumeration of the locomotives at work on American railroads. In 1838 the combined roster for all New England lines was forty-five. Of this number eight were American locomotives built outside New England, twelve had been imported from Great Britain, and the remaining twenty-five had been built in New England shops.[123] But these relative totals must not conceal the decisive importance of the English locomotives. They were the pace-makers; they set the style.

It is unfortunate, therefore, that the experts in the field of loco-motive history, a field almost as recondite as genealogy which it in some respects resembles, cannot agree upon the characteristics or the types of these earliest locomotive immigrants. Since neither models nor engines survive and the technical accuracy of available pictures is usually conjectural, so wide a latitude is given for interpretation that the first *Stevenson* on the Boston and Lowell has been identified as a *Samson* type, a *Northumbrian* type, and a *Planet* type.[124] There is no doubt, however, that the *Planet* type became in the thirties the favorite pattern for the New England roads. From Stephenson and from others came its characteristic features — the multi-tubular boiler and the draught forced by a steam exhaust, both devices essential for maintaining steam pressures in so compact a power plant. On Stephenson's earlier locomotives, the cylinders had been placed at an angle and driving rods had been connected to the wheels; this arrangement gave a shimmying motion to the engine and every down-stroke was a blow upon the track. In the *Planet* type the cylinders were horizontal, were placed inside the engine frame, and were connected, not with the wheels, but with the axle which was cranked, though of course less intricately, like the crank shaft of an automobile. These inside-connected locomotives rode

---

[122] *Dictionary of American Biography*, I, 541–542, XIII, 555–556, XVI, 112–113.
[123] *House Executive Documents*, 25 Cong., 3 Sess., no. 21 (s.n. 345), pp. 30, 49, 51, 59, 86.
[124] *Bulletin of the Railway and Locomotive Historical Society*, XXII (1933), 39–41, XXXIV (1934), 58–63.

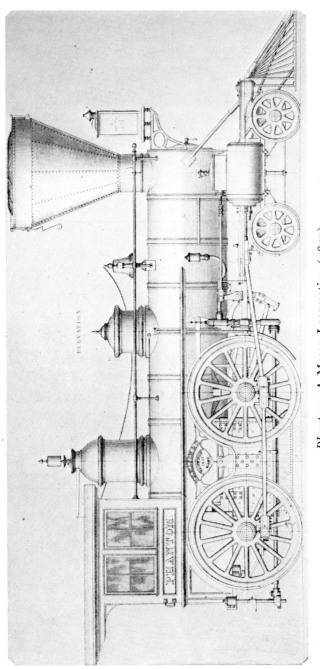

Phantom: A Mason Locomotive (1857)

smoothly. The first *Planet* type in New England had one set of 5-foot drivers, a set of somewhat smaller lead wheels, — hence they were 2–2–0's in the nomenclature of the locomotive classifiers — and weighed somewhat over ten tons.[125]

Within a decade, however, the *Planet* and other types, foreign and domestic, acquired some striking American features. One was the lead truck of four wheels connected with the engine framework by a swivel. This device served for the locomotive the same function that it did for long cars.[126] Then the number of drivers was doubled — an innovation generally attributed to Henry R. Campbell — and the rear pair were driven by ties coupled to the forward two. At first the drivers were mounted so rigidly that the locomotives in use tore both themselves and the track to pieces. Joseph Harrison prevented this destruction by his equalizer. The bearing between the engine and the drivers was a fulcrum centered between the forward and rear drivers which were thus enabled to tilt up or down and conform easily to the irregularities of the rails.[127] The resulting engine, a 4–4–0 whether inside or outside connected, was known as the American type. The innovators who had made it so, however, were not New Englanders.

By 1840 the more foresighted among the latter were becoming aware that different traffics required engines of different characters. In the transport of passengers, speed, convenience, and comfort were the desiderata; frequent trains drawn by light engines, with large drivers, — every rotation of the driver sending the engine forward farther with less vibration — and inside con-

[125] Zerah Colburn, *Locomotive Engineering, and the Mechanism of Railways: A Treatise on the Principles and Construction of the Locomotive Engine, Railway Carriages, and Railway Plant, with Examples* (London and Glasgow: William Collins, Sons, and Company, 1871), I, 31–32.

[126] Angus Sinclair, *Development of the Locomotive Engine. A History of the Growth of the Locomotive from Its Most Elementary Form* (New York: Angus Sinclair Publishing Company, 1907), pp. 200–201; William H. Brown, *The History of the First Locomotives in America. From Original Documents, and the Testimony of Living Witnesses* (New York: D. Appleton and Company, 1871), pp. 213–214.

[127] Sinclair, *Development of the Locomotive Engine*, p. 639; E. G. Young, "Historical Notes on Locomotive Design, 1769–1840," *Bulletin of the Railway and Locomotive Historical Society*, XVI (1928), 21–22.

nected, served such purposes well. In the carriage of freight there were obvious economies in fuel and repairs in long trains pulled at slower speeds with more powerful engines. More power also was essential upon a road with grades, for on such the effectiveness of the engine collapsed with disheartening rapidity. A solution was not easy. The tractive power of a locomotive depended upon its grate area, the size of its boiler, the number and length of boiler tubes, the dimensions of the cylinder, and the stroke of the piston; if all of these were enlarged, the result was a heavier engine. Superficially such weight was all to the good. The portion of it brought to bear upon the track through the drivers meant an increase in the engine's adhesion and its consequent effectiveness in operation. But immense weights on single drivers broke axles and pounded the light rails of New England roads to pieces. The answer was the distribution of the weight through a multiplication of drivers.[128]

Apparently in search of perfection on this score, the Western in the early forties, on the advice of its engineer, Major Whistler, purchased for $11,000 apiece seven Winans engines. All their eight wheels were drivers; the engines weighed 22 tons; their power plant was a vertical boiler. It was thought they could haul 80 tons of merchandise and 60 tons of cars. "Engines of this capacity," wrote the road's president, "with a greater adhesion than any others known, are indispensable to our heavy freighting business over high grades." Unfortunately their parts broke easily and they failed to keep up steam. The whole experiment expired miserably in the recriminations of investigations by stockholders and the state legislature.[129] Ironically enough, fifteen years later a leading American locomotive engineer was berating

---

[128] *Report of the Directors of the Boston and Worcester Rail Road, to the Stockholders, at Their Annual Meeting, June 1, 1840* (Boston: Samuel N. Dickinson, 1840), pp. 12–15; *Report of the Directors of the Boston & Worcester Rail Road Corporation to the Stockholders at Their Tenth Annual Meeting, June 7, 1841* (Boston: Samuel N. Dickinson, 1841), pp. 9–19; Zerah Colburn, *The Locomotive Engine: Including a Description of Its Structure, Rules for Estimating Its Capabilities, and Practical Observations on its Construction and Management* (Philadelphia: Henry Carey Baird, 1853), pp. 171–178.

[129] *Proceedings of the Western Railroad Corporation with a Report of the Committee of Investigation* (Boston: Freeman and Bolles, 1843), pp. 17–27, 49–68, 111–120; *A Letter to the Majority of the Joint Committee of the Legislature, on the*

the Western for its conservatism in running small and frequent passenger trains. It should have heavier engines, a "concentration of power." [130]

Nonetheless engines had increased steadily in size and power. These changes also consigned inside connections to oblivion. It was impossible to secure room for the rotation of the cranked axle beneath the larger boilers without turning the engine into a top-heavy structure. Indeed, one of the arguments for Maine's broad-gauge system was that it could carry larger engines and perpetuate inside connections. Aside from the fundamental difficulty of space, inside connections were a mechanical weak spot, and they were hard to reach for repair. Improvements in counter-balancing the drivers at the same time removed the need which had once called inside connections into existence.[131] By 1855 the New England engines had usually discarded this characteristic, though not universal trait. Like those in the rest of the country, its locomotives were now outside connected.[132]

But the locomotives of the region still presented a fascinating variety when in 1851 the New England Association of Railway Superintendents and the Middlesex Mechanics Association put them on view and provided opportunity for appraising their qualities. Perhaps inspired by the country fair, these two groups arranged a trial of speed and of "power of draft" by locomotives from the New England railroads. Seven passenger and three freight engines were entered; all had been either built or rebuilt between 1849 and 1851; one indeed was fresh from the shops. The track for both freight and passenger tests mingled straights and curves, but never exceeded a gradient of nine feet. The increase in weight since the day of the *Planet*, if the mechanics had been historically minded, was impressive. One-half of the engines weighed over 45,000 pounds. Although there were still engines

---

Affairs of the Western Rail Road with Some Additional Testimony Proposed by the President of the Corporation (Boston: Eastburn's Press, 1843), pp. 6–20.

[130] Zerah Colburn, "The Economy of Railroads, as Affected by the Adaptation of Locomotive Power — Addressed to the Railroad Interests of New England," *American Railroad Journal*, XXVII (1854), 241–245.

[131] *American Railroad Journal*, XXVI (1853), 406, 765.

[132] Colburn, *Locomotive Engineering and the Mechanism of Railroads*, I, 80.

with only two driving wheels, the majority had either four or six. The winning passenger engine was the *Addison Gilmore* of the Western Railroad. The heaviest locomotive entered, 50,885 pounds, it had two immense driving wheels, 6.9 feet in diameter, and two carrying wheels; it traversed the contest distance of 9 miles in 12 minutes, 18.2 seconds. The *Nathan Hale* of the Boston and Worcester, 47,095 pounds, with four drivers of 5.6 feet, covered it in 12 minutes and 55.3 seconds. The winning freight engine was the *Milo* of the Boston and Lowell. Comparatively speaking a light engine, 38,900 pounds, it had six drivers, each four feet in diameter.[133]

As this display was taking place, New England railroads were on the verge of changing from wood to coal fuel. From the very beginning the advantages of coal had been realized. In 1832 Loammi Baldwin, writing to his brother, James F. Baldwin, covered this subject in observations upon his railroad experiences in New Jersey and southward: "The locomotives burn pine wood, & the sparks, from the velocity of the cars, fall upon, round, & into the cars so as to endanger the cloths. Great patches are already burned in the lining & curtains of the cars. A bag of biscuits on the top of one car took fire, & the man thru it off to prevent the car from taking fire. I hope you will avoid this in the Lowell railroad. You must burn coke or Lehigh coal, & I would provide for it in the outset, for I want your road and travelling to be perfect from the first start." [134] Some New England railroads made an effort to follow such advice.[135] However by 1840 they had generally abandoned the experiment. Wood was the chosen fuel.

It was said that anthracite engines, since both the mineral and chemical action of the coal wore out the fire-boxes, ran up larger repair bills and that engine drivers preferred wood since it was the easiest fuel of all to manage. With wood, no crusted fires had

---

[133] *New England Association of Railway Superintendents. Report of the Trial of Locomotive Engines, Made upon 1st and 2d October, 1851* (Boston: J. B. Yerrinton & Son, 1852).

[134] Loammi Baldwin to James F. Baldwin, December 2, 1832, Ms., Baldwin Papers, XXXVI, Harvard Business School Library.

[135] Proceedings of the Directors and Stockholders of the Boston and Worcester Railroad, II, 1.

to be broken, no clinkers removed, no variable drafts deftly manipulated.[136] More fundamental, however, were the relative costs of wood and coal. In the early forties when the Western Railroad began its experiments with the Winans locomotives, originally designed to burn coal, the road insisted that they be altered for wood, since "coal would be a less economical kind of fuel than wood." [137] Those who liked to scold found other reasons for the New England conservative preferences. In the use of coal, as in changes of locomotive design, "there was in New England a deliberate resistance to real improvement. . . . Such real and now unquestioned improvements as were open to all, had to fight their way, inch by inch, for five years, before railway men would be convinced." [138]

In the fifties change got under way. Cheaper supplies of high grade bituminous were brought to New England by the coasting trade from the Middle Atlantic states, where canals and railroads moved the new fuel to tidewater. Among others, the gifted master mechanic of the Boston and Providence, George S. Griggs, equipped the firebox of locomotives with a deflector just below the tubes and thus formed a combustion chamber where air was mixed with the coal gases. Such engines burned bituminous advantageously.[139] At the same time the rising prices of cordwood, particularly in southern New England, turned attention to coal. The directors of the Boston and Worcester complained that the cost of fuel was "a subject of much anxiety," and the Boston and Providence, alarmed at a fuel shortage, bought 1,753½ acres of woodlands in Virginia and built a railroad and sawmill to utilize it. An exponent of railroad efficiency calculated that burning coal would save the Boston railroads $355,886 a year and be equivalent to a dividend of 1.51 per cent upon their stocks.[140]

[136] Colburn and Holley, *The Permanent Way*, pp. xvi–xxi, 117; Jonathan Amory, *Economy in the Generation of Steam, with Some Suggestions upon the Proposed Substitution of Coal for Wood upon Railroads* (Boston: Bazen and Chandler, 1857), pp. 4–7, 12–14.

[137] *Proceedings of the Western Railroad Corporation . . . 1843*, pp. 50–51.

[138] Colburn and Holley, *The Permanent Way*, p. xxi.

[139] Alexander L. Holley, *American and European Railway Practice in the Economical Generation of Steam* (New York: D. Van Nostrand, 1861), p. 94.

[140] *Twenty-fifth Annual Report of the Directors of the Boston and Worcester*

Road after road made experiments. On the Providence and
Worcester, for instance, the *Slater*, burning bituminous coal from
Cumberland, was pitted against the *Grafton*, burning wood. The
Slater saved one-half the fuel bills.[141] The Old Colony, the Bos-
ton and Providence, the Boston and Worcester, the New Haven,
the Eastern, the Fitchburg, even the Boston and Maine, which
used to get "wood cheaper than any other railroad leading out of
Boston," all found coal superior to wood by 1860.[142]

IX

As the census of locomotives taken by the Secretary of the
Treasury had shown, New England in 1838 built the majority of
the locomotives used upon her roads. By the fifties this tendency
was even more pronounced. Some railroads built engines in their
own shops; the shop foremen or master mechanics on the Boston
and Providence and on the Western, George S. Griggs and Wilson
Eddy, were among the foremost designers in the nation.[143] More
numerous were the engines from New England's merchant builders. The Mill Dam Foundry, which built the *Yankee* for the
Boston and Worcester in 1834, the first locomotive built in New
England, had no continuous history in the new industry.[144] A

Railroad Corporation, for the Year Ending November 30, 1854 (Boston: David
Clapp, 1855), p. 12; *Report of the Committee for Investigating . . . the Boston
and Providence Railroad . . . 1856*, p. 24; Grant, *Boston Railways*, pp. 128–129.
   [141] Grant, *Boston Railways*, pp. 120–127; *Report on Fuel Used in Locomotives
on the Boston and Maine Railroad, for Charles Minot . . . and Ross Winans*
(Boston: Stacy, Richardson & Co., 1850).
   [142] *Report of the Directors of the Boston and Maine Railroad to the Stockholders. Wednesday, Sept. 14, 1859* (Boston: Henry W. Dutton & Son, 1859), pp.
8–10; *Report of the Directors of the Boston and Maine Railroad to the Stockholders. Wednesday, Sept. 11, 1861* (Boston: Henry W. Dutton & Son, 1861), pp.
6–7; *The Twenty-fifth Annual Report of the Eastern Rail-Road Company, for the
Year Ending May 31st, 1860* (Boston: Henry W. Dutton & Son, 1860), p. 9; *Report of the Board of Directors to the Stockholders of the New York & New Haven
Railroad Company. May 12, 1859* (New York: Wynkoop, Hallenbeck and Thomas,
1859), pp. 5–6; *Fifth Annual Report of the Directors of the Old Colony and Fall
River Rail Road Company, to the Stockholders January, 1859* (Boston: Crocker
and Brewster, 1859), p. 5; *Eighteenth Annual Report of the Directors of the
Fitchburg Railroad Company, Made at Their Annual Meeting, January 31, 1860*
(Boston: 1860), p. 9; Boston & Providence Railroad Locomotive and Repair
Works, Coal Consumed, Miles Run, &c., Year Ending Nov. 30th, 1859 (Broadside).
   [143] John W. Merrill, "Eddy Clocks," *Bulletin of the Railway and Locomotive
Historical Society*, II (1921), 13–18; Sinclair, *Development of the Locomotive En-
gine*, pp. 199–209.   [144] *Report . . . of the Boston & Worcester . . . 1841*, p. 16.

more important pioneer was the Locks and Canal Company of Lowell, which in 1834 summoned Major George W. Whistler to that city to construct engineering works and locomotives. This arrangement, tying together the Boston and Lowell Railroad, the cotton mills of Lowell, and engine building, forecast a common New England phenomenon.[145] The building of locomotives, in one fashion or another, was usually connected with the shops devoted to the construction and repair of cotton machinery. Such shops had equipment; their workers had training and skill. Locomotive building at Manchester fell into the same pattern.[146] South of Boston, at Taunton, long a center of iron working in New England, there were two producers, the Taunton Locomotive Works and William Mason and Company. Before he made locomotives, Mason won a reputation as the inventor of a self-acting mule and operated a large plant devoted to the manufacture of textile machinery.[147] As time went on, however, the connection between textiles and locomotives weakened or disappeared. The most prolific manufacturer in New England was the Boston Locomotive Works. By 1855 it had turned out somewhat over 500 engines. Its founder was Holmes Hinkley, an itinerant carpenter, pattern maker in machine shops, and builder of steam engines.[148] At least this establishment had an artisan background. The Portland Locomotive Works, chartered in 1848 by John A. Poor to build engines for the Atlantic and St. Lawrence, did not have even that.[149]

Greater than Whistler, Griggs, or Eddy, was William Mason. Of all the New England builders, his thought left the sharpest image upon the American locomotive. Although he emphasized interchangeable parts, Mason was not interested in quantity pro-

[145] Edwin R. Clark, "Early Locomotive Building in Lowell, Mass.," *Bulletin of the Railway and Locomotive Historical Society*, VII (1924), 29–31, 42–57.

[146] Charles E. Fisher, "Locomotive Building at Manchester, New Hampshire," *Bulletin of the Railway and Locomotive Historical Society*, XXVI (1931), 9–14.

[147] Charles E. Fisher, "The Rival Builders," *Bulletin of the Railway and Locomotive Historical Society*, II (1921), 27–42.

[148] Engine Book of Hinkley and Drury, Ms., Boston Public Library; Charles E. Fisher, "The Hinkley Locomotive Works," *Bulletin of the Railway and Locomotive Historical Society*, XXV (1931), 6–11.

[149] Charles S. Given. "The Portland Company," *Bulletin of the Railway and Locomotive Historical Society*, IX (1925), 6–18.

duction; he emphasized precision and beauty. The counterbalances on the wheels of his outside-connected engines were not ugly iron plates, but lead poured into the hollowed spokes and rim of the wheel. He spaced apart the wheels of the swivel truck; he leveled the cylinders; he arranged the steam dome, sand-box, and smokestack symmetrically above the boiler. "The chimney, which although comparatively light, has necessarily the appearance of great weight, was thus brought directly over the truck, which supported its load with the symmetry of a pedestal in architecture. Mason discarded all outward incumbrances . . . thus leaving all the working parts in full view, and a clear range from end to end and under the boiler. The horizontal lines of his running board, hand rail, feed pipe, etc., heighten the symmetry of the design, while the graceful forms and disposition of the details give a finished expression to the whole sufficient to raise it to the dignity of a work of genuine art." [150] It was no accident that this distinguished New England builder was also an accomplished painter and musician.[151]

Although New England-built locomotives were sold to the trans-continentals and were shipped to foreign countries, their greatest employment was naturally in New England itself. North of the Boston and Worcester and the Western, their use was almost universal.[152] Probably the most conspicuous exception was the Vermont Central, whose engineer, Henry R. Campbell, came from Pennsylvania and was associated with the engine builders of that region. Besides, the Rutland and Burlington had purchased New England engines; they could not be good.[153] Of the seventy-two engines on the long roster of the Western Railroad in 1860, only two came from outside New England — from W.

---

[150] Bishop, *A History of American Manufactures from 1608 to 1860*, III, 322.

[151] Charles E. Fisher, "William Mason," *Bulletin of the Railway and Locomotive Historical Society*, XV (1927), 28.

[152] Charles E. Fisher, "Locomotives of the Boston & Maine Railroad," *Bulletin of the Railway and Locomotive Historical Society*, XXVI (1931), 18–22, XXVIII (1932), 13–23, XXXI (1933), 7–9, XXXII (1933), 30–38, XXXV (1934), 52–76, XXXVIII (1935), 40–46.

[153] Inglis Stuart, "Charles Christopher Rowell," *Bulletin of the Railway and Locomotive Historical Society*, XXIX (1932), 18–19.

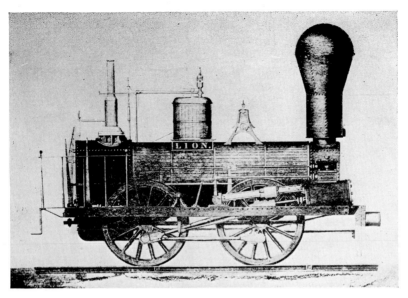

Lion (1844), Hinkley and Drury
Nashua and Lowell Railroad

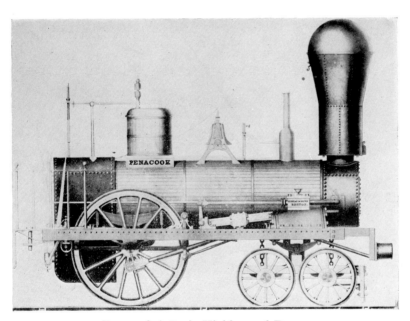

Penacook (1842), Hinkley and Drury
Concord Railroad

THE EVOLUTION OF THE LOCOMOTIVE

General Stark (1849), Amoskeag
Concord Railroad

Attleboro (1855), Boston and Providence Shops

Norris and Company.[154] Though on New England's roads, built in the New York interest, New England engines had some share, the favorite builder for the New Haven was Rogers, Ketchum, and Grosvenor. After all, Thomas Rogers, the founder of this concern, was a New Englander, a Connecticut exile to New Jersey.[155]

X

To formulate a system of operation for the railroad was as great a triumph of the human mind as to invent its equipment. Men, who for centuries had ridden or driven horses or traveled in boats, were suddenly called upon to devise orderly arrangements for the passage of powerful engines over a fixed track. Up to that time this was the most revolutionary and novel burden ever imposed in the field of transportation upon manual skill and administrative imagination. One task was to keep the roads running the year round, to make sure that they were not like the derided canals and rivers, a seasonal means of transportation. Their enemy was snow. While the optimistic hoped for a remedy in milder winters or a snow like that of Maine dry, fine, and easily handled, the realistic devised measures.[156] On one line the directors apparently first resolved to shovel out with men and with scrapes drawn by horses; on another, the engineer proposed, as a less obvious solution, laying the road with greatly elevated chairs in order to be above the snow.[157] But eventually all roads came to the snowplow. A few boards on the front of the engine sufficed for flurries; but for heavier falls superintendents designed huge

[154] *Twenty-sixth Annual Report of the Directors of the Western Rail Road Corporation, to the Stockholders, January, 1861* (Springfield: J. F. Tannatt and Company, 1861), p. 29.

[155] Charles E. Fisher, "Locomotives of the New Haven Railroad," *Bulletin of the Railway and Locomotive Historical Society*, XL (1936), 62–67, XLIII (1937), 60–63, XLIV (1937), 64–65.

[156] James Hall, *Report of a Reconnoisance of a Route for a Railroad from Portland to Montreal* (Portland: A. Shirley & Son, 1844), pp. 14–15.

[157] Proceedings of the Directors and Stockholders of the Boston and Worcester Railroad, I, 238, 239, 258; Knight and Latrobe, *Report upon the Locomotive Engines*, appendix H; John M. Fessenden, *Report on the Surveys and Definite Location of the Eastern Rail Road* (Boston: Freeman and Bolles, 1836), p. 13.

implements as high as the headlights, bolted to the engines.[158]
Still with the light locomotives of the day, only repeated spasms
of withdrawal and attack could pierce the drifts.

A snow-blown track was a battlefield. Thoreau meditated:

> "I am less affected by their heroism who stood up for half-an-hour
> in the front line of Buena Vista, than by the steady and cheerful
> valour of the men who inhabit the snow-plough for their winter quar-
> ters; who have not merely the three o'clock in the morning courage,
> which Bonaparte thought was the rarest, but whose courage does not
> go to rest so early, who go to sleep only when the storm sleeps or the
> sinews of their iron steed are frozen. On this morning of the Great
> Snow, perchance, which is still raging and chilling men's blood, I
> hear the muffled tone of their engine bell from out of the fog-bank of
> their chilled breath, which announces that the cars *are coming*, with-
> out long delay, notwithstanding the veto of a New England north-
> east snow-storm, and I behold the ploughmen covered with snow and
> rime, their heads peering above the mould-board which is turning
> down other than daisies and the nests of field-mice, like boulders of
> the Sierra Nevada, that occupy an outside place in the universe." [159]

Yet New England weather sometimes vetoed heroism. For three
days in 1840 snow and ice delayed the trips of the Boston and
Worcester and "part of them were entirely defeated." [160] Improved
equipment, however, diminished the frequency of such embar-
goes.

Before the railroads were built, some felt that the New England snow would enforce a shutdown for the winter. Others dis-
couragingly speculated on the impossibility of operating numerous trains in both directions over a single track. Railroads might
be feasible when they were so short that one train, shuttling back
and forth, provided sufficient service, or the tracks were so
straight that the engine crew could, at least in daylight and fair
weather, see the dangers ahead.[161] But even the pioneers recog-

[158] Chevalier de Gerstner, "Letters from the United States," p. 291; James H.
French, "Early Railroad Times," *Bulletin of the Railway and Locomotive Historical Society*, VI (1923), 53.

[159] Henry D. Thoreau, *Walden* (Boston: Houghton, Mifflin & Co., 1889), I,
186–187.

[160] Ninth Annual Report of the Boston and Worcester Rail Road Corporation,
Massachusetts *Senate Documents*, 1841, no. 17, p. 15.

[161] Nathan Hale, *Remarks on the Practicability and Expediency of Establishing
a Rail Road on One or More Routes from Boston to the Connecticut River* (Bos-

nized these instances as exceptions. Luckily the solution was easy and early. In 1828 the Board of Commissioners of Internal Improvements for Massachusetts had solved the problem by foreseeing the start, simultaneously from Boston and Providence, of "caravans" of coaches and of wagons which proceeding at fixed rates of speed could pass at calculated spots through the use of "movable rails." [162] Thus early were the "fixed meeting" orders of the New England railroads anticipated. Difficulties, however, at once arose; the solution could not apply to loose trains, like the "steamboat trains" leaving the terminals of the southern New England roads the moment the boat arrived. Such, though they were advertised as expresses, felt their way along. Early running instructions on the Boston and Providence enjoined the "greatest care" and the sounding of a bell on curves, and instructed the conductor to "keep a good look-out, sending one of his Brakemen ahead to *look round* curves, if he have any doubt with respect to the vicinity of a train which may be expected approaching him." [163] Even for ordinary trains, a completely rigid system of fixed meetings was undesirable. Accident or prolonged delay might bring all operations to a standstill. Running instructions, therefore, provided for waits of a certain length, gave rights of way to certain categories of trains, and permitted them to proceed on occasion with caution.

The best cure for the inflexibility of running rules or for the occasional disasters, sure to arise from the exercise of individual judgment, was a double track.[164] Lines like the Boston and Lowell had been graded for a road of that sort at the outset.[165] By 1860, although some of the dowager lines in Massachusetts

---

ton: William L. Lewis, 1827), pp. 7–8; *Reports Made to the Directors of the Massachusetts Rail Road Association; on the Practicability of Conducting Transportation on a Single Set of Tracks* (n.p., 1829).

[162] *Report of the Board of Commissioners of Internal Improvements in Relation to the Examination of Sundry Routes for a Railway from Boston to Providence. With a Memoir of the Survey* (Boston: Dutton & Wentworth, 1828), pp. 31–36.

[163] Knight and Latrobe, *Report upon the Locomotive Engines*, appendix A.

[164] *Report . . . of the Boston & Worcester . . . 1840*, p. 9; *Report . . . of the Boston & Worcester . . . 1841*, pp. 5–9.

[165] Third Annual Report of the Boston and Lowell Railroad, 1834, Massachusetts *Senate Documents*, 1834, no. 26, p. 7.

had done little in this direction, the Fitchburg was double-tracked and the route to the Lakes and the route to Albany had been thus improved as far as Concord and Springfield, respectively. In Connecticut the great central thoroughfare from New York to New Haven, Hartford, and Springfield was nearly all double-tracked.[166] Even on lines thus equipped, the problem of maintaining proper intervals between trains remained. "Many of the roads of Massachusetts . . . made use of appliances more or less crude and antiquated, such as semaphore signals, dials, sand glasses and green flags." In other cases the conductor as he ran read the number of fingers held up by a station agent or glanced at the figures chalked on a board.[167] Railroad operation by telegraph was the real key to flexible operation on both single and double-track lines. Indeed it was a less expensive alternative to double-tracking. Though some companies in the late fifties made a partial and discretionary use of this new instrument, most New England roads did not. In instances it was met with outright hostility.[168] In short, the slow speeds and the sparse number of trains on New England lines was the greatest assurance of railroad safety.

XI

The state also took a hand as people were injured or killed at highway crossings or while riding in the cars. To be sure, such unfortunate individuals or their heirs had recompense under the common law. Railroads could be sued for damages if they were guilty of negligence and the injured party had observed due diligence and carefulness.[169] These traditional devices, however,

[166] Poor, *History of the Railroads and Canals of the United States*, pp. 45, 104, 122–127, 135, 160, 197, 210; *Nineteenth Annual Report of the Directors of the Western Rail-Road Corporation, to the Stockholders. January, 1854* (Boston: Crocker and Brewster, 1854), p. 6.

[167] Massachusetts *Third Annual Report of the Board of Railroad Commissioners. January, 1872*, p. cxxxix; Zerah Colburn, "Safety System of the New York and New Haven Railroads," *American Railroad Journal*, XXVII (1854), 37–39.

[168] Charles E. Fisher, *The Story of the Old Colony Railroad* (Charles E. Fisher, 1919), p. 24; Charles F. Adams, Jr., *Notes on Railroad Accidents* (New York: G. P. Putnam's Sons, 1879), pp. 64–65.

[169] Commonwealth *v.* Boston and Worcester Railroad Corporation, 101 *Massachusetts*, 202.

were not preventive and major accidents, piled with drama, compelled the passage of safety laws. It is no mere coincidence that the first major enactments on the subject came in the fifties. The Norwalk disaster in 1853 directly inspired Connecticut's "Act to Prevent Injuries and the Destruction of Life upon Railroads and by Railroad Trains," of its sort the most systematic statute passed by any New England state. By the fifties, moreover, the railroads had been long enough in operation to reveal their defects and dangers. It was a decade of appraisal by legislators as well as investors.

For safeguards at crossings, legislation early prescribed a bell for every engine, the length of its tolling, and the erection of warning boards over the highways — "RAIL ROAD CROSSING — LOOK OUT FOR THE ENGINE WHILE THE BELL RINGS." [170] The erection of gates, the employment of flagmen, or the elimination of crossings were not mandatory except on petition or complaint, usually to the county commissioners. The railroad bore all the expenses of such improvements or alterations.[171] Such legislation accomplished little. For the protection of passengers, statutes required a brakeman for every two cars and a full stop before trains crossed drawbridges or other railroads.[172] Finally the Connecticut statute of 1853, already mentioned, appointed a board of three railroad commissioners. Then and later they were given extensive powers to inspect roads to determine if their construction and operation were consistent with the public safety and to make recommendations for repairs, the employment of additional workers, and the adoption of

[170] *The Statutes of the State of Connecticut . . . 1854*, p. 753; *The Revised Statutes of the Commonwealth of Massachusetts, Passed November 4, 1835; to Which are Subjoined an Act in Amendment Thereof and an Act Expressly to Repeal the Acts Which are Consolidated Therein, Both Passed in February, 1836*, p. 347; Webb, *The Railroad Laws of Maine*, p. 583.

[171] *The General Statutes of the Commonwealth of Massachusets Enacted December 28, 1859, to Take Effect June 1, 1860. Second Edition, 1873*, pp. 356, 361; *The Compiled Statutes of the State of New Hampshire . . .* [1851], pp. 348, 351.

[172] *Public Acts Passed by the General Assembly of the State of Connecticut, May Session, 1853*, pp. 132, 134; *Public Acts Passed by the General Assembly of the State of Connecticut, May Session, 1854*, p. 119; *The General Statutes of the Commonwealth of Massachusetts . . . 1860*, p. 360; Webb, *The Railroad Laws of Maine*, pp. 587, 613.

safety devices.[173] In 1860 Maine imitated such legislation.[174]

All states, according to their varied lights, sought to determine and punish the parties responsible for accidents. It was not enough to admit the corporation could be sued; guilt should be personal. Officials who knowingly permitted certain forbidden practices or employed any conductor, engineer, brakeman, or switchman "who shall make use of intoxicating liquors as a beverage," might be fined or imprisoned; employees if they violated certain rules or caused injury or death to others might be punished for negligence or manslaughter.[175] Although provisions in this legislation on occasion effected operational innovations, it was often nothing more than the legalization of rules and practices already in force upon the most progressive railroads.[176]

Within the framework of the operating rules, equipment, and natural circumstances, the railroads achieved speeds surpassing the expectations of the railroad schemers of the twenties. Nothing much was demanded of freight trains; they were bound in any case to be faster than freight wagons or coasting vessels. By 1860 their average speed in Massachusetts approximated thirteen miles an hour.[177] As for passenger trains, the inevitable dream was a speed of a mile a minute, sixty miles an hour. Though some of the earliest engines in England and America attained that rate on short stretches, New England waited to the forties to show that it could be done. An engine built at Lowell for the Western in 1842 was capable of three miles in two minutes,[178] and six years later, when the president of the Vermont Central offered

[173] *Public Acts . . . of Connecticut, May Session, 1853,* pp. 132–139; *Public Acts Passed by the General Assembly of the State of Connecticut, May Session, 1856,* p. 9.

[174] Webb, *The Railroad Laws of Maine,* pp. 630–631.

[175] *Public Acts . . . of Connecticut, May Session, 1853,* pp. 133–134; *The General Statutes of the Commonwealth of Massachusetts . . . 1860,* p. 362; *Acts and Resolves Passed by the General Assembly of the State of Vermont, at the October Session, 1851,* p. 43; Webb, *The Railroad Laws of Maine,* pp. 597–598.

[176] Fifth Annual Report of the Directors of the Boston and Worcester Rail-Road Corporation, 1837, Massachusetts *Senate Documents,* 1837, no. 43, pp. 28–29; Proceedings of the Directors and Stockholders of the Boston and Worcester Railroad, I, 191, 223–225, II, 13–14.

[177] Returns of the Railroad Corporations in Massachusetts, 1860. Together with Abstracts of the Same, Massachusetts *Public Documents,* 1861, no. 46, Abstract.

[178] Portland *Eastern Argus,* March 21, 1842.

Baldwin $10,000 for an engine capable of pulling a passenger train at the rate of sixty miles per hour, the builder responded with the leviathan *Governor Paine*, weighing 50,000 pounds, which reputedly ran a mile in 43 seconds.[179] But, after all, these were exceptions. The average rate of speed for passenger trains on the Massachusetts roads in 1860 was 23 miles an hour.[180] Still this was progress. At the beginning of the century it had taken days to get out of New England. On the eve of the Civil War, travelers could escape from Boston to Montreal, if they were willing to pay the price of spending the night in White River Junction, Vermont, in 17 hours running time. Fugitives from the capital of Massachusetts could reach Albany in 8 hours and 55 minutes, and New York, by the all-rail route, in 8 hours and 10 minutes.[181] But who would want to be a fugitive from Boston?

[179] R. H. Sanford, "A Pioneer Locomotive Builder," *Bulletin of the Railway and Locomotive Historical Society*, VIII (1924), 17.

[180] Massachusetts *Public Documents*, 1861, no. 46, Abstract.

[181] *Snow's Pathfinder Railway Guide, for the New England States and Part of Canada . . . January, 1860*, pp. 14, 19, 20, 21.

X

THE RAILROAD CRISIS

"We have invested in these Railroads millions on millions of dollars, and a great portion of the money is at this moment useless to those who invested it, while the public is a gainer. Towns and neighborhoods have been brought to life without the stockholders receiving even their legal interest." — Proceedings of the Convention of the Northern Lines of Railway . . . 1850, p. 20.

I

In 1851 Boston celebrated the final completion of her railroads to the West and Canada and the inauguration by her own citizens of steamboat communication with Liverpool. Both events, interconnected, provided the occasion for retrospective rejoicing and unchecked prophecies of a glorious future. Although just twenty years earlier the charters for the pioneer railroads of Massachusetts had been granted and sixteen years had passed since the first railroad had been completed, Massachusetts, according to as sound calculations as any available, had now over a thousand miles of railroad within her boundaries and another thousand miles of tributaries elsewhere in New England; Boston railroads reached to Portland, Montreal, Ogdensburg, Albany, and New York City, and were groping toward more remote destinations. So three days, September 17, 18, and 19, were set aside for the Great Railroad Jubilee and invitations were issued. Outside Boston the response was not wholly satisfactory. State governors were too busy to attend. But the governor of New York sent a graceful and generous message declaring that the great prize for which both Boston and New York were striving, the trade of the West, was large enough for all. "After yielding to you a share sufficient to satisfy any but an inordinate and grasping ambition, enough will remain for us. . . . A manly and generous competition is beneficial to every interest." [1] From the British North American colonies came the governor general, Lord Elgin, and an entourage which included railroad statesmen like Francis Hincks, the prime minister, and Hon. Joseph Howe, provincial secretary of Nova Scotia. From Washington came no less a personage than Millard Fillmore, the President of the United States, to congratulate the city on "the intelligence of your citizens, who have also opened avenues of commerce to the western world, which is now, through them, pouring into your lap her rich treasures. You have stretched, too, your Briarean arms to the capital of my own State, and laid her under contribution, and have now reached even to the Canadas, and made them also contributors to your still increasing wealth." [2]

For three sunlit, happy days the city surrendered to joy. On the first day there was the reception to the President, at which the large attendance of ladies was in the fashion of the day a subject of remark. On the second day guests and hosts sailed about the harbor and welcomed Lord Elgin at the Western Railroad Station. Although his throat was full of dust from a day of railroad travel, he was glad to celebrate "the conjugal union of the Canadas with the Ocean." The third day was distinguished by the "Procession, the Dinner on the Common and the Fireworks and Illuminations in the evening." The President was unable to ride in the procession owing to "a sudden, though happily not serious, indisposition," [3] but Harvard students and mechanics both marched through streets alive with flags, bunting, and printed sentiments; the dinner on the Common was served in a huge pavilion, 250 by 90 feet, decorated with flags, representations of trains in motion, and maps of Boston's railroad system. It all seemed a magnificent fulfillment of the magisterial prophecy

---

[1] *The Railroad Jubilee. An Account of the Celebration Commemorative of the Opening of Railroad Communication between Boston and Canada, September 17th, 18th, and 19th, 1851* (Boston: J. H. Eastburn, 1852), p. 208.

[2] *Ibid.*, p. 65.　　　　　　　　　　　　　　　[3] *Ibid.*, pp. 95, 102–103.

made two years earlier in the mayor's inaugural address: "The long winter of New England isolation is broken; — she now warms and flourishes in friendly and thrifty intercourse with the luxuriant West; and it is not too much to anticipate that the day will come, when there will be no greater or more prosperous city upon the American continent than the City of the Pilgrims." [4]

Yet the last day of the Boston Railroad Jubilee closed with an ominous but unarranged symbolism. As the celebrant orators at the great banquet talked the afternoon away, the autumn evening settled over Boston. The flags, the banners printed with happy sentiments, even the huge railroad maps grew dim. Darkness took possession of the pavilion. The impatient chairman called upon Josiah Quincy, Jr., to *"enlighten* the audience." In a brief paragraph of response he assured the stockholders and officers of the new railroads of the importance of their labors "whatever might be the pecuniary results." A moment later the mayor adjourned the meeting with the traditional exhortation, "GOD SAVE THE COMMONWEALTH OF MASSACHUSETTS." [5] A few months later Quincy was a bankrupt, the railroad depression, already in being, tightened its grip, and the darkness of the pavilion on Boston Common covered the railroad network of New England.

The surface indications of collapse were read in the quotations of railroad securities. The year 1850 may serve as a point of departure for by then most of the through roads were in operation. Generally the decline reached its nadir in 1856. Within these years on the pioneer three of Massachusetts, the stock of the Boston and Lowell sank from a minimum value of 111 to one of 52; that of the Boston and Worcester from 91¾ to 74½; and that of the Boston and Providence from 79¼ to 60. Among roads of the middling sort, the stock of the Eastern declined from 93¾ to 38¾; the Fitchburg from 105½ to 67. At the periphery of New England, the stock in the Northern of New Hampshire nearly halved in value between 1850 and 1857, while that of the Vermont Central and the Rutland and Burlington fell, respectively, from highs of 45¼ and 69 in 1850 to lows of 1¼ and 3

Ibid., p. 11.   [5] *Ibid.*, pp. 185–186.

in 1854. Little wonder that neither stock was quoted on the Boston market after that year.[6] Perhaps the destruction of values is better illustrated by totals. Between 1845 and 1856 the value of the stock of the seven railroads leading out of Boston fell from $18,539,000 to $12,279,000 in spite of the fact that the number of shares increased from 164,000 to 278,000.[7]

Of course this decline in security prices was not mirrored precisely in the dividend columns. The Hartford and New Haven and the Boston and Worcester were hardly affected. In 1855, on the other hand, the Boston and Lowell reduced its traditional 8 per cent dividends to 3 per cent; the Boston and Providence, which had averaged 6 per cent for a decade, passed its dividend; and both the Eastern and the Fitchburg, which had once paid 8 per cent or better, did likewise. In the previous year the Northern of New Hampshire had ceased payment of its modest dividends. The Rutland and Burlington and the Vermont Central never paid anybody anything at any time.[8] Soon in the hinterland the long process of receiverships and bankruptcies was to begin. By the end of the decade, in New England as a whole, dividends on well over a third of the stock and interest on a third of the funded debts had stopped.[9] No wonder that the railroad crisis, deeper in New England than elsewhere in the nation, left its severest mark upon the region. No wonder speakers, writers, pamphleteers, newspaper correspondents, railway officials, and experts tried to understand and explain the cessation of dividends and the deflation of railway securities. No wonder investigating committees, appointed by the stockholders, pried into books when they could find them, scrutinized accounts, and interviewed officials. Nearly every railroad of importance had at least one such examination; several had more.

[6] Joseph G. Martin, *A Century of Finance. Martin's History of the Boston Stock and Money Markets, One Hundred Years. From January, 1798, to January, 1898* (Boston: Joseph G. Martin, 1898), pp. 146, 148.

[7] William Appleton and W. H. Swift, *Massachusetts Railroads. 1842 to 1855* (Boston: J. H. Eastburn, 1856), p. 15.

[8] Martin, *A Century of Finance*, pp. 147, 149.

[9] Henry V. Poor, *History of the Railroads and Canals of the United States of America, Exhibiting Their Progress, Cost, Revenues, Expenditures and Present Condition* (New York: John H. Schultz & Co., 1860), pp. 11, 39, 69–71, 91, 193.

II

Though every aspect of railroad construction and operation underwent appraisal, it was natural to turn first to the methods of railroad financing. After all, it was securities which had declined in value; it was dividends that were missing. The analysts, therefore, sought to determine the costs of the New England railroad system, to discover beneath the oratorical strata of "millions upon millions" the realities of railroad financing. For the end of the fifties Henry Varnum Poor was printing reliable totals. The face value of the stock was $92,347,526, of the funded debt or bonds $46,883,600, and of floating debt $6,506,755.[10]

Of this sum, state or local governments had provided a considerable proportion. In New England, Massachusetts was the only state to join the ranks of the Middle Atlantic and Western states usually more solidly associated with the policy of financial assistance to railroads. Rhode Island and Maine, soon after the railroad age got under way, included in their constitutions a virtual prohibition against using state credit directly or indirectly for paying "the obligations of others" and set a limit upon the size of their state debts;[11] the other New England states simply did not imitate the Massachusetts pattern. Massachusetts herself was no niggard. By 1860 she had authorized contributions of $8,200,000 to eight railroads.[12] From time to time efforts had been made to base this procedure upon proper principles. At the beginning of the successful drive for state aid, a legislative committee had warned that railroads must rely primarily upon private capital, that state funds should be supplementary, and that they must never be invested in an enterprise likely to relapse into

[10] *Ibid.*, pp. 12, 40, 71, 93, 186, 194.

[11] *General Laws of Rhode Island, Revision of 1909*, p. 26; *The Revised Statutes of the State of Maine, Passed April 17, 1857; to Which are Prefixed the Constitutions of the United States and of the State of Maine*, pp. 49–50.

[12] *Supra*, I, 130–134, 193–194, 196–198; *Laws of the Commonwealth of Massachusetts, Passed by the General Court, in the Years 1837 and 1838*, pp. 75–77, 196–198, 200–202, 392–394, 413–415; *Acts and Resolves Passed by the Legislature of Massachusetts, in the Year 1839*, pp. 75–76; *Acts and Resolves Passed by the General Court of Massachusetts, in the Year 1854*, pp. 149–153.

the hands of the state.[13] Neither then nor later was the state willing to participate in management. In only two corporations did it appoint directors. Since the state legislature rarely instructed them in policy they acted as individual business men and not as delegates.[14] In brief, the Commonwealth was chiefly concerned in measures to protect its investments. To that end railroads were to establish sinking funds, give bonds secured by their franchise and property, and transfer to the state railroad stock, usually to the amount of the loan.[15]

Fifteen years later, in 1853, when a constitutional convention assembled, a large minority supported proposals forbidding state assistance without a popular referendum or a two-thirds majority in the General Court.[16] Normally the resulting debate should have proceeded on the high ground of principle informed by experience. Indeed, on occasion supporters of the suggestions declared that private capital was now sufficient to finance all railroads promising profits; opponents, that the state should encourage competition and the further development of the state by grants to railroads. However, the contemporary campaign by the Troy and Greenfield Railroad for state assistance in tunneling Hoosac Mountain and the resulting opposition of the Western colored every phase of the discussion; around this antagonism gathered the interests of localities, benefited or unbenefited.[17] At least the controversy revealed, as had a similar one in the late twenties, that it was folly to approach the question of state assistance from the ground of principle. Local and corporate rivalries were the determining factors, unless overridden by a clear failure

---

[13] Report of Joint Committee on Railroad Petitions for State Aid, Massachusetts *Senate Documents*, 1838, no. 39, p. 2.

[14] *Acts and Resolves Passed by the Legislature of Massachusetts, in the Year 1843*, pp. 81, 410–411, 625; Report of a Minority of the Committee on Finance on the Sale of the State Stock in the Western, Massachusetts *House Documents*, 1848, no. 91, pp. 3–6; *General Laws and Resolves Passed by the Legislature of Massachusetts During the Session of 1866*, pp. 113–114.

[15] *Laws of the Commonwealth of Massachusetts Passed by the General Court, in the Years 1837 and 1838*, pp. 75–76, 197–198, 201–202, 509–511.

[16] *Official Report of the Debates and Proceedings in the State Convention, Assembled May 4th, 1853, to Revise and Amend the Constitution of the Commonwealth of Massachusetts*, II, 312–314, 657, 664, 682–683, III, 25–26.

[17] *Ibid.*, II, 282–283, 295, 647–649, 650–654, 665–667, III, 7–10, 12.

of the policy. In the early fifties it was still too early to appraise the financial success of Massachusetts policy.

But more than state governments had a financial stake in New England railroads — for if and when the state did not aid, towns and cities did. In Rhode Island, Connecticut, and Maine the process was widely and lavishly used. Portland, Hartford, Bridgeport, New London, Norwich, and Providence contributed generously to the railroads which were to make them great emporiums. In Massachusetts, though the General Court had once brusquely reproved those who felt it was a function of municipalities to finance railroads, the disapproval finally melted away. In 1852 Nantucket was permitted to subscribe to the stock of the Cape Cod Branch Railway and three years later towns along the Troy and Greenfield were authorized to pour money down that financial drain.[18] By 1860 municipal and town assistance in Massachusetts totaled $228,000.[19] Only Vermont and New Hampshire held aloof. In the latter, the railroad antipathies of the railroad war of 1840 accomplished the repeal of a previous act authorizing Concord to subscribe to the Concord Railroad.[20] The unfortunate history of most railroad enterprises in these two states certainly rewarded their self-restraint.

III

However crucial government assistance may have been for individual enterprises, in New England as a whole private individuals furnished directly the means of construction. They purchased stock, the only securities that the early railroads issued. Their burden was eased by the privilege of installment buying, for in fact the requirement of only a small down-payment upon subscription and the levy of later assessments, whatever its origin, constituted such an arrangement. The device had immense advantages for raising funds in a dynamic community with a

[18] *Acts and Resolves Passed by the General Court of Massachusetts, in the Year, 1852*, p. 110; *Acts and Resolves Passed by the General Court of Massachusetts, in the Year, 1855*, pp. 781–782.

[19] Massachusetts *Second Annual Report of the Board of Railroad Commissioners. January, 1871*, pp. lxxxix–xc.

[20] *Laws of the State of New-Hampshire, Passed June Session, 1840*, p. 433.

slowly accumulating capital. At once, however, it revealed defects; as the years passed, these snowballed to the proportions of
an evil. Individuals made preliminary subscriptions to get the
road started or to impress other potential subscribers, and then
ceased further payments; others, when their personal fortunes
made payment inconvenient or their estimates of the road's profitableness grew less rosy, withdrew from the enterprise.[21]
Though the road could sell at public auction the stock of delin-
quent subscribers and, if the sale did not meet the assessment, sue
the stockholder in some jurisdictions for the remainder of his
debt, such protective measures were useful only in prosperous
times, precisely when they were least needed.[22] If pursued rig-
orously in periods of depression, they glutted the treasury with
forfeited stock and the legal staff with potential civil actions.[23]
Under such circumstances boards and officers found it politic to
adjourn assessments.

Directors by vote or stockholders by agreement gave other
favors. Assessments were limited to small sums and spread over
years; [24] payments were made by personal notes for which the
stock was often left with the company as security; [25] and interest
was paid on assessments if met in advance or if made at all,
though the latter return waited upon the opening of the road.[26]

[21] *Report of the Directors of the Rutland and Burlington Rail-Road Company, at
Their Annual Meeting, at Rutland, Held 20th June, 1849* (Burlington: Free Press,
1849), pp. 12–13; *First Annual Report of the Board of Directors, to the Stockholders of the Hartford and New-Haven Rail-Road Company* (New Haven: Hitchcock & Stafford, 1836), p. 7.

[22] *The General Statutes of the Commonwealth of Massachusetts, Enacted December 28, 1859, to Take Effect June 1, 1860*, p. 351; The Danbury and Norwalk
Railroad Company *v.* Wilson, 22 *Connecticut*, 456; Rutland and Burlington Railroad Company *v.* Reuben R. Thrall, 35 *Vermont*, 546.

[23] Report of the Commissioners of the Housatonic Rail Road, Connecticut
General Assembly Documents, 1843, no. 7, p. 4; *Report of Directors of Housatonic
Rail Road Company, to the Stockholders, 20th June, 1844* (New York: H. Cogs-
well, 1844), pp. 4–5.

[24] *Brief Statement of Facts in Relation to the Proposed Rail-Road from Boston
to Plymouth* (Plymouth: James Thurber, 1844), p. 16.

[25] *First Annual Report of the Board of Directors to the Stockholders of the
Housatonic Rail-Road Company* (New Haven: Hitchcock & Stafford, 1838), p. 8;
Proceedings of the Directors and Stockholders of the Boston and Worcester Rail-
road, Ms., Harvard Business School Library, I, 174, 253, IV, 65.

[26] Proceedings of the Directors and Stockholders of the Boston and Worcester
Railroad, I, 139; Andrew J. Waterman *v.* Troy and Greenfield Railroad Company,

When neither pains nor rewards sufficed, directors resorted to homilies on "honor" and "duty." [27] In brief, installment buying immeasurably increased the costs of raising money. By the fifties it was also clear that it contributed to the launching of purely speculative enterprises. On a "shoe string," promoters started railroads without prospects, other than verbal ones, or without assurance they would ever be completed. Massachusetts, which had once permitted railroads to start on the basis of a prospectus and a down-payment on a portion of the stock, forbade in 1852 any enterprise to begin construction until "responsible parties" had subscribed to all the stock and paid into the treasury 20 per cent of the par value of each and every share.[28] The laudable intentions of this statute were easily evaded.[29] In spite of such handicaps, stock built New England railroads. In 1859 it constituted two-thirds of all security issues.[30]

This percentage, nonetheless, was not so high as it had been earlier. Financial desperation had driven railroads to other methods of raising money. When further stock issues were prevented by charter limitations or when the market would not absorb, except at extreme discounts, permissible issues, corporations resorted to short-time loans. For individual roads, like the Vermont Central, these reached impressive proportions; for Massachusetts railroads as a whole, on the eve of the railroad depression, over 25 per cent of the cost of construction had been borrowed largely on a short-time basis.[31] Prudent presidents, treasurers, and directors realized that such methods compelled a dangerous dependence upon a vacillating money market. They

---

8 *Grey*, 433, 435; *Opinion of J. Barrett, Chancellor in Suit by Richardson et al. v. Vt. & Mass. R. R. Co., In Chancery. Windham Co., Sept. Term, 1869*, pp. 3–4; *In Chancery. Windham County Court, February Term. 1871. Joseph Richardson et al. v. Vermont & Massachusetts Railroad Company. Brief for Defendants.*

[27] *Report . . . of the Rutland and Burlington Railroad . . . 1849*, p. 14; *First Annual Report . . . of the Hartford and New-Haven*, p. 7.

[28] *Acts and Resolves Passed by the General Court of Massachusetts, in the Year 1852*, p. 208.

[29] Massachusetts *Eighth Annual Report of the Board of Railroad Commissioners. January, 1877*, p. 43.

[30] Poor, *History of the Railroads and Canals of the United States*, pp. 12, 40, 71, 93, 186, 194.

[31] *Hunt's Merchants' Magazine and Commercial Review*, XIX (1848), 636–637.

sought to fund such debts or to avoid them entirely by the issue of securities more tempting than stock. One answer was preferred stock with a guaranteed dividend, a prior lien upon the earnings of the enterprise. Though such issues did not usually disfranchise their owners and might bring about a regrettable clash of interest among shareholders, they were sometimes inescapable.[32] But most railroads "struggling upon a turbulent sea of debt" pre- ferred to resort to bonds, a revolutionary means of railroad fi- nance. As such, it required definition. One commentator de- scribed bonds as "a convenient form of preferred stock, entitled to a fixed dividend." The Supreme Judicial Court of Massachu- setts defined them as "notes under seal."[33]

The judicial characterization best accorded with historical de- velopment. On railroad after railroad, short-time loans were first transformed into short-time bonds, really notes having one to five years rather than a few months to run. Such were stamped with the corporation's seal. Then these short-time bonds were transformed into long-term bonds, with ten, fifteen, or even twenty years before maturity.[34] Such notes or bonds had a prior claim, as any creditor did, upon the property of the corporation. But this common law right was frequently given more explicit- ness. As early as the thirties, for instance, the Massachusetts railroads aided by the state executed in return a "bond" upon their franchises and property and established sinking funds for

[32] 35 *Vermont*, 540, 545; *Acts and Resolves Passed by the General Court of Massachusetts, in the Year 1850*, p. 375; *Acts and Resolves Passed by the General Court of Massachusetts, in the Year 1853*, pp. 351–353.

[33] James P. Kirkwood, "Railroad Enterprises and Their Detractors," *Hunt's Merchants' Magazine and Commercial Review*, XXXII (1855), 407; Common- wealth *v.* Jerome V. C. Smith & Others, 10 *Allen*, 455.

[34] *Sixth Annual Report of the Directors and Treasurer of the Vermont Central Railroad Company, Prepared for the Stockholders Meeting, August 27, 1851* (Montpelier: E. P. Walton & Son, 1851), p. 6; *Report of the Investigating Com- mittee of the Vermont Central Railroad Co. to the Stockholders, July 1, 1853* (Boston: George C. Rand, 1853), pp. 58–63; *Fourth Annual Report of the Direc- tors of the Rutland & Burlington Rail Road Company, Submitted to the Stock- holders, June 18, 1851* (Boston: T. R. Marvin, 1851), pp. 8–9; *Report of the Stockholders' Committee Appointed at the Annual Meeting of the Vermont and Massachusetts Rail-Road Company, February 14th, 1849* (Boston: Crocker and Brewster, 1850), pp. 6–7; *Annual Report of the Directors of the Vermont and Massachusetts Railroad to the Stockholders, February 13th, 1850* (Cambridge: Metcalf and Company, 1850), pp. 7–8.

the repayment of the loans.[35] Twenty years later, when the Boston and Lowell issued $500,000 of bonds, its stockholders, for the security of the purchasers, established a sinking fund, although they persistently rejected the advice of their treasurer to place a mortgage upon the property as a means of heightening the salability of the issue.[36] Nevertheless a bond issue usually became an issue of mortgage bonds. Sometimes mortgage was piled upon mortgage.[37]

This protean instrument became increasingly popular. First employed by the precarious enterprises in the back country of New England, the bond spread finally to the careful dowager roads of Massachusetts. By 1850 the Boston and Maine, the Eastern, and the Old Colony, of the roads entering Boston, had issued this form of security. Within the decade the Boston and Providence, Boston and Lowell, Boston and Worcester, and the Fitchburg had all created funded debts to finance their construction or expansion.[38] Meanwhile the perils of the depressed fifties had led everywhere to the spawning of the new securities. In that decade the totals of railroad bonds in Maine and Connecticut tripled, those in New Hampshire multiplied four times, those in Vermont eight times. In Maine the funded debt of the railroads exceeded the share capital by roughly $2,000,000; in Vermont the railroad debt, funded and unfunded, equaled the capitalization of the state's roads.[39] In Vermont and Connecticut, every railroad, with the exception of two, had issued bonds, in some instances to huge amounts.[40]

Such figures did more than mirror the issue of securities "to relieve financial embarrassments." They were evidence of a new method of railroad financing. According to a contemporary, bonds

[35] *Laws .... of Massachusetts ... 1838 and 1839*, pp. 75–76, 197–198, 201–202, 509–511.

[36] *Report of the Directors of the Boston and Lowell Railroad, for the Year Ending November 30, 1856* (Boston: J. H. Eastburn, 1856), pp. 15–18.

[37] *The General Statutes of the State of Connecticut . . .* [1866], p. 195; *The General Statutes of the State of Vermont . . . 1862*, p. 237; Edmund F. Webb, *The Railroad Laws of Maine*, p. 596.

[38] Martin, *A Century of Finance*, p. 163; Returns of the Railroad Corporations in Massachusetts, 1860, Massachusetts *Public Documents*, 1861, no. 46, *passim*.

[39] Poor, *History of Railroads and Canals of the United States*, pp. 12, 40, 71, 194.

[40] *Ibid.*, pp. 72–82, 193.

were no longer an afterthought; they were part of the original
design. Those who subscribed to stock along the line did not ex-
pect it would either build the road or maintain its par value. They
took shares because they believed in the enterprise or expected
"to be distinctly benefitted by it in their business or in their property, or in the shape of comfort, help, or convenience of some
kind." If the stock went down, they really lost nothing; indirect
benefits were compensation. "After stock subscriptions, the next
step in the process of financiering for railroads, is that of issuing
bonds — in other words, borrowing money on the pledge of the
railroad works and properties, in their finished or unfinished
state." By this device, they could, depending upon the character
of the road, meet between one-fifth and four-fifths of the construction costs. Even though railroads met principal and interest payments, bonds might decline in value. "The railroad companies
cannot control the fluctuating price of their securities. . . . The
necessities of the holders are the cause of the sacrifice in price."
To the critics complaining that this financial realpolitik was in
fact synonomous with "swindling, cheating, deceiving," the
Olympian expositor of the new doctrine made an old reply, *caveat
emptor.*[41]

How far such doctrines were consciously adopted in New England, it is impossible to say. Everywhere roads conformed to the
pattern. As bonds grew commonplace, however, the more alert
states became aware that their issue, like that of stocks, required
some regulation. The motive was not, entirely, a preference for
accustomed ways of financing. If a road were largely financed by
bonds, the property which secured them might prove inadequate,
and the stock was reduced to a speculative level. Conservative
opinion announced that roads built by stock were more "profitable," those built "mostly on loans will, in most cases, prove a
nuisance, and a lure to the unfortunate holders" of their stock.[42]

[41] Kirkwood, "Railroad Enterprises," pp. 405–409; *Hunt's Merchants' Magazine
and Commercial Review*, XXXI (1854), 209.
[42] David M. Balfour, "How Should Railroads Be Managed?" *Hunt's Merchants' Magazine and Commercial Review*, XXIII (1850), 199; *Twenty-fifth Annual Report of the Directors of the Boston and Worcester Railroad Corporation,
for the Year Ending November 30, 1854* (Boston: David Clapp, 1855), p. 14.

Besides, bond financiering had developed in a legal half-light. In some instances railroad corporations had sought special enactments from the state authorizing the issue of bonds; the state had coupled its permission with varied restrictions.[43] On other occasions railroad enterprises had acted under the assumption that their corporate rights to make contracts, mortgage their property, and borrow money were sufficient legal basis for an issue of bonds.[44] By the fifties a spate of statutes ensued. Typical was the Connecticut act of 1849 specifying that bond issues must not exceed one-third of the amount "actually expended upon the road."[45] Five years later a Massachusetts statute, authorizing roads to issue bonds to fund floating debts or for any other lawful purpose, specified that their amount should not exceed the capital stock actually paid in. Also they could not be issued in denominations of less than $100, for more than twenty years, or for interest over 6 per cent.[46]

Even novel and guaranteed securities could not always find a market in a community where investment opportunities clamored for capital. An intricate system of barter therefore arose. Securities were exchanged for the necessities of construction. Stock or bonds paid the land damages, bought the ties and purchased the rails and the rolling stock.[47] Soon those who contracted to build the road arranged to take a portion of their pay in securities. In Connecticut, Alfred Bishop, the Atlas of the Housatonic, the Naugatuck, and the New York and New Haven, illustrated the tendency. Elsewhere in New England, S. F. Belknap, later saluted by E. H. Derby as the "prince of contractors," thus built, in whole or in part, the Fitchburg, the Northern of New York, the Rutland and Burlington, the Sullivan, and the Vermont Central.[48] For the last enterprise, prior to his contract, he made a

[43] *Resolves and Private Laws of the State of Connecticut from the Year 1836 to the Year 1857*, pp. 910, 1010, 1045.
[44] 10 *Allen*, 455; *Acts and Resolves . . . of Massachusetts . . . 1850*, p. 422.
[45] *The General Statutes of the State of Connecticut . . .* [1866], p. 195.
[46] *Acts and Resolves . . . of Massachusetts, . . . 1854*, pp. 206–207.
[47] Thelma M. Kistler, *The Rise of Railroads in the Connecticut River Valley* (Northampton: 1938), p. 73; *Fourth Annual Report of the Directors of the Boston, Concord and Montreal Railroad. 1850* (Concord: Asa McFarland, n.d.), p. 7.
[48] *Report to the Stockholders of the Fitchburg Rail-Road Company. January,*

subscription for 5,000 shares, one-fourth the original capital of the concern.[49] The Portland contractors for the Atlantic and St. Lawrence received one-quarter of their dues in bonds of the company and one-quarter in stock.[50] It is not known what arrangements such contractor-subscribers utilized to raise money through the hypothecation or sale of the securities that they took. Clearly the Schuyler brothers, George L. and Robert, who were together or singly contractors for the New York and New Haven and for other shorter New England roads, could utilize their brokerage house and banking concerns for that purpose.[51] In their instance there is a close approximation, if not more, to the noisome construction companies of a later era.

IV

Whatever the form of security, New Englanders by and large provided the funds for their purchase. Foreign capital played only a minor part. The Western, to be sure, marketed abroad somewhat over two-fifths of the state scrip it received from Massachusetts.[52] In 1843 at a special meeting of the corporation it was "ordered, unanimously, that the thanks of the stockholders . . . be presented to Messrs. Baring Brothers and Company of London, for the confidence evinced by them, in the unstained credit of the Commonwealth of Massachusetts when that of several States in our Federal Union was impaired to an alarming degree, and for their judicious exertions in disposing of the Massachusetts Bonds entrusted to them by this corporation." [53] The Barings had distributed these securities in Great Britain and on

---

1844 (Boston: Dutton and Wentworth, 1844), p. 4; Montpelier *Vermont Watchman and State Journal*, November 4, 1847.

[49] *Report of the Investigating Committee of the Vermont Central . . . 1853*, pp. 63–76, 81.

[50] *Report of the Directors to the Stockholders of the Atlantic & St. Lawrence Rail Road Company. Presented August 6, 1850* (Portland: Thurston & Co., 1850), p. 6.

[51] *Hunt's Merchants' Magazine and Commercial Review*, XXXI (1854), 207.

[52] Report of the Joint Special Committee on the Sale of State Stock in the Western Railroad, Massachusetts *Senate Documents*, 1863, no. 199, p. 13.

[53] Records of the Western Rail Road Corporation, Ms., Harvard Business School Library, p. 115.

the continent.[54] These were state securities, albeit dedicated to a railroad enterprise. In the early fifties the same house underwrote directly at the solicitation of William Sturgis $650,000 of the bonds of the Eastern Railroad.[55] But these were unusual instances. Within America, moreover, it was exceptional for New Englanders to go outside New England for investment funds. This was not entirely true, as we have seen, for the New York and New Haven and other roads in the New York interest. Still these enterprises also depended upon the "monied men" and those of the middling sort in Connecticut and Massachusetts.

Throughout New England the geographical distribution of investments followed the pattern already hinted. Local roads depended upon local subscriptions. Hartford, Providence, Concord, Portland, Worcester, and Springfield thus constituted a group of minor investment centers. Larger enterprises depended also upon subscriptions along the line — here a few shares, there a few more. Then their sponsors descended upon the Boston investment market. By the late thirties Boston subscribers held nearly 80 per cent of the stock in the Western; in the next decade nearly 60 per cent of the stock in the Connecticut River Railroad and 43 per cent of the Boston and Maine.[56] From the sales of these multiplying securities, though the daily totals were often trivial, the Boston Stock Exchange drew its chief nourishment.[57]

Though the hundreds of small stockholdings scattered through New England gave to railroad enterprises a local character and abated to some extent antagonisms directed against absentee ownership, far more important was the distribution of stock among individual owners. On this score, whenever railroads desired state assistance or fought against restrictions, a familiar litany was raised. From the thirties to the fifties, listeners were informed,

[54] Proceedings of the Board of Directors of the Western Railroad Corporation, Ms., Harvard Business School Library, I, 219–220.

[55] Ralph W. Hidy, "A Leaf from Investment History," *Harvard Business Review* XX (1941), 73.

[56] Kistler, *The Rise of Railroads in the Connecticut River Valley*, pp. 244, 246; *Report of the Committee of Investigation Appointed by the Stockholders of the Boston and Maine Railroad, May 28, 1849* (Boston: Eastburn's Press, 1849), pp. 10–11.   [57] *Boston Shipping List & Prices Current*, January 30, July 6, 1850.

The stockholders belong, for the most part, to classes and descriptions of persons, who have the strongest claims upon the goodwill and particular care of the Legislature. . . . It seems to be supposed that they consist of large capitalists, of the rich, of persons extensively engaged in business operations, of speculators, and the makers and holders of fortunes. It is not so. . . . I am inclined to think it would be found, that by far the largest part of the stock of these institutions is held in small numbers of shares, by persons belonging to the middling and even humble conditions of life. . . . The great bulk of the stockholders are persons of limited means — not much engaged in trade or commerce — retired from the prominent movements of society — widows, single women, charitable institutions, institutions for savings, and the like.[58]

On occasion such observations were even made the basis for suggesting that the state should aid railroads in order that stockholders might sooner enjoy dividends and not have to sell their tiny holdings to wealthy investors! [59]

Though the point was pressed often to extravagance, there was considerable evidence that owners of railroad shares were of the middling sort. Ownership was widely diffused. It became more so. In 1831 there were 241 original subscribers to the Boston and Worcester; by 1865 the shareholders numbered 2,359. On the Western, somewhat less typical since the state owned 10,000 shares, the original subscribers in 1836 numbered 1,863; in 1865 there were 2,383 shareholders. It was such figures that led the unwary or the interested to assert that railroad stockholders were not persons of wealth. Admittedly a test of riches is hard to formulate, particularly for a different time than one's own. In the fifties and sixties, days of small fortunes, small investments were proportionately large ones; holdings of $2,500 to $3,000 in an enterprise did not come from ordinary folk. In the period under discussion, holders of between twenty-five and thirty shares owned a majority of the stock in three sample railroad corporations. In each enterprise this group constituted roughly between one-seventh and one-tenth of the total shareholders.[60] Owner-

---

[58] *Supra*, I, 132; *Speech of Honorable Charles W. Upham, President of the Senate, on the Bill for the Extension of the Credit of the Eastern Railroad Corporation. April 11, 1857* (n.p., n.d.), pp. 7–8. [59] *Ibid.*, p. 9.
[60] *List of Stockholders in the Fitchburg Railroad Company, 1863* (n.p., n.d.);

ship was diffused; control — at least potential control — was concentrated.

As for widows and orphans, available data afford no answer. Evidence on institutional holdings is also incomplete. For the Boston and Worcester at the somewhat later date of 1865, however, dividend books reveal that banks received dividends on 536 shares and insurance companies on 1,400.[61] The total capitalization of the road was then 45,000 shares. In Massachusetts, as distinguished from other states, legislation had been liberalized to let savings banks first loan upon and then invest in bonds, and insurance companies to place a portion of their funds in the bonds or stock of roads of which the capital was paid in and which met certain other financial standards.[62]

V

Though the decline in securities and dividends demonstrated in the fifties the existence of the railroad crisis, it did not entirely explain the situation. Indeed there were some perfectionists who informed the unenlightened that if only the roads had cost more and hence been better built, they would have cost less to operate.[63] In the high level of operating expenditures the diagnosticians of the fifties had already detected the cause of railroad prostration. The cure was the reduction of excessive costs. Railroads should institute a prudent management to put an end to losses and to check extravagance. The first and most obvious step was to get

Records of the Directors and Stockholders of the Boston and Worcester Railroad, I, 19–29; Dividend Books of the Boston and Worcester Railroad, Ms., Harvard Business School Library, XI; Stock Ledger of the Western Railroad, Ms., Harvard Business School Library; Dividend Books of the Western Railroad, VII, Ms., Harvard Business School Library.

[61] Boston and Worcester Dividend Books, XI, Ms., Harvard Business School Library.

[62] *Acts and Resolves Passed by the Legislature of Massachusetts, in the Year 1841*, pp. 355–356; *Acts and Resolves Passed by the Legislature of Massachusetts, in the Year 1845*, pp. 418–419; *General Statutes and Special Acts of Massachusetts. 1863*, p. 491; *The General Statutes . . . of Connecticut . . .* [1866], pp. 159–160.

[63] Zerah Colburn and Alexander L. Holley, *The Permanent Way and Coal-Burning Locomotive Boilers of European Railways; with a Comparison of the Working Economy of European and American Lines, and the Principles upon Which Improvement Must Proceed* (New York: Holley and Colburn, 1858), pp. 1–31.

rid of dishonest men. Apparently such had penetrated every grade of the hierarchy. Conductors, unchecked by systematic surveillance, were appropriating fares that belonged to the company, wood agents were buying fuel from themselves at huge prices, and higher officials were enriching themselves through sales of property to the corporation and the collection of commissions for performing duties for which they were already paid a salary. These customary peccadillos did not account for large sums. From time to time, however, financial wrong-doing on a larger scale plundered treasuries and shook the confidence of investors. Presidents overissued stock and treasurers defaulted. On the Eastern Railroad embezzlement took on the character of recurrent costs; it might have been discounted. The last defalcation, that of William S. Tuckerman, the eminently respectable treasurer, "burst forth in the full effulgence of a QUARTER OF A MILLION DOLLARS." In order to finance his speculations in a half a dozen railroads, particularly those of northern New England, he muddled accounts, overissued stock, and pocketed the proceeds of notes issued as treasurer of the company. Finally his wife induced him to confess.[64]

New England railroad men, less given to interpreting life in terms of melodrama or human sin, searched for more systematic ways of cutting costs than raising the bonds of treasurers. They considered possible reductions in salaries and wages, reductions often checked by the realization that a decent compensation was itself an economy: it lured ability to the enterprise.[65] They advocated the adoption of more modern and more economical ways of doing things. The use of coal fuel was a case in point.[66] Finally they suggested the curtailment of extravagances in train operation. Locomotives and cars traveling at high speeds ran up heavy

---

[64] E. B. Grant, *Boston Railways: Their Condition and Prospects* (Boston: Little, Brown, and Company, 1856), pp. 30–31; *Report of the Investigating Committee of the Stockholders of the Eastern Railroad Company. July 30th, 1855* (Boston: C. C. P. Moody, 1855), pp. 15–30; Commonwealth *v.* William S. Tuckerman, 10 *Gray*, 174.

[65] Grant, *Boston Railways*, p. 129; *Report of Committee of Investigation, Appointed at Annual Meeting of Fitchburg Railroad Company, January 29, 1856* (Boston: Henry W. Dutton & Son, 1857), pp. 31–32.

[66] Grant, *Boston Railways*, pp. 50–60, 114–129.

operating costs and wore out the inferior iron rails. Since the
roads, moreover, ran too many trains, a reduction in schedules
would save labor, fuel, and wear of the rails.[67] Finally, extremists,
calculating the costs of doing each classification of business, recommended that the roads drop traffic which did not yield some
return. Here there was no response, perhaps because of the highly
tentative nature of the figuring involved. Anyway, these economies, proposed and actual, had their limits. They might easily
degenerate into a "morbid disposition towards petty savings,
stoppage of free-passes, dismissals of agents, reductions of salaries already small enough, — dismissal of laborers often needed
to maintain the track, great savings in oil, waste, stationary, advertising, etc., and other items, well enough considered alone, but
utterly insignificant when compared with the enormous, resistless tide of expense in maintenance of way and works, and in
power." [68]

In truth, not until the fifties did most railroads appreciate "the
resistless tide of expense in maintenance of way and works" and
illuminate this shapeless charge by breaking it down into repairs, depreciation, and perhaps obsolescence. Usually their
earlier failure on this score was not due to the fact they did not
keep accounts. Among the first acts of directors was always the
opening of a set of books. Those of the Boston and Worcester,
for instance, were "kept in a strictly mercantile style, according
to the Italian method of book-keeping by double entry." [69] Managers, however, did not know what items to include and, if they
did, what amounts to allot to them, for railroads were a new kind
of property, different from shops or mills. From their brief opera-

[67] *Report of Committee of Investigation, . . . of Fitchburg Railroad . . . 1856,*
p. 31; *Thirteenth Annual Report to the Stockholders of the Vermont and Massachusetts Railroad. February 11th, 1857* (Boston: 1857), pp. 14–16; Appleton and
Swift, *Massachusetts Railroads,* pp. 10–11.

[68] Colburn and Holley, *The Permanent Way,* pp. xv–xvi; *Annual Report of
the Directors of the Fitchburg Railroad Company, to the Stockholders of That
Corporation. At Their Meeting, January 29, 1856* (Boston: Bazin and Chandler,
1856), pp. 22–25.

[69] *Report of the Directors of the Boston and Worcester Railroad, Presented at
the Annual Meeting of the Stockholders, June 4, 1849. Together with a Report of
the Committee of Stockholders, Presented at the Same Time* (Boston: Eastburn's
Press, 1849), p. 20.

tions no generalizations could be drawn. Even if precise information had been available, it was not politic to reveal it; it might have discouraged construction. "To get [railroads] afloat is the problem. Once afloat, and with rare exceptions, they will not have long to wait for a full cargo." [70] Consequently engineers underestimated the costs of operation as consistently as costs of construction.

Still the early promoters had a partial foresight. They recognized the inescapability of repairs. The Massachusetts Board of Internal Improvements in 1829, while admitting that no estimates had been made of maintenance costs, anticipated that the durable and solid character of their proposed granite construction would keep them down to 1 or 1½ per cent upon the first cost of the road.[71] For the pioneer lines of the Commonwealth more particular specifications were forthcoming. The committee for the Boston and Lowell, relying largely upon English experience, announced that the cost of annual repairs would be £40 a mile and the repairs upon engines and cars would be annually 25 per cent. Since, unlike other property, the railroad "is not subject to loss by fire or other like casualties," costs would be lower.[72] For the Worcester, Fessenden, its engineer, calculated repairs at $150 a mile, less than 1 per cent upon the estimated cost, and depreciation and repairs of the rolling stock at 18 per cent per year.[73] To such sanguine calculations, the contemporary facts of the turnpikes should have been an antidote. At every hand these enterprises were abandoning their property because they could not afford to keep it in repair. The gloomy example went unheeded.

Still, the foresighted among railroads took precautions. On the Boston and Worcester the directors established at once a re-

---

[70] Kirkwood, "Railroad Enterprises," p. 404.

[71] *Report of the Board of Directors of Internal Improvements of the State of Massachusetts, on the Practicability and Expediency of a Rail-Road from Boston to the Hudson River and from Boston to Providence. Submitted to the General Court, January 16, 1829* (Boston: W. L. Lewis, 1829), p. 69.

[72] *Report of a Committee on the Boston and Lowell Rail Road* (Boston: 1831), pp. 9, 13–14.

[73] *Report of the Directors of the Boston and Worcester Rail-Road Corporation to the Stockholders, Together With the Report of John M. Fessenden, Esq.* (Boston: W. L. Lewis, 1832), pp. 35–36.

serve fund upon the resources of which they drew for replacing ties, depreciation of locomotives and cars, and other extraordinary expenditures. When it was exhausted, they met the recurring repairs and depreciation from income.[74] Roads not as careful waked quickly to the dangers of their situation. Eight years after the opening of the Boston and Lowell, its directors wrote: "At the close of the accounts of the corporation for the present year, the directors, aware that a depreciation must have been going on in their stock of engines and cars, many of which have been in use ever since . . . 1835, have caused a valuation of the same to be made, to ascertain the amount of this depreciation." They discovered the rolling stock to be overvalued by a third. "To meet a part at least of this depreciation, the directors have ordered $30,000 to be charged to expenses, and credited to this account." [75]

Meanwhile circumstances put in the hands of management an alternative method for handling these items. Young roads, in course of borning, naturally opened a construction account the total of which should have coincided theoretically with the capitalization and loans incurred for construction. Most New England roads, however, were built in haste, and, as soon as they were opened, the endless course of reconstruction and extension began. It was easy to believe these new expenses should be added to the construction account and met by a floating debt and the eventual creation of additional stock or bonds. It was also difficult to draw a sharp cleavage between repairs and depreciation, on the one hand, and additions and extensions, on the other. The former items stole into the construction account. The convenience of this process became increasingly alluring. To maintain the credit of the corporation among lenders, to convince stockholders that the road was yielding suitable earnings, to maintain the value of

[74] *Report of the Directors of the Boston and Worcester Rail-Road Corporation, to the Stockholders, at Their Eleventh Annual Meeting, June 6, 1842* (Boston: I. R. Butts, 1842), p. 7; *Report of the Directors of the Boston and Worcester Rail-Road, to the Stockholders, at Their Annual Meeting, June 3, 1844* (Boston: I. R. Butts, 1844), pp. 4–5; *Report . . . of the Boston and Worcester Railroad, . . . June 4, 1849*, pp. 30–31.

[75] Fourteenth Annual Report of the Boston and Lowell Railroad Corporation, Massachusetts *House Documents*, 1845, no. 46, p. 6.

the securities in the market, it was only necessary to detach certain items from the current expense column and bury them in construction account. Thus not only did repairs of stations and replacements of rails and rolling stock come to rest in this capacious half-lit area; more obvious running expenses on occasion enjoyed the hospitality of the construction account.[76]

By the fifties uninformed and careless methods of accounting no longer went unchallenged and unnoticed. Distress was a grim teacher. The New England roads built in the late thirties and forties suddenly wore out, and the device of an open construction account wore out too. Fortunately the railroads had now been long enough in operation so that workable generalizations could be drawn from their experience. A revolution in accounting got under way. Though state legislation, by specifying detailed reports, partially prodded the transformation, the real drive came from management or from stockholders, curious to have explained the reasons for the declining value of their property and energetic enough to organize investigations, order inventories and appraisals, make recommendations, and turn out incompetent boards of directors. One achievement, treated in a later chapter, was the adoption of careful auditing methods. A second was a sounder realization of the meaning and rapidity of depreciation. "It was formerly supposed that railroads, and even their equipments, had the durability of real estate, and that once provided for and paid for, there was an end to that expense. But later experience has shown that railroads consist of two classes of property; the land, buildings and road-bed, which have the permanency of real estate; and the equipment and superstructure, which, like ships, or other similar property, perish rapidly in the use. This depreciation or waste is at least ten per cent per annum." A sum must be spent "or set apart to supply this waste,

[76] *Report of Committee of Investigation, . . . Fitchburg Railroad . . . 1856*, pp. 25–26; *Annual Report of the Directors of the Vermont and Massachusetts Railroad to the Stockholders, at Their Meeting, February 12th, 1851* (Cambridge: Metcalf and Company, 1851), pp. 4–5; *Annual Report to the Stockholders of the Vermont and Massachusetts Railroad. February 8, 1854* (Boston: 1854), p. 8; *Report of the Committee for Investigating the Affairs of the Old Colony Railroad Company. Appointed by the Stockholders, December 26, 1849* (Boston: Eastburn's Press, 1850), pp. 14, 16–17.

independent and beyond the expense of ordinary repairs." [77]   On rare occasions, some realized that beyond repair and depreciation lurked the shadowy expense of obsolescence.[78]   Far more common was the demand that a contingent fund be accumulated from expenses to meet the unpredictable losses from fire, defalcation, or accident.[79]   This, like other "funds," was often a mere bookkeeping item; the money was invested in materials or loaned to other accounts.

These detailed changes attacked from every side that useful repository, the construction account.   Its angry critics declared categorically that such accounts must be "closed" and occasionally insisted that they be reduced to the amount of stocks and bonds or the appraised value of the property.   Such reduction must be by appropriations from income, even if dividends were sacrificed.[80]   After this return to fundamentals, investigators recommended that "all repairs of the Road, and the appurtenances thereto, and all alterations, improvements, and reconstructions of buildings, bridges, engines and cars, hereafter made, be charged to running expenses." [81]   Stockholders' committees and new boards

[77] *Report of the Committee for Investigating the Affairs of the Boston and Providence Railroad Corporation, Appointed by the Stockholders, January 9, 1856* (Boston: J. H. Eastburn, 1856), pp. 20–21; *Report of the Committee of the Stockholders of the Western Railroad Corporation, Appointed at the Annual Meeting in February, 1851, to Examine into the System of Accountability . . . and also the Condition and Value of the Property of the Corporation . . . February, 1852* (Boston: Eastburn's Press, 1852), pp. 17–29.

[78] *Report of the Committee for Investigating . . . the Old Colony . . . 1849*, p. 53.

[79] *Report of the Committee for Investigating . . . the Boston and Providence . . . 1856*, pp. 21–22; *Report of the Directors of the Eastern Rail Road Company, to the Stockholders, at Their Annual Meeting, Held at Boston, July 9, 1849* (Salem: Observer Office, 1849), p. 7; *Report of the Directors of the Boston and Maine Railroad to the Stockholders, September 13th, 1854* (Boston: Dutton and Wentworth, 1854), pp. 7–8.

[80] *Thirty-second Annual Report of the Directors of the Boston & Worcester Railroad Corporation, for the Year Ending November 30, 1861* (Boston: David Clapp, 1862), pp. 5–6; *Report of the Board of Directors of the Boston and Providence Railroad Corporation, for the Year Ending November 30, 1863; Presented at the Annual Meeting, January 13, 1864* (Boston: J. H. Eastburn, 1864), p. 5; *Annual Report of the Directors of the Fitchburg Railroad Company, to the Stockholders, at Their Meeting, January 30th, 1855* (Boston: Bazin & Chandler, 1855), pp. 15–16.

[81] *Report of the Committee of Investigation Appointed by the Stockholders of the Boston and Maine Railroad, at a Meeting Held at Exeter, N. H., May 28, 1849* (Boston: Eastburn's Press, 1849), pp. 55–56.

of directors were peculiarly prone to such dicta. More experienced officials, though they gave general assent, advanced the puzzle of exceptions. Some directors thought that "for a road which is completed" no recourse should be had to further stock issues for expenses "except in the case of a large sum being at once required to secure a corresponding amount of new business." [82] Others pointed out that a reformation which lumped together all varieties of expenses and charged them to income without new particularities might be as misleading as the old evils.[83] There were also differences over the further argument that a closed construction account and the reinvestment of earnings prevented the dilution of share capital by new issues and assured dividends based upon a richer investment.[84]

As the debate went on, the outlines of improved procedure became clearer and roads in comfortable circumstances sought to introduce them. Among these fortunate corporations, to take an illustration, the Boston and Providence determined upon a system that was uniform from year to year and apparently infallible. In the first place the directors assumed an "annual decay" of structures and rolling stock; then a separate account was set up for each variety of property. "We have endeavored to ascertain, so far as is practicable, from the experience of years, what may be expected, with a given amount of business, to be the amount of expenses chargeable to each account, annually; and if in any year the amount actually expended falls short of the estimate, we do not rely upon a permanent reduction of these expenses but charge the expenses of the year with the *estimated* amount, and carry the difference to a fund to meet what may be the expenditures of another year on that account beyond the estimate." [85] In

[82] *Report of the Directors of the Boston and Lowell Railroad, 1849* (Boston: Eastburn's Press, 1849), p. 6.

[83] *Report of the Directors of the Boston and Maine Railroad, to the Stockholders, September 10th, 1856* (Boston: Henry W. Dutton, 1856), pp. 9–10; Grant, *Boston Railways*, p. 49.

[84] *Report of the . . . Boston and Lowell . . . 1849*, p. 7; *Report . . . of the Eastern Rail Road . . . 1849*, p. 6.

[85] *Report of the Board of Directors of the Boston and Providence Railroad Corporation, at the Annual Meeting, January 11, 1860* (Boston: J. H. Eastburn, 1859), pp. 3–4; *Report of Committee of Investigation, . . . Fitchburg Railroad . . . 1856*, pp. 26–27.

addition to this rigorous budgeting, the road paid for ten miles of double track from annual income.[86] There were other corporations which could not afford so extravagant a devotion to the fetish of a closed construction account. Indeed there were some who derided the whole structure of judicious innovation. From its perch in the Green Mountains, the Vermont Central commented, "It has recently been stated by some writers of undoubted experience and science, that large amounts, never before anticipated or imagined, will be required to cover a new account in Railroad matters, termed *Depreciation*, and many holders of Railroad securities have become alarmed at this new phantom. . . . Is not a more serious difficulty to be found in the charge called *Competition?*"[87] In spite of skepticism, defiance, and exceptions, the experimental period of railroad accounting had, by the fifties, settled into a stabler age. The sounder financial structure, built by improvements in method, explained in part the extraordinary prosperity which the next decade brought to New England roads.

VI

As the railroad crisis came to New England, more discussion and polemics gathered about the question of rates than of capital stock and depreciation. "In the mercantile world," sneered Derby, "the great specific for profits is an advance of prices. If the merchant can sell at an advance, his profit is certain, and this is the first remedy which occurs to merchants for a railway."[88] To this or any other general policy on rates there was certainly little legal impediment, for aside from occasional requirements that railroads should post their rates and raise them only at stated intervals,[89] and aside from relying upon charter or statute limitations of profits, the beneficent action of competition, and imprecise common-law conceptions of reasonableness, the states left rate deci-

---

[86] *Report . . . of the Boston and Providence . . . January 13, 1864*, p. 5.

[87] *Tenth Annual Report of the Directors of the Vermont Central Railroad Co. to the Stockholders, Presented at the Annual Meeting, Oct. 31, 1855* (Montpelier: E. P. Walton, Jr., 1855), pp. 14, 16.

[88] E. H. Derby, "The Railways of Massachusetts," *Hunt's Merchants' Magazine and Commercial Review*, XXIII (1850), 306.

[89] *Laws of the State of New Hampshire. Passed June Session, 1850*, pp. 430–431; Webb, *The Railroad Laws of Maine*, pp. 605–606.

sions to managers and owners. Nor did a concert of railroads shape the rate structures. "Pooling agreements" and "conventions" on rate policy were still infrequent. So each railroad decided upon its own rates. Though variety and not uniformity was the rule, certain common influences operated upon all railroad enterprises. Thus at the outset of the railroad age, since little experience was available, lines set their railroad fares at levels below those charged by stage coach, wagon, or boat.[90]

Let us begin with passenger fares, for until 1860 returns from them played the larger part on the railroads of southern New England. On the pioneer railroads in Massachusetts, the Boston and Lowell originally charged $1.00 for its twenty-six miles, the Boston and Worcester $1.50 for its forty-five, and the Boston and Providence $2.00 for its forty-three.[91] For such railroads as New England had in 1835, a generalization of 4 cents a mile was accurate enough.[92] In the forties the drive to develop more business and to meet competition induced such rapid reductions that by the end of the decade the through fare of the Boston and Lowell was 50 cents, of the Boston and Worcester $1.00, and the Boston and Providence $1.25.[93] Taking New England as a whole, with the single exception of the road from New Haven to Hartford, through fares were below 3 cents a mile, some roads charged as low as 2, the average was not far from 2½. Generally they were the lowest in the country.[94]

Though such figures are useful as evidence of a trend, they do not reveal the real complexity of the passenger-fare structure. To the distress of theorists patiently explaining that long distance

[90] *Report of the Directors of the Boston & Worcester Rail Road, to the Stockholders at Their Ninth Annual Meeting, June 1, 1840* (Boston: S. N. Dickinson, 1840), pp. 7–8; *Proceedings of the Convention of the Northern Lines of Railway, Held at Boston, in December, 1850, and January, 1851* (Boston: J. B. Yerrinton & Son, 1851), pp. 15, 18.

[91] *Report . . . of the Boston and Lowell . . . 1849*, p. 3; Proceedings of the Directors and Stockholders of the Boston and Worcester Railroad, II, 48, 180; E. H. Derby, "Administration of the Railroads of Massachusetts: with Reference to the Rates of Freight and Fare," *Hunt's Merchants' Magazine and Commercial Review*, XV (1846), 238.

[92] Derby, "Administration of the Railroads," p. 236.

[93] *Pathfinder Railway Guide for the New England States, . . . October 1st to 8th, 1849* (Boston: Geo. K. Snow, n.d.), pp. 18–19, 28, 46–47.

[94] *Hunt's Merchants' Magazine and Commercial Review*, XVIII (1848), 97.

passenger travel was not mass travel and that long distance travelers were precisely those who could afford to pay more, single tickets for through travel were cheaper per mile than those for local distances. Not all the speculations of those who knew better could adjourn the necessity of meeting competition.[95] That the contrasting treatment of local and through traffic did not arouse more frequent disfavor than it did, was due to the development of commutation, a device for granting lower fares to regular travelers. Stagecoach and ferry had inaugurated this practice.[96] As soon as railroads were opened they were asked to copy it. The first response was not always favorable. When a petitioner prayed the Boston and Worcester in 1837 for a season or annual ticket — the cost was $400 — a committee of directors reported, "It is inexpedient to sell season tickets. Should it be done in this case, others would ask for similar arrangements, which would finally result in making separate contracts with each regular customer, & at reduced rates of fare." [97] A year later the directors reversed their position and from time to time sold such tickets to individuals and their families. Either personal favoritism or response to pressure from shippers of merchandise probably explained this reversal of principle.[98] In the forties many roads, including the Boston and Worcester, systematically extended the privilege to all comers. To annual tickets were first added those sold for a half or a quarter year; then package tickets bought in amounts of a 100 and over at progressive discounts, and scholars' tickets at half price.[99] Though there were season-ticket holders

[95] Grant, Boston Railways, pp. 67–68.

[96] Report of the Committee Appointed at a Meeting of the Stockholders of the Eastern Rail-Road Company, to Examine into the Past Doings and Present Condition of Said Company, and to Report at an Adjourned Meeting, to be Held at Boston, May 21, 1840 (Boston: Dutton and Wentworth, 1840), p. 12.

[97] Proceedings of the Directors and Stockholders of the Boston and Worcester Railroad, II, 236–237.

[98] Ibid., pp. 32–33; Twenty-eighth Annual Report of the Directors of the Boston and Worcester Railroad Corporation, for the Year Ending November 30, 1857 (Boston: David Clapp, 1858), p. 7.

[99] Proceedings of the Directors and Stockholders of the Boston and Worcester Railroad, IV, 158–159, V, 7; Twenty-eighth Annual Report . . . of the Boston and Worcester, . . . 1857, p. 7; Pathfinder Railway Guide . . . 1849, p. 48; Hunt's Merchants' Magazine and Commercial Review, XV (1846), 324–325.

on long runs, the immense majority of users lived within a radius of fifteen miles of Boston. In the mid-fifties the Boston railroads were selling about 6,500 season tickets.[100]

For so extensive a practice, some other rationale than favoritism was necessary. First it was claimed that the holders of special tickets filled up the seats otherwise empty in the regular trains. Through their friends and families they brought an additional traffic upon the line, and, by populating suburbs, built new communities to patronize it.[101] When the roads unexpectedly discovered that this supplementary business had become a regular one requiring its own accommodations, outsiders explained that suburban trains were cheap trains. They used light engines, ran at low speeds, and the cars were crammed.[102] Such reassurances hardly stilled the renewed misgivings of railroad enterprisers. Commuting fares, they felt, had sunk too low. Season-tickets rates were a quarter to a half less than regular ones; savings on package tickets ranged from 12½ to 45 per cent; probably the average commuting fare was a trifle less than one cent a mile.[103] That was below cost, asserted managers and stockholders. Such a system was "unsound" in principle, "unjust," "unreasonable," and "injurious"; surely passengers would realize it. "It cannot be supposed that any inhabitant of Dedham or West Roxbury, would knowingly put his hand into the pocket of a fellow passenger, simply because he was a Stockholder in the road, for the money to pay his fare." [104] To which the citizens thus addressed replied, they were unwilling to pay fares to recompense the Boston and Providence "for losses in carrying freights at losing rates,

---

[100] Grant, *Boston Railways*, p. 98.

[101] *Report of the Committee for Investigating . . . the Boston and Providence . . . 1856*, p. 4; Grant, *Boston Railways*, pp. 95–96.

[102] Grant, *Boston Railways*, pp. 92–94.

[103] *Ibid.*, p. 90; *Twenty-eighth Annual Report . . . of the Boston and Worcester, . . . 1857*, p. 8; *Hunt's Merchants' Magazine and Commercial Review*, XV (1846), 325; *Report of the Investigating Committee of the Boston and Maine Railroad, to the Stockholders, September 29th, 1855* (Boston: Dutton and Wentworth, 1855), pp. 44–45 insert; *Report of the Investigating Committee of the . . . Eastern . . . 1855*, p. 39; *Report of the Committee for Investigating . . . the Boston and Providence . . . 1856*, pp. 4–5.

[104] *Report of the Committee for Investigating . . . the Boston and Providence . . . 1856*, pp. 5–6; Appleton and Swift, *Massachusetts Railroads*, p. 14.

for loose and extravagant management of corporation officers, or for unprofitable investment of their money and credit." [105] The railroads' experiment with low local rates certainly produced a waspish vested right. Still it must have been worth retaining. As horse railways pushed their lines into the suburbs, the menaced railroads fought back with their weapon of commutation.[106]

There were other variations than season or package tickets. Second-class fares, where they existed, were two-thirds of the first-class rate. Immigrant fares gave contracts for mass transportation in merchandise or second-class cars. Excurson trains — at times their universality reaching the stage of a "mania" — gave lower fares to militia and engine companies and other associations or provided general transportation for hordes of pleasure seekers at half price. Such trains, it was said, brought a new class of travel upon the roads, heightened its popularity, and in wholesome railroad travel presented an alternative to dissipation in "country taverns," "beer shops," and "gin palaces." One railroad president, altering the bibulous argument, claimed, "The arguments" in favor of excursion trains "were like those for intoxicating drinks — they gave an occasional stimulus, but diminished its [i.e., the railroad's] vital strength in the end." [107]

The free passage system did away with fares entirely. The opprobrium generally visited upon this device was partially undeserved. Officials and employees of the granting road were always the most numerous recipients. Passes, like stock, took the place of money. They entered into the payments for land damages, they were an unacknowledged portion of official salaries, and they were granted "to men connected with the Telegraph" in return for a free use of the wires. They were a form of rebate to large shippers, expressmen, and forwarders of passengers. Imperceptibly passes merged into favors for an amorphous good

---

[105] *Report of a Committee of Citizens of Dedham, Relative to the Advance in Fares, upon the Boston and Providence Railroad, at a Meeting in Temperance Hall, Dedham, March 12, 1856* (Dedham: Cox & Hutchins, 1856), p. 11.

[106] *The Twenty-fourth Annual Report of the Eastern Railroad Company, for the Year Ending May 31st, 1859* (Boston: Henry W. Dutton & Son, 1859), pp. 10–11.

[107] *Proceedings of the Convention of the Northern Lines . . . December, 1850,* pp. 29–44; *Annual Report of the Fitchburg . . . 1855,* p. 13.

will. They were granted to directors of connecting roads, innkeepers, drivers of hacks, captains of steamboats, and immigrant-aid agents. From them it was only a short step to "editors and the Fraternity," state officials, and to Daniel Webster, who received a pass from the Old Colony, perhaps because he was the most eminent statesman living on its line.[108] Other motives inspired largess. Passes were given from politeness and sentiment — for instance, to retiring directors who had rendered distinguished service to the corporation and to widows of officers. Thus the Boston and Worcester gave Mrs. George Bond, relict of a former director, "and her son Edward, & her two daughters who live with her," a free ticket for use on the Newton train. A month later, when the directors learned that Mrs. Bond had five minor children rather than three, the privilege of the pass was extended to the other two.[109] Mercy and charity played their role: "It is difficult to refuse the shipwrecked sailor." [110]

The system soon got out of hand. As they yielded to pressure after pressure, directors lost count of the number of passes. One Boston road in the mid-fifties calculated that probably three thousand persons now had free passage on it by right and an unestimated number by "loose general custom." [111] In that critical decade such performances were unlikely to go unchallenged. Free passes, it was now often asserted, were an "evil." They were unjust to the stockholders for they diminished the revenue; they were unfair to passengers who were paying their own way as well

[108] Proceedings of the Directors of the Western Railroad, II, 288; *The Twenty-first Annual Report of the Eastern Railroad Company, for the Year Ending May 31st, 1856* (Salem: Wm. Ives & Geo. W. Pease, 1856), pp. 15–16; *Report of the Committee of Investigation . . . of the Boston and Maine . . . 1849*, pp. 52–54; *Report of the Committee for Investigating . . . the Old Colony . . . 1849*, pp. 74–77; *Report of the Committee for Investigating the Affairs of the Boston and Providence Railroad Corporation. Appointed by the Stockholders, January 14, 1857* (Boston: Henry W. Dutton and Son, 1857), p. 18.

[109] Proceedings of the Directors and Stockholders of the Boston and Worcester Railroad, II, 245–246, V, 33, 38.

[110] *Annual Report of the Directors of the Eastern Rail Road Company, to the Stockholders, for the Year Ending June 30, 1850* (Salem: Observer Office, 1850), p. 15; Proceedings of the Directors and Stockholders of the Boston and Worcester Railroad, VI, 322.

[111] *Report of the Committee for Investigating . . . the Boston and Providence . . . 1856*, pp. 17–18.

as an additional sum for those who were not; they menaced any system for enforcing accountability.[112]

Though the individual railroads made stabs at reformation, concerted action was preferred, since directorates wished to divide the odium of an unpopular curtailment. Since even co-operative measures broke down,[113] railroads were not averse to help from the state. New Hampshire in 1850 forbade free passes except to stockholders going to the annual meeting, officials of the railroad or those with whom it had connections or contracts, employees, express and mailmen, and poor people who could not afford to travel but must.[114] In 1855 Rhode Island adopted a similar restriction but only after an anti-railroad campaign which in the course of five years produced some of the most cogent arguments for equality and so unusual an apologia for free passes as to suggest the ironic. "Liberality" was "so unusual in corporations it should be encouraged when shown, instead of being made the cause of distrust," declared the railroad commissioners of the state.[115]

VII

As the pre-Civil-War decades passed, freight receipts increased percentage-wise more rapidly than those from passengers. They had always been the traffic mainstay in Vermont and New Hampshire; by the end of the fifties, in spite of the ubiquity and efficiency of a rival water transportation, they surpassed passenger receipts in Maine, and even in southern New England their re-

---

[112] *Report of the Committee for Investigating . . . the Boston and Providence . . . 1857*, pp. 14–17; *Twenty-first Annual Report . . . of the Boston and Worcester . . . 1850*, p. 26.

[113] *Ninth Annual Report of the Directors of the Old Colony Rail Road Corporation, to the Stockholders. January, 1853* (Boston: Crocker & Brewster, 1853), pp. 3–4; *Twenty-first Annual Report of the Eastern . . . 1856*, pp. 14–16.

[114] *Laws of the State of New Hampshire, Passed June Session, 1850* pp. 429–430; *Ninth Annual Report of the Directors of the Concord Railroad Corporation, May, 1850* (Concord: Asa McFarland, n.d.), p. 11.

[115] Report of the Board of Railroad Commissioners, *Acts and Resolves of the General Assembly of the State of Rhode-Island and Providence Plantations. Passed at the October Session, 1851*, p. 81; *Acts and Resolves of the General Assembly, of Rhode Island and Providence Plantations, Passed at the January Session, 1855*, p. 13.

spectable totals had the pace setters in sight.[116] Such facts led railroad managers to think it more important to discuss freight than passenger rates.[117] The former, indeed, had fallen more precipitately. Unparticularized averages — perhaps guesses — revealed the trend. According to Derby, the rate per mile was in 1835 around 9 cents a ton, and in the late forties it was between 3 and 4 cents. In the mid-fifties averages of through and local rates on three roads placed the figure near 3 cents; on the Western it was 2.4 cents.[118] These figures, nonetheless, are extremely inconclusive. Freight rates rarely received the printed formalization of passenger fares; and the area for experimentation and differentiation was larger, for here experience gave little precedent for fixed rates. On wagon and boat, freights were determined by bargain, season, and circumstance. Daunted by the arcana of the problem, the directors of the Boston and Worcester, before their road opened, debated and differed over "what measures shall be adopted touching the transportation of merchandise on the Rail Road & what shall be the respective rates or prices for transportation &c &c." When they could not decide, they voted "that the superintendent be authorised in the mean time to contract for the transportation of merchandise with any person or persons, who shall offer the same, at such rates and on such terms as he shall deem expedient, provided that no merchandise shall be taken at a rate less than two dollars per ton." [119] Here in germ was a forecast of the complexity of the freight-rate structure and even the methods used to build it.

However unflattering it may be to the concept of numberless human personalities all different from each other, the distinctions between freights are sharper and more significant for the rail-

[116] Poor, *History of the Railroads and Canals of the United States*, pp. 12, 40, 71, 93, 186, 194; Balfour, "How Should Railroads be Managed?", p. 193.
[117] *Proceedings of the Convention of the Northern Lines . . . December, 1850*, p. 15.
[118] Derby, "Administration of the Railroads of Massachusetts," p. 236; Derby, "The Railways of Massachusetts," p. 309; Zerah Colburn, "The Economy of Railroads, as Affected by the Adaptation of Locomotive Power — Addressed to the Railroad Interests of New England," *American Railroad Journal*, XXVII (1854), 241.
[119] Proceedings of the Directors and Stockholders of the Boston and Worcester Railroad, I, 226, 227–228.

road-rate maker. Goods of different quality could bear different freight rates, while goods in bulk assured cargoes and did not require detailed handling. Freight classifications appeared. In the forties when the Worcester and the Western were worrying over rates, two classifications and a third category for goods subject to special treatment — bulky articles like flour, lime, plaster, lumber, and coal — were sufficient. A decade later refinements delineated four classes but still retained the extra group carried at negotiated rates.[120] Meanwhile the minimum quantity winning special rates had declined. On the Boston and Worcester the original decision had been fifty tons, within a year it was ten, within three years a carload. Later "the 6,000 lb. rule" was the determinant of reductions.[121]

As in the case of passengers, through rates were lower than local ones and partly for the same reason, competition. Since in the freight, as distinguished from the passenger business where the cargo handled itself, there were charges for loading and unloading no matter what the distance traveled, the disparity was increased. Through rates on a mileage basis might be, therefore, anywhere from a third to two-thirds lower than local ones; frequently the total for the shorter was greater than for the longer distance.[122] While managers realized this outcome incited suspicion and irritation among the road's patrons, and cleared the way for the charge that the local traffic was made to support the through, they pled for an appreciation of the realities. "It is no injustice to our other customers, who have not the advantages of . . . competition, if we take a higher price from them for doing the same work, — provided always that this higher price is rea-

---

[120] Proceedings of the Board of Directors of the Western Railroad Corporation, I, 28–29, 164, 218–219, II, 273, 288; Colburn, "The Economy of Railroads," p. 241.

[121] Proceedings of the Directors and Stockholders of the Boston and Worcester Railroad, II, 250, III, 4, 54–55, 197; Proceedings of the Board of Directors of the Western Railroad Corporation, I, 28, 219.

[122] Colburn, "The Economy of Railroads," p. 241; *Report of the Investigating Committee of the Concord Railroad, to the Stockholders, December, 1857* (Concord: McFarland & Jenks, 1857), p. 31; *Considerations for the Stockholders of the Providence & Worcester Railroad Co.* (Woonsocket: S. S. Foss, 1861), p. 7, table; *Mr. Harris Reviewed. Being an Examination of His "Further Considerations for the Stockholders of the Providence and Worcester Railroad." By a Rhode Islander* (Providence: Alfred Anthony, 1864), pp. 7–10.

sonable in itself. It is not only not unjust to our local customers on the other parts of our road, to take these minor rates from others, — but it redounds to their advantage: for, if we refuse to take this business which comes to us at a less profitable rate, the road must be sustained by the other business, — and our local customers would have a just ground of complaint against us, that we did not use all proper means to lighten their burdens." [123]

Just as easy and just as natural were the favors shown individual shippers. Even before the road was opened to Worcester, some paper manufacturer requested the directors of the Boston and Worcester for a "special bargain" on his goods. Soon "special bargains," "drawbacks," and "special contracts" were made for quantity shipments, business out of season, the exclusive carriage of a concern's output, and to meet competition.[124] They were a flexible response to a wide variety of pressures and needs. In 1845, for instance, the directors of the Boston and Worcester were informed that Messrs. J. & C. Washburn were about to remove from Worcester and erect a rolling mill at or near Boston "on account of the expense of transportation." The board responded by authorizing the superintendent, if expedient, "to place iron rods & iron wire in the 2d class of freight." [125] In this or other forms, rebates were ubiquitous. Factories at Lowell, Biddeford and Saco, Fall River, Worcester, and along the Blackstone received them.[126] How much lower than regular rates these special ones were, it is impossible to say. On the Fall River Railroad, reductions ranged from 20 to well over 30 per cent; the directors of the corporation thought the latter figure excessive.[127]

[123] *Report . . . of the Boston and Maine . . . 1856*, pp. 12–13.

[124] Proceedings of the Directors and Stockholders of the Boston and Worcester Railroad, II, 14–15, III, 33, 114, V, 37, 179–180; Proceedings of the Board of Directors of the Western Railroad Corporation, II, 108.

[125] Proceedings of the Directors and Stockholders of the Boston and Worcester Railroad, V, 198.

[126] *Report of the Investigating Committee of the Boston and Maine . . . 1855*, pp. 41–43; *Report of the Committee for Investigating . . . the Old Colony . . . 1849*, appendix, p. 118; *Mr. Harris Reviewed*, pp. 10–12; Fourteenth Annual Report of the Boston and Lowell Railroad, Massachusetts *House Documents*, 1845, no. 46, pp. 4–5; *Report of the Committee for Investigating . . . the Boston and Providence . . . 1856*, p. 16.

[127] *Report of the Committee for Investigating . . . the Old Colony . . . 1849*, appendix, p. 118; *Report of the Committee for Investigating the Affairs of the Fall*

Sometimes officers criticized this rebate system. Thus a delegate to the Boston Convention of Northern Lines informed his colleagues:

> Means are used to get business from *other roads*, which any one would be ashamed to resort to in the transactions of private business; which shows that the Managers as well as the Corporation, have but *small* souls, if any. We make solemn bargains with each other to be governed by certain principles and rules, and violate them the same day, by a secret bargain with an individual, to obtain a small pittance of freight from another road. The people, seeing this, lose all respect for us, and we seem to have none for ourselves; and they approach us to *dicker* with us, like jockies, without even thinking that we might deem it an insult. In this way we have already sunk our characters so low, that the term '*Railroad man*' is one of reproach, and at once destroys his influence in legislative halls, and jeopardizes his rights, and the rights of the corporation, even in our courts of justice.[128]

Sometimes also stockholders protested arrangements by which directors granted rebates to themselves as shippers.[129]

Gradually popular disapproval of the railroad-rate structure grew strong enough in Vermont, New Hampshire, and Rhode Island to pass regulatory legislation. These were states traversed by routes which under the impact of competition lowered the rates for through business until they stood in sharp contrast with local charges. Perhaps more than the other states, these were at the moment the repository of equalitarian sentiment. In any case they adopted a variety of statutes groping toward a mileage basis for rates, prohibiting a greater charge for a short than for a long haul, and, with appropriate exceptions for season tickets and excursion trains, specifying that the "rates . . . shall be the same for all persons and for the like descriptions of freight between such stations." [130] In Rhode Island the movement for controls of this

River Railroad Company. Appointed by the Stockholders, January 17, 1850 (Boston: Eastburn's Press, 1850), p. 34.
[128] Proceedings of the Convention of the Northern Lines . . . December, 1850, p. 23.   [129] Mr. Harris Reviewed, pp. 10–12.
[130] Statutes of New Hampshire, Public and Private. 1850–1855, pp. 926–927; Laws of the State of New Hampshire: Passed June Session, 1852, p. 1214; The Acts and Resolves Passed by the Legislature of the State of Vermont, at the October Session, 1850, p. 34; Proceedings of the Convention of the Northern Lines . . . December, 1850, pp. 77–78.

sort began earlier and engendered more debate than anywhere else in New England. The situation there was unique. The alliance of railroads and steamship companies and the subsequent severe competition for the commerce between New York and Boston, — and to a less extent with Worcester — pushed down the through rates and left the local ones high. In addition, the New York, Providence and Boston had a thirty-year monopoly of its route.

As early as the thirties, ill-worded provisions in charter or statute might be interpreted to prohibit any difference in rates between individuals and localities except on a mileage basis. Thus the act of 1838 establishing the railroad commission in Rhode Island gave it powers of investigation and report in order to secure for citizens of that state "the full and equal privileges of the transportation of persons and property . . . and rateably in proportion to the distance any such persons or property may be transported." [131] No imperative, this suggestion was observed in the breach. Later, in the early fifties, the campaign against discrimination reached crescendo. It was led by a remarkable crusader, Rowland G. Hazard. He blended political liberalism, wool manufacturing, and sufficient philosophical ability to refute Jonathan Edwards on "The Will" and excite the admiration of John Stuart Mill.[132] His factory village lay off the main line of the New York, Providence and Boston. Although his attack on the railroads contained the expected shibboleths — a sulphurous picture of Wall Street that a Granger might envy, an assertion Rhode Islanders never shall be slaves, and an envy of foreigners, meaning shippers from Massachusetts [133] — it was the most trenchant analysis of the disadvantages arising from contemporary rate practices, at least those of special contracts and high local rates.

In support of his bill for regulation, Hazard declared, "The several succeeding sections provide for equality of service and of compensation." The community had a right to this equality for,

[131] Acts and Resolves of Rhode-Island and Providence Plantations. Passed at the June Session, 1839, pp. 23–24.

[132] Dictionary of American Biography (New York: Charles Scribner's Sons, 1928–1936), VIII, 471–472.

[133] Rowland G. Hazard, Economics and Politics. A Series of Papers upon Public Questions Written on Various Occasions from 1840 to 1885 (Boston and New York: Houghton, Mifflin and Company, 1889), pp. 54–56, 59–60, 70–71, 111–114.

The corporations can have the power to take private property, only on the condition of public benefit. . . . Neither the corporation nor the State have any right to make a privileged class which shall have exclusive claims to this benefit, due to the whole public. . . . Suppose that the general government should say that the city of New York, importing more largely than any other city, might import for twenty-five per cent. duty, Boston for thirty, and Providence for forty per cent.; and then that some of the most extensive merchants in New York might have a further advantage over their fellow-citizens, and import for fifteen per cent. Under such a rule the large cities would swallow up the smaller, and men of large capital destroy those of more limited means. It is evident, too, that the exercise of such powers by the government would inevitably lead to despotism; and are they safer in the hands of irresponsible corporations? I think I might safely rest this right of equality on this fundamental principle.[134]

Although Hazard and his allies kept the railroad commissioners in turmoil with investigations and the legislature busy passing and repealing laws, the final result, the General Act of 1855, did little more, as far as rates were concerned, than restrict the list of free passes.[135]

While Rhode Island and other states were pointing a trend, if not passing effective legislation, the Supreme Judicial Court of Massachusetts had occasion to review the inequalities of the rate structure. In this instance the judges were concerned not with the expediency or idealism of policy but with its legality under the common law. Their decision placed differences in treatment upon a firm basis. Railroads must give "equal justice to all," but this equality consisted in charging not the same rate but "a reasonable compensation. . . . If, for special reasons in isolated cases, the carrier sees fit to stipulate for the carriage of goods or mer-

[134] *Ibid.*, pp. 93–94.

[135] *Ibid.*, p. 74; *Acts and Resolves . . . of Rhode Island . . . January Session, 1852*, pp. 5–6; *Acts and Resolves . . . of Rhode Island . . . January Session, 1853*, p. 262; *Acts and Resolves . . . of Rhode Island . . . Passed at the January Session, 1855*, pp. 13–16; Report of the Railroad Commissioners, *Laws of Rhode Island, October, 1851*, pp. 79–80; Report of the Railroad Commissioners, *Acts and Resolves . . . of Rhode Island . . . May Session, 1854*, pp. 147–150; *Report of the Railroad Commissioners to the General Assembly of Rhode Island, at its January Session, 1854*; Report of the Majority and Minority of the Rhode Island Railroad Commissioners, October Session, 1854, *Railroad Commissioners' Report.*

chandise of any class for individuals for a certain time or in certain quantities for less compensation than what is the usual, necessary and reasonable rate, he may undoubtedly do so without thereby entitling all other persons and parties to the same advantage and relief." [136] This dictum consecrated existing rate practices, on the whole wisely. Freedom in making rates had given the corporations the opportunity to experiment. With drawbacks, special contracts, and local discriminations the railroads felt their way and discovered, not too expensively, their potentialities and limitations. Frequently privileges granted to a few were generalized for the many.[137] That discrimination and rebates thus had a benign aspect in the early period was no argument for hardening them into a permanent system. For the future Hazard's criticism was unanswerable.

VIII

The railroad crisis of the fifties was immediate; it called for action as well as for philosophical reflection. The roads, therefore, turned to the possibility of salvation through increased fares and freights. At once the old debate between advocates of high and low rates was resumed. It was a debate in the dark. The controversialists did not resort to refined economic analysis for they were partisans; they could not have employed it, if they would, for without the improved accounting methods of a later period the requisite data were not at hand. The leading protagonist of low fares was naturally E. H. Derby. He had championed them on the Worcester and the Western and, as counsel for the Fitchburg, regarded with approval the low-fare experiments of that railroad. Scarred by his earlier skirmishes but not suppressed, he now fought in a state-wide arena for the theory that low fares meant a greater business. He focused upon passenger traffic. During the forties when rates were falling, both the numbers of passengers and the totals of passenger receipts increased; experience could not have been more explicit. The dilemmas raised for

---

[136] Fitchburg Railroad Company *v.* Addison Gage and Others, 12 *Gray*, 398, 399.
[137] Proceedings of the Directors and Stockholders of the Boston and Worcester Railroad, III, 105, 116.

stockholders and managers by the large expenditures and rising costs of the fifties did not disturb his writing. He forgot difficulties as he stressed the primary objects of a railroad: "creating new value, giving a new impulse to industry and wealth and promoting social intercourse;" or took refuge in the comfortable and meaningless compromise, "It is sincerely to be hoped that that rate will be most successful which gives the greatest good to the greatest number." In practice he recognized that reductions carried too far were damaging.[138] His sanguine faith — for it was little more — while useful during the early period to prod cautious men to bold experiment in an untried business was not adapted to the crisis of the fifties.

One of Derby's intellectual heirs, E. B. Grant, therefore went somewhat deeper. Although bemused with the inexorability and universality of the "law of low fares," Grant advocated "moderate" ones, granted the right of stockholders to earn 8 per cent, and reconciled the attainment of these twin objectives through technical and other economies.[139] Grant had partially allied with the enemy. Some of the latter crew were content to expatiate upon the absolute folly of the low-fare advocates and the preposterous character of their proposals. The more reasonable made the discovery that what might have been sound in the forties was not necessarily sound in the fifties. This group focused upon the rising tide of expenditures, the higher prices of materials like fuel and oil, the heavy appropriations, belatedly made, for depreciation, and the large capital expenditures for the increased services and extensions demanded by the public. To meet these, neither the low-rate level of the forties nor its projected trend into the future sufficed.[140]

---

[138] Derby, "The Railways of Massachusetts," pp. 304–308; *Proceedings of the Annual Meeting of the Western Rail-Road Corporation, Held, by Adjournment, in the City of Boston, March 12, 1840, Including the Report of the Committee of Investigation Appointed by the Stockholders* (Boston: Dutton and Wentworth, 1840), pp. 55–56.

[139] Grant, *Boston Railways*, pp. 77–87.

[140] *Annual Report of the Fitchburg Railroad . . . 1855*, pp. 8–10; *Report of the Committee for Investigating . . . the Boston and Providence . . . 1856*, pp. 8–10; Appleton and Swift, *Massachusetts Railroads*, pp. 11–14; Balfour, "How Should Railroads be Managed?", pp. 189–194.

To raise rates, however, would be certain to arouse public clamor and abuse. Concerted action promised protection.[141] It was, alas, unattainable. Although on details of technical operation it had been possible to effect a measure of agreement,[142] rates were a matter of high policy and the competitive situation was too volatile for co-operation. Nevertheless the pressures were inescapable. In 1849–1850 the trend of rates turned. Through passenger fares first reflected the difference. Within a decade, dowager roads like the Boston and Lowell and Boston and Worcester had raised theirs a third; a new management on the Fitchburg, Derby's laboratory, angry at the "suicidal reduction of prices for railroad services," raised them 55 per cent. The Concord raised its fares 85 per cent.[143] The tide spread to commutation and freights.[144] To outsiders the unanimity of action suggested a "combination"; to low fare advocates, a desertion. Perhaps the worst traitor was the Fitchburg. Once liberal, it now "treated the public as a many-headed monster whose sole delight, desire, and aim was to ruin shareholders." [145]

In truth the advocates of higher rates exalted the rights of the stockholders. Sometimes the appeal was sentimental, more often it stressed the contributions which the railroads, those veins and arteries of commerce, had made to New England. The productions of the earth had been doubled and quadrupled in value and

[141] Appleton and Swift, *Massachusetts Railroads*, pp. 6–7; *Annual Report of the Fitchburg . . . 1855*, p. 9; *Twenty-fifth Annual Report . . . of the Boston and Worcester . . . 1854*, p. 15.

[142] *Records of the New-England Association of Railway Superintendents. Reprinted from the Original Records in 1910* (Washington: D. C. Gibson Bros., 1910), pp. 16, 28, 31; *Reports and Other Papers of the New-England Association of Railway Superintendents from the Commencement of the Society to January 1st, 1850* (Boston: Stacy, Richardson & Co., 1850), pp. 23, 29–32, 37–41, 47–48.

[143] *Pathfinder Railway Guide for the New England States . . . 1849*, pp. 28, 47, 40, 50; *Snow's Pathfinder Railway Guide, for the New England States and Part of Canada: Containing Official Time-Tables of the Railway Companies, with Stations, Distances, Fares, etc., . . . January, 1860* (Boston: Geo. K. Snow, n.d.), pp. 12, 16, 18, 19.

[144] *Report . . . of the Boston and Maine . . . 1856*, p. 13; *Eleventh Annual Report of the Fitchburg Railroad Company. January 25th, 1853* (Charlestown: W. W. Wheildon, 1853), p. 12; Grant, *Boston Railways*, p. 19; *Twenty-fifth Annual Report . . . of the Boston and Worcester . . . 1854*, p. 15.

[145] Grant, *Boston Railways*, p. 41; *Report of a Committee of Citizens of Dedham*, p. 15.

remote country towns quickened by enterprise. The old-school squire "of formal manners and of formal dress" had become "as extinct as the dodo." [146] Above all, the railroads had saved New England's metropolis, Boston. Rivers of statistics flowed to prove it. Between 1830 and 1860 the valuation of real and personal property multiplied between four and five times and population nearly three. These warming figures were surpassed by the towns surrounding Boston. In the ten years before the Civil War some of these communities attained rates of increase which the Dallas and the Los Angeles of the twentieth century might have envied. Somerville, Brookline, and Melrose all had growths of over one hundred per cent.[147] Bostonians who lived through the era could hardly believe that Roxbury, Charlestown, and Waltham, once regions of farms and graceful country estates, were taking on the aspects of the city; that Lowell, Worcester, and Salem were almost suburbs. When even the partisans of low fares admitted the railroad to be responsible for these miracles, it was not surprising that management and shareholders looked upon themselves as "in some good sense, public benefactors, and as such entitled, whenever their Roads are judiciously located, to a fair and adequate compensation from the public for the use of their money." [148] Although they might have aimed for the 10 per cent which charters fixed as a maximum return, "the legal rate," most would have been content with 7 or 8 per cent.[149] Whatever the figure, there was here no admission that shareholders invested in railroads for incidental advantages. These were rationalizations

[146] Charles F. Adams, Jr., "The Railroad System," *North American Review*, CIV (1867), 488; *Speech of Honorable Charles W. Upham . . . April 11, 1857*, pp. 3–4; *Fourteenth Annual Report of the Fitchburg . . . 1856*, pp. 27–28; *Report of a Committee of Stockholders of the Concord Railroad, May, 1851* (Concord: McFarland & Jenks, n.d.), p. 11.

[147] Report of Israel D. Andrews on the Trade and Commerce of the British North American Colonies, *Senate Executive Documents*, 32 Cong., 1 Sess., no. 112 (s.n. 622), pp. 286–287; *Hunt's Merchants' Magazine and Commercial Review*, XLIII (1860), 463; *Abstract of the Census of Massachusetts, 1860, From the Eighth U.S. Census, with Remarks on the Same*, pp. 208, 313.

[148] *Report of a Committee . . . of the Concord . . . 1851*, p. 11.

[149] *Report . . . of the Boston and Lowell . . . 1849*, pp. 5–6; Grant, *Boston Railways*, p. 86; *Annual Report of the Fitchburg . . . 1855*, pp. 9–10; *Report of the Committee for Investigating . . . the Boston and Providence . . . 1856*, p. 22.

after the event — when capital failed to earn dividends — permissible for apostles of the new methods of financiering, visionaries of the Derby stripe, and railroad commissioners. In the fifties stock owners were asking a fundamental and ancient question — whether the laborer was worthy of his hire.

XI

THE BOSTON AND ALBANY RAILROAD

"When you can't stem the current, get in and steer." Reputed
motto of Chester W. Chapin. Margaret E. Martin, Merchants and
Trade of the Connecticut River Valley, p. 198.

I

With the sixties renaissance came to the New England railroad
system. As soon as the first dislocations of the Civil War were
past, prosperity poured upon the railroads; earnings and stock
values shot upward. The end of the war was another fillip to op-
timism and the region embarked upon a new era of construction.
The timidities and the despair of the fifties vanished; plans and
promotions took their place. In mood and in action New England
returned to the decade of the twenties; she stood again on the
verge of a new railroad era where nothing was impossible.

Since the region seemed destined to recapitulate the history of
an earlier and hopeful decade, attention was once again primarily
focused upon a route to the West. The resulting diagnosis of the
situation might have been written by the Board of Directors of
Internal Improvement or by Nathan Hale. Boston was failing to
maintain her commercial hold upon the West and even upon her
hinterland. Worcester and Pittsfield drew their grain from ports
along the Sound rather than by rail direct from Albany, and merchants in the interior of Massachusetts preferred, in view of the
rapidity of deliveries, to make their purchases in New York rather
than in Boston. Western Vermont and Massachusetts were in the
sixties less dependent upon Boston than when the railroad had

first demonstrated its capacity to mount the highlands between Boston and the Connecticut.[1] As for the service to the West, the Grand Trunk, two hundred miles north of Boston, carried grain to Portland, one hundred miles east of Boston, and then derisively shipped it back to the Massachusetts metropolis. The Pennsylvania took goods from Maine, New Hampshire, and central Massachusetts, transported them to Philadelphia and then west in a successful rivalry with Boston's direct route to the Hudson.[2] As for New York's railroads, the Erie and the New York Central, the crescendo in their business overshadowed the smaller increases on the Boston and Worcester and the Western.[3] The consequent complaints from Boston merchants, manufacturers, importers, and forwarders were intense. "There is immense competition for the Western business. Philadelphia, Baltimore, New York and Portland are all striving for it. It is impossible to deny that Boston is falling in the rear, and that other cities and states are securing the advantages."[4] Of these rivals, New York was, as it had been earlier, the most deadly and the most successful.

Critics universally ascribed Boston's misfortunes to the defects and the delinquencies of the Boston and Worcester and the Western. Though physically they embodied the early vision of a route to the Hudson, actually they had not fulfilled the aims of early railroad schemers and later sponsors. Yet measures to redress the situation aroused differences of view. Some pinned their hopes upon the route to the Lakes, but the prosperous post-war years did not lighten its embarrassments. Others backed the line through Fitchburg and Greenfield to Troy. In the sixties this route had as yet no Hoosac tunnel and the vacillating and ineffective policy of the state gave little promise of one. Even the hope-

[1] *Seventeenth Annual Report of the Boston Board of Trade, for the Year Ending January 11, 1871* (Boston: Barker, Cotter & Co., 1871), p. 38; Report of the Joint Special Committee of the Legislature on the Failures of the Western Railroad, Massachusetts *House Documents*, 1866, no. 330, pp. 44–45, 98.

[2] Peleg W. Chandler, *Argument in Favor of the Proposed Consolidation of the Western and Worcester Railroad Corporations, before the Committee on Railways and Canals, March 16th, 1864* (Boston: Geo. C. Rand & Avery, 1864), p. 4.

[3] Charles F. Adams, Jr., "Railroad Legislation," *Hunt's Merchants' Magazine and Commercial Review*, LVII (1867), 347–348; Massachusetts *House Documents*, 1866, no. 330, pp. 99–101.

[4] Chandler, *Argument in Favor of the Proposed Consolidation*, p. 4.

ful realized usefulness of this road could come only in a dim and distant future. The reformation of the Boston and Worcester and the Western, therefore, promised the most immediate salvation. Besides, this route had behind it the sanctity of history and experience.

Since reformation was a vague prescription, the railroad schemers of the sixties bent themselves to definition. Undoubtedly preponderant opinion advocated the consolidation of the two roads — a cure as old as the forties. To the customary arguments for all consolidations — economies in operation through the concentration of direction and equipment — advocates implied that union would be followed by lower freight rates — the Western's scale was to be imposed upon the Boston and Worcester — and an end to the "buck-passing" characteristic of a segmented line. Above all, consolidation would terminate the continual quarrel over a division of receipts which had too long engulfed the abilities and energies of both corporations.[5] Advantageous as this accomplishment might be, there were skeptics to assert that a cessation of inter-corporate quarrels did not necessarily ensure gains to the public good.

Perhaps these and other doubts might be quieted by a new conception of the function of the state directors. In 1866, before consolidation was accomplished, the General Court resolved, "That the large contribution from the treasury of the Commonwealth in aid of the construction of the Western railroad, was made for the promotion of the prosperity of the people of the Commonwealth generally; and it is the duty, therefore, of the state directors of said road to exert themselves to promote that object by the increase and enlargement of facilities of travel, trade, and commerce rather than by the return of a larger percentage of pecuniary profit to the Commonwealth as stockholder." Henceforth state directors could be neither stockholders nor em-

---

[5] *Statements and Arguments in Behalf of the Petitioners before the Committee on Railroads and Canals of the Legislature of Massachusetts, 1864, on the Petition of the Boston and Worcester and Western Railroad Corporations for the Consolidation of Those Roads* (Boston: Geo. C. Rand & Avery, 1864), pp. 65–71; *Twenty-eighth Annual Report of the Directors of the Western Rail Road Corporation, to the Stockholders, January, 1863* (Springfield: J. F. Tannatt, 1863), pp. 8–9.

ployees of the road nor members of the legislature; they were
to submit an annual report to the General Court.[6] This resolution envisaged an increased and independent participation in
management by the state.

On the other hand, a minority scoffed at the inadequacy of
these proposals. In behalf of a more thorough and effective policy E. H. Derby and Josiah Quincy, Jr., raised ancestral voices
for state ownership. Their cause echoed overtones from the
twenties, from Sedgwick, and from the earlier Hale. Their task
was easier. They did not have to build a railroad; they simply had
to acquire one in being. Briefly they proposed that the state purchase the Boston and Worcester and the Western under the recapture provisions stated in the original charters, later enactments, and general statutes.[7] It is not necessary to appraise the
heated calculations of various costs, for the effectiveness of state
ownership and of the proposed methods of operation was the
point at issue. Though Derby and Quincy agreed on the wisdom
of state purchase, they advanced different programs of operation. With many a citation from Belgian and French experience,
the former advocated operation by a new corporation in which
"the State would remain as a partner." [8] Quincy sympathized
with the dread of state ownership: "The people have justly a
want of confidence in the administrative ability of government
officials. They demur at the vast increase of patronage which
would thus be given to the government. Of course management
by government would never be allowed." To escape from this
dilemma, he would have the Commonwealth lease the road to
Boston and entrust management to seven directors, four chosen
by the city on nomination from the Board of Trade, and one each
by Worcester, Springfield, and Pittsfield.[9] Though Quincy stirred
a terrific hullabaloo, he failed to win support from the Boston

[6] *Acts and Resolves Passed by the General Court of Massachusetts, in the Year
1866*, p. 319.

[7] Legislative Hearing on the Matter of the Western Railroad, Massachusetts
House Documents, 1866, no. 330, pp. 58–65, 70–74, 77–78; Josiah Quincy, Jr., *The
Railway System of Massachusetts. An Address Delivered before the Boston Board
of Trade, . . . November 19, 1866* (Boston: Mudge & Son, 1866), p. 21.

[8] Massachusetts *House Documents*, 1866, no. 330, pp. 72–73.

[9] Quincy, *Railway System of Massachusetts*, pp. 21–22.

City Council, the Board of Trade, or the General Court.[10] As the Springfield *Republican* patronizingly and dogmatically put it, "The State will buy no more railroads, nor will the city of Boston hire and run them. America doesn't organize states and cities to run railroads any more than barber shops. It is foreign to our philosophy and purposes."[11]

The campaign for consolidation, however, enrolled impressive interests. One was the organized merchants of Boston. The Board of Trade, the motive for whose establishment had been the wretched access of Boston to the West, demanded, "UNION — EARLY, PERPETUAL UNION, ON TERMS OF EXACT JUSTICE." [12] The Western Railroad, under the driving leadership of President Chester W. Chapin, advocated consolidation, and, if it were not forthcoming, threatened to extend its tracks into Boston when the Worcester's thirty-year monopoly expired.[13] Yet frictions slowed the realization of the program of combination. Though parallel lines were not involved, doctrinaire exponents of competition dreaded consolidation; foes of corporate monopoly feared the overwhelming political and economic power of an immense corporation; "manifest-inferior-destiny men" declared it was impossible for Boston to rival New York and the attempt should be abandoned; and communities along the line of the proposed consolidated line apprehended the lowering of through rates at the expense of local charges and interests.[14] To the opposition cause most of the directors in the Boston and Worcester also gave adherence. With them an emotional preference for running their own railroad supplemented economic analysis, just as with the city of Worcester civic pride in its ter-

[10] Springfield *Daily Republican*, March 15, November 21, 1866, February 6, March 14, 1867; Boston *Journal*, January 24, February 5, 12, March 12, 14, 1867.
[11] Springfield *Daily Republican*, January 12, 1867.
[12] *Boston Board of Trade. Report of the Select Committee of the Board of Trade, on the Controversy between the Boston and Worcester and Western Railroads. August 1862* (Boston: Wright & Potter, 1862), p. 27.
[13] *Twenty-sixth Annual Report of the Directors of the Western Rail Road Corporation, to the Stockholders, January, 1861* (Springfield: J. F. Tannatt & Company, 1861), p. 19.
[14] Massachusetts [E. H. Derby], *Consolidation of the Boston & Worcester and Western R.Rs.* (n.p., n.d.); Report of the Joint Standing Committee on Railways and Canals, Massachusetts *House Documents, 1864*, no. 294 pp. 9–10.

minal position joined the fear of local rate discrimination to arouse opposition to consolidation.[15] Even the Boston and Worcester, however, realized that it could not forever meet "the petitioning and protesting" of others with a policy of "promising and postponing." Though directors were loath to accept union, stockholders were not — a development which Chapin and his friends hastened through large stock purchases in the road.[16] In 1864 stockholders of both corporations petitioned the legislature for the right to consolidate. The committee on railways reported adversely and the House defeated the bill by a narrow margin.[17] For this reversal of universal expectations the Boston and Worcester was primarily responsible. At the annual meeting of 1864, consolidation and anti-consolidation tickets for directors were put in the field. The latter won. Forthwith they maneuvered the defeat of pending legislation for union.[18]

While intrigue delayed the movement for consolidation, it could not permanently prevent success. The city government pressed for action. The Board of Trade, after rejecting Quincy's proposals, memorialized the legislature in behalf of legislation.[19] The Western remained its persistent advocate. Finally in 1867 the legislature empowered the two roads to consolidate with a capital equal to that of the two roads combined and apportioned between them by agreement or by adjudication of commissioners appointed by the Supreme Judicial Court. In case the Boston and Worcester refused to consolidate, the Western could build its own line to Boston or unite with any other road which would provide such a route in whole or in part. However effected, the new line was to be called the Boston and Albany Railroad. Other provi-

---

[15] Chandler, *Argument in Favor of the Proposed Consolidation*, pp. 12–20; Massachusetts *House Documents*, 1864, no 294, pp. 6–8.

[16] *Statements and Arguments . . . on the Petition of the Boston and Worcester*, pp. 46–47.

[17] *Ibid.*, pp. 46–47; Massachusetts *House Documents*, 1864, no. 294, pp. 1, 4–6.

[18] *Twenty-ninth Annual Report of the Directors of the Western Rail Road Corporation, to the Stockholders, January, 1864* (Springfield: J. F. Tannatt & Co., 1864), pp. 18–22; *Thirty-fourth Annual Report of the Directors of the Boston and Worcester Railroad Corporation, for the Year Ending November 30, 1863* (Boston: David Clapp, 1864), p. 7; Boston *Advertiser*, March 26, May 14, 1867.

[19] *Fourteenth Annual Report of the Boston Board of Trade, for the Year Ending January 8th, 1868* (Boston: J. H. Eastburn's Press, 1868), pp. 31–33, 78–80.

sions preserved the public interest in the new corporation or regulated its procedures. Of the thirteen directors, the Commonwealth was to appoint five. The consolidated road, furthermore, "shall furnish . . . accommodations or facilities for local traffic and business not less than are now furnished by either of the corporations" and should not charge "for the transportation. . . of freight to any station upon its road, a greater sum than is at the same time received by it for the transportation of the like class and quality of freight from the same original point of departure to a station at a greater distance on its road in the same direction; *provided*, that the sum received in any case for the transportation of joint freight shall not be taken as the standard for charges on local freight." [20]

By the end of the year the two roads agreed upon terms of union. The capitalization of the new company equaled that of the combined corporations and was exchanged share for share. Security holders in the Boston and Worcester received a bonus of $10 a share. On the Western the stockholders had, somewhat earlier, foresightedly increased their capitalization by $2,000,000 and distributed the amount to themselves as a dividend "in part representing the sum which had been expended in the construction of the road, and which had been doubly provided for in the accumulated earnings of the road." [21] Though this gratuity may not have been water, the resulting stock inflation was, in fact, a method by which the corporation might transfer to its shareholders' pockets higher earnings than the 10 per cent permitted by the charter.

II

The Boston and Albany, thus brought into being, was the wealthiest corporation in Massachusetts. Although its stock was for

[20] *Acts and Resolves Passed by the General Court of Massachusetts in the Year 1867*, pp. 667–672.

[21] *Thirty-third Annual Report of the Directors of the Western Railroad Corporation, to the Stockholders. January, 1868* (Springfield: Samuel Bowles & Company, 1868), pp. 6–7; *Third Annual Report of the Directors of the Boston and Albany Railroad Co. to the Stockholders. January, 1871* (Springfield: Samuel Bowles & Company, 1871), p. 7.

Chester W. Chapin
President

Hudson River Bridge at Albany (1866), Howe Truss

FEATURES OF THE BOSTON AND ALBANY

Herman Haupt   Alvah Crocker

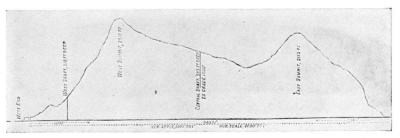

Profile of Hoosac Mountain

Drilling Machine at Work

TUNNELERS AND TUNNELING

the day widely distributed, management remained the prerogative of a small traditional group. Directors held office for decades; often death alone, accompanied with dignified black-bordered resolutions in annual reports, pried them loose. Without exaggeration the road could be called a family corporation. Its first president, Chester W. Chapin of Springfield, served for twelve years; then, after an interlude of two years, his son-in-law, Major William Bliss, gained that office and held it until the end of the century. A second son-in-law, James A. Rumrill, was vice-president and director. Chapin, the founder of this dynasty, was one of the great railroad capitalists of New England, indeed of the nation. A former stage driver and steamboat man, he was called by Addison Gilmore into the Western. He became a large investor in the New York, New Haven and Hartford, the Connecticut River Road, and the New York Central, as well as the Boston and Albany. Characterized by one of his associates as "one of the hardest men I ever knew," he exemplified the policy of presidential management, if not dictation. He determined the composition of the board of directors, assembled it at his pleasure "when anything happened," and secured the succession to the throne.[22]

Thus captained, the road took its place as the most progressive technically in Massachusetts; in New England its only rival was the New York, New Haven and Hartford. The specifications for advance had been stated in the long discussion over consolidation and, though the Boston and Worcester and Western had begun their modernization before 1867, the program was now pushed forward with new resolution and imagination. Within two years double tracking, often postponed during the Civil War, was completed between Boston and Albany. Then the replacement of iron rails with steel went with such speed that a decade later the change had been made for the entire length of the main line. In the 1890's these seventy-five pound rails were superseded by ones of ninety-five. A year before consolidation, a long wooden

---

[22] Report of the Committee on Railroads on Matters Relating to the Boston & Albany Railroad, Massachusetts *House Documents*, 1876, no. 355, appendix, pp. 23–24, 65–68, 206–208; Hartford *Courant*, January 24, April 21, 1876.

bridge, financed in part by the Western, took the place of the ferries across the Hudson River. Although a toll, authorized by the state legislature, did not repay the capital investment, a parallel bridge was almost immediately constructed and the wooden superstructure of the first one replaced by one of iron. Along the whole route wooden bridges came down; structures of iron and stone took their place. In the adoption of safety devices, such as the air brake, the block system, and the steam heating of passenger cars, the Boston and Albany was always at the front.[23]

At Boston, meanwhile, the road provided modern facilities, the lack of which, merchants and shippers had long complained, choked and constricted the through business from the West. In the city it enlarged its freight houses and built a grain elevator for 500,000 bushels. The properties which the Boston and Worcester had acquired on the East Boston waterfront and connected with their line by the Grand Junction Railroad, were greatly improved by new storage houses, by dredging, and by the erection of an elevator with a capacity of 1,000,000 bushels.[24] An organized effort by the Boston and Albany and others induced the Cunard line to resume the sailings to Liverpool abandoned a few years earlier. The railroad guaranteed Cunard weekly cargoes and, with the assistance of the New York Central, devised eastbound rates on grain and flour for export which made this guarantee feasible.[25] These arrangements, as Boston's foreign commerce

---

[23] *Thirty-second Annual Report of the Directors of the Western Rail Road Corporation, to the Stockholders. January, 1867* (Springfield: Samuel Bowles & Company, 1867), p. 6; *Sixth Annual Report of the Directors of the Boston and Albany Railroad Co. to the Stockholders. January, 1874* (Springfield: Clark W. Bryan, 1874), p. 7; *Twelfth Annual Report of the Directors of the Boston and Albany Railroad Co. to the Stockholders. January, 1880* (Springfield: Powers Paper Company, 1880), p. 7; *Twenty-first Annual Report of the Directors of the Boston and Albany Railroad Company to the Stockholders* (Boston: Rand, Avery Supply Company, 1888), pp. 7-8; *Twenty-fourth Annual Report of the Directors of the Boston & Albany Railroad Company to the Stockholders* (Boston: Rand, Avery Supply Company, 1891), p. 7.

[24] *First Annual Report of the Directors of the Boston & Albany Railroad Co., to the Stockholders. January, 1869* (Springfield: Samuel Bowles & Company, 1869), p. 6; *Fifth Annual Report of the Directors of the Boston and Albany Railroad Co. to the Stockholders. January, 1873* (Springfield: Clark W. Bryan and Company, 1873), pp. 8-9.

[25] *Fourth Annual Report of the Directors of the Boston and Albany Railroad*

revived, were extended to other steamship lines. In return for its progressiveness, the Boston and Albany enjoyed until the mid-seventies a preferred or monopolistic position in shipping products eastward for export and carrying back products imported from abroad and consigned to interior destinations.[26]

While such achievements were gratifying, Ginery Twichell, once president of the Boston and Worcester and now a director of the Boston and Albany, summoned his stagecoach experience to provide a commonsense parable. He recalled a fellow stage driver once saying "something that impressed itself on me very strongly, while he was running a very fine stage, with six beautiful white horses, and his opponent running very poor horses. He said one day: there, sir, I will take my coach, and run it with my team straight from here to heaven, and he will run his straight to hell; and I will run empty and he will run full; and all at half price. It is the price in the end that governs." More fundamental than technical progress was the level of rates. On the through business with the West which the Boston and Albany had been consolidated to develop and expand, Boston soon learned that she need not worry about absolute rate levels. Thus in the mid-fifties, according to the recollections of Ginery Twichell, the tariff to Chicago from Boston was $2.15 a hundred pounds and every one was satisfied; in 1876 the rate had lost the two dollars, and was only fifteen cents.[27] As for rates from the West, the Massachusetts Railroad Commission announced in 1871 that they were "very low," an assertion reiterated throughout the decade.[28] Cheaper rates were of little advantage if other ports were also benefiting by their reduction. Boston was, therefore, more interested in comparative rate structures; her demand was not neces-

---

Co. to the Stockholders. January, 1872 (Springfield: Samuel Bowles & Company, 1872), p. 9.

[26] Joseph Nimmo, First Annual Report on the Internal Commerce of the United States . . . Being Part Second of the Annual Report of the . . . Bureau of Statistics on the Commerce and Navigation of the United States . . . 1876, appendix, p. 100; Massachusetts Tenth Annual Report of the Board of Railroad Commissioners. January, 1879, p. 411.

[27] Massachusetts House Documents, 1876, no. 355, pp. 202, 203.

[28] Massachusetts Second Annual Report of the Board of Railroad Commissioners. January, 1871, pp. xxxvi.

sarily for lower rates but for equal ones. She bitterly resented the fact that New York, her closest and traditional rival, succeeded in securing generally lower rates, a variety of differentials.

No New England road possessed the power to determine independently through rates with the West, for none had touched or traversed that section; all relied upon connections — built, financed, and controlled by others. Thus the Boston and Worcester and the Western had been thrown across Massachusetts to reach the Hudson and the Erie Canal, dug by the enterprise of New York State. The Boston and Albany still tapped the latter but, as railroad transportation conquered waterways, it relied increasingly upon the New York Central, a consolidation in 1853 of the small roads crossing New York. In the next decade, Vanderbilt, once a steamboat king, turned to the new world of the railroads. By 1869 he merged the Central and the Hudson River Railroad, both roads which he controlled, into the New York Central and Hudson River Railroad and secured extensions to Chicago over the Lake Shore and Michigan Southern. Wherever located, these were obviously New York enterprises, forged by an outstanding capitalist of Wall Street and running in an unbroken line from the mouth of the Hudson to the foot of Lake Michigan. At Albany this giant became the western connection of New England's first transectional railroad.

An alliance between the two was inescapable. Interlocking stockownership and directorates were one tie. Chapin, who at one time owned at least 3,400 shares in the Central, sat on its board after 1867. An intimate of Vanderbilt, New Yorkers often suspected him of exerting over the Commodore a sinister influence in favor of New England.[29] In the eighties William Bliss held the Chapin chair on the Central's direction and Chauncey M. Depew, president of the Central, was elected to the board of the Boston and Albany.[30] These exchanges of personnel were but evidence of agreements that had existed from the late sixties. In

[29] Massachusetts *House Documents*, 1876, no. 355, p. 24; Henry V. Poor, *Manual of the Railroads of the United States for 1868-1869*, p. 35; Springfield *Daily Republican*, September 20, 1899.

[30] Henry V. Poor, *Manual of the Railroads of the United States for 1885*, p. 158; Henry V. Poor, *Manual of the Railroads of the United States for 1889*, p. 7.

1880, at a time when most railroads preferred to keep their arrangements covert, the Boston and Albany and the Central announced publicly that they were a joint line from New England to the West. They were to operate as if they were consolidated except that the property and earnings of each company should be kept distinct.[31] It has been ordinarily assumed that in this partnership the Boston and Albany occupied a suppliant's position; that the interests of New England's transectional line were sacrificed to the great Vanderbilt monopoly, whose primary interest was New York City. Undoubtedly when freights were divided on a pro-rata basis, the New York Central gained by ignoring its New England ally. Since the distance from Chicago to New York was 981 miles by the Lake Shore route and that to Boston was 1,038, and the length of the New York Central's carriage was in both instances 298 miles, the Central would have 298/981 of the rate between Chicago and New York. Nor did those calculations take into account the further gain made by the Central on the carriage between Albany and New York City. When these considerations were applied to a ten-ton car of wheat, at a rate of 45 cents a hundred, the Central would earn $40.00 if the car went to New York and only $25.83 if transferred to the Boston and Albany at Albany.[32]

On the other hand, the Boston and Albany had at its disposal an immense tonnage originating in New England. The westbound totals over the road mounted from 480,688 tons in 1868 to 852,-867 in 1880, although it is impossible to disentangle the proportion carried to Albany.[33] The products it shipped in that direction were boots, shoes, cottons, woolens, hardware, and tools—all in the first or second freight classifications paying the higher rates. The Central hardly cared to contemplate the diversion of this

[31] Edward Hungerford, *Men and Iron. The History of New York Central* (New York: Thomas Y. Crowell, 1938), p. 391.

[32] [Daniel W. Lincoln] *Reply to the Complaints Urged Before the Legislative Committee on Railroads, in Relation to the Management of the Boston & Albany Railroad. By the Vice-President of the Company. February 25, 1875* (Boston: Wright & Potter, 1875), pp. 20-21.

[33] *Thirteenth Annual Report of the Directors of the Boston and Albany Railroad Co. to the Stockholders, January, 1881* (Springfield: Powers Paper Company, 1881), p. 12.

traffic to other routes, for after all the Boston and Albany was not the only exit from New England. On eastbound goods, while the Central might prefer to ship to New York the portion destined for export, it had to deliver to the Boston and Albany the raw materials and the food distributed along the latter's main line or routed to other New England markets and producers. Rough and ready calculations showed that in the seventies 60 to 70 per cent of the Central's through business crossed into New England; the proportion reaching Boston as compared to New York was estimated as 30 to 103.[34] Two decades later, in 1898-1899, 53 per cent of the tonnage brought east from western termini by the New York Central was delivered to the Boston and Albany.[35]

Those who believed the New York Central was indifferent or hostile to Boston's interests should have stopped harkening to their own subjective promptings and listened to the criticism heaped by New Yorkers upon the Central. They would have been startled to discover that in New York City the Central was frequently regarded as in the Boston interest. The remark of the general agent of the Cheap Transportation Association of New York in 1876 was typical: "The interest of the New York Central Road in New England business induces a policy which heretofore has operated against the commercial interests of New York."[36] Commodore Vanderbilt and his son, successive overlords of the Central's empire, occupied a delicate position. They could not neglect the demands of New York City, for it did a much greater east- and west-bound business than Boston; and at New York the Erie Railroad and the Pennsylvania were only too glad to

[34] Nimmo, *First Annual Report on the Internal Commerce of the United States . . . 1876*, p. 75, appendix, pp. 71, 76; *Resolves of the Town of Weymouth, in Favor of the Purchase of the Boston & Albany Railroad by the State of Massachusetts and the Address of Nath'l Blanchard, Chairman of the Town Committee, before the Railroad Committee of the Legislature, Feb. 5, 1874, in Favor of a Public Road from Boston to Albany* (Weymouth: Weekly Gazette Press, 1874), p. 6.

[35] *Lease of the Boston & Albany R. R. to the New York Central R. R. Hearing by the Committee on Railroads* (n. p., n. d.), p. 107.

[36] New York *Proceedings of the Special Committee on Railroads, Appointed under a Resolution of the Assembly to Investigate Alleged Abuses in the Management of Railroads Chartered by the State of New York* [Hepburn Committee], I, 454-456, II, 1249-1251; Nimmo, *First Annual Report on the Internal Commerce of the United States . . . 1876*, appendix, pp. 70-71.

serve merchants and shippers who thought the Central false to their prosperity. Nor could the Vanderbilts antagonize Boston too flagrantly. As already suggested, the Boston and Albany and the Central were not New England's only avenue to the West.

In spite of its achievements, the Boston and Albany saw no rest. The general anti-railroad ferment of the seventies and the continuous demand that New England's first transectional accomplish the impossible furnished the background. As differentials persisted, as officials admitted they could not overawe Vanderbilt, as the Boston and Albany apparently made its peace with the competitive tunnel route, welcoming from this once dreaded competitor "a reasonable conservatism" rather than a "profitless competition," the demand grew for a more exacting state policy toward the Boston and Albany. Once again the agitators—scamps and idealists—vexed the management with proposals for state acquisition and operation. Edward Crane, a dubious promoter, and the Bay State Transportation League sketched the attractive lineaments of the Boston and Albany Railway Trust Company, in which a group of incorporators were to select a board of directors who in turn would arrange for the eventual ownership by the state of all securities in the line; Wendell Phillips, who roved oratorically among the reform movements of the day, declared that the state ought to take the roads at a price of $16,000,000; and in 1871 a measure for state assumption actually passed one branch of the legislature.[37] More prosaic folk sought merely the remedy of grievances—"Boston on perfect equality with New York, in every respect so far as freight is concerned," and local rates pro-rated "with the through freight, allowing of course, a fair price extra, for the loading and unloading of such freight."[38] In 1875 the uproar forced a legislative investigation "to inquire . . . whether the Boston & Albany is furnishing proper facilities

---

[37] Report of the Committee on the Hoosac Tunnel and Troy & Greenfield Railway, Massachusetts *Senate Documents,* 1877, no. 170, p. 26; *Report of the State Commission on Cheap Railway Transportation between Boston and Lake Ontario, to the Legislature of Massachusetts. 1870* (Boston: Wright & Potter, 1870), pp. 5–15, 37–54; Hartford *Courant,* May 20, 1871.

[38] Report of the Committee on Railroads on the Boston and Albany Railroad, Massachusetts *House Documents,* 1875, no. 338, p. 51.

for the transportation of merchandise and for the promotion of
the trade and commerce of the Commonwealth, and particularly
whether its rates of freight and other arrangements are properly
adjusted so as to encourage the shipping of freight to and from
the port of Boston." To these interrogations the Railroad Committee of the General Court gave a generally affirmative reply.[39]

III

Calm might have settled over the scene if a state director on the
road had not seen fit in an annual report of 1876 to disclose the
procedures by which the Boston and Albany leased the Ware
River Railroad.[40] This short line running northward from the
Boston and Albany's main line at Palmer and connecting with
the decrepit Massachusetts Central, a cross-state enterprise from
Boston which paralleled the Boston and Albany on the north,
apparently threatened the domain of President Chapin's road.
He bestirred himself. He bought a majority control of the Ware
River Railroad, sold the road at auction, bought it in, and completed the construction to the northern line of the state. This
maneuver was a family affair. The president of the Ware River
Railroad was J. A. Rumrill, a son-in-law, and the money for the
performance was provided by the Chapin Banking and Trust
Company, whose stockholders were Chapins of all varieties and
the two sons-in-law, William Bliss and J. A. Rumrill. Finally in
1873 the Boston and Albany Railroad leased the Ware River
Railroad with an eventual guarantee of 7 per cent upon an agreed
valuation of $750,000. The transaction placed the forceful
Chapin in an unfavorable light. Although the lease was a wise
protective measure for the Boston and Albany and although
Chapin apparently informed some of his associates on the railroad as to what he was doing and observed certain other proprieties, he placed himself in the vulnerable position of acting as
principal for two concerns whose interests as buyer and seller
were hardly identical and of being a stockholder in the Ware

---

[39] *Ibid.*, pp. 1-2.
[40] Massachusetts *House Documents*, 1876, no. 355, pp. i-xiv.

whose securities, purchased at an average of 70 cents on the dollar, rose happily after the lease.[41]

Compared to the contemporaneous plunder raids on other railroads, Chapin's activities hardly constituted a great sin. The real sensation of the episode and of the subsequent investigation was the revelation of the rôle played by the state directors in the management of the Boston and Albany. These appointments had customarily gone to businessmen who had often served in the legislature.[42] Incidental to the consolidation, the General Court had sought to improve the character of its appointees and to use them as instruments for imposing a public policy upon this private enterprise. State directors must submit annual reports; no employee or shareholder of the Boston and Albany or legislator during his term of office could serve as a state director.[43] In 1876 the state was abruptly informed that none of these objectives had been realized—quite the contrary. The informer was a state director, F. B. Hayes. A one-time member of the legislature and a railroad lawyer, he had been, in the eyes of his critics, connected with railroad enterprises of "questionable character" and he was tainted with "Butlerism," a word loosely used by conservatives to ascribe self-seeking or dishonesty to the liberal movements of the era. As a state director he certainly departed from the rôle traditionally played by the state directors of the Boston and Albany.[44] His charges against his colleagues compelled legislative investigation.

As the testimony accumulated, the committee on railroads learned that, in spite of prohibitions, state directors were, in instances, still stockholders. Furthermore, as state directors they never held meetings, they neglected to make the required annual reports, they did not vote the state stock at annual meetings, they took little responsibility. Unwittingly a counsel wrote a fit

[41] *Ibid.*, pp. 7–18, appendix, pp. 17–40, 54–58, 63–76, 373–381, 471–488; Springfield *Daily Republican*, February 11, 12, March 2, April 25, 1876; Hartford *Courant*, February 10, March 29, 1876.

[42] Hartford *Courant*, April 22, 1876.

[43] *Acts and Resolves Passed by the General Court of Massachusetts, in the Year 1873*, p. 632.

[44] Hartford *Courant*, January 24, 29, 1876; Massachusetts *House Documents*, 1876, no. 355, pp. ix-x, xii.

epitaph for the whole experiment with state representation when he characterized the position of one state director relative to the Ware River Railroad lease, "Feeling it was not right, doubting whether it was honest, . . . your share was silence." [45] The most flagrant dereliction of proprieties was exhibited by Moses Kimball, Boston businessman, donor to the city of a statue of Abraham Lincoln freeing the slaves, and, more to the purpose in hand, one-time state director in the Troy and Greenfield Railroad and long-time state director in the Western and then its successor, the Boston and Albany. The dean of state directors and their real policy maker, he owned, directly or indirectly, stock in the Boston and Albany; he was a member of the finance committee prominent in the negotiation of the lease of the Ware River Railroad; he advanced money to Chapin for its purchase and secured in return Ware River Railroad securities; and he was financially interested in the Chapin bank. Taxed for serving as both buyer and seller, Kimball replied, "I don't think it is a parallel case. I own Ware River stock, and the Boston & Albany lease the road. I am not the Boston & Albany road." [46] Members of the investigating committee submitted three separate reports. They differed only in the degree of opprobrium which they saw fit to distribute. The majority, the most lenient, declared Kimball's actions "indefensible."[47]

Although the Commonwealth, on advice of learned counsel, instituted no suit against the officials of the road, the latter were frightened. Kimball, casting aside his rôle as state director, became a director in his own right. Chapin, an old man, resigned the presidency in 1878 and D. W. Lincoln, popular in Boston and dissociated from the inner circle which ran and was to run the road, took his place.[48] Finally the episode spurred the railroad to extinguish the state's right to interfere in its management. Though measures against the general power to regulate were, of course, impossible, the specific basis for a shared control, the state's financial stake in the corporation, was more vulnerable.

[45] Massachusetts *House Documents*, 1876, no. 355, pp. 242-260, 296-301, 385-387.
[46] *Ibid.*, appendix, pp. 105-130.
[47] *Ibid.*, pp. 1-36.
[48] Boston *Journal*, April 18, 1878, July 8, 1879.

Legislation of the thirties and forties had forged the tie. Perhaps its severance now was possible. Such a solution would have the further advantage of disposing in some fashion of a "surplus" and an "improvement fund," the amounts of which were increasing at an embarrassing rate. In 1882 the total of these two accounts was $3,385,393.[49] The crux of the situation was, of course, the state's investment in the Boston and Albany. In the late sixties and seventies, the sinking funds of the Western and payments by the road canceled the indebtedness of the road to the state, an indebtedness "which dates from the building of the road: an indebtedness rendered necessary in the beginning by the magnitude of the enterprise, and by a want of confidence at that time felt in the value of the stock."[50] Stockholding by the state remained. The original investment of 10,000 shares had grown by gradual accretions and by the stock dividend of 1866 to 24,115.[51]

In 1882 the inaugural address of Governor John D. Long described the true doctrine for the relations between state and railroad. After some specific illustrations, he indulged in a generalization: the state should be separated "from all railroad partnerships. Such alliances always are, or are liable to be, entangling, embarrassing to legislation and the public finances, and satisfactory to neither party. Unless Government is to assume the business of railroading, it is better to leave it altogether to private enterprise."[52] Forthwith a bill was introduced and passed permitting the Boston and Albany to issue 5 per cent bonds and exchange these bonds for stock held by the Commonwealth in the railroad. Since the state was to receive $160 in 5 per cent bonds for each share, it actually secured a guaranteed income of 8 per cent. With the conclusion of the transaction, "the

---

[49] *Fifteenth Annual Report of the Directors of the Boston and Albany Railroad Company to the Stockholders* (Boston: Franklin Press, 1882), pp. 5, 16.

[50] *Fourth Annual Report . . . of the Boston and Albany . . . 1872*, p. 7.

[51] Report of the Joint Special Committee on the Sale of State Stock in the Western, Massachusetts *Senate Documents*, 1863, no. 199, pp. 5-6; Boston *Journal*, January 18, 1882.

[52] *Acts and Resolves Passed by the General Court of Massachusetts in the Year 1882*, p. 263; Report of Committee on Expenditures on the Sale of the Commonwealth's Stock, Massachusetts *House Documents*, 1882, no. 122.

Commonwealth shall not be represented in the board of directors." [53] Stockholders were hardly unanimous in favor of this
arrangement. A powerful minority protested the price was too
high and argued with unconscious irony that it was not necessary
at such cost to eliminate the state directors when they were in a
minority and had never caused any trouble. But the majority
ratified the arrangement.[54] Soon after, the state received $3,858,-
000 in bonds and $400 in cash and the road reacquired 24,115
shares of stock.[55]

For a decent interval the Boston and Albany permitted the
stock to repose in its treasury; then the road began to distribute
it, as a gratuity, among the stockholders on a basis of one share
for ten, and to reduce the surplus by an equal amount.[56] A cry of
rage rose through the state. The bonded indebtedness of the railroad upon which it had to earn interest had been increased by
$3,858,000, the only basis for these bonds was the surrendered
stock, this stock was given to shareholders for nothing. Although
the surplus was proportionately reduced, that surplus had been
built not from contributions of stockholders but from payments
by shippers. At one stroke the railroad had increased the amount
of its annual payments and obliterated a surplus. Whatever the
subterfuge, this distribution was a stock dividend or a stock
watering, a procedure which the legislature, acutely aware of the
problem, had long ago specifically forbidden. The legislators at
once empowered the attorney general to proceed against the
Boston and Albany Railroad.[57] He filed two suits, one to render
void the distribution already effected, another to prevent a further
division of the shares. In 1886 the Supreme Judicial Court rendered its decision. Though "literally" the distribution was a stock

---

[53] *Acts and Resolves . . . of Massachusetts . . . 1882*, pp. 90-91.

[54] Boston *Journal*, April 7, 13, 27, 1882.

[55] *Sixteenth Annual Report of the Directors of the Boston & Albany Railroad Company to the Stockholders* (Boston: Rand Avery Supply Company, 1883), p. 8; *Seventeenth Annual Report of the Directors of the Boston & Albany Railroad Company to the Stockholders* (Boston: Rand Avery Supply Company, 1884), pp. 6-7.

[56] *Seventeenth Annual Report . . . of the Boston & Albany*, p. 8.

[57] Springfield *Daily Republican*, September 29, 1883; Boston *Journal*, April 23, 1884; *Acts and Resolves Passed by the General Court of Massachusetts, in the Year 1884*, p. 387.

dividend, actually the stock had been twice paid for, once by the state, again by the railroad. Furthermore the law of 1882 had made the state stock, once transferred, the "absolute property" of the corporation. Its action, therefore, had been perfectly legal.[58] The directors at once proceeded to distribute most of the remaining shares at a ratio of one for thirty.[59] Thus an adroit *coup d'état* was both consecrated and achieved.

IV

Until the end of the nineties no other untoward incident disturbed the serene prosperity so characteristic of the Boston and Albany. Then, in 1900, for all practical purposes New England's first and greatest transectional railroad ceased to have a history of its own: the New York Central leased it for ninety-nine years. A railroad era, built upon commercial rivalry with New York City, thus came to an end. Not the states nor the cities involved accomplished this result, but the railroads—and for perfectly comprehensible reasons. For Vanderbilt's Central, the Boston and Albany was a prize in its own right. With a record of 8 per cent dividends uninterrupted by the panic or prosperity of the eighties and nineties, with stock quoted on the market at 260, and with an improvement fund of $3,465,084 and a surplus of $331,072, the road was a valuable property.[60] The Central wished to bind its ally tighter to meet threatened renewals of trunk-line competition. As the Supreme Court in the late nineties was breaking down by a vigorous application of the Sherman Anti-Trust Act the partial harmony among competitors achieved by the trunk-line association, the trunk lines individually responded by

[58] Commonwealth *v.* Boston and Albany Railroad Company, 142 *Massachusetts*, 146.

[59] *Nineteenth Annual Report of the Directors of the Boston and Albany Railroad Company to the Stockholders* (Boston: Rand Avery Supply Company, 1886), pp. 8-9.

[60] *Thirty-third Annual Report of the Directors of the Boston & Albany Railroad Company to the Stockholders* (Boston: Rand Avery Supply Company, 1900), pp. 5, 26; Joseph G. Martin, *A Century of Finance. Martin's History of the Boston Stock and Money Markets. One Hundred Years. From January, 1798, to January, 1898* (Boston: J. G. Martin, 1898), pp. 152-153, 156-157; *Statement of the Directors. To the Stockholders of the Boston and Albany Railroad Company* (n. p., n. d.).

acquiring new lines and linking allies by closer and stronger ties. In 1898, for instance, the Central purchased the capital stock of both the Lake Shore and Michigan Southern and the Michigan Central, lines already leased, to establish "on a permanent basis, the unity of interests of the three companies." [61] The lease of its traditional New England outlet was a logical step in the same policy.

For the Boston and Albany the lease meant security. It would put an end to the occasional dalliance between the New York Central and the Fitchburg. It would provide a fixed income in a future already shadowed by the competition of electric railways. It would afford fiduciary stockholders, who held between a third and a fourth of the common stock, a gratifiably certain income.[62] It would terminate vexations: "They can sit down under the fig tree and have nothing to worry them. If two or three more populists come up here it will not worry them then: they have got the lease. That is just where the whole thing is. They don't want the trouble. They are too conservative." [63] It was an old charge. Old, too, were the intimate commercial relationships with the New York Central. Figures for an earlier period have been given; in 1899 the Central still provided 62 per cent of the revenue and 60 per cent of the tonnage of the Boston and Albany's freight business. "It is to that system that this Company naturally belongs," wrote the directors of the Massachusetts road.[64]

Twenty years earlier the railroad commissioners of the state, that is to say Charles Francis Adams, advocating the advantages of such a consolidation, observed: "The mere suggestion of it will be looked upon as visionary, if not denounced as in some

[61] *Twenty-ninth Annual Report of the Board of Directors of the New York Central and Hudson River Railroad Company and Its Leased Lines to the Stockholders for the Year Ended June 30, 1898* (n. p., 1898), pp. 5-6.

[62] Report of the Railroad Commissioners in Response to an Order of the House of Representatives, Massachusetts *House Documents*, 1900, no. 1090, p. 9; *Statement . . . To the Stockholders of the Boston and Albany*.

[63] *Hearings in Opposition to the Approval of the Lease of the Boston & Albany Railroad to the New York Central & Hudson River Railroad Company before the Joint Standing Committee on Railroads. 1900* (n. p., n. d), p. 300.

[64] *Statement . . . To the Stockholders of the Boston and Albany*.

way unpatriotic." [65] In 1900 Massachusetts did the incredible; she made visions come true. The opposition of other railroads to such an alliance subsided. Since at the very moment the Fitchburg and the Boston and Maine were seeking consolidation, they would hardly provide arguments and passion that could be directed with deadly effect upon their own petition. Nor did massed merchants descend upon the legislature with demands that the General Court repel the "Vanderbilt monopoly" at the state line. Instead, the Boston Chamber of Commerce and other like organizations marched up capitol hill to give their testimony on behalf of the lease.[66] But mercantile opinion has often been manufactured. In the past railroads had bought it by rebates, by "protection" as it was called, or intimidated it by threatening reprisals. In this instance the Central offered the efficiencies of a consolidated line, promised to improve terminal facilities, and announced that it was reaching toward Boston because its New York outlet was inadequate and more expensive.[67] Although there was a specious air about many of these statements, it was true that the Central could not in any case divert from the road traffic destined for New England and that, as Adams pointed out in 1879, it would derive from the export trade a greater return on a pro-rata basis from goods carried to Boston rather than New York if its line were lengthened to the former city.[68] Thus fears were soothed. The railroad schemers of the thirties and the apostles of consolidation in the sixties would not, however, have been thus easily satisfied. In truth the ardent temper of those earlier days had wilted. Nathan Hale and Josiah Quincy, Jr., would have shuddered to hear a Boston merchant announce, "I do not think Boston is superior. I think Boston is much smaller

[65] Massachusetts *Tenth Annual Report of the Board of Railroad Commissioners. January, 1879*, p. 67.

[66] *Lease of the Boston & Albany R. R. to the New York Central R. R. Closing Argument of Samuel Hoar, a Director of the Boston & Albany Railroad Company, before the Committee on Railroads of the Legislature of Massachusetts* (n. p., n. d), pp. 11-12, 33-55.

[67] *Argument of Samuel Hoar, Esq. before the Committee on Railroads on the Several Propositions of State Purchase of the Boston & Albany Railroad Company, March 21, 1900* (n. p., n. d), pp. 5-6, 8.

[68] Massachusetts *Tenth Annual Report of the Board of Railroad Commissioners. January, 1879*, p. 66.

than the port of New York, and always will be; but we can approximate to the size of New York." [69]

Still there was opposition. A powerful minority of stockholders in the Boston and Albany, although willing to lease on principle, thought the offered payments too niggardly.[70] The Boston city government demanded that the lease should be made only on terms that guaranteed the expenditure of funds for harbor improvement and an equality of rates between New York and Boston.[71] The Democrats made an ambiguous opposition a party program. For them F. J. Stimson, who managed to combine his strange political faith with a good family background and a Harvard degree, sounded the authentic tocsin. The New York Central could pay the rental from the Boston and Albany's local traffic and divert the through business to New York City; the papers of that metropolis were hailing the lease as a means of regaining lost ground. "I feel that the tendency towards having all New England corporations, and especially our railroads which are absolutely the nerves of the country, controlled in New York, will end in making New England merely a rich and prosperous province to support New York City." [72] Such opponents, however, had no common program. Some merely wished the preservation of the status quo; others were willing to countenance the lease on terms. Some argued that the question should be submitted to a popular referendum; others revived for the last time the project of state acquisition. The attorney-general informed the last group that, while the right to acquire had been carefully safeguarded throughout the involved history of previous legislation, the act of consolidation in 1867 had raised the annual net profit assured the stockholders from 7 to 10 per cent.[73] Counsel for the Boston and Albany handled opposition less genteelly. Stimson was dismissed as a "lawyer and poet of Dedham and New York," and advocates

[69] *Lease of the Boston & Albany R. R. to the New York Central R. R. Hearing by the Committee on Railroads*, p. 63.

[70] Springfield *Daily Republican*, August 17, 29, 30, 1899.

[71] *Hearings in Opposition to the . . . Lease of the Boston & Albany Railroad . . . 1900*, pp. 248, 281.

[72] *Ibid.*, pp. 235-241.

[73] Opinion of the Attorney-General, Hosea M. Knowlton, Massachusetts *House Documents*, 1900, no. 1107, pp. 11-19.

of state purchase were "men of socialistic tendencies," "doctrinaires or experimenters in public policies." [74]

Though the legislature beat down all proposals for drastic amendments, pressures brought about considerable modification of the original agreement. Stockholder opposition accounted for some of them. As a result the final lease guaranteed a return of 8 per cent upon the common stock of the Boston and Albany and the Central purchased certain property of the Boston and Albany for five and a half million dollars rather than four.[75] Opposition outside the company accounted for other changes. Though many were willing to rely upon the "honor" of the Central to make improvements, and to follow the policies which its representatives had outlined, the legislature took a somewhat more hard-headed view. The Boston and Albany was to remain subject to Massachusetts law and the New York Central was to make to the state the complete annual reports required hitherto. Over a period of years the latter railroad was to spend $2,500,000, derived either from earnings or from the sale of Boston and Albany bonds, on the improvement of the Grand Junction Railroad and the East Boston terminals and waterfront. Finally "the New York Central and Hudson River Railroad shall not . . . charge . . . a greater sum for transportation by it of freight from any point of origin, to the port of Boston for export to foreign countries, than is at the time received by it for transportation of the like class and quantity of freight from the same point to the port of New York for export to foreign countries; or charge . . . a greater sum for transportation from the port of Boston of freight from foreign countries through said port to any point, than is at the time received by it for transportation of the like class and quantity of freight through the port of New York to the same point: *provided, however,* that if the aforesaid provisions of this section shall conflict with any regulations made by act of congress this section shall be null and void." [76] Certainly the protection given

[74] *Closing Argument of Samuel Hoar,* p. 28; *Argument of Samuel Hoar,* . . . *on the . . . State Purchase,* pp. 2, 4.

[75] *Thirty-third Annual Report . . . of the Boston & Albany,* pp. 9–15; Springfield *Daily Republican,* November 15, 1899, July 12, 1900.

[76] *Acts and Resolves Passed by the General Court of Massachusetts, in the Year 1900,* pp. 464–467.

Boston was explicit enough. As far as rates were concerned, however, it simply froze a situation that had existed for thirty years.

In 1867 when the Boston and Worcester disappeared into the greater corporate sea of the Boston and Albany, the directors of the former bade a nostalgic farewell to their own enterprise. Their saddened delight in its past achievements was understandable.[77] The report of the directors of the Boston and Albany in 1900, however, contained no comparable ritual. Perhaps loyalty and affection for a corporation had gone out of existence. Certainly the Boston and Albany had results to celebrate. As Boston's through route to the West, it had served the metropolis well. In a little over thirty years, the tonnage of goods carried westward from Boston to Albany multiplied twice; the tonnage in the opposite direction between the same termini nearly seven times.[78] Furthermore the consolidated road continued the earlier tendency of its two components: it was a road with an immense local traffic.[79] Its financial success had been exceptional. Still the route to the Hudson had not accomplished what Hale, Quincy, De Grand, and Derby had hoped from it. It had not made Boston the equal or superior of New York. For this failure enthusiasts and sectional zealots blamed the road severely. When its performance was placed in the larger setting of urban rivalries, trunk-line competition, and geographical factors, the expectations of the railroad schemers of Massachusetts were clearly impossible of fulfillment. That these national considerations were overwhelming, the act which permitted the lease of the New York Central at last recognized. The proviso on rates admitted that competition between New York and Boston was no longer merely the concern of either of these cities or of the states in which they were located. It was a matter of national moment, policy, and decision.

[77] *Thirty-eighth Annual Report of the Directors of the Boston & Worcester Railroad Corporation. For the Year Ending November 30, 1867* (Boston: David Clapp & Son, 1868), pp. 10-13.

[78] *Thirty-third Annual Report . . . of the Boston & Albany*, p. 22.

[79] Springfield *Daily Republican*, October 16, 1895.

XII

"THE GREAT BORE"

"When publishers no longer steal,
And pay for what they stole before,
When the first locomotive's wheel,
Rolls through the Hoosac tunnel's bore;—

Till *then let Cummings blaze away,*
And Miller's saints blow up the globe;
But when you see that blessed day,
Then *order your ascension robe!"*

Oliver W. Holmes, Poems, 1882, p. 168.

I

In 1854 Massachusetts embarked anew upon a policy of financial assistance to railroads by granting a $2,000,000 state loan to the Troy and Greenfield Railroad. This enterprise was the third in a chain of five railroads arching northward from Boston, moving westward through the northern tier of Massachusetts townships, and eventually coming down to the Hudson River at Troy. The Troy and Greenfield was also the critical link in this new transectional railroad, for across its chartered route lay the immense bulk of Hoosac Mountain. Only a tunnel could carry the rails from the Deerfield Valley on the east of this barrier to the Hoosic Valley on the west. The state's largess of 1854 soon proved but a beginning. Step by step Massachusetts was drawn deeper into the business until finally a state constitutional convention, the General Court and its committees, the governor and council, the Board of Railroad Commissioners, and other assorted commissions were giving counsel and formulating policy; some of these agencies were actually engaged in the construction and operation of a railroad. The whole episode had neither precedent nor parallel in all New England.

The Hoosac or "tunnel" route, as it came to be called, followed the historic line which in 1825 Loammi Baldwin had selected as the most fit for the proposed cross-state canal. The failure to construct this waterway and the later location of the railroad to the Hudson along a more southern route left the area between the Lowell-Concord and the Boston and Worcester and Western routes without improved means of transportation. It was a "God-forsaken country." The explanation for this neglect varied. Some ascribed it to accident. Others inferred a tacit conspiracy; the wealth of Lowell on the one hand and the pressure of Worcester and Springfield on the other had secured for themselves a location on the routes to the West in face of the fact that the most suitable was the one chosen by Baldwin's "eye of genius." [1] In any case the result was the creation in northern Massachusetts of a region intensely conscious of its need for railroads and of a grievance at the lack of them. Its spokesmen and politicians formed a bloc which sought to utilize issues, many of them remote from the point at hand, to advance the transportation interests of the region. In a later phrase, "they had tunnel on the brain." Such zealots were not to be placated by the construction of branch lines from the Boston and Worcester, the Western, or the route to the Lakes. Like other places they craved direct access to the capital of Massachusetts and a location upon a through route to some ill-defined West. Besides branches were demeaning.[2] An

[1] *The Argument of E. H. Derby, Esq. in Favor of a State Loan to the Vermont and Massachusetts Railroad Co. before the Joint Committee on Railways and Canals of the Legislature of Massachusetts. March, 1855* (Boston: Dutton and Wentworth, 1855), pp. 4–7; *Brief Statement of Facts Relative to the Proposed Rail-Road from Fitchburg to Brattleborough, under Charters Lately Obtained for the Same in the States of Massachusetts and Vermont* (Boston: Dutton and Wentworth, 1844), p. 3; *Report of a Committee of the Directors of the Fitchburg Rail-Road Company on the Statistics and Prospects of the Proposed Rail-Road* (Boston: Dutton and Wentworth, 1842), pp. 3–4, 6.

[2] *To the Stockholders of the Vermont and Massachusetts Rail-Road* (n.p., n.d.), pp. 3–4.

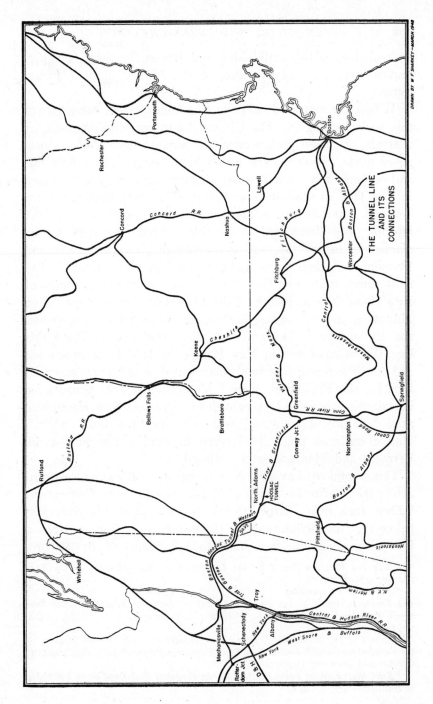

THE TUNNEL LINE
AND ITS
CONNECTIONS

DRAWN BY W. F. SHARKEY — MARCH 1946

[389]

appreciation of this unthinking and fervent localism is a pre-requisite for an understanding of the history of the Hoosac route.

At first the state did only the minimum to meet the wants of this neglected region. The General Court received petitions for charters, discussed perfunctorily the public exigency of the pro-posed roads, and responded with acts of incorporation—only this and nothing more. The first two charters came early in the boom forties. One, in 1842, incorporated the Fitchburg Railroad to run between Charlestown, across the river from Boston, to the interior town designated in its title.[3] From the start it was planned to extend the road into southern New Hampshire and Vermont and then on to Lake Champlain and Canada.[4] The most direct route was that crossing the southwestern corner of New Hampshire to Bellows Falls and continuing over the Green Mountains to Rutland and Burlington. Though the Cheshire and the Rutland and Burlington railroads eventually utilized this line, the railroad war in New Hampshire halted the promotion and construction of new roads between 1840 and 1844, a crucial time for the Fitchburg's plans.[5] Consequently the sponsors for its extension, pausing long enough to stigmatize New Hampshire as a "non-productive state" with a "heavy snowfall" and "an illiberal railroad policy,"[6] secured in 1844 a charter for the Vermont and Massachusetts Railroad.

This second road avoided New Hampshire. It swung westward across the interior highlands of Massachusetts to the Connecticut Valley, then bent sharply to the north, crossed the river just below the Massachusetts-New Hampshire state line, and ran a few miles along the west bank to a terminus at Brattleboro,

[3] *Acts and Resolves Passed by the Legislature of Massachusetts, in the Year 1842*, pp. 535–537.

[4] *Report of a Committee . . . of the Fitchburg Rail-Road . . . on the Statistics and Prospects*, pp. 4–5, 14; *Brief Statement of Facts in Relation to the Pro-posed Rail-Road from Boston to Fitchburg* (Charlestown: Caleb Rand, 1842), pp. 4–21.

[5] *Report of the Stockholders' Committee Appointed at the Annual Meeting of the Vermont and Massachusetts Rail-Road Company, February 14th, 1849* (Boston: Crocker and Brewster, 1850), p. 16.

[6] *Brief Statement of Facts Relative to the Proposed Rail-Road from Fitchburg to Brattleborough*, pp. 4, 8.

Vermont.[7] Still far from Lake Champlain or Canada, the road was confused as to how to reach either for, no matter how fondly such possibilities were cherished, a railroad crossing of the Green Mountains in southern Vermont was a formidable undertaking. As early as the thirties Loammi Baldwin, after a survey of suggested routes, had written a cold report on their possibilities.[8] Now engineers somewhat less careful and less scrupulous examined the ground. Though tunnels were necessary, the rock was happily suited for easy excavation; and, aside from the final ridge of the Green Mountains, singularly direct valleys traversed these wild mountain fastnesses and promised grades of sixty feet to the mile, less than those of the Western.[9] As it turned out, neither the Vermont and Massachusetts nor any other road attempted this pathway across the mountains. For a route to the West the former relied upon other railroads up the Connecticut Valley and upon connections with the Rutland and Burlington and the Vermont Central.

Not only were the Fitchburg and the Vermont and Massachusetts parts of a single conception; they were promoted and built by Alvah Crocker, president of both corporations. Put to work in a paper mill when eight years old, Crocker owned his own plant in Fitchburg by the time he was twenty-five. He went on to become the chief businessman of the town and one of its most active politicians.[10] Voluble with tongue and pen, an incorrigible optimist, a pungent controversialist who neither gave nor asked quarter in his frequent business or political battles, perhaps the single word which best describes him was one which he frequently employed—"electric." In his railroad promotions he soon enlisted as ally the eminent railroad counsel and fellow director, Elias Hasket Derby, who needs no further introduction. Their mating was a most congenial one. The two troubadours at once began

---

[7] *Acts and Resolves Passed by the Legislature of Massachusetts, in the Year, 1844*, pp. 227–231.

[8] Loammi Baldwin to John Holbrook and others, January 9, 1836, Ms., Baldwin Papers, XXXVII, Harvard Business School Library.

[9] *Brief Statement of Facts Relative to the Proposed Rail-Road from Fitchburg to Brattleborough*, pp. 6–8, 17–18.

[10] *Dictionary of American Biography* (New York: Charles Scribner's Sons, 1928–1936), IV, 551.

chanting of the new road as one with low fares and engaged in the carriage of bulky freights.

The granite of Fitchburg, as fine as that of Quincy, was to come by rail down-hill to Boston to construct her warehouses and increase her exports; ship timbers, lumber, and charcoal, already depleted elsewhere, would find there a ready market; a tide of metals and minerals from soapstone to copperas would aid old industries or establish new ones; untamed water powers, as great as those at Lowell, would be harnessed. The tyranny of New York City over the Connecticut Valley and Vermont would be broken.[11] Nor was the poetry of promotion Crocker's only contribution. By sheer energy and will he seemed to lift the railroads over financial and physiographic obstacles. The Fitchburg was completed in 1845 and the Vermont and Massachusetts five years later.[12] Shortly thereafter, as the railroad depression deepened, the hold of Crocker and Derby on the management of the two corporations somewhat weakened. Other talents than theirs were called for by the new times.[13]

The further construction of the New England network had meanwhile undermined the original assumptions upon which the line had been founded. The Fitchburg, as a local road between Boston and Fitchburg, was not seriously affected; if it did not quite become one of the dowager roads like the Boston and Worcester, Boston and Lowell, and Boston and Providence, it so artfully concealed its *arriviste* nature as to be practically indistinguishable from them.[14] As for the Vermont and Massachusetts, the construction of the Cheshire to Bellows Falls and of the Rutland and Burlington to Lake Champlain, and the organiza-

[11] *Report of a Committee . . . of the Fitchburg Rail-Road . . . on the Statistics and Prospects*, pp. 5–10; *Brief Statement of Facts in Relation to the Proposed Rail-Road from Boston to Fitchburg*, pp. 4–21; *Brief Statement of Facts Relative to the Proposed Rail-Road from Fitchburg to Brattleborough*, pp. 13–15.

[12] Henry V. Poor, *History of the Railroads and Canals of the United States of America, Exhibiting their Progress, Cost, Revenues, Expenditures, & Present Condition* (New York: John H. Schultz, 1860), pp. 122, 158.

[13] *Annual Report of the Directors of the Vermont and Massachusetts Railroad to the Stockholders, at Their Meeting, February 13, 1850* (Cambridge: Metcalf and Company, 1850), pp. 5–6, 24; E. B. Grant, *Boston Railways: Their Condition and Prospects* (Boston: Little, Brown, and Company, 1856), p. 40.

[14] Joseph G. Martin, *A Century of Finance. Martin's History of the Boston*

tion of a route to the Lakes through Concord and White River
Junction gave more direct and effective routes to northern Vermont, Canada, and the West. "Since the charter of the Vermont
and Massachusetts was granted, the whole face of things has
changed. . . . Neither Lake Champlain or Canada is now looked
to as a terminus of the road. A better route by which to reach
these places has been discovered." [15] Thus a convention at Greenfield brutally informed the Vermont and Massachusetts. The
remedy was plain. The terminus of the road must be swung to the
south. The branch which the Vermont and Massachusetts
projected to Greenfield must become its main line. That main
line must be extended to Troy.[16] In 1848 the Massachusetts
General Court at the solicitation of Crocker and others chartered
the Troy and Greenfield Railroad to build westward from Greenfield "to some point on the line of the State of New York or of
Vermont, convenient to meet or connect with any railroad that
may be constructed from any point at or near the city of Troy,
on the Hudson River, in the State of New York." [17] At once New
York incorporated the Troy and Boston, a road which ran eastward along the Hoosic River to the Vermont state line, and
Vermont did likewise for the Southern Vermont, an eight-mile
link to connect the Troy and Boston with the Troy and Greenfield
at the Vermont-Massachusetts line. Thus charters sketched the
shape of things to come.[18]

One result of the decision to shift to the Hudson the western
terminus of this half-completed road was to crystallize the
apprehensions of the Western Railroad into a deep-rooted hos-

---

*Stock and Money Markets, One Hundred Years. From January, 1798, to January,
1898* (Boston: Joseph G. Martin, 1898), pp. 146–149; *Annual Report of the Directors of the Fitchburg Railroad, to the Stockholders, at Their Meeting, January
27, 1852* (Charlestown: W. W. Wheildon, 1852), p. 14.

[15] *Address to the Stockholders of the Vermont and Massachusetts Rail Road
Company, Adopted by the Convention Held at Greenfield, Oct. 25, 1845* (Greenfield: Merriam & Mirick, 1845), pp. 4–6.

[16] *Ibid.*, pp. 5, 12, 16.

[17] *The Tunnel Hearing in 1854. A Brief Report of the Evidence of the Petitioners
for a Loan to the Troy and Greenfield Railroad Company of Two Millions, before
a Joint Special Committee of the Legislature of Massachusetts* (Boston: Thurston,
Torry, and Emerson, 1854), p. 5.

[18] Poor, *History of the Railroads and Canals of the United States*, pp. 77, 318.

tility. It had regarded the original proposals of the Fitchburg and the Vermont and Massachusetts with some trepidation. Though the Fitchburg in turn somewhat muted the possibilities of rivalry and was soon on harmonious terms with the Boston and Worcester,[19] the extension of the route to the Connecticut definitely offered the possibility of intercepting higher up that valley the trade which flowed down to Springfield and then followed the Western to Boston. The promoters of the Vermont and Massachusetts had no doubt of their superior advantages. They were explained by a figure of speech quite common in this promotional era: "The good people of Boston have a project of bringing soft water into the city; if you were reduced to the necessity of taking it from the Connecticut river and were desirous of obtaining the largest possible quantity, you would dam the stream at the lowest point at which you could command the water, knowing that if you struck the river too high, you would lose the tributaries which fell in below that point; and if you struck it too low, you would not have sufficient head to bring the water to the city." [20] Or more particularly the railroad which would command the trade of the Connecticut River must reach it between Greenfield and Brattleboro and not at Springfield.

Though the Western might tolerate such creeping encroachments upon its territory, a new route to the Hudson was a different matter. When the Committee on Railroads and Canals debated a charter for the Troy and Greenfield, Addison Gilmore, the competent captain of the Western, addressed a remonstrance to the General Court; his arguments against incorporation of a competitor were so cogent that the majority of the committee adopted them almost verbatim.[21] On the other hand, the Troy and Greenfield in order to secure its charter had to stress the

[19] *Report of a Committee . . . of the Fitchburg Rail-Road . . . on the Statistics and Prospects*, pp. 6, 14; Records of the Directors and Stockholders of the Boston and Worcester Railroad, V, 230, Ms., Harvard Business School Library.

[20] Charles Hudson, *Letters on the Vermont and Massachusetts Railroad, Addressed to Hon. Thomas H. Perkins* (Boston: White, Lewis & Potter, 1844), pp. 4–8.

[21] *Memorial of the Western Railroad to The Honorable Senate and House of Representatives, in General Court Assembled* (n.p., n.d.); Report of the Second Joint Special Committee on Railways and Canals on the Charter of the Troy and Greenfield, Massachusetts *Senate Documents*, 1848, no. 120.

inadequate achievements of Massachusetts' first transectional railroad. Fortunately for the immediate success of the former, its case was launched on the rising tide of a popular belief in competition. The General Court rejected the notion that the "doctrine of free trade, free competition" did not apply to railroads as well as to manufacturing; it granted the charter.[22] Therewith it unloosed a thirty-year war between the Western and the Troy and Greenfield. Each moved mountains, though not the Hoosac, to discredit and checkmate the other. This hostility, like the intense local patriotism of northern Massachusetts, was a continuous and fundamental factor in the history of the tunnel route.

II

The incorporation of the Troy and Greenfield also amplified difficulties already confronted on a tinier scale in the construction of its eastern connections. Some of these difficulties were technical. The building of the Fitchburg had raised few problems; it followed convenient river valleys to its interior destination. In the golden phrase of Crocker and Derby, it "requires little more grading than a turnpike." [23] The Vermont and Massachusetts was a far different proposition. Like the Western, it had to cross the wide highlands between the Connecticut and the coastal plain. Engineering talent, including that of James Hayward, was mobilized for the task; the best it could produce was a route with grades going westward of 58 feet to the mile and crossing a height of land 1,106 feet above sea level, two hundred feet higher than the comparable crossing farther south by the Western. The line then followed Millers River to the Connecticut. In spite of the numerous bridges, this stretch had somewhat more favorable grades; the heavy traffic eastward-bound confronted maximum grades of 48½ feet to the mile.[24]

---

[22] Massachusetts *Senate Documents*, 1848, no. 120, p. 24; *Fifth Annual Report of the Vermont & Mass. . . . 1849*, p. 11; *Acts and Resolves Passed by the General Court of Massachusetts, in the Year 1848*, pp. 789–791.

[23] *Report of a Committee . . . of the Fitchburg Rail-Road . . . on the Statistics and Prospects*, p. 13.

[24] Charles Hudson, *Vermont and Massachusetts Railroad. To the Stockholders*

The topography west of Greenfield made these handicaps pale. The Deerfield River, which the projected route must follow, was not a valley but a defile. Hoosac Mountain — only the shysters felt it could be avoided — had to be pierced by a tunnel at least four miles long. The committee of the General Court in 1848 commented, "It appeared, that no work of this magnitude had ever been undertaken in this country, or abroad, in the construction of a railroad. No one of the witnesses could give opinions founded on any extensive experience in the construction of tunnels. Few works of this character have been performed in this country. In Great Britain, and on the continent, numerous tunnels through rock and earth, at a much less distance below the surface, and less in length, have been constructed." [25] Such sober truths did not daunt Crocker. "The Hoosuc or Green mountain chain," he announced in 1849, "is believed to be the only barrier between Boston and the Pacific. To say it will not be demolished, is to say that the feudal, time-worn institutions of Europe, develop and mature the will of man *more fully* than the free air and more free institutions of our own youthful republic." [26] Old Hoosac still stood.

Naturally a second problem was that of finance. The opinion of experts, if the designation can be applied to those inexperienced in tunnel construction, differed as to costs of the tunnel: the minimum guess was $1,600,000; the maximum was $3,000,000.[27] Funds for a forty-mile railroad from Greenfield to the Vermont state line had, in addition, to be secured. To meet these combined expenses, the charter of the Troy and Greenfield provided for a capitalization of $3,500,000. This fantastically petty figure is so

of the Vermont and Massachusetts Railroad Corporation (n.p., n.d.), pp. 3–7; Hudson, *Letters on the Vermont and Massachusetts Railroad,* pp. 9–13; *Second Annual Report of the Vermont and Massachusetts Railroad Company, February 11, 1846* (Boston: White & Potter, 1846), pp. 4–10; *Fifth Annual Report of the Directors of the Vermont & Mass. Railroad Co., February 14, 1849* (Fitchburg: W. J. Merriam, 1849), pp. 3–6; Eighth Annual Report of the Vermont and Massachusetts Railroad, Massachusetts *Senate Documents,* 1852, no. 9, p. 195; Report of the Commissioners of the Troy and Greenfield Railroad and Hoosac Tunnel, Massachusetts *Senate Documents,* 1863, no. 93, p. 75, folded chart, p. 100.

[25] Massachusetts *Senate Documents,* 1848, no. 120, pp. 8–9.

[26] *Fifth Annual Report . . . of the Vermont & Mass. . . . 1849,* p. 11.

[27] Massachusetts *Senate Documents,* 1848, no. 120, pp. 9–10.

close to that stated by Loammi Baldwin for his canal as to suggest
that the promoters of the railroad must have turned to his archaic
document for estimates of cost.[28] Certainly they could not have
derived them from contemporaneous experience. The Western,
which ran *over* the mountains without benefit of tunnel, had cost
$6,000,000 between Springfield and Albany.[29] Nor had the Fitch-
burg and Vermont and Massachusetts, with far fewer technical
uncertainties, found it easy to raise money. To build the former,
it had been necessary to whittle construction costs penuriously
and to induce the contractor to subscribe to a large fraction of
the stock.[30] The Vermont and Massachusetts, when faced with
an appalling discrepancy between funds in hand and costs of
construction, had first appealed to the Commonwealth for assistance; when its plea went unanswered, the corporation sold
its bonds at 90 and the stock at 50 cents on the dollar.[31] The
Troy and Greenfield at once demonstrated that it belonged in the
same category. Within three years of its chartering the corporation had collected roughly $56,000 of its capital; within six
years, $100,000. Only three and a half times as much had been
subscribed.[32]

The dates were significant, since in 1851 the Troy and Greenfield first applied to the Massachusetts legislature for financial
assistance and in 1854 secured its grant of $2,000,000. In the
course of the three-year campaign there were three engagements
in the legislature[33] and a major battle in the State Constitutional

[28] *Supra*, I, 98.

[29] Massachusetts *Senate Documents*, 1848, no. 120, p. 4.

[30] Second Annual Report of the Fitchburg Railroad Company, Massachusetts
Senate Documents, 1844, no. 19, pp. 85–86; *Report to the Stockholders on the Affairs
of the Fitchburg Rail-Road Company, January, 1844* (Boston: Dutton and Wentworth, 1844), pp. 3–15; *Report of the Fifth Hearing on the Hoosac Tunnel Consolidation, before the Committee on Railways, February 6, 1873*, pp. 16–17.

[31] *Fifth Annual Report . . . of the Vermont & Mass. . . . 1849*, pp. 7–9; Report
of the Joint Special Committee on Aid to the Vermont and Massachusetts Railroad,
Massachusetts *Senate Documents*, 1847, no. 55.

[32] Second Annual Report of the Troy and Greenfield Railroad, Massachusetts
Senate Documents, 1852, no. 9, p. 192; Fifth Annual Report of the Troy and Greenfield Railroad Company, Massachusetts *Senate Documents*, 1855, no. 2, p. 258.

[33] *Hoosac Tunnel. The Memorial of the Western Railroad Corporation, Relating
to the Application of the Troy and Greenfield Railroad for a State Loan of Two
Million Dollars* (Boston: Eastburn's Press, 1853), p. 4.

Convention of 1853, when an attempt was made to include in the prohibitions of the proposed constitution one upon state loans to private enterprises. The last struggle was not over general principles. One member of the convention rightly discovered, "There are two great things in this Convention, but I did not really suppose that either of these two great things were present. One of the creatures, the invisible creatures present, is the great Hoosac Tunnel. The second invisible creature is the great Western Railroad." [34] In the end, the tunnel won. It enlisted the gifts of the most able soothsayers and manipulators in Massachusetts. Though the Western and its henchmen from Springfield and elsewhere opposed, though Boston capitalists were cool, the Troy and Greenfield had in its service the nestor of promoters and popularizers, P. P. F. De Grand, the persuasiveness of its counsel, E. H. Derby, the subterranean political manipulations of Crocker, and the railroad ambitions of such localities as existed in the northern wilderness from Greenfield to North Adams or lined the route of the Fitchburg and the Vermont and Massachusetts.

Their case could hardly be reduced to logic. It was hot with imagination and, in the ensuing haze, beyond the summits of the Berkshires, shimmered the mirage of an immense western commerce. The new route would bring this commerce more cheaply to Boston than did the Western, because its costs of operation would be lower. On the whole the tunnelites tended to correlate costs with a mere mileage basis. Their route was fourteen miles shorter than the Western. They made it shorter still by calculating the Western should run to Troy rather than the tunnel road to Albany, and, finally, through pseudo-scientific formulas, they "equated" curves and grades into mile equivalents and wiped more miles away.[35]

[34] *Official Report of the Debates and Proceedings in the State Convention, Assembled May 4th, 1853, to Revise and Amend the Constitution of the Commonwealth of Massachusetts*, II, 467.

[35] *Speech of T. G. Cary, on The Use of the Credit of the State for the Hoosac Tunnel, in the Senate of Massachusetts, May 18, 1853* (Boston: J. M. Hewes & Co., 1853), pp. 10–11; Elias H. Derby, *A Brief Review of the Speech of Hon. Thomas G. Cary, a Senator from Suffolk County, against the Loan of State Credit, for the Hoosac Tunnel, May, 1853* (Boston: Damrell & Moore, 1853), pp. 5–7.

Skeptics who felt these hypothetical savings might be lost through high costs of construction were answered by bringing low the costs of tunneling Hoosac Mountain. Though most witnesses on this point were ignorant and partisan, competent experts did little better. James Hayward, one of New England's pioneer railroad engineers and now president of the Boston and Maine, concluded on the basis of existing costs, "I think two millions of dollars will be *ample* to tunnel the Hoosac, — it leaves a large margin," [36] and President Edward Hitchcock of Amherst, intimate of Benjamin Silliman, Congregationalist clergyman, chemist, naturalist, and state geologist *extraordinaire*, announced, "If there is any confidence to be placed in the principles of geology, then we may rely upon the rock's proving to be the same throughout the mountain." The rock was mica slate in thin perpendicular layers, without granite or trap intrusions. It would be "easier to work after you get down through the edges"; in fact the mountain was composed of "soft" rock. It was also the presidential impression, that "this tunnel will be found to be dry after penetrating a considerable distance from the surface." [37]

When, to such hypothetical calculations of intangibles, the anti-tunnelites declared the new route could not charge lower rates than those on the Western, on the route to the Lakes, and on the eastern connection of the Troy and Greenfield,[38] they were met with the assertion that such rate levels were the result of wilfulness. "The commerce and growth of Boston seem to be the victims of an idea, ... We are now reaping the fruits of the inflexible workings of this policy; a policy based upon the idea of doing a comparatively small amount of business at a large profit, instead of a large amount of business at a small profit." [39] Other objections to a program of state aid — that it

[36] *The Hoosac Tunnel. A Brief Report of the Hearing of the Troy and Greenfield Railroad Company Petitioners for a Loan of Two Millions, before a Joint Special Committee of the Legislature of Massachusetts* (Boston: Thurston, Torry, and Emerson, 1853), pp. 24–26.

[37] *The Tunnel Hearing in 1854*, pp. 8–9; *Dictionary of American Biography*, IX, 70–71.

[38] *Speech of T. G. Cary, . . . May 18, 1853*, pp. 22–24; *Hoosac Tunnel. The Memorial of the Western Railroad Corporation,* . . . [1853], pp. 12–14.

[39] Otis Clapp, *A Letter to the Hon. Abbott Lawrence and the Hon. Robert G.*

induced log-rolling, legislative carelessness and corruption, and unloosed the irresistible influence of railroad corporations upon the General Court [40] — were unanswered. The final demurrer, that the state should not aid a corporation to rival and injure another in which it had an investment of $5,000,000, was brushed aside with the plea that it was now the turn of northern Massachusetts to stand at the public trough. The Commonwealth, "a parent worth six hundred million dollars," should "indorse a piece of paper like this, for the benefit of her own children." [41]

As the state government yielded to these interests and arguments, it followed in part the pattern of the earlier grants to the Western. The state was to transfer to the Troy and Greenfield Railroad $2,000,000 in its own scrip. To protect the loan, Massachusetts was to have a mortgage on the property, to appoint state directors, and to be repaid from a sinking fund, for which 10 per cent of the loan was immediately set aside for a nucleus. After the road was open, annual payments of $25,000 were to be added to the fund. The loan was to "construct a tunnel and railroad under and through the Hoosac Mountain"; private capital was to build the rail approaches from east and west. The state transferred its scrip in installments, the first of which was to be paid when $600,000 had been subscribed to the stock, of which 20 per cent must be "actually paid" in, and when one thousand feet of tunnel and seven miles of railroad had been completed. Further footage and further mileage won further installments. [42]

Shaw on the Present Condition and Future Growth of Boston, 1853 (Boston: John Wilson & Son, 1853), p. 3.

[40] *Official Report of the . . . State Convention . . . 1853 . . . to Amend the Constitution of Massachusetts*, II, 283, 299, 305, 666–667.

[41] *Speech of Hon. Whiting Griswold, On the Bill for Loaning the Credit of the State to the Amount of Two Million Dollars to the Troy and Greenfield Rail Road Corporation for the Purpose of Tunneling the Hoosac Mountain.*——*In the Senate of Massachusetts, Wednesday and Friday, April 9th and 11th, 1851* (n.p., n.d.), pp. 12–14.

[42] *Acts and Resolves Passed by the General Court of Massachusetts, in the Year 1854*, pp. 149–153; *Argument on the Petition of the Troy & Greenfield Railroad Company, for a Change in the Conditions of the Loan Act, before the Joint Committee of Railways and Canals, of the Legislature of Massachusetts, January 12th, 1859* (Boston: Alfred Mudge and Son, 1859), pp. 3–4.

III

At last provided with prospective assistance, the corporation sought contractors for the construction of its immense works. The respondents had to provide not only technical skill but also, in view of the small subscription by private investors, sufficient funds to carry the work until the construction prerequisites for the state installments were met. After these joint tasks had defied the engineering ingenuity and financial resources of a firm or two, Herman Haupt undertook in 1856 to meet the challenge. A Pennsylvanian, a graduate of West Point, railroad engineer, professor at Gettysburg, an expert on bridges — his *General Theory of Bridge Construction* was a pioneer investigation of stresses and strains — he came to Massachusetts from the Pennsylvania Railroad on which he had been first general superintendent and later chief engineer.[43] His technical competence seemed unquestioned. His relations with Pennsylvania capitalists and his own modest fortune promised that magic "large capital" for the lack of which the Troy and Greenfield was stagnant.[44]

Haupt's successive contracts with the railroad revealed the desperate status of the corporation. The first set the price of railroad and tunnel at $3,883,000. Though the totals did not jibe, he was to receive $2,000,000 in Massachusetts scrip, $900,-000 in 6 per-cent, second mortgage bonds of the company, $598,000 in capital stock, and only $382,000 in cash! For the stock payment to which he technically "subscribed" he was to pay in work or as it was called in "stock credits."[45] Two years later a second contract gave Haupt even more imperial powers.

[43] Herman Haupt, *Reminiscences of General Herman Haupt . . . Giving Hitherto Unpublished Official Orders, Personal Narratives of Important Military Operations . . . with Notes and a Personal Sketch by Frank Abial Flower* (Milwaukee: Wright & Joys Co., 1901), pp. xiii–xx; [Herman Haupt], *Remarks on the Present Position of the Hoosac Tunnel Enterprise* (Boston: Alfred Mudge and Son, 1858), pp. 3–6.

[44] Report of the Joint Special Committee on the Petition of the Troy and Greenfield Railroad, Massachusetts *House Documents*, 1856, no. 174, p. 11; *Report of the Committee of the Executive Council on the Memorial of the Troy and Greenfield Railroad Co., With the Evidence before Said Committee* (Boston: William White, 1861), pp. 26–27.

[45] Report of the Special Committee of Five — the Kimball Committee — on the Payments to the Troy and Greenfield Railroad, Massachusetts *House Documents*, 1862, no. 194, pp. 19–20, 44–48.

The price of the job was now increased to $4,000,000; the Massachusetts scrip and second mortgage bonds of the railroad constituted a part payment, the remainder was in such cash subscriptions as had or would be made, and in capital stock.[46] Even in an age when shrewd and ingenious men were perfecting the fine art of railroad contracting, these two documents were unique. Haupt was chief promoter and largest stockholder, he sat on the board of directors, and his firm was to pay into the treasury of the Troy and Greenfield annually $500 to defray the necessary expenses of organization and printing. The Troy and Greenfield Railroad was a myth.[47] Its alpha and omega were Herman Haupt.

The engineering methods of the time did not promise the speedy excavation of the tunnel; they were still the old ones of hand drilling and black powder upon which Loammi Baldwin had based his calculations. Promoters, investors, engineers, and the tunnel faction could not wait for hand labor thus to chip a hole through the mountain from both ends; the sinking of vertical shafts to secure additional faces for attack was only a palliative.[48] Machines were the answer. Haupt and his predecessors were hypnotized by the possibilities of huge contraptions run by steam power; such "Excavators" or "Boring Machines" were to ream great circular holes through Hitchcock's "mica slate" as if it were cheese. Technically all failed to meet expectations. The "character of the rock" forbade their use.[49] Housed or left in the open, they stood "a crumbling and rusting monument of sanguine, but wild and delirious expectations" in the phrase of a Massachusetts governor.[50] Probably they were intended primarily for advertising purposes. Meanwhile, in 1856 France and Sardinia

[46] *Ibid.*, pp. 20–21, 49–51.

[47] F. W. Bird, *The Road to Ruin: or, the Decline and Fall of the Hoosac Tunnel* (Boston: Wright & Potter, 1862), pp. 25, 31.

[48] Haupt, *Remarks on the Present Position of the Hoosac Tunnel*, pp. 10–11.

[49] *Ibid.*, pp. 11–12; *Answer to Some of the Objections Made against the Memorial of the Troy and Greenfield R.R. Company* (Boston: William White, 1857), pp. 13–14; *The Hoosac Tunnel. A Brief Report of the Hearing of the Troy and Greenfield* . . . [1853], p. 7; Report of the Joint Special Committee on the Troy and Greenfield, Massachusetts *House Documents*, 1856, no. 174, p. 44.

[50] Veto Message of Governor Henry J. Gardner, Massachusetts *House Documents*, 1862, no. 214, pp. 9–10.

had undertaken the construction of the eight-mile Mt. Cenis
tunnel under the Alps. Experiments there with small batteries of
power drills turned Haupt's attention in this direction. The
technical problems were intricate, as the drills had to reciprocate,
rotate, and advance in continuous operation. For power the
European devices used compressed air. Haupt elected steam.[51]
To get the steam near the heading, he planned a series of mobile
boilers, advancing into the tunnel as the work progressed; a
"vacuum pipe" was to withdraw their smoke and fumes and at
the same time provide a draft for the fires.[52] These perfections,
if they can be so called, were designed, however, only after Haupt
was no longer in a position to apply them.

During this period of fruitless engineering, Haupt and his allies
also fought for money by one desperate foray after another.
Private investment was hardly to be thought of, when Derby
owned one share, Otis Clapp two, and Alvah Crocker fifteen, and
when partisans of the route, who glowed most feverishly in public
over its prospects, took largely verbal chances.[53] After
Massachusetts in 1855 authorized towns along the route to
subscribe upon a favorable vote of two-thirds of their inhabitants,
only a half of the communities availed themselves of the privilege
and their total subscriptions, some hedged with conditions, were
only 1,456 shares.[54] Then Haupt, like earlier promoters, dreamed
of a loan from Boston — a stroke which he, like his predecessors,
never brought off.[55] By 1859 the paid-in capital amounted to

[51] *Argument on the Petition of the Troy & Greenfield Railroad Company*, . . .
1859, pp. 12–13; *Annual Report of the Troy and Greenfield Railroad Company, for
the Year 1860* (n.p., n.d.), pp. 8–9.

[52] Statements before the Joint Special Committee on the Troy and Greenfield
Railroad, Massachusetts *House Documents*, 1862, no. 235, p. 17; Memorial of
Haupt to the General Court of Massachusetts, Massachusetts *Senate Documents*,
1863, no. 95, pp. 21–38.

[53] Stockholders of the Troy and Greenfield Railroad, Massachusetts *Senate Documents*, 1859, no. 31, pp. 5, 6.

[54] *Acts and Resolves Passed by the General Court of Massachusetts, in the Year
1855*, pp. 781–782; Massachusetts *House Documents*, 1862, no. 194, pp. 100–105.

[55] *Annual Report of the Troy and Greenfield* . . . *1860*, p. 10; *Report of the
Committee of the Executive Council on the Memorial of the Troy and Greenfield*,
p. 27; *Reasons Why Boston Should Aid in the Construction of the Hoosac Tunnel.
Letters from J. Edgar Thomson, Benjamin H. Latrobe, Major Gen'l J. E. Wool,
and Others*, . . . (Boston: Alfred Mudge & Son, 1860); *Acts and Resolves Passed
by the General Court of Massachusetts, in the Year 1860*, pp. 143–145.

only $385,206, part of it in "stock credits" from H. Haupt & Co.[56]

Haupt, meanwhile, had turned once more to a complacent state. Only state aid would enable him to meet the conditions for collecting the installments of the state loan of 1854. The audacious suggestion that the state facilitate this process by subscribing to the road's stock failed for once to meet legislative approval.[57] In the next year, 1858, however, the state transferred the first $100,000 of its scrip. By one method or another Haupt had hacked enough footage out of old Hoosac and built enough railroad. In doubt whether his contributions in "stock credits" met the statutory requirements for capital "actually paid" in, he transferred $100,000 in bank notes to the treasurer of the Troy and Greenfield; that official immediately returned the sum in partial payment for Haupt's work on the contract. "A mere form," observed Haupt.[58] To ease further construction, Haupt and his tunnelites continually sought to liberalize the original loan act. In 1860, after a governor favorable to the Hoosac had been elected, they won a real victory. Of the remaining state scrip — now $1,770,000 — part, $650,000, was appropriated for the completion of the railroad and the rest, $1,120,000, for the tunnel. Payments on the latter account were to be made at the rate of $50 for each lineal foot, and those for the railroad were to to be based upon the proportion which the value of the work done bore to the total estimated cost of the railroad.[59] Settlements were to be made monthly. In short, the contractors were released from

[56] Ninth Annual Report of the Troy and Greenfield Railroad, Massachusetts *Public Documents*, 1860, no. 39.

[57] Report of the Joint Special Committee on a State Subscription to the Troy and Greenfield, Massachusetts *House Documents*, 1856, no. 174, pp. 1–20; *The Hoosac Tunnel. Argument of E. Hasket Derby, Esq., Delivered Feb. 29th, 1856. Before a Joint Special Committee of the Legislature of Massachusetts, in Behalf of the Troy and Greenfield Railroad Company; Petitioners for a State Subscription to Their Stock* (Boston: Bazin & Chandler, 1856); Massachusetts *Senate Documents*, 1863, no. 93, appendix, p. 147.

[58] *Committee of Investigation on the Hoosac Tunnel Loan. Communication of H. Haupt, to the Governor and Council of the State of Massachusetts, Containing a Review of the Report of the Committee* (Greenfield: H. D. Mirick & Co., 1860), p. 9; Massachusetts *House Documents*, 1862, no. 194, pp. 22–24.

[59] *Acts and Resolves Passed by the General Court of Massachusetts, in the Year 1859*, pp. 283–288; *Acts and Resolves . . . of Massachusetts . . . 1860*, pp. 157–162.

building the railroad with their own funds, the payments from the state came at frequent intervals, and the possibility that the state would be left with an unfinished railroad and tunnel and exhausted funds was brought measurably nearer.

Whether tunneling or borrowing, drilling or peddling stock, Haupt had to find time to fight the tunnel's foes. They were vigorous, vigilant, and resourceful. There were some opposed to state aid on the ground of principle. Of the others, who united principle to self-interest, the Western Railroad and the localities which it served, particularly Springfield, formed a solid phalanx. It had the assistance of an able press in the Springfield *Republican*, spokesman for the city of the Chapins, and in the Boston *Advertiser*, the heir of Nathan Hale.[60] The hatchet man for this group was D. L. Harris. No one could have been better fitted — railroad engineer, director and president of the Connecticut River Railroad, always closely allied with the Western, city councilman and mayor of Springfield, and a member of a bridge firm committed to the excellencies of the Howe patent, perhaps menaced by Haupt's innovations.[61] To Haupt he was this "ever vigilant Cerberus," "this kind friend, whose personal attachment to me and my fortunes has made him, as he himself declares, my constant attendant for a period of five years, following my tracks incessantly." [62]

Then there were creditors and allied lawyers. At one time Haupt played with the idea "that the most expeditious way of

[60] *Troy and Greenfield Railroad. Speech of Hon. Alvah Crocker, on the Bill for the More Speedy Completion of the Troy and Greenfield Railroad, in the Senate of Massachusetts, April 15, 1862* (Boston: Wright & Potter, 1862), pp. 4–12; *Brief Review, by H. Haupt of the Errors, Inconsistencies and Mis-Statements Contained in a Pamphlet Dated March 8th, 1862, Distributed amongst Members of the Legislature of 1862, by D. L. Harris* (n.p., n.d.), pp. 9–10; *Reply to Articles in the Springfield Republican, and Other Papers, in Opposition to a Change in the Tunnel Loan Act* (Boston: Alfred Mudge and Son, 1859).

[61] *Closing Argument of H. Haupt on Behalf of the Troy and Greenfield Railroad Co., before the Joint Special Committee of the Senate and House of Representatives of Massachusetts, at a Public Hearing on Thursday, March 6, 1862* (Boston: Wright & Potter, 1862), p. 6; Charles E. Fisher, "Daniel L. Harris," *Bulletin of the Railway and Locomotive Historical Society*, XXXII (1933), 7–14; John J. Piper, *Facts and Figures Concerning the Hoosac Tunnel* (Fitchburg: John J. Piper, 1866), pp. 31–32.

[62] *Closing Argument of H. Haupt . . . March 6, 1862*, p. 26.

getting a hole through the mountain, would be to wall up a dozen lawyers at one end of the tunnel, and put a good fee at the other." [63] Finally there were the state directors, one of whom was Moses Kimball. In 1860 this redoubtable merchant headed a legislative investigating committee whose report questioned whether Haupt had fairly earned the state scrip already given to his company.[64] Early the next year he was advising the new governor, John A. Andrew, to appoint a new state engineer to appraise what had been done. This appointee must be "able to stand up against the blandishments of Mr. Haupt, who is one of the smartest men *in his way* in all New England." [65] Andrew adopted the suggested policy. When the new engineer certified that Haupt's work on the railroad did not meet the specifications of the various loan acts, further payments from the state stopped. So did the work on the Troy and Greenfield Railroad and the Hoosac Tunnel.[66]

Though the Civil War shook the nation, a smaller struggle but one just as passionate convulsed Massachusetts. Some opposed Haupt, some opposed the tunnel, and always those opposing the second opposed the first. Some favored Haupt, some favored the tunnel, and in the beginning those who favored the latter favored the former also. The tunnelites, therefore, exerted every effort to restore him to the enterprise. In this cause their most effective ally was Haupt himself. He had not been successful as promoter and engineer. The situation was too desperate, his connection with the enterprise too short, and his ambition, pride, and perhaps naiveté had blinded him to the grim realities of the Deerfield River route and of Hoosac Mountain.[67] Besides, he seems to have relied overmuch upon President Hitchcock's insight into the interior of the latter barrier. But now, to protect his reputa-

[63] *Argument on the Petition of the Troy and Greenfield Railroad Company,* . . . *1859,* p. 12.

[64] Massachusetts *House Documents,* 1862, no. 194, pp. 34–35.

[65] Moses Kimball to John A. Andrew, April 8, 1861, May 8, 1861, Ms., Andrew Papers, Massachusetts Historical Society.

[66] *Report of the Committee of the Executive Council on the Memorial of the Troy and Greenfield Railroad Co.,* pp. 29–45, 83–89; Massachusetts *House Documents,* 1862, no. 235, pp. 3–8.

[67] Massachusetts *House Documents,* 1862, no. 235, pp. 11, 19.

tion and secure repayment for the funds he had advanced, he fought with singular persistence, dignity, candor, and restraint. For a while he sought to conduct his Massachusetts campaign for vindication and serve in the Union army at the same time. Eventually, however, he refused an appointment as Brigadier General and was thereupon dismissed from his part-time labors by Secretary of War Stanton. "No doubt the extraordinary character of the offence called for punishment, for no other individual, perhaps, was ever guilty of the crime of refusing to be made a general." [68]

The pro-tunnel warriors confronted an intractable governor and also F. W. Bird. The latter, a Walpole paper manufacturer, was originally in favor of state aid to the tunnel and to other railroads.[69] An abolitionist gadfly, a sincere and inconsistent zealot, he was convinced that Haupt was a scoundrel and he employed all the vituperative techniques of his tribe against him. In comparison, Harris was a tyro. In Bird's pamphleteering phrases, Haupt was "a Uriah Heep," a "Shylock and Pecksniff by turns," "squandering in wild speculations and visionary excitements, the money he made out of the Pennsylvania Railroad—the road which has had to be built over almost entirely new since he left it — leaguing himself with the most unscrupulous political gamblers and profligate adventurers in the State, he has corrupted and influenced the legislature of the State to an extent which would be impossible to one less unscrupulous and indefatigable." [70]

Gradually the tunnelites realized they must sacrifice their idol for the realization of their expectations. When they promised to protect his interests, he complied.[71] After years of waiting he won only partial reimbursement.[72] Meanwhile, "wearied and dis-

[68] *Statement of Herman Haupt Presented to the Joint Special Committee on Troy and Greenfield Railroad and Hoosac Tunnel. February, 1864* (n. p., n. d.), pp. 40–41.

[69] Report of F. W. Bird, Minority Member of the Committee on Finance on Sale of State Stock in the Western, Massachusetts *House Documents*, 1848, no. 91; Bird, *The Road to Ruin*, p. 3.

[70] Bird, *The Road to Ruin*, p. 37.

[71] *Statement of Herman Haupt . . . February, 1864*, p. 26.

[72] *Reminiscences of General Herman Haupt*, p. xxvii.

gusted," he shook the dust of Massachusetts from his feet "as a testimony against the robbery which has been perpetrated by a State which prides itself upon its high financial credit, and whose politicians boast of an 'unsullied honor' " [73] — a state to which he had come "with the greatest veneration . . . and admiration of her intelligence, public spirit, and liberality in every great and good work" but a state in which he had always felt alien.[74] In Haupt's mind, his battle for the Hoosac was a struggle between Pennsylvania and Massachusetts.

IV

When Haupt ceased work, he had completed about a half-mile of tunnel at the eastern end and about six hundred feet at the west facing where the material was loose and difficult. Roughly four miles of mountain were untunneled. The Trojans had built the Troy and Boston to the New York-Vermont line, and Massachusetts and Haupt had built the Southern Vermont. Of the Troy and Greenfield, the section west of the Hoosac Mountain was done, that east far from complete. State expenditures had totaled $1,162,041.[75] What should be done with the ruin? If the anti-tunnelites believed that the downfall of Haupt meant the end of the Hoosac, they were speedily undeceived. Northern Massachusetts, upset by Haupt's dismissal, went Democratic in the state election of 1861 and thus served notice that the tunnel must be built. In alliance with the Boston merchants, convinced of the necessity of a competitive route to the West, and with other localities and promoters clamoring for financial assistance to pet railroad projects, they formed a determined minority bloc which gubernatorial and other candidates and interests had to conciliate.[76] In 1862, after a terrific legislative battle, a statute in effect transferred the decision on future policy to the governor

---

[73] Herman Haupt, *The Hoosac Tunnel. Final Settlement of the Claim of H. Haupt & Co. Against the State of Massachusetts. The Liberality of "A Generous and Opulent Commonwealth" Exhibited* (Boston: Wright & Potter, 1869), p. 18.

[74] *Closing Argument of H. Haupt . . . March 6, 1862*, p. 5.

[75] Massachusetts *Senate Documents*, 1863, no. 93, pp. 151–153, 155.

[76] H. B. Crandall to John A. Andrew, July 29, 1861, Ms., Andrew Papers; Bird, *The Road to Ruin*, p. 3.

and council.[77] They were to appoint three "able, impartial and skillful" commissioners who in turn were to investigate the cheapest way of completing the project, to assess its value as a completed thoroughfare, and to spend the remainder of the $2,000,000 in completing the railroad from Greenfield to the eastern end of the tunnel.[78]

Undoubtedly the commission in ability met the requirements of the act. One member was John W. Brooks, the railroad engineer and builder, who, in alliance with J. M. Forbes, had constructed and operated the Michigan Central; the second, Samuel M. Felton, was the heir of Loammi Baldwin as a teacher of engineers and the official who, after leaving various New England enterprises, transformed the Philadelphia, Wilmington, and Baltimore Railroad into one of the best organized, technically advanced, and financially sound railroads of the East; the third, Alexander Holmes, was president of the Old Colony Railroad.[79] Their report, submitted in 1863, was supplemented by opinions of other engineers to whom even Haupt had to pay tribute. Though it was the most sober appraisal of the tunnel route up to that time, it did not entirely escape the tag of promotional literature. The commissioners approved of the tunnel project. It could not compete with the Western for passengers nor divert heavy freights from New York to Boston when the Erie Canal and Hudson River were open, but, as a freight carrier within New England, it was superior to the Western. Its slightly shorter distances and its more favorable grades on eastbound traffic would enable it to shade the operating costs of the latter by 10 per cent. It might even earn something upon the cost of construction, though the completion of Haupt's flimsy Troy and Greenfield Railroad would require $572,060 and the tunnel $3,218,323. Since the interest charges on the latter sum were a wasteful accumulation until the bore was opened, the commissioners were heartened

[77] F. W. Bird, *The Hoosac Tunnel: Our Financial Maelstrom* (Boston: Wright & Potter, 1866), pp. 6–11; *Report of the Second Hearing on the Hoosac Tunnel Consolidation, before the Committee on Railways, January 30, 1873*, pp. 6–8.

[78] *Acts and Resolves Passed by the General Court of Massachusetts, in the Year 1862*, pp. 101–103; *Acts and Resolves Passed by the General Court of Massachusetts, in the Year 1863*, pp. 510–512.

[79] Bird, *The Hoosac Tunnel: Our Financial Maelstrom*, pp. 11–13.

by the belief that seven and a half or eight years were sufficient for its construction if the machines contemporaneously used on the Mt. Cenis tunnel were employed. In conclusion, the commissioners announced that they had taken control of the property under the various mortgages executed to the state, that approximately $1,200,000 in scrip remained available for their operations, and "that the work should be undertaken by the Commonwealth." [80]

The substitution of the state for Haupt stunned the opponents of the tunnel. Once more Bird let fly a polemical discharge. Brooks was "arrogant, insolent, and domineering," "plausible, deferential, and obsequious;" "we needed a master; we got a lackey." [81] When the original state appropriation was exhausted in 1866 and the state legislature granted additional funds to the enterprise,[82] the resulting reaction by F. W. Bird required citation only by title: *The Hoosac Tunnel: Our Financial Maelstrom. Beyond the Lowest Depth, a Lower Deep.* It concluded with the admonition, "Abandon the work, pocket the loss, and let the resources of the State be henceforth applied to legitimate functions." [83]

Meanwhile the work went on. From 1863 to 1868, the state commissioners labored at their herculean tasks, first under the virtual direction of J. W. Brooks, then of Alvah Crocker, who brusquely shoved his associates aside to become the one-man superintendent of the work.[84] There was action aplenty, but meagre accomplishment. To be sure, nitroglycerin manufactured at the site, since the railroads refused to transport it, took the

[80] Massachusetts *Senate Documents*, 1863, no. 93, pp. 2–5, 22–25, 31–33, 57, 61–88, 95–100.

[81] Bird, *The Hoosac Tunnel: Our Financial Maelstrom*, pp. 11–12.

[82] *Acts and Resolves Passed by the General Court of Massachusetts, in the Year, 1866*, pp. 274–275; *Acts and Resolves Passed by the General Court of Massachusetts, in the Year, 1867*, pp. 649–650.

[83] Bird, *The Hoosac Tunnel: Our Financial Maelstrom*, p. 62.

[84] Annual Report of the Commissioners on the Troy and Greenfield R. R. and Hoosac Tunnel, Massachusetts *House Documents*, 1867, no. 30, p. 10; Statement of Governor Bullock and J. M. Shute, Massachusetts *House Documents*, 1868, no. 87; Letter of Hon. Charles Hudson, Massachusetts *House Documents*, 1868, no. 359, pp. 9–12; J. M. Shute, *Rejected Papers in Relation to the Hoosac Tunnel* (Boston: Wright & Potter, 1868), pp. 4–9.

place of black powder.[85] Power drilling superseded hand labor —
but only belatedly. The Mt. Cenis drills, under whose destructive advance that tunnel was completed in 1871, the commissioners neither imported nor imitated. Instead, at state expense
they financed a series of experiments at a Fitchburg machine
shop; the resulting Burleigh drill, not entirely automatic, when
put to use wore out rapidly and made less progress and cost more
than hand labor. A year passed before it was perfected.[86] This
extraordinary performance was never satisfactorily explained.
Perhaps it was another illustration of the faith, held by American
engineers and inventors, that they could always improve upon
Europeans. Perhaps it was political jobbery. As soon as the
drill was ready, a private company, including members of the
state legislature, was organized to take over the patents.[87]

In the tactics of construction, the state commissioners decided
upon a vertical shaft sunk 1,033 feet to the grade of the tunnel.
Its sponsors claimed this great innovation opened two new facings
for cutting and provided essential ventilation for the tunnel.
Without improvements the shaft later failed to fulfill the second
purpose, and as a means of hastening excavation it was handicap
rather than help. Its construction and operation required expensive hoisting and pumping apparatus, while the excavation at its
base increased the expense of the tunnel. But this was a later
development. The shaft did not reach grade during the Brooks-
Crocker period.[88] At the west end of the tunnel the commission

---

[85] Report on the Hoosac Tunnel and Troy and Greenfield Railroad, by the Joint
Standing Committee of 1866, Massachusetts *Senate Documents*, 1867, no. 59, pp.
38–41; Annual Report of the Commissioners of the Troy & Greenfield R. R. and
Hoosac Tunnel, Massachusetts *House Documents*, 1867, no. 30, pp. 6, 21–23;
Report of the Hon. Alvah Crocker, Commissioner, Acting as Superintendent of
Work upon the Troy & Greenfield Railroad and Hoosac Tunnel, Massachusetts
Senate Documents, 1868, no. 20, pp. 19–20.

[86] Report of the Commissioners of the Troy and Greenfield R. R. and Hoosac
Tunnel, Massachusetts *House Documents*, 1865, no. 4, pp. 8–9; Report of the
Commissioners of the Troy and Greenfield R. R. and Hoosac Tunnel, Massachusetts *House Documents*, 1866, no. 4, pp. 7–8; Massachusetts *House Documents*,
1867, no. 30, pp. 18–21, 32–38; Massachusetts *Senate Documents*, 1868, no. 20,
pp. 56–57; Report of the Joint Standing Committee on the Troy and Greenfield
Railroad and Hoosac Tunnel for 1872, Massachusetts *Senate Documents*, 1873, no.
201, pp. 14–15.   [87] Shute, *Rejected Papers*, p. 11.

[88] Report on the Troy and Greenfield Railroad and Hoosac Tunnel, by the

was confronted with water and porous rock, which the opponents of the tunnel described as "quicksand" and "porridge." First the builders abandoned Haupt's entrance, raised the grade of the railroad, and attacked a facing somewhat farther to the east; then they returned approximately to Haupt's location, decided upon an open cut, and when the cut caved in, arched it; they ended by letting a contract to a private contractor who succeeded in meeting the difficulties.[89] By 1869 the headings or adits for this entrance penetrated 4,056 feet into the mountain. On the east end, with hand labor and power drill, the heading was pushed to a distance of 5,282 feet into the mountain.[90]

These measurements were not those for a completed cross section of the tunnel. The veteran consulting engineer, B. H. Latrobe, condemned as technically unwise this pushing of the headings "wildly on" so far in advance of their enlargement *"under the specious idea that popular favor will be best propitiated by a mere progress in running feet."* [91] As for the railroad, which the commissioners practically completed to the eastern tunnel entrance, a later survey showed it to be carelessly constructed and recommended the relocation of three-quarters of the line in order to avoid the excessive curvatures adopted.[92] In sum, the era of state construction was one of inertia, false starts, engineering mistakes, and incompetence. Its expenditures were $3,229,530, a sum between three and four times the sum received by Haupt from the Commonwealth.[93] For once the emotionalism of F. W. Bird was judicious, *"Oh, for one year of Herman Haupt!"* [94]

Joint Special Committee of 1864, Massachusetts *Senate Documents*, 1865, no. 50, pp. 27–28; *Arguments of Stillman B. Gaston and William Gaston Relative to the Petition of Walter Shanly before the Committee on Claims of the Massachusetts Legislature. 1882* (Boston: Wright & Potter, 1882), pp. 6–7.

[89] Massachusetts *House Documents*, 1867, no. 30, pp. 66–68.

[90] Report of the Commissioners of the Troy and Greenfield Railroad and Hoosac Tunnel for the Year 1868, Massachusetts *House Documents*, 1869, no. 192, diagram, p. 26.

[91] Massachusetts *Senate Documents*, 1868, no. 20, p. 53.

[92] Massachusetts *House Documents*, 1869, no. 192, p. 31; Report of Edward S. Philbrick on Surveys of the Troy and Greenfield Railroad, Massachusetts *House Documents*, 1874, no. 9, pp. 4–6, 8–9.

[93] Report of the Commissioners of the Troy and Greenfield Railroad and Hoosac Tunnel, Massachusetts *Senate Documents*, 1874, no. 150, pp. 50–51.

[94] Bird, *The Hoosac Tunnel: Our Financial Maelstrom*, p. 65.

Clearly, if the enterprise were to continue, new direction and new methods were needed. In the late sixties the tunnelites, therefore, determined to let the completion of the work to "enterprising and skillful men, who, while they may enrich themselves, will save to the State a very large proportion of the outlay which is certain to result from the present unsystematic and constantly changing method of operation." [95] Calculating that $5,000,000 would turn the trick, they introduced a bill to that effect. The open demand for this huge sum precipitated a legislative battle unequaled since that of 1862. Although Bird and his fellow purists dressed up old arguments with new vituperation, circumstances were against them. It was an election year and the managers of the tunnel case, scattering manna to those hungry for bridges, harbors, and other railroads, skillfully collected votes by the familiar process of log-rolling. Their bill passed the House by 115 to 91; in the Senate, which had "tunnel on the brain," opposition was negligible. [96] In 1868 Massachusetts chose to issue not more than $5,000,000 in 5 per-cent state scrip and authorized its expenditure under a single contract. The contractors must guarantee to finish the tunnel within seven years; to enforce this provision the last million dollars was to be withheld until the road was completed. [97] Members of the tunnel crew had already selected their contractors, the brothers, Walter and Francis Shanly. Walter Shanly was a Canadian businessman, engineer, politician, and contractor. He had acquired experience on the Canadian canals and a diversity of railroads, of which the Grand Trunk was the most important. [98] Although their bid of $4,623,069 was not the lowest, the governor and council in 1868 awarded them the construction contract; it specified in great detail the

[95] Massachusetts *House Documents*, 1868, no. 87, p. 5.

[96] F. W. Bird, *The Modern Minotaur* (Boston: Wright & Potter, 1868), *The Intolerable Burden* (n. p., 1868), *The Last Agony of the Great Bore* (Boston: E. P. Dutton & Co., 1868), pp. 35–39, 60–66, 72–81; William S. Robinson, *"Warrington," Pen-portraits: A Collection of Personal and Political Reminiscences from 1848 to 1875* (Boston: Mrs. W. S. Robinson, 1877), pp. 326–329; *Death of our Minotaur by Theseus* (Boston: 1868).

[97] *Acts and Resolves Passed by the General Court of Massachusetts, in the Year 1868*, pp. 249–250, 265–266.

[98] George M. Rose, ed., *A Cyclopedia of Canadian Biography: Being Chiefly Men of the Time* (Toronto: Rose Publishing Company, 1886), p. 617.

character of the tunnel and the engineering procedures to be followed.[99]

The Shanlys for the first time applied system to the project. For a year they were busy with preparations, recruiting and training a labor force, providing additional sources of power, rebuilding defective hoisting and pumping apparatus. Then they swung into action. Their labor force of nine hundred men, divided into three shifts, worked a twenty-four-hour day; the power drills, four on a carriage and two carriages to a heading, could drill holes four or five feet deep in an hour and in record instances worked three months without replacement. In 1869 they excavated a distance of 1,688 feet; and in 1872, the year of greatest advance, 4,456. The pattern of their difficulties was by now familiar. The east facing involved few problems; work at the western end, whether from the central shaft or from outside, was hampered by a deluge of water. Once again President Hitchcock's insight had proved defective. Finally, on November 27, 1873, the last rock barrier was holed through and the advancing ends of the tunnel were found to be only 9/16ths of an inch out of the way. In 1875 the first passenger and freight trains passed through the mountain. "The great bore," so ancient a Massachusetts institution that many believed that the Hoosac Tunnel had come over with the *Mayflower*, was at last an accomplished fact. No legislative committee busied itself with investigations into the circumstances attending the loss of 136 lives in its construction; that was an accepted hazard of peace.[100]

But the Shanlys, announcing through attorneys that their loss on the contract was $276,495 and that they had only $500 in

[99] Remonstrance of Carpenter, Odiorne & Gardner, Massachusetts *House Documents*, 1869, no. 145; Massachusetts *House Documents*, 1869, no. 192, pp. 127–142; F. W. Bird, *The Hoosac Tunnel Contract* (Boston: Wright & Potter, 1869), pp. 4–20.

[100] E. S. Martin, *History of the Hoosac Tunnel* (Boston: Alfred Mudge & Son, 1878), pp. 3, 8–15; Report of the Joint Standing Committee on the Troy and Greenfield Railroad and Hoosac Tunnel for 1869, Massachusetts *Senate Documents*, 1870, no. 58, pp. 4–7; Massachusetts *Senate Documents*, 1873, no. 201, pp. 13, 22–23; Evidence and Arguments on the Petition of Walter and Francis Shanly before the Committee on the Hoosac Tunnel and Troy & Greenfield Railroad, Massachusetts *Senate Documents*, 1874, no. 300, pp. 41–43; Robinson, *"Warrington," Pen-portraits*, p. 330.

their pockets, dispatched to the General Court for over a decade a succession of petitions asking reimbursement either for work done beyond contract stipulations or for unforeseen or unjustified losses. In the last category they emphatically placed the state's rigorous insistence upon excavation from the central shaft. Six legislative committees heard them with sympathy, extolled their "fidelity" and "energy" and recommended appropriations. Two appropriations, aggregating $210,495, were made in 1875 and 1887.[101]

V

If it were worthwhile, an imaginative statistician could work out a Hoosac Tunnel cyclical theory, since there was so regular a rhythm to its history. Now in 1873, as in 1854 and 1862, its affairs came to one of their periodic crises. The holing-through in that year compelled a determination as to how the tunnel route was to be operated. A full-dress performance of hearings and legislative battles ensued. All informed opinion realized the necessity of a consolidated route. Since the dreary example of the Boston and Worcester and the Western had demonstrated the folly of end-to-end roads on a through route, the newer route to the West to be successful must have "a vigorous and powerful connection, a formidable and incessant competition, and a heavy individual traffic." [102] If private enterprise were to accomplish this union, theoretically any of four railroad corporations might have been the instrument of it. The Southern Vermont, however, was a mere connection without corporate vigor; the Troy and Boston was a New York corporation, the plaything of a speculative tribe, and a road with a poor dividend record; [103] the Vermont and Massachusetts was a weakling at birth and years had

[101] *Acts and Resolves Passed by the General Court of Massachusetts, in the Years 1874, '75*, p. 884; *Acts and Resolves Passed by the General Court of Massachusetts, in the Years 1886-87*, p. 1173.

[102] Report of the Corporators of the Boston, Hoosac Tunnel and Western Railroad Company, Massachusetts *House Documents*, 1875, no. 9, p. 21.

[103] *Second Hearing on the Hoosac Tunnel Consolidation . . . January 20, 1873*, p. 28; *Report of the Twelfth Hearing on the Hoosac Tunnel Consolidation, before the Committee on Railways. February 20, 1873*, p. 40; Springfield *Daily Republican*, January 31, 1879.

not strengthened it. Only the Fitchburg qualified for the task. Suddenly the Boston and Lowell appeared as the Fitchburg's ally; it sought an amendment to its charter by which it might lease or purchase the roads to Troy.[104] The hearings cast doubt upon the candor and good faith of both of these petitioners. The interest of the Boston and Lowell in the tunnel route, it was said, was merely strategic. It wished to brandish this alternative route before its more direct connections on the route to the Lakes and force them thereby into a workable consolidation.[105] On its part the Fitchburg ostensibly disdained the tunnel route because it did not reach Lake Ontario. Probably it would have been willing to acquire the route to Troy on its own terms. It did not propose to be an evangelist of consolidation at its own expense.[106]

These selfish and trivial maneuvers hardly concerned those who in the great debate of 1873 turned their backs upon private enterprise and advocated state ownership and operation of the new route to the West. As usual they were a strange amalgam. On the one hand were such "practical men" as Otis Clapp, leader of the tunnel ring, and Edward Crane, the dubious railroad promoter. Once more the latter revived his perennial design of a railroad trust, state financed, to hold the stock and operate the railroads from Boston to the golden West.[107] At the other extreme were the railroad reformers, Josiah Quincy, Jr., President Chadbourne of Williams College, and the Massachusetts Board of Railroad Commissioners, for whom Charles Francis Adams, Jr., was the spokesman. This second group believed that the state could acquire the Fitchburg and the Vermont and Massachusetts

---

[104] Report of the Sixth Hearing on the Hoosac Tunnel Consolidation, before the Committee on Railways. February 11, 1873, pp. 3–31; Report of the Tenth Hearing on the Hoosac Tunnel Consolidation, before the Committee on Railways. February 18, 1873, pp. 7–14.

[105] Report of the Thirteenth Hearing on the Hoosac Tunnel Consolidation, before the Committee on Railways. February 26, 1873, pp. 3–20, 26–27.

[106] Report of the Fourth Hearing on the Hoosac Tunnel Consolidation, before the Committee on Railways. February 5, 1873, pp. 20–33; Report of the Fifth Hearing on the Hoosac Tunnel Consolidation, . . . February 6, 1873, pp. 3–19.

[107] Report of the Fourteenth Hearing on the Hoosac Tunnel Consolidation, before the Committee on Railways. February 27, 1873, pp. 16–40; Report of the Fifteenth Hearing on the Hoosac Tunnel Consolidation, before the Committee on Railways. February 28, 1873, pp. 3–10.

either under the recapture provisions of their charters or through the exercise of public domain and unite the roads with the state's property. The most trenchant justification for such a proposal came from the young Adams. Vigorously admitting his allegiance to the doctrine "that our governments should have the least possible connection with industrial enterprises," he nevertheless advocated this "innovation" of state enterprise because the railroad was not in actuality "subject to the laws of supply and demand and of competition." Except at a few points "transportation by rail is a pure, absolute monopoly." One protection against this unhappy condition was regulation; Adams, though chairman of the Board of Railroad Commissioners, stigmatized this device as a "panacea." The other escape from monopoly was state ownership and operation, not of all the railroads, but of enough roads to furnish a competitive measuring rod to private enterprise. Such a dual system would enhance the purity and efficiency of both its parts. "We rely on competition to preserve us from red tape on one side and corruption on the other, and so we do not want to destroy competition by State ownership, but we want to get back to it through mixed ownership. When we stand upon competition, we feel the solid ground under our feet." [108]

To such exposition of "those fundamental laws upon which what is known as the science of political economy is based," the railroads replied only with platitudes about corruption, mismanagement, and business "a football for politicians." [109] A more searching analysis of the issue came from the Massachusetts apostles of *laissez faire*. Edward Atkinson, cotton-mill manufacturer and free trader, presented a memorial, sanctified by the signatures of industrialists and bankers, against the further construction, purchase, acquisition, or operation by the state of "any railroad whatsoever." [110] Part of the accompanying defence was

[108] *Report of the Eighth Hearing on the Hoosac Tunnel Consolidation, before the Committee on Railways. February 14, 1873*, pp. 3–31.

[109] *Report of the Tenth Hearing on the Hoosac Tunnel Consolidation,* . . . *February 18, 1873*, pp. 13, 25–26; *Report of the Eleventh Hearing on the Hoosac Tunnel Consolidation, before the Committee on Railways. February 19, 1873*, pp. 7–11.

[110] *Report of the Fifteenth Hearing on the Hoosac Tunnel Consolidation,* . . . *February 28, 1873*, p. 11.

pure theoretical assertion. Much more convincing was his statistical analysis of some of the original assumptions of railroad schemers. For decades the people of Massachusetts had heard the chatter of how "cheap living" for her factory operatives was a necessary protection for her industrial economy. On this point, with almost the depressing carefulness of a pre-bellum slave-owner, Atkinson had investigated the food costs of his workers. For three months the cost of flour and meat for six hundred and fifty adults was $645; in the same period they produced cloth worth $250,000. Of the food costs perhaps $100 was the cost of transportation over the Boston and Albany; if it had been entirely removed, he could have produced his cloth "either five one-thousandths, or five ten-thousandths of a cent a yard" cheaper — "I don't know which — the decimal was so long I couldn't find the point." Still the issue was the tunnel route. If it reduced freight as much as it promised, Atkinson's firm would pay more in taxes than it saved in transportation costs on food. In reality that route put the "great wheat fields of the West one thousand miles farther off" from Massachusetts. "Therefore, we pray you, confine your statutes to the enforcement of justice, and let each man work out his material welfare under that Great Power which has not arrayed men in selfish antagonism, but who has so ordered our way of life that from the seeming clash of self-interests will surely come that practical coöperation and harmony in society which will ultimately yield abundance to all, and yet harm none." [111]

Bewildered by the whirlwinds of economic theory and railroad tactics, the legislature could not hear the voice of experience. Unwilling to force consolidation under public ownership, it rejected Crane's proposals and all their variants. Loath to surrender its railroad and tunnel to private enterprise, the state in 1875 finally chose to retain them as a link in a disconnected through route and to allow all connecting roads to "enter upon and use" them with their cars and their own motive power at

[111] *Ibid.*, pp. 10–30, 36–37; *Report of the Sixteenth Hearing on the Hoosac Tunnel Consolidation, before the Committee on Railways. March 4, 1873,* pp. 3–11.

"just and reasonable tolls" to be set by the governor and council. Under this arrangement the governor and council were to act as a board of directors; they were to select a state manager to oversee actual operations.[112] Within a few years these arrangements were the subject of contracts between the state and the railroads operating over its property.[113] Whatever the form, the system was a most clumsy and ineffective device. It was an anachronism; its concepts stemmed from the pioneer era of Massachusetts railroad history. With an ironic appropriateness, it was designated the "toll-gate system."

VI

Not only did this policy prevent the effective consolidation which every student recognized as essential for the success of the route, it also completely frustrated all efforts to extend the line farther west. After all, the most aggressive and honest sponsors of the Hoosac always saw that its route must press beyond Troy unless, like the Boston and Albany, a despised and timid servitor, it wished merely to exchange traffic with the New York Central and Vanderbilt. Though this much was clear, a confusion of counsel and tongues arose over the proper route and destination. There were those still under the spell of waterways. Of this archaic clan, some advocated an extension of the road from the Hoosac to Ogdensburg to shorten the unnecessarily long journey over the mosaic of lines between the Boston and Lowell and the Northern of New York. Others fixed their eyes upon ports farther west: Sackett's Harbor, which had "become a great port during the Civil War," or Oswego with its immense grain and flour business. These glib proposals ignored the excessive grades, the ease with which the projected roads could be tapped by connections from New York City, and the complete futility of reaching Lake Ontario until the Welland Canal had been enlarged. As long as three-quarters of the tonnage on the lakes, particularly

[112] Report of the Joint Special Committee on the Hoosac Tunnel and Troy and Greenfield Railroad, Massachusetts *Senate Documents*, 1877, no. 170, pp. 7–9, 25–47; *Acts and Resolves . . . of Massachusetts . . . 1874, '75*, pp. 460–462, 652–655.

[113] *Acts and Resolves Passed by the General Court of Massachusetts, in the Years 1880–81*, p. 237.

the huge vessels that carried single cargoes of 80,000 bushels of grain, could not pass the Niagara barrier, Ogdensburg, Sackett's Harbor, and Oswego were all of a piece — inferior. Still others derided the necessity of reaching the Great Lakes at all. Since the Erie Canal could still carry bulky commodities more cheaply than the railroads, the Hoosac route simply had to tap it at a more convenient spot than Albany or Troy. Schenectady was the favored spot. It was farther west, it was above the tiers of locks descending to the Hudson, it was fifteen miles nearer Boston by the Hoosac route than by the Boston and Albany.[114] Such arguments were reminiscent of the 1820's when Nathan Hale and P. P. F. De Grand chanted the expediency of a railroad to the Hudson.

Those more sensitive to the shadow which the railroads were casting across the waterways of the nation advocated all-rail extensions to the West. From Sackett's Harbor or Oswego the tracks must press on to Buffalo, cross the Niagara River, come to terms with the Great Western, and at last reach the railroad network built or projected by New Englanders in the West — the Michigan Central, the Milwaukee and St. Paul, the Northern Pacific. If the destination were Schenectady, a further route must utilize existing charters to parallel the New York Central to Oswego or Buffalo, or, turning south, connect with the Delaware and Hudson, the great anthracite road, or with the Erie Railroad at Binghamton, or, through eighty miles of new construction, with the great Pennsylvania Railroad. Both the Erie and the Pennsylvania were western roads, enemies of the New York Central whose grip upon the New England roads must be broken.[115]

Discouragements accumulated. Such proposals antagonized

[114] Massachusetts *House Documents*, 1875, no. 9, pp. 17–19, appendix, lxxx–xcii; Edward Crane, *An Abstract of an Address of Edward Crane, Esq., on the Subject of Transportation, at the Green Room, State House, February 13th, 14th, and 18th, 1868* (Boston: Wright & Potter, 1868), pp. 10–17, 37–40; George P. deT. Glazebrook, *A History of Transportation in Canada* (New Haven: Yale University Press, 1938), pp. 416, 417, 420; Charles F. Adams, Jr., "Boston," *North American Review*, CVI (1868), 566–576.

[115] Massachusetts *House Documents*, 1875, no. 9, pp. 12–17, appendix, lxxviii–lxxx; *Railroad Gazette*, XII (1880), p. 23.

powerful railroad interests in Massachusetts; the solicitude of
the Boston and Albany lest the merchants and capitalists of
Boston spend "their own and the State's money in extending new
roads over untried territory," [116] was touching. This westward
extension, furthermore, must pass through a New York State
hardly attuned to encourage a promising New England invasion
and must challenge New York railroads hardly likely to accept
passively an inferior status. The financial outlay ran into the
millions. Adams showed in 1868 that it should be easy to raise
the capital in a community that had in the previous seven years
sunk more than fifty millions in bubble schemes — coal, oil,
copper and gold — but he overestimated the gullibility of Boston's investors and of course had not anticipated the financial
punishment inflicted by the crisis of 1873.[117] Nor was the Commonwealth, however generous it may have been with the tunnel,
likely to tax its citizens to finance a road outside its borders.

At last, in the seventies a group of private investors determined
to undertake the project. The list of original promoters included
Oliver and F. L. Ames, a family forever associated with the Union
Pacific; Elisha Atkins, Boston merchant trading to the West
Indies and prominent follower of Edward Crane; William Claflin,
a somewhat more discriminating disciple; and George R. Blanchard, of the Erie Railroad. The president of the enterprise was
General William L. Burt, former postmaster of Boston and Civil
War veteran, in short, politician, lawyer, soldier, and railroad
official, a common type in the era.[118] In New York this group
chartered the Boston, Hoosac Tunnel and Western. Their line
ran from the Southern Vermont to Schenectady and thence along
the Mohawk Valley to Lake Ontario. They also petitioned Massachusetts for permission to lease, purchase, or build a railroad from
Greenfield to Boston and, under restrictions protecting other

---

[116] *Seventh Annual Report of the Directors of the Boston and Albany Railroad
Co. to the Stockholders, January, 1875* (Springfield: Clark W. Bryan & Company,
1875), p. 10.

[117] Adams, "Boston," p. 575.

[118] Abstract of the Proceedings before the Joint Special Committee of the Legislature on the Hoosac Tunnel and Troy and Greenfield Railroad, Massachusetts
House Documents, 1877, no. 201, pp. 4, 32–34; Hartford *Courant*, March 17, 1877.

roads, for the right to operate the tunnel and Troy and Greenfield Railroad.[119]

Frustration dogged the enterprise. Massachusetts legislators, affecting to believe the Boston, Hoosac Tunnel and Western a potential Trojan horse for designing New Yorkers, gave it no privileges in their Commonwealth.[120] "It is better to try the safe experiments first, and this toll-gate system is a safe experiment." [121] The New York railroads fought the New England interloper. The Troy and Boston and Mr. Vanderbilt compelled Burt to build, amidst a pressure of law suits and injunctions, a route parallel to the Southern Vermont, a road under perpetual lease to the Troy and Boston.[122] When the Boston, Hoosac Tunnel and Western had crossed the Hudson and come down into the Mohawk Valley, hopeful of consolidating existing charters into a line to Buffalo or Oswego or of connecting with the famous parallel to the Central, the New York, West Shore and Buffalo and the New York, Ontario and Western, the New York courts broke up the former procedure and the Central leased the New York, West Shore and Buffalo when it emerged from bankruptcy in 1885.[123] Thus Burt's vision of a route to the West went glimmering. It had always sounded like "stage thunder." [124] Still the Boston, Hoosac Tunnel and Western retained a connection with the Erie Railroad and with a newcomer farther south, the Delaware, Lackawanna and Western.

For the tunnel route, therefore, the New York Central remained the chief connection with the West. The alliance had begun in the sixties when the Troy and Boston, even before the completion of the tunnel, had formed a through line with its western neigh-

[119] Massachusetts *House Documents*, 1877, no. 201, pp. 3–18, 155–156, 166–184.
[120] Massachusetts *Senate Documents*, 1877, no. 170, pp. 47–66.
[121] *Ibid.*, p. 68.
[122] *An Appeal to the Legislature of the State of New York by the Boston, Hoosac Tunnel, and Western Railway Company of New York. An Infamous Bill! ! !* (n. p., n. d.) ; The Troy & Boston Railroad Company *v.* The Boston, Hoosac Tunnel & Western Railway Company et al., 86 *New York*, 107; Springfield *Daily Republican*, February 16, March 7, 1878, July 4, 8, 1879.
[123] H. V. Poor, *Manual of the Railroads of the United States for 1883* (New York: Henry V. Poor, 1883), p. 123; H. V. Poor, *Manual of the Railroads of the United States for 1886* (New York: H. V. & H. W. Poor, n. d.), pp. 489–490.
[124] Springfield *Daily Republican*, February 10, 1881.

bor.[125] It was cemented in 1875 when a number of roads established the Hoosac Tunnel Fast Freight Line, which in two years had over three thousand freight cars in operation and agents soliciting and forwarding freight throughout the West. The Central and its allied lines contributed heavily to the car pool of this organization; in turn the eastern members, particularly the Troy and Boston, discriminated in rates against the Central's competitors.[126] In this setting Vanderbilt's assurances to Massachusetts inquirers that "no discrimination whatever should be made by the Central Road, as between the Boston & Albany and the Tunnel routes" was understandable and charmingly ingenuous.[127] If the Tunnel route consorted with the Central's enemies, punishment was swift and condign. In 1884, when the Fitchburg and others dallied with the Erie, the West Shore, and the Delaware, Lackawanna and Western, the New York Central abruptly withdrew its passenger and freight services from the tunnel line.[128] Such disharmony did not last long. In the nineties the Fitchburg co-operated willingly. For all practical purposes it withdrew from the through passenger business to the West; it was content with the freight business which the Central turned over to it.[129] These friendly relationships were reinforced by purchases of stock in the Troy and Boston and the Fitchburg by the Vanderbilts and the Central interests.[130]

Meanwhile the state owned and partially operated a railroad property. Expenses heaped up from every side. For one thing,

[125] *Report of the Second Hearing on the Hoosac Tunnel Consolidation,* . . . *January 30, 1873,* p. 30; *Report of the Fourth Hearing on the Hoosac Tunnel Consolidation,* . . . *February 5, 1873,* p. 3.

[126] Massachusetts *House Documents,* 1877, no. 201, pp. 41–46, 48, 55–75, 93–100; Report of the Manager of the Troy & Greenfield Railway and Hoosac Tunnel, Massachusetts *Senate Documents,* 1877, no. 44, pp. 25–27.

[127] Massachusetts *House Documents,* 1875, no. 9, pp. 11–12.

[128] *Forty-third Annual Report of the Directors of the Fitchburg Railroad Company, for the Year Ending Sept. 30, 1884* (Boston: Rand Avery Supply Company, 1885), p. 6.

[129] *Argument of George A. Torrey, Counsel of the Fitchburg Railroad before the Railroad Committee of the Massachusetts Legislature in Favor of an Act to Authorize a Lease of the Fitchburg Railroad Company to the Boston and Maine Railroad, April 30 and May 18, 1900* (Boston: Rand Avery Supply Co., 1900), pp. 18–19.

[130] *Ibid.,* p. 21; Springfield *Daily Republican,* July 4, 8, 1879, July 13, 1887, December 22, 1899.

it was soon discovered that, though the tunnel was done, it was far from complete, and that, though the Troy and Greenfield Railroad ran, it was in a deplorable state of dilapidation.[131] To re-grade the railroad for double tracks, to lay the roadbed with steel rails, and to relocate the line to avoid excessive curvatures, more millions must follow the millions already spent. Between 1873, when the Shanlys transferred the finished property, and 1884, when the last appropriations were made, the state spent approximately $4,640,000 on the tunnel. Included in this sum were further issues of $3,372,500 in state scrip.[132] The expenses of operation, as the toll-gate acts had enjoined, were a matter of contracts between the state manager and the connecting roads. By the terms of such instruments the Troy and Boston and the Boston, Hoosac Tunnel and Western operated the line west of North Adams, and the Fitchburg and the New Haven and North-ampton operated the route east of that city.[133] By leasing the Vermont and Massachusetts in 1874, the Fitchburg reached the state's road at Greenfield; by building northward, the New Haven and Northampton connected at Conway Junction.[134]

Of the gross receipts from the traffic over the state's railroad, one-half was given to the railroads—their pressure had forced the proportion to this figure — and the other half went to Massachusetts. The railroads' share was estimated to equal the cost of their operations; the Commonwealth from its remainder bore the expenses for maintenance and administration and financed a trivial fraction of its more permanent expenditures.

[131] Massachusetts *House Documents*, 1875, no. 9, pp. 4–8.

[132] *Acts and Resolves . . . of Massachusetts, . . . 1872, '73*, pp. 869–870; *Acts and Resolves . . . of Massachusetts, . . . 1874, '75*, pp. 459, 842–843; *Acts and Resolves . . . of Massachusetts, . . . 1876, '77*, pp. 662–664; *Acts and Resolves . . . of Massachusetts, . . . 1878–79*, pp. 266–268, 275, 278, 614–615; *Acts and Resolves . . . of Massachusetts, . . . 1880–81*, pp. 194–195, 611–612; *Acts and Resolves . . . of Massachusetts, . . . 1882–1883*, pp. 174, 462–463; *Acts and Resolves . . . of Massachusetts, . . . 1884–85*, p. 186.

[133] Report of the Manager of the Troy & Greenfield Railroad and Hoosac Tunnel, Massachusetts *House Documents*, 1884 no. 5, p. 11.

[134] *Thirty-third Annual Report of the Directors of the Fitchburg Railroad Company, Made at the Annual Meeting of That Corporation, January 26, 1875* (Boston: 1875), pp. 3–8; *Forty-fourth Annual Report of the New Haven & Northampton Railroad Company. Eleventh Since the Expiration of the Leases, September 30, 1880* (New Haven: Tuttle, Morehouse & Taylor, 1881), pp. 6–7.

The state's income was never sufficient to pay the interest on the debt incurred for construction of railroad and tunnel.[135] The prospect before the Commonwealth was dismal. Although the sinking fund had accumulated sufficiently to discharge the portion of the debt maturing before July, 1891, taxation or other devices would have to meet payments after that date.[136] If these grim details were not enough to compel a change in the system, the failure of the toll-gate arrangement to forge an effective route to the West was an additional one. As critics had foreseen, the toll-gate system condemned the "state property to lie idle, like a village common, accessible to all passers-by and everybody's cow, but the very antipode of successful farming."[137]

VII

By the eighties all signs pointed to the likelihood that this dismal experiment was over. The reigning Republican party believed in a divorce between the state government and railroad enterprises. The note had already been sounded in the case of the state stock in the Boston and Albany. Nor were those outside the party fold convinced that any other policy was wise. In 1885 Governor Robinson informed the General Court that the toll-gate system had failed. To its costliness there was no end. One alternative, an exclusive management by the state, was unsound. "A republican government cannot safely and efficiently manage" a railroad business. The frequent changes in public office, "salutary as they may be in point of political advantage, are radically destructive in the management of business affairs, for which experience, sagacity and unity of action are essential." Only a sale to private interests was feasible.[138] Consequently, in 1885 the legislature passed an act to embody the recommended pro-

[135] Report of the Manager of the Troy & Greenfield Railroad and Hoosac Tunnel, Massachusetts *Senate Documents*, 1878, no. 95, pp. 22–25; Report of the Manager of the Troy & Greenfield Railroad and Hoosac Tunnel, Massachusetts *House Documents*, 1884, no. 5, pp. 6–11, 12, 16–23; Springfield *Daily Republican*, January 4, December 17, 1879, February 2, August 18, 1880, March 25, 1881; *Acts and Resolves . . . of Massachusetts, . . . 1886–87*, pp. 1202–1203.

[136] *Acts and Resolves Passed by the General Court of Massachusetts, in the Year 1885*, p. 967.

[137] Springfield *Daily Republican*, April 21, 1877.

[138] *Acts and Resolves . . . of Massachusetts, . . . 1884–85*, pp. 969–978.

gram. The state prescribed two procedures. Either a new corporation could purchase the Hoosac, the Troy and Greenfield Railroad, and other companies to form a continuous route from the coast to the Massachusetts state line, or an existing corporation or corporations could fulfill that requirement. This consolidation was authorized to carry its road by lease of other roads as far as Buffalo, there to make connections with roads still farther west. The road could not issue stock beyond certain prescribed quotas, charge roads connecting with the Troy and Greenfield rates above a certain maximum, nor sell nor lease its road or franchise without the consent of the legislature.[139]

Then the state sought purchasers. A sale to New York capitalists was not to be thought of. Governor Robinson gave warning that the state's valuable property would not be sold "to any management that should prevent or destroy competition, or should regard chiefly the promotion of commerce with other seaports instead of our own capital city, or that should subordinate the interests of Massachusetts to the advancement of any other state or community."[140] Massachusetts buyers were coy. Finally, in 1887, after two years of rumor, maneuver, and delay, the Fitchburg bought the tunnel and railroad for $5,000,000 in its bonds, on which interest was to rise from 3 to 4 per cent over the years, and for $5,000,000 in common stock. Of the latter securities, the state held the entire issue, since the pre-existing common stock of the Fitchburg was transformed into preferred.[141] The common stock was worth little. Not entitled to a return until the preferred had earned 4 per cent, it never paid the state a dividend; it was generally quoted in the market at a maximum of $25 a share.[142] In short, this second $5,000,000 was a graceful gesture to impress public opinion. The state was to have three representatives upon the Fitchburg directorate.[143]

[139] *Ibid.*, pp. 747–753.

[140] *Ibid.*, p. 975.

[141] *Forty-sixth Annual Report of the Directors of the Fitchburg Railroad Company, for the Year Ending September 30, 1887* (Boston: Cashman, Keating & Co., 1888), pp. 27–31; *Acts and Resolves . . . of Massachusetts, . . . 1886–87*, pp. 1203–1204.

[142] Martin, *A Century of Finance*, pp. 154–157.

[143] *Forty-sixth Annual Report . . . of the Fitchburg . . . 1887*, p. 33.

Then the Fitchburg proceeded to the acquisition of the Troy and Boston and of the Boston, Hoosac Tunnel and Western. Whereas the state had received considerably less than its property had cost it, these New York roads were handsomely rewarded. The Troy and Boston, whose capitalization and bond issues totaled $4,278,600, whose stock had not paid a dividend in eight years, and which was operating with a deficit, received $4,000,000 — contingently somewhat more — in bonds and preferred stock of the consolidated Fitchburg.[144] The stocks and bonds of the Boston, Hoosac Tunnel and Western, totaling $5,551,000, the Fitchburg in effect purchased for $7,000,000. To be sure, $2,000,000 of the price was in Fitchburg common stock an entity of dubious value; on the other hand, the common stock of the Boston, Hoosac Tunnel and Western was currently quoted at from $3 to $4 a share and the preferred stock of the Fitchburg for which it was exchanged at varied ratios never sold under $90 the year of its issue.[145] Finally, in 1891 the Fitchburg purchased the Southern Vermont from the Commonwealth of Massachusetts for $175,000 in 4 per-cent bonds. The annual return to the state from the road was thus $7,000. Massachusetts had originally paid $200,000 for the Southern Vermont and leased it to the Troy and Boston for an annual rental of $12,000.[146] The dichotomy between the returns to the state and to private corporations inevitably stirred comment. Though there were some who excoriated the governor for selling the state's property at a loss, the general opinion was relief that the state had at last "cast the old elephant off." [147] On the other hand, the high prices for the Troy and Boston and the Boston, Hoosac Tunnel and Western, roads which the Fitchburg had once looked upon "as a

[144] *Ibid.*, pp. 35–41; H. V. Poor, *Manual of the Railroads of the United States for 1887* (New York: H. V. & H. W. Poor, n. d.), p. 333.

[145] *Forty-sixth Annual Report . . . of the Fitchburg . . . 1887*, pp. 42–46; Poor, *Manual of the Railroads . . . 1887*, p. 115; *Commercial and Financial Chronicle*, XLIV (1887), 620; Martin, *A Century of Finance*, p. 154.

[146] *Fiftieth Annual Report of the Directors of the Fitchburg Railroad Company, for the Year Ending June 30, 1891* (Boston: E. L. Drisko, n. d.), pp. 9–10; Poor, *History of the Railroads and Canals of the United States*, p. 77.

[147] Hartford *Courant*, January 3, 8, 1887; Springfield *Daily Republican*, June 28, 1883, December 29, 1886, January 6, 7, 1887.

countryman looks upon a ghost," convinced a minority of the latter's stockholders that its president or his family made speculative gains by the transaction.[148]

Though personal gain by officials was not a reason, the sudden transformation of the Fitchburg from a road quite satisfied with the toll-gate system into an aggressive apostle of expansion and consolidation required explanation. No sudden revelation that a united line to the West was required for Boston's good or the state's welfare accounted for the change. No more in the eighties than in the seventies did the Fitchburg feel called upon to sacrifice itself for visions of railroad statesmen. On the other hand, by the eighties the pioneering period of the route was over. Technically the state had brought its property to as near a state of completion as any railroad ever reached; the purchaser would have neither to trim the tunnel walls nor lay a double track. Ten years of actual operation had demonstrated that the road would have a traffic. The Fitchburg was uneasy, moreover, lest it lose the fruits of this experimental decade. Recall that in the mid-eighties the Central knocked it sharply across the knuckles for its waywardness. Furthermore it was conceivable that the Central or others might inspire the Troy and Boston or the Boston, Hoosac Tunnel and Western to coalesce with the Boston and Lowell and its leased Central Massachusetts, projected across that state to Northampton and a junction with the Troy and Greenfield. By the purchase of the state's works a new tunnel line without the Fitchburg could then come into being. Whether the Fitchburg was to be worthy friend or foe of the Central, consolidation was prelude. "Your directors," wrote those of the Fitchburg in 1888, "are satisfied that all of those roads were necessary, and that they were obtained at the lowest possible price." [149]

---

[148] *Caution. "Common" Stockholders Will Please Not Ask These Questions of their Forty-Dollars-a-Day President as "It Makes Him NERVOUS to Be Questioned," Besides, if Truthfully Answered "Common" Stockholders Might Get Awfully NERVOUS Themselves!!* (n. p., n. d.); Springfield *Daily Republican*, January 30, May 7, 1889.

[149] *Forty-seventh Annual Report of the Directors of the Fitchburg Railroad Company, for the Year Ending September 30, 1888* (Boston: Cashman, Keating & Co., n. d.), p. 11; Springfield *Daily Republican*, December 6, 12, 1886, March 9,

Once under way consolidation did not stop. Throughout the nineties there were rumors and rumors of rumors of further combination. Then at the end of the decade the Boston and Maine stepped forth an avowed suitor for the Fitchburg's hand. The Commonwealth was in a strategic position to forbid or bless the banns. Through the state directors it had representation on the Fitchburg's board, it was the largest holder of the capital stock, and by statute its assent was required for the consolidation of all railroads entering Boston. Governor Winthrop Murray Crane utilized these advantages to the full. First the Boston and Maine had to give assurances that it was not the agent for some shadowy New York capitalist or corporation; then it had to raise its preliminary offer of $1,000,000 for the state's stock to one of $5,000,000 payable in 3 per-cent Boston and Maine gold bonds.[150] This bonanza was hailed by the railroad commission as "a rare instance of the application to a public transaction of a business sagacity exceptional even in private affairs." [151]

Though this arrangement quieted the opposition of the threatened state, it did not still the factional differences among the Fitchburg stockholders — indeed it heightened them — over the expediency of the lease. In the end, an energetic protective committee secured an affirmative vote.[152] With the Commonwealth's permission the Boston and Maine, itself an accumulation of consolidations, began in 1900 the operation of the Fitchburg.[153]

July 13, 1887; H. V. Poor, *Manual of the Railroads of the United States for 1886* (New York: H. V. & H. W. Poor, n. d.), p. 170; *Argument of George A. Torrey, Counsel of the Fitchburg Railroad before the Railroad Committee of the Massachusetts Legislature in Favor of an Act to Authorize a Lease of the Fitchburg Railroad Company to the Boston and Maine Railroad. April 30 and May 18, 1900* (Boston: Rand Avery Supply Co., 1900), pp. 4–5.

[150] *Statement of Mr. Lucius Tuttle, President of the Boston and Maine Railroad, Before the Railroad Committee of the Massachusetts Legislature in Favor of an Act to Authorize a Lease of the Fitchburg Railroad Company to the Boston and Maine Railroad. April 23 and 24 and May 15, 1900* (Boston: Rand Avery Supply Co., 1900), pp. 5–8; *Argument of George A. Torrey,* pp. 15–17, 52.

[151] Massachusetts *Thirty-second Annual Report of the Board of Railroad Commissioners. January, 1901,* p. 46.

[152] *Statement of Mr. Lucius Tuttle,* pp. 8–10, 39–40; *Argument of George A. Torrey,* pp. 7–10.

[153] *Acts and Resolves Passed by the General Court of Massachusetts, in the Year 1900,* pp. 364–366.

The arguments for union were impressive. The Boston and Maine had unsatisfactory connections with the West, the Fitchburg filled the need; the Fitchburg had little westbound traffic with which to tempt the western connections, the Boston and Maine gathered goods and commodities from northern and eastern New England; the Fitchburg had a cramped Boston waterfront, the Boston and Maine had extensive facilities. Such considerations, coupled with a slightly higher return under the lease upon the Fitchburg securities, won the benign assent of the Vanderbilt stockholdings to the arrangement.[154] Anyway the Central was leasing the Boston and Albany.

VIII

Now comes the time to appraise the accomplishments of seventy-five years of dreams and effort. Although attempts to make it a through passenger line met with continued frustration, the Hoosac became a great freight route. Before the tunnel was opened, the Fitchburg had had a tiny western business, — for instance, in 1875 it carried 718,262 tons of freight from and to Massachusetts stations as compared to 8,504 tons to and from other states.[155] The completion of the tunnel revolutionized the situation. Ten years later, in 1885, the Fitchburg was bringing to Boston over a million barrels of flour, approximately three and three-quarter million bushels of corn, over a million bushels of wheat.[156] By 1895 it had become the bulk carrier *par excellence:* as the grain and livestock of the West poured down its rails to Boston, it provided 60 per cent of the commodities for the export trade of the city.[157] These achievements were secured through the secular growth of imports into New England and through a diversion of traffic from other New England roads.

[154] *Statement of Mr. Lucius Tuttle*, pp. 13–18, 34–37; *Argument of George A. Torrey*, pp. 12–15.

[155] *Statement of Mr. Lucius Tuttle*, pp. 28–29; Massachusetts *Seventh Annual Report of the Board of Railroad Commissioners. January, 1876*, p. 170.

[156] Massachusetts *Seventeenth Annual Report of the Board of Railroad Commissioners. January, 1886*, pp. 65–66, 68.

[157] Massachusetts *Twenty-seventh Annual Report of the Board of Railroad Commissioners. January, 1896*, pp. 77–79; Annual Report of the State Directors of the Fitchburg Railway, Massachusetts *House Documents*, 1900, no. 47, p. 2.

In order to create a new traffic beyond that which would normally accrue to Boston, the Hoosac route would have had to steal commodities away from the roads serving the other Atlantic ports. For this accomplishment the one certain device was lower rates. The sponsors of the route had for decades proceeded on the assumptions that the Hoosac could carry freights more cheaply than the Boston and Albany, that this ability would be mirrored in lower rates, and that the competition of the tunnel route would bring about general reductions. All proved to be false. By the mid-nineties the funded debt of the Fitchburg was three times that of the Boston and Albany and the operating expenses per train mile practically identical.[158] As a competitor, the combination of the Grand Trunk and its New England extensions was a more desperate slasher of charges. Finally, the Hoosac did not determine its own rates. On through business from the West, the prize for which the road was built, the rate, as the Fitchburg report of 1883 confessed, "is fixed by the managers of the great trunk lines, and is virtually beyond our control." [159] The Fitchburg had to accept its share of this return and by cutting costs make the best possible profits for itself. As a through route, though it did little for Boston which would not otherwise have been done, its availability made unnecessary the enlargement of the other routes to carry an increased business. As a through route, it gave stations along its lines west of Fitchburg lower rates than they might otherwise have enjoyed. To this extent northern Massachusetts, the locale of the tunnel ring, had correctly foreseen its own advantage.

At what cost had the state bought this limited accomplishment? By 1885, when the General Court passed the act for the sale of the tunnel and railroad, the state had incurred a funded debt of $14,198,028 on their behalf.[160] As Edward Atkinson never

[158] Massachusetts *Twenty-seventh Annual Report of the Board of Railroad Commissioners. January, 1896*, appendix, pp. 12,100; *Argument of George A. Torrey*, p. 27.

[159] *Forty-first Annual Report of the Directors of the Fitchburg Railroad Company, Made at the Annual Meeting of That Corporation, January 30, 1883* (Boston: Franklin Press, Rand, Avery, & Company, 1883), p. 16.

[160] Report of the Auditor of Accounts, Massachusetts *Public Documents*, 1885, no. 6, p. 383.

tired of pointing out, the taxes of every man were increased to pay a 5 per-cent interest on this debt.[161] The principal turned out not to be an eternal burden. Though the original sinking fund was not enough to discharge the state's indebtedness, the money received from the Fitchburg in 1886 and deposited to the sinking fund made it possible for all practical purposes to discharge the entire state debt at maturity.[162] Meanwhile the state had been paying interest on its investment. By 1885 such payments had totaled $9,975,210.[163] Before the last state securities were liquidated in 1897, an additional interest payment of $4,683,-157 had been made. The cost of the tunnel, principal and interest, by January 1, 1898 was $28,856,396.[164] Since the state debt was met by sinking funds and the Commonwealth received an unexpected bonus of $5,000,000 in 1900, the net loss was approximately $9,500,000. The income from the Boston and Maine bonds might further reduce this deficit.

A half-century earlier, the counsel of the Western had anticipated the unhappy outcome. "If Massachusetts ever embarks in this enterprise, I would suggest the propriety of a little ornamental work at the entrance of the Hoosac tunnel and on this I would place a marble slab with this inscription: — 'A Monument to the Folly of Massachusetts.'"[165] The inscription was just enough if applied to the whole period of state aid, construction, and operation. In the twentieth century, however, New England could have ill afforded to dispense with this gateway opened to the West through Hoosac Mountain.

[161] Abstract of the Proceedings of the Joint Special Committee of the Legislature, on the Hoosac Tunnel and Troy and Greenfield Railroad, Massachusetts *House Documents*, 1877, no. 200, pp. 97–102.

[162] *Acts and Resolves . . . of Massachusetts*, . . . *1886-87*, p. 1205.

[163] Massachusetts *Public Documents*, 1885, no. 6, p. 10.

[164] Report of the Auditor of Accounts, Massachusetts *Public Documents*, 1898, no. 6, pp. 576–577.

[165] Ansel Phelps, Jr., *Hoosac Tunnel. Speech of Ansel Phelps, Jr., Counsel for Remonstrants, before the Joint Special Committee of the Legislature, on Petition of the Troy and Greenfield Railroad Corporation, for State Aid, April 6, 1853* (Boston: Eastburn's Press, 1853), p. 33.

XIII

THE FAILURE OF A ROUTE

"The same class of people are afraid of consolidation that are afraid of ghosts; it is they who have never seen ghosts that are afraid of them; they are not familiar with ghosts; they never happened to meet a ghost; they are entirely unacquainted with ghosts; and consequently they are afraid of a ghost. Now whenever you find a man who is scared of consolidation, or what is here called consolidation, he is a man who knows nothing of the practical working operations and savings to the people by the union of roads." — A. W. Sulloway, quoted in Ira D. Colby, The Railroad Question (1887) p. 31.

I

When the Boston and Lowell was pleading for a program of consolidation at the Hoosac Tunnel hearings of 1873, its manager, speaking of the northern line of railroads to the West, admitted they had "not been able to compete with the Boston and Albany." [1] There were many reasons for this inability, but at the forefront stood the number of independent and quarrelsome corporations comprising the route. After all, between Boston and Albany there had been only two different corporations, between Boston and Troy only five; while between Boston and Montreal or Boston and Ogdensburg there were seven. Their rails traversed five different jurisdictions — Massachusetts, New Hampshire, Vermont, New York, and Canada. To an extraordinary degree

[1] *Report of the Tenth Hearing on the Hoosac Tunnel Consolidation, before the Committee on Railways. February 18, 1873*, p. 9.

the character of the segmented enterprises changed as state lines were crossed.

The base of the line was the Boston and Lowell, one of the pioneer three of Massachusetts. A short line, it looked on the map a mere local enterprise; instead, it excited the incredulous admiration of observers by carrying, on rare occasions, more wheat than the Boston and Albany and the Grand Junction Railroad combined.[2] Of its Massachusetts connections, the most important was a virtual amalgamation with the Nashua and Lowell, by which both roads had the same general manager and president. Indeed the joint roads were often denominated the Boston, Lowell and Nashua. With the expiration of its thirty-year monopoly between Boston and Lowell, the long dreaded competition by a parallel from the Boston and Maine was open and unhampered. The Boston and Lowell retaliated with the construction of branches into its rival's territory. This competition, however, always stopped short of a war of extermination; instead it assumed a bland and reasonable air.[3] Meanwhile at Boston the road expanded its terminal facilities. In the metropolis it erected a magnificent and costly passenger station. Across the harbor it bought the Mystic flats and built thither a connection crossing only two streets at grade rather than the forty or fifty of the Boston and Albany's Grand Junction. On the new site the railroad was erecting seawalls and wharves, dredging channels and filling the low land.[4] The financial strain of the mid-seventies shattered an eleven-year record of 8 per-cent dividends; the upswing of the eighties never brought complete recovery on this score.[5] Still the Boston and Lowell was a dowager enterprise.

In New Hampshire, at Nashua, the line of the Concord Rail-

[2] Massachusetts *Second Annual Report of the Board of Railroad Commissioners. January, 1871*, pp. xxxvi–xxxvii; Massachusetts *Seventh Annual Report of the Board of Railroad Commissioners. January, 1876*, p. 122.

[3] *Report of the Directors of the Boston and Lowell Railroad Corporation, for the Year 1873, with Statements of Twelve Months Accounts to September 30, 1873* (Boston: James F. Cotter & Co., 1873), pp. 9–10; *Report of the Directors of the Boston and Lowell Railroad Corporation, for the Year 1874, with Statements of Twelve Months Accounts to September 30, 1874* (Boston: James F. Cotter, 1874), pp. 7–10.

[4] *Report of the Sixth Hearing on the Hoosac Tunnel Consolidation, before the Committee on Railways. February 11, 1873*, pp. 20–23.

[5] Joseph G. Martin, *A Century of Finance. Martin's History of the Boston*

road began. One of its admirers at the Hoosac Tunnel hearing described the route with justified superlatives. "There is no richer piece of railroad property in the United States than the Concord Railroad. I think its earnings are something like seventy per cent on its capital. From the peculiar formation of the country the railroads pour into the Valley at Concord the whole business of the northern and western part of the State. From Concord it runs down a perfectly level road to Nashua." [6] Its capital stock with a par value of $50 often had the highest market appreciation of any railroad stock in New England; its annual dividends of 10 per cent were never threatened.[7] It was an indigenous enterprise. Two-thirds of its stockholders lived in New Hampshire; two-thirds of its stock was held there.[8] Such facts gave reality to the tiresomely reiterated statements of its officials that the Concord was the fortress of New Hampshire virtues and interests, always in danger of attack from alien capitalists. The assertion, however, was made not because of its truth but because of its usefulness.

From Concord the route to the West could continue over the Boston, Concord and Montreal to Wells River and thence over the Connecticut and Passumpsic and other roads to Montreal. Not content with this mileage, the Boston, Concord and Montreal filled the White Mountain region with its tracks and pushed northward a tentacle to a junction with the Grand Trunk.[9] But the traditional connection beyond Concord was the Northern which cut across the state to White River Junction, where it connected with the Vermont roads leading to Canada and to Ogdensburg on Lake Ontario. Neither the Boston, Concord and Montreal nor the Northern was in the Concord's image. As far as the law permitted, their boards of directors gave representation to the Boston interests that financed them. The counsel for the

Stock and Money Markets, One Hundred Years. From January, 1798 to January, 1898 (Boston: J. G. Martin, 1898), pp. 149, 152–153.

[6] *Report of the Thirteenth Hearing on the Hoosac Tunnel Consolidation, before the Committee on Railways. February 26, 1873,* p. 18.

[7] Martin, *A Century of Finance,* pp. 149, 152–153, 161.

[8] *Forty-first Annual Report of the Railroad Commissioners of the State of New Hampshire, 1885,* p. 150.

[9] Henry V. Poor, *Manual of the Railroads of the United States for 1880* (New York: H. V. & H. W. Poor, 1880), p. 20.

Northern in 1873 informed a committee of the Massachusetts General Court, "the Northern railroad was mainly built, and is now owned, by Massachusetts capital. Of its directors, four are citizens of Massachusetts. At least three-quarters of its capital is held within this State." [10] There was, however, one distinction between the Northern and the Boston, Concord and Montreal. The former generally paid dividends; the latter did not.[11]

II

At White River Junction the through route touched that perpetual bankrupt and debtor, the Vermont Central. The latter's first receivership, the earliest large-scale one in the nation, had got under way in the later fifties; the early sixties finally gave this receivership shape. A board of receivers and managers ran both the Vermont Central and the Vermont and Canada, leased by the Central for a guaranteed rental, presumably a first lien upon the earnings of the lessee. The receivers and managers were assisted and advised by trustees of the first and second mortgage bonds, committees appointed by bondholders, and the directors and officials of the corporations involved. Whatever transitory shape the phantasmagoria of organization assumed, the same individuals were in charge. Always in the ranks of receivers and managers was J. Gregory Smith, president of the Central, a trustee of its first mortgage bonds, and its largest stockholder. His brother, W. C. Smith, was from time to time a director and president of the Vermont and Canada, treasurer and second vice-president of the Vermont Central, trustee of the second mortgage bonds, and eventually a receiver and manager. G. G. Smith, a son of J. Gregory Smith, was clerk of the Vermont Central, and Lawrence Brainerd, his father-in-law, was a perpetual receiver and manager.[12] Such outsiders as were associated with the Smiths were

[10] *Report of the Thirteenth Hearing on the Hoosac Tunnel Consolidation,* . . . *February 26, 1873,* p. 3.

[11] Martin, *A Century of Finance,* pp. 160–161, 162a.

[12] *Report of Special Masters in the Case of Vermont and Canada R. R. Co. vs. Vermont Central R. R. Co. and Others. Filed April 24, 1877* (St. Albans: Advertiser Print, 1877), pp. 17, 29, 32, 36, 46–47, 55, 77, 78; *Report of the Joint Special Committee to Investigate the Vt. Central Railroad Management. Ordered by Joint Resolution Adopted at the Biennial Session, 1872,* p. 80.

John Smith

J. Gregory Smith

W. C. Smith

A VERMONT RAILROAD DYNASTY

A Trestle on the Portland and Ogdensburg

THE CONQUEST OF CRAWFORD NOTCH

soon taken into the family circle and given a share in the perquisites of power.

Aside from labyrinth entwined with labyrinth, the receivership had another aspect of novelty. Referees, special masters, and puzzled justices never tired of asserting it was not as other receiverships were: it was to wear a corporate air and manage its properties as a corporate enterprise.[13] A more formal materialization of this concept occurred in 1872, after managers and receivers failed to meet payments on their notes and ceased paying the rents on their leases and the interest on their bonds. The stocks of the Vermont and Canada and the bonds of the Vermont Central plummeted dramatically. In this extremity the Vermont Central gang turned to the legislature and secured their incorporation, still in the capacity of receivers, as the Central Vermont Railroad Company.[14] After an interval of some years they asked the courts for permission to sell this property, assertedly theirs, to pay the debts of themselves as receivers and managers, debts holding precedence over the rent to the Vermont and Canada and the bonds of the old Vermont Central. A veritable *"hydra* of contention, bitterness, loss and litigation" ensued.[15]

After passing upon the issue three times, the justices of the Vermont Supreme Court finally brought themselves to the position advanced by learned counsel of the receivers.[16] Two years later, in 1884, the long receivership was over. From another corporation, the Consolidated Railroad Company, formed under the general laws of the state, the Central Vermont leased its own roads as well as the Vermont and Canada. Some years later the Central

[13] The Vermont & Canada Railroad Company *v.* The Vermont Central Railroad Company and Others, 50 *Vermont*, 561; James R. Langdon and Others *v.* The Vermont & Canada Railroad Company and Others, 53 *Vermont*, 290; *Report of Special Masters . . . April 24, 1877*, p. 169.

[14] The Vermont & Canada Railroad Company *v.* The Vermont Central Railroad Company et al., 46 *Vermont*, 794; Hartford *Courant*, September 24, 1872; *Report of Special Masters . . . April 24, 1877*, pp. 50–51; *Acts and Resolves Passed by the General Assembly of the State of Vermont, at the Second Biennial Session, 1872*, pp. 335–342.

[15] Vermont & Canada R. R. Co. *v.* Vermont Central R. R. Co. and Others, 50 *Vermont*, 594.

[16] 50 *Vermont*, 533; 53 *Vermont*, 236; James R. Langdon and Others *v.* The Vermont & Canada Railroad Co. and Others, 54 *Vermont*, 597.

Vermont consolidated with both the others.[17] In the late nineties, however, the dismal cycle again came round: in 1896 E. C. Smith, a son of J. Gregory Smith and president of the Central Vermont, was appointed a receiver for the property. He shared this office with a representative from the Grand Trunk,[18] for the development of decades had finally brought new interests into control. But the collapse, whoever was in charge, caused only "mild surprise in financial circles." [19]

Indebtedness and poverty were no bar to expansion. Indeed the receivers and managers felt it was their duty to acquire additional trackage and lease other corporations in order to protect their "trust" and wring concessions from connections. With Vermont as a center, they pushed in every direction except the east. Northward they persistently sought connections with Montreal. Though they built and leased and bought control, the vigilance of the Grand Trunk denied the Central success in this direction. Over its own lines the latter could get no nearer to Montreal than St. Johns.[20] To the west, affrighted lest the Rutland snap up the former Northern of New York, now the Ogdensburg and Lake Champlain, the Central leased in 1870 this rambling railroad to Lake Ontario.[21] To the south the receivers early in the sixties, by leasing the Sullivan Railroad between Windsor and Bellows Falls, secured connections with the Cheshire-Fitchburg line and thus an alternate route to Boston.[22] Finally, in 1870 it turned to the Rutland, its ancient rival both in commerce and in financial disaster. Though in after years recriminations broke out between the two companies over the circumstances of the lease, the Central sought the agreement and guaranteed a rental which in the light of the acknowledged defects of the Rut-

[17] *Report to the Stockholders of Central Vermont Railroad Co. for the Year Ending June 30th, 1886* (St. Albans: Messenger Job Office, 1886), pp. 3–4; *Central Vermont Railroad Co. Report of the Directors to the Stockholders for the Year Ending June 30th, 1892* (St. Albans: Messenger Job Office, 1892), pp. 6–7.

[18] *United States Circuit Court, District of Vermont. Grand Trunk Railway of Canada, v. The Central Vermont Railroad Company. In Equity. Record of Proceedings* (n. p., n. d.), I, 22–28.

[19] Springfield *Daily Republican*, March 24, 1896.

[20] *Report of Special Masters . . . April 24, 1877*, pp. 109–114, 119–121.

[21] *Ibid.*, pp. 74–77, 130–133.

[22] *Ibid.*, pp. 93, 96.

land was sure to accumulate immense losses for the Central.[23]

On the map the arrangement opened a tempting future, for the Rutland was no longer a local road. Like the Central, it had expanded through the lease of roads down the Connecticut Valley from Bellows Falls to a point on the Vermont and Massachusetts.[24] Here it connected with the New London Northern Railroad, the outgrowth of New London's pride, ambition, and wealth, which, first conceived in the forties, had grown slowly inland amidst misfortune and discouragement.[25] The Vermont Central leased the New London in 1871.[26] By then the Central had for all practical purposes consolidated the railroads of Vermont; only a few around the edges were not within its empire. Its main line extended from Ogdensburg on Ontario to New London on the Sound, and from the latter port steam vessels carried the route to New York City. Thus extended, the Central was one of the seven largest railroad systems in the nation; it was certainly the greatest in New England.[27] Later, hard times dislodged the structure piece by piece. By the late seventies the Central had dropped its leases in southwestern Vermont and returned, though only for a moment, the Ogdensburg and Lake Champlain to its owners.[28] The lease of the Rutland, at first modified, was given up in the financial disaster of the nineties. First the Delaware and Hudson and then the interests related to the Vanderbilts succeeded to the discarded property.[29]

For the funds required in operation and expansion, the receiv-

[23] *Ibid.*, pp. 127–130.

[24] Henry V. Poor, *Manual of the Railroads of the United States for 1873–74* (New York: H. V. & H. W. Poor, 1873), p. 137.

[25] Thelma M. Kistler, *The Rise of Railroads in the Connecticut River Valley* (Northampton: n. d.), pp. 66–70, 73–79, 183.

[26] Henry V. Poor, *Manual . . . for 1873–74*, p. 188.

[27] Charles J. Forbes, "History of the Vermont Central–Central Vermont Railway System, 1843–1933," *Vermonter*, XXXVII (1932), p. 251.

[28] *Central Vermont Railroad Co. Report of the Directors to the Stockholders for the Year Ending June 30th, 1889* (St. Albans: Messenger & Advertiser, 1889), pp. 5–6.

[29] Julius I. Bogen, *The Anthracite Railroads, a Study in American Enterprise* (New York: Ronald Press, 1927), pp. 189–197; Report of the Public Service Commission Relative to the Capital Expenditures, Investments and Existing Contingent Liabilities of the New York, New Haven, and Hartford Railroad Company, Massachusetts *House Documents*, 1916, no. 1900, pp. 194–198.

ers and managers resorted to a variety of expedients. The rents due to the Vermont and Canada were transformed into additional stock in that corporation until its capitalization had more than doubled. On this expanding sum the Vermont Central had to pay 8 per cent under the terms of the lease. The interest on the bonds of the Vermont Central was funded by the issuance of new bonds to the amount of $1,000,000, an increase of 50 per cent. Also the receivers issued four equipment loans to a total of $2,000,000, and other bond issues, some based upon the securities of leased roads. In addition the trust had by the middle of 1872 a floating debt of $2,878,164.[30] Though a Vermonter, a race supposedly prudent in financial affairs, occasionally protested that "you can never pay a debt by borrowing money to pay the interest," nothing effectively stayed the course of the Smiths and their allies. They were the official spokesmen for most of the interests that might have protested. Nor did the court, under whose protection the property lay, raise doubts or impose restraints.[31] Perhaps its aloofness was due to perplexity over the novel procedures in which it participated. As the judges of the Supreme Court confessed when they attempted to unravel the priority of debts and payments, "We have not been much aided by precedents in the determination of the questions involved in this controversy. We have not discovered any case so analogous to this in its facts as to be authoritative." [32]

Though the road lived on in the shaded half-light of financial illness, its managers and receivers had the best of health. By sorcery they turned corporate misfortune into individual gain. One device was the discriminating manipulation of leases. Thus Smith and his associates leased the Sullivan Railroad not as receivers and managers but as individuals. Almost immediately the traffic from the Vermont Central routed over the leased road increased. In twelve years the Sullivan paid aggregate profits of

[30] *Report of Special Masters . . . April 24, 1877*, pp. 50–55.

[31] *The Vermont Central and Vermont and Canada Railroads. Report of Trustees and Managers, and Action of the Stock and Bond Holders, at Horticultural Hall, Boston, Oct. 2, 1872* (Boston: Rand, Avery, & Co., 1872), p. 30.

[32] *Report of the Joint Special Committee to Investigate the Vt. Central . . . 1872*, pp. 15–16; 53 *Vermont*, 276.

$391,187 to its three lessees, one of whom was J. Gregory Smith. The three shared this sum with others who entered the charmed circle of receivers and managers.[33] At the northern edge of their empire the Montreal and Vermont Junction Railroad ran from the international boundary to St. Johns. J. G. Smith and Joseph Clark completed its construction, bought most of the stock and all of the bonds at low prices, and then entered into an arrangement with themselves as trustees of the Vermont Central by which in the latter guise they should operate the road and in the former guise, that of owners of the connection, receive half the gross earnings. Since operators of a road customarily received 70 rather than 50 per cent for their services and since the length of the road, twenty-four miles, was thoughtfully entered as thirty-five in the through pro-rating, the returns were handsome. In six years, until some bondholders protested the arrangement, Smith and Clark divided between them $405,807.[34] No wonder the Hartford *Courant* declared that "the directors of the Vermont Central follow the Fisk and Gould plan of conducting railroad operations." [35]

The ring enjoyed other perquisites. J. Gregory Smith and W. C. Smith, brothers and owners of the St. Albans Foundry, leased the enterprise to the former's son, Edward C. Smith, and a partner. With the proprieties thus observed, the St. Albans Foundry received contracts for wheels and castings from the trustees or receivers and managers, including, of course J. Gregory and W. C. Smith. Of the latter two, W. C. Smith received from the lessees of his foundry a royalty on each wheel and casting sold the trust. Although his more distinguished brother apparently did not share in these payments, both of course enjoyed the rental from the foundry they patronized.[36] A few years later, in 1868, J. Gregory Smith, W. C. Smith, Edward C. Smith, and their perennial associates, in order to provide rolling stock for the

[33] *Report of Special Masters . . . April 24, 1877*, pp. 99–102; *Report of the Joint Special Committee to Investigate the Vt. Central . . . 1872*, pp. 346–354.
[34] *Report of Special Masters . . . April 24, 1877*, pp. 104–109, 116–117; *Report of the Joint Special Committee to Investigate the Vt. Central . . . 1872*, pp. 355–373.
[35] Hartford *Courant*, September 25, 1872.
[36] *Report of Special Masters . . . April 24, 1877*, pp. 149–156; *Report of the Joint Special Committee to Investigate the Vt. Central . . . 1872*, pp. 8–10, 264–270, 275–294, 403–407.

through route, chartered the National Car Company, of whose capital of $1,000,000 about three-fifths was paid in. This company contracted for, but did not construct, one thousand cars; these cars when run over the road of the trust originally received from it a rental of three cents a mile, twice the customary rate on other through lines.[37] Then the Vermont Central clique chartered the Vermont Iron and Car Company, with a capital stock of $1,000,-000, half of which was paid in. Its specialty was lumber cars of an unusual length. Built in the shops of the Vermont Central, their wheels were bought from the St. Albans Foundry Company.[38]

Investors in the National Car Company and the Vermont Iron and Car Company were well rewarded for the chances they took: both corporations paid 10 per-cent dividends on their book capital.[39] When these profitable arrangements compelled an investigation by the Massachusetts Railroad Commission that body reported, "The cars of these companies, running at fixed rates per mile, whether full, partially full, or empty, have been kept in motion at rates for the carriage of goods which, at times, have caused the railroad to pay more for car service than the entire amounts they have secured as freights . . . In yet other cases, preference has been given to the cars of these private companies over the cars of the corporations, — the last being kept standing on sidings, while all merchandise was reserved for the first . . . Stockholders and railroad corporations were the victims, and were reduced, it may be, to bankruptcy."[40]

For their legerdemain the Vermont Central gang required a co-operative state. The legislature had to grant, extend, withhold or amend charters and to pass or defeat other legislation. The

---

[37] Report of Special Masters . . . April 24, 1877, pp. 142–144; Report of the Joint Special Committee to Investigate the Vt. Central . . . 1872, pp. 78–90; Massachusetts Fourth Annual Report of the Board of Railroad Commissioners. January, 1873, p. 35.

[38] Report of Special Masters . . . April 24, 1877, pp. 144–145, 147–148; Report of the Joint Special Committee to Investigate the Vt. Central . . . 1872, pp. 90–99, 109–122, 146–150, 158–159.

[39] Report of Special Masters . . . April 24, 1877, pp. 143, 145.

[40] Massachusetts Fourth Annual Report of the Board of Railroad Commissioners. January, 1873, pp. 35–36.

courts had to apply and interpret railroad statutes and oversee the receiverships to which these enterprises were prone. Though directors belonged to both political parties and officials gave free passes to the delegates to the Democratic state convention, the Vermont Central became synonomous with the Republican party.[41] J. Gregory Smith was Vermont's Civil War governor and served as Republican national committeeman; Edward C. Smith, his Republican son, occupied the governorship at the close of the century.[42] More covert and extensive relationships between the Central and the politicians were partially revealed on occasion. Thus a fierce legislative battle with the Rutland in 1869 led to charges of corruption and an investigation.

Evidence showed that the Central collected from odds and ends of revenue a secret service fund and that J. D. Hatch, a genial member of the Central's directorate, a "general agent," and its most vigilant and active lobbyist, generally dispensed this accumulated fund. One of his vouchers showed the disbursement of $1,000 in the session of 1869 to the lieutenant governor, senators, the railroad commissioner, speaker of the house of representatives, members of railroad committees, and others. Hatch couldn't remember why their names were on the list; J. Gregory Smith said the recipients were lawyers, retained as counsel for possible suits against the railroad.[43] Though the investigators found no causal connection between these payments and the fate of any legislation, they characterized the retainer system as a means of winning influential friendships rather than a method of employing legal talent. In Vermont the legislature also elected the judges. These brethren of the bench possessed free passes on the Smith roads and usually had been "retained" at one time or another.[44] Whether their objectivity was warped by this generosity can never be determined. The Springfield *Republican*, prob-

---

[41] Springfield *Daily Republican*, May 1, 15, 1873, March 29, 1876, June 27, 1878, July 21, 1882.

[42] Springfield *Daily Republican*, October 7, 1898.

[43] *Report of the Joint Special Committee to Investigate the Vt. Central . . . 1872*, pp. 122–123, 175–204, 222–243.

[44] *Report of the Joint Special Committee to Investigate the Vt. Central . . . 1872*, pp. 15–16; Springfield *Daily Republican*, August 28, 1873, September 1, 1875.

ably over-suspicious, thought court decisions so extraordinary that they must reflect some influence. The judges "caught the burglar, locked him in the house he wanted to rob, kept out the owners, and now say the bar can do nothing about it when the Legislature lets loose the fatted monster!" [45]

III

At its best the Vermont Central did not reach the West; it simply tapped Lake Ontario. In the early days of New England railroading that had been deemed enough and, though members of the route to the Lakes were later undeceived, they retained over the decades some organizational relationship with a steamboat line running propellers to the ports of the Great Lakes.[46] Such a connection, however, was a purely seasonal one; its interruption when the lakes were frozen greatly hampered the line. Still the competition of this water route discommoded the Grand Trunk which had pushed its rails westward, north of Lake Ontario, to Detroit and beyond, and which was seeking to develop a trade between the West and Boston by way of Portland, Maine. Perhaps these rivalries might be adjusted by an alliance. Such a proposal appealed not only to the railroads but to the Boston Board of Trade, which regarded the Portland terminus of the Grand Trunk and the transfer there "to steam vessels, of merchandize laden in cars at the West for Boston, as in direct contravention of the laws of trade, and as sure, therefore, to come to an end in the natural course of things." [47]

In 1862 this observation was being fulfilled. The railroads of the route to the Lakes and the Grand Trunk came to an agreement about rates, a car ferry was thereafter placed in operation

---

[45] Springfield *Daily Republican*, August 9, 1873, December 16, 1880, November 22, 1882.

[46] *Tenth Hearing on the Hoosac Tunnel Consolidation, . . . February 18, 1873*, pp. 8, 17–18; *Central Vermont Railroad Co. Report of the Directors, to the Stockholders, for the Year Ending June 30th, 1887* (St. Albans: Messenger & Advertiser, 1887), pp. 6–7; *Central Vermont Railroad Co. Report . . . June 30th, 1889*, pp. 7–8.

[47] *Boston Board of Trade. 1863. Ninth Annual Report of the Government, Presented to the Board at the Annual Meeting, on the 14th January, 1863* (Boston: Alfred Mudge & Son, 1863), pp. 30–31; *Report of Mr. Thomas E. Blackwell, Vice-President and Managing Director of the Grand Trunk Railway Company of Canada, for the Year 1859* (London: Waterlow and Sons, 1860), pp. 1–4, 8–9, 14–15.

between Prescott on the Grand Trunk and Ogdensburg, and later there was an interchange by way of Montreal.[48] Relations, once begun, strengthened. First the National Dispatch, the fast freight line on the route, built "compromise cars" which could adjust to either the standard gauge of the American or the broad gauge of the Grand Trunk's tracks; then the Grand Trunk changed to standard gauge in 1874.[49] A few years later, when the trunk line association came into being, the Central Vermont and the Grand Trunk acted as a unit. "The Vermont Central and the Grand Trunk have always been as intimate as if they were interchangeable owners," complained Chauncey M. Depew, of the New York Central.[50]

Financial interrelationships accompanied this commercial cooperation. Debt paved the way. After the reorganization of the seventies the Central Vermont kept going by borrowing from the Grand Trunk the traffic balances which it owed the latter and paying interest upon them.[51] Then the Grand Trunk began purchasing common stock in the Central, its "main connection" with the New England states. By 1885, when it owned a majority of the stock in the Central Vermont, not to mention its holdings of bonds, preferred stock, and stock in the Consolidated Railroad of Vermont, the two roads formed a traffic agreement preventing interchange of traffic with competitive lines without mutual consent. The Grand Trunk could continue its Portland business and the interchange of traffic at the Niagara frontier, and the Central Vermont was permitted rail and water traffic via Ogdensburg.[52]

[48] *Boston Board of Trade. 1863. Ninth Annual Report*, p. 31; *Testimony before Special Masters, 1875*, pp. 84, 315; *Argument of Hon. J. G. Abbott, before the Committee on Railways and Canals, February 18, 1864, on the Petition of the Boston and Lowell Railroad for a Union with Certain Railroads in Massachusetts and New Hampshire with the Evidence for the Petitioners* (Boston: Wright and Potter, 1864), pp. 42–43.

[49] *Report of Special Masters . . . April 24, 1877*, pp. 143, 145–146; *Half-Year Ended June 30th, 1875. Grand Trunk Railway Company of Canada. Report of the Directors to the Proprietors and Statement of the Revenue and Capital Accounts for the Half-Year Ended June 30th, 1875* (London: Waterlow & Sons, 1875), p. 8.

[50] Report of the Committee on Interstate Commerce on Canadian Roads, *Senate Reports*, 51 Cong., 1 Sess., no. 847 (s. n. 2706), p. 60.

[51] 54 *Vermont*, 596, 597.

[52] *Half-Year Ended 30th June, 1883. The Grand Trunk Railway Company of Canada. Report of the Directors . . .* (n. p., n. d.), p. 8; *Half-Year Ended 30th*

Finally in 1889, when the Vermont road again emerged from reorganization, the Grand Trunk controlled two-thirds of the Central's common stock and guaranteed, within certain limits, to pay the 4 per-cent interest on its funded debt of $12,000,000. Though there were Vermont names still upon the directorate, representatives of the Canadian road wielded the power.[53]

To fuse the discordant roads, from the dowager Boston and Lowell to the ne'er-do-well Central Vermont, into an effective route to the Lakes daunted the most sanguine railroad official. Still the task had to be undertaken. Since 1850 when a railroad convention of the northern roads met in Boston, agreements had been one way to secure the necessary unity of action.[54] First the Northern Railroad, later the Boston and Lowell took the lead in bringing about their formulation.[55] Two decades of experimentation finally crystallized into the agreement of 1870. It was to run for twenty years. In charge of the through business of this Vermont Central line was a board of directors consisting of a representative from each of the six roads. The companies furnished the cars for the line, helped pay the rent of the Ogdensburg and Lake Champlain, under lease to the Vermont Central, and financed the propellers on the Great Lakes. The managers of the line were J. Gregory Smith and General Stark of the Boston and Lowell and the Nashua and Lowell. The latter, as manager

---

June, 1884. The Grand Trunk Railway Company of Canada. Report of the Directors . . . (n. p., n. d.), p. 7; *Half-Year Ended 30th June, 1885. The Grand Trunk Railway Company of Canada. Report of the Directors* . . . (n. p., n. d.), pp. 21–23; *Half-Year Ended 31st December, 1885. The Grand Trunk Railway Company of Canada. Report of the Directors* . . . (n. p., n. d.), p. 13.

[53] *Half-Year Ended 31st December, 1899. The Grand Trunk Railway of Canada. Report of the Directors* . . . (n. p., n. d.), p. 9; Charles M. Wilds, *Central Vermont R. R. Reorganization. House Bill no. 70. Hearing Before the Railroad Committees of the Senate and House of Representatives Sitting Jointly. Argument in Behalf of the Bill. Nov. 10, 1898* (Montpelier: Argus and Patriot, 1898), pp. 7–18; *Acts and Resolves Passed by the General Assembly of the State of Vermont at the Fifteenth Biennial Session, 1898*, pp. 125–128; Springfield *Daily Republican*, October 27, 1898, March 22, April 29, 1899, October 10, 1900.

[54] *Supra*, I, 181–186.

[55] *Report of the Tenth Hearing on the Hoosac Tunnel Consolidation,* . . . *February 18, 1873*, p. 8; *Report of the Thirteenth Hearing on the Hoosac Tunnel Consolidation,* . . . *February 26, 1873*, pp. 5–7; *Argument of Hon. J. G. Abbott,* . . . *February 18, 1864, on the Petition of the Boston and Lowell Railroad*, pp. 41–44.

and chairman, sometimes fixed the rates from Boston to Chicago without consulting anyone. The division among the companies, however, was provided by the agreement.[56] However detailed such documents became, they were unsatisfactory. Single roads held aloof; others drove hard bargains; financial embarrassments of individual members upset calculations. In essence the successful functioning of such agreements depended upon the will or whim of a single corporation.[57]

IV

Consolidation was better. Naturally the Vermont Central could not undertake it. The feeble could lease only the feebler; the bankrupt could hardly guarantee a return upon the securities of the prosperous. To be effective the impulse for combination had to come from an enterprise with resources as well as ambition. Suddenly in 1864 the Boston and Lowell, by petitioning the Massachusetts General Court for permission to unite with the Nashua and Lowell and the Concord, stepped forward as the protagonist of at least a limited consolidation. Naturally the purposes of the program were stated in colorful ultimates: "A great many cities in the Middle Ages were built up simply by the commerce which they carried on between Europe and the East; but to-day, here in Boston, here in Massachusetts, anywhere upon the railroad, instead of its being the 'golden East' it is really the

[56] *Report of the Tenth Hearing on the Hoosac Tunnel Consolidation* . . . *February 18, 1873*, pp. 8, 17–18, 21–22; *Report of the Twelfth Hearing on the Hoosac Tunnel Consolidation,* . . . *February 20, 1873*, p. 33; *Report of the Thirteenth Hearing on the Hoosac Tunnel Consolidation,* . . . *February 26, 1873*, pp. 7–13; *Charters of the Vermont Central, Vermont and Canada, and Central Vermont Railroads. The Vermont and Canada Lease. The First and Second Mortgages and Deeds of Surrender of the Vermont Central Railroad Company. Orders and Decrees in the Cause Vermont and Canada R. R. Co. vs. Vermont Central R. R. Co. et al.*, pp. 348–363.

[57] *Report of the Sixth Hearing on the Hoosac Tunnel Consolidation,* . . . *February 11, 1873*, pp. 6–8; *Report of the Tenth Hearing on the Hoosac Tunnel Consolidation,* . . . *February 18, 1873*, pp. 8–9, 28–29, 31–32; *Report of the Directors of the Boston and Lowell Railroad Corporation, for the Year 1875, with Statements of Twelve Months Accounts to September 30, 1875* (Boston: James F. Cotter & Co., 1875), p. 7; *Report of the Directors of the Boston and Lowell Railroad Corporation, for the Year 1876, with Statements of Twelve Months Accounts to September 30, 1876* (Boston: James F. Cotter & Co., 1876), pp. 11–12.

golden West to which we are to look as the source of our prosperity and increase." [58] As a step toward this promise the consolidation of the three lower roads offered possibilities of efficiency, savings, and of pooled funds for terminals in Boston.[59] By this petition the Boston and Lowell discarded its provincial role of an earlier decade when it was quite content with a local traffic. It embarked upon a career of expansion. This new direction reflected the contemporary trend to consolidation and aggressive leadership. Into the Boston and Lowell had come as president F. B. Crowninshield, a practical railroad man who had seen on the Old Colony the advantages of consolidation, and as manager George Stark, "not only the *captain* of the Boston and Lowell Railroad, but about as near the entire rank and file as I ever knew any one man to be, connected with any corporation." Like Crowninshield a practical railroad man, he was the apostle of expansion.[60]

Though the General Court proved as unwilling to authorize this consolidation as it had that of the Boston and Worcester with the Western in the same year, Massachusetts opposition was actually short lived. The hard core of resistance to the Lowell's program was New Hampshire. Of all the New England states the most consistently suspicious of railroad enterprises, and those who ran them, her railroad law allowed consolidation only on the narrowest terms and for short periods. Professedly she was wedded to the doctrine of competition. The Lowell's program, furthermore, collided with powerful interests and personalities in the Granite State. In the first category was the Concord Railroad, or rather the succession of Concord officials and owners who would assent to the dread fate of consolidation only if they were paid enough.

Among the individuals was William E. Chandler, controller of the Concord *Daily Monitor* and its weekly edition, the *Independent Statesman*, and one of the outstanding Republican "radicals"

---

[58] *Argument of Hon. J. G. Abbott, . . . February 18, 1864, on the Petition of the Boston and Lowell Railroad*, pp. 3–4.

[59] *Ibid.*, pp. 9–19, 37–38.

[60] *Ibid.*, pp. 30–32, 59–68; *Argument of John H. George, Esq., in Behalf of the Petition of the Boston and Lowell Railroad for an Increase of Terminal Facilities in Boston, before the Railroad Committee of the Massachusetts Legislature, Thursday Evening, February 4, 1869* (Boston: Wright & Potter, 1869), p. 25.

in the nation.[61] A foe of railroad consolidation, there was about his case more instinct than consistency or logic. Thus at times he opposed the consolidation on provincial grounds: it would take the control of the railroads out of the state and result in higher local rates. In other moods, abjuring a belief in competition as such, he would tolerate consolidation only if accompanied with stricter regulation of fares and finance.[62] Since the lodestar of his life was Republican partisanship, his approach to railroad problems was primarily political and his thinking on the subject highly colored by the association of railroad enterprises with his political opponents. Thus, while he did valuable work attacking abuses, he was a less penetrating critic on railroad matters than Charles F. Adams, Jr., in Massachusetts or Henry L. Goodwin in Connecticut. Of course, in a state more litigatious, if possible, than Vermont, consolidation or its methods were always before the courts· Hence both objectives and procedures came under the surveillance of Charles Doe, Chief Justice of the New Hampshire Supreme Court. One of the most eminent jurists in New England, Doe was a Dartmouth graduate, a judicial reformer, an original and penetrating legal scholar, and a distinctive individual.[63] Whether he cared if consolidation were voted up or down, his decisions did not state directly; but, by condemning the short cuts taken to secure it as a violation of the laws of the state and of more fundamental equities, he did his judicial best to postpone it for years.

The difficulties of the New Hampshire situation were partially revealed in the early seventies. The Boston and Lowell, not long discouraged by the opposition of the Massachusetts General Court, returned to the campaign in 1869, — this time with success. It secured a charter for the Great Northern Railroad Company. The Boston and Lowell, Nashua and Lowell, Concord, and Northern, or any of them could form within six years a "consolidated corporation." The new enterprise was authorized, furthermore, to

[61] *Dictionary of American Biography* (New York: Charles Scribner's Sons, 1928-1936), III, 616-618.
[62] Concord *Independent Statesman*, October 6, 27, 1881.
[63] *Dictionary of American Biography*, V, 354-355.

purchase or lease the Vermont Central and all its appanages, the Boston, Concord and Montreal, the Connecticut and Passumpsic, and "steamships running in connection with said trunkline between Ogdensburg and Chicago." Its capitalization was limited to the total of the consolidated lines and such additional amounts for expansion as a board of commissioners permitted. The maximum in any case was $50,000,000. Rates for passengers and freight could never "exceed the local rates of charge, as now established," and "charges for transportation on through freight, discharged within thirty miles of Boston, shall not exceed the rates of through freight to said city." [64] Prospects for success were auspicious. That Judge Josiah Minot, for three years a director of the Northern Railroad, was now as well president of the Concord and that a common interest suffused both corporations was a particularly encouraging omen.[65] Less reassuring was the provision of the charter requiring the assent of New Hampshire to the projected procedures.

As the scene shifted in 1870 to that peculiar state, a group of New Hampshire men, small-city luminaries, sensed the possibilities of making money through purchasing a controlling stock interest in the key road, the Concord, and blackmailing either the Boston and Lowell or the Northern or both into repurchasing it from them. The resulting maneuvers produced a piquant mingling of politics, railroading, and banking. J. W. Johnson, a wool and produce merchant and former railroad commissioner of New Hampshire, and Boston brokers, one of whom was William A. Tower, bought up the stock and then redistributed it to those who formed the ring.[66] Mixed motives animated its members. Some hated President Minot and his "dirty work"; others aspired to office on the Concord Railroad; a conductor, against whom the

[64] *Acts and Resolves Passed by the General Court of Massachusetts, in the Years 1868, '69*, pp. 767–772.

[65] *Twenty-sixth Annual Report of the Directors of the Concord Railroad Corporation. March 31, 1867* (Concord: McFarland & Jenks, 1867), p. 3; *Northern Railroad vs. Concord Railroad. S. J. Court. Merrimack County, June Term, 1870. In Chancery. Evidence on the Part of Complainants* (Concord: McFarland & Jenks, 1870), pp. 32, 45–46.

[66] *Northern Railroad vs. Concord Railroad . . . Evidence . . . of Complainants*, pp. 1–9.

Concord was pushing a case for short-changing, wanted the case withdrawn; ex-Governor Smyth, inveigled into the contest, continued because he "did not like to be beaten. . . . [He] felt a desire to be in control of the road, for the same reasons that men usually have, to be in power"; and John H. Pearson, Concord grain merchant, was an ingrained foe of consolidation. Like a threnody through all their testimony runs the expressed desire to make "a safe, sound, and good investment." [67] Eventually the ring controlled between seven and eight thousand shares, a good portion of which was purchased, according to their tell, at an average price of $84 to $85 a share.[68] The par value, be it remembered, was $50.

To meet the financial strain, they borrowed practically all the money from various banks in Concord, Manchester, and Nashua in which they were presidents, trustees, directors, treasurers, or cashiers. Usually they followed the methods outlined to ex-Governor Smyth by one of his associate investors: "I should like to hire some money at your bank, and I will loan you from our bank." [69] Occasionally, with a nonchalant disregard for the proprieties and the banking laws, they borrowed from banks in which they were officers.[70] However they got the money, the borrowers paid higher interest rates to the banks than they received on the inflated values of the Concord securities. Such sacrifices were necessitated for the purpose of financing "an investment" in the Concord road. Justice Doe later paid his sardonic compliments to this explanation: "As the investment was made in expectation of a loss of principal and a loss of interest, and was chiefly of money hired for the purpose of being invested at a loss, it is evident that, on this vital point, their testimony is highly figurative. On their oaths, explaining conduct that so much needs explanation, they declare their object was an investment, which, in the ordinary meaning of the term, was inconsistent with any rational system of finance. The use of so common and plain a word in a

---

[67] *Ibid.*, pp. 10–13, 94–96, 176–181, 195–196, 249, 256.
[68] *Ibid.*, pp. 83–85, 153–154, 217, 220.
[69] *Ibid.*, p. 186.
[70] *Ibid.*, pp. 13–21, 100–102, 107–120, 169–171, 185–194, 237–240.

sense so eccentric and obscure, agrees with other evidence in pointing to an investment with mysterious profits." [71] If Doe ever strayed from his customary diet of law books, he must have just finished reading C. F. Adams' *A Chapter of Erie.*

Whatever the motives of these interlocking borrowers, James W. Johnson was in search of buyers for their holdings. General Stark of the Boston and Lowell, furiously angry at the hold-up, refused to participate either in counter-measures or purchases; Judge Minot, discouraged by Stark's attitude, abandoned designs to maintain control of the Concord; but Onslow Stearns, president of the Northern, felt compelled to make an offer. He feared the ring might charge higher freights to his road and in union with the lower roads or the Vermont Central punish it for contumacy. He was willing to purchase the ring's stock at $85 a share and toss in a bonus of $100,000; the ring was to vote for directors favored by the Northern and use its influence in the directorate to make a business contract with the Northern and in the legislature to secure the necessary ratification.[72] Some speculators had qualms about selling their "influence," others thought a better price might be secured, still others felt the offer too "conditional." "We wanted the greenbacks on the table," said one with refreshing candor.[73] Understandably suspicious of each other, they loyally signed a pledge to stand together and obtain control of the Concord at the forthcoming annual meeting in May, 1870.[74]

A month before this projected revolution, Onslow Stearns and Josiah Minot executed a *coup de main.* The Northern and the Concord signed an agreement patterned after that between the Boston and Lowell and Nashua and Lowell. The document provided for a joint management of the two roads and guaranteed the Concord an annual dividend of 10 per cent. This business arrangement had to have the assent of the railroad commissioners, the council, and the governor. These were immediately forthcoming. In fact, Onslow Stearns, president of the Northern, assented to

[71] Fisher et al. *v.* The Concord Railroad et al., 50 *New Hampshire,* 207.
[72] *Northern Railroad vs. Concord Railroad . . . Evidence . . . of Complainants,* pp. 22–25, 46–53, 80–83, 86–87, 131, 156–157.
[73] *Ibid.,* pp. 23–24, 182–183, 250–254.
[74] *Ibid.,* pp. 97–99, 184, 241–244.

the lease as governor of New Hampshire and forthwith became the first agent for the Concord and Northern Railroads.[75] "When he wanted anything," said Johnson, "and put his foot down, he had things in his own way, and that things would be as he said." [76] This time Stearns was in error. At the annual meeting of the Concord the angry ring triumphantly elected a new board of directors, and in resolutions, righteous with indignation, declared the contract between the Concord and Northern "wholly unauthorized, illegal, and in violation of our rights and the rights of the public, and we thefore [sic] pronounce the same null and void." [77] When the Northern brought an injunction to compel the enforcement of contract, the case came before the New Hampshire courts. In December, 1870, the Supreme Court of New Hampshire declared the Northern-Concord contract illegal on the ground that the purpose of the old board in making it "was, by substantially transferring the management of the Concord for five years, to the Northern, to prevent the management from going into the hands of their own successors." [78]

Thus legally secure, it remained for the investors in the Concord to realize upon their energy and foresight. Once again James W. Johnson began his amiable exploratory sales trips. Not only the Northern but also the Boston, Concord and Montreal was interested since it had certain local traffic agreements with the Concord to readjust. As a consequence, in 1872-1873, Johnson sold approximately eight thousand shares to Onslow Stearns of the Northern and to John E. Lyon, president and virtual owner of the Boston, Concord and Montreal. The price, $105 to $106 a share, rewarded the Concord ring almost as generously as the projected bargain of 1870.[79] Still there were hard feelings. James

---

[75] *Ibid.*, pp. 41–42, 66–67, 77, 123–126, 145–146; *Report of the Railroad Commissioners of the State of New Hampshire, June Session, 1871*, pp. 22–26.

[76] *Pearson v. Concord Railroad et als., Testimony* (n. p., n. d.), J. W. Johnson, p. 7.

[77] *Northern Railroad vs. Concord Railroad . . . Evidence . . . of Complainants*, p. 267.

[78] Northern Railroad *v.* Concord Railroad et al., 50 *New Hampshire*, 175, 179, 181.

[79] *Pearson v. Concord Railroad, Testimony*, J. T. Vose, p. 2; J. W. Johnson, pp. 2–5, 8–45; Charles F. Choate, pp. 9–10, 12–13.

W. Johnson fared somewhat better than his associates, since he deftly collected a $50,000 bonus for his retail services.[80] Furthermore, J. H. Pearson, owner of 1,848 shares in the Concord, filling the air with assertions of his own righteousness, characterized the sale "as a breach of faith, of honor, and of solemn promises," and asked his former leader, William A. Tower, "if a few paltry thousands can compensate for the loss of position and self respect which you must incur by the act which you are about to consummate?" [81] We have here another example of those Galahads who enlisted in speculative enterprises for the most spiritual of reasons.

V

Disregarding the racket, Lyon went ahead to become the largest individual owner of Concord stock. Stearns and Minot made further purchases for themselves, or as trustees, and distributed the purchases to associates, banks, the Northern Railroad, and to the Old Colony, of which Stearns became president in 1866. Somewhat later, Stearns became president of the Concord; together with Lyon, he constituted the executive committee of the road. They were given the "power to direct the operation of the railroad, and make all necessary purchases and contracts therefor, subject to the approval of the board," which was itself overwhelmingly recruited from the officials and other directors of the Northern and the Boston, Concord and Montreal.[82] These New Hampshire doings had, meanwhile, driven the Boston and Lowell to exasperation. Its failure, under the terms of the Great Northern Railroad charter, to secure authority in New Hampshire even to unite with the Nashua and Lowell simply added to the desperation.[83] Suddenly the 1873 debate in Massachusetts over

---

[80] *Ibid.*, J. W. Johnson, pp. 15–18; Charles F. Choate, pp. 12–13.

[81] [J. H. Pearson] *To the Stockholders of the Concord Railroad* (n. p., n. d.), p. 7.

[82] *Pearson v. Concord Railroad, Testimony*, J. T. Vose, pp. 3–10; G. E. Todd, pp. 3–5; J. P. Pitman, pp. 1–3; Nathan Parker; pp. 1–8, 13–16; J. W. Fellows, p. 3; Charles F. Choate, pp. 10–12.

[83] *Report of the Sixth Hearing on the Hoosac Tunnel Consolidation,* . . . *February 11, 1873*, pp. 7–8; *Report of the Tenth Hearing on the Hoosac Tunnel Consolidation,* . . . *February 18, 1873*, p. 19; *Report of the Thirteenth Hearing on the Hoosac Tunnel Consolidation,* . . . *February 26, 1873*, pp. 20–22.

the disposition of the Hoosac Tunnel pointed an avenue of escape. At the hearings the representatives of the road requested the amendment of the Great Northern Railroad charter to permit the Boston and Lowell to lease or purchase the Fitchburg, the Cheshire, and the Rutland railroads. Although the old authorization to join with the roads by way of Concord and White River was continued, and although there were many vague words uttered on the Hoosac route, the real purpose was obvious: to afford the Boston and Lowell the choice of an alternate road not across Massachusetts but through New Hampshire or Vermont.[84] Sighting the danger signals from afar, Onslow Stearns, president of the Northern, and his counsel, repaired to Boston with a protest.[85] The total conflict of interests in the Hoosac Tunnel, of which this was but a single strand, prevented the action sought by the Boston and Lowell. This defeat was the high water mark in this first effort of the road to consolidate the route to the Lakes. When the depression of the middle seventies caught the Boston and Lowell off balance and dividends were passed, the apostles of a narrower and more economical policy secured the resignation of General Stark.[86] His work was so far threatened that in 1878, when the joint agreement with the Nashua and Lowell ran out, the roads temporarily parted.[87]

Two years later, however, the Boston and Lowell resumed its career of expansion. Chancing New Hampshire law and New Hampshire "demagogues," it leased the Nashua and Lowell for

[84] *Report of the Sixth Hearing on the Hoosac Tunnel Consolidation, . . . February 11, 1873*, pp. 4–5, 8–31.

[85] *Report of the Thirteenth Hearing on the Hoosac Tunnel Consolidation, . . . February 26, 1873*, pp. 3–30.

[86] George Stark, *The Nashua & Lowell Railroad Company: Some of Its Unpublished History and Reasons Why Every Stockholder Should Attend the Next Annual Meeting on the Last Wednesday of May, 1879, and Investigate the Management* (Nashua: 1879), p. 1; *Answer to the Attack of Geo. Stark, on the Management of the Nashua & Lowell R. R.* (Nashua: O. C. Moore, 1879).

[87] *Forty-third Annual Report of the Directors of the Nashua & Lowell Railroad Corporation, for the Year Ending May 29, 1878* (Nashua: O. C. Moore, 1878), pp. 3–10; *Forty-fourth Annual Report of the Directors of the Nashua & Lowell Railroad Corporation, for the Year Ending May 28, 1879* (Nashua: O. C. Moore, 1879), pp. 3–8; *Forty-fifth Annual Report of the Directors of the Nashua & Lowell Railroad Corporation, for the Year Ending May 26, 1880* (Nashua: O. C. Moore, 1880), pp. 3–6.

ninety-nine years.[88] Then, as the dread word of "consolidation" flew about New Hampshire, the citadel of the Concord was stormed. In August, 1881, the two roads signed a five-year business agreement patterned upon the earlier one between the Nashua and the Boston and Lowell. There were to be a common general manager and a common cashier; the operation of the two roads was to be pooled; and the "net income, after payment of all expenses incident to the operation of the joint roads including rentals . . . shall be divided . . . in the proportion of sixty per cent to the Boston and Lowell Railroad, and forty per cent to the Concord Railroad." [89] At one stroke this gave a unified line from Boston to the Connecticut River, for, be it remembered, the Northern Railroad and the Boston, Concord and Montreal at this time controlled the Concord Railroad. The Northern still owned over four thousand shares of Concord stock and on the latter's board representatives of the Northern and of the Boston, Concord and Montreal constituted a majority. The new union of the roads was fittingly symbolized in Henry C. Sherburne: already president of the Northern, a director of the Concord, he now became the general manager of the combined Boston and Lowell and Concord.[90]

This brilliant realization of consolidation dreams rested upon insecure foundations. It did not coincide with the intricate formalities of New Hampshire railroad law. The lease of the Nashua and Lowell, though it met the requirements of Massachusetts legalities, was not validated by New Hampshire officials. Though the business contract with the Concord, as that document insisted, was in no sense "a lease of one road to the other, or . . . a union of their corporate powers or privileges," [91] New Hampshire

---

[88] Massachusetts *Twelfth Annual Report of the Board of Railroad Commissioners. January, 1881*, pp. 368–371.

[89] *Report of the Directors of the Boston and Lowell Railroad Corporation, for the Year 1881. With Statements of Twelve Months Accounts to September 30, 1881* (Boston: James F. Cotter & Co., 1881), pp. 11–19.

[90] *Report of the Directors of the Boston and Lowell Railroad Corporation, for the Year 1882. With Statements of Twelve Months Accounts to September 30, 1882* (Boston: James F. Cotter & Co., 1882), p. 2; *Thirty-eighth Annual Report of the Railroad Commissioners of the State of New Hampshire, 1882*, pp. 14, 27.

[91] *Report . . . of the Boston and Lowell . . . 1881*, p. 12.

opponents were not put off by the subterfuge. This agreement, too, required validation by New Hampshire officials. As for the interlocking stockownerships and directorates between the Northern, the Boston, Concord and Montreal, and the Concord, they clearly defied the spirit of the laws in a jurisdiction committed by statute to competition. "To the courts," shouted the foes of these alliances. The response to this cry by governors and attorney-generals was reluctant, though W. E. Chandler shrieked against "consolidationists," "free-pass legislatures," "the reckless defiance of law . . . marked by corruption and seduction," and prophesied, if the Republican party did not harken to the call of duty, it was headed for oblivion.[92]

Quicker to take action was the minority of the Concord's stockholders opposed to the whole development. They were led by John H. Pearson, one of the Concord "investors" who had excited the derision of Justice Doe. Pearson purchased a paper, the *New Hampshire People and Patriot*, more effectively to vent his griefs and assail his enemies, and turned the Concord's annual meetings into campaigns against alien consolidations.[93] When these maneuvers failed, he or his confederates sought assistance from the legislature and entered two suits in the courts.[94] Of the latter, one challenged the validity of the business agreement between the Concord and the Boston and Lowell; the other, the control of the Concord by the Northern and the Boston, Concord and Montreal.

In 1882 and 1883 the Supreme Court chopped down the painfully built structure of consolidation. Chief Justice Doe struck one blow. To his mind the business agreement between the Boston and Lowell and the Concord was of the sort requiring govern-

---

[92] Concord *Independent Statesman*, October 6, 13, 20, 27, November 17, 24, December 15, 1881.

[93] Springfield *Daily Republican*, February 23, 1879; Concord *Independent Statesman*, May 26, 1881, July 29, 1886; *Closing Argument of Hon. Irving W. Drew, before the Railroad Committee of the House of Representatives, August 3, 1887* (Concord: Republican Press Association, 1887), p. 24.

[94] Concord *Independent Statesman*, May 19, 1881; *Journals of the Honorable Senate and House of Representatives of the State of New Hampshire, June Session, 1881*, p. 808; *Closing Argument of Hon. Irving W. Drew . . . August 3, 1887*, pp. 24–26.

mental sanction. The roads had not secured it. Furthermore, the contract in effect established a partnership. Losses in New Hampshire might be counterbalanced by gains in Massachusetts, losses in Massachusetts by gains in New Hampshire. All this was business possibility: "No legal reason appears, for compelling the plaintiffs," — the abused minority on the Concord — "to exchange their share of the risks of their own road for an equal or greater or less share of the risks of the whole line." Somewhat later Justice Smith reflected hostilely upon the Concord's ties with its northern connections. Though interlocking directorates were often "convenient and desirable" among roads forming parts of a continuous line, directors in one corporation could not make contracts with themselves as directors in another. This confusion of interests, this serving of two masters, this conflict between duty and self-interest was sure to strain the conscience beyond endurance and deprive the stockholders in at least one of the corporations of honest action by their officials. As for interlocking stock-ownerships, since no charter provision permitted the Northern to own stock in the Concord or in any other form of enterprise, the purchase of Concord shares by the former was a "misapplication of corporate funds." [95] The Boston and Lowell and the Concord dropped their agreement.[96] The Pearson clique on the Concord succeeded in ejecting from its board representatives of the upper roads. The Concord was no longer "in the hands of the Philistines." Pearson's purge had triumphed.[97]

VI

Turned back by the judicial power, the Boston and Lowell openly renounced its larger ambitions: "The rapid development

[95] Burke et al. v. Concord Railroad et al., 61 *New Hampshire*, 160; Pearson v. Concord Railroad Corporation et al., 62 *New Hampshire*, 537.

[96] *Report . . . of the Boston and Lowell . . . 1882*, p. 11; *Report of the Directors of the Boston & Lowell Railroad Corporation, for the Year 1883, With Statements of Twelve Months Accounts to September 30, 1883* (Boston: Huse, Goodwin & Co., 1883), p. 14.

[97] John M. Mitchell, *Opening Argument of John M. Mitchell before the Railroad Committee of New Hampshire Legislature, Monday, June 29, 1887, in Support of House Bill no. 67, Entitled "An Act to Secure to the State of New Hampshire the Control of Its Railroads."* (n. p., n. d.), pp. 10–11.

of our local traffic and such other business as is necessarily tributary to our road, has fully occupied our terminals, and relieved
us from the necessity of making such concessions to obtain or
retain such contributive business as has been in the past of very
questionable value." [98] Still cherishing in actuality the consolidation program, it took heart from the comprehensive revision of
railroad law and policy effected in 1883 by the New Hampshire
legislature. The body passed two bills. One, the Colby Act, provided for railroad incorporation by general law; the second
reorganized the railroad commission. Included among the many
provisions of the first statute was one which declared that "two
or more railroad corporations may contract that either corporation
shall perform all the transportation of persons and freight upon
and over the road of the other . . . and any railroad corporation
may lease its road, railroad property, and interests to any other
railroad corporation upon such terms and for such time" as the
directors agreed and two-thirds of the stockholders present
approved. It also provided that "no competing railroads now
prohibited by law from leasing or uniting shall have a right under
the provisions of this act to unite with or lease each other unless
said roads, or one of them, has heretofore leased or united with
other road or roads for the purpose of forming a continuous line,
or shall hereafter, or at the time of such lease or union, unite with
or lease some other road for such purpose." [99] However this verbal
obeisance to the principles of the past did not conceal the real
reversal of New Hampshire policy.

Parties responded to the change, each in his fashion. Chandler
growled against measures for "unlimited consolidation," the railroad commissioners prayed for peace and stability and an end to
agitation and aggrandizement, and railroad officials and learned
counsel appraised the practical effects of the new measures upon
the many proposals for consolidation brewing throughout the
state.[100] The Boston and Maine and the Eastern Railroad, already
in the preliminary stages of union, found the act to their liking.

[98] *Report . . . of the Boston & Lowell . . . 1883*, pp. 14–15.
[99] *Laws of the State of New Hampshire, Passed June Session, 1883*, pp. 70–81.
[100] *Fortieth Annual Report of the Railroad Commissioners of the State of New Hampshire, 1884*, pp. 4–5.

The consolidationists on the Concord, the Northern, and the Boston, Concord and Montreal were pleased. Whether the Colby Act benefited the Boston and Lowell was less certain. Apparently it could avail itself of the privileges of the policy even though it was a foreign corporation. A proviso of the Colby Act stated: "Railroad Corporations created by the laws of other states, operating roads within this state, shall have the same rights for the purposes of operating, leasing, or uniting with other roads as if created by the laws of this state." [101]

Unleashed by the new measures, the scramble for leases began. A year later, 1884, the Boston and Lowell succeeded in capturing the Northern and the Boston, Concord and Montreal, an objective it reached just ahead of the Concord.[102] The Boston and Lowell had acted with more dispatch, offered higher rentals, and probably had a preliminary understanding with its acquisitions.[103] The Concord appreciated too slowly the necessity of expansion. After all, the mood of the Pearson crowd was epitomized in their own assertions — *"The Concord is all right as it is now,"* — "We are out of debt and sure of our dividends for the next one hundred years as we have been for the past twenty, if we keep out of these doubtful schemes. It is always best to let well enough alone." [104] Then the Boston and Lowell, with the Northern and the Boston, Concord and Montreal, purchased control of the St. Johnsbury and Lake Champlain Railroad across northern Vermont, united with the Canadian Pacific to secure connections across the border,

[101] *Laws of the State of New Hampshire, Passed June Session, 1883*, pp. 70–81; *Journals of the Honorable Senate and House of Representatives of the State of New Hampshire, June Session, 1883*, pp. 1050–1056; Ira Colby, *The Railroad Question, Speech of Hon. Ira Colby, Representative from Claremont, in the House of Representatives in Favor of the Hazen Bill, September 21, 1887* (Concord; Republican Press Association, 1887), pp. 4–9; E. P. Jewell, *Argument of E. P. Jewell, before the Railroad Committee of the House of Representatives, July 7, 1887* (Concord: N. H. Democratic Press Company, n. d.), pp. 4–10.

[102] Massachusetts *Sixteenth Annual Report of the Board of Railroad Commissioners. January, 1885*, pp. 411–419.

[103] Harry Bingham, *Closing Argument of Hon. Harry Bingham, before the Railroad Committee of the New Hampshire Legislature, Wednesday, August 10, 1887, in Favor of the "Atherton Bill" and in Opposition to the "Hazen Bill"* (Concord: N. H. Democratic Press Company, 1887), pp. 16–17; Colby, *The Railroad Question*, pp. 9–10; Drew, *Closing Argument, . . . August 3, 1887*, pp. 28–32.

[104] Drew, *Closing Argument, . . . August 3, 1887*, pp. 25–26.

and finally in 1887 leased the Connecticut and Passumpsic.[105] The Boston and Lowell was at last a system. It had a considerable Massachusetts network, operated two-fifths of the mileage of New Hampshire, and tapped Canada without relying upon the Central Vermont. The various roads were placed in divisions, traffic was re-routed over the most advantageous routes, rates were reduced and made uniform, and extensive technical improvements were undertaken.[106] The Concord, however, still held apart the mother and her children.

The Concord, nonetheless, confronted an emergency. If it were to extricate itself from the pressure at both extremities and avoid the construction of a connection between the roads it kept apart, it would have to abandon its traditional role of a "plethoric corporation." For once it acted in positive fashion. From its large stockholders, directors, and others, including "investors" Pearson, Johnson, and Smyth, a "syndicate" of twenty coalesced and undertook the purchase of stock in the Boston, Concord and Montreal. "They have thrown themselves into the hot gates of Thermopylae and are heroically stemming the tide of foreign invasion." [107] As an investment the securities which these "Spartans" were buying were hardly attractive, for the new and the old common stock did not pay dividends, the preferred stock had only the $300,000 rental under the lease from the Boston and Lowell, and the buyers had to pay prices far above the market quotations. Later, after the syndicate had secured control, these new stockholders of the Boston, Concord and Montreal demanded from the Boston and Lowell the return of their property. Their ultima-

[105] *Testimony Offered in Support of the "Hazen Bill" before the Railroad Committee of the New Hampshire House of Representatives June Session, 1887* (Concord: Republican Press Association, 1887), pp. 57, 72–73, 187–188.

[106] *Forty-third Annual Report of the Railroad Commission of the State of New Hampshire, 1887*, pp. 46, 53–54, 60; James F. Briggs, *Speech of Hon. James F. Briggs, before the Railroad Committee of the House of Representatives, July 20, 1887* (Concord: Republican Press Association, 1887), p. 6; *Report of the Directors of the Boston & Lowell Railroad Corporation, for the Year 1886, with Statements of Twelve Months Accounts, to September 30, 1886* (Boston: Rockwell & Churchill, 1886), p. 14.

[107] Edgar Aldrich, *Argument of Hon. Edgar Aldrich, before the Railroad Committee of the House of Representatives, July 5, 1887* (Concord: Republican Press Association, 1887), p. 31.

tum declared the "instrument purporting to be a lease" was "illegal and void." [108] This unprejudiced appraisal drew strength from a recent decision by Justice Doe in the case of Dow et al. *v.* Northern Railroad et al. Eventually, therefore, the Boston and Lowell lost the Boston, Concord and Montreal.

To break the bonds between the Concord and the Northern, the Pearson strategy had once again involved an appeal to the courts. The argument had been foreshadowed when a Concord spokesman, who held stock in the Northern road, rose to protest, at a meeting of the Northern's shareholders, the projected lease by the Boston and Lowell. Aside from questions of expediency, he asserted, the lease was illegal. Although the Colby Act apparently authorized it, no provision in the act protected the property of the dissenting stockholders: furthermore, the Boston and Lowell was not authorized to lease New Hampshire roads, for it was neither a New Hampshire corporation nor legally operating a railroad within the state.[109] A week later S. H. Dow, who owned 110 shares in the Northern and much more in the Concord, started these arguments on the path through the courts.[110] Though for two years lawyers, referees, and judges poured over briefs and answers, Justice Doe in 1887 settled the issue in a single cryptic paragraph. The lease was invalid—the reason, by implication, was because it did not protect the rights of dissenting stockholders.[111]

Because of Doe's ill health and the pressure of other business, a statement of full judicial wisdom waited twelve years. When finally reported in 1899, the decision embraced long excursions on the true meaning of the Dartmouth College Case, portions of a

[108] *Testimony . . . in Support of the "Hazen Bill,"* pp. 130–133, 143–144; *Testimony Introduced before the Railroad Committee, of the New Hampshire Legislature, in Favor of the "Atherton Bill" and in Opposition to the "Hazen Bill"* (Concord: N. H. Democratic Press Company, n. d.), pp. 60–61; Henry McFarland, "Concord as a Railroad Center," J. O. Lyford, ed., *History of Concord, New Hampshire, from the Original Grant in Seventeen Hundred and Twenty-five to the Opening of the Twentieth Century* (Concord: 1903), II, 894–895.

[109] Drew, *Closing Argument, . . . August 3, 1887,* p. 32.

[110] Mitchell, *Opening Argument . . . June 29, 1887,* p. 12; *Circuit Court of the U. S. New Hampshire District. Boston, Concord & Montreal R. R. vs. Boston & Lowell R. R. Corporation. Hearings and Evidence* (n. p., n. d.), p. 53.

[111] Samuel H. Dow et al. *v.* Northern Railroad et al., 67 *New Hampshire,* 2.

manuscript previously published in the *Harvard Law Review*, and
more than the customary erudition. Neither the original succinct
decision of the court nor the printed opinion chose to discuss the
legal position of the Boston and Lowell, a foreign corporation, as
a lessor of New Hampshire railroads; instead, the judges brooded
upon the nature of corporations, charters, and directorial obligations. The charter of the Northern was a contract between the
stockholders of the company. Although the legislature could alter
such charter-contracts, "no alteration has authorized a part of
the company to suspend the company's performance of the contract by transferring their road and business to other principals
for ninety-nine years. . . . The lease violates the partnership contract, and takes from the plaintiffs an equitable estate of ninety-
nine years without their consent, and without prepayment of the
value of the estate taken." [112] In brief, leases must have unanimous consent or protesting stockholders must receive compensation.

In 1887, after three years of operation, the system of the Boston and Lowell confronted disintegration. Once again the roads
north of Concord were thrown into the pot. In its extremity the
Lowell turned to an alliance with the Boston and Maine. A
union with that road had several advantages. It would put a stop
to the competition between the two roads in Massachusetts. The
Boston and Maine, a New Hampshire corporation, might assume
the New Hampshire leases of the Boston and Lowell and set at
rest the accusation of "foreignness." Besides, the Boston and
Lowell was tired. With the prospect of a guaranteed return upon
its securities greater than it could earn, the Lowell was "willing
somebody else should fight the fight and we take the money." [113]
Consequently, in the latter part of April the Boston and Lowell
executed a new lease of the Northern with the understanding that
the Boston and Maine pay the rental and itself lease the Northern
if the first understanding was declared invalid.[114] In June the
Boston and Lowell system as a unit was leased to the Boston

---

[112] *Ibid.*, 3, 9, 20–21, 63–64.
[113] *Testimony . . . in Support of the "Hazen Bill,"* pp. 84–87.
[114] *Ibid.*, pp. 37–41.

and Maine.[115] Except as a skeleton organization, the career of this pioneer railroad of New England was done. Even its opponents were moved to express an emotion asserted as genuine: "The Boston and Lowell is no more! Never, while the mountains lift themselves under our northern New Hampshire skies, will that splendid corporation be resurrected." [116] Its departure, to be sure, settled no immediate problems. But the chaos and contention which followed in New Hampshire belong to the history of the consolidation of the Boston and Maine.[117]

VII

In spite of hearings and injunctions, court decisions and broken agreements, speculative raids and stormy annual meetings, the roads still ran, and running helped transform the economy of northern New England. The raw material industries were quickened and expanded and lumbering, in particular, moved to the new wilderness areas of upper New Hampshire and Vermont.[118] Agriculture under the impact of western competition turned to dairying and away from cereal production. To the surprise of those who had lived through a different era, it was no longer possible for a grist mill in every town to make a living for its owner by grinding local grain.[119] The milk car or train was the symbol of the transformation. The old self-sufficiency disappeared. "New Hampshire is to a certain extent a dependent state. While we have within our borders a diversity of interests, we are largely dependent upon Massachusetts for our market in which both to buy and sell. London is no more the centre of England than is Boston the centre of all that portion of New England east of the Connecticut River. All our railroads centre in that city." [120]

Though the Grand Trunk-Central Vermont route — or to use

---

[115] Massachusetts *Nineteenth Annual Report of the Board of Railroad Commissioners. January, 1888,* pp. 467–473.

[116] Jewell, *Argument . . . July 7, 1887,* p. 9.

[117] *Forty-fourth Annual Report of the Railroad Commissioners of the State of New Hampshire, 1888,* pp. 6–10.

[118] Concord *Independent Statesman,* September 22, 1881.

[119] *Ibid.,* July 10, 1883; *Senate Reports,* 51 Cong. 1 Sess., no. 847 (s. n. 2706), pp. 415–416.

[120] Concord *Independent Statesman,* May 31, 1883.

the appellation of its fast freight, the National Dispatch line —
was of immense importance to northern New England, its tonnage
figures apparently proved its inferiority as an instrument for
promoting metropolitan commerce and greatness. Though in the
quarter century after 1875 the amount of corn it brought to Boston
multiplied twelve times and of wheat eight, its totals were still
far below the receipts of the same products over either the Boston
and Albany or the Tunnel route.[121] As for westbound traffic from
New England, it carried in the late eighties about 13 per cent of
the total.[122] Such statistics revealed only partially the contributions of the route. Through its enterprise or need, it developed
the dressed-beef and the dairy-product trade between the West
and Boston.[123] Since its mileage to Chicago was longer and its
deliveries slower, since in the Grand Trunk and the Central
Vermont the line always hovered at the edge of financial disaster,
the managers of the route were more aggressive, independent, and
unprincipled in the matter of rates. They undercut, seized differentials, crawled out of rate agreements, and brought on some of
the major competitive battles among the trunk lines. New
England shippers, receivers, and merchants were convinced that
the mere existence of this independent route through Canada prevented other lines from neglecting New England business. It
operated as a beneficent "regulator" of rates.[124] Those who
owned bonds in the Vermont Central or shares in the Vermont
and Canada or both in the Grand Trunk could have this recompense as consolation.

[121] Massachusetts *Seventh Annual Report of the Board of Railroad Commissioners. January, 1876*, pp. 119, 120, 122; Massachusetts, *Thirty-second Annual
Report of the Board of Railroad Commissioners. January, 1901*, pp. 35–36.
[122] *Senate Reports*, 51 Cong., 1 Sess., no. 847, p. 14.
[123] *Ibid.*, pp. 259, 261, 388–389.
[124] *Ibid.*, pp. 302, 322, 367, 400, 402–406.

XIV

MAINE'S EXPERIMENT WITH GOVERNMENT AID

"Why should private individuals be called upon to make a useless sacrifice of their means, when railroads can be constructed by the unity of public with private interests, and made profitable to all?"
— Portland Press, March 13, 1867.

I

In 1870 Governor Joshua L. Chamberlain diagnosed for the legislature the peculiar position of the State of Maine. Declaring she was not like other New England states, he concluded, "She reminds me more of the Western States in her condition and needs, — a virgin soil, undeveloped powers, vast forests, and vigorous men, but no money. Like them she is trying to build railroads, invite immigration and develop her resources." [1] Although few could match the gubernatorial rhetoric, Chamberlain's pride in the state and his dreams of her golden future were shared by a host of fellow citizens. They, too, felt the impulse to reverse the state's habit of decline and labored to inaugurate a day of redemption. In the sixties "an act to encourage manufactures" permitted towns to exempt manufacturing enterprises from taxation for ten years; a hydrographic survey, directed by the energetic John A. Poor, described the waterpower resources of Maine; and the state promoted on a small scale the immigration of Scandinavians.[2] Communities and the state alike embarked

---

[1] Address of Governor Chamberlain to the Legislature, January, 1870, Maine *Public Documents*, 1870, no. 2, p. 9.

[2] *Ibid.*, pp. 26–31; Address of Governor Chamberlain to the Legislature, January, 1869, Maine *Public Documents*, 1869, no. 2, pp. 18–20; *Acts and Resolves Passed by the Forty-third Legislature of the State of Maine.* 1864, p. 175.

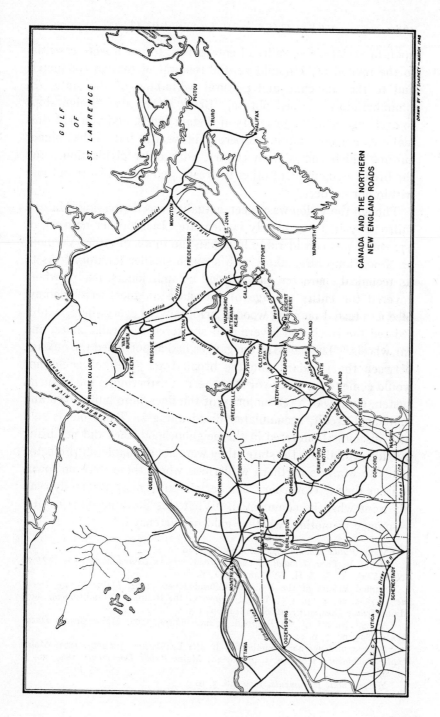

CANADA AND THE NORTHERN
NEW ENGLAND ROADS

DRAWN BY W.F. SHARKEY — MARCH 1948

upon financial aid to railroad enterprises, for such were essential to the revival of shipbuilding, the renewal of foreign commerce, and to the economic and cultural rekindling of the state. In Chamberlain's strained phrase, "Bring hither also foreign ships to exchange here the products of distant lands, and you will thus make us not only more prosperous in wealth, but in that higher culture which comes from contact with older civilizations, and the broad recognition of other interests, and other men than those within our borders." [3]

Though the vision was sweet, actuality was depressing. Maine's railroad system was utterly inadequate. In 1860 her network of 472 miles was considerably less than the totals of either Vermont or New Hampshire, states with a much smaller territory.[4] As to its technical character, the railroad commissioners, one of whom covered the entire mileage of the state on foot, were gloomy. Sleepers rested on clay, wooden bridges were everywhere, winter twisted the track and severe cold shattered iron rails, axles, and car wheels.[5] The battle of the gauges had apportioned the mileage between the standard and the broad track; neither could nor would come to the rescue of the other.[6] Furthermore, the financial system upon which the majority of the lines were built, town and municipal credit, accumulated disadvantages. Town bonds sold at a discount; marketed in the neighborhood, they did not bring outside capital into the state; they were not available for projected roads to Maine's northern wilderness where there were no towns to issue them.[7] Governor Chamberlain put it more succinctly than his wont when he commented, "What this State needs is capital — money in motion, whether gold or currency." [8]

[3] Maine *Public Documents*, 1869, no. 2, p. 20.
[4] Henry V. Poor, *Manual of the Railroads of the United States, for 1871–72* (New York: H. V. & H. W. Poor, 1871), p. xxxiii.
[5] Annual Report of the Railroad Commissioners, 1864, Maine *Senate Documents*, 1865, no. 4, pp. 3–5; Annual Report of the Railroad Commissioners, 1865, Maine *Senate Documents*, 1866, no. 12, pp. 3–5.
[6] Annual Report of the Railroad Commissioners, 1868, Maine *Senate Documents*, 1869, no. 7, p. 20.
[7] Address of Governor Chamberlain to the Legislature, January, 1867, Maine *Public Documents*, 1867, no. 3, pp. 39–40; Maine *Public Documents*, 1869, no. 2, pp. 19–20.
[8] Maine *Public Documents*, 1870, no. 5, p. 9.

Between 1860 and 1875, however, the railroad mileage of the state somewhat more than doubled, a rate of increase unmatched elsewhere in New England.[9] As for its technical qualities, the constant complaints of railroad commissioners against excessively heavy rolling stock or excessively fast speeds revealed indirectly that both roadbeds and rails were still frail and insubstantial.[10] Still the broad gauge had been shifted to the standard one. Though the costs for altering cars were not excessive, those for moving the track were large and for altering locomotives so excessive that new motive power generally came upon the rails. The convenience of interchange within the state and the advantage of connections outside drove the state to this expensive penance for her earlier craving for railroad independence.[11] In this period, also, the old methods of private finance, generously assisted by town and municipal aid, were made into a system. Unwilling or unable to repeal constitutional limitations upon state assistance, the legislature in 1867 passed an act permitting two-thirds of the voters at a legal meeting in town or city to appropriate, in any form they saw fit, a sum in aid of railroad construction, not greater than 5 per cent of the community's valuation.[12] When this statute seemed a restriction, the legislature annually altered its limitations by special enactment, and for particular enterprises, notably the European and North American, discovered other means of state assistance. The railroad mania of the times did the rest. Significantly enough, in 1878 the state wrote into its constitution an amendment prohibiting any community from incurring a debt greater than 5 per cent of its valuation.[13] For the moment the frenzy for expansion was over.

[9] Henry V. Poor, *Manual of the Railroads of the United States, for 1881* (New York: H. V. and H. W. Poor, 1881), p. lxxviii.

[10] *Report of the Railroad Commissioners of the State of Maine, for the Year 1873*, pp. 8–10; *Report of the Railroad Commissioners of the State of Maine, for the Year 1874*, pp. 10–12.

[11] *Report of the Railroad Commissioners of the State of Maine, for the Year 1877*, pp. 4–5.

[12] *Acts and Resolves Passed by the Forty-sixth Legislature of the State of Maine. 1867*, pp. 68–69.

[13] *Fourth Revision. The Revised Statutes of the State of Maine, Passed August 29, 1883, and Taking Effect January 1, 1884*, p. 53.

II

From this era of railroad promotion and construction, Bangor, previously a mere railhead for Portland's network, emerged as a minor railroad center. Fired by the railroad fever, she dreamed of independence, discarded her "old fogginess," and permitted John A. Poor, the railroad prophet, to resurrect the time-worn vision, the European and North American.[14] Poor and everyone else realized that public assistance alone could build it. Whence to obtain such aid was the problem. The national government, lavishly endowing western projects with land grants and occasional loans, had in Maine no public domain to bestow. Though Maineites as eminent as Governor Chamberlain saw beyond the international boundary dark political doings full of foreboding, — the governor believing "the scheme for the consolidation of the British Provinces on our border . . . along with the French Empire of Mexico, a part of the great conspiracy against Liberty on this youthful continent" — [15] few in Washington were impressed with such fears and fewer still with the wisdom of national assistance for a railroad built to protect Maine and the nation against them.[16] Nonetheless a subterfuge was at hand. For decades Massachusetts and Maine had pressed various claims against the national government. Both felt entitled to sums which the former had spent during the War of 1812 and to compensation for the timber carried away by interloping Canadians and for lands transferred under the provisions of the Webster-Ashburton Treaty to owners holding titles from New Brunswick or Quebec. For years reports of Congressional committees had regarded these claims favorably; for years nothing important was done.[17] At last, in 1868 Congress appropriated $146,593 for the land claims and two

[14] John A. Poor, *No Restrictions on Railway Transit. Argument of John A. Poor, before the Joint Standing Committee on Railroads, Ways and Bridges* (Bangor: David Bugbee & Co., 1865), pp. 65–66.

[15] Maine *Public Documents*, 1867, no. 3, p. 32; Maine *Senate Documents*, 1869, no. 7, p. 20; Poor, *No Restrictions on Railway Transit*, pp. 51–52.

[16] Petition of John A. Poor to the National Congress, Maine *Senate Documents*, 1864, no. 1, pp. 2–4.

[17] Report of the Committee of Claims on Land Titles in Maine, *House Reports*, 36 Cong., 1 Sess., no. 458 (s. n. 1069); Report of the Committee on Foreign Rela-

years later $678,362 for interest on money spent by Massachusetts in the War of 1812.[18]

It was comparatively easy to persuade Maine to transfer these sums to the road. Massachusetts was a tougher problem — for the European and North American had originally been planned as a part of Maine's independent network. It was to be built on the broad gauge of the Grand Trunk rather than on the standard gauge of the Boston roads, and the whole broad-gauge network was legally stiffened into an anti-Boston system by the act of 1860 forbidding any railroad west of the Grand Trunk road to change its gauge or lay a third rail without the assent of the legislature.[19] Unless this act was repealed, the Boston Board of Trade, the Massachusetts General Court, and influential investors made it quite clear that Massachusetts would transfer no claims against the national government to the European and North American Railway or even consider the more generous forms of state assistance Poor was suggesting. The measure had to go.[20] It was simple for the governor to declare the statute was no longer "indispensable"; it was far harder for John A. Poor to reconcile his previous insistence upon the broad gauge with his present advocacy of its repeal. He made the effort.[21] Portland cried out at the betrayal, and the steamboat, commercial, and railroad interests of the city, which Poor had once taught to look upon Boston as an enemy, now moved upon Augusta determined to prevent the legislature from surrendering to their hated rival.

---

tions on Land Titles under the Washington Treaty, *Senate Reports*, 37 Cong., 3 Sess., no. 88 (s. n. 1151); Report of a Select Committee on the Defences of the Northeast, *House Reports*, 38 Cong., 1 Sess., no. 119 (s. n. 1207), pp. 14–32, 64–83.

[18] *The Statutes at Large, Treaties, and Proclamations of the United States of America*, XV, 120, XVI, 197–198; Maine *Public Documents*, 1869, no. 2, p. 16.

[19] *Acts and Resolves Passed by the Thirty-ninth Legislature of the State of Maine*. 1860, p. 135.

[20] Portland *Press*, January 16, 1865; Memorial of the European and North American Railway, Massachusetts *Senate Documents*, 1866, no. 9, pp. 8–9, 30–34; Report of the Committee on Finance on Aid to the European and North American, Massachusetts *House Documents*, 1866, no. 423; Report of the Joint Standing Committee on Railways and Canals, Massachusetts *Senate Documents*, 1866, no. 227, pp. 33–37.

[21] Poor, *No Restrictions on Railway Transit*, pp. 53, 55–56, 66; Address of Governor Cony to the Legislature, January 5, 1865, Maine *Public Documents*, 1865, no. 3, pp. 25–26; Portland *Press*, January 16, 27, April 19, 1865.

After a fierce legislative battle, the capitulation was made.[22] Thereupon the Massachusetts General Court, though it could not appropriate state money for railroads outside the Commonwealth, detected no comparable illegality in transferring a state claim against the nation to the European and North American Railway. The dowry was given.[23]

Meanwhile the architects of the road sought from Maine a tangible endowment of land and timber. Muting, except for imaginative men like Governor Chamberlain, the glories of the "Atlantic Ferry," they pictured their enterprise as of immediate benefit to the state. The European and North American was to weld the trade of the Maritime Provinces to Maine, stop the drain of commerce eastward from Aroostook into the alien land of New Brunswick, enhance the value of the wild lands in northern Maine, and serve as a means of military defense.[24] The state was sufficiently impressed to transfer to the road its claims against the national government and to grant the timber on certain townships. It conditioned a lavish grant of state lands upon Massachusetts' willingness to grant favors to the road and to the state.[25] Surveying the highly conjectural nature of such assistance, the Portland *Press*, mouthpiece for a city opposed to the whole program, observed, "In making a good chowder, one of the first things is to *catch* the cod." [26]

In 1868 the state legislature abandoned further dalliance. With the exceptions of lumber or timber already set aside for public schools, lots designated as "settlement lands" — the Maine equivalent of the homestead — and all previous grants of timber and land, the state gave the railroad "all the timber and lands . . . situated upon the waters of the Penobscot and of the St. John

[22] *Acts and Resolves Passed by the Forty-fourth Legislature of the State of Maine. 1865*, p. 284; Portland *Press*, February 6, 8, 15, 18, 19, 20, 24, 25, 1865.

[23] *Acts and Resolves Passed by the General Court of Massachusetts, in the Year 1865*, p. 631.

[24] Maine *Public Documents*, 1867, no. 3, pp. 39, 41; Address of Governor Chamberlain to the Legislature, January, 1868, Maine *Public Documents*, 1868, no. 3, pp. 39–41.

[25] *Acts and Resolves . . . of the State of Maine. 1864*, pp. 387–390.

[26] Portland *Press*, quoted in Portland *Argus*, September 25, 1865.

rivers." On its part the state required the railroad to divide such of its holdings as were suitable for settlement into lots not greater than 160 acres; to set as a requirement for individual title a maximum price of not over $1.00 an acre, residence for five years, and the performance of certain "settling duties"; and to stimulate immigration into the state through an agent and other forms of publicity. The road could sell the land or timber or use it as a security for mortgage bonds.[27] In the same year the legislature also brought to a conclusion a series of acts authorizing Bangor to assist this enterprise by an appropriation of $1,000,000 with the assent of three-fourths of the voters present at the referendum and two-thirds of both aldermen and council. Mortgages upon the road and the right to select three directors were relied upon to protect the loan.[28] The city's money was to assist construction northward from Bangor along the Penobscot Valley, the returns from the land grant bonds were to assist the construction eastward to the Maine-New Brunswick boundary.

At the moment when the European and North American at long last entered the promised land, John A. Poor, whose "original, aggressive, and peculiar" character so much accounted for the miracle, was dismissed from the enterprise.[29] As on the Atlantic and St. Lawrence and the Penobscot and Kennebec, the occasion was an obscure quarrel over a construction contract, which Poor as president of the European and North American had awarded to Pierce and Blaisdell, a contracting group in which he was financially interested and in which Pierce and Blaisdell sold the controlling interest to individuals largely identified with the Pennsylvania Railroad.[30] As law suits attempted to appraise the tangled fiduciary relationships concerned, construction proceeded apace. By mid-October, 1871, the road was ready to celebrate its

---

[27] *Acts and Resolves . . . of Maine, 1864*, pp. 388–389; *Acts and Resolves Passed by the Forty-fifth Legislature of the State of Maine, 1866*, pp. 117–118; *Acts and Resolves of the Forty-seventh Legislature of the State of Maine. 1868*, pp. 524–526.

[28] *Acts and Resolves . . . of Maine, 1864*, pp. 411–415; *Acts and Resolves . . . of Maine. 1866*, pp. 96–101; *Acts and Resolves . . . of Maine. 1868*, pp. 493–499.

[29] Portland *Press*, September 6, 1871.

[30] John A. Poor *v.* European & North American Railway Company, 59 *Maine*, 270; European & North American Railway Company, in equity *v.* John A. Poor, 59 *Maine*, 277; Portland *Press*, January 3, 11, 23, 1868, December 19, 1871.

official opening. In a Bangor bedizened with decorations, the usual civic celebration of parades, drills, and firemen's muster unrolled. Then the dignitaries — President Grant and the governor general of Canada, and the governors of Maine and of New Brunswick — proceeded over the rails to Vanceboro on the boundary, there to lend "their presence at festivities commemorative of the completion of a work which . . . is yielding to the country a royalty of employment and prosperity, . . . beyond prediction of seer or enthusiast." [31] Just a month earlier Poor had died suddenly in Portland.[32]

Although a few gaps in the Provinces broke temporarily the through line to Halifax, Maine's portion of the European and North American Railroad was done. It was a frontier road. Cuts were narrow; embankments were not up to grade; culverts were of wood rather than of stone; and sleepers, of less than standard size and spaced too far apart, enabled the builders to skimp 400 ties and 1,600 spikes to the mile. Occasionally fills over bogs sank so rapidly that work trains kept the route open with difficulty. The superintendent who brought to "the discharge of his duties the advantage of much familiarity with the workings of Western railroads," must have felt at home on this Maine enterprise.[33]

According to Poor's *Manual*, "The officers of this company have always refused to furnish any information as to its operations or financial condition." [34] In spite of their policy of concealment, the financial imperfections of the road could not be hidden. Apparently the cost of building and equipping the road had been met by a "paid-in" capital stock of $522,300 — how nominal this was there is no means of knowing, — by $824,956 in cash from the

[31] *Report of the Railroad Commissioners of the State of Maine, for the Year 1871*, pp. 6, 9–10; Portland *Press*, October 12, 20, 1871.

[32] Portland *Press*, September 6, 1871.

[33] Report of the Railroad Commissioners, 1869, Maine *Senate Documents*, 1870, no. 1, p. 11; *Report of the Railroad Commissioners . . . of Maine, . . . 1871*, pp. 7–8; *Report of the Railroad Commissioners of the State of Maine, for the Year 1880*, pp. 12–14; *Report of the Railroad Commissioners of the State of Maine, for the Year 1881*, pp. 14–15.

[34] Henry V. Poor, *Manual of the Railroads of the United States for 1875–76* (New York: H. V. & H. W. Poor, 1875), p. 7.

national government via Massachusetts and Maine, $1,000,000 from the city of Bangor, represented by first mortgage bonds, $2,000,000 in bonds based on the land grant and the road itself, and a large floating debt "hovering over it, like a bird of prey." [35]

The road was soon at war with the state over the exact extent of the latter's benefactions. To politicians it seemed a "princely domain." To a jerry-built road, advised by ingenious counsel, it was clear that the state had in reality given greater favors and more land than the local statesmen would admit. The European and North American claimed the right to timber already granted to the Maine Wesleyan Seminary and Female College, with the understanding this institution would establish five perpetual scholarships "for returned soldiers or their children, or the children of such as had fallen in defense of their country," [36] and later it asserted that settlement lands, or at least the timber upon them, had not in fact been reserved by the state but given to the road.[37] These contentions the court in the mid-seventies brusquely rejected.[38] The railroad meanwhile had enlarged its unpopularity.

All in all, the state's generosity to the road greatly benefited neither party to the arrangement. The railroad neglected its obligation to stimulate immigration and, when an angry legislature compelled action on the premises, the compliance was merely nominal.[39] Nor had the railroad fulfilled its promise of developing northern Maine. Built part-way up the Penobscot, it turned sharply east to the Maritimes and left aside the whole northern peninsula of the state. On its part the European and North American received apparently about 734,000 acres, on a third of which the timber was reserved by the state. In the early eighties the land commissioner of the railroad had sold land and stumpage

[35] *Report of the Railroad Commissioners of the State of Maine, for the Year 1875*, pp. 11, 13; Henry V. Poor, *Manual of the Railroads of the United States, for 1872–73* (New York: H. V. & H. W. Poor, 1872), p. 395.

[36] European & North American Railway Company *v.* E. G. Dunn, 60 *Maine*, 454n.

[37] Address of Governor Perham to the Legislature, January, 1872, Maine *Public Documents*, 1872, no. 4, pp. 9–10.

[38] Elbridge G. Dunn *v.* Parker P. Burleigh and Another, 62 *Maine*, 24.

[39] *Acts and Resolves of the Fiftieth Legislature, of the State of Maine. 1871*, pp. 150–151.

for $102,870; after various deductions, $55,466 of this sum had been spent in the repurchase of the land-grant bonds and $28,015 had been transferred to the railroad.[40] Curiously enough from the experiment of government aid, Bangor emerged comparatively untouched. Though the road collapsed and was reorganized in the mid-seventies, Bangor had to pay the interest on its bonds for only a few months and received in the new company a first mortgage to protect its $1,000,000 loan.[41] This the Maine Central, when it finally leased the European and North American in the early eighties, undertook to pay, both interest and principal.[42] Private investors fared much worse.

So far Bangor had been fortunate. The Maine Central had underwritten the city's pre-Civil-War advances to the Penobscot and Kennebec [43] and its loan to the European and North American. The city's experience with a third and smaller enterprise, the Bangor and Piscataquis, was, however, both unlucky and vexatious. This road, chartered in 1861 and completed in 1884, ran northward from Oldtown on the European and North American to the foot of Moosehead Lake.[44] According to its projectors it traversed a region surfeited with natural resources and embryo water powers; it also was the link in a through route to Canada and the Great West.[45] For a time the planners hoped their line might be constructed by the European and North American and

[40] Address of Governor Dingley to the Legislature, January 7, 1875, Maine *Public Documents*, 1875, no. 4, p. 27; Henry V. Poor, *Manual of the Railroads of the United States for 1882* (New York: H. V. & H. W. Poor, 1882), p. 5.

[41] *City of Bangor. Mayor's Address; Also, the Annual Reports of the Several Departments, and the Receipts and Expenditures for the Municipal Year 1875-'76*, p. 6; *City of Bangor. Mayor's Address; . . . Annual Reports . . . for the Municipal Year 1878-'79*, p. 12.

[42] *City of Bangor. Mayor's Address; . . . Annual Reports . . . for the Municipal Year 1882-83*, p. 12; *City of Bangor. Mayor's Address; . . . Annual Reports . . . for the Municipal Year 1892-93*, pp. 8-9.

[43] *City of Bangor. Mayor's Address, . . . Annual Reports . . . for the Municipal Year 1874-75*, p. 6.

[44] *Acts and Resolves Passed by the Fortieth Legislature of the State of Maine. 1861*, pp. 43-49; *Report of the Railroad Commissioners of the State of Maine. 1884*, p. 12.

[45] Report of a Special Committee on Railroad Communication into Piscataquis County, Maine *House Documents*, 1861, no. 19; Maine *Senate Documents*, 1869, no. 1, pp. 7-8.

share in the bounty given the latter by the state.[46] When these
expectations failed, Bangor undertook to provide the finances.
Authorized at the outset to subscribe at the rate of $15,000 a
mile, the city eventually owned $925,000 worth of the road's bonds
and $200,000 of common stock out of an issue of $356,920.[47]
Actually Bangor built and managed the road.[48]

The Bangor and Piscataquis was an unhappy adventure for
municipal finance. In spite of occasional interruptions, the
deficits mounted and the shaky enterprise did little to help the city
meet the obligations incurred in the former's behalf.[49] Year after
year railroad issues, relevant and irrelevant, disturbed the course
of Bangor politics. Some candidates for the mayoralty reluctantly proposed increased taxation. Others advocated economy,
for taxation was "a great hardship upon the middle class, . . . We
are here but for a short time at the most and it is not our duty to
be forever burdened with high taxes that the future inhabitants of
this city may live in luxury." [50] The possibility of repudiation
was, however, beaten back by the cry, "No legacy is so rich as
honesty." [51]   As the arguments went on, proposals for sale or
lease were accepted by the citizens and rejected by the city government or accepted by the city government and rejected by the
citizens. Bangor officials had to keep their eyes open to prevent
the chartering of parallel roads.[52] Finally in the late nineties an

[46] *Acts and Resolves . . . of Maine. 1864*, pp. 389–390; *Acts and Resolves . . .
of Maine. 1867*, pp. 314–315.
[47] *Acts and Resolves . . . of Maine. 1868*, pp. 406–411; *City of Bangor. Mayor's
Address; . . . Annual Reports . . . for the Municipal Year 1876–'77*, pp. 16–17;
Report of the Railroad Commissioners of the State of Maine, for the Year 1876,
p. 8; Portland *Press*, April 20, 1867.
[48] *City of Bangor. Mayor's Address; . . . Annual Reports . . . for the Municipal
Year 1883–84*, pp. 25, 210.
[49] *City of Bangor. Mayor's Address; . . . Annual Reports . . . for the Municipal
Year 1889–'90*, p. 37.
[50] *City of Bangor. Mayor's Address, . . . Annual Reports . . . for the Municipal
Year 1895–6*, pp. 6–7.
[51] *City of Bangor. Mayor's Address; . . . Annual Reports . . . for the Municipal
Year 1879–'80*, p. 18.
[52] *City of Bangor. Mayor's Address; . . . Annual Reports . . . for the Municipal
Year 1883–84*, p. 7; *City of Bangor. Mayor's Address; . . . Annual Reports . . . for
the Municipal Year 1885–86*, p. 7; *City of Bangor. Mayor's Address; . . . Annual Reports . . . for the Municipal Year 1888–89*, pp. 8–10; Portland *Press*, June
1, 1870, February 13, 1880.

adroit mayor compelled a newcomer, the Bangor and Aroostook, to assume the bonds of the Bangor and Piscataquis owned by the city. Bangor secured no compensation for the arrears of interest.[53]

III

While Bangor thus realized her limited ambition to be a center of Maine railroads, Portland still sought the status of a great Atlantic port — amidst the gathering gloom. For her first-born, the Grand Trunk, once the Atlantic and St. Lawrence, had grown to disappointing manhood. As might have been foreseen, this Canadian, this "foreign" enterprise, was more devoted to Montreal than to its Maine mother.[54] Furthermore it now behaved like other trunk lines. Though originally conceived for the benefit of a single metropolis, it promoted commerce to any port or along any route that offered promise and profit. In the sixties the Grand Trunk was already turning to the Vermont Central and the route to Boston.[55] To despoil the latter, the Atlantic and St. Lawrence had been built — at least so thought the more loyal Portlanders. There was even considerable doubt whether the road could fill its diminished rôle as a supplier of the Maine market and a connection between Montreal and its winter port. The passage of heavy freights had worn out the roadbed; iron rails, recently installed, were of inferior quality; sleepers were rotten and defective.[56] In 1868 the Maine Railroad Commission forbade passenger trains to run faster than fifteen miles an hour and during the ensuing quarrel threatened to close the road entirely unless improvements were made.[57] Nor was the financial prospect reassuring. As the Portland scrip issued for the Atlantic and St. Lawrence came due

---

[53] *City of Bangor. Mayor's Address; . . . Annual Reports . . . for the Municipal Year 1898–99*, pp. 3–4, 6–7.

[54] Portland *Press*, May 9, 1865, December 11, 12, 1866.

[55] Portland *Press*, June 23, 1862, January 17, February 4, 1867, January 16, 1868; *Half Year Ended December 31st, 1871. Grand Trunk Railway Company of Canada. Report of the Directors to the Bond and Stockholders* (London: Waterlow & Sons, 1872), p. 12.

[56] Report of the Railroad Commissioners, 1865, Maine *Senate Documents*, 1866, no. 12, pp. 10–11; Maine *Senate Documents*, 1868, no. 6, pp. 12–13.

[57] Maine *Senate Documents*, 1869, no. 7, pp. 9–13; Maine *Senate Documents*, 1870, no. 1, p. 10.

between 1868 and 1871, the sinking funds previously accumulated for its redemption were sufficient to meet only half the total. The city had to refund the remainder with a new issue of its securities.[58] These were finally discharged in 1888.[59]

Under the circumstances, Portland again saw "the necessity of stretching out her iron arms as Boston had done, and bringing to her embrace the West," [60] and in the post-Civil-War railroad era it was as logical to plan for this purpose two new routes as one. Since both required municipal assistance, both repaired to the state legislature for enactments permitting Portland to bestow it. Their noisy rivalry was one explanation for the enactment in 1867 of the general law, already noted, permitting cities and towns to subscribe up to 5 per cent of their valuation to railroad enterprises. Thus badgered legislators avoided the embarrassment of determining which road was the better and transferred the choice to Portland's citizens. The latter could decide whether to aid the Portland and Rochester or the Portland and Ogdensburg if they could pierce the golden mist of promotion obscuring both projects.

The first, the Portland and Rochester, an old corporation with a long history of broken promises and financial mismanagement, was really designed as a new route to Boston or as a cross-country one through Nashua and Worcester to New York.[61] Under the excitement of the moment, it now prated of extensions westward by way of the Vermont Central or the Hoosac Tunnel. In either case the selected route was not precise and the necessary links to complete it were not built, much less chartered.[62] No wonder

---

[58] *City of Portland. Mayor's Address and Annual Reports of the Several Departments of the City Government, for the Financial Year 1869–70*, pp. 87–90; *City of Portland. Mayor's Address and Annual Reports . . . for the Financial Year 1871-72*, pp. 64–67.

[59] *City of Portland. Auditor's Thirtieth Annual Report . . . with the Mayor's Address, and Annual Reports . . . March, 1889*, p. 70.

[60] Portland *Press*, January 30, 1867.

[61] *Acts and Resolves Passed by the Twenty-sixth Legislature of the State of Maine, A. D. 1846*, pp. 447–454; *Acts and Resolves Passed by the Thirty-second Legislature of the State of Maine, A. D. 1853*, pp. 180–181; *Acts and Resolves . . . of Maine, 1866*, pp. 91–92.

[62] Portland *Press*, February 2, 1867, November 9, 1870; Portland *Argus*, December 20, 1866.

the partisans of the Portland and Ogdensburg derided the detours of the projected line and hinted that it traversed territory irrevocably linked to the Boston interest.[63]

On the other hand the Portland and Ogdensburg was chartered in 1867 at the insistence of Portland citizens.[64] It had a rugged independence. Moving westward along a new route from Portland, it hit the Saco Valley; followed that stream northward through Crawford Notch, where a grade of 65 feet to the mile was possible since "the Great Architect of the Universe left open a passage through the White Hills, to be found when wanted for a worthy purpose"; attained the Connecticut; crossed northern Vermont and at Lake Champlain made connection with the railroad to Ogdensburg. There Portland's railroad would touch the steamer traffic of the Great Lakes or proceed by other roads along Lake Ontario's southern shore, it is not quite clear how far.[65] The route would quicken the development of the water powers which lined it, save for Portland the trade of western Maine, gain for it the commerce — copper, iron, lumber, and maple sugar — from northern New Hampshire and Vermont, win the markets of a people who were all "good livers," and make available the scenery of the White Mountains.[66] "This tendency of travel in the summer, accelerated by the combined forces of desire to escape the heat of large cities, and a wish to enjoy the air and scenery of the mountains is a phase of our social life, that has within a few years enlarged into importance in economical statistics." [67] Portland even had transcontinental ambitions. "To complete an all-rail communication across the continent, by the most direct line, from Portland to San Francisco, there is needed only the 150 miles more or less" of the Portland and Ogdensburg.[68] That this route relied upon the Vermont Central, a Boston road, and upon lake transportation, at the very moment the latter's inferiority was being realized, was not emphasized.

[63] Portland *Press*, February 4, 7, 8, 1867.   [64] *Ibid.*, January 15, 1867.
[65] *Ibid.*, April 30, July 23, August 27, 1867.
[66] *Report of the Railroad Commissioners of the State of Maine, for the Year 1870*, pp. 6–7; Portland *Press*, March 28, April 11, 16, 1867, October 9, 1871.
[67] *Report of the Railroad Commissioners of the State of Maine, for the Year 1872*, pp. 19–20.   [68] Portland *Press*, July 24, 1867.

These two fantastic enterprises, the Portland and Rochester and the Portland and Ogdensburg, now combined for an assault upon the city. Since 5 per cent of Portland's valuation was $1,400,000, each of the roads was ultimately entitled to $700,000, $250,000 of which was to be granted at once and the remainder when the city government was convinced western connections were assured. At least that was the suggested compromise.[69] Since both roads, moreover, desired to hasten the flow of private investment, they unloosed a promotional campaign blending the romance of the circus with the evangelical ardor of the camp-meeting. If doubts were expressed, Portlanders of vision dismissed the voices as those of "timid conservatives," "retired gentlemen of wealth, usurers, constitutional croakers, and grumblers."[70] There were excursions. One over the projected route from Portland to Ogdensburg carried ex-governors, mayors, journalists, congressmen, and capitalists worth $5,000,000.[71] There were picnics. In July, when Portland entertained her "western friends," speeches soared to the zenith, as orators contemplated the union of the Great Lakes and Casco Bay, "a marriage more significant than the wedding of Venice and the Adriatic,"[72] and in the general glow Boston, now more pitied than feared, was told there was trade enough for all. One wit christened the monster clambake a "coup de Maine."[73] If John A. Poor had not always been in earnest, his descent upon the city the following year with a third proposal, the Portland, Rutland, Oswego and Chicago Railroad, would have added simply an appropriately comic note to the general din.[74]

Meanwhile Portland met the obligations expected of her; she voted aid to both the Portland and Rochester and the Portland and Ogdensburg. The original grants or their later modifications, however, gave the loans little protection. On the Portland and

[69] *Ibid.*, April 19, 26, 1867.
[70] *Ibid.*, May 15, 1868.
[71] *Ibid.*, June 7, 10, 11, 12, 13, 14, 16, 17, 18, 25, 1867.
[72] *Ibid.*, July 18, 23, 1867.
[73] *Ibid.*, July 19, 1867.
[74] *Ibid.*, February 20, March 22, 1868, January 15, October 8, 9, 11, 13, 1869, January 11, March 17, 18, December 16, 1870, February 24, 28, 1871.

Rochester the mileage prerequisites to the receipt of municipal credit were soon waived, and for the $700,000 granted the Portland and Ogdensburg the city received common stock rather than first mortgage bonds.[75] Both roads picked up additional funds by the sale of first mortgage bonds to private investors and by exceedingly limited subscriptions to their common stock. By the end of 1871 neither was complete. Though the Portland and Rochester had staggered into Rochester, the vital connecting links to New York City were not yet built, and an excursion on the Portland and Ogdensburg carried the directors within sight of the mountain scenery but left them daunted by Crawford Notch. Neither road could find a market for its bonds.[76]

Once more they put Portland under siege. The first maneuver was an appeal to the legislature for an exception to the General Act of 1867. Without much ado the solons in 1872 authorized the city to subscribe $450,000 to the Portland and Rochester and its western extensions and to subscribe not more than $2,500,000 to the Portland and Ogdensburg. In both instances two-thirds of the city's voters must give their assent to the loans and the city be protected by collateral — mortgage bonds and common stock each to the amount of the loan — and by sinking funds.[77] The next operation was an appeal to the city. The prospect was not promising. The city government was surly and Thomas Brackett Reed, attorney-general of the state and a citizen of Portland, effectively analyzed for the city council and a committee of the legislature the unsoundness of the whole promotion.[78]

As it turned out the time for common sense had not yet arrived. When the voters granted the modest request of the Portland and Rochester,[79] when the larger sums asked by its contemporary gave the electorate pause, there was a perfect fever of mass meetings, personal abuse, and successive ballotings.[80] Before the citizens

[75] *Ibid.*, May 1, 1867, February 4, May 28, 29, 1868, May 21, 1869, October 11, 1870.
[76] *Ibid.*, January 18, August 16, October 6, 1871, January 17, 1872.
[77] *Acts and Resolves of the Fifty-first Legislature of the State of Maine. 1872*, pp. 150–155, 173–176.
[78] Portland *Press*, February 5, 7, 14, March 6, 1872.
[79] *Ibid.*, June 26, July 1, 1872.
[80] *Ibid.*, March 19, June 21, 24, 25, 26, July 8, 1872.

the Portland and Ogdensburg flourished a final contract for construction through the Notch to the Connecticut. Of the price, $2,300,000, the contractors were to take half in bonds and half in cash; Portland was to raise the latter sum by the loan of $1,350,000 of its scrip.[81] Those who still felt Portland should not take this "new departure in the race for wealth" [82] were confronted once again with the teleological argument. The "God of Nature" had not "forbidden the use of the mountain gorge for business purposes, and affixed the penalty of the storm and the avalanche" but instead had "cleft the mountain asunder for a channel through which the vast products of the West might flow to the sea." [83] By such considerations a two-thirds majority was convinced.

Thus succored, the two roads were at last completed. To what advantage was not clear. Of course the Portland and Rochester never reached the West. As a route to New York it was of trivial service; as a somewhat longer route via the Boston and Lowell to Boston it irritated the Boston and Maine and the Eastern and occasionally "demoralized" rates to the gratification of Portland shippers.[84] The Portland and Ogdensburg, on whose Vermont division the final silver spike was driven in 1877, had broken its contractors and had been built in a flimsy and impermanent fashion.[85] Its route through Crawford Notch proved in actuality no God-given way to the West, but a severe handicap to effective transportation. Though travelers admired this portion of the line as "truly one of the wonders of the world" bidding fair to "surpass all other works of art and nature," [86] the curves had short radii and the promised maximum of 65 feet to the mile became a nearly continuous grade of 116 feet to the mile for 7.4 miles. While these grades were down-hill for heavy freights Portland-bound, trains, before beginning the

[81] *Ibid.*, May 8, June 13, 1872.
[82] *Ibid.*, July 9, 1872.
[83] *Ibid.*, July 10, 1872.
[84] *Ibid.*, September 8, November 23, 1874, October 7, 1875, November 7, December 4, 1878.
[85] *Report of the Railroad Commissioners . . . of Maine, . . . 1876*, p. 19; Portland *Press*, January 20, December 23, 1875, February 8, July 18, 1877.
[86] Portland *Press*, September 15, 1875.

descent, had to climb grades of 85 feet to reach the head of the Notch.[87] In New Hampshire the Portland and Ogdensburg depended upon the Boston, Concord and Montreal for a link with its more western portion; in Vermont it depended upon the Vermont Central for a connection with the Ogdensburg road.[88] Both were roads in the Boston interest. So was the Eastern Railroad, with which it connected in New Hampshire and with which it had a traffic agreement not to divert Boston-bound business to other ports.[89]

For years the cost of these empty triumphs was concealed from the commonalty of Portland by reticent municipal bookkeeping, the silence of city officials, and the apparently iron-clad guarantees tendered by the claimant railroads. In the mid-seventies the crust cracked. The Portland and Rochester was the first to declare that it could no longer meet the interest on the city loan; in 1876, soon after receiving the last installment of its $1,350,000 of city scrip, the Portland and Ogdensburg announced it could no longer pay the interest on the city's advances. Of course it had never paid any dividends on Portland's $700,000 subscription to its common stock, although the city had always paid the interest on its bonds issued for that purpose. For a while the city sought to postpone the day of reckoning by issuing new securities to pay the interest on the old. Railroads which could not pay interest on the former municipal indebtedness were relied upon to do so on the newest installment.[90] When these subterfuges in turn collapsed, Mayor Francis Fessenden spoke plainly. To meet the city's indebtness he predicted an increase in the tax rate from $5.00 to $6.50 on each thousand of valuation. A few months later the city government appointed commissioners to appraise the actual situation.[91]

[87] *Report of the Railroad Commissioners . . . of Maine, . . . 1875*, pp. 25–26.
[88] Portland *Press*, January 19, 1876, April 26, 1882, January 18, 1883, January 16, 1884, February 24, 1885. [89] *Ibid.*, November 27, 1873.
[90] *Ibid.*, September 8, 1874; *City of Portland. Auditor's Seventeenth Annual Report . . . with the Mayor's Address, and Annual Reports . . . .March, 1876*, p. 10.
[91] Portland *Press*, October 4, 1877; *City of Portland. Auditor's Seventeenth Annual Report . . . with the Mayor's Address, and Annual Reports . . . March, 1876*, p. 11.

Entitled, "The Rise and Fall of Two Railroads. Our Burdens and How to Bear Them," the commission's report belatedly revealed realities. Toward construction of the Portland and Rochester, private capitalists had provided a small subscription to the stock and $350,000 to the bonds; Portland contributed $1,150,000 to the latter form of security and an additional $207,000 of bonds to pay the interest on its bonds. The annual interest charges of the road were over $100,000; net earnings did not exceed $20,000. On the Portland and Ogdensburg, private investors subscribed to 3,165 shares of stock; Portland to 7,143. Private investors or contractors took $1,031,600 worth of bonds, often at a discount; Portland held $1,350,000 bonds, bought dollar for dollar. The road had a large floating debt and had not paid employees for their labors. The interest payments on the road's debt were double the net income from its operations. Though for this mountain of misfortune city and railroad officials were in part to blame, the citizens of Portland could not escape responsibility. When the Portland and Rochester sought municipal aid, the commission commented, "A fond mother could hardly have been more indulgent to a favorite child. To ask was to receive; to knock and the doors of the city treasury flew open. . . . The city and its authorities seem to have been as ready to give as the managers of the road were to ask." [92] So much for the past. After the publication of the report, one of the commissioners, Moses M. Butler, was elected mayor of the city. He described the proper course for the future. To meet the annual interest charges on its railroad loans, a sum of $150,000, Portland could not increase taxes "without exerting a disastrous influence upon the growth and prosperity of the city." The alternative was "retrenchment pure and simple," the sale of the city's interest in the two roads, and the transfer of the resultant gains to the sinking funds. Under no circumstances should the municipality own or manage railroad enterprises.[93]

The sale of the city's securities in these two enterprises in-

[92] Portland *Press*, February 8, 1877.
[93] *City of Portland. Auditor's Eighteenth Annual Report . . . . with the Mayor's Address, and Annual Reports of the Several Departments, Made to the City Council, March, 1877*, pp. 14–17, 19–21.

volved a sacrifice both of capital and of the fancied competitive advantages which these roads had been built to supply. Perhaps the city council, legally empowered to dispose of Portland's holdings, might chance the political hazard involved. If it did, some critic was sure to suspect improper influences or official malfeasance and demand the submission of the issue to the voters. Such was the outcome in 1877 when the council sold the city's interest in the Portland and Rochester for $236,500 in cash, a sum about one-sixth of that which Portland had placed in the enterprise, and the Portland and Rochester at once allied itself with the Boston and Maine.[94] Clearly municipal divestment from the Portland and Ogdensburg must be more circumspect. So over the years as the road went through bankruptcy and reorganization, the city's securities were reduced to the level of common stock, and the road's business withered away to pleasure travel through the White Mountains.[95] Nothing was done. Finally in 1888 the citizens, tired by vicissitude and frustration, voted to lease the road to the Maine Central. For the first three years the railroad was to pay 1 per cent on the city's stock; thereafter 2.[96] In 1893 Portland was annually receiving from the road $47,122, paying annually on the municipal securities loaned to it $79,590 in interest, and still appointing directors.[97]

IV

While the folly and ambition of Bangor and Portland had multiplied the mileage of Maine's railroads, the region east of the Penobscot and north of the Piscataquis remained comparatively untouched by the improved means of transportation, except for the line of the European and North American. To be sure Hancock and Washington, the seacoast counties in question, had

[94] *City of Portland. Auditor's Twenty-first Annual Report . . . with the Mayor's Address, and Annual Reports . . . March, 1880*, pp. 10, 16, 77; Portland *Press*, May 1, June 24, July 9, November 14, 1879.

[95] Portland *Press*, February 9, 21, June 8, 1883, September 8, 1884, April 11, 17, June 5, October 14, 1885, July 15, 1887.

[96] *Ibid.*, February 21, 23, 1885, April 30, July 19, 20, 26, August 3, 1888.

[97] *Ibid.*, January 19, 1893, March 12, 1895; *City of Portland. Auditor's Thirty-fourth Annual Report . . . with the Mayor's Address and Annual Reports . . . March, 1893*, pp. 64, 72–73.

an already highly developed coastwise water transportation, and the eastern edge of Aroostook was connected by branch lines with the New Brunswick railroad system. This was insufficient. There must be more railroads. As a result, between 1885 and 1900 Maine had a final spurt of railroad construction. The relative increase of her mileage, 70 per cent, and its absolute increase, 800 miles, were unmatched in New England.[98] As in the earlier day, Maine turned once again to public assistance and with much the same result. However widespread the disillusionment with the policy,[99] the persistence of frontier conditions within the state compelled a resort to it.

Along the rough coast east of Portland, the chief ports had in the 1830's dreamed of building railroads into the interior, perhaps as far as some Canadian entrepôt. The vision, once held, was surrendered with reluctance; and throughout the nineteenth century it still stirred communities with an ample harbor and little capital to measures for its realization. They always fell short.[100] A similar fate haunted the efforts to construct a railroad along the coast. Before the Civil War the rails had reached the Kennebec at Bath. When the war was over, the Knox and Lincoln extended the line as far as Rockland. It crossed drawbridges and trestles galore, it curved around obstacles when it could and charged through rocks and ridges when it couldn't. The expense of construction was on a comparative basis "much the most costly in the State." [101] Town bonds built it; towns paid the interest on its debt; town taxpayers writhed under the resulting burdens; and the recalcitrancy of town meetings prevented, until the nineties, its sale or its lease.[102] No wonder the road never continued to Bangor. Beyond the latter city the various proposals for a coastal route had resulted by the mid-eighties in a line south and east to the Mount Desert Ferry. Plans for a connection

[98] *Infra*, II, 352.
[99] *Report of the Railroad Commissioners of the State of Maine. 1883*, p. 3.
[100] *Report of the Railroad Commissioners . . . of Maine, . . . 1871*, p. 23.
[101] *Ibid.*, pp. 22–23.
[102] Portland *Press*, March 30, 1874, March 11, 1875, November 22, 1879, May 25, 1881, March 1, 1883, April 24, May 29, September 18, 1890, April 25, December 16, 1891; Aretas Shurtleff *v.* Inhabitants of Wiscasset, 74 *Maine*, 130.

through Washington County to Calais foundered on the rock of finance.[103] In the nineties Washington County, announcing it could wait no longer, secured a charter for the Washington County Railroad, bought out the individuals previously interested in the route, and after the customary referendum invested $500,000 in the preferred stock of the enterprise.[104] Construction at last began. Open in 1899, the road soon collapsed into bankruptcy and reorganization.[105] The original stockholders, including the County of Washington, lost their entire investment. Eventually the Maine Central absorbed the enterprise.[106]

The failure of Maine railroads, particularly the European and North American, to penetrate northern Maine was far more deplorable than their neglect of the Maine coast. It was understandable, perhaps, for rails to pass by the forests, lakes, and streams of this remote wilderness, but to leave unsown and untended Aroostook, the "Garden of Maine," was inexcusable.[107] Lamentably, furthermore, the county's little settlements communicated by rail with New Brunswick. Though these lines eventually led to Bangor and Portland, they were indirect and passed through an alien land. The railroad commissioners of Maine regretted that the "enlightened foresight" of the citizens of these northern communities "had not seen their interest in a railroad looking toward the commercial centres and the ancestral hearthstones of the State to which they owe allegiance, rather than in a diversion of their business toward provincial towns, and into a foreign government." [108]

[103] *Report of the Railroad Commissioners . . . of Maine. 1883,* p. 21; Portland *Press,* July 3, 1871, August 18, December 31, 1875, June 6, 1882, July 21, 1885, July 7, 1898.
[104] Portland *Press,* November 8, 1890, May 6, 1891, January 6, 1893, January 5, February 14, July 26, 30, 1895; *Acts and Resolves of the Sixty-fifth Legislature of the State of Maine. 1891,* pp. 391–395; *Acts and Resolves of the Sixty-sixth Legislature of the State of Maine. 1893,* pp. 705–707, 848–855; *Acts and Resolves of the Sixty-seventh Legislature of the State of Maine. 1895,* pp. 111–114; Lewis D. Greene in equity *v.* William M. Nash and Others, 85 *Maine,* 148.
[105] *Forty-first Annual Report of the Railroad Commissioners of the State of Maine . . . Decisions and Rules of the Board Made During the Year Ending November 30, 1899,* pp. 45–46; Portland *Press,* January 1, 1899.
[106] Edward E. Chase, *Maine Railroads. A History of the Development of the Maine Railroad System* (Portland: E. E. Chase, 1926), pp. 96, 99, 106.
[107] Portland *Press,* November 24, 1881, December 30, 1883.
[108] *Report of the Railroad Commissioners . . . of Maine, . . . 1873,* p. 22.

Unhappily for state pride, "foreign capitalists" first breached this wilderness and gave Bangor, incidentally, an avenue to the Great Lakes. The Canadian Pacific was the deliverer. Trumpeting from the West its defiance of the Grand Trunk, the "C.P." announced an invasion of eastern Canada. On it came, to Ottawa, to Toronto, to Montreal and Quebec, and then, drawn by the irresistible magnet of the Atlantic, it sought a winter port. Neither Portland nor Boston, reached by an alliance with the Boston and Maine, would do; the ports of the Maritime Provinces, St. John and Halifax, insisted that the Canadian Pacific come to them and they had the political power to make their wish come true.[109] The road consequently proceeded to acquire in Maine a charter, previously granted to others, for the International Railway of Maine. This line was to enter the state at the Quebec border near Lake Megantic, build eastward to the Penobscot, connecting with the Bangor and Piscataquis along the way, and then proceed to Vanceboro on the New Brunswick boundary over the tracks of the European and North American, now a part of the Maine Central.[110]

Ordinarily Maine would have bristled at the prospect of becoming a mere right of way between Montreal and Halifax. Powerful interests, however, calmed hostility. The Maine Central was reconciled, in view of the arrangements for the use of its tracks between the Penobscot and Vanceboro. Bangor, if only the Canadian Pacific connected with the Bangor and Piscataquis, had a short route to the West and the promise of more traffic over its languishing municipal railroad.[111] Even Portland took comfort in a competitor to the Grand Trunk and felt its harbor, fog-free and ample, was so much better than St. John that "laws of commerce" would direct the Canadian Pacific to it.[112] To

[109] George P. de T. Glazebrook, *A History of Transportation in Canada* (New Haven: Yale University Press, 1938), pp. 294–296.

[110] *Acts and Resolves of the Sixtieth Legislature of the State of Maine. 1881*, Part II, pp. 59–61; *Acts and Resolves of the Sixty-second Legislature of the State of Maine. 1885*, Part II, pp. 563–565; H. V. Poor, *Manual of Railroads of the United States for 1886* (New York: H. V. & H. W. Poor, n.d.), p. 897.

[111] Report of the Committee on Interstate Commerce, *Senate Reports*, 51 Cong., 1 Sess., no. 847 (s. n. 2706), pp. 424–427; Portland *Press*, September 26, 1883.

[112] Portland *Press*, November 12, 17, 1886, January 3, 1887, July 17, December 6, 1889.

make sure the newcomer did not discriminate against Maine, the charter of the International Railroad compelled it to "make and maintain their rates with all connecting railroads in this State, their lessees and assigns, pro rata and according to the distance carried on the railroad of said corporation, its lessees and assigns." [113]

Surveyors and trackmen descended upon northern Maine.[114] When construction was done in 1889, Maine discovered that the builders had laid through the wilderness 145 miles of a genuine transcontinental; some of the trestles in length and height were truly western.[115] With a lavishness that Maine cities and towns. could only envy, the Dominion granted an annual subsidy of $186,000 for twenty years.[116] Scornfully the Portland papers commented, "Canada has a magnificent railroad and a magnificent debt." [117] To the misgivings aroused by a road essentially a foreign enterprise, the decade of the nineties gave no clear answer.

V

The Bangor and Aroostook Railroad was, however, a Maine native. Its line lay wholly within the state of Maine; it connected the largest county, Aroostook, with the rest of the state, and its builders were not English lords or apostate Americans. A. A. Burleigh, the road's president, came from a Maine family long associated with Aroostook as state land agents, promoters of settlement, surveyors, and great land owners.[118] F. W. Cram, successively general manager, vice-president, and president, was born in Bangor, trained as a railroader on the Maine Central, European and North American, and the New Brunswick Railroad Company. Like Poor, he was a promoter with enthusiasm

---

[113] *Senate Reports*, 51 Cong., 1 Sess., no. 847, p. 425.

[114] Portland *Press*, June 14, 1887.

[115] *Thirty-first Annual Report of the Railroad Commissioners of the State of Maine . . . Decisions of the Board Made During the Year. 1889*, pp. 5–6, 29–30; Portland *Press*, December 12, 1887, May 8, 1889.

[116] *Senate Reports*, 51 Cong., 1 Sess., no. 847, p. 233.

[117] Portland *Press*, August 14, 1888.

[118] George T. Little, ed., *Genealogical and Family History of the State of Maine* (New York: Lewis Historical Publishing Company, 1909), III, 1089–1092.

and vitality; unlike Poor he was a practical railroad man.[119] To the road the state gave most liberal assistance. During the nineties the legislature prohibited for thirty years any parallel line within fifteen miles of the Bangor and Aroostook, repealed for twenty years 95 per cent of the road's taxes in exchange for the empty obligation of carrying troops and military material free of charge "in times of war, insurrection, or civil commotion"; and, in the new tradition of county aid, authorized Aroostook to subscribe not more than $728,000 to the preferred stock of the railroad and elect, through its legislative delegation, three representatives on the directorate.[120] Most of the private capital in the road was raised outside the state through the agency of the Aroostook Construction Company which secured loans on the basis of the road's securities or on the personal credit of the incorporators.[121]

Trade, present and potential, rather than topography determined the route of the Bangor and Aroostook. Discarding the old idea of taking off for the north from some junction on the European and North American, Burleigh and Cram started their route from a point on a branch of the Bangor and Piscataquis, breached the upper Penobscot Valley from the west to tap its potential water powers, and then proceeded, by 1899, to a northeastern terminus at Van Buren on the St. John. Branches splayed through the north country. Its partially unballasted roadbed, its fills that sank into bogs perpetuated the pioneer tradition. Its heavy steel rails, iron bridges, and easy gradients and curves gave it a modern air.[122] In the same decade, the nineties, the Bangor and Aroostook brought under its own control the Bangor and Piscataquis, for the legislature made quite clear its expectations that the newcomer should relieve the city of this

[119] *Ibid.*, II 574–575

[120] *Acts and Resolves . . . of Maine, 1891*, pp. 213–214, 268–269, 374–379; *Acts and Resolves . . . of Maine. 1893*, pp. 595–596; *Acts and Resolves of the Sixty-seventh Legislature of the State of Maine. 1895*, pp. 254–258.

[121] Portland *Press*, January 16, 1892, February 2, 1893; Chase, *Maine Railroads*, pp. 123–125, 128.

[122] Portland *Press*, September 13, 1894; *Forty-first Annual Report of the Railroad Commissioners of the State of Maine . . . Decisions and Rules of the Board Made During the Year Ending November 30, 1899*, pp. 36–38.

ancient burden. After years of troublesome negotiations, the Bangor and Aroostook in 1898 bought the railroad and issued its own bonds to replace those of this unhappy enterprise. Bangorians were delighted.[123] First the B. and A. rebuilt its acquisition. Then with typical thoroughness it extended a by-pass west of Bangor to tidewater terminals, open the year round, at Searsport.[124]

For northern Maine the road was a savior. A traveler in the mid-nineties described its main line as traversing swamps, bogs, and small growth; it was mostly stations, "brand new little stations in the midst of tiny clearings in the wilderness." [125] Statistics of autumn shipments of deer, caribou, and moose furthered the impression it was a huntsman's road.[126] Soon the great paper companies moved into the area, bought the spruce lands, and erected modern mills of permanent character.[127] The potato vied with the spruce, for after the arrival of the railroad, Aroostook's production of this vegetable spurted ahead. In the nineties the acreage in Maine sown to potatoes increased 44.6 per cent and the Maine potato, once marketed primarily in New England, invaded the stores of New York and even in remote Texas challenged the harvest of southern and western growers.[128]

In spite of occasional bickerings with potato growers over railroad rates,[129] most Maineites were content to hail the Bangor and Aroostook as the infant prodigy of American railroads. Between 1893 and 1900 its freight traffic, the road's chief resource, increased from 80,305 to 638,974 tons.[130] Nor was the

---

[123] *City of Bangor. Mayor's Address . . . Annual Reports . . . 1892–93*, p. 8; *City of Bangor. Mayor's Address, the Annual Reports . . . for the Municipal Year 1896–7*, pp. 5–6; *City of Bangor. Mayor's Address . . . Annual Reports . . . for the Municipal Year 1898–99*, pp. 3–4; Henry V. Poor, *Poor's Manual of the Railroads of the United States, 1899* (New York: H. V. & H. W. Poor, n.d.), p. 3; Portland *Press*, February 18, 1892.

[124] Chase, *Maine Railroads*, pp. 129–131.

[125] Portland *Press*, April, 2, 1894.

[126] *Ibid.*, May 1, 1895.

[127] *Thirteenth Annual Report of the Bureau of Industrial and Labor Statistics for the State of Maine. 1899*, pp. 43–44.

[128] *Twelfth Census of the United States. Taken in the Year 1900*, VI, Part 2, pp. 282–283, 326–327; Portland *Press*, February 16, 1898.

[129] Portland *Press*, December 11, 1896.

[130] *Thirty-fifth Annual Report of the Railroad Commissioners of the State of*

investment of Aroostook County in its preferred stock ever in jeopardy. Furthermore, in the language of a somewhat earlier period, "the trade of this border county, like Rip Van Winkle's dog Snyder," recognized its "old master and followed him back into the market places of the State and the Union." [131]

Maine . . . Decisions and Rules of the Board Made During the Year 1893, appendix, p. 15; *Forty-second Annual Report of the Railroad Commissioners of the State of Maine . . . Decisions and Rules of the Board Made During the Year Ending November 30, 1900,* p. 16.

[131] *Report of the Railroad Commissioners . . . of Maine, . . . 1875,* p. 22.

XV

BOSTON'S RATES WITH THE WEST

"Boston, Philadelphia, and Baltimore can extort from the railroads running into New York terms unfavorable to its commerce, but as long as the Erie Canal is secure, New York will have a channel through which freight can be carried to it, cheaper than to any competing point." — New York Annual Report of the State Engineer and Surveyor on the Canals of the State, . . . 1881, pp. 5–6.

I

New England lay at the outermost edge of trunk-line territory, a territory stretching from the Great Lakes and the St. Lawrence to the Potomac and the Ohio, from the Mississippi to the Atlantic coastline. Scattered through its western areas were the great shipping centers of St. Louis, Peoria, Cincinnati, Cleveland, and above all Chicago. Along the eastern edge lay the Atlantic rivals — Baltimore, Philadelphia, New York, and Boston. Before the great east-west railroads had been constructed and the area had been christened after the existing trunk lines, water transportation dominated its commerce. From Chicago goods flowed eastward along the Great Lakes to Buffalo, followed the Erie Canal to Albany, and finally with the current dropped down the Hudson to New York City. It was to tap this great artery that Boston conceived and built its first transectional railroad. But neither Boston nor New York thought in the first part of the nineteenth century to supersede it. Railroad rates could not possibly be as low as those by water. As late as 1869, with an awe unusual in his family, Charles Francis Adams, Jr., was chronicling the

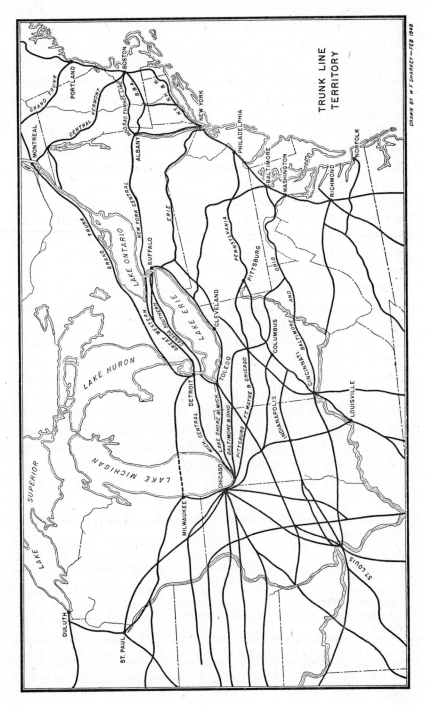

TRUNK LINE
TERRITORY

DRAWN BY W. F. SHARKEY — FEB. 1948

departure of two tows aggregating 300 barges from Albany for New York City. Their cargo was 440,000 bushels of grain; their total freight rate was only $8,800. To carry the same amount over the hills to Boston would require 1,100 freight cars and cost in charges $27,500.[1]

The striking evidence of such specific instances tended to obscure the inroads rail transportation was already making. In the fifties the railroads had taken over the carriage of high grade commodities; in the sixties, though flour, wheat, and other grain products still came east to Buffalo by water, the railroads began to take these bulky products away from the Erie and the Hudson. Finally the Lakes succumbed to the new competitor, as all-rail shipments of grain between Chicago and Buffalo proved practicable. Undertaken for the first time in 1864, this practice rapidly accelerated.[2] By the end of the seventies, when the tonnage shipped east from Chicago by rail was greater than that shipped by water and the cargoes carried by the New York Central were 2,500,000 tons greater than on the Erie Canal, a government report justly observed: "The diversion of grain and other products of the West from the lake and canal route to the various rail routes connecting the West with the seaboard constitutes one of the most important features of the internal commerce of the United States."[3] A few years later New York State recognized the novelty of the situation. In 1883 she abolished the tolls on the Erie; only a free canal could survive in competition with the railroads, only a free canal could protect New York's commerce.[4]

---

[1] Massachusetts *First Annual Report of the Board of Railroad Commissioners. January, 1870*, p. 35.

[2] Joseph Nimmo, Jr., *First Annual Report on the Internal Commerce of the United States. Being Part Second of the Annual Report of the Chief of the Bureau of Statistics on the Commerce and Navigation of the United States, for the Fiscal Year Ending June 30, 1876*, pp. 67–68, appendix, p. 65; Joseph Nimmo, Jr., Treasury Department, *Report on the Internal Commerce of the United States. Submitted December 1, 1879. Commerce and Navigation*, pp. 99–102.

[3] Nimmo, *Report on the Internal Commerce of the United States . . . 1879*, p. 103.

[4] David A. Wells, L. J. N. Stark, William Thurstone, *Report of the Commissioners Invited by the Canal Board of the State of New York, July 10th, 1877, to Consider and Report on the Subject of Revenues and Acts to Increase the Commerce of Canals* (Albany: Weld, Parsons & Company, 1878), pp. 38–39, 59–67;

As this revolution in transportation took place, New York's rivals felt a thrill of satisfaction and of hope. Gone were the days when their only emotion was an envy of the latter's superior access by the Erie to the West. Like New York, Philadelphia, Baltimore, and Boston could have railroads. Their delight was premature. They did not realize that the mere existence of water transportation between Chicago and New York set the rail rates between the two termini, and that the rail rate between Chicago and New York was the standard by which all rates from the West to the Atlantic seaboard were to be determined.[5]

Of the railroads which had accomplished the diversion from waterways, the most remote from New England geographically was the Baltimore and Ohio. It secured a Chicago connection in 1874.[6] Farther to the north lay the Pennsylvania Railroad. Before the Civil War, it formed a through line between Philadelphia and Chicago, following in the Middle West the tracks of the Pittsburgh, Fort Wayne and Chicago.[7] New York was served by two western railroads of its own. One was the malodorous Erie Railroad, variously renamed as it escaped from a succession of rascals and receiverships.[8] The other was the New York Central and Hudson River Railroad, the consolidation which Commodore Vanderbilt had formed in the sixties. He extended it westward to Chicago by the Lake Shore and Michigan Southern Railroad, the controlling interest in whose stock he

---

Annual Report of State Engineer and Surveyor on Canals, New York *Senate Documents*, 1882, no. 74, pp. 14–15; Noble E. Whitford, *History of the Canal System of the State of New York together with Brief Histories of the Canals of the United States and Canada, Supplement to the Annual Report of the State Engineer and Surveyor of the State of New York*, 1905, I, 316.

[5] Massachusetts *Eighth Annual Report of the Board of Railroad Commissioners. January, 1877*, pp. 47–48; Nimmo, *Report on the Internal Commerce . . . 1879*, p. 106; Albert Fink, *Testimony of Albert Fink before the Select Committee on Interstate Commerce of the United States Senate. New York, May 21, 1885* (Washington: Government Printing Office, 1885), pp. 14–15.

[6] Henry V. Poor, *Manual of the Railroads of the United States for 1875–76* (New York: H. V. & H. W. Poor, 1875), p. 212.

[7] Henry V. Poor, *History of the Railroads and Canals of the United States of America, Exhibiting Their Progress, Cost, Revenues, Expenditures & Present Condition* (New York: John H. Schultz & Co., 1860), pp. 493–494.

[8] Henry V. Poor, *Manual of the Railroads of the United States for 1880* (New York: H. V. & H. W. Poor, 1880), pp. 186–187.

owned by 1869 and whose presidency he added to his collection in 1874.[9] This route was south of Lake Erie.

But the Central's empire was always threatened. Between Buffalo and New York City it had to meet and contain, as best it could, the competition of such veterans as the Erie and such inter-lopers as the Delaware, Lackawanna and Western and the West Shore. The Grand Trunk was a greater and more enduring menace. This through route from Portland and Montreal had pushed westward, north of the Lakes to the St. Clair River at Sarnia, crossed by a car ferry to Port Huron, arched southward to Detroit, and reached Chicago first by the Michigan Central and then by an extension of its own, completed in 1880.[10] The Grand Trunk was not only a through line in its own right, but also, by the acquisition of a route between Detroit and the Niag-ara River, it connected with the Central's rivals crossing New York State to New York City and New England.[11] The Central had meanwhile acquired its own link north of Lake Erie to Detroit and in 1878 the Vanderbilts took over the Michigan Central.[12]

In varying degrees all these trunk lines served New England. The Baltimore and Ohio, although "a Baltimore railroad," had by the seventies a water connection via the Merchants' and

[9] Henry V. Poor, *Manual of the Railroads of the United States for 1874–1875* (New York: H. V. & H. W. Poor, 1874), pp. 578, 582; Edward Hungerford, *Men and Iron. The History of the New York Central* (New York: Thomas Y. Crowell Company, 1938), pp. 213–214.

[10] *Grand Trunk Railway of Canada. Accounts for the Half-Year Ending 30th June, 1858, and Report of Mr. T. E. Blackwell, Vice President and Managing Director in Canada. September 30th, 1858* (London: Waterlow & Sons, 1858), pp. 21–22; *Report of Mr. Thomas E. Blackwell, Vice-President and Managing Director of the Grand Trunk Railway Company of Canada, for the Year 1859* (London: Waterlow and Sons, 1860), pp. 1–2; *Half-Year Ended 30th June, 1880. Grand Trunk Railway Company of Canada. Report of the Directors and State-ments of the Revenue, Capital, and Expenditure Accounts* (n.p., n.d.), p. 7.

[11] *The Grand Trunk Railway Company of Canada. Report of the Directors and Statements of Accounts of the (Late) Grand Trunk Railway Company of Canada, from the 1st January to the 11th August, 1882, and of the (Late) Great Western Railway Company (of Canada), from the 1st February to the 11th August, 1882. December, 1882* (n.p., n.d.), pp. 3, 9.

[12] Hungerford, *Men and Iron*, pp. 215–216; *Report of the President and Direc-tors of the Michigan Central Railroad Company, to the Stockholders. Together with Reports of the General Manager, Treasurer, and Sinking Fund Trustees, for the Year Ending December 31st, 1878* (Detroit: Richmond, Backus & Co., 1879), pp. 3, 5.

Miners' Transportation Company; there were three sailings a week. The Pennsylvania Railroad could reach Boston through a coastwise steamer service from Philadelphia or could lighter cars around New York harbor to docks owned by New England railroads. The Erie Railroad sent goods to Boston by the Metropolitan Steamship Company or to ports in southern New England by the boat lines on Long Island Sound. Though such routes were circuitous and burdensome, because of transshipments and the necessity of paying marine insurance, they were a competitive factor of some importance.[13] The intimate relation between the New York Central or the Grand Trunk and the New England railroad system needs little reiteration. The former was the ally of the Boston and Albany; the latter was the westward extension of the route to the Lakes.

The mere existence of the trunk lines did not, however, explain their victory over the water route to the West. The reason lay in their superior functioning. One measure of their effectiveness was the perfected arrangements for through shipments. In the days of end-to-end railroads, goods had to be transhipped from the cars of one corporation to those of another. Such costs on the traffic between Boston and Chicago were annually $500,000. Bills of lading were generally issued only by the receiving roads and, where through bills were granted, the reservations governing payments for loss and damage crippled their effectiveness and put shippers to intense inconvenience. The latter often had to employ commission merchants to effect transfers of shipments where a genuine interruption, as at Buffalo, occurred in their carriage. Through rates were not known in advance; times of delivery were incalculable.[14] These vexations were abated or

[13] Nimmo, *First Annual Report on the Internal Commerce of the United States . . . 1876*, appendix, pp. 101, 113; *State of New York. 1879. Proceedings of the Special Committee on Railroads, Appointed under a Resolution of the Assembly to Investigate Alleged Abuses in the Management of Railroads Chartered by the State of New York* [Hepburn Committee], I, 426–429.

[14] *Boston Board of Trade. 1866. Twelfth Annual Report of the Government Presented to the Board at the Annual Meeting, on the 10th January, 1866* (Boston: George C. Rand and Avery, 1866), pp. 67–70; New York *Proceedings of the Special Committee on Railroads* [*Hepburn Committee*], IV, 2959–2960; *Seventh Annual Report of the Interstate Commerce Commission. December 1, 1893*, pp. 43–44.

eliminated by the through freight lines which undertook to receive and forward on their own responsibility. Although the first of such lines antedated the Civil War, most were established in the sixties.

Roughly these freight lines fell into two varieties. In some instances, of which the National Dispatch Company over the Vermont Central-Grand Trunk was an example, officials as private individuals created a corporation which built or bought cars and ran them over the line, charging the railroads a rental for each mile. The abuses of this device have already been illustrated.[15] The other category was denominated the co-operative fast freight line. Within New England its first illustration was the Red Line, between Boston and Chicago, whose members were the Boston and Worcester, the Western, the New York Central, and four roads west of Buffalo.[16] Other color lines for other routes soon appeared on the Boston and Albany. The Hoosac Tunnel Line, already mentioned, belonged to the same category.[17] In such organizations the railroad corporations contributed cars to the line pool. Though the line received a mileage rental for each car, the railroads were actually paying it to themselves and there was no division of interest between the managers in their capacity as managers of the road and of the line.[18] This valuable innovation was introduced at the insistence of New England railroad officials, probably those on the Western Railroad.[19]

[15] Massachusetts *Fourth Annual Report of the Board of Railroad Commissioners. January, 1873*, pp. 35–37.

[16] *Boston Board of Trade. 1886. Twelfth Annual Report*, p. 69.

[17] Petition of the Boston, Hoosac Tunnel and Western Railroad Company. Abstract of Proceedings before the Joint Special Committee of the Legislature on the Hoosac Tunnel and Troy and Greenfield Railroad, Massachusetts *House Documents*, 1877, no. 201, pp. 93–94; Nimmo, *First Annual Report on the Internal Commerce of the United States . . . 1876*, appendix, pp. 49–50; Massachusetts *Second Annual Report of the Board of Railroad Commissioners. January, 1871*, pp. xxxv–xxxvi.

[18] Massachusetts *Fourth Annual Report of the Board of Railroad Commissioners. January, 1873*, pp. 31–37; New York *Proceedings of the Special Committee on Railroads, . . .* [Hepburn Committee], V, appendix, pp. 10–15; Nimmo, *First Annual Report on the Internal Commerce of the United States . . . 1876*, appendix, pp. 50–51.

[19] Charles F. Adams, Jr., "Railway Problems in 1869," *North American Review*, CX (1870), 130–132.

Fast freight lines of whatever variety had agents soliciting freight and overseeing its carriage.[20] Not content with these fundamental advances, the fast freight lines, at first on the payment of a slight additional fee, promised the delivery of goods within a certain time.[21] They also introduced through bills of lading, an instrument few merchants saw before 1860, and in the seventies guaranteed as accurate the quantities listed on the bill.[22] Under their aegis the shipment of goods from the heart of the American West to European markets was greatly facilitated.[23] Not only did guaranteed bills of lading lower costs of transportation. They also "furnish a safe and desirable basis of bank credits, and in this way they have become an important instrumentality in the finance of commerce, supplying an extensive medium of exchange in commercial operations." [24]

In the last analysis, however, the railroads triumphed over the Great Lakes, Erie, and Hudson waterway, because they drastically lowered their through rates. They took this essential step partly from design and partly because their intense competition with one another and with the waterways compelled them to it. The best measure of the decline in freight rates was that on grain between Chicago and New York. By adding or subtracting fixed figures or percentages to or from this fundamental measure, rates could be determined to Baltimore, Philadelphia, or Boston, or from St. Louis, Cincinnati, or any one of several western shipping points. In 1865 the rates per hundred pounds of grain from Chicago to New York varied between $1.60 and 62½

[20] Nimmo, *First Annual Report on the Internal Commerce of the United States* . . . *1876*, appendix, pp. 67–68.

[21] *Boston Board of Trade. 1866. Twelfth Annual Report*, p. 69.

[22] Massachusetts *Seventh Annual Report of the Board of Railroad Commissioners. January, 1876*, pp. 70–71; Nimmo, *First Annual Report on the Internal Commerce of the United States* . . . *1876*, appendix, p. 104; *Twenty-fifth Annual Report of the Boston Board of Trade, January 1, 1879* (Boston: James F. Cotter & Co., 1879), pp. 20, 22.

[23] Nimmo, *First Annual Report on the Internal Commerce of the United States,* . . . *1876*, pp. 130–132; *Report of Mr. Thomas E. Blackwell* . . . *1859*, p. 3; Nimmo, *Report on the Internal Commerce of the United States* . . . *1879*, appendix, pp. 29–30.

[24] Nimmo, *Report on the Internal Commerce of the United States* . . . *1879*, pp. 148–149.

cents — in terms of gold, between 83 and 43 cents; a decade later they were 45 and 30 cents — in terms of gold 38 and 27. In 1885 the variation was between 25 and 20 and in 1895 between 20 and 15. Sporadically in the early eighties they sank to 12½ cents.[25] No wonder the railroads complained that they were doing business at less than cost. No wonder railroad commissioners assured their readers that the absolute level of rates need not worry them. Thus in 1876 the Massachusetts board summarized a theme which it had frequently emphasized: "The community has been so accustomed to hearing the cry for cheap transportation of Western produce raised, that it fails to realize how much cheapness has been secured. The fact is, however, that rates have now fallen so low that not only this, but all other descriptions of through merchandise, are habitually carried on more favorable terms than the most sanguine anticipated a few years ago."[26] In later years the observation was often restated.[27]

II

However helpful to the economy of New England lowered rates were, the real problem for Boston, and for the region of which it was the commercial center, was its position vis-à-vis Baltimore, Philadelphia, and New York. If its rates to the West were higher than from these Atlantic rivals, it suffered a relative disadvantage as importer or manufacturer. If its rates from the West were higher, it suffered as an exporter of commodities, a consumer of food, or a converter of raw materials. Such elementary facts were appreciated as early as the twenties by the Massachusetts railroad schemers. Such elementary facts underlay the agitation for

[25] Department of Commerce and Labor. Bureau of Statistics, *Monthly Summary of Commerce and Finance of the United States, April, 1904,* p. 3968; *Railroad Gazette,* XVII (1885), p. 25; Massachusetts *Seventh Annual Report of the Board of Railroad Commissioners. January, 1876,* p. 62.

[26] Massachusetts *Second Annual Report of the Board of Railroad Commissioners. January, 1871,* p. xxxviii; Massachusetts *Seventh Annual Report of the Board of Railroad Commissioners. January, 1876,* p. 61.

[27] Massachusetts *Eighth Annual Report of the Board of Railroad Commissioners. January, 1877,* p. 47; Massachusetts *Tenth Annual Report of the Board of Railroad Commissioners. January, 1879,* pp. 15–18; In the Matter of Alleged Excessive Freight Rates and Charges on Food Products, 4 *Interstate Commerce Commission,* 48.

a route to the Hudson and the years of effort and expenditure invested in the Boston and Albany, the Hoosac line, and the route to the Lakes. The aim of all these dreams and plans had been to secure for Boston advantages, or, at least, an equality. Since no New England route reached unaided to these western regions, it participated at one remove in the endless arguments between the trunk lines over the proper standards for determining the rates between the West and the eastern cities.

All granted that the rate between Chicago and New York was the base of every calculation. There agreement ended, and the railroads elevated to the level of high policy the childish statements, made time out of mind in their prospectuses. The Baltimore and Ohio and the Pennsylvania railroads claimed for Baltimore and for Philadelphia a lower rate to and from the West than New York. They based their right to a differential upon their shortness; they were the partisans of rates based solely upon mileage. To the New York Central such fantasies did not appeal. Though its rivals might be shorter, the Central was entitled to as low a rate as any because of its absence of grades and curves, its superb rolling stock, its high technical finish, and the huge business it carried. No differentials must operate against New York.[28] Such formulas at least were based upon strength. The Grand Trunk built its case upon weakness. Its route to the West was long; its track traversed a region locked in snow and ice; its costs, including its fuel costs, were high; it confronted water competition along its route. If the Grand Trunk were to have its proper share of the through business, it must, therefore, charge lower rates to and from its termini than did the more fortunately situated roads to the south. Not the shortest but the longest, not the strongest but the frailest, must have the advantage. This was the basis of its plea for a differential for Montreal, Portland, and Boston.[29] Such was the ideological setting in which merchants,

---

[28] Alden G. Thurman, E. B. Washburne, and Thomas M. Cooley, *Report of Messrs. Thurman, Washburne & Cooley, Constituting an Advisory Commission on Differential Rates by Railroads between the West and the Seaboard* (New York: Russell Brothers, 1882), pp. 13–29.

[29] New York *Proceedings of the Special Committee on Railroads, . . .* [Hepburn Committee], I, 455–458; Nimmo, *First Annual Report on the Internal Com-*

shippers, importers, exporters, consumers, producers, boosters, urban patriots, and railroads — singly or organized — quarreled over differentials. There were differentials on goods going west, differentials on goods coming east. The prosperity, even the survival of Boston, New York, Philadelphia, and Baltimore was alleged to depend upon differentials.

Although they could not agree on overarching generalities, the railroads in search of harmony or stability or law soon discovered that the settlement of details involved different degrees of difficulty. Tariffs on goods westbound were a comparatively simple problem. The commodities were in the upper freight classification; the distinction between imported and domestic goods bound for the interior raised few quarrels; and the small number of trunk lines, radiating from the eastern ports, had the right, as initial receivers, to set the through rates. Agreement was relatively easy. The most disturbing factor was the discrepancy between the transport space required by eastbound and westbound tonnage; the great tide of agricultural products that flowed from the interior demanded far more cars than the shipment thither of the less bulky commodities of the East and Europe. To fill their empty westbound cars the eastern railroads undercut each other with rate reductions.[30]

Rates on eastbound tonnage were a matter of far more complexity and concern. In the grain trade, for instance, there were wheat, flour, and corn destined for domestic consumption or for export or for either market. In the first instance, the railroads found it relatively easy to come to an agreement; but the eastern movement of grain for foreign shipment, whether at first or second hand, sharpened the rivalry of railroad with railroad and port with port. When the grain put to sea, comparative charges between Boston, New York, Philadelphia, or Baltimore, and Europe complicated solutions, for ocean rates were a science or a mythology in themselves. They differed for sailing vessel and

merce of the United States . . . *1876*, appendix, p. 70; Nimmo, *Report on the Internal Commerce of the United States . . . 1879*, appendix, p. 106.

[30] Thurman, Washburne, and Cooley, *Report*, pp. 22–24; Massachusetts *Seventh Annual Report of the Board of Railroad Commissioners. January, 1876*, pp. 66–67.

steamship, for cargo rates, when the product filled the hold, or
for "berth rates," when it formed only a part of the manifest;
and they fluctuated wildly and inexplicably as harbors were
crammed with vessels or empty of sail. Finally, there were the
costs of bringing rail and vessel together — costs of elevating and
storing, docking, and lighterage. Those who advocated the same
through rate between Chicago and Liverpool, by whichever American port the grain traveled, confronted all these variables.[31]
They also faced the fact that the Atlantic ports and their railroads
were willing to talk and occasionally suffer at the barricades for a
quarter-of-a-cent difference in rates and charges.

Not analysis but experience, not dogma but action, set the original pattern of differentials. They appeared as soon as the
through routes were completed to Chicago in the mid-fifties.
Through the next twenty years competition between the trunk
lines hammered them into shape. This competition was not un-
remitting. No trunk line, however favorably situated or well financed, could long endure a war of rates. There were intervals
of exhaustion; intervals even of limited agreement. When they
passed, the struggle was resumed. It is not unjust, therefore, to
designate the two decades before 1877 as those of cut-throat competition. Such was the period which gave to the differentials so
impregnable a character that later years, though they might mod-
ify them, effected no full alterations. Even upon rate levels history laid its ineluctable curse.

On westbound traffic New England suffered no handicaps that
were not also New York's. Though Baltimore and Philadelphia
enjoyed lower rates to the West, the trunk lines as early as the
fifties conceded that westbound rates from New York City and
from Boston should be identical.[32] In the next decade such an understanding was a feature of the treaty of alliance between the

---

[31] Nimmo, *First Annual Report on the Internal Commerce of the United States
. . . 1876*, pp. 69–71; New York *Proceedings of the Special Committee on Railroads,* . . . [Hepburn Committee], I, 664–675, 777; New York Produce Exchange *v.*
Baltimore & Ohio Railroad Company and Others, 7 *Interstate Commerce Commission,* 624.

[32] New York *Proceedings of the Special Committee on Railroads,* . . . [Hep-
burn Committee], I, 428, II, 1490–1491, IV, 3043, 3046.

Boston and Albany, newly consolidated, and the New York Central and of the promises advanced by the Grand Trunk as it sought a Boston connection.[33] The last road, however, soon felt the impact of its "peculiar" situation; to get its share of the traffic, it would have to reduce fares and freights, reductions which only misguided competitors would regard as "cuts." The Grand Trunk demanded and inaugurated a differential on westbound goods. Its rivals, to keep the peace, reluctantly tolerated the resulting lower charges of 5 to 20 cents a hundred pounds on through freights.[34]

In 1875 the other trunk lines, convinced that they were powerful and united enough to discipline the Canadian maverick, served notice that such concessions were at an end. The Grand Trunk retaliated with a slash in rates; the Boston and Albany, far from indifferent, struck back. Soon the rates from Boston to the West were 10 per cent lower than from New York; later they were 100 per cent lower. Gradually the other trunk lines, the Erie and the Pennsylvania, were embroiled in what was originally a local quarrel and shipped goods westward from Boston by water and rail routes through New York more cheaply than by railroad from the latter city. Imports of heavy articles destined for interior points were diverted to the Massachusetts metropolis in order to take advantage of its cheaper rates. As New York lost trade and prestige the anger of its merchants knew no bounds. Railroads groaned at the "utter demoralization" of rates.[35] Finally, in December 1875 an agreement divided the westbound traffic between the Boston and Albany and the Grand Trunk on the basis of what each had done during the previous two years.[36] It was but a truce, soon shattered. The Grand Trunk demanded and received a differential. While the Boston and Albany, urged by the Central, submitted openly to this sacrifice for the cause of

---

[33] *Ibid.,* IV, 3048–3049.

[34] Massachusetts *Seventh Annual Report of the Board of Railroad Commissioners. January, 1876,* p. 65.

[35] *Ibid.,* pp. 65–68; Nimmo, *First Annual Report on the Internal Commerce of the United States . . . 1876,* appendix, pp. 71–73, 102–103.

[36] Massachusetts *Eighth Annual Report of the Board of Railroad Commissioners. January, 1877,* p. 46.

peace in trunk-line territory, it secretly granted the Grand Trunk rates to its own patrons.[37]

Since the carriage of grain, flour, and livestock dwarfed by its immensity the mere transport of boots, shoes, cottons, woolens, and hardware, the struggle over eastbound differentials was both frequent and intense. By the end of the sixties, the episodic and tentative statement of rate differences to the Atlantic ports had crystallized into a system. New York had a differential of 5 cents over Boston, Philadelphia one of 5 cents over New York, and Baltimore one of 5 cents over Philadelphia. But exceptions soon developed. The agreement between the Boston and Albany, the New York Central, and the Cunard Line, by which the Cunarders resumed their sailings from Boston, provided that exporters of grain, provisions, and cotton at Boston received a drawback of 5 cents a hundred pounds and exporters of flour one of 10 cents a barrel.[38] Only goods for export were placed on terms of rate equality with New York. Grain, flour, and livestock for domestic consumption still paid 5 cents more than if they had gone to the New York metropolis. Aside from the justice of any differential whatever, its amount, 5 cents, aroused criticism. The Massachusetts Railroad Commission in 1876 stigmatized it as an "arbitrary" exaction, since the "additional charge of 5 cents a hundred represents an increased rate of 12 per cent to meet 5 per cent of increased distance." [39] This assertion certainly advanced the mileage hypothesis of rates in its baldest form. It was an unsafe argument for New England.

Early in 1876, however, the New York roads permitted themselves to be talked into differentials based upon a percentage basis. On shipments from Chicago to Philadelphia and Baltimore, for instance, the reduction from the New York rate was 10 to 13

---

[37] Nimmo, *First Annual Report on the Internal Commerce of the United States . . . 1876*, appendix, p. 70.

[38] Massachusetts *First Annual Report of the Board of Railroad Commissioners. January, 1870*, p. 37; Nimmo, *First Annual Report on the Internal Commerce of the United States . . . 1876*, appendix, p. 71; Albert Fink, *Report upon the Adjustment of Railroad Transportation Rates to the Seaboard* (New York: Russell Brothers, 1882), p. 47.

[39] Massachusetts *Seventh Annual Report of the Board of Railroad Commissioners. January, 1876*, p. 69.

per cent, respectively; on goods from Cincinnati the agreement permitted reductions of 12 and 24 per cent. Boston rates remained unchanged.[40] Since the differentials to Philadelphia and Baltimore were sufficient to pay the higher ocean freights from those ports to Europe, the New York roads soon saw the traffic of the West shifting to the Baltimore and Ohio and the Pennsylvania railroads, and New York merchants cried with anguish at the growing commerce of Baltimore and Philadelphia. The New York Central forthwith announced that such differentials must cease. A competitive war ensued. During this "fiercest, the most determined, and perhaps the most wasteful contest ever known in the history of railroad management," rates sank with a dismaying directness. On the New York Central, passenger fares between Boston and Chicago dropped from $25.85 to $14.00 and on the Grand Trunk from $23.85 to $12.50; freights on agricultural products from Chicago to New York fell from 50 cents a hundred pounds to 18. By the end of the year the managers were willing to compromise. All railroads, including the Central which had managed to continue its dividends, had suffered.[41]

After some experimentation a peace treaty, dated April 5, 1877, settled terms that endured on paper for a decade. The underlying concept of this document felt justice was best served if charges from the West to Liverpool, for instance, should be identical no matter through what Atlantic port the shipment went. Since the shorter voyage to England made marine rates from Boston and New York less than from Philadelphia and Baltimore, the latter cities were given a compensation in lower railroad rates. On eastbound goods, whether for export or domestic use, Philadelphia possessed a differential of 2 cents over New York, Baltimore one of 3 cents. The second provision of the contract read "that the rates to Boston shall at no time be less than those to New York on domestic or foreign freights." This clause simply set a minimum. Actually the 5 cent distinction in rates between

[40] Fink, *Report upon the Adjustment of Railroad Transportation Rates*, p. 6.
[41] Massachusetts *Eighth Annual Report of the Board of Railroad Commissioners. January, 1877*, pp. 50–55; Nimmo, *First Annual Report on the Internal Commerce of the United States . . . 1876*, p. 62.

goods for export and for domestic use continued. To assure absolute equality between all ports in the foreign trade the charges for transferring grain from road to vessel were made uniform — 1¼ cents a bushel.[42] As it turned out this settlement fell at the end of a highly competitive era. Within a year or two the trunk railroads introduced new methods to fix and enforce orderly and stable rates. Meanwhile Boston had not done badly. Though two decades of competition had not given her the same rates as New York with the West, they had shrunk the area in which differentials operated.

III

Throughout this competitive era most of the trunk lines made efforts at common action. As the years went by such experiments increased in frequency and complication. First had come the "railroad convention" debating "general principles" and often formulating concrete procedures; later the freight and ticket agents of the interested roads assembled, set rates, and authorized their publication; finally in the seventies Vanderbilt of the Central proposed the appointment of disinterested commissioners to determine rates and arbitrators to secure obedience to them. Such efforts broke down whenever roads detected advantages in a relapse to the individualistic competitive pattern. Furthermore these agreements were unpopular; they were attacked as monopolies.[43] Evidently such critics did not read the annual reports of the Massachusetts Railroad Commission or, if they did, were not impressed by their reasoning. Adams and his colleagues welcomed the openness, orderliness, and certainty of concerted action. The commission, for instance, noted with open delight that 1877 was the "pooling" year and during it "arrangements for the

[42] New York *Proceedings of the Special Committee on Railroads,* . . . [Hepburn Committee], II, 1247–1251, IV, 3041–3043; Fink, *Report upon the Adjustment of Railroad Transportation Rates,* pp. 23, 26.

[43] Hungerford, *Men and Iron,* pp. 109–111, 115–116; Charles S. Langstroth and Wilson Stilz, *Railway Co-operation. An Investigation of Railway Traffic Associations and a Discussion of the Degree and Form of Co-operation That Should Be Granted Competing Railways in the United States* (Philadelphia: University of Pennsylvania, 1899), pp. 20–27; Charles F. Adams, Jr., *Railroads: Their Origin and Problems* (New York: G. P. Putnam's Sons, 1878), pp. 148–164.

division of business by competing railroads reached a point of development which had never before been known." [44]

In truth the trunk lines, wearied and worn from their battles, were at last determined to discard their "systematic bad faith" for a system of co-operation and control. A similar aim had succeeded elsewhere, notably in the South where the Southern Railway and Steamship Association had brought peace to some twenty-five warring railroads. The successful administrator and indeed the creator of that organization had been Albert Fink. The trunk lines brought him north to lead them. Fink was a German immigrant, a practical railroad man, and a pioneer in the field of railroad economics and statistics.[45] Now he became commissioner and secretary of the Eastern Trunk Line Executive Committee formed in June 1877 by the Central, Baltimore and Ohio, Pennsylvania, and Erie. Somewhat later the roads in the western half of trunk-line territory formed the Western Executive Committee. United with its eastern colleague, the two formed the Joint Executive Committee. Of this body Fink was chairman.[46] The whole structure was justly described as a "trunk-line protectorate" or a "trunk-line confederation." [47] Within it power was centralized. The representatives of the roads voted on policy and practice; if they were not unanimous, Fink decided the issue and his decision was to have the force of a unanimous one. Though there could be an appeal to disinterested arbitrators, Fink was actually the "Napoleon" or the "Caesar" for whom commentators, like Adams, and railroad men had been calling.[48]

[44] Massachusetts *Sixth Annual Report of the Board of Railroad Commissioners. January, 1875,* p. 41; Massachusetts *Seventh Annual Report of the Board of Railroad Commissioners. January, 1876,* pp. 68–72; Massachusetts *Tenth Annual Report of the Board of Railroad Commissioners. January, 1879,* pp. 50, 53–56, 65–68.

[45] Massachusetts *Ninth Annual Report of the Board of Railroad Commissioners. January, 1878,* pp. 67–75; *Dictionary of American Biography* (New York: Charles Scribner's Sons, 1928–1936), V, 387–388.

[46] New York *Proceedings of the Special Committee on Railroads, . . .* [Hepburn Committee], I, 481–483.

[47] Adams, *Railroads: Their Origin and Problems,* pp. 179, 200.

[48] Nimmo, *Report on the Internal Commerce of the United States . . . 1879,* p. 168; *Organization of the Joint Executive Committee, as Adopted Dec. 18 and 19, 1878 with Additions and Amendments to June 18, 1878* (New York: Russell Brothers, 1879), pp. 3–8; Adams, *Railroads: Their Origin and Problems,* p. 194.

In the northeast Fink preached primarily a new method of enforcing the rates upon which the roads had decided. His organization would divide the traffic at its source between the competing roads. The lines which carried more than their share would transfer the receipts, after deducting the expense of haulage, into a common fund which would in turn be distributed among the railroads according to the agreed percentages.[49] Thus the temptation to violate the fixed rates disappeared. As the twelve years of Fink's railroad viziership passed by, it was found necessary to bring more and more roads into the organization. The Grand Trunk became a member of the Joint Executive Committee in 1880.[50] It was found necessary, also, to add to Fink's simple scheme a host of administrative refinements. Passenger agents formed a Passenger Department and published proceedings of their own.[51] As for freight, at each of the shipping centers, committees, specializing either in livestock or dead freight, labored to divide the traffic. Then, when the roads to which it was assigned did not always forward the freight according to rule, Fink's agents had to chaperon the goods from one end of the line to another. They were to handle all waybills, prevent surreptitious underbilling and false billing, and throw traffic from roads that were "over" to roads that were "short" and, if this proved difficult because of intractableness of shippers, make calculations for the transfer of money from one member of the pool to another. After certain railroads disclosed a tendency to retain these funds, a peremptory rule required monthly settlements.[52]

[49] Nimmo, *Report on the Internal Commerce of the United States . . . 1879*, pp. 166–170; Adams, *Railroads: Their Origin and Problems*, pp. 174, 176–177.

[50] *Proceedings of the Joint Executive Committee at Its Meeting in New York, Aug. 26 and 27, 1880* (New York: Russell Brothers, 1880), p. 151.

[51] *Proceedings and Circulars of the Joint Executive Committee, 1882* (New York: Russell Brothers, 1883), pp. 36–37, 42–45; *Proceedings and Circulars of the Joint Executive Committee, (Passenger Department), 1883* (New York: Russell Brothers, 1884).

[52] *Proceedings and Circulars of the Joint Executive Committee, 1882*, pp. 20–24; *Proceedings and Circulars of the Joint Executive Committee, 1883* (New York: Russell Brothers, 1884), pp. 117–118; *Proceedings and Circulars of the Joint Executive Committee, (Freight Department), 1885*, (New York: Russell Brothers, 1886), pp. 139–142.

At other times the differential system came under fire. For one thing the situation was so complicated and changing that it was difficult to administer the underlying concept: that through rates between American interior cities and European ports should be the same whether the commodities traveled through Baltimore, Philadelphia, New York, or Boston. Even the sagacity of a Solomon could not have applied this rule. Ocean rates were like quicksilver. At a single port they varied from steamship to sailing vessel, from day to day, from hour to hour. Publicized rates differed from offered rates. The averages, which calculators liked to depend upon, were delusions. In desperation Fink finally retreated to the faith that if the trunk roads would only observe the railroad differentials to the Atlantic ports, ocean rates would so adjust as to assure a combined ocean-and-land rate equal through all the Atlantic ports.[60] Actually to effect this result the railroads would have had to control ocean transportation. At a time when they could hardly control themselves, the likelihood was implausible.

Though the attainment of general ends proved impossible, the details of the differential system were not seriously modified by the Fink regime. As soon as it was established, his organization undertook at each of the Atlantic ports to divide the westward traffic among the various trunk lines. When Fink's janissaries tackled Boston, the Grand Trunk, which was not yet in the association, served notice that it would adhere to no apportionment which did not recognize its customary differential rate. The other lines demurred. The Grand Trunk reacted with a characteristic foray. It cut westbound rates; other railroads followed suit. Forthwith, all along the coast, traffic for the West converged upon Boston. Goods from New York were even shipped to Boston and

---

p. 7; *Report of the Directors of the Boston & Lowell Railroad Corporation, for the Year 1885 with Statements of Twelve Months' Accounts, to September 30, 1885* (Boston: M. R. Warren, 1885), p. 12.

[60] Fink, *Report upon the Adjustment of Railroad Transportation Rates,* pp. 22–46; Joint Executive Committee, *Plan Proposed for Making Rates to Foreign Points the Same via all the North Atlantic Ports* (New York: Russell Brothers, 1880), pp. 39–41; The New York Produce Exchange *v.* The New York Central & Hudson River Railroad Company, and Others, 3 *Interstate Commerce Commission,* 172; 7 *Interstate Commerce Commission,* 661.

remote from the West than New York and the Boston and Albany had heavier grades, greater fuel costs, shorter trains, and a smaller traffic than the New York roads. The rejoinder of the Boston Chamber of Commerce that the higher rates, excused by these costs of service, were given not only to the Boston and Albany, which had to bear them, but also to the Lake Shore and the New York Central which did not, was brushed aside with the remark that these were "through rates" and it was not the Commission's business to adjudicate the proper basis of pro-rating them.[73]

Although the principle of differentials was reaffirmed, the further question of whether the existing differential relative to Boston was "undue or unreasonable" divided the Commission. The minority felt that a fixed differential of 10 and 5 cents, depending upon classification, was probably just when the general level of rates was higher; now that rates were lower, the burden was proportionately much greater. Originally the differential was an approximate advance over New York rates of 10 per cent; now it was 20. They advocated, therefore, a percentage differential.[74] Four years later, when the issue was raised again, the majority of the Commission adopted this reasoning. The existing fixed differentials were unlawful. "Hereafter the Boston rate from Chicago and points west of Buffalo to Boston and New England points shall be made by adding to the New York rate (as differential) an increase of 10 per cent." [75] Though this decision was highly unsatisfactory to the railroads, they tardily but voluntarily reduced the Boston differential from 5 to 2 cents.[76]

Perhaps elated by their success and the demonstration that the Commission did change its mind, persistent Bostonians continued to attack the fortress of differentials from other quarters. At the end of the nineties the Commission was invited to ponder,

[73] 1 *Interstate Commerce Commission*, 436.

[74] 1 *Interstate Commerce Commission*, 463.

[75] The Toledo Produce Exchange, The Cleveland Board of Trade *v.* The Lake Shore & Michigan Southern Railway Company and Others; Edward Kemble *v.* The Lake Shore & Michigan Southern Railway Company and Others, 5 *Interstate Commerce Commission*, 166.

[76] Massachusetts *Twenty-fourth Annual Report of the Board of Railroad Commissioners. January, 1893*, pp. 17–18.

somewhat more formally than it had, whether one rate for export and another for domestic use violated the Interstate Commerce Act. The Commission, easily discerning that this was no attack upon the export rate but upon the differentials as such, dealt at length with the subject. Probably because they had received some tart instruction on the premises from the Supreme Court in other cases, the Commissioners now emphasized more than previously the rôle of competition in forming the differential structure, a structure built not capriciously but by the slow, historical, competitive process of trial and error. Consequently, like Thurman, Washburne, and Cooley in 1882, the Commissioners were predisposed to find reasons for preserving in general the seaboard rates, a large and complicated system the relations and inter-relations of which were such that any material change in one rate involved numerous other changes.[77] So the differentials stood. Surveying the long array of decisions which had consecrated this structure, some of course explained the outcome in terms of law and its application. Others sought to penetrate beneath the legal surface to the sinews of pressure and response. One of this inquiring tribe came to the conclusion in 1900: "The whole problem seems to be based upon giving each city some part of what it asks and refusing some other part, although the principle formally proclaimed is to create an equality between various railroads or various ports, equalizing their respective advantages and disadvantages."[78]

Meanwhile the railroads, as the Interstate Commerce Act intended they should, continued to set rates in the first instance; and, though the act prohibited pooling, they still sought to assure stability and profit through co-operative action. Their methods, however, were less effective. In 1889 when Fink resigned, the personality holding the members of the association to some modicum of unity and good faith departed. Furthermore the Interstate Commerce Act was explicit on the illegality of divisions of

[77] 7 *Interstate Commerce Commission*, 658; Edward Kemble *v.* Boston & Albany Railroad Company and Others, 8 *Interstate Commerce Commission*, 110.

[78] Treasury Department, Bureau of Statistics. *Monthly Summary of Commerce and Finance of the United States. January, 1900*, p. 1985.

freights and traffics. In 1887 competition flared. The perpetual
rebel, the Grand Trunk, not content with receiving the differentials on westbound traffic now granted to it almost without question, demanded differentials on eastbound shipments of dressed
beef and goods for export. Rates fell and only when the Grand
Trunk was bought off by a favorable allowance of 3 cents per
hundred on dressed beef to Boston did peace come.[79] Then followed through the early nineties an interval of comparative harmony. After 1893, however, competition broke out anew. Even
the directors of the Grand Trunk saw fit to characterize the situation as "insane"; they also prophesied "an agreement . . . containing some novel and drastic conditions which, it is hoped, will
ensure its observance." [80]

In 1896 thirty-one railroad companies, most of the companies
engaged in transportation between Chicago and the seaboard,
formed the Joint Traffic Association. With the usual unctuous
words, the preamble announced the association was "to aid in
fulfilling the purpose of the Interstate Commerce Act, to co-oper-
ate with each other and adjacent transportation associations to
establish and maintain reasonable and just rates, fares, rules, and
regulations," and "to prevent unjust discrimination." The managers of this association could recommend changes in rates and
fares and no railroad could deviate from their recommendations
without a vote of the directors of the railroad. When unauthorized changes were made, the managers of the association were
"to act promptly upon the same for the protection of the parties."
The managers also were to secure to each party "equitable proportions of the competitive traffic . . . as far as it could be le-

[79] *Proceedings and Circulars of the Joint Committee (Freight Department),
1887*, pp. 104–106; *Proceedings and Circulars of the Joint Committee (Freight
Department), 1890* (New York: Russell Brothers, 1891), pp. 96–100; *Proceedings
and Circulars of the Joint Committee (Freight Department.), 1891* (New York:
Russell Brothers, 1892), pp. 13–15, 16–17, 55.

[80] *Half-Year Ended 30th June, 1894. The Grand Trunk Railway Company of
Canada. Report of the Directors and Statements of Accounts* (n.p., n.d.), p. 9;
*Half-Year Ended 31st December, 1894. The Grand Trunk Railway Company of
Canada. Report of the Directors and Statements of Accounts* (n.p., n.d.), pp. 9–13;
*Half-Year Ended 30th June, 1895. The Grand Trunk Railway Company of Can-
ada. Report of the Directors and Statements of Accounts* (n.p., n.d.), pp. 8–9.

gally done." [81] The government forthwith brought suit against the association under the Interstate Commerce Act and the Sherman Anti-Trust Act. Although the inferior courts upheld the agreement, the Supreme Court in 1898 reversed the finding. Basing their decision in large part upon the similarities between this association and that already condemned by the Court in United States *v.* Trans-Missouri Freight Association, the august justices declared that the agreement under review "affects interstate commerce by destroying competition and by maintaining rates above what competition might produce." Since Congress sought to preserve competition, the Joint Traffic Association was illegal. Sound as the reasoning was, it had little practical effect upon the pool's operations. [82]

Certainly Boston's experience with national regulation hardly justified her earlier apprehensions. It was a disadvantage, no doubt, to have differentials stiffly institutionalized upon "principles" sanctified by the Interstate Commerce Commission. On the other hand, Boston had placed upon a firm legal foundation the rebate on exports. By securing an extension of that rebate to goods destined for domestic consumption and then re-exported, it won a needed flexibility and easiness for its coastwise and foreign commerce. Finally, by placing the Boston differential in a percentage relationship to New York rates and securing a reduction in its amount, it shattered a differential system that had existed essentially unchanged from 1877 to 1892. Such were the considerable achievements of a series of complaints before the Interstate Commerce Commission.

V

A somewhat larger problem, however, remains to be considered, that of appraising the impact upon New England, particularly Boston, of the revolution in transportation and commerce effected by the construction and development of through routes to the

[81] United States *v.* Joint Traffic Association, 171 *United States,* 506, 507.
[82] 171 *United States,* 558; *Tenth Annual Report of the Interstate Commerce Commission. December 1, 1896,* pp. 41–43; *Fifteenth Annual Report of the Interstate Commerce Commission. January 17, 1902,* p. 16.

West. Differentials were but a part of this more extensive picture. As far as domestic commerce was concerned, no noticeable disadvantage handicapped New England in the competition with her rivals along the Atlantic seaboard. Her industries poured their boots, shoes, textiles, and hardware westward at the same rates as did New York, and the import trade at Boston, a port surpassed in this respect along the Atlantic coast only by New York, had a similar equality. In return the railroads brought back the wheat, flour, corn, livestock, and dressed beef required by New England's industrial and commercial population. On these imports New England indeed paid a higher rate than did the Middle Atlantic states. On analysis this burden was not a decisive handicap. Edward Atkinson had disposed of this matter in impressive fashion at the Hoosac Tunnel hearings and elsewhere.[83] In 1888 the Interstate Commerce Commission reinforced his findings. Discussing the differentials, it concluded: "There is no reason to believe that the consumption would be larger or the prices to consumers materially less if the rates were on a par with those to New York." [84] Although this was merely an official surmise, the differentials were actually an infinitesimal burden upon New England industry.

The desire to build Boston as a great seaport had always been the pressing incentive for improved transportation to the West. The crux of the question was exports. Although goods for Boston were occasionally imported through New York, the former city never doubted her advantages as a channel for imports; vessels would come thither if only they could be assured of a back cargo. Hence her merchants and shippers had been insistent that Boston enjoy parity of interior rail rates with her nearest and greatest rival, New York; she had achieved her desires on goods intended for export. The original limitation of this equality to commodities consigned abroad on through bills of lading undoubtedly tethered Boston's expansion. Coupled with the earlier limited elevator capacity at Boston, it prevented the accumulation at Boston of stores of grain which could be used either for domestic

[83] *Supra*, pp. 417–418.
[84] 1 *Interstate Commerce Commission*, 458.

purposes or for foreign delivery. Lacking these reserves Boston did not become to any extent a grain market; tramp steamers preferred to make New York where they could always be sure of supplies.[85] In the seventies when Boston railroads and merchants were conducting their energetic and successful campaign to bring back the Cunarders and to establish other lines, the railroads had to guarantee a return cargo for vessels; on occasion the Boston and Albany had itself to buy grain to fulfill its obligations. Fortunately this procedure later became unnecessary.[86]

In spite of handicaps, sheer figures showed the resurrection of Boston port. In 1860 she exported 839,376 bushels of flour, wheat, and corn; New York, Baltimore, and Philadelphia all surpassed this figure. Boston's exports were somewhat less than 6 per cent of the total exported through the four Atlantic ports.[87] In the early seventies, though the absolute figures increased and cries of ecstacy arose in the reports of the Boston Board of Trade, her relative position was worse. After 1875 when her shipments formed 4.9 per cent of the total grain exports, an almost uninterrupted improvement got under way and continued through the eighties. In the nineties Boston held her own.[88] In 1899 she exported 13.8 per cent of the total grain exports from the Atlantic ports.[89] She had commenced other trades. Shipments of fresh meat began in 1880 and by the mid-nineties had reached 164,381,243 pounds; exports of live cattle, undertaken in a small way in 1877, had reached such importance that twenty years later they were the largest from any single port in the United States.[90] Naturally this resurrection affected the carrying trades. At the

[85] Nimmo, *First Annual Report on the Internal Commerce of the United States . . . 1876*, appendix, pp. 103–104, 137; 7 *Interstate Commerce Commission*, 627; Massachusetts *Twenty-ninth Annual Report of the Board of Railroad Commissioners. January, 1898*, pp. 41–42.

[86] Nimmo, *First Annual Report on the Internal Commerce of the United States . . . 1876*, appendix, pp. 100, 103.

[87] Nimmo, *Report on the Internal Commerce of the United States . . . 1879*, p. 119.

[88] 7 *Interstate Commerce Commission*, 636; *Eighteenth Annual Report of the Boston Board of Trade, for the Year Ending January 10, 1872* (Boston: Barker, Cotter & Co., 1872), pp. 17–21.

[89] *Monthly Summary of Commerce and Finance, . . . January, 1900*, p. 1986.

[90] Massachusetts *Twenty-ninth Annual Report of the Board of Railroad Commissioners. January, 1898*, pp. 42–43.

end of the sixties Boston was bewailing the loss of the Cunarders and admitting that only ninety-seven steamers cleared "foreign" in any one year and not a single steamer left for Europe.[91] But the Cunarders came back, and in the seventies the Warren and the Leyland lines were established; in 1880 Boston had on the average a departure every day of the week for England and Scotland; fifteen years later the number of her foreign entrances and clearances surpassed Baltimore's and Philadelphia's.[92] The Interstate Commerce Commission, after juggling columns of statistics, announced in 1898, "It is pretty apparent that of these four ports as compared with one another Boston has been a decided gainer, Baltimore has made a small gain, while New York and Philadelphia have both lost. . . . Compared with the entire group New York has lost." [93]

Such an achievement would have been impossible if the differentials had been a massive burden upon Boston. Clearly in the thirty years after the Civil War, they were not. It is well to remember that they were in large part a paper system, and even on paper many exceptions existed. Whether for export or the domestic market, lumber for Boston did not always carry the full differential and apparently live hogs and cattle had the same rates as to New York.[94] Entirely aside from such refinements in published rates, it must be remembered that competition was continually undermining them. In 1893 the Massachusetts Railroad Commission, which earlier sang a different tune, admitted, "For

[91] Massachusetts *Eleventh Annual Report of the Board of Railroad Commissioners. January, 1880*, p. 20; Hamilton A. Hill, *Boston's Trade and Commerce for Forty Years 1844–1884* (Boston: T. R. Marvin & Son, 1884), p. 17; Nimmo, *First Annual Report on the Internal Commerce of the United States, . . . 1876*, appendix, p. 103.

[92] Henry Fry, *The History of North Atlantic Steam Navigation with Some Account of Early Ships and Shipowners* (London: Samuel Low, Marston and Company, 1896), pp. 265–266; Hill, *Boston's Trade and Commerce*, pp. 16–17; 7 *Interstate Commerce Commission*, 640.

[93] 7 *Interstate Commerce Commission*, 676.

[94] *Proceedings of the Joint Executive Committee, at Its Meeting in New York, September 16, 1880* (New York: Russell Brothers, 1880), p. 195; Joint Executive Committee, Circular no. 187, May 5, 1880; Joint Executive Committee, Circular no. 219, October 11, 1880; *Proceedings and Circulars of the Joint Committee (Freight Department), 1887,* p. 27; *Proceedings and Circulars of the Joint Executive Committee 1882*, p. 58.

some years prior to the enactment of the interstate commerce law, this excess of rates on goods destined to Boston was in great measure absorbed by the active competition between the railroad lines, so that the difference between the rates to New York and Boston was more nominal than real." [95] This observation could have been justly repeated at the end of the nineties.[96] Furthermore the universal habit of making "special rates" or "contract rates" eroded every rate structure, including the differentials. Substantial evidence is hard to obtain, for recipients of rebates were not given to publicizing such favors and non-recipients were given to exaggerated generalizations.[97] Certainly no one appreciated better than Fink the ubiquity and extent of such deductions. According to his estimate, the rebate was inherent in the rate-making *mores* of the trunk lines: "The stockholders, in the first place, surrender their control to a board of directors; the board of directors surrender it to the president; the president surrenders it to a general manager, who in turn surrenders it to the general freight agents of his own and a great number of other roads, who again surrender it to a large number of soliciting agents, and finally these soliciting agents surrender it to the shippers. The shippers practically make their own rates. The result is utter confusion and demoralization of tariffs, and no end of unjust discrimination between shippers and localities." [98]

Differentials were, however, a fact, and Boston was inferior to New York. New Englanders, being what they were, grieved over inferiorities and censured themselves for the outcome. Charles F. Adams, Jr., was peculiarly prone to this habit and all through the seventies the Massachusetts Railroad Commission, under his

[95] Massachusetts *Twenty-fourth Annual Report of the Board of Railroad Commissioners. January, 1893*, p. 17; Nimmo, *First Annual Report on the Internal Commerce of the United States, . . . 1876*, appendix, p. 103; Fink, *Report upon the Adjustment of Railroad Transportation Rates*, pp. 11, 31; New York *Proceedings of the Special Committee on Railroads, . . .* [Hepburn Committee], I, 486.

[96] 7 *Interstate Commerce Commission*, 630, 649, 673.

[97] Nimmo, *First Annual Report on the Internal Commerce of the United States, . . . 1876*, appendix, pp. 103–104, 138; *Fifteenth Annual Report of the Interstate Commerce Commission. January 17, 1902*, pp. 12–13.

[98] *Proceedings of the Joint Executive Committee at Its Meeting in New York, August 10, 1881*, pp. 88–89.

leadership, rode the old theme that Massachusetts lagged behind others because she had no line of her own to the West. Baltimore and Philadelphia each had but one route, but that was a through one; Massachusetts had a number of competing roads all ending at the Hudson. This policy she followed "from a popular inability to adopt any other and more positive line of action, than any particular faith in it." The through business had entered "a new phase, — that of competition between rival termini instead of between rival lines to the same terminus." [99] Time and time again since Adams' day, the theory has been repeated. It has been as unquestioned as a revelation. In spite of the high authority which consecrates it, the dogma was not strictly accurate in fact. Boston did have a line of her own, the Central Vermont-Grand Trunk. Adams realized it, but dismissed it as unimportant. Boston was "wholly dependent on such chance and suicidal competition as the Grand Trunk may be disposed to wage with its more powerful and direct rivals." [100] The eighties and nineties showed, on the contrary, that the competition from the Grand Trunk was frequent and effective, and that New England merchants, manufacturers, and shippers valued the strategic rôle of the Grand Trunk.

More fundamental was the unsoundness of the assumption that after the Civil War the railroads between the West and the Atlantic ports were run each in the interest of a particular eastern terminus. Surface activity might create that impression. Boards of trade and committees of more specialized shippers, often with the connivance of legislators, paraded their woes and demanded that their roads should build New York, Philadelphia, Baltimore, or Boston, as the case might be, into markets and emporia and should discriminate against rivals. To such pressures the roads apparently responded with promises of protection and other pla-

[99] Massachusetts *Seventh Annual Report of the Board of Railroad Commissioners. January, 1876*, pp. 68–69; Massachusetts *Eighth Annual Report of the Board of Railroad Commissioners. January, 1877*, pp. 47–50, 52, 58–60; Massachusetts *Tenth Annual Report of the Board of Railroad Commissioners. January, 1879*, pp. 65–67; *Twenty-third Annual Report of the Boston Board of Trade. January 1, 1877* (Boston: James F. Cotter & Co., 1877), pp. 14, 48.

[100] Massachusetts *Eighth Annual Report of the Board of Railroad Commissioners. January, 1877*, p. 58.

catory utterances. Actually, as those equipped with cold statistics were pointing out, two-fifths of the eastbound tonnage brought to Baltimore was brought there by the Pennsylvania Railroad and a similar percentage of the tonnage to Philadelphia was carried thither by New York roads.[101] Since railroad managers sought traffic even if it went beyond their line and sought it for the longest possible hauls, the Pennsylvania would carry freight past Philadelphia if it were paid for it. Both the Pennsylvania and the Baltimore and Ohio bent every effort to secure connections with New York and to participate in its traffic. If a powerful through route to the West in the Boston interest could have been constructed, it would have followed the same pattern. For railroads were not city roads, they were national roads, "commercial highways" each operating "upon the strictly business principle of making its interests paramount to all other considerations in the conduct of its affairs." [102] Railroads sought maximum profits, not the urban hegemony of the cities that promoted them. Such was the discipline of the private capitalist system. It was wise and natural for Boston to build a series of connections to trunk lines which she saw fiercely competing with one another and to rely upon the commercial and national character of the railroad network.

[101] Fink, *Report upon the Adjustment of Railroad Transportation Rates*, p. 45.
[102] Nimmo, *First Annual Report on the Internal Commerce of the United States,* . . . *1876*, pp. 74–77; Nimmo, *Report on the Internal Commerce of the United States,* . . . *1879*, pp. 146–147; Thurman, Washburne, and Cooley, *Report*, pp. 7–12.